THE CRIMINAL PROCESS

THE CRIMINAL PROCESS

Third Edition

ANDREW ASHWORTH AND
MIKE REDMAYNE

OXFORD
UNIVERSITY PRESS

OXFORD
UNIVERSITY PRESS

Great Clarendon Street, Oxford OX2 6DP

Oxford University Press is a department of the University of Oxford.
It furthers the University's objective of excellence in research, scholarship,
and education by publishing worldwide in

Oxford New York

Auckland Cape Town Dar es Salaam Hong Kong Karachi
Kuala Lumpur Madrid Melbourne Mexico City Nairobi
New Delhi Shanghai Taipei Toronto

With offices in

Argentina Austria Brazil Chile Czech Republic France Greece
Guatemala Hungary Italy Japan South Korea Poland Portugal
Singapore Switzerland Thailand Turkey Ukraine Vietnam

Oxford is a registered trade mark of Oxford University Press
in the UK and in certain other countries

Published in the United States
by Oxford University Press Inc., New York

First published 1994
Second edition 1998

British Library Cataloguing in Publication Data

Data available

Library of Congress Cataloging in Publication Data

Data available

ISBN 0–19–927338–3
978–0–19–927338–6

3 5 7 9 10 8 6 4 2

Typeset by RefineCatch Limited, Bungay, Suffolk
Printed in Great Britain
on acid-free paper by
Ashford Colour Press, Gosport, Hampshire

PREFACE

Some seven years have elapsed since the second edition of this work was published. Andrew Ashworth, author of the previous editions, has now been joined by Mike Redmayne, and we have expanded the book from 10 to 13 chapters. This increased coverage reflects not just the vibrancy of debates about the criminal process but also a burgeoning volume of legislation—most notably, for this edition, the Criminal Justice Act 2003. The book has always recognized the centrality of European human rights law to debates about the shape of the criminal process, and it seems that there are more criminal process, evidence and procedure cases raising arguments under the Human Rights Act 1998 than cases in any other category. However, the hope (or fear) that that Act would presage the arrival of a 'rights culture' has not been realized. There have been occasional gestures by the legislature and the courts to human rights arguments—with the Joint Committee on Human Rights becoming a significant influence on the former—but the notion that the Government would 'bring rights home' seems to have been exaggerated. So far as the criminal process is concerned, the focus has rather been on finding reasons for overriding or making exceptions to the declared rights.

The aim of the book remains that of providing a thoughtful treatment of practical and normative issues in criminal processes and procedures, drawing on arguments from the law, research, policy and principle. It does not purport to be a textbook, but rather to subject a number of key issues to deeper examination than would be possible if the book were to aim for wider coverage. For this edition, five new chapters have been added, and the remaining chapters have been substantially re-written.

The book opens with a chapter setting out the context of recent changes to the English criminal process. A theoretical framework is advanced in Chapter 2. This chapter retains its emphasis on the European Convention on Human Rights, and seeks to develop a human rights approach to resolving issues in the criminal process. Chapter 3 focuses on the occupational cultures of criminal justice professionals and on questions of legal ethics that arise at various stages. The book then goes on to deal with nine key issues in the criminal process, integrating and commenting upon the latest developments in law and practice. Thus Chapter 4 examines the questioning stage of the criminal process, looking at the role and powers of the police. This is followed in Chapter 5 by an analysis of powers and practices in relation to the gathering of evidence. Chapter 6 turns to the decision about whether a suspect should be prosecuted or diverted from the formal criminal process, in the light of recent changes to the role of the Crown Prosecution Service. While the emphasis in that chapter is upon diversion out of the criminal process, Chapter 7 looks at cases that are charged and then subjected to prosecutorial review, and there is detailed consideration of the functions and performance of the Crown Prosecution Service. In Chapter 8 there is an analysis of remand decisions, scrutinizing the justifications for taking away liberty before trial. Chapter 9 reviews a number of pre-trial rights and duties, including contentious issues such as the disclosure of evidence. In Chapter 10 the law and practice on plea negotiation is examined in the light of recent judicial decisions, legislative changes and other proposals. Chapter 11 turns to the criminal trial itself, raising questions about the roles of judge and jury. Chapter 12 examines the appeals system. The book closes with a final chapter in which general conclusions about the criminal process are elaborated.

The writing of the text was completed in early November 2004, and we hope to have taken into account major legal and policy changes up to that date. However, the pace of change in criminal process has been so rapid—on one count, 27 law and order bills since the last general election—that just keeping abreast of developments threatens to become a full time job. Our plea in mitigation of any oversights is one we hope others working in this area will have sympathy for: we have been too busy writing about the criminal process to keep up to date with it.

A.A.,
Oxford, November 2004
M.R.,
London, November 2004

CONTENTS

Preface   v

Table of Cases   xi

Table of Statutes   xvii

Table of International Statutes   xx

Table of Treaties and Conventions   xxi

Table of Statutory Instruments   xxii

1 INTRODUCTION TO THE ENGLISH CRIMINAL PROCESS   1

  1.1 Key stages in decision making   2

  1.2 Distinguishing types of decision   8

  1.3 Reforms of the criminal process   9

  1.4 Process and system   16

2 TOWARDS A FRAMEWORK FOR EVALUATION   19

  2.1 A theory of criminal process   19

  2.2 Internal and external values   26

  2.3 Fundamental rights and the European Convention   28

  2.4 Evaluating the criminal process   37

  2.5 Developing the rights perspective: the State and victims   48

  2.6 Dispositive values   52

  2.7 Conclusion: the criminal process and the limitations of human rights   55

3 ETHICS, CONFLICTS AND CONDUCT   59

  3.1 Rules, roles and ethics   60

  3.2 Identifying 'unethical' practices   63

  3.3 Understanding 'unethical' behaviour   66

  3.4 Justifying 'unethical' behaviour by challenging the ethics   71

  3.5 Discretion and accountability   75

  3.6 Criminal justice reform through ethics   77

4 QUESTIONING   81

  4.1 Questioning and confessions: psychological research   83

  4.2 The context of questioning   84

4.3   Interviews   93

4.4   Interviewing victims   99

4.5   Confessions in court   101

4.6   Conclusions   104

5 GATHERING EVIDENCE: RELIABILITY, PRIVACY AND
   BODILY INTEGRITY   106

5.1   Stop and search   106

5.2   Surveillance   113

5.3   Eyewitness identification evidence   115

5.4   Voice identification   124

5.5   DNA samples   124

5.6   The privilege against self-incrimination   129

6 GATEKEEPING AND DIVERSION   138

6.1   Reporting and enforcing   140

6.2   The range of formal responses   146

6.3   The police and selective enforcement   150

6.4   The role of prosecutors   159

6.5   Accountability   161

6.6   Values and principles   164

6.7   Conclusions   169

7 PROSECUTIONS   173

7.1   The Crown Prosecution Service   174

7.2   Evidential sufficiency   178

7.3   The public interest   184

7.4   CPS policies and their implementation   186

7.5   The role of the victim   199

7.6   Accountability   201

7.7   Prosecutorial ethics   203

7.8   Conclusions   205

8 REMANDS BEFORE TRIAL   207

8.1   Remands, rights and risk   208

8.2   The law relating to remands   213

8.3   The treatment of unconvicted defendants   218

8.4 The treatment of victims and potential victims 224

8.5 Procedural justice and remand decisions 227

8.6 Equal treatment in remand decisions 230

8.7 Conclusions 232

9 PRE-TRIAL ISSUES: DISCLOSURE, DELAY AND ABUSE
OF PROCESS 236

9.1 Filtering cases prior to trial 237

9.2 Pre-trial disclosure 238

9.3 Delay 249

9.4 Entrapment 260

10 PLEA 264

10.1 The rate of guilty pleas 266

10.2 Pleading not guilty 268

10.3 Charge bargains 269

10.4 Fact bargains 274

10.5 Plea bargains 275

10.6 Policies and principles 285

10.7 Conclusions 292

11 THE TRIAL 297

11.1 Modes of trial 297

11.2 Crown Court trial: judge and jury 312

11.3 The exclusion of unfairly and illegally obtained evidence 314

11.4 Other exclusionary rules of evidence 333

12 APPEALS 338

12.1 Restrictions on appeal rights 340

12.2 Challenging jury verdicts 344

12.3 Due process appeals 354

12.4 Post-appeal review of convictions: The Criminal Cases Review
Commission 358

12.5 Prosecution appeals 360

12.6 Double jeopardy 364

13 CRIMINAL PROCESS VALUES 369

13.1 The avoidance of criminal trials 369

13.2   The principled approach   375

13.3   Discrimination and non-discrimination   376

13.4   Promoting the principles   379

13.5   The criminal process of the future   382

Bibliography   385

Index   403

TABLE OF CASES

A v Secretary of State for Home Affairs (2004) *The Times*, 17 December . . . 15 (n. 47), 32 (n. 32)

A, C, D v Secretary of State for the Home Department [2004] EWCA Civ 1123 . . . 333 (n. 192)

Adams [1996] 2 CR App R 467 . . . 306 (n. 48)

Ahmed v Birmingham Magistrates' Court and the CPS [2003] EWHC Admin 72 . . . 258

Alladice (1998) 87 Cr App R 380 . . . 321, 329

Allen v United Kingdom (2002) 35 EHRR CD 289 . . . 136 (n. 177)

Amann v Switzerland (2000) 30 EHRR 843 . . . 114 (n. 67)

Argent [1997] 2 Cr App R 27 . . . 95 (n. 101), 96 (n. 104)

Assenov v Bulgaria (1999) 29 EHRR 652 . . . 212 (n. 24)

Associated Provincial Picture Houses Ltd v Wednesbury Corporation [1948] 1 KB 223 . . . 77, 202 (n. 124)

Attorney-General's Guidelines on the Acceptance of Pleas [2001] 1 Cr App R 425 . . . 273 (n. 43), 282, 285

Attorney-General's Reference (No 1 of 1990) [1992] QB 630 . . . 255 (n. 84)

Attorney-General's Reference (No 3 of 1999) [2001] 2 AC 91 . . . 324, 330, 331

Attorney-General's Reference (No 2 of 2001) [2003] UKHL 68 . . . 256, 259

Attorney-General's Reference (No 3 of 2000) [2001] UKHL 53 . . . 261 (n. 109), 322 (n. 141)

Attorney-General's Reference (No 4 of 2002) [2004] UKHL 43 . . . 33 (n. 40)

Attorney-General's Reference (No 44 of 2000) (Peverett) [2001] 1 Cr App R 416 . . . 274 (n. 46), 281 (n. 69), 282 (n. 74)

B v UK [1981] Com Rep . . . 31 (n. 28)

Bailey [1993] 3 All ER 513 . . . 321, 325 (n. 154), 331 (n. 186)

Barber [2002] 1 Cr App R (S) 548 . . . 279, 288 (n. 102)

Barbera, Messegue and Jabardo (1989) 11 EHRR 360 . . . 287 (n. 96)

Barry (1992) 95 Cr App R 384 . . . 102 (n. 144)

Beckles v United Kingdom (2002) Crim LR 917 . . . 95 (n. 100)

Beedie [1998] QB 356 . . . 364 (n.109)

Bell v DPP of Jamaica [1985] AC 937 . . . 255 (n. 83)

Benham v UK (1996) 22 EHRR 293 . . . 33 (n. 39, 41)

Bennett, ex parte, see R v Horseferry Road Magistrates Court, ex parte Bennett

Berger v United States (1935) 294 US 78 . . . 204 (n. 135)

Beswick [1996] 1 Cr App R (S) 343 . . . 274, 275 (n. 49)

Betts and Hall [2001] 2 Cr App R 185 . . . 96

Blackwell [1995] 2 Cr App R 625 . . . 320, 321 (n. 125), 329

Bowden [1993] Crim LR 379 . . . 122 (n. 110)

Brennan v United Kingdom (2002) 34 EHRR 18 . . . 227 (n. 85)

Brian M [2000] 1 Cr App R 49 . . . 251 (n. 61)

Brogan v United Kingdom (1988) A.145-B . . . 32 (n. 35), 48 (n. 84)

Brown v Stott [2001] 2 WLR 817 . . . 41 (n. 63), 46, 131, 135

Buffrey (1993) 14 Cr App R (S) 511 . . . 266 (n. 11)

Buhay [2003] SCC 30 . . . 326 (n. 165)

Bunkate v Netherlands (1993) 19 EHRR 477 . . . 259 (n. 102)

Bunning v Cross (1978) 141 CLR 54 . . . 326

Caballero v United Kingdom (2000) 30 EHRR 643 . . . 208, 217

Cameron v R (2002) 209 CLR 339 . . . 276 (n. 51), 278 (n. 55)

Canavan and Kidd [1998] 1 Cr App R (S) 243 . . . 272 (n. 39)

Castorina v CC Surrey (1988) *The Times*, 15 June . . . 85 (n. 19)

CC v United Kingdom [1999] Crim LR 228 . . . 208 (n. 7)

Chalkley [1998] QB 848 . . . 322, 323, 353, 354, 357–59

Chatwood [1980] 1 WLR 874 . . . 313 (n. 92)

Chenia [2003] 2 Cr App R 6 . . . 96 (n. 102)

Christie v United Kingdom (1994) 78–A DR 119 . . . 114 (n. 67)

Christou and Wright (1992) 95 Cr App R 264 . . . 262

Clingham v Kensington and Chelsea Borough

Council [2003] 1 AC 787 . . . 14, 33 (n. 39),
    377 (n. 20)

Clooth v Belgium (1991) 14 EHRR 1159 . . . 209
    (n. 10)

Collins [1987] 1 SCR 265 . . . 318 (n. 118), 326
    (n. 164)

Condron and Condron [1997] 1 Cr App R 185,
    [1997] 1 WLR 827 . . . 96 (n. 106), 356 (n. 77)

Condron v United Kingdom [2001] 31 EHRR 1
    . . . 95 (n. 99), 134 (n. 173), 312 (n. 86)

Connelly v DPP [1964] AC 1254 . . . 364
    (n. 109))

Connor [2004] UKHL 2 . . . 309 (n. 67)

Cooke [1995] 1 Cr App R 318 . . . 332

Coombs [1985] 1 NZLR 318 . . . 327 (n. 170)

Cooper [1969] 1 QB 267 . . . 348

Crampton (1991) 92 Cr App R 369 . . . 102

Crawford v Washington (2004) 124 S Ct 1354 . . .
    45 (n. 74), 336 (n. 209)

Curry [1983] Crim LR 737 . . . 122 (n. 110)

Davis [2001] 1 Cr App R 115 . . . 355, 356

Deweer v Belgium (1980) 2 EHRR 30 . . . 256,
    257, 288

Doorson v Netherlands (1996) 22 EHRR 330 . . .
    34 (n. 46), 47 (n.79)

DPP v Ara [2002] 1 Cr App R 16 . . . 98 (n. 121),
    151 (n. 45), 160 (n. 72), 163

DPP v Williams and O'Hare (1994) 98 Cr App R
    206 . . . 263

Du Plooy v HM Advocate (2003) SCCR 640 . . .
    278 (n. 55), 289

Edwards v UK (1993) 15 EHRR 417 . . . 33
    (n. 42)

Edwards and Lewis v United Kingdom [2003]
    Crim LR 891 . . . 33 (n. 43), 47 (n. 83), 246,
    247 (n. 52)

Ellis [2003] EWCA Crim 3930 . . . 359 (n. 87)

Engel v Netherlands(1979) 1 EHRR 647 . . . 13,
    33 (n. 39)

Everett [1988] Crim LR 826 . . . 102 (n. 141)

Fergus (1994) 98 Cr App R 313 . . . 64 (n. 25)

Forbes [2001] 1 AC 473 . . . 63, 116–18, 121, 122

Ford [1989] 2 All ER 445 . . . 308 (n. 59)

Foster [2003] EWCA Crim 178 . . . 92 (n. 83),
    102

Fox, Campbell and Hartley v United Kingdom
    (1990) 13 EHRR 157 . . . 32 (n. 33)

Friend [1997] 2 Cr App R 231 . . . 96 (n. 105),
    183 (n. 34)

Fulling [1987] QB 426; [1987] 2 All ER 65 . . . 92
    (n. 83), 315 (n. 103)

Funke, Cremieux and Miailhe v France (1993) A.
    256, (1993) 16 EHRR 297 . . . 130–132

Galbraith [1981] 1 WLR 1039 . . . 198, 237,
    (n. 5), 252, 312–14, 348 (n. 38), 349, 352,
    363

Gayle (1986) The Times, 16 May . . . 341 (n. 13)

Gentry [1956] Crim LR 120 . . . 214 (n. 29)

Gerald [1999] Crim LR 315 . . . 359 (n. 87)

Ghosh [1982] QB 1053 . . . 303 (n. 36)

Gill [2001] 1 Cr App R 160 . . . 96 (n. 103)

Gleeson [2004] Crim LR 579 . . . 62 (n. 9),
    243–45

Goldenberg (1989) 88 Cr App R 285 . . . 102

Goodwin [1993] 2 NZLR 153 . . . 326 (n. 171)

Govell v United Kingdom [1999] EHRLR 121 . . .
    113 (n. 63)

Gowland-Wynn [2002] 1 Cr App R 231 . . . 96
    (n. 103)

Gray [2003] EWCA 1001 . . . 350 (n. 49)

Gummerson [1999] Crim LR 680 . . . 124
    (n. 116)

H v France (1990) 12 EHRR 74 . . . 256 (n. 86)

H and C [2004] 2 WLR 335 . . . 47 (n. 83), 247

Hakala [2002] EWCA Crim 730 . . . 349, 350, 355
    (n. 66)

Halford v UK (1997) 24 EHRR 523 . . . 113
    (n. 63)

Hanratty [2002] 3 All ER 534 . . . 349 (n. 44)

Harper [1968] 2 QB 108 . . . 288 (n. 99)

Harris [2003] EWCA Crim 174 . . . 63 (n. 20)

Heaney and McGuinness v Ireland (2000) 33
    EHRR 12 . . . 41 (n. 64), 46 (n. 78), 48 (n. 84),
    131, 136, 256, 257

Hewitt and Harman v United Kingdom (App No
    20317/92) . . . 114 (n. 67)

Hickey, unreported CA 30 July 1997 . . . 349
    (n. 44)

Hill (1993) Cr App R 456 . . . 313 (n. 91)

Holgate-Mohammed v Duke [1984] 2 WLR 660
    . . . 85 (n. 22)

Howarth v United Kingdom (2001) 31 EHRR 861
    . . . 256, 257

Howell [2003] Crim LR 405 . . . 96–99, 243
    (n. 37)

Howells [1999] 1 Cr App R (S) 335 . . . 288
    (n. 103)

IJL and others v United Kingdom (29522/95)
    19 September 2000 . . . 131 (n. 157)

Ireland v United Kingdom (1978) A.25 . . . 31
    (n. 26)

Jablonski v Poland (2003) 36 EHRR 455 . . . 32 (n. 38), 209 (n. 10)

Jago v District Court (NSW) (1989) 87 ALR 577 . . . 255 (n. 83)

Jasper v United Kingdom (2000) 30 EHRR 1 . . . 246

JB v Switzerland [2001] Crim LR 748 . . . 131 (n. 152), 132, 136, 290

Jeffries [1998] 2 Cr App R 79 . . . 354

Jenkins (2004) *The Independent*, 20 July . . . 351

Jespers v Belgium (1981) 27 DR 61 . . . 241

Jones [1997] 1 Cr App R 86 . . . 351

Jones [2002] UKHL 5 . . . 211 (n. 20)

Jones v United Kingdom, 9 September 2003 . . . 211 (n. 20)

Keane [1994] 1 WLR 746 . . . 248

Keenan v United Kingdom (2001) *The Times*, 18 April . . . 31 (n. 30)

Kelly v United Kingdom (1993) 74 DR 139 . . . 30 (n. 25)

Khan [1996] 3 WLR 162; [1996] 3 All ER 289 . . . 316, 321, 322, 325, 331 (n. 186), 332

Khan v United Kingdom (2000) 31 EHRR 1016 . . . 34 (n. 48), 113, 322 (n. 137)

King v United Kingdom (2004) STC 911 . . . 132, 136 (n. 177)

Knight [2004] 1 Cr App R 9 . . . 96 (n. 109)

Konig v Germany (1978) 2 EHRR 170 . . . 258 (n. 97)

Kopp v Switzerland (1999) 27 EHRR 91 . . . 114 (n. 66)

Kudla v Poland (App 30210/96) (2000) 26 October . . . 259 (n. 103)

Lambert [2002] 1 AC 545 . . . 33 (n. 40)

Latif and Shahzad [1996] 1 WLR 104 . . . 325 (n. 154)

Latimer 92004) 9 February, CA . . . 351 (n. 57)

Law-Thompson [1997] Crim LR 674 . . . 321 (n. 127)

Leatham (1861) 8 Cox CC 498 . . . 320

Letellier v France (1992) 14 EHRR 83 . . . 213 (n. 26)

Looseley [2001] 1 WLR 2060; [2001] UKHL 53 . . . 261–63, 322 (n. 141), 332 (n. 187), 380 (n. 28)

Luca v Italy (2003) EHRR 46 . . . 335 (n. 207)

M [2000] 8 Archbold News 2 . . . 88 (n. 59)

M and La Rose v Metropolitan Police Commissioner [2002] Crim LR 215 . . . 227 (n. 85)

McCann v United Kingdom (1996) 21 EHRR 97 . . . 30 (n. 24)

McGovern (1991) 92 Cr App R 228 . . . 101 (n. 136), 102 (n. 141)

McIlkenny v CC West Midlands Police Force [1980] 2 All ER 227 . . . 353 (n. 61)

McIlkenny et al (1991) 93 Cr App R 287 . . . 10 (n. 27)

MacKenzie (1993) 96 Cr App R 98 . . . 314 (n. 95)

Maihi (2002) CA181/02 . . . 327

Malone v UK (1985) 7 EHRR 14, (1984) A.82 . . . 113

Maloney [2003] EWCA Crim 1373 . . . 350

Mapp v Ohio 367 US 643 (1961) . . . 326

March [2002] 2 Cr App R (S) 448 . . . 272

Mason [1988] 1 WLR 139 . . . 103, 315, 321, 322

Mason [2002] 2 Cr App R 38 . . . 321, 322 (n. 138), 325 (n. 154), 331 (n. 186), 332 (n. 187)

Mellors v United Kingdom (App 57836/00) (2003), 17 July . . . 257

Miller (1992) 97 Cr App R 99 . . . 315

Mills and Another (No 2) [2004] 1 Cr App R 7 . . . 350 (n. 51), 351

Mirza [2004] UKHL 2 . . . 309 (n. 67)

Monnell and Morris v UK (1988) 10 EHRR 205 . . . 341 (n. 18), 342

Morales (1993) 77 CCC (3d) . . . 211 (n. 22)

Morgan Smith [2001] 1 AC 146 . . . 270

Morley (1995) *The Times*, 25 January . . . 341 (n. 14)

Mountford [1999] Crim LR 75 . . . 96 (n. 103)

Mullen (1999) 2 Cr App R 143 . . . 355

Muller v France (1999) 17 March . . . 209 (n. 9)

Murray (John) v UK (1996) 22 EHRR 29 . . . 27 (n. 17), 28 (n. 19), 34 (n. 44), 46 (n. 76), 90 (n. 71), 95, 97, 98, 134 (n. 173), 290 (n. 111)

Nangle [2001] Crim LR 506 . . . 62 (n. 12)

Nathaniel [1995] 2 Cr App R 565 . . . 245 (n. 44), 323, 324, 330

Newton (1982) 4 Cr App R (S) 388 . . . 264 (n. 2), 274, 275

Nikolova v Bulgaria (2000) 31 EHRR 64 . . . 32 (n. 36), 227 (n. 86)

Nix v Williams 467 US 431 . . . 326 (n. 160)

Oakwell [1978] 1 All ER 1223 . . . 122 (n. 110)

Offen (No 2) [2001] 1 WLR 253 . . . 217 (n. 51)

O'Hara v United Kingdom [2003] Crim LR 493 . . . 32 (n. 34), 183 (n. 35)

Okafor [1994] 3 All ER 741 . . . 89 (n. 65)

Oliphant [1992] Crim LR 40 . . . 321 (n. 127)

Omar v France (2000) 29 EHRR 210 . . . 342

Orkem v Commission [1989] ECR 3283 . . . 132 (n. 170)

Osman v United Kingdom (1998) 29 EHRR 245 . . . 212 (n. 25)

Ozturk v Germany (1984) 6 EHRR 409 . . . 53 (n. 98), 372 (n. 8)

Paris, Abdullahi and Miller (1992) 97 Cr App R 99 . . . 81 (n. 2)

Pendleton [2001] UKHL 66 . . . 345 (n. 27), 346 (n. 34), 348–53, 357, 359

People (Attorney-General) v Callaghan [1966] IR 426 . . . 211 (n. 21)

PG and JH v United Kingdom [2002] Crim LR 308 . . . 34 (n. 48), 113 (n. 63)

Phillips (1947) 32 Cr App R 47 . . . 214 (n. 29), 216

Pitman [1991] 1 All ER 468 . . . 281

Porter v Magill [2002] 2 AC 357 . . . 258

Practice Direction (Bail: Failure to Surrender and Trial in Absence) (2004) The Times, 26 January . . . 233 (n. 111)

Practice Direction (Bail Pending Appeal) [1983] 1 WLR 1292 . . . 208 (n. 3)

Practice Direction (Criminal: Consolidated) [2002] 3 All ER 904 . . . 341 (n. 15)

Practice Direction (Mode of Trial Decision-making) [2002] 3 All ER 904 . . . 300

Practice Direction (Victim Personal Statements) [2002] 1 Cr App R 69 . . . 51 (n. 92), 199 (n. 111)

Preston (1994) 98 Cr App R 405 . . . 281 (n. 68)

Price v United Kingdom (2001) 34 EHRR 53 . . . 31 (n. 29)

Puddick (1865) 1 F&F 497 . . . 79 (n. 71)

Punzelt v Czech Republic (2001) 33 EHRR 1159 . . . 209 (n. 11)

Quereshi [2002] 1 WLR 518 . . . 309 (n. 67)

R (Bannister) v Crown Court at Guildford [2004] EWHC 221 . . . 253, 254

R (Gibson) v Winchester Crown Court [2004] 2 Cr App R 14 . . . 253

R (on the application of Gillan and another) v Commissioner of Police for the Metropolis [2004] 3 WLR 1144 . . . 107 (n. 6)

R (on the application of Joseph) v DPP [2001] Crim LR 489 . . . 202 (n. 126)

R (on the application of Lloyd) v Bow Street Magistrates' Court [2004] Crim LR 136 . . . 257, 258

R (McCann) v Manchester Crown Court [2003] 1 AC 787 . . . 33 (n. 39), 377 (n. 20)

R (Sullivan) v Crown Court at Maidstone [2002] 1 WLR 2747 . . . 242 (n. 32)

R v A [2002] 1 AC 45 . . . 356

R v B [2003] EWCA Crim 319 . . . 251 (n. 66), 313 (n. 89), 347, 348

R v Bow Street Magistrates' Court, ex parte Proulx [2001] 1 All ER 57 . . . 101 (n. 137), 102

R v Brentford JJ, ex parte Wong [1981] QB 445 . . . 255 (n. 84)

R v CC South Yorkshire [2002] 1 WLR 3223 . . . 128

R v Central Criminal Court, ex parte Johnson (Orleander) [1999] 2 Cr App R 51 . . . 253

R v Chichester Justices, ex parte Crowther [1998] All ER (D) 457 . . . 257 (n. 96)

R v Chief Constable of Kent, ex parte L (1991) 93 Cr App R 416 . . . 162 (n. 81), 202, 203

R v Chief Constable of South Yorkshire, ex parte LS/Marper [2004] UKHL 39 . . . 126 (n. 130), 127, 128, 324 (n. 153), 330 (n. 182)

R v Criminal Cases Review Commission, ex parte Farnell [2003] EWHC 835 . . . 350

R v Criminal Cases Review Commission, ex parte Pearson [2000] 1 Cr App R 141 . . . 359 (n. 84), 360 (n. 90)

R v Crown Court at Harrow [2003] 1 WLR 2756 . . . 217 (n. 49)

R v Croydon Justices, ex parte Dean [1993] QB 769 . . . 323 (n. 148)

R v Director of Public Prosecutions, ex parte C [1995] 1 Cr App R 136 . . . 163 (n. 89)

R v Director of Public Prosecutions, ex parte Jones [2000] Crim LR 858 . . . 202 (n. 127)

R v Director of Public Prosecutions, ex parte Kebilene [2000] 2 AC 326 . . . 163 (n. 85), 203

R v Director of Public Prosecutions, ex parte Lee [1999] 2 All ER 237 . . . 227 (n. 86)

R v Director of Public Prosecutions, ex parte Manning [2001] QB 330 . . . 202 (n. 126)

R v General Council of the Bar, ex parte Percival [1990] 3 All ER 137 . . . . . . 163 (n. 87), 202 (n. 123)

R v H [1995] 2 AC 596 . . . 313 (n. 90)

R v Horseferry Road Magistrates Court ex parte Bennett [1994] 1 AC 42, [1993] 3 WLR 90 . . . 236, 259, 380 (n. 28)

R v Inland Revenue Commissioner, ex parte Mead [1993] 1 All ER 772 . . . 163 (n. 84), 203

R v Leeds Crown Court, ex parte Wardle [2001] UKHL 12 . . . 65 (n. 31), 254, 255

R v Liverpool Stipendiary Magistrates, ex parte Ellison [1989] Crim LR 369 . . . 65 (n. 31)

R v Manchester Crown Court, ex parte McDonald [1990] 1 WLR 841 . . . 253 (n. 76)

R v Metropolitan Police Commissioner, ex parte Blackburn (No 1) [1968] 2 QB118 . . . 161 (n. 78), 202 (n. 121)

R v Metropolitan Police Commissioner ex parte Blackburn (No 3) [1973] 1 QB 241 . . . 202 (n. 122)

R v Metropolitan Police Commissioner, ex parte P (1995) 160 JP 367 . . . 163 (n. 88)

R v Metropolitan Police Commissioner, ex parte Thompson [1997] 1 WLR 1519 . . . 156 (n. 57), 158 (n. 65), 160 (n. 71), 163, 168

R v M(KJ) (2003) 2 Cr App R 322 . . . 335

R v Stratford JJ, ex parte Imbert [1999] 2 Cr App R 276 . . . 239 (n. 13)

R v Telford Justices, ex parte Badhan [1991] 2 QB 78 . . . 251, 252, 255

R v United Kingdom (2003) 37 EHRR 9 . . . 217 (n. 50)

R v Warley Justices, ex parte DPP [1998] 2 Cr App R 307 . . . 278 (n. 56)

Reid v United Kingdom (2003) 27 EHRR 9 . . . 229 (n. 97), 257

Rennie (1982) 74 Cr App R 207 . . . 102, 104

Rice v Connolly [1966] 2 QB 414 . . . 137 (n. 179)

Roberts [1997] 1 Cr App R 161 . . . 321

Robinson (1854) 23 LJQB 286 . . . 213

Rollinson (2003) CA434/02 . . . 327

Rose (1898) 78 LT 119 . . . 213

Rossborough (1985) 81 Cr App R 139 . . . 245 (n. 44)

Rowe and Davis v UK (2000) EHRR 1 . . . 47 (n. 81), 355

Salabiaku v France (1989) 13 EHRR 379 . . . 33 (n. 40)

Smith[2003] 1 WLR 2229 . . . 308 (n. 59)

Smith [2003] EWCA Crim 927 . . . 82 (n. 5)

Samuel [1988] 1 QB 615 . . . 316 (n. 108), 321, 322, 329, 88 (n. 47)

Saunders v UK (1997) 23 EHRR 313 . . . 46 (n. 76), 130–133, 136, 290 (n. 111)

Sawoniuk [2000] 2 Cr App R 220 . . . 250

SC v United Kingdom [2005] Crim LR 130 . . . 377 (n. 18)

Senior and Senior [2004] Cr App R 215 . . . 89 (n. 65)

Shaheed [2002] 2 NZLR 377 . . . 327

Sharp [2003] EWCA Crim 3870 . . . 359

Sheldrake v DPP [2004] UKHL 43 . . . 33 (n. 40)

Simpson [1998] 1 Cr App R (S) 197 . . . 272 (n. 40)

Slippey [1988] Crim LR 767 . . . 313 (n. 88)

Smith (1990) 90 Cr App R 413 . . . 281 (n. 68)

Smith (1999) 2 Cr App R 238 . . . 355 (n. 68)

Smurthwaite and Gill [1994] Crim LR 53; (1994) 98 Cr App R 437 . . . 321 (n. 134)

Stack v Boyle (1951) 342 US 1 . . . 209 (n. 15)

Stafford v DPP [1973] 3 All ER 763 . . . 348–50, 352, 353

Stillman [1997] 1 SCR 8 . . . 326 (n. 163)

Stogmuller v Germany (1979) 1 EHRR 155 . . . 256 (n. 85)

Stone [2001] Crim LR 465 . . . 346

Strawhorn v McLeod 1987 SCCR 413 . . . 288 (n. 104)

Tait and Bartley (1979) 24 ALR 473 . . . 292 (n. 123)

Teixeira de Castro v Portugal (1998) 28 EHRR 101 34 (n. 45), 48 (n. 84), 261 (n. 113), 262 (n. 115), 323 (n. 146)

Thompson and Venables (2000) 30 EHRR 121 . . . 356

Tibbs [2000] 2 Cr App R 309 . . . 242 (n. 32)

Togher and Others [2001] 3 All ER 463 . . . 356 (n. 71) 357, 358

Turnbull [1977] QB 224 . . . 122–124, 313

Turner [1970] 2 QB 321 . . . 281, 286, 292

Turner [1975] QB 834 . . . 313 (n. 90)

Underwood [2003] EWCA 1500 . . . 356 (n. 74)

United States v Havens 466 US 620 (1980) . . . 326 (n. 161)

United States v Leon 468 US 897 (1984) . . . 326 (n. 159)

United States v Salerno (1987) 481 US 739 . . . 210 (n. 18)

V and T v UK (2000) 30 EHRR 121 . . . 28 (n. 21), 377

Valenzuela v Spain (1998) 28 EHRR 483 . . . 114 (n. 67)

Van Mechelen v The Netherlands (1997) 25 EHRR 547 . . . 47 (n. 80)

Wadsworth [2004] 1 Cr App R (S) 109 . . . 283 (n. 80)

Ward [2003] EWCA Crim 3191 . . . 350 (n. 49)

Wahab [2003] 1 Cr App R 15 . . . 102

Walsh (1990) 91 Cr App R 161 . . . 321 (n. 128)

Wanklyn (1984) *The Times*, 12 November . . . 341 (n. 13)

Wardle v United Kingdom (2003) 4 EHRLR 459 . . . 65 (n. 31)

Weeks v United Kingdom (1988) 10 EHRR 293 . . . 54 (n. 102)

Wharton [1955] Crim LR 565 . . . 214 (n. 29)

Wheeler [2001] 1 Cr App R 10 . . . 242 (n. 32)

Wilkinson [1996] 1 Cr App R 81 . . . 251, 252

Williams [2003] EWCA Crim 3200 . . . 122 (n. 108) 123

Wood [1996] 1 Cr App R 207 . . . 312 (n. 84)

X v United Kingdom (1972) 40 CD 64 . . . 287 (n. 97), 292 (n. 124)

Yagci and Sargin v Turkey (1992) 20 EHRR 505 . . . 209 (n. 8)

TABLE OF STATUTES

Anti-Terrorism, Crime and Security Act 2001 . . .
  7, 15, 372
  ss 21–29 . . . 209 (n. 13)

Bail Act 1976 . . . 5, 182, 214, 217, 218, 222, 223,
  230 (n. 100), 232
  s 3(6) . . . 214
  s 4 . . . 215
  s 4(1) . . . 215
  s 5(3) . . . 230 (n. 100)
  Sch 1 . . . 215
  Sch 1, para 2 . . . 215, 222
  Sch 1, paras 3–6 . . . 215
  Sch 1, para 9 . . . 220, 222
Bail (Amendment) Act 1993 . . . 225 (n. 77), 230
Bail Reform Act 1966 (US) . . . 214
Bail Reform Act 1984 (US) . . . 210, 214, 215

Courts Act 2003 . . . 15
Crime and Disorder Act 1998 . . . 4, 12, 149, 154,
  157, 162, 165, 168, 169, 249, 371, 377
  s 1 . . . 13
  s 28 . . . 270
  ss 29–32 . . . 188, 270
  s 51 . . . 238 (n. 8)
  s 56 . . . 217 (n. 48)
  s 65 . . . 153
  Sch 3 . . . 238 (n. 10)
Criminal Appeal Act 1968 . . . 346, 348
  s 2(1) . . . 346
  s 23 . . . 346
  s 29 . . . 341 (n. 11)
Criminal Appeal Act 1995 . . . 11, 16, 130, 346,
  354, 355, 258, 359
  s 2(1) . . . 354
  s 13 . . . 358 (n. 82), 359 (n. 83)
Criminal Justice Act 1967 . . . 214
  s 11 . . . 244 (n. 41)
Criminal Justice Act 1972—
  s 36 . . . 339 (n. 4)
Criminal Justice Act 1987 . . . 7, 280, 372
  s 9 . . . 33 (n. 3)
Criminal Justice Act 1991—
  s 1(2) . . . 222 (n. 64)
Criminal Justice Act 2003 . . . 1, 4, 6, 15, 16, 42,
  54 (n. 100), 56, 57, 62, 85, 87, 126, 147, 149,
  154, 159, 162, 165, 168, 169, 173, 178, 193,
  205, 218, 230, 238, 239, 241, 242–44, 279,
  300, 302, 304, 305, 314, 333–36, 339, 340,
  360, 362, 363, 364, 365–67, 371
  s 1 . . . 107 (n. 3)
  s 3 . . . 111 (n. 49)
  s 4 . . . 85, 218
  s 9 . . . 57
  s 10 . . . 57, 126 (n. 128)
  Part 2 . . . 5 (n. 5)
  s 13 . . . 215 (n. 40)
  s 14 . . . 217
  s 15 . . . 217
  s 16 . . . 57
  s 18 . . . 225 (n. 77)
  s 22 . . . 149
  s 22(3) . . . 160
  s 23 . . . 149, 159
  s 24 . . . 149, 160
  s 24(2) . . . 161
  ss 25–27 . . . 149
  ss 28–30 . . . 177
  s 40 . . . 242 (n. 31)
  s 41 . . . 238 (n. 9)
  s 43 . . . 304
  ss 44–46 . . . 304 (n. 39)
  s 58 . . . 362
  s 62 . . . 340 (n. 6), 362, 364
  s 64 . . . 362 (n. 98)
  s 67 . . . 362 (n. 97)
  s 68 . . . 340 (n. 6)
  Part 10 . . . 364 (n. 111)
  s 78 . . . 57, 364 (n.112)
  s 78(3)(c) . . . 364 (n.112)
  s 79 . . . 57, 368 (n. 126)
  s 79(2)(c) . . . 365 (n. 114)
  s 101 . . . 334 (n. 198)
  s 103 . . . 334 (n. 199)
  s 114 . . . 57, 333 (n. 196)
  s 114ff . . . 333 (n. 195)
  s 125 . . . 314 (n. 96)
  s 143(3) . . . 232 (n. 110)
  s 144 . . . 266, 275
  s 152(2) . . . 222
  s 154 . . . 302 (n. 26)

s 309 . . . 339 (n. 3)
s 330(5) . . . 304 (n. 40)
Sch 2 . . . 177
Sch 3 . . . 238 (n. 9), 278 (n. 58), 279 (n. 61)
   Para 5 . . . 302 (n. 30)
   Para 6 . . . 302 (n. 29)
   Para 22 . . . 302 (n. 28)
Sch 4, Part 1 . . . 362 (n. 99)
Sch 5, Part 1 . . . 365 (n. 115)
Criminal Justice and Police Act 2001 . . . 126
   ss 1–11 . . . 5 (n. 12)
Criminal Justice and Public Order Act 1994 . . . 11, 72, 82, 93, 95, 98, 99, 110, 134, 218, 242, 243
   s 7 . . . 87 (n. 36)
   s 25 . . . 216, 217
   s 26 . . . 217
   s 34 . . . 72 (n. 57), 82 (n. 9), 93, 96–99
   s 35 . . . 96 (n. 105)
   s 36 . . . 93
   s 37 . . . 93
   s 48 . . . 266 (n. 10)
   s 60 . . . 107, 110
   s 60(5) . . . 107 (n. 5)
Criminal Procedure and Investigations Act 1996 . . . 11, 62, 94 (n. 93), 136, 239, 242–45, 247, 248, 264, 339, 367
   s 3(1)(a) . . . 240 (n. 18)
   s 5 . . . 242 (n. 30)
   ss 6C, 6D . . . 245 (n. 46)
   s 6E . . . 243 (n. 33)
   s 7 . . . 241 (n. 24)
   s 9 . . . 240 (n. 19)
   s 11 . . . 243 (n. 33)
   s 24 . . . 239 (n. 17)
   Part III . . . 280
   ss 28–38 . . . 6 (n.22)
   ss 35, 36 . . . 339 (n. 3)
   Part IV . . . 280
   ss 39–43 . . . 6 (n.21)
   s 54 . . . 339 (n. 5), 364 n. 110)
Criminal Procedure (Scotland) Act 1995—
   s 196 . . . 288 (n. 104)

Domestic Violence, Crime and Victims Act 2004 . . . 15, 18, 49, 51, 200
   s 13 . . . 225 (n. 75)

Fireworks Act 2003 . . . 5 (n.12)

Homicide Act 1957 . . . 351
   s 3 . . . 351 (n. 53

Human Rights Act 1998 . . . 13, 29, 30, 35, 40, 41, 45, 47, 131, 217, 227 (n. 87), 256, 319, 322, 331, 354, 375, 381, 383
   s 2 . . . 29, 257
   s 3 . . . 29, 375
   s 4 . . . 29
   s 6 . . . 29
   s 172 . . . 41

Interception of Communications Act 1985 . . . 113, 114

Legal Aid Act 1988 . . . 5

Magistrates' Courts Act 1980 . . . 250
   s 19 . . . 302 (n. 30)
   s 20 . . . 279 (n. 61)
   s 108 . . . 340 (n. 9)
   s 127 . . . 250 (n. 56)
Mental Health Act 1983. . . . 231
Misuse of Drugs Act 1971 . . . 107
   s 23 . . . 107 (n. 4)

Offences Against the Person Act 1861 . . . 191
   s 18 . . . 191, 269, 270, 272, 274
   s 20 . . . 270, 272
   s 47 . . . 270
Official Secrets Act 1989 . . . 299

Police Act 1996 . . . 142
Police and Criminal Evidence Act 1984 (PACE) . . . 3, 9, 10, 16, 60, 63, 64, 71, 82, 84, 86–88, 93, 102–104, 110, 116, 122, 126, 135, 218, 315, 316, 319–21, 324, 325, 329, 330–33, 347, 380
   s 1 . . . 106
   s 2(9)(a) . . . 107 (n. 8)
   ss 24, 25 . . . 85
   s 28 . . . 86 (n. 30)
   s 29 . . . 87 (n. 45)
   s 30 . . . 86 (n. 31)
   s 30A . . . 85
   s 37 . . . 3 (n. 9), 63 (n. 16)
   s 38 . . . 5 (n. 14)
   ss 40–44 . . . 3(n. 10), 87
   s 58 . . . 88, 320
   s 61 . . . 126 (n. 126)
   s 62 . . . 126 (n. 124), 135 (n. 176)
   s 63 . . . 126 (n. 125)
   s 64 . . . 126 (n. 129), 330
   s 64(3) . . . 324
   s 67(1) . . . 3 (n. 11)
   s 76 . . . 3 (n. 11), 92 (n. 83), 101, 102, 313, 314, 315
   s 76(2) . . . 101 (n. 135)

s 76(2)(a) . . . 101
s 76(2)(b) . . . 101, 102
s 77 . . . 101
s 78 . . . 3 (n. 11), 92 (n. 84), 101, 102, 121,
    320–22 (n. 139), 323–26, 329, 330, 331, 357
s 78(1) . . . 324 (n. 150)
s 116 . . . 87 (n. 40), 317 (n. 111)
Sch 1A . . . 84 (n. 18), 111 (n. 49)
Code of Practice A . . . 107, 108, 112
    1.2 . . . 107 (n. 7)
    1.4 . . . 112 (n. 60)
    1.5 . . . 108 (n. 18)
    2.2 . . . 107 (n. 11)
    2.3 . . . 108 (n. 14)
    2.4 . . . 108 (n. 15)
    2.11 . . . 107 (n. 10)
    2.15 . . . 108 (n. 16)
    3.1 . . . 112 (n. 54)
    3.3 . . . 107 (n. 7)
    3.5 . . . 107 (n. 7)
    3.6 . . . 107 (n. 8)
    3.7 . . . 107 (n. 9)
    4.11 . . . 108 (n. 19)
Code of Practice C . . . 9, 86, 89–92, 98, 102,
320
    3.21 . . . 87 (n. 45)
    3.22 . . . 87 (n. 45)
    10.1 . . . 89 (n. 66)
    10.3 . . . 86 (n. 30)
    10.4 . . . 86 (n. 31)
    10.5 . . . 89 (n. 67)
    11.1 . . . 89 (n. 60)
    11.1A . . . 89 (n. 62)
    11.4 . . . 89 (n. 63)
    11.5 . . . 92 (n. 82), 315 (n. 102)
    11.6 . . . 91 (n. 80)
    11.7 . . . 90 (n. 73)
    Annex C . . . 90 (n. 72)
Code of Practice D . . . 9, 116–122, 124, 151
    2.3 . . . 116
    3.2 . . . 120 (n. 98)
    3.4 . . . 117 (n. 81)
    3.5 . . . 118 (n. 84)
    3.11 . . . 121 (n. 104)
    3.12 . . . 118 (n. 82)
    3.14 . . . 118 (n. 86)
    3.16 . . . 119 (n. 93)
    3.17 . . . 119 (n. 95)

    3.20 . . . 120 (n. 97)
    3.23 . . . 119 (n. 94)
    3.30 . . . 128 (n. 139)
    5.22 . . . 128 (n. 139)
    Annex A, 11–12 . . . 119(n. 89)
    Annex B, 9 . . . 117 (n. 78)
    Annex B, 18 . . . 124 (n. 115)
Code of Practice E . . . 90 (n. 74)
Code of Practice F . . . 90
Code of Practice on Questioning and
    Identification . . . 63
Police Act 1997—
    Part III . . . 113, 114
Police Reform Act 2002 . . . 76, 161
    Part 1 . . . 161
Powers of Criminal Courts (Sentencing) Act 2000
    s 91 . . . 272 (n. 42)
Prosecution of Offences Act 1985 . . . 9, 175, 178,
    201, 253
    s 10 . . . 175
    s 22 . . . 6(n. 20),
    s 22(3) . . . 253
    s 23 . . . 6(n. 18), 65 (n. 29), 175 (n. 7),
    193
Public Order Act 1986 . . . 142

Regulation of Investigatory Powers Act 2000 . . .
    34, 114, 115, 260, 262, 331, 332
    s 5(2), (3) . . . 114
Road Traffic Act 1988 . . . 131, 132, 135, 136, 325,
    329
    ss 6, 7 . . . 131 (n. 159)
    s 172(2)(a) . . . 131 (n. 160)

Sex Offenders Act . . . 149, 170 (n. 120)
Sexual Offences Act 2003 . . . 14, 164, 371
    Part 2 . . . 149

Terrorism Act 2000 . . . 7, 15, 110
    s 38B . . . 137
    s 43 . . . 107 (n. 6)
    s 44 . . . 107 (n. 6), 110
    ss 45–47 . . . 107 (n. 6)
    Sch 8 . . . 87 (n. 43)

War Crimes Act 1991 . . . 250

Youth Justice and Criminal Evidence Act 1999
    . . . 13, 377
    s 59 . . . 131 (n. 156)

TABLE OF INTERNATIONAL STATUTES

AUSTRALIA

Evidence Act 1995 . . . 326
   s 138 . . . 327 (n. 167)

CANADA

Charter of Rights and Freedoms . . . 318,
   326
   s 24(2) . . . 326
Criminal Code . . . 214

GERMANY

Code of Criminal procedure–
   s 152 . . . 147
   s 153a . . . 147

NEW ZEALAND

Bill of Rights . . . 327, 332

UNITED STATES

Constitution . . . 45
   Fourth Amendment . . . 319 (n. 121),
   326
   Sixth Amendment . . . 336

TABLE OF TREATIES AND CONVENTIONS

Charter of Fundamental Rights . . . 28

European Convention on Human Rights . . . 13,
15, 21, 28–30, 35, 37, 38, 41, 45, 46, 55, 60,
74, 95, 131, 168, 204, 216, 234, 256, 264, 287,
290, 292, 303, 321, 323, 356, 370, 373, 375,
376, 381, 383
  Art 2 . . . 30, 36
  Art 2(1) . . . 30
  Art 2(2) . . . 30
  Art 2(2)(b) . . . 30
  Art 3 . . . 30, 31, 36, 54
  Art 4(1) . . . 36
  Art 5 . . . 15, 31, 32, 34, 37, 46–48, 57, 58, 78,
    84, 207, 208, 220, 232, 252, 254, 256, 373
  Art 5(1) . . . 31, 183, 208, 210, 261, 341
  Art 5(1)(a) . . . 342
  Art 5(1)(c) . . . 32, 208
  Art 5(2) . . . 31
  Art 5(3) . . . 31, 32, 208 (n. 5), 215, 217,
    256
  Art 5(4) . . . 31, 32 (n. 38), 256, 257
  Art 5(5) . . . 31, 221 (n. 62)
  Art 6 . . . 32–34, 37, 41–43, 46–49, 53 (n. 98),
    58, 78, 90, 95, 98, 130, 132, 134, 211 (n. 20),
    239, 256, 258, 260, 287, 288, 290, 322, 335,
    354, 356, 357, 370, 373, 375
  Art 6(1) . . . 32, 47, 150, 256–59, 291, 292, 335,
    341
  Art 6(2) . . . 32, 33, 208, 287, 290
  Art 6(3) . . . 32, 33, 57
  Art 6(3)(b) . . . 227

  Art 6(3)(c) . . . 33
  Art 6(3)(d) . . . 33, 34, 57, 335
  Art 7 . . . 34, 36
  Art 8 . . . 34, 37, 41, 43, 48, 57, 113, 114, 126,
    316, 322, 331, 375
  Art 8(1) . . . 34, 113, 114
  Art 8(2) . . . 34, 35, 113, 114, 316
  Art 9 . . . 35–37, 41, 43, 48, 375
  Art 10 . . . 35–37, 41, 43, 48, 375
  Art 11 . . . 35–37, 41, 43, 48, 375
  Art 13 . . . 355 (n. 70)
  Art 14 . . . 35, 126, 290, 376
  Art 15 . . . 36
  Art 15(1) . . . 36
  Art 40 . . . 48
  Art 49(3) . . . 54
  Protocol 7, Art 4 . . . 365
  Protocol 12 on Non-Discrimination . . .
    376

Inter-American Convention on Human Rights–
  Art 8 . . . 129 (n. 143)
International Covenant on Civil and Political
  Rights (UN) . . . 28, 365, 367
  Art 14 . . . 129 (n. 143), 290 (n. 111)
  Art 14.7 . . . 57, 58

Treaty Establishing a Constitution for Europe
  2004 . . . 29

United Nations Convention on the Rights of the
  Child 1990 . . . 28, 45, 48, 377

TABLE OF STATUTORY INSTRUMENTS

Crime and Disorder Act 1998 (Dismissal of Charges Sent) Rules 1998 (SI 1998 No 3048) ... 238 (n. 10)

Criminal Justice and Police Act 2001 (Amendment) Order 2002 (SI 2002 No 1934) ... 5

Criminal Justice Act 2003 (Conditional Cautions: Code of Practice) Order 2004 No 1683 ... 154 (n. 50), 159 (n. 69), 160, 168, 171

    para 2.3 ... 160 (n. 73)

    para 2.6 ... 160 (n. 75)

    para 3.3 ... 154 (n. 50)

    para 4.1 ... 160 (n. 71)

    para 4.1(ii) ... 160 (n. 72)

    para 5.1 ... 160 (n. 74)

    para 7.1 ... 168 (n. 112)

    para 8.2 ... 160 (n. 75)

Police Reform Act 2002 (Modification) Order 2004 (SI No 2540) ... 5

Prosecution of Offences (Custody Time Limits) Regulations 1987 (SI 1987 No 299)—

    reg 5 ... 253 (n. 71)

Magistrates' Courts (Advance Information) Rules 1985 (SI 1985 No 601) ... 239 (n. 12)

Misuse of Drugs Act 1971 (Modification) (No 2) Order 2003 (SI 2003/3201) ... 111 (n. 48)

1

INTRODUCTION TO THE ENGLISH CRIMINAL PROCESS

Issues of criminal process are rarely out of the news. In the months before work on the third edition of this book was begun, one could have read the following stories in the newspapers. The Court of Appeal quashed the convictions of Anthony Poole and Gary Mills, as well as that of George Kelly. Poole and Mills had spent fourteen years in prison for murder, whereas Kelly had been hanged in 1950. In both cases the Court of Appeal found that the prosecution had failed to disclose important evidence to the defence.[1] Some months prior to this the Metropolitan Police Commissioner, Sir John Stevens, gave a public lecture in which he launched a scathing attack on criminal justice institutions. The criminal process, he argued, fails to protect the victims of crime: street robbers are repeatedly released on bail, only to rob again, while the criminal trial is simply an 'uneven game of tactics'. A major problem was said to be that 'the development of the legal system in our time has tended to be to the advantage being given to the defendant.'[2] This attack quickly met with a response from the Bar Council, which drew attention to the fundamental importance of requiring the prosecution to prove its case beyond reasonable doubt, and warned of the dangers of sliding into a police state.[3] Later, in another lecture, the Home Secretary, David Blunkett, echoed one of Stevens' themes: 'despite our recent efforts to redress it, the balance of justice is still tipped against victims'.[4] The subject of his lecture was civil renewal, a topic which allowed him to stress 'the principle of lay involvement in the criminal justice system' and the need to make it harder for people to avoid 'their civic duty of jury service.'[5] While all this was going on, a major piece of criminal justice legislation was making its way through Parliament. Among many others, the bill (which was to become the Criminal Justice Act 2003) contained provisions extending

---

[1] 'Pair Win Appeal Against Murder Conviction' *The Guardian*, 18 June 2003; 'Man Hanged 50 Years Ago Was Innocent', *The Guardian*, 11 June 2003.

[2] 'Sir John Stevens Calls for Criminal Justice Reform' *The Guardian*, 6 March 2002.

[3] 'Sir David Bean Replies to Sir John Stevens' *The Guardian*, 8 March 2002.

[4] David Blunkett MP, *Civil Renewal: A New Agenda*, CSV Edith Kahn Memorial Lecture (2003), 38.

[5] *Ibid.*, 39.

the amount of time suspects can be held in police detention, restricting the use of jury trial in serious fraud cases, and giving new rights of appeal to prosecutors.

This is a rather bewildering set of topics, but each is relevant to the criminal process. The aim of this book is to explore topics such as these and to critically assess the relevant law and practice and the debates around them. In Chapter 2, more will be said about what is understood here by 'the criminal process', what its functions are, and what principles or other criteria should be used to assess it. The present chapter gives a brief sketch of the key decision-making stages of the criminal process and their significance. It also provides the reader with some orientation by summarizing some of the main events in the reform agenda that has moulded the criminal process in the past quarter century.

1.1 KEY STAGES IN DECISION MAKING

The criminal process is part of the State response to crime, part of the mechanism by which the State applies substantive criminal law to its citizens. At its most expansive, it covers a range of decisions and procedures from the investigation and questioning of people as possible suspects through to appeals against conviction and other means of challenging convictions or acquittals. The criminal process forms part of the wider criminal justice system, which includes all the agencies and institutions (police, prosecutors, public defenders, judges, probation officers, prison officers and so on) as well as the criminal law itself and the sentencing system. In this book we focus on the criminal process, but it is not easy to define exactly what this is. Our chief concern lies with the processes and procedures whereby the system deals with potential suspects, suspects and defendants.

Before drawing attention to the key stages in the criminal process, it is important to put it in perspective. It is sometimes presented as if it were a vital tool of crime control in society, but the figures demonstrate that the majority of crime never comes to the attention of the police or other enforcement agencies, and that even when offences are brought to official attention they do not always elicit a formal response. Thus the British Crime Survey has for some 20 years attempted to measure the amount of crime suffered by members of households. It suggests that only some 43 per cent of crimes are reported to the police, and of those, only two-thirds are recorded.[6] This means not only that figures of crimes recorded by the police may significantly underestimate the amount of crime in society, but also that the number of offenders detected and prosecuted starts from a low base. In fact, the Home Office estimates that the 'attrition rate', i.e. the percentage of alleged crimes that do not result in a

---

[6] Home Office, *Crime in England and Wales 2002/2003*, 9; it should be noted that the British Crime Survey does not purport to measure all crimes, and concentrates on crimes against the property or person of those aged 16 or over.

conviction, is considerable. If we start with the British Crime Survey figures just mentioned, then only two-thirds of 43 per cent of crimes are recorded by the police, i.e. some 28 per cent. Of these, fewer than a quarter are 'cleared up' by the police, which means that only six per cent of all crimes are traced to a suspected offender. About half of those result in a conviction or a caution. In other words, the percentage of alleged crimes that end up in a conviction is between two and three per cent (albeit higher for some offences, such as violent and sexual crimes, and lower for others).[7] The Government has now drawn attention to what it has labelled 'the justice gap': 'in 2000–2001, 5.17 million crimes were recorded, but only 19.8 per cent of them resulted in an offender being brought to justice.'[8] It is promoting various strategies to reduce the gap by improving the practices of agencies involved.

The above figures show that, even when crime is reported to and recorded by the police, the police will not be able to identify a suspect in about three-quarters of cases. Although it is not easy to define exactly what the criminal process is, we take it as starting with the identification of one or more suspects by the police. It is at this stage that serious issues of criminal procedure arise. If the police have identified someone whom they suspect has committed a crime, they will often wish to take steps towards initiating a prosecution. In minor cases, the police are likely to proceed by issuing a summons against a suspect, which will require him to attend court. In more serious cases, the police are likely to take the course of arresting the suspect and taking him to a police station. A police officer is entitled to arrest any person whom he or she has reasonable grounds to suspect of having committed or being about to commit an 'arrestable offence'. The regime in the police station is intended to offer the suspect certain protections—for example, against unnecessary detention or unduly aggressive questioning. In all police stations where suspects may be detained, a police officer is given the role of 'custody officer'. This person should play an important role in ensuring that the protective regime operates properly. When the suspect is brought to the police station, the custody officer has to decide whether the suspect should be released without charge, charged, or (if it is thought necessary to obtain further evidence by questioning) detained for questioning.[9] That detention may be for up to six hours in the first place, and there are procedures for renewal.[10] The custody officer must record these and other decisions on a custody sheet, and the suspect must be informed of the right to free and confidential legal advice. The Codes of Practice issued under the Police and Criminal Evidence Act 1984 (PACE) set out standards for the conduct of police investigations. For example, they impose restrictions on the manner in which the police may question a suspect,[11] and on the handling of identification procedures. Many details of these procedures will be examined in Chapter 4, where actual practice as well as the letter of the law will be discussed. The police will

---

[7] Home Office, *Digest 4: Information on the Criminal Justice System in England and Wales*, 29.

[8] Home Office, *Narrowing the Justice Gap* (2002), quotation at p. 5.   [9] PACE, s 37.

[10] PACE, ss 40–4.

[11] Taken in conjunction with ss 76, 78 and 67(1) of PACE. For the latest version of the Codes and general discussion, see M. Zander, *The Police and Criminal Evidence Act 1984* (2003).

seek to question the victim at an early stage, and should inform victims of violent offences of the existence of the Criminal Injuries Compensation Board. The police may also put the victim in touch with Victim Support or other similar agencies. Inquiries in a case may be completed quickly or may spread over a considerable time, in which case the police have a duty to keep the victim informed of the progress of the case.

The outline in the previous paragraph focused on police procedures. Other investigating agencies, such as HM Customs and Excise, are subject to the Codes of Practice, although there are fewer controls over investigations by the many so-called regulatory agencies. The general principle throughout, however, is that a person may only be questioned before charge and not after charge. Once there is sufficient evidence, the suspect should be charged. However, it must not be thought that charging is the only way of commencing a prosecution. The alternative method is for a police officer to lay an information before a magistrate or justices' clerk, as a result of which a summons will be issued and served on the defendant. The summons procedure is more commonly used for minor offences: the power of arrest, which places considerable discretion in the hands of the police, is typically used for more serious offences, but can also be deployed for relatively minor offences against public order.

One of the things which is occurring at this stage of the criminal process is that the police are trying to build a case against the suspect. Even if a suspect has been caught 'red-handed', a conviction will not be probable, should the case come to court, unless the case can be made to look strong, first to the prosecutor who decides on the charge or reviews the file, and then to the court. In a 'red-handed' case the police will want to take statements from any witnesses and write up their own reports of the incident. A confession from the suspect will also strengthen the case. In other cases the police may want to gather further evidence by, for example, holding an identification parade, taking a DNA sample from a suspect or searching his house. Some of these evidence-gathering activities are regulated in various ways. In the case of confessions and identity parades, the regulation is largely intended to secure the reliability of any evidence produced. With DNA samples and searches of property, other values—such as privacy and bodily integrity—are at stake.

It has been assumed so far that the progression from sufficient evidence to charge or summons is natural or inevitable, but that is far from being true. An authority with the power to prosecute may decide to take no formal action at all, perhaps believing that the experience of detection or an informal warning is sufficient, or it may decide that a formal caution or warning is appropriate. During the twentieth century the police developed the practice of issuing a formal caution to certain offenders, particularly the young, the elderly, and those whose offences were very minor. The Crime and Disorder Act 1998 replaced police cautions for young offenders with a statutory scheme of reprimands and final warnings. The Criminal Justice Act 2003 introduces a statutory caution for adults, the 'conditional caution,' discussed further in Chapter 6. Many regulatory agencies also have powers to issue formal warnings to employers, companies, farmers, and others in respect of offences, and most of them prefer to adopt this approach in the hope of maximizing compliance with the law. Some agencies have powers to exact financial penalties from offenders without bringing a prosecution: the Inland Revenue may offer citizens the opportunity to pay, say, double the amount of tax evaded as a condition of non-prosecution. Recently, the police have been given powers to impose on the spot fines on minor offenders.[12]

If the prosecution proceeds by way of summons, the defendant will be given a date for first appearance in a magistrates' court. If it proceeds by arrest, the police officer now has a power to grant bail to the suspected offender without going to the police station—a power known colloquially as 'street bail'.[13] However, in many arrest cases the officer will take the suspect to the police station and, if it is decided that the suspect is to be charged, he or she must then decide whether the suspect is to be bailed or remanded in police custody after charge. There is a duty to ensure that a defendant is brought before a court as soon as practicable, which is often the morning after arrest (or on Monday morning, if the arrest takes place on a Saturday). The defendant may be bailed to appear in court or, if there are reasonable grounds for believing that detention is necessary for certain purposes, the police may keep the defendant in custody until the first court appearance.[14] At first appearance the magistrates' court must either dispose of the case or, if not (and particularly in serious cases which will be committed to the Crown Court for trial), the court must decide whether to release the defendant on bail or to make a custodial remand. The Bail Act 1976 proclaims a presumption in favour of bail, but also sets out various reasons for the refusal of bail: see Chapter 8 below.

Legal assistance is available at several stages in the process. Not only is there a right to free legal advice at the police station, but there are duty solicitor schemes to facilitate this and to advise on representation in court. A new Public Defender Service was established in 2001 on an experimental basis and by 2004, offices in eight areas were undertaking criminal defence work in police stations, courts and prisons.[15] More generally, the Legal Aid Act 1988 provides that magistrates' courts must grant legal aid to defendants who are going to the Crown Court, and may grant legal aid for summary trials. Defendants with means are expected to make contributions, but a majority of defendants are unemployed or otherwise in receipt of State assistance. The exercise of the discretion to grant legal aid differs between courts.[16] The organization of legal aid and advice in criminal cases has been altered with the advent of the

---

[12] Criminal Justice and Police Act 2001, ss 1–11, and the Police Reform Act 2002, Sch 4. See, e.g., the Criminal Justice and Police Act 2001 (Amendment) and the Police Reform Act 2002 (Modification) Order 2004, which sets out the powers of the police to issue on the spot fines for a number offences, including contraventions of the Fireworks Act 2003 and theft.

[13] Criminal Justice Act 2003, Part 2; see A. Hucklesby, 'Not Necessarily a Trip to the Police Station: the Introduction of Street Bail', [2004] Crim LR 803.

[14] PACE, s 38.

[15] The Public Defender Service was established under the auspices of the Legal Services Commission. For its latest report, *Putting Clients First: Public Defender Service, Annual Report 2003–04*, see www.legalservices.gov.uk

[16] R. Young and D. Wall (eds), *Access to Criminal Justice* (1996), esp Ch. 7.

so-called Criminal Defence Service, with contracts being awarded only to firms who fulfil certain requirements.[17]

Until recently it has been the police who take the decision whether or not to charge the defendant. However, under the Criminal Justice Act 2003 the Crown Prosecution Service (CPS) now determines the charge in most cases—sometimes working alongside the police in a local criminal justice unit, or at other times by telephone. Once the file is completed, it is passed to the CPS so that there can be a review of the strength of the evidence and whether the 'public interest' favours prosecution. The CPS has the power to discontinue prosecutions in magistrates' courts,[18] and may drop a case when it is brought to trial in the Crown Court. They may decide to continue with the prosecution on the charges preferred by the police, or may alter the charges. If it is a Crown Court case it will be necessary to draft the indictment.[19] If the defendant has been remanded in custody, time-limits now apply to the period between first appearance in the magistrates' court and committal (70 days), and between committal to the Crown Court and trial (112 days).[20] The prosecution may apply for an extension, but if there are insufficient grounds the accused must be released on bail until the trial.

The choice of charge determines the mode of trial. Most minor offences are triable summarily only, in the magistrates' courts. Most serious offences are triable only on indictment, in the Crown Court. The intermediate category of offences triable either way may be tried in a magistrates' court or at the Crown Court. In these cases a defendant is asked by the magistrates whether he intends to plead guilty. If he indicates his intention to plead guilty, the magistrates' court becomes seized of the case (under the 'plea before venue' procedure) and may proceed to pass sentence or, if it believes its sentencing powers are inadequate, may commit the case to the Crown Court for sentence. If, on the other hand, the defendant indicates an intention to plead not guilty, the magistrates have to decide, having heard representations, whether to commit the case to the Crown Court for trial. Even if they decide not to do so, taking the view that the case is suitable for summary trial, the defendant has an unfettered right to elect Crown Court trial.

If a defendant indicates an intention to plead not guilty, there may be various exchanges between prosecution and defence before the date set for trial. In some magistrates' courts there may be a pre-trial review, and in the Crown Court there will be a Plea and Directions hearing, intended to define the issues for trial and to facilitate rulings on the admissibility of evidence in advance of the trial.[21] In long or complex cases the Crown Court judge has the power to order a preparatory hearing, with similar powers.[22] In many cases there will be discussion between prosecuting counsel and defence counsel on the day before, or the very day of, the Crown Court trial. In

---

[17] For details, see www.legalservices.gov.uk   [18] Prosecution of Offences Act 1985, s 23.

[19] For details, see J. Sprack *Emmins on Criminal Procedure* (2002), Ch. 6.

[20] Prosecution of Offences Act 1985, s 22; for analysis of the amended regulations and cases, see *Blackstone's Criminal Practice*, D10.4.

[21] Criminal Procedure and Investigations Act 1996, ss 39–43.

[22] *Ibid.*, ss 28–38.

some cases there may be a preliminary discussion with the judge. Defence counsel may then discuss the case with the defendant, and a change of plea to guilty may take place. This part of the process, sometimes described as 'plea bargaining,' is unregulated by statute and little regulated by the Court of Appeal. The many issues arising are discussed in Chapter 10 below.

A defendant who pleads guilty will be sentenced by the magistrates or by the Crown Court judge, after hearing a statement of facts from the prosecution and a plea in mitigation from the defence, and in non-minor cases after receiving a pre-sentence report. A defendant who pleads not guilty will be tried in the appropriate court. Magistrates' courts tend to be less formal, with less strict adherence to the laws of evidence but also with a greater sense of briskness. In the Crown Court the trial will be before judge and jury, and matters are unfolded in greater detail.

A defendant convicted by a magistrates' court may appeal against conviction or sentence to the Crown Court, where the appeal takes the form of a rehearing. If either the defence or the prosecution wish to appeal on a point of law, the magistrates may be asked to state a case to the Divisional Court. A defendant convicted in the Crown Court may appeal against conviction and/or sentence to the Court of Appeal (Criminal Division). After the appeal process has been exhausted there is provision for a case to be referred to or taken up by the Criminal Cases Review Commission and, if the Commission so decides, to be referred back to the Court of Appeal. This system is intended to remedy the defects that led to the long delays in dealing with what became the notorious cases of miscarriage of justice uncovered in the late 1980s and early 1990s. These issues are further examined in Chapter 12.

The various stages in decision making outlined above apply generally, although reference was made to differences between the powers and practices of the police and of the regulatory agencies. However, there are differences of approach to cases involving certain types of suspect or defendant and certain types of alleged offence. Where the suspect or defendant is a juvenile, aged between 10 and 18, there are special procedures and safeguards. There is also special provision for mentally disordered suspects and defendants. Persons requiring interpreters or suffering from deafness, etc., should also be treated differently. As for types of offence, brief mention may be made of the different legal regimes for motoring offences and for persons suspected of terrorist offences or of serious fraud. Many motoring offences may be dealt with by a fixed penalty without a court appearance, and some of those that have to be brought to court do not require the appearance of the defendant. There are also several other differences of procedure, including particular time-limits for commencing a prosecution. The Terrorism Act 2000 and the Anti-Terrorism, Crime and Security Act 2001 give considerably greater powers to the police in the investigation of suspected terrorist offences. The Criminal Justice Act 1987 (as amended) gives enhanced powers to the Serious Fraud Office when investigating persons suspected of involvement in frauds involving millions of pounds, including a special procedure for bringing cases of serious fraud to trial.

Before leaving this outline of decisions, their context within a system needs to be emphasized. They are not discrete individual decisions taken in laboratory conditions. Rather, they should be viewed as decisions taken either by individuals or by courts, working within a given professional context. The individual police officer or Crown Prosecutor is likely to be affected, for example not only by the working practices and expectations of colleagues, but also by decisions taken by others beforehand and decisions likely to be taken at subsequent stages. The factual basis for the decision may well have been constructed by others, in a way that depends partly on selection and interpretation. This point is developed in several chapters of the book, but it is important to avoid from the outset the dominance of a 'rationalist' notion of decisions taken by individuals independently and based on objective information.[23]

1.2 DISTINGUISHING TYPES OF DECISION

The various legal procedures and practices described in the previous section combine to affect the ways in which particular suspects and defendants are processed by officials. Formal procedures do not necessarily determine that treatment, since the working practices of officials are what suspects and defendants actually experience. Those practices may be more or less faithful to the rules, and in some instances the law may leave discretion rather than imposing rules.

It is noticeable, however, that the various decisions outlined above are not all of the same kind. Most of them might be described as 'processual', in that they are decisions about the processing of the case from initial charge through to trial and appeal. But there are two or three decisions that may be described more accurately as 'dispositive', in that they are concerned more with the disposal of the case. One strong example of this is the decision whether to give a police caution, conditional caution or warning or to take no formal action, rather than to prosecute. This decision, whether taken by the police, the CPS or a regulatory agency, may be regarded as analogous to sentencing. It disposes of the case, which goes no further in the system, and it does so with a form of censure. The weakness of the analogy is that no court is involved. Diversion is premised on the belief that the case does not warrant full processing and a court appearance. A second example is the later review of a case by the CPS, followed by a decision to discontinue the prosecution on grounds of insufficient public interest—although such cases should be fewer if the CPS brings the right charge(s) in the first place. In addition to these two examples of dispositive decisions, there are other stages in the criminal process which have a dispositive element—for example, the decision on mode of trial and, more especially, the decision to accept a guilty plea to a lesser offence or to fewer charges than originally preferred.

The point of making this distinction is that different considerations will apply to processual decisions and to dispositive decisions—as is clear from the analogy

---

[23] Cf. R. Baldwin and K. Hawkins, 'Discretionary Justice: Davis Reconsidered', [1984] *PL* 570, at 581.

between dispositive decisions and sentencing, which has no application to decisions on the processing of cases. None the less, in practice questions of evidential sufficiency and of public interest often intermingle in the minds of decision makers, and so the distinction may be less sharp in practice than in theory. Moreover, there is at least one type of decision that is neither processual nor dispositive: the remand decision, whether to grant bail or to remand in custody. This has no direct bearing on whether the prosecution will be continued or discontinued, nor on mode of trial or plea, although in practice it may be affected by these other decisions. Nor is it a means of taking a case out of the system and dealing with it otherwise. It is *sui generis*, and is perhaps best described as a temporizing decision, in that it arises solely if and when a case cannot be dealt with at the first court appearance. The adjective 'temporizing' refers only to why this decision is necessary rather than to the nature of the issues it raises, and these are discussed further in Chapter 8.

1.3 REFORMS OF THE CRIMINAL PROCESS

Criminal procedure reform often occurs in response to a miscarriage of justice of some sort. So it was with the Philips Royal Commission, which reported in 1981.[24] The Commission had been set up in 1977, at a time when it was becoming apparent from the inquiry by Sir Henry Fisher into the *Confait* case that there were systemic problems that could not be examined within the confines of the review of a single case.[25] What had happened in the *Confait* case was that three young men were convicted of murder on the basis of confessions later shown to be false. The case highlighted the lack of regulation in the police station as well as the extent to which false confessions could seal an innocent defendant's fate. The Philips report ranged widely over police powers and prosecutions, and formed the basis of the Police and Criminal Evidence Act 1984 (PACE), a piece of legislation which remains important to this day. PACE gave the police wider powers of arrest and stop and search than they had previously possessed; it also formalized the regime for detention in the police station, giving the police specific time limits in which they could detain suspects and introducing the role of the custody officer. For the first time the legislation clearly provided suspects with a right of access to legal advice while in police custody. PACE was accompanied by a series of Codes of Practice which add considerable detail to the legislative provisions, explaining how certain powers and procedures are to be given effect: examples are Code C on the detention and questioning of suspects and Code D on identification procedures. The other major piece of legislation to result from the Philips report was the Prosecution of Offences Act 1985, which took responsibility for

---

[24] Royal Commission on Criminal Procedure, *Report* (1981).

[25] *Report of an Inquiry by the Hon. Sir Henry Fisher into the circumstances leading to the trial of three persons on charges arising out of the death of Maxwell Confait and the fire at 27 Doggett Road, London SE6* (1977).

the prosecution of offences away from the police and gave it to the newly established Crown Prosecution Service.

The next significant event in the reform process was a series of miscarriage of justice cases, recognized as such in the late 1980s and early 1990s. The cases of the Birmingham six, the Guildford four, the Maguire family and Judith Ward highlighted many issues.[26] The defendants in these cases had all been convicted of offences arising out of the bombing campaign conducted by Irish nationalists during the 1970s. As in *Confait*, some of the defendants had falsely confessed. There were allegations that they had confessed because of considerable pressure—including violence—from the police. Several of the cases also involved forensic science evidence, and highlighted issues about the independence and neutrality of forensic scientists. There had also been failures to disclose evidence to the defence and, in some cases, failure by the police to disclose evidence to the prosecutor. Another disturbing feature was that in several cases the allegations of false conviction had been long-running. The Birmingham six, for example, had had their case heard twice by the Court of Appeal before the convictions were quashed in 1991.[27] Issues about how the criminal process deals with appeals and allegations of miscarriage of justice were brought to the fore, as well as many questions about the operation of the early stages of the criminal process.

The official response to these cases was to set up another Royal Commission to consider their implications and to suggest reforms. The Runciman Commission reported in 1993.[28] Its proposals were nowhere near as far-reaching as those of Philips. Perhaps this is not surprising. The miscarriage of justice cases that were generally seen as setting its agenda involved convictions secured before the protections of the PACE regime were brought in.[29] Runciman recommended new procedures for appeals against conviction and for post-appeal review of alleged miscarriages of justice, but many of its proposals involved fine-tuning the existing PACE regime rather than radical reform. Others addressed issues unconnected to the miscarriage of justice cases: there were proposals on the way cases are allocated between Crown and magistrates' court and on plea-bargaining, both of which were controversial.

To understand the legislation and other developments which followed the Runciman report it is important to know something about the political climate surrounding criminal justice reform. Histories of criminal justice policy suggest that for much of the twentieth century, criminal justice was not politically controversial.[30] There was a broad consensus between the main political parties as to how policy should develop. That changed at the 1979 general election, which the Conservative Party fought partly

---

[26] J. Rozenberg, 'Miscarriages of Justice', in E. Stockdale and S. Casale, *Criminal Justice under Stress* (1993).

[27] *McIlkenny et al* (1991) 93 Cr App R 287.

[28] Royal Commission on Criminal Justice, *Report* (1993).

[29] There were exceptions, such as a number of cases involving the West Midlands Serious Crime Squad. See T. Kaye, *'Unsafe and Unsatisfactory'? Report of the Independent Inquiry into the Working Practices of the West Midlands Serious Crime Squad* (1991).

[30] See D. Downes and R. Morgan, 'The Skeletons in the Cupboard: The Politics of Law and Order at the Turn of the Millenium' in M. Maguire, R. Morgan and R. Reiner (eds), *The Oxford Handbook of Criminology* (2002).

on 'Law and Order' issues. In the 1980s the police made clear their support for a Conservative rather than Labour administration, a move which helped to confirm the Conservatives as the party of law and order. The 1980s thus marked the end of the bipartisan consensus: criminal justice had become a political and therefore an electoral issue. In the aftermath of the Runciman report, this was perhaps most clearly visible when the then Home Secretary, Michael Howard, gave a speech to the 1993 Conservative Party annual conference detailing 27 'ways to crack crime'. Among them was reform of the defendant's right to silence, something which had actually been rejected by Runciman.[31] A significant part of the political rhetoric around this time was a shift to emphasizing concern for victims and their treatment within the criminal justice system.

The first major piece of criminal justice legislation after Runciman was the Criminal Justice and Public Order Act 1994. This contained provisions—advocated by the Government but not supported by the Royal Commission's report—allowing juries to draw inferences against defendants who are silent at trial or during police questioning. The following year some of the Runciman reform agenda was enacted: the Criminal Appeal Act 1995 contained reforms of the appeals and post-appeals process. The next year saw more Runciman proposals translated into legislation. The Criminal Procedure and Investigations Act 1996 made significant changes to the disclosure regime. This responded in part to a campaign by senior police officers who argued that their disclosure obligations were far too onerous—a good example of how the police will sometimes actively campaign for criminal justice reform.[32] The Act restricted prosecution disclosure obligations and at the same time introduced the requirement that the defence disclose the outline of its case before trial in the Crown Court.

Two other aspects of the political climate surrounding criminal justice reform are worth highlighting at this stage. A number of commentators on the Runciman report drew attention to what they perceived to be its excessive concern with increasing the efficiency of the criminal justice system: the mode of trial and plea-bargaining recommendations provided examples. This reflects a wider shift in emphasis in criminal justice policy during the 1990s, towards prioritizing managerial concerns, in particular, the need to make the system run as efficiently as possible. A second issue of significance relates to what was said above about the politicization of criminal justice policy. During the 1980s, the Conservatives were able to position themselves as the party of law and order, a strategy which probably put Labour at an electoral disadvantage. When, after its electoral defeat in 1992, the Labour party began to rethink its policies—the process from which 'New Labour' emerged—criminal justice was among them. 'Tough on crime, tough on the causes of crime' was the new Labour slogan. Labour was now prepared to embrace criminal process reforms which it would once have vehemently opposed. Its relatively muted opposition to the reforms of the right to silence in the Criminal Justice and Public Order Act 1994 was a first sign of this.

---

[31] See n 26 above, para 4.22.

[32] See R. Morgan, 'The Process is the Rule and the Punishment is the Process' (1996) 59 *MLR* 306.

More recently, Labour criminal justice policy has often been presented as toughening the criminal justice system and promoting the interests of victims rather than those of defendants. It was noted above that David Blunkett, as Home Secretary, has spoken of the criminal process being tipped too far against the interests of victims. Tony Blair has gone even further, talking of the need to replace the criminal justice system with a victim justice system.[33]

Returning to the reform chronology, the mid 1990s saw other significant events. The efficiency-driven agenda could be seen in a report on aspects of the trial process written by a Home Office civil servant.[34] The Narey report highlighted the need to bring cases to trial as quickly as possible; it also endorsed Runciman's proposals on the removal of the defendant's right to elect trial by jury. Some of Narey's proposals became law in the Crime and Disorder Act 1998. Removal of the right to elect jury trial, however, proved too controversial, and after two failed attempts the Labour Government has abandoned this as a reform priority. Soon after the 1997 election, the new Government announced a review of the Crown Prosecution Service by Sir Iain Glidewell, and the managerialist reform agenda can also be seen in his report published in 1998.[35] Although there have been concerns about the way in which the CPS reviews cases—there is some evidence that it is too ready to prosecute weak cases—the Glidewell report had almost nothing to say about this, nor about other broad issues of prosecution policy. The report's main focus was upon various managerial issues within the CPS, but it did recommend that police officers and prosecutors should work together in Criminal Justice Units to determine whether to prosecute and on what charge(s), and also in Trial Units to prepare files for cases going to trial.

The 1990s also saw concern about a miscarriage of justice of a different kind, one not involving allegations of wrongful conviction. Stephen Lawrence, a young black man, had been killed in an apparently racist attack in 1993. There were police enquiries, and five young white men were interviewed, but no prosecution was brought as a result. Eventually the Lawrence family launched a private prosecution against those five individuals, but the case was stopped when the judge ruled the evidence against them insufficient. The Government set up an inquiry into the case chaired by Sir William Macpherson, a High Court judge. It reported in 1999 with the conclusion that the investigation into the murder was 'marred by a combination of professional incompetence, institutional racism and a failure of leadership by senior officers.'[36] Much of the report was concerned with police investigative procedures and criticisms of what took place in that particular case, but two other points are of particular importance here. First, the report found what it termed 'institutional racism' in the police: the definition of institutional racism is controversial, in that it elides racist behaviour and attitudes with practices that unintentionally have the effect of

---

[33] 'Victims Now Priority of Justice System', *The Guardian*, 14 November 2002.

[34] M. Narey, *Review of Delay in the Criminal Justice System* (1997).

[35] *Review of the Crown Prosecution Service: A Report* (1998), reviewed at [1998] Crim LR 517.

[36] *The Stephen Lawrence Inquiry: Report of an Inquiry by Sir William Macpherson of Cluny* (1999): quotation at 46.1.

disadvantaging members of minority ethnic groups,[37] but the report succeeded in drawing attention to deep-seated problems of race in criminal justice. More will be said about these in later chapters, notably on remands (Chapter 8) and on plea (Chapter 10). Secondly, the report argued in favour of a re-examination of the double jeopardy rule that prevented the prosecution of a person already acquitted. That issue was referred to the Law Commission, which reported in favour of relaxing the double jeopardy rule,[38] and Part 10 of the Criminal Justice Act 2003 broadly implements that report. The Macpherson report therefore shows how concern about unmerited acquittals and the treatment of victims and their families can motivate reform of the criminal process, just as much as concern about false convictions.

The growing concern about the experiences of victims and witnesses in the criminal process can also be seen in *Speaking up for Justice*, the report of a Home Office Working Party in 1998.[39] The report focused on the treatment of children and vulnerable witnesses. It raised concerns about the way in which the process of giving evidence in court may be unduly stressful for such witnesses. Many of its proposals found their way into the Youth Justice and Criminal Evidence Act 1999, subsequently developed in Part 8 of the Criminal Justice Act 2003.[40]

Perhaps the most significant legislative reform of the 1990s was one that was not specifically focused on criminal justice. The Human Rights Act 1998 gives effect to the European Convention on Human Rights in English law. More will be said about the Convention, and its importance to criminal justice, in Chapter 2. For the moment, it is worth noting that the Convention has implications for many areas of the criminal process: detention and questioning in the police station, the right to silence and the privilege against self-incrimination, remand decision making, disclosure, and the rules of evidence. Assessing the actual and potential impact of the Convention on the criminal process is a major concern of this book.

However, one early sign of Government ambivalence about human rights in their application to the criminal process was the introduction of the anti-social behaviour order by s 1 of the Crime and Disorder Act 1998. The European Convention and the European Court adopt the approach that, where proceedings are in substance criminal because of what is at stake (even though the domestic law treats them as civil), they should be treated as criminal for the purpose of the safeguards that the Convention applies to those charged with criminal offences.[41] The whole point of the anti-social behaviour order is to circumvent this, or at least to press the point as far as it can go. Thus the Government promoted the measure as a way of avoiding the 'problem' of the criminal process: an application is made to a court under civil procedure, and if

---

[37] See, e.g. the critique by M. Tonry, *Punishment and Politics* (2004), Ch. 4.

[38] Law Com No 267, *Double Jeopardy and Prosecution Appeals* (2001).

[39] Home Office, *Speaking Up for Justice* (1998).

[40] For a detailed account of the background to the 1999 Act and related legislation, see P. Rock, *Constructing Victims' Rights: the Home Office, New Labour and Victims* (2004).

[41] *Engel v Netherlands* (1979) 1 EHRR 647; see generally B. Emmerson and A. Ashworth, *Human Rights and Criminal Justice* (2001), Ch.4.

they find evidence of anti-social behaviour they may make an order imposing conditions on the defendant (sometimes more than ten conditions) restricting his behaviour in the coming years. Breach of an order is a criminal offence carrying up to six months' imprisonment in a magistrates' court or up to five years in the Crown Court. Although the House of Lords held that the standard of proof in the civil proceedings is so high as to be indistinguishable from the criminal standard, the main thrust of its decision was that the Government had succeeded in its circumvention and that the proceedings for making an order are not to be treated as criminal.[42] While that decision is the subject of an application to Strasbourg, it appears that the Government has been able to by-pass the protections for criminal charges and to open up a way of dealing with crimes (many orders being made in respect of conduct that is clearly criminal, not simply non-criminal nuisances) that avoids the safeguards. The same tendency is evident in other preventive orders that it is possible for courts to make (e.g. risk of sexual harm orders under the Sexual Offences Act 2003) without proof of an offence having been committed.[43]

These developments highlight two recent tendencies affecting the criminal process. The first concerns the slippage between criminal and civil procedures. Not too long ago it was a mark of enlightenment to suggest that some forms of misconduct should be taken out of the criminal law and dealt with only through civil processes. Now it seems that that route is being exploited as a means of avoiding the protections of criminal procedure, while ensuring that, by means of making breach of the civil order an offence of strict liability with a high maximum penalty, severe sanctions are available. The second and related tendency is the increased focus on risk, and not just objective risk but also subjectively perceived risk of harm. Many of the preventive orders that can now be made—in particular, risk of sexual harm orders, anti-social behaviour orders—respond to contemporary insecurities about the risks we face and, more particularly, the risks that some people think they face (since prediction in these matters is a difficult task).

The continual process of review and reform has not abated in the new century. The year 2001 saw the publication of the Auld review of the criminal courts.[44] The remit of the Auld review was, to say the least, wide ranging. Yet, unlike the Runciman Commission, the task was given to a single person with relatively little opportunity to commission research on the problems he was meant to solve. Some parts of the report did not break new ground. The mode of trial issue was again considered, with Auld broadly endorsing the Runciman and Narey proposals. Auld's main recommendation was for a unified criminal court with three levels of jurisdiction, a proposal that has not survived. The report also contains a mass of detailed recommendations on aspects of evidence and criminal procedure, including prosecution appeals, double jeopardy,

---

[42] *Clingham v Kensington and Chelsea LBC* [2003] 1 AC 787.

[43] See further A. Ashworth, 'Social Control and "Anti-Social Behaviour": the subversion of Human Rights?', (2004) 120 LQR 263.

[44] *Review of the Criminal Courts of England and Wales: Report* by Rt. Hon. Lord Justice Auld (2001).

disclosure and several aspects of case management. It was Auld who recommended the transfer of the power to charge suspects from the police to the CPS. The Auld report also contained significant proposals on jury trial, including recommendations for trial by judge alone in serious and complex fraud cases and in other cases in which a defendant so elects. There was some indication during the inquiry that the Government had already made its mind up about certain issues to which Auld's proposals could have made little difference.[45]

Shortly after the publication of the Auld report (and of the Halliday report on sentencing, also commissioned by the Government), the world was rocked by the events of 11 September 2001. The British Government, like its American counterpart, was not slow in coming forward with new legislation extending the powers of the State in many directions. Although the Terrorism Act 2000 had consolidated and extended state powers in respect of persons suspected of 'terrorist' activities,[46] the Anti-Terrorism, Crime and Security Act 2001 introduced sweeping powers to detain without trial persons labelled as 'suspected international terrorists,' in respect of which it was necessary for the Government to enter a derogation from Article 5 of the European Convention on Human Rights. In a landmark decision, the House of Lords has held that these provisions and the derogation from Article 5 are incompatible with the Convention.[47] It is not yet clear what the Government's response to this will be.

Reforms of the general criminal process did not cease while terrorism dominated public discussion. On the contrary, the Government pressed ahead with a number of schemes—notably two that tested the co-ordination of different parts of the system, the Street Crimes Initiative in early 2002[48] and various schemes targeted at persistent or prolific offenders. Some months after the Auld report, the Government published its plans on criminal justice reform in a White Paper, *Justice for All*.[49] The proposed reforms were presented as part of an ambitious plan to modernize the criminal justice system and include changes to the jurisdiction of magistrates' courts, major reform of the double jeopardy rules, provisions allowing trials without juries in the Crown Court in various circumstances, as well as very significant changes to the rules of evidence. Some of the recommendations in the Auld report, though not those relating to the three-tier unified criminal court, were incorporated into the White Paper's proposals. Most of these reforms were enacted in the Criminal Justice Act 2003 and the Courts Act 2003—the reforms relating to the rights of victims of crime are to be found in the Domestic Violence, Crime and Victims Act 2004. At the level of political rhetoric, one interesting aspect of the debates surrounding the Criminal Justice Act is

---

[45] A number of reform proposals were revealed in *Criminal Justice: The Way Ahead* (2001), published six months before Auld reported. See also 'Blunkett Plans Big Working Changes for Police' *The Guardian*, 21 June 2001.

[46] For a general assessment, see C. Walker, 'Terrorism and Criminal Justice—Past, Present and Future', [2004] Crim LR 311.

[47] *A v Secretary of State for Home Affairs* [2004] *The Times*, 17 December.

[48] For a summary, see [2002] Crim LR 851.   [49] Home Office, 2002.

a reversal of the traditional positions of the Conservative and Labour parties with respect to criminal justice. While Labour has presented its reforms in the language of modernization and the promotion of victims' interests, the Conservative opposition has on occasion stressed principles such as the double jeopardy rule and trial by jury as important protections for defendants against the might of the State.[50]

The pace of criminal process reform seems unlikely to abate, and in mid-2004 there was discussion of a new agency called the Serious and Organised Crime Agency, together with the publication of a further White Paper calling for special measures and special procedures in respect of those suspected of a particular group of offences.[51] Among the many points raised are the need for new powers to compel suspects and witnesses to answer questions relating to organized crime—as has become typical, the White Paper offers no evidence that such measures would be effective, and refers, without analysis, to decisions of the European Court of Human Rights on compulsory questioning and the privilege against self-incrimination. It also claims that there is a need for changes in pre-trial and trial procedures in order to prevent tactical ploys by the defence in this type of case—again, without evidence that this is happening, or that it is the fault of the defence rather than inadequate prosecution preparation, or why it is that fewer people are willing to give evidence for the prosecution. This White Paper simply confirms the current trend of gung-ho proposals for which the public are not given proper evidence or proper analysis of the issues.[52]

1.4 PROCESS AND SYSTEM

The overview of criminal process reform sketched in the preceding paragraphs has two goals. One is to familiarize readers with some of the major reports and pieces of legislation which will be discussed in later chapters. The other is to give some sense of the forces which shape criminal justice policy. The reform process is often event-driven, with proposals responding to particular problems in the criminal process which have gained publicity. The *Confait* case led on to Philips and PACE; the Birmingham Six and other miscarriage of justice cases led to Runciman and the Criminal Appeal Act 1995. At times this can make the reform process seem somewhat haphazard: if the failed prosecution of the suspects in the Stephen Lawrence case had not received the media attention that it did, it seems unlikely that the double jeopardy rule would have been the subject of provisions in the Criminal Justice Act 2003. It would be wrong, however, to suggest that there is some simple causal process whereby a failing in the system leads to reform. The account above has drawn attention to the

---

[50] 'Tories and Lib Dems Home in on Civil Rights' *The Guardian*, 13 November 2002.

[51] Home Office, *One Step Ahead: a 21st century strategy to Defeat Organised Crime* (Cm 6167 of 2004).

[52] For a general critique of this Government's reluctance to set out the evidence (although pre-dating this particular White Paper), see Tonry, above, n 37, Chs 1 and 2.

increasingly politically charged climate in which reforms of the criminal process take place. Both major political parties seek to sell their criminal justice policies to the electorate; there is an important populist element in the way in which criminal justice policy is framed. The shared assumption of the parties seems to be that being seen to be tough on crime, and claiming to promote the interests of victims rather than defendants, will bring electoral success. This assumption plays an important part in moulding the criminal process as it undergoes a seemingly continual round of reforms.

It will be evident that we refer to the criminal process, rather than to 'the criminal justice system.' This is because it is not a 'system' in the sense of a set of co-ordinated decision making bodies. Even from the broad survey above it will be apparent that many groups working within criminal justice are relatively autonomous and enjoy considerable discretion. None the less, the inappropriateness of the term 'system' should not be allowed to obscure the practical interdependence of the various agencies.[53] Many depend on other agencies for their case-load or for their information, and decisions taken by one agency can impinge on those taken by others. Thus, to take a few examples, the Crown Prosecution Service depends almost entirely on the police for the information on which it must take its decisions. Those CPS decisions in turn affect the case-load of the courts, and may constrain the powers of magistrates' courts and of defendants to determine mode of trial. Many other examples of interdependence and influence will be found throughout the book, and in the first section of this chapter it was emphasized that decisions should be viewed in this context rather than as discrete and objectively based determinations.

References to systems and interdependence are, however, very much in the managerial mode. The criminal process impinges directly on victims, suspects, and defendants. It impinges on them in the form of one or more contacts and decisions. A defendant who has been questioned by the police, charged, kept in police custody, remanded by the court, perhaps offered a plea bargain, and then tried in court is already likely to feel 'punished' irrespective of whether a guilty verdict and sentence follow. A person who is acquitted after such a sequence of events may well feel 'punished' by the process to which he or she has been subjected, even if relieved at the outcome. Of course this is a misuse of the term punishment, which is properly confined in the present context to sentences imposed by courts after findings of guilt. But it accords with the results of American research by Malcolm Feeley, encapsulated in the title of his book *The Process is the Punishment*.[54] Suspects and defendants often feel that the way in which they are treated is equivalent to punishment, in the sense that it inflicts on them deprivations (of liberty, of reputation) similar to those resulting from a sentence. This is particularly true for defendants who have been remanded in custody, and may flow from a single decision such as the decision to prosecute. Alternatively it may be a consequence, not so much of decisions taken in their case,

---

[53] For discussion, see the essays by Pullinger and by Feeney in D. Moxon (ed), *Managing Criminal Justice* (1985).

[54] M. Feeley, *The Process is the Punishment* (1979).

but rather of what they regard as disrespect for their rights by the officials dealing with them. For present purposes, it is sufficient to make the point that the criminal process is a process to which defendants are subjected by officials who have considerable *de facto* power as well as the power of law behind them. It amounts to an exercise of State power—necessary, as part of the political system, but no less real for that. It is therefore appropriate to consider proper standards, fair procedures, accountability, and other issues relevant to dealings between the State and individual citizens.

It is not just defendants but also victims and witnesses whose interests should be protected. There is no shortage of empirical research findings that victims have been and are being treated in the criminal process in ways that can be described as 'punishment'. In the language of victimologists, victims who report crimes often experience 'secondary victimization' at the hands of police, prosecutors, and courts.[55] While some steps have been taken to reduce these effects (for example) by improving techniques of police questioning, by granting anonymity to victims of certain offences, and by introducing video links into courts, there is little doubt that some victims still suffer psychologically and socially from their involvement in the criminal process, in addition to the crime itself. Although efforts are being made to reduce this secondary victimization—for example, through the work of the Witness Service and the provisions of the Domestic Violence, Crime and Victims Act 2004—our point here is that the criminal process can be said to be a process to which victims of crime, too, are subjected by officials.

If one adds to these processual elements the fact that the one 'temporizing' decision—remand before trial—may result in loss of liberty, and also the effects that dispositive decisions such as conditional cautions may have (as a form of sentence without trial), it is evident that there are many elements of the criminal process that call for clear and careful justification. We now move, in Chapter 2, towards an exploration of the sources of justification and of critique of the English criminal process. The examination of principles continues in Chapter 3, where we look particularly at ethical issues in relation to the working practices of criminal justice professionals. Those general chapters are then followed by a sequence of chapters on particular stages of the criminal process—questioning; gathering evidence; diversion; charging and prosecutorial review; remands; pre-trial rights and duties; plea changing; trial procedures; and appeals.

---

[55] See L. Zedner, 'Victims', in M. Maguire, R. Morgan and R. Reiner (eds), *Oxford Handbook of Criminology* (3rd ed., 2002), 428–432.

2

TOWARDS A FRAMEWORK FOR EVALUATION

What should we expect of a criminal process? What aims should it pursue and what values ought it to respect? In answering these questions the links between the different parts and aspects of the criminal justice system must be kept in view. The purpose and scope of the criminal law itself have a bearing on pretrial matters such as powers of arrest and even plea negotiation. The rules of evidence at trial may place some limits on the investigative powers of the police and other enforcement agencies. And the principles of sentencing are strongly related both to the criteria for diversion from the criminal process and to the system of plea negotiation. This chapter will keep those wider relationships in view while focusing on a framework for evaluating criminal procedure, chiefly in relation to pre-trial justice.

2.1 A THEORY OF CRIMINAL PROCESS

The preceding chapter has provided an outline of the criminal process. It depicts a sequential process, with suspects being identified by the police and the case then moving on to further stages. At various points suspects may drop out of the system, perhaps because the evidence is thought not to be strong enough, or it is decided that the case is suitable for diversion, or because the CPS decides on review that the case should be discontinued. The process potentially continues up to trial, which may result in conviction or acquittal. After trial, there are further stages of the process, involving appeals. More now needs to be said on what this process is about and what values should underpin it.

The sort of theory we aim to develop here is a normative one. We are trying to develop a framework which can be used to understand and evaluate the criminal process; this is different to the descriptive account of the criminal process which was given in Chapter 1. Account must be taken of the complexity of the criminal process as an institution that embodies a number of different aims and values. Another problem is that the criminal process varies between jurisdictions: some systems are inquisitorial and some adversarial (though it is not easy to pin down what these terms mean); some use juries as fact-finders and some rely on professional judges. Perhaps it would be possible to develop a single normative model of criminal process that would have sufficient detail to show that certain actual criminal processes (perhaps all adversarial ones) are in some way deficient. This would be an ambitious enterprise, and there must be doubts as to whether it would actually be possible to develop so detailed a theory—not least because some aspects of the criminal process (such as the type of fact-finder used) may reflect values which have relatively little to do with the criminal process itself. Institutions such as the jury may exist for historical and political reasons which make them more appropriate for some jurisdictions than for others.

One way of proceeding would therefore be to draw a distinction between internal and external values in the criminal process. Internal values would be the core values of criminal process, ones which all systems of criminal process should embody. One would expect such a theory to be relatively thin and lacking in detail. Something could then be said about the external values which, in a particular jurisdiction such as England and Wales, might fill in the details of this thin account. There is some merit in this approach, but there are also problems. One is that it may prove difficult to distinguish between internal and external values. The criminal process is part of the wider criminal justice system, and there are many theories of criminal justice. A theory of criminal justice may be related to some wider political theory, at which stage there are further choices of approach to be made. The situation is rather like a set of Russian dolls, where the core values of the political theory at the centre play a role in shaping the outer layers such as the criminal process. It may therefore be difficult to find agreement on internal values of criminal process that may be claimed to apply across all jurisdictions.

Because of this problem, we should say a little more about the basic values we believe should play a role in shaping the criminal process. The thin, internal account we start with reflects the values of a liberal state, where State power is limited and citizens are viewed as bearers of rights. In terms of criminal justice—and this will become important as we add detail to the thin theory—we subscribe to a retributive, or desert-based, rationale for punishment. On this view the institution of punishment is justified by the moral appropriateness of visiting censure on citizens for crimes as wrongs, and the need to reinforce that with sanctions in order that the censure be taken seriously. It is appropriate that the State should maintain a system for enforcement and adjudication, so as to ensure a public, authoritative and consistent approach to the imposition of censure. But a proper relationship between the coercive State and its citizens as rational and rights-bearing subjects means that a punishment should always be proportionate to the seriousness of the crime, and not disproportionate so as to fail to respect the offender.[1] Those principles of proportionality and respect for the suspect/defendant/offender as a rational rights-bearing subject should also underpin the criminal process. A criminal process based on deterrence, or on principles of restorative justice, might differ significantly from one based on desert.[2]

---

[1] For elaboration, see A. von Hirsch and A. Ashworth, *The Proportionate Sentence* (2005), Ch. 2.

[2] See further part 5 of this chapter, below.

What, then, are the purposes of the criminal process and what values should it reflect? One simple point can be made at the outset. The laws, regulations and institutions that make up the criminal process provide a set of rules, standards and areas of discretion for decision making. These rules or procedures have an immediate value, no matter what their content. Rules are intended to guide decision makers and to exert some control over their discretion. In a complex institution such as the criminal process, which involves many different actors, procedure has a co-ordinating function. It allows different decision makers to work together by giving them some knowledge of what other actors will have done. Set procedures also allow for transparency: they allow rules to be made accessible to the public as well as to the actors in the process. Thus procedure should serve the rule of law, by making decisions more consistent, more predictable, and less arbitrary. These simple points do not say anything about the contents of the rules and standards; they merely suggest the basic value of having some set of procedures. This emphasis on proper procedures rather than arbitrariness lies, as we shall see, at the core of the European Convention on Human Rights.

Moving beyond this, it is obvious that the criminal process is part of the State response to crime. There are, however, many ways in which the State responds to crime which do not invoke criminal procedure. Much of the State's strategy against crime is preventive: it includes things as diverse as education, street lighting, and the maintenance of a visible police presence. The criminal process (as we understand the term, for the purposes of this book) is far narrower than this. It is the mechanism that allows the State to apply the criminal law to its citizens. It is only invoked when it is suspected that a crime has been committed. Again, though, the State can respond to suspected crime in many ways. Minor offences may be ignored, or met with a warning. Some offences, such as driving offences, are dealt with by way of fixed penalty notices. The point is even more obvious where criminal justice agencies other than the police are involved. Agencies such as the Health and Safety Executive often respond to breaches of the criminal law through processes designed to ensure future compliance; prosecution is only used as a last resort.[3] We will say more about these responses to crime in Chapter 6; the discussion of 'dispositive values' in Part 6 of this chapter is also relevant. That many of these responses are said to involve 'diversion' from the criminal process suggests that there is only a minimal sense in which the criminal process is involved. Nevertheless, the principles underlying diversion are important, in part because of the light they shed on those cases which do enter the criminal process more fully. The full criminal process becomes involved where a relatively formal response to crime is taken: where—to concentrate on the central case of the police— the police respond to a suspected offence with a view to possible prosecution. The possible end result of the process is adjudicative: a trial. Whether a trial will result will depend on many other factors. As has been emphasized, many suspects drop out of the process for a variety of reasons. But what matters is the potential, not the probability. Criminal procedure is a process that may lead to a trial.

[3] K. Hawkins, *Law as Last Resort* (2003).

This characterization of criminal procedure enables something to be said about its purposes. The function of criminal procedure is to regulate and facilitate the preparation of cases for trial; this suggests that the purposes of criminal trials will determine in a little more detail the functions of criminal procedure. The twin objects of the criminal trial are accurately to determine whether or not a person has committed a particular criminal offence and to do so fairly. This suggests that one important focus of criminal procedure is, broadly speaking, investigation. Criminal procedure should provide mechanisms to regulate the gathering of evidence so as to allow adjudicative decisions to be made accurately. Note that this account is already being moulded by some of the presuppositions identified earlier. The principle of proportionality in sentencing makes it especially important to obtain accurate information about the offence, so that the sentence can reflect the gravity of wrongdoing. Such detailed information might not be so important, for example, in a criminal process based on principles of restorative justice.

An investigation into a suspected criminal offence is unlikely to get very far unless the police are given certain coercive powers over suspects. Justifications may therefore be found for giving the police various powers enabling them, for example, to detain suspects in the police station and to take fingerprints and DNA samples from them. Trials, as enquiries into a defendant's guilt or innocence and as venues for sentence, are likely to be most effective if the defendant is present. This gives some basis for other coercive powers, such as the power to remand in custody, to ensure that the defendant is present at trial, and powers to summon witnesses to attend trial.

An obvious, but important, point should be made at this stage. Although criminal procedure exists to ensure a particular end result—an effective criminal trial—it is not like a mechanized assembly line in a car factory. Whether or not an assembly line is good can be judged largely in terms of its end results: whether the car it produces is of good quality. It does not matter how the metal, plastic, paint etc. is treated during the process of achieving that end. Criminal procedure is different because it deals with people. It matters how people are treated. They should be treated with dignity, in other words, their rights should be respected. Note that we are again drawing here on the wider principles of justice within which our account of the criminal process is embedded. Given that effective criminal procedure requires that prosecuting agencies be given coercive powers, it seems that a key facet of criminal procedure will be the provision of limits on those powers to ensure that the human interests connected to the respect for dignity are not unnecessarily infringed. This is in fact one of the central problems of criminal procedure: the need to reconcile a process which will bring cases to effective trial with the protection of human rights and the fundamental requirement of a fair trial. More will be said about the factors in play here later; for the moment, it is more helpful to concentrate on the relatively abstract theory of the criminal process which is being developed.

The recognition that criminal procedure infringes human interests has several implications. If cases could be brought to effective trial without affecting human interests, then it might make sense to bring all cases to trial in order to enable some definitive determination of criminal liability. However, because human interests are much affected, one function of criminal procedure should be to provide for the filtering of cases, to make sure that they are not kept in the system without good reason. Waiting for trial imposes considerable stress on people, especially those remanded in custody. The criminal process also deals with people suspected of crimes of widely varying levels of seriousness. In the least serious cases the principle of proportionality suggests that the pressures and effects of a trial may not be justified. Here, again, we can see why the topic of diversion is important in an account of the criminal process. However, the need for filtering is not just to ensure that coercive procedures are not applied more widely than they should be, or to minimize the considerable stress suffered by people awaiting trial. Filtering is also important because trials, by their nature, are fallible and somewhat unpredictable; sometimes they produce erroneous verdicts. The danger that a mistake will be made at trial provides a further reason for filtering cases during the pre-trial stage, to remove cases where there is little evidence that the suspect has committed an offence. Moreover, efficiency, the costs of procedure and trials, provide further reasons for filtering out cases which do not merit prosecution.

A convincing normative theory of the criminal process needs to be properly connected to facts about actual criminal processes. Thus, reference to the stress of waiting for trial was made in order to explain the importance of filtering cases which are in the system. There are other facts about the system which it is important to take into account. In Chapter 1, reference was made to miscarriages of justice which have played a role in shaping the system. Familiarity with these cases suggests that sometimes the police are over-eager to secure the conviction of those they believe to be guilty. Police officers have been prepared to put considerable pressure on suspects in order to extract confessions from them—at one time the use of violence was not uncommon, whereas now various interrogation techniques (including deception) may be deployed. It is known that suspects sometimes confess falsely.[4] Other sources of evidence too are fallible: eyewitness evidence is an example.[5] The frailty of such types of evidence can be difficult to detect at trial. A primary function of criminal procedure is to provide rules to ensure that reliable evidence is produced which can form the basis of an effective trial. Criminal procedure should therefore provide safeguards against especially unreliable forms of evidence. Concern for human dignity is an additional reason for this: aggressive or violent questioning infringes legitimate human interests.

This theory of criminal procedure is trial-centred; it assumes that preparation of cases for possible trial is the principal objective of the investigative and pre-trial stages. It was suggested above that the objects of the criminal trial are accurately and fairly to determine whether or not a person has committed a particular criminal offence. But this may be too simple; saying a little more about trials generates a slightly richer theory of criminal process. Accurate decision making is an important

---

[4] Royal Commission on Criminal Justice, *Report* (1993), 57, and Ch. 4 below.   [5] See Ch. 5.3 below.

function of criminal trials, but complete accuracy is unattainable: trials are fallible.
Of the two sorts of errors a criminal trial can make—acquitting a guilty person or
convicting an innocent person—the latter is more serious, since it involves a mon-
strous wrong against an individual whereas the former does not, although it reflects
badly on the system and may reduce the community's confidence in it. To protect
against convicting the innocent, a heavy burden of proof is placed on the prosecution.
The prosecution must prove its case beyond reasonable doubt. The implication of this
is that, all else being equal, of the errors that criminal courts make, more will involve
acquitting the guilty than convicting the innocent. Criminal trials thus incorporate an
error preference; one type of error is preferred to another. This is a cardinal value of
the criminal process. This might be thought to have important implications for pre-
trial criminal procedure. Perhaps this error preference should mould the pre-trial
process just as it moulds the trial. In fact, it is not obvious that it should, and
one should actually be wary of seeing criminal procedure as an obstacle course the
purpose of which is to make it difficult for the prosecution to secure a conviction.[6]
There are features of English criminal procedure which might appear to apply the
error preference in the pre-trial stage: the rules protecting defendants against false
confession or mistaken eyewitness identification, for example. But a perfectly good
explanation for these rules was suggested above: that they help to ensure an effective
trial by safeguarding the reliability of evidence. The important filtering function was
also explained without reference to error preference. While it is true that the decision
by the prosecution whether or not to continue a prosecution is informed by the high
standard of proof at trial, this is due to the predictive nature of the CPS decision at
this stage which necessarily refers to the standard of proof at trial.[7]

The trial is not just about accurate fact-finding: as we have insisted, principles of
fairness lie at the heart of the trial in particular, as well as the criminal process in
general. Thus, the trial is not just a diagnostic procedure, of which the sole purpose
is to establish as accurately as possible (subject to the standard of proof) what happened. As Antony Duff argues, the trial should also be seen as a communicative
process, whereby the State tries to let the convicted defendant know, in terms which he
can understand, why he is to be subjected to the censure of the criminal sanction. In
Duff's terms, the trial is about calling the defendant to account.[8] Another influential
strand of commentary on the criminal trial makes a similar point in terms of legitimacy. It is said that it is important for the trial verdict to be legitimate, and this is taken
to have consequences for the use of devices such as entrapment in the pre-trial stage of
criminal procedure. Ian Dennis goes so far as to say that the production of legitimate
verdicts is the key aim of the criminal trial, and that this takes priority over—although
it usually coincides with—the aim of securing accurate verdicts.[9]

---

[6] This obstacle course depiction of the pre-trial process is one problem with Packer's due process model,
discussed further below.

[7] See Ch. 7 below.   [8] R.A. Duff, *Trials and Punishments* (1986).

[9] I.H. Dennis, *The Law of Evidence* (2nd ed., 2002), Ch. 2.

We would certainly endorse the view that the trial is not simply about accurate fact-finding. As with our account of the criminal process as a whole, we would stress the concomitant aim of respecting rights and other important values. We revisit this issue in the context of the exclusion of improperly obtained evidence in Chapter 11. For the moment, we suggest that there is some reason to be sceptical of the legitimacy-based account of the criminal trial, and therefore of accounts of the criminal process more generally which stress legitimacy. Legitimacy is a rather elusive concept: once one has excluded the most obviously problematic senses of legitimacy (where legitimacy is seen in terms of whatever the general public desires at a particular point in time[10]) it is not obvious how legitimacy differs from an account which emphasizes accuracy and respect for rights. And there is a danger in legitimacy-based accounts: they seem to be in some way consequentialist, with legitimacy being the value to be maximized. This might allow the argument that it does not matter whether the criminal process reaches accurate outcomes, or respects the rights of defendants and victims, so long as it *appears* to do so. On our account, reality is more important than appearances. Duff's account is in important ways different from this. The claim that the criminal trial is about calling the defendant to account reflects a particular theory of punishment.[11] On our account of the criminal process, the purposes of criminal process can only be understood in the light of a theory of punishment, retributive justice being the theory which grounds our particular account. The concept of calling the defendant to account is not necessarily incompatible with retributivism and desert theory,[12] and therefore Duff's communicative notion of the trial may not be in tension with our own. Moreover, this notion of the trial might add to an understanding of the wider criminal process: one of the most obviously coercive aspects of the criminal process occurs when defendants are remanded in custody prior to trial in order to ensure that they attend trial. If the trial were a simple fact-finding process, this practice might be particularly difficult to justify, for it might be possible to hold a reasonably effective trial in the defendant's absence. If, however, the trial is seen as an essentially communicative process, the power to remand in custody may be, at least in theory, somewhat easier to justify.

An obvious objection to a trial-centred theory of criminal process is that in reality the criminal process in England and Wales (and, increasingly, in other jurisdictions too) is centred round trial-avoidance.[13] The guilty plea is the normal method of disposing of criminal cases. Guilty pleas are discussed in detail in Chapter 10, and the analysis there is relevant to the brief response to the 'trial avoidance' objection offered here. Guilty pleas do not avoid trial completely. Bearing in mind the retributive

---

[10] 'Public attitude legitimacy', in Mirfield's terms: P. Mirfield, *Silence, Confessions and Improperly Obtained Evidence* (1997), 23–28.

[11] For the most recent account, see R.A. Duff, *Punishment, Communication and Community* (2001), Ch. 3.

[12] A.E. Bottoms, 'Five Puzzles in von Hirsch's Theory of Punishment', in A. Ashworth and M. Wasik (eds), *Fundamentals of Sentencing Theory* (1998).

[13] M. Langer, 'From Legal Transplants to Legal Translations: the Globalization of Plea-Bargaining and the Americanization Thesis in Criminal Procedure', (2004) *Harvard Int. L.J.* 1.

background to our account of criminal process, an important function of the trial is sentencing, and the court still plays a role as a sentencing venue after a guilty plea. Further, the dependence on guilty pleas does not undermine the importance of the criminal process as an investigative mechanism. A desert-based theory of sentencing emphasizes that sentences should be proportional to wrongdoing, which makes accurate investigation important, even if there will be no contested trial. In fact, one of the problems of the system of guilty pleas in England and Wales is that it may allow sentencing to be carried out without accurate knowledge of the facts of the offence: the gravity of the offending may be down-played as part of a charge-bargain, or a defendant may plead guilty when innocent in order to take advantage of a sentence discount. But the emphasis on trials, and accurate fact-finding, allows us to criticize the emphasis on guilty pleas for these very reasons. That is one of the themes of Chapter 10.

2.2 INTERNAL AND EXTERNAL VALUES

We have argued that the purposes of the criminal process are accurate determinations and fair procedures at all stages, and have suggested that the criminal trial should be regarded as the focus of the process, even though the majority of cases do not go to trial. Our theory is partly instrumental, giving an account of the sorts of things the criminal process will need to do and the sorts of powers (to arrest and detain suspects, to filter cases) that will be needed to achieve these ends. But just as important are the values—respecting human rights—that should mould the way in which these ends are achieved. The theory is thin and relatively generic—an 'internal' theory in the sense outlined above. We now turn to consider external values, and how they inform a theory of criminal process.

Some external values are reasonably jurisdictionally specific. An example, mentioned earlier, is the use of lay fact-finders in the English criminal process (lay magistrates and juries). English criminal procedure is fairly unique in the extent to which it relies on lay fact-finders.[14] Many other systems of criminal procedure make some use of lay fact-finders, whereas some do not use them at all. Much has been written about the value that lay justice—particularly trial by jury—brings to the criminal process. The point of identifying lay justice as an external value is to suggest that those systems which rely on it do so partly for particular historical and political reasons, and that there is not necessarily anything deficient, as systems of criminal procedure, in those systems which do not. Perhaps such jurisdictions can be criticized on other grounds: perhaps, as polities, they accord insufficient value to citizen involvement in decision making. But this is a much wider point than one about criminal procedure.

Another example of an external value in criminal procedure is adversarialism. Although the classification of systems of criminal procedure is a complex topic, the

---

[14] S. Doran and R. Glenn, *Lay Involvement in Adjudication* (2000).

basic point is that adversarial systems, such as those operating in the UK and the US, give a far greater role to the parties in developing the case and conducting the trial than do 'inquisitorial' systems, such as those operating in continental Europe. In some ways, these different systems reflect competing political philosophies. In French criminal procedure, for example, the role of the State in protecting its citizens' interests is emphasized. Giving too great a role to defence lawyers is seen as disruptive and potentially inegalitarian, and also as something for which there is little need because the State can be trusted to look out for the accused.[15] This sort of view is anathema in Anglo-American criminal procedure. Damaška has also suggested that Anglo-American criminal procedure differs from continental criminal procedure in the extent to which it is 'policy-implementing'. An example is that in England and the United States, criminal procedure is prepared to forego effective fact-finding at trial, either to uphold the integrity of the system or in the hope of exerting some influence over the way in which the police gather evidence. Unfairly or illegally obtained evidence may thus be ruled inadmissible at trial. Continental systems, historically at least, have tended to see control over the police as being better exercised in other ways.[16] This example will be discussed in more detail in Chapter 11. For now the point is that the way the criminal process responds to improperly obtained evidence seems best identified as an external value: there is nothing in the theory of criminal process itself which tells us whether or not courts should exclude improperly obtained evidence.

We have emphasized the importance of rights in this account of criminal process. The fact that the criminal process should respect rights is an internal aspect of criminal process, but the content of the rights which the criminal process should respect is often best seen as being set externally to the criminal process. A theory of criminal process cannot always tell us very much about what rights people have. While some rights are specific to the criminal process (the presumption of innocence is an example) many rights which place important constraints on criminal process (the right to bodily integrity and the right to respect for private life, for example) have significance well beyond the criminal process. But saying that such rights are determined externally to the criminal process is not the same as saying that the rights are jurisdictionally specific. While there may be some things which we refer to as rights which have a particular significance in certain jurisdictions (the right to legal advice in the police station, for example[17]), there are many rights which any criminal process should respect. This is reflected in the fact that many international human rights documents include rights

---

[15] See J. Hodgson, 'Human Rights and French Criminal Justice: Opening the Door to Pre-Trial Defence Rights', in S. Halliday and P. Schmidt (eds), *Human Rights Brought Home: Socio-Economic Perspectives on Human Rights in the National Context* (2004); J.L. Sauron, 'Les Vertus de l'inquisitoire, ou l'Etat au service des droits' (1990) 55 *Pouvoirs* 53.

[16] See R. Frase, 'France', in C. Bradley (ed), *Criminal Procedure: A Worldwide Study* (1999), 161–162; C. Bradley, 'The Emerging International Consensus as to Criminal Procedure Rules', (1993) 14 *Michigan J. Int. Law* 171.

[17] The European Court of Human Rights has held that the right of access to legal advice takes on particular importance when inferences may be drawn from silence at police interview: *Murray v United Kingdom* (1996) 22 EHRR 29. On the different attitude to legal advice in France, see n 15 above.

which have immense significance to the criminal process. A good way of adding more detail to our so far rather thin account of the criminal process is to examine these documents and the rights contained in them. In the next section, then, the discussion will be more descriptive. We will concentrate on the European Convention on Human Rights, which has particular significance for the criminal process in England and Wales and therefore provides a foundation for the analysis of the criminal process in the chapters which follow. The material remains relevant to a normative account of criminal process, however, for it identifies the most important of the rights which should shape the criminal process. The discussion also starts to analyse the way in which we should think about rights by showing some of the problems in the claim that rights can be balanced against other values.

2.3   FUNDAMENTAL RIGHTS AND THE EUROPEAN CONVENTION

(a)   HUMAN RIGHTS OBLIGATIONS

So far as this country's international obligations go, there are several international declarations of human rights to which we are subject. Three of them may be mentioned before we go on to consider the European Convention in detail. One is the International Covenant on Civil and Political Rights, drawn up by the United Nations and monitored by the ICCPR Human Rights Committee. The extent and formulation of rights in the ICCPR differ in some respects from those in the European Convention on Human Rights, which is considered in detail below. Although less frequently discussed in this country, the ICCPR remains a document of some importance,[18] not least because reference has been made to it (in view of its wider international status) when interpreting the European Convention.[19]

A second instrument of importance is the United Nations Convention on the Rights of the Child. This does not primarily have reference to criminal proceedings, but it does declare a number of rights of children who are either defendants in criminal cases or sentenced following a finding of guilt.[20] As with the ICCPR, the Convention on the Rights of the Child has been used by the Strasbourg Court as a source of rights applicable to young children.[21]

A third instrument, yet to exert its force, is the Charter of Fundamental Rights approved by the European Union in 2000, brought into force in 2003, and forming

---

[18] See the essays in D.J. Harris and S. Joseph (eds), *The International Covenant on Civil and Political Rights and United Kingdom Law* (1995).

[19] See, e.g. *John Murray v UK* (1996) 22 EHRR 29.

[20] G. van Bueren, *The International Law on the Rights of the Child* (1998).

[21] See, e.g. *V and T v UK* (2000) 30 EHRR 121.

part of the Treaty establishing a Constitution for Europe signed in Rome in 2004. This contains several Articles devoted to safeguards in the criminal justice system, some of which go further than those currently recognized under the Convention.[22]

Those three rights instruments should be kept in mind as we turn to the European Convention on Human Rights and Fundamental Freedoms, now the foremost authoritative source of rights in this country both generally and for the criminal process. The Convention was signed in 1950, ratified by the United Kingdom in 1951, and came into force in 1953. It has been ratified by all member states of the Council of Europe. Since 1966 the United Kingdom has allowed individual petition to Strasbourg. Thus any individual may make an application to the European Court of Human Rights, provided that domestic avenues of challenge have been exhausted. The Court will adjudicate on whether or not the complaint is admissible. Admissible cases are then heard by a section of the Court. If the Court rules against the member state, the State will usually alter the law so as to comply with the judgment, but there is no absolute obligation to do so. The Committee of Ministers monitors State responses to findings of the Court.

(b) THE HUMAN RIGHTS ACT 1998

The United Kingdom has been the subject of many adverse judgments in Strasbourg, and has been found by the Court to be in breach of the Convention in over forty cases in the last decade. One reason for this was that the British courts were unable to apply the Convention when hearing domestic cases. When the Labour Government was elected in 1997, it quickly adopted the view that it was frustrating, embarrassing, and unnecessary that individuals should have to go outside the UK to secure the enforcement of rights to which the British Government committed itself long ago. The Human Rights Act was passed in 1998, and came fully into force in 2000. For present purposes, there are four principal provisions. The first is s 6, which requires all courts and public authorities (such as the police and the CPS) to conform with the Convention in all their decisions and policies. Then comes s 3, which requires courts to interpret statutes so far as possible in a way that gives effect to Convention rights—a strong interpretive duty. Sections 3 and 6 should be read together with s 2, which requires courts to take account of the decisions of the Strasbourg Court. This does not require courts always to follow decisions of the Court in interpreting the Convention, although it does suggest that good reasons should be given for not doing so.[23] Unlike some constitutions such as that of the United States, the Convention does not (under the Human Rights Act) have priority over legislation. If a higher court finds that a UK statute cannot be interpreted so as to be compatible with the Convention, the court may make a 'declaration of incompatibility' under s 4; there is then provision for

---

[22] See A. Ward and S. Peers (eds), *The EU Charter of Fundamental Rights* (2004).

[23] As stated by the senior Law Lord, Lord Bingham, in *Anderson v Home Secretary* [2002] 4 All ER 1089, at [18].

the Government, if it wishes, to initiate a fast-track procedure for parliamentary amendment of legislation which falls foul of the Convention. We will note, at appropriate points in the following chapters, how the courts have adapted to the duties and powers given to them by the Human Rights Act.

(c) CONVENTION RIGHTS AND THE CRIMINAL PROCESS

For present purposes, a general overview of those Convention rights chiefly relevant to the criminal process will be given. Each of the relevant Articles will be set out, and a few illustrative comments added.

'Article 2   1. Everyone's right to life shall be protected by law. No one shall be deprived of his life intentionally save in the execution of a sentence of a court following his conviction of a crime for which this penalty is provided by law.

2. Deprivation of life shall not be regarded as inflicted in contravention of this Article when it results from the use of force which is no more than absolutely necessary:

(a) in defence of any person from unlawful violence;

(b) in order to effect a lawful arrest or to prevent the escape of a person lawfully detained;

(c) in action lawfully taken for the purpose of quelling a riot or insurrection.'

This Article's relevance here resides in paragraph 2(b) and its impact on the use of force in arrest or the prevention of escape. The leading Strasbourg case is *McCann v United Kingdom*.[24] An undercover team of specially trained soldiers were keeping three IRA members under surveillance in Gibraltar, in the belief that the latter were about to carry out a bombing. When they thought that the three were about to detonate the bomb, they shot and killed them. In fact there was no detonator and no bomb. The European Court of Human Rights found that the planning of the operation was so defective that it made the killings foreseeable, although avoidable, and that this breached the victims' right to life under Article 2.1. Controversially, the majority of the Court held that the shooting did not fall within the 'absolute necessity' exception in Article 2.2, and therefore held the UK in violation of the Article. Some years earlier in *Kelly v United Kingdom*,[25] the European Commission had held that the action of a soldier in shooting at a car that had failed to stop at a checkpoint in Northern Ireland, killing one of the occupants, was 'absolutely necessary . . . in order to effect an arrest.' Article 2 is not well drafted in this respect: it contains no reference to the purpose of the arrest, and fails to confront the obvious point that one cannot arrest a person who has just been killed.

'Article 3 No one shall be subjected to torture or to inhuman or degrading treatment or punishment.'

---

[24] (1996) 21 EHRR 97.
[25] (1993) 74 DR 139, on which see the critical discussion by Sir John Smith at (1994) *New LJ* 354.

Perhaps the best-known case on this Article is *Ireland v United Kingdom*,[26] in which the Court ruled that the notorious 'five techniques'[27] used in the interrogation of suspected terrorists by the authorities in Northern Ireland did not amount to 'torture', but did amount to 'inhuman and degrading treatment'. This Article is also relevant to the conditions in which people are detained on remand pending court proceedings: in one case the European Commission referred to 'deplorable overcrowding' in prison, but concluded that there was no inhuman treatment.[28] Since then, the Court has been developing the positive duties that flow from Article 3, holding the UK to account for failing to provide proper facilities for disabled prisoners[29] and for failing to provide proper medical care for prisoners who present a known risk of suicide.[30] One difficulty is that many of those in detention are unable to pursue claims in order to draw attention to the conditions, and so the European Committee on the Prevention of Torture and Inhuman and Degrading Treatment has been established, with authority to inspect the prisons and police stations of all member states. It has inspected British prisons on three occasions, and has made critical reports.[31]

'Article 5   1. Everyone has the right to liberty and security of person. No one shall be deprived of his liberty save in the following cases and in accordance with a procedure prescribed by law . . . c) the lawful arrest or detention of a person effected for the purpose of bringing him before the competent legal authority on reasonable suspicion of having committed an offence, or when it is reasonably considered necessary to prevent his committing an offence or fleeing after having done so . . .

2. Everyone who is arrested shall be informed promptly, in a language which he understands, of the reasons for his arrest and of any charge against him.

3. Everyone arrested or detained in accordance with the provisions of paragraph 1(c) of this Article shall be brought promptly before a judge or other officer authorised by law to exercise judicial power and shall be entitled to trial within a reasonable time or to release pending trial. Release may be conditioned by guarantee to appear for trial.

4. Everyone who is deprived of his liberty by arrest or detention shall be entitled to take proceedings by which the lawfulness of his detention shall be decided speedily by a court and his release ordered if the detention is not lawful.

5. Everyone who has been the victim of arrest or detention in contravention of the provisions of this Article shall have an enforceable right to compensation.'

This Article covers a great deal of ground, and has been developed considerably by the Court. Since one of its purposes is to guarantee the right to liberty, it has high relevance to those stages of the pre-trial process at which liberty is curtailed—i.e. arrest, remand by the police and by a court, and trial within a reasonable time. Although Article 5 does provide (circumscribed) exceptions to deal with detention for

---

[26] (1978) A.25.

[27] Wall standing, hooding, subjection to noise, deprivation of sleep, and deprivation of food and drink.

[28] *B. v United Kingdom* [1981] Com Rep 26.   [29] *Price v United Kingdom* (2001) 34 EHRR 53.

[30] *Keenan v United Kingdom, The Times*, 18 April 2001.

[31] R. Morgan, 'International Controls on Sentencing and Punishment' in M. Tonry and R. Frase (eds), *Sentencing and Sanctions in Western Countries* (2001), esp at 393–399.

those purposes, it makes no allowance for detention without charge or trial. For this reason the Government had to derogate from Article 5 of the Convention when Parliament enacted the Anti-Terrorism, Crime and Security Act 2001, sections 21–23 of which provide for the indefinite detention of persons certified to be 'suspected international terrorists'. The House of Lords has now held this provision and the derogation from Article 5 to be incompatible with the Convention,[32] and the Government's response to this is not yet known.

That apart, Article 5 does provide for the detention of a person on reasonable suspicion of having committed an offence. In the leading case of *Fox, Campbell and Hartley v United Kingdom*,[33] the Strasbourg Court held that:

'the exigencies of dealing with terrorist crime cannot justify stretching the notion of reasonableness to the point where the essence of the safeguard secured by Article 5(1)(c) is impaired.'

In that case the UK was held to have violated the Article, because the only grounds for arrest were that two of the three had previous convictions for terrorist offences. However, in *O'Hara v United Kingdom*,[34] the Court held that the requirement of reasonable suspicion was fulfilled when the police arrested the applicant on information received, even though that information was not revealed to the Court. Article 5 requires an arrestee to be brought promptly before a court, and in *Brogan v United Kingdom*,[35] the Court held that detention for longer than four days violated this provision. In order to determine whether it is justifiable to detain a defendant before trial, under Article 5(3), the Court has developed an extensive jurisprudence which emphasizes the presumption of liberty and the presumption of innocence, and which requires courts to avoid stereotypical reasoning (e.g. that someone with previous convictions will therefore commit offences if granted bail) and to assess each case on its facts.[36] The Court has also sought to place limits on the length of time for which a person may be detained before trial (in conjunction with the right to trial within a reasonable time under Article 6, below),[37] and has insisted on the importance of regular review of the continued justification for detention.[38]

'Article 6 1. In the determination of his civil rights and obligations or of any criminal charge against him, everyone is entitled to a fair and public hearing within a reasonable time by an independent and impartial tribunal established by law . . .
2. Everyone charged with a criminal offence shall be presumed innocent until proved guilty according to law.
3. Everyone charged with a criminal offence has the following minimum rights:

  (a) to be informed promptly, in a language which he understands and in detail, of the nature and cause of the accusation against him;

---

[32] *A v Secretary of State for Home Affairs* [2004] *The Times*, 17 December.
[33] (1990) 13 EHRR 157.   [34] [2002] CrimLR 493.
[35] (1989) 11 EHRR 117; a breach of this provision was also found in *O'Hara v U.K.* (last note).
[36] Discussed further in Ch.8 below; see generally the decision in *Nikolova v Bulgaria* (2000) 31 EHRR 64.
[37] See Ch. 9 below on delay.
[38] E.g. *Jablonski v Poland* (2003) 36 EHRR 455; cf. also Article 5(4) on review of detention.

(b) to have adequate time and facilities for the preparation of his defence;

(c) to defend himself in person or through legal assistance of his own choosing or, if he has not sufficient means to pay for legal assistance, to be given it free when the interests of justice so require;

(d) to examine or have examined witnesses against him and to obtain the attendance and examination of witnesses on his behalf under the same conditions as witnesses against him;

(e) to have the free assistance of an interpreter if he cannot understand or speak the language used in court.'

This Article has many different implications, but its central aim is to guarantee the right to a fair trial. Thus the opening words of the Article, which apply also to civil proceedings, guarantee three free-standing rights—to a fair and public hearing; to trial within a reasonable time; and to an independent and impartial tribunal. The remaining rights in Article 6 apply only to criminal proceedings, but this in itself has become a matter of controversy. The Strasbourg Court has insisted that the phrase 'charged with a criminal offence' has an autonomous meaning, thereby preventing member states from subverting the special protections in Article 6 by framing proceedings as civil.[39]

Article 6(2) declares the presumption of innocence, and this might be thought to indicate that placing burdens of proof on defendants would be very much restricted. However, this provision has been the subject of one of the loosest and least convincing judgments of the Strasbourg Court.[40] The minimum rights in Article 6.3 can be seen as non-exhaustive elaborations of the basic right to a fair trial. Many of these specific rights will be discussed at the appropriate places in later chapters. The boundaries of the right to free legal aid (Article 6.3(c)) have not yet been fully established, but it should certainly be provided when a person is in danger of being committed to prison.[41] Article 6.3(d) has a bearing not only on changes to the hearsay rule but also on the use of anonymous witnesses and of statements from witnesses unable to attend court.

No less significant have been the rights the Strasbourg Court has implied into Article 6 as concomitants of the general right to a fair trial. Probably the foremost example of this is the principle of equality of arms, which has recently crystallized as the right of a defendant to have disclosure of 'all material evidence for or against the accused,'[42] subject to circumscribed exceptions.[43] The Court has also implied into Article 6 the right of silence and the privilege against self-incrimination, describing

---

[39] Compare the leading cases of *Engel v Netherlands* (1979) 1 EHRR 647 and *Benham v United Kingdom* (1966) 22 EHRR 293 with the decision of the House of Lords in *Clingham v Kensington and Chelsea LBC; R (McCann) v Manchester Crown Court* [2003] 1 AC 787.

[40] *Salabiaku v France* (1989) 13 EHRR 379; cf. the interpretation of the English courts in *Lambert* [2002] 1 AC 545 and *Attorney General's Reference No.4 of 2002; Sheldrake v DPP* [2004] UKHL 43.

[41] See *Benham v United Kingdom*, above, n. 39.

[42] *Edwards v United Kingdom* (1993) 15 EHRR 417.

[43] *Edwards and Lewis v United Kingdom* [2003] Crim LR 891.

them as 'generally recognised international standards which lie at the heart of the notion of fair procedure under Article 6.'[44] In *Teixeira de Castro v Portugal*,[45] the Court confirmed that the right to a fair trial extends to the right to fair pre-trial procedures, and found a violation when a court had received and acted upon evidence obtained by entrapment. However, both express and implied rights may occasionally have to give way to countervailing rights of others involved in criminal proceedings: thus in the landmark decision in *Doorson v Netherlands*,[46] the Court held that a defendant's right of confrontation under Article 6(3)(d) may have to give way in cases where witnesses have been threatened with violence and therefore ought to be questioned by the judge in the presence of counsel (but not the accused). The rights of the witnesses under Article 5 (security of person) and Article 8 (respect for private life) were rightly protected in those circumstances.

We will not give detailed consideration to Article 7, which declares the right not to be convicted or punished as a result of a law coming into force after the relevant act or omission. Suffice it to say that it has important implications for the criminal law, and that it is an aspect of the general requirement that criminal offences be defined with sufficient certainty.[47]

'Article 8 1. Everyone has the right to respect for his private and family life, his home and his correspondence.

2. There shall be no interference by a public authority with the exercise of this right except such as is in accordance with the law and is necessary in a democratic society in the interests of national security, public safety or the economic well-being of the country, for the prevention of disorder or crime, for the protection of health or morals, or for the protection of the rights and freedoms of others.'

This Article sets out the right to privacy. Once the right is engaged, it is still possible for the State to justify interfering with it, so long as the requirements of Article 8.2 are fulfilled. Innocuous as the first requirement of Article 8.2 ('in accordance with the law') may appear, the fact is that the United Kingdom has lost many cases in Strasbourg because of the absence—at least until the Regulation of Investigatory Powers Act 2000—of a proper statutory framework for electronic and other forms of surveillance.[48] Even if the 2000 Act is held to have removed the objections of 'arbitrariness' from the previous English approach, an interference with the right to privacy must also be held to be 'necessary in a democratic society' and required for one of the reasons set out in Article 8.2. The Court has developed various general principles for interpreting the exceptions to declared rights. Not only must the exception be prescribed by law, but account must also be taken of the principles of proportionality (significant intrusions into privacy only for serious offences), subsidiarity (intrusive techniques must be the last resort), accountability (prior independent

---

[44] *John Murray v United Kingdom* (1996) 22 EHRR 29, at para 45.

[45] (1998) 28 EHRR 101, discussed below, Ch. 9.4.   [46] (1996) 22 EHRR 330.

[47] See further B. Emmerson and A. Ashworth, *Human Rights and Criminal Justice* (2001), Ch. 10.

[48] E.g. *Khan v United Kingdom* (2000) 31 EHRR 1016; *P.G. and J.H. v United Kingdom* [2002] Crim LR 308.

authorization for intrusions on the declared right, supported by record-keeping and monitoring), and finality (information obtained by exceptional means should be used only for the purpose for which it was obtained).

These principles lend greater concreteness to the exceptions to the declared rights, not only to the right to respect for private life in Article 8 but also to the right of freedom of thought and religion (Article 9), the right to freedom of expression (Article 10), and the right to freedom of assembly and association (Article 11). Articles 9–11 are all followed by a second paragraph along the same lines as Article 8.2, and all have been subject to interpretation by the Court.[49]

'Article 14   The enjoyment of the rights and freedoms set forth in this Convention shall be secured without discrimination on any ground such as sex, race, colour, language, religion, political or other opinion, national or social origin, association with a national minority, property, birth or other status.'

This does not amount to a general right not to be discriminated against: its terms are restricted to discrimination in relation to Convention rights, and therefore it can only be used in a situation where a violation of one of the other Convention rights is found.

This brief introduction to the key Convention rights should be sufficient to give an outline of the interaction between the Convention and the rules of the criminal process. Detailed consideration of that interaction will be found in the relevant chapters below: what is plain from their inclusion in the Convention and from the enactment of the Human Rights Act is that they should have a special place in English law generally and in the criminal process specifically—they are more fundamental than other rights not so recognized, and have what might be termed a 'constitutional' dimension of added weight. In this context there are two other particular aspects of the Convention which are crucial to the arguments of this chapter, and to a theory of the criminal process. The first concerns the ranking of rights under the Convention, in terms of their differing strengths. The second, to which we will return later, concerns the patterns of reasoning when applying Convention rights.

(d) PRIORITY AMONG CONVENTION RIGHTS

A problem with rights-based accounts of the criminal process is that rights may conflict with each other or with other social values. Some rights may also seem to be more important, or weightier, than others. This may give the impression that rights can be traded off against one another and against other values. This, in turn, might lead one to conclude that because rights do not have an absolute value, they have no special value at all, and that a rights-based approach is in fact no different from a consequentialist approach (discussed further below). This line of reasoning is mistaken. It is correct in so far as rights can conflict, and can be roughly ranked in

---

[49] For a full-length discussion, see Parts III and IV of D. Feldman, *Civil Liberties and Human Rights in England and Wales* (2nd ed., 2002).

terms of importance. But it is wrong in concluding that rights can simply be traded off against other values, or that rights-based approaches are not distinctive. All this raises some complex issues, but we suggest that insight on some of these questions can be gained by looking at how they are dealt with within the framework of the European Convention on Human Rights. This intensely practical scheme contains considerable wisdom about how to reason about rights.

It may already have become apparent that some of the Convention rights have different strengths, or have larger or more flexible exceptions, but the key to the ranking of Convention rights is to be found in Article 15:

'Article 15 1. In time of war or other public emergency threatening the life of the nation any High Contracting Party may take measures derogating from its obligations under this Convention to the extent strictly required by the exigencies of the situation, provided that such measures are not inconsistent with its other obligations under international law.
2. No derogation from Article 2, except in relation to deaths resulting from lawful acts of war, or from Article 3, 4 (paragraph 1) and 7 shall be made under this provision . . .'

The thrust of Article 15 is that it is permissible for States to derogate from various Convention rights if the conditions for doing so are satisfied, but that no derogation at all is allowed from four rights. This immediately establishes an order of priority. The non-derogable rights are:

- the right to life (Article 2),
- the right not to be subjected to torture or inhuman or degrading treatment (Article 3),
- the right not to be subjected to forced labour (Article 4.1), and
- the right not to be subjected to retrospective criminal laws or penalties (Article 7).

The fact that they are non-derogable indicates that they are the most basic of the fundamental rights in the Convention. Of course, their meaning and reach are subject to interpretation, and in that sense they are not *absolute* rights—or, at least, not until the scope of their application has been finally determined. But it is plain that they are not intended to give way to 'public interest' considerations: the metaphor of 'balancing' should not be applied here.

Another category of Convention rights might be termed qualified or *prima facie* rights—the right is declared, but it is also declared that it may be interfered with on certain grounds, to the minimum extent possible. We have already noted examples of this in the right to respect for private life (Article 8), the right to freedom of thought and religion (Article 9), the right to freedom of expression (Article 10), and the right to freedom of assembly and association (Article 11). All these qualified rights are subject to interference, if it can be established that this is 'necessary in a democratic society' on one of the stated grounds. As outlined above,[50] the Strasbourg Court has

---

[50] For a full-length discussion, see Parts III and IV of D. Feldman, *Civil Liberties and Human Rights in England and Wales* (2nd ed., 2002), pp. 34–35.

interpreted the second paragraphs of these Articles in such a way as to impose meaningful limitations on state interference with the rights.

Situated between non-derogable rights and qualified rights is an intermediate category, which is less easy to label and less easy to assess. In the European Convention this category includes the right to liberty and security of the person (Article 5) and the right to a fair trial (Article 6). One might refer to the rights in this intermediate category as 'strong rights', to demonstrate that they have a strength which is not qualified to the extent that the rights in Articles 8–11 are qualified. Indeed, the rights in Articles 5 and 6 are not at all qualified on the face of the Convention. In the internal logic of the Convention, this may prove to be quite a significant distinction. What it suggests is that, although strong rights are less fundamental than the non-derogable rights, any arguments for curtailing a strong right must at least be more powerful than the kind of 'necessary in a democratic society' argument that is needed to establish the acceptability of interference with a qualified right.

More will be said in Part 4 below about rights-based reasoning. The important point here is that it would not be accurate to state that human rights can be 'balanced' against public interest considerations, for that would be to corrupt the more demanding processes of reasoning outlined here. In the jurisprudence of the Strasbourg Court, at least, that vague notion of balancing does not dominate the interpretation of the Convention. Unfortunately, as we will see, the same is not true of the British courts, where some judges have seized on the notion of balancing and a corrupted version of the proportionality requirement to make significant inroads into the protection of rights.

Although we have concentrated on rights in this section, there are many values which mould criminal procedure which are not to be found in documents such as the European Convention and which are not usually thought about in terms of rights but which play an important role in shaping the criminal process. Several of these values have been alluded to already. There are the values associated with the involvement of lay people in criminal justice decision making, and the values associated with adversarialism. There are the values reflected in treating the defendant as an integral part of the process—as someone who is being called to acount, in Duff's terms—rather than as a simple object of the process, about whom judgments can be made without his being involved in the process in any significant way. Complex societies may also recognize a wide range of other values, and it is quite proper for these to be reflected in an institution such as the criminal process.

2.4 EVALUATING THE CRIMINAL PROCESS

Thus far in this chapter we have sought to develop and to justify a theory that accords twin purposes to the criminal process—accurate determinations and fair procedures. The trial has been treated as the focus of the criminal process, and in that respect we have argued for the importance of regulating preparation for an effective criminal trial and of ensuring respect for rights and other important values. We have added a certain amount of detail to the theory by situating it in an analysis of the rights to be found in the European Convention on Human Rights. We now go on to show how and why our approach differs from certain other accounts of the criminal process.

(a) HERBERT PACKER'S TWO MODELS

The best-known framework for evaluating the criminal process is that of Herbert Packer, developed in the 1960s.[51] It has been subjected to considerable criticism and modification in subsequent years, and will not be adopted as a starting point here. It should be noted at the outset that Packer did not advance it as a normative theory: he advanced two models which would help in interpreting trends in criminal procedure. Thus he suggested that tendencies in criminal justice might be evaluated by reference to two models, the Crime Control model and the Due Process model. 'The value system that underlies the Crime Control model is based on the proposition that the repression of criminal conduct is by far the most important function to be performed by the criminal process.'[52] This calls for 'a high rate of apprehension and conviction', placing a 'premium on speed and finality', and therefore preferring informal to formal procedures, with minimal opportunity for challenge. To work efficiently, the Crime Control model should ensure that weak cases are discarded at the earliest opportunity and that strong cases are taken forward to conviction and sentence as expeditiously as possible. The police are in the best position to judge guilt, and, if they form the view after their investigation that a person is guilty, the subsequent stages of the process should be as truncated as possible.

Packer contrasts with this the Due Process model, which takes cognizance of the stigma and loss of liberty that might result from the criminal process, and which insists on fairness criteria and other protections for the suspect or defendant. Thus the emphasis should be on formal and open adjudication of the facts in court, with the possibility of appeal, in order to give maximum protection to the innocent. Some proponents of the Due Process model would claim that it is a more accurate method of discovering the truth than the Crime Control model, but others would emphasize its recognition that errors do occur and its attempt to erect safeguards against mistaken judgments.

These models are, of course, artificial constructs which list the features of a 'pure' or extreme form of a particular approach. They are designed as interpretive tools, to enable us to tell (for example) how far in a particular direction a given criminal justice system tends, and they do not of themselves suggest that one approach is preferable to the other. But even as models they are open to a number of objections, of which five may be mentioned briefly here.

---

[51] H. Packer, *The Limits of the Criminal Sanction* (1968).   [52] *Ibid.*, 158.

(1) Packer failed to give a clear explanation of the relationship between his models. He recognized that 'the polarity of the two models is not absolute',[53] and stated that the ideology of Due Process 'is not the converse of that underlying the Crime Control model', since 'it does not rest on the idea that it is not socially desirable to repress crime'.[54] His models might be reconstructed so as to suggest that Crime Control is the underlying purpose of the system, but that pursuit of this purpose should be qualified out of respect to Due Process; or so as to suggest that Crime Control and Due Process should be recognized as the two main objectives of the system. Any such reconstruction would need to be supported by careful arguments.

(2) Packer assumed that the system of pre-trial justice is capable of affecting the crime rate, since he used the term Crime Control. It is true that Packer included powers of arrest and detection rates in his discussion of pre-trial justice, but evidence is needed of a significant relationship between the extent of police powers and the crime rate.[55] Variations in the crime rate may be influenced more greatly by social and economic factors, and it would need to be established that the different styles of policing have a significant effect on the rate of convictions. The notion that different methods of processing defendants before trial might affect crime rates is not only unproven but also question-begging at a more fundamental level: surely Packer's models would be more realistic if he posited, as the primary State interest in pre-trial processes, convicting the guilty rather than controlling crime.

(3) Related to this, Packer underestimated the importance of resource management as an element in the criminal process. This may have assumed greater significance in the years since Packer wrote, as governments have come under much greater financial pressure, and have brought this pressure to bear on criminal justice agencies.[56] But any contemporary model of criminal justice ought to take account of the influence of targets, performance indicators and other bureaucratic goals on the workings of the main agencies (e.g. police, prosecutors).[57]

(4) Packer's models make no allowance for victim-related matters. Again, this may be because there was far less consciousness of victims' interests and rights in the 1960s, but it is a significant drawback in using Packer's models today. Indeed, the models could probably not be adapted to accommodate this perspective: a new model would need to be added.

---

[53] *Ibid.*, 154.   [54] *Ibid.*, 163.

[55] For a review of the evidence up to the mid-1990s, see D. Dixon, *Law in Policing* (1997), 81–88.

[56] However, A.E. Bottoms and J.D. McClean took this point only eight years after Packer had written: *Defendants in the Criminal Process* (1976), Ch.9.

[57] I. Loader and R. Sparks, 'Contemporary Landscapes of Crime, Order and Control', in M. Maguire, R. Morgan and R. Reiner (eds), *Oxford Handbook of Criminology* (3rd ed., 2002).

(5) It is possible to mount various internal critiques of the two models. One
     example is the premium on speed, which Packer describes as an element in
     the Crime Control model. However, delays are also a source of considerable
     anxiety and inconvenience, and occasionally prolonged loss of liberty, to
     defendants. A properly developed notion of Due Process would surely insist
     that there be no unreasonable delay.[58]

Consideration of Packer's models begins to demonstrate the complexity of the criminal process and the problems of devising a satisfactory theoretical framework. The
models may help us to identify elements of two important strands, but they neglect
other, conflicting tendencies. One could try to remedy the defects by constructing
further possible models: Kent Roach, for example, has developed two models incorporating victims' rights, the construction of which amply demonstrates the politicization
of victims' rights rather than the rational pursuit of victim-centred objectives.[59] But all
of these are merely models to assist in interpreting trends in criminal justice, and they
are less important than the pursuit of a framework of values for the criminal process.

(b) THE METAPHOR OF BALANCING

Much discussion of criminal justice by governments, courts and official bodies gives a
central role to the notion of balance. Three clear examples in recent times are to be
found in the report of the Royal Commission on Criminal Justice in 1993, in some of
the leading British judgments under the Human Rights Act, and in Government
claims about the rights of victims of crime. In our view, the metaphor of balancing is
a rhetorical device of which one must be extremely wary. At worst, it is a substitute for
principled argument: 'achieving a balance' is put forward as if it were self-evidently a
worthy and respectable goal, rather like 'achieving justice.' Who, after all, would argue
in favour of injustice or an unbalanced system? Of course it is important to recognize
that the criminal process is the scene of considerable conflict between diverse aims
and interests. The difficulty is that many of those who employ this terminology fail to
stipulate exactly what is being balanced, what factors and interests are to be included
or excluded, what weight is being assigned to particular values and interests, and so
on. There were many examples of this vitiating vagueness throughout the report of
the Runciman Royal Commission in 1993,[60] and this may indicate either self-delusion
or intellectual dishonesty. For how can one properly invoke the notion of balance
without having prepared the ground conscientiously? In this connection the most
glaring omission from the Runciman report was the failure even to mention, let alone
to consider and to draw upon, the rights enshrined in the European Convention on
Human Rights. Nor did the Royal Commission conduct a systematic assessment of
other relevant interests and claims—those of defendants, victims, potential victims,

---

[58] See the discussion in Ch. 9.3 below.
[59] K. Roach, *Due Process and Victims' Rights: the New Law and Politics of Criminal Justice* (1999).
[60] Royal Commission on Criminal Justice, *Report* (1993).

corporations, economic constraints, and so forth. By resting recommendations on the criminal justice system on notions of balance, without taking any account of human rights, the Royal Commission report laid bare its utter inadequacy on matters of principle.

A second example comes from a number of decisions of the British courts applying the Convention under the Human Rights Act 1998. By far the most significant was the first judgment handed down by the Privy Council after the 1998 Act came into force. In *Brown v Stott*,[61] an appeal from Scotland raised the question whether the privilege against self-incrimination, recognized as an implied right under Article 6,[62] protects the owner of a car from having to declare who was driving it at a given time and place. Of greater interest than the Privy Council's conclusion that the privilege should not apply in this situation was the reasoning of Lord Bingham, the senior Law Lord. Having explained that motoring laws are socially important because of the risk of death and injury from bad driving, he went on:

'If one asks whether section 172 [requiring owners to declare who was driving] represents a disproportionate response to the problem of maintaining road safety, whether the balance between the interests of the community at large and the interests of the individual is struck in a manner unduly prejudicial to the individual, whether (in short) the leading of this evidence would infringe a basic human right of the respondent, I would feel bound to give negative answers.'[63]

This is a crucial passage, setting the tone for many of the subsequent decisions under the Human Rights Act. Yet it is flawed. The plausibility of the reasoning derives from the reliance on two key concepts, 'balance' and 'proportionality', which seem to be understood in terms of some kind of trade-off between a conception of the public interest (in which human rights apparently have no part) and the rights of the individual. Even if those concepts can be constructed in a defensible way, the point is that they do not belong here. As argued above, the right to a fair trial in Article 6 is a strong right under the Convention, and its component rights cannot simply be traded off by reference to the public interest. The Strasbourg jurisprudence gives little support to that mode of reasoning in Article 6 cases (as compared with Articles 8–11, where it can be used), and indeed within a week of the decision in *Brown v Stott*, the Strasbourg Court held that the privilege against self-incrimination could not be outweighed by the social importance of anti-terrorist laws.[64] There is a role for the concept of proportionality in Convention cases, but that is chiefly in respect of Articles 8–11. Moreover, the concept of proportionality forms part of a specified mode of reasoning under the second paragraph of those Articles: proportionality is relevant in considering whether the interference with the individual's right can be justified as 'necessary in a democratic society' for one of the listed reasons. Lord Bingham's use of the concept in relation to Article 6 was far less disciplined and more vague, whereas

[61] [2001] 2 WLR 817.   [62] See n 39 above and accompanying text.   [63] [2001] 2 WLR 817.
[64] *Heaney and McGuinness v Ireland* (2000) 33 EHRR 12.

(because the Article 6 right is stronger) it should have been more refined. We will return to this point at pp. 46–48 below.

A third example involves the rights of victims. These will be discussed in more detail below, but at this point the debate about victims is a useful illustration of how the balancing metaphor is sometimes simply misleading. The Government has claimed that a major purpose of the various reforms introduced by the Criminal Justice Act 2003 is to re-balance the criminal justice system in favour of victims. It may be disputed whether any of the provisions in the Act will achieve this,[65] but the point to be made here is that this general metaphor of balancing advantages between defendants and victims is misleading in several respects. Here, the metaphor implies that the lot of defendants has to be made worse in order to make that of victims better. But many victim-centred reforms—giving victims better courtroom facilities, better support, and keeping them properly informed of the progress of their cases—do not affect defendants in any way. Other reforms have affected defendants, for example, reforms restricting the ways in which vulnerable witnesses can be cross-examined. Here the rebalancing metaphor is more appropriate, though it may still mislead. It might be taken to suggest that there is a clash between the rights of defendants and those of witnesses when in fact there is not. The reforms centred around vulnerable witnesses are generally intended to allow such people to give their 'best evidence'. But no defendant has a legitimate interest in a witness giving unreliable evidence, or in their feeling intimidated. Even in the most controversial of these reforms, that involving a restriction on the ability of defendants to cross-examine witnesses in sexual assault cases about their sexual history, there is a shared assumption on both sides of the debate that defendants have a right to adduce all relevant evidence; the dispute has been over just what is relevant. These various reforms do not affect defendants' rights, then. If there is balancing going on here, it does not involve balancing two rights. A further reason why the rebalancing metaphor may mislead is that it tends to suggest that victims have an interest in increased conviction rates, no matter how that increase is produced. One of the reforms introduced by the Criminal Justice Act 2003 is to enlarge the cirumstances in which juries can be informed of a defendant's previous convictions. Critics of this reform fear that it will lead to an increase in false convictions. If this is right, then the reform will not improve the lot of victims in any way: victims have no legitimate interest in seeing defendants falsely convicted. Reflection on this sort of example suggests that defendants share many of the interests of victims: interests in fair and dignified treatment, and in accurate fact-finding. This is something that the rebalancing metaphor only serves to obscure.

Our criticisms here are aimed at a vague and unprincipled use of the concept of 'balancing'—one that fails to examine the interests involved, to give reasons for assigning them particular weight, and so forth.[66] We are not arguing that there is no

---

[65] J. Jackson, 'Justice for All: Putting Victims at the Heart of Criminal Justice?' (2003) 30 *JLS* 309.

[66] For a somewhat similar perspective, see J. Waldron, 'Security and Liberty: the Image of Balance', (2003) 11 *J. Political Philosophy* 191.

place for the notion of 'balance', or 'proportionality', in reasoning about the criminal process. It is evident that such concepts do have limited relevance to human rights arguments: under Articles 8–11 of the Convention there is a structured form of balancing in order to determine whether interference with the right is 'necessary in a democratic society', and occasionally the rights of two persons conflict (e.g. the Article 8 rights of a witness may conflict with the Article 6 right of a defendant, or with the Article 10 right of a broadcaster or writer). But we are also arguing that there are certain rights that are too fundamental to be 'balanced'; and that even where balancing is proper, the exercise should be conducted in a particular way. That is, the concept of 'balance' should be reserved for the conclusion of a lengthy and careful process, whereby rights and interests are identified; arguments for including some and excluding others are set out; appropriate weights or priorities are assigned to particular rights and interests, either generally or in specific contexts; and so forth. Above all, this must be a properly researched, reasoned, and principled course of argument, not simply the pronouncement of a conclusion. We will pursue this argument below. Prior to that, it will be helpful to illustrate some of the problems of balancing with reference to consequentialist theories of criminal process, which tend to rely heavily on this device.

(c) CONSEQUENTIALISM IN THE CRIMINAL PROCESS

Jeremy Bentham and John Stuart Mill are well known for their espousal of utilitarianism. The theory may take more or less sophisticated forms, but in essence social policies both generally and in respect of criminal justice should be determined by calculating what approach would conduce to the greatest happiness of the greatest number of people.[67] A felicific calculus, measuring pain and pleasure, would be used to determine the approach that would overall produce least pain. An obvious criticism of such a consequentialist approach is that its chief concern is with aggregate benefits, and that it may therefore ride roughshod over particular individuals (or minorities) in order to benefit the majority. The most provocative example would be torture: human rights instruments typically prohibit it absolutely, whereas utilitarians might accept it when it seems likely to yield a benefit for the majority. More prosaically, human rights instruments often proclaim the presumption of innocence in criminal proceedings, whereas on a utilitarian calculus it may often benefit the community more if defendants were required to prove, for example, any defence that they wished to raise.

Rights theories, on the other hand, are essentially anti-consequentialist: the whole point of recognizing a right is to uphold the claim of an individual to protection from treatment of certain kinds, even though such treatment may accord with the wishes of the majority or be for the overall benefit of the community. This does not mean that consequentialist reasoning is always inappropriate, but it does carve out certain

---

[67] A good account of consequentialism is W. Kymlicka, *Contemporary Political Philosophy: An Introduction* (2nd ed., 2002), Ch. 2.

spheres of activity in which it must give way to recognized rights. There has been a recent revival of consequentialist theories in criminal justice, and two may be mentioned briefly here. John Braithwaite and Phillip Pettit argue that the ultimate determinant should be the republican ideal of liberty: the difficult clashes between individual rights and public interests should be resolved by calculating which approach advances 'dominion' on a greater scale—dominion meaning non-interference by others, secured by society and the community so as to become the expectation of each individual.[68] One difficulty with this form of republican theory is that it appears not to recognize anything other than vague outer limits on state intervention in individual lives. Thus its authors refer to the need to provide reassurance to the community, and espouse incapacitative penal strategies: 'crucial to the promotion of community reassurance' is the power to 'escalate responses' as 'an offender displays more and more intransigence about offending against others.'[69] Although primarily directed at sentencing rather than at pre-trial processes, this approach provides no principled restraints on state intervention, and it is unclear whether and to what extent it would recognize individual rights. Whatever the merits of the republican ideal, the absence of principled limits means that the theory leaves individuals too much at the mercy of the state.

Andrew Sanders and Richard Young adopt a different form of consequentialism, though one that has marked similarities to Braithwaite and Pettit's. For Sanders and Young, it is 'freedom', rather than dominion, which is the value to be maximized. They find a place for human rights, but evidently regard them as an ingredient to be put into some kind of balancing process with others. Thus they argue that when human rights and other interests are being compared, the approach 'that is likely to enhance freedom the most' should be chosen, since the various conflicting considerations (human rights, protecting the innocent, convicting the guilty, protecting victims, maintaining public order, etc) should be seen 'as means to achieving the overriding goal of freedom.' Thus 'all we have to do is to prioritise the goal that is likely to enhance freedom the most.'[70] Two difficulties with this approach concern the definition of freedom and the approach to balancing that it requires. The meaning of freedom is highly contestable—as the classic essay by Isaiah Berlin on negative liberty and positive liberty shows[71]—and when the authors state that they would include the freedom 'of the community at large' the glass becomes rather dark.[72] Not only is their fundamental concept thus under-determined, but it is not clear how they would deal with the weighting of 'competing goals, interests and rights' that is necessary.[73] They

---

[68] J. Braithwaite and P. Pettit, *Not Just Deserts: A Republican Theory of Criminal Justice* (1990).

[69] For brief contributions to the debate, see P. Pettit with J. Braithwaite, 'Republicanism in Sentencing: Recognition, Recompense and Reassurance', and A. Ashworth and A. von Hirsch, 'Desert and the Three Rs', both in A. von Hirsch and A. Ashworth (eds), *Principled Sentencing: Readings on Theory and Policy* (2nd ed., 1998).

[70] A. Sanders and R. Young, *Criminal Justice* (2nd ed., 2000), 52.

[71] I. Berlin, 'Two Concepts of Liberty', in A. Quinton (ed), *Political Philosophy* (1967).

[72] Sanders and Young, above n 70, 58.   [73] *Ibid.*, 62.

certainly recognize the need to assign weights to them, but their confidence in 'the language of freedom' to smooth the path by providing a 'common currency' may be overdone. However, the merit of their analysis is to recognize the sheer range of relevant interests to be considered, and to recognize that assigning weight to each of them in particular contexts is an essential precondition of any kind of 'balancing' operation.

To summarize: the principal problem with consequentialist theories is that they allow rights to be overridden in pursuit of some other value. Even the reasonably sophisticated consequentialist theories of Braithwaite and Pettit and Sanders and Young would seem to allow violations of human rights if to do so would ultimately promote dominion or freedom. Moreover, these theories try to reduce everything to a single value. When one considers the sheer number of different values recognized in a complex society, many of which conflict, it is difficult to believe that they can all be reduced to a single core value. To mention, once again, examples we have already used: the choice between an adversarial or inquisitorial system, or between lay or professional fact-finders, cannot sensibly be made in terms of which better promotes dominion or freedom. Or, to take another example, the value of confrontation between defendant and witness, which is contained in the US Constitution and has recently been accorded significant importance by the Supreme Court,[74] cannot easily be conceptualized or assessed in those terms either. One should be suspicious of theories that attempt, as consequentialist theories do, to reduce all human values to a single metric.

(d) DEVELOPING THE RIGHTS PERSPECTIVE

Our approach to criminal process differs from those just described in that it is rights-based. This is not to say that the purpose of the criminal process is to implement human rights, but that in the pursuit of retributive justice respect for rights is essential. Respect for rights should be seen as a concomitant aim of criminal process—not merely a side-constraint on the pursuit of accuracy or 'rectitude' in convicting the guilty and acquitting the innocent, but an objective to be attained while pursuing that aim. Thus the European Convention on Human Rights is taken to be part of the normative framework for the criminal process, as indeed it is in terms of both United Kingdom law (following the Human Rights Act) and the country's international obligations. But the Convention does not exhaust our normative arguments. We recognize that it has shortcomings: it has been supplemented by various Protocols over the years, and there are good arguments for further Protocols on, for example, discrimination. Like Packer's models it says nothing about the rights of victims and witnesses, although there are several Council of Europe recommendations dealing with those issues. The Convention also needs supplementing in respect of young suspects and defendants, and the UN Convention on the Rights of the Child achieves that. Furthermore, as we have noted, values beyond those contained in such documents play a legitimate role in shaping the criminal process.

[74] *Crawford v Washington* (2004) 124 S Ct 1354.

The human rights perspective can make a particular contribution through its subtle weighting of different rights, and its structuring of arguments for making exceptions to rights. We noted above that certain rights do provide for interference and for a balancing process to determine whether the interference is justified. But the kind of balancing that is permitted under the Convention is a far cry from the vague and undisciplined concept often used by politicians, exemplified by Lord Bingham's landmark judgment in *Brown v Stott.*[75]

Our starting point is the hierarchy of Convention rights (sketched at p. 36) which distinguishes between non-derogable rights, strong rights, and qualified rights. The non-derogable rights permit no balancing of the public interest. For example, arguments that torturing certain people would be in the public interest cannot be entertained. On the other hand, the qualified rights are self-evidently open to balancing. But what we noted was that this is not some vague exercise of trying to measure the individual's right against the wider public interest, but rather a structured process of reasoning indicated by the wording of the second paragraph of those rights and developed in the jurisprudence of the Court. This is not to deny that courts can reach different conclusions about whether an interference is 'necessary in a democratic society,' or that there are grounds for contesting some judgments of this kind. The argument is that the structure of reasoning required in order to justify interference with a qualified right provides a guide to the weighting of the right and the circumstances in which it can be outweighed.

More difficult are the two strong rights declared by Articles 5 and 6. It must be said that the Strasbourg Court has not been entirely consistent in its judgments. There are some decisions on Articles 5 and 6 where it has stated either that a particular right is not absolute, or that it may be necessary to balance a right against some other interest. Now this proposition must be treated with care, and not as a licence for vague and undisciplined 'balancing'. Thus the Strasbourg Court has said that both the right of silence and the privilege against self-incrimination are not absolute,[76] yet that emphatically does not mean that they can be freely 'balanced' against public interest considerations. What it means in respect of the right of silence is that there may be 'situations calling for an explanation from' the accused, in which adverse inferences may justifiably be drawn from the accused's silence: this is a significant qualification, but it refers to the evidential situation, and not at all to the seriousness of the crime charged or the complexity of the investigation.[77] Thus the fact that a power is believed to be essential in the fight against terrorism has been held insufficient to justify an exception to the privilege against self-incrimination.[78]

As for balancing an Article 6 right against another Convention right, the principal

---

[75] Above, p. 41.

[76] E.g. in *John Murray v U.K.* (1996) 22 EHRR 29 and in *Saunders v UK* (1997) 23 EHRR 313.

[77] For further discussion of this point, see A. Ashworth, *Human Rights, Serious Crime and Criminal Procedure* (2002), 108–118, and J. Waldron, 'Security and Liberty: the Image of Balance', (2003) 11 *J. Political Philosophy* 191, at 203–204.

[78] *Heaney and McGuinness v Ireland* (2000) 33 EHRR 12.

example of this is *Doorson v Netherlands*,[79] where the Court held that the defendant's right to examine witnesses against him has to be balanced against the rights of the witnesses themselves, notably where a witness has reason to fear violent reprisals if her or his identity is revealed. But, again, this decision does not licence some vague kind of 'balancing.' In the first place, the interests 'balanced' were both rights of individuals, not any public interests. Moreover, the process of 'balancing' was quite rigidly structured: thus the Court insisted that, although it was proper to protect the identity of the witness, the rights of the defence must be curtailed as little as possible. Thus the 'handicaps under which the defence laboured [must be] sufficiently counterbalanced by the procedures followed by the judicial authorities', such as appropriate directions from the judge; and any conviction should not be based 'solely or mainly' on the evidence of the witnesses who were thus allowed to give their evidence anonymously.[80] All these requirements, indeterminate as they may be in their application, constitute an advance on general notions of 'balancing,' by showing how a right can continue to exert its influence even where its application is curtailed.

Another example of a structured approach may be found in the Court's judgments on the prosecution's duty to disclose documents to the defence, and the claim of 'public interest immunity' from having to disclose certain evidence. In the leading decision of *Rowe and Davis v United Kingdom*,[81] the Court held that the principle of equality of arms is a requirement of fairness under Article 6, but that:

'the entitlement to disclosure of relevant evidence is not an absolute right. In any criminal proceedings there may be competing interests, such as national security or the need to protect witnesses at risk of reprisals or keep secret police methods of investigating crime. In some cases it may be necessary to withhold certain evidence from the defence so as to preserve the fundamental rights of another individual or to safeguard an important public interest. However, only such measures restricting the rights of the defence which are strictly necessary are permissible under Article 6(1). Moreover, in order to ensure that the accused receives a fair trial, any difficulties caused to the defence by a limitation on its rights must be sufficiently counterbalanced by the procedures followed by the judicial authorities.'[82]

There may be room for debate about whether the Court has insisted on sufficient 'counterbalancing' procedures in these cases of public interest immunity—is the deployment of 'special counsel' sufficient, and are there circumstances in which even this should not be allowed?[83]—but what is clear is that the reasoning must be structured, and the essence of the defendant's right must be safeguarded.

These examples therefore demonstrate that, on the rare occasions when the Strasbourg Court has recognized that a degree of balancing may enter into the determination of certain rights under Articles 5 and 6, it has insisted on structured

---

[79] (1996) 22 EHRR 330.

[80] *Ibid.*, para 72; cf. *Van Mechelen v Netherlands* (1997) 25 EHRR 547.   [81] (2000) 30 EHRR 1.

[82] *Ibid.*, para 61.

[83] See now the decision in *Edwards and Lewis v United Kingdom* [2003] CrimLR 891, and the resolute curtailment of that decision by the House of Lords in *H and C* [2004] 2 WLR 335.

reasoning. It has not allowed a right simply to be 'balanced away', but has concentrated on preserving the essence of the defendant's right while giving some weight to pressing public interest considerations. If English courts and politicians are to continue to adopt the metaphor of 'balancing', it is submitted that they should at least move to a more rigorous and structured approach. As argued earlier, even the justifications for interfering with the qualified rights under Articles 8–11 of the Convention must be reasoned according to a particular structure of requirements: this renders all the more cogent the argument that rigorous and structured reasoning should be used when there is a question of 'balancing' certain rights (not all) under the stronger Articles 5 and 6 against some public interests.

Structured reasoning only takes one so far. It offers a procedure, but no ultimate criterion for making choices. Human rights standards have areas of open texture, perhaps more than some rules of domestic law. Because human rights are as much political as legal, their reach will inevitably generate controversy. But we have argued that the structure of the Convention sets certain markers and establishes an order of priority, which may be used as a basis for reasoned argument. In respect of Articles 5 and 6, which are the rights primarily relevant to the criminal process, it should be recognized that they are essentially 'trumps' over considerations of public interest. There may be limited circumstances in which certain rights may be 'over-trumped' by extreme and urgent considerations of public interest. But, even then, the Strasbourg court has shown that policies such as the fight against terrorism or the war on drugs cannot be taken as sufficient for these purposes.[84] Consequentialist approaches might well lead to other conclusions in these types of case, and that marks a significant difference in emphasis.

2.5 DEVELOPING THE RIGHTS PERSPECTIVE: THE STATE AND VICTIMS

What we have described as a theory of the criminal process—one that has the twin goals of regulating the processes for bringing suspected offenders to trial so as to produce accurate determinations, and of ensuring that fundamental rights are protected in those processes—still needs to be supplemented and adapted in several ways. Differences of approach may be necessary when dealing with young suspects, for example. It is necessary to look to the United Nations Convention on the Rights of the Child (1990), whose wide-ranging list of rights includes those in Article 40 on 'the administration of juvenile justice'. A different question is whether all the rights in the Convention ought to apply to corporate bodies as well as to individuals: how ought the right to liberty and security of the person (Article 5) or the right to a fair trial

---

[84] E.g. *Heaney and McGuinness*, above, n 78; *Brogan v UK*, above n 35; and, on drugs, *Teixeira de Castro v Portugal*, above n 45.

(Article 6) to apply to companies? It is also necessary to assess the relevance of what are claimed to be victims' rights. In 1985 the Council of Europe approved recommendations on *The Position of the Victim in the Framework of Criminal Law and Procedure*, and the United Nations approved a *Declaration of Basic Principles of Justice for the Victims of Crime and Abuse of Power*. No amendment was made, however, and no protocol added to the European Convention. Does that mean that victims' rights ought to be placed in some fourth, lower category of rights, beneath those enumerated above? Surely not. A more likely historical explanation, in terms of practical politics, is that no-one dared to begin the process of amending the Convention for fear that it would prove counter-productive, or even so controversial as to undermine the consensus that exists around the existing rights. Victims' rights should therefore be assessed on general principles, unlimited by the restricted list of rights in the Convention, and this will inevitably raise the question of the proper role of the State in criminal procedure.

It is a commonplace that, until the final quarter of the last century, there had been a relative neglect of victims' needs for support, respect and compensation. Since then, there has been increasing recognition that the victims of crime have rights to respectful and sympathetic treatment from law enforcement agents; to support and help in the aftermath of the offence; to proper information about the progress of their case; to facilities at courtrooms that separate them from other members of the public; and to compensation for the crime, either from the offender or (if that is not possible) from the State, at least for crimes of violence.[85] These rights to services should be regarded as an important element in social provision for the disadvantaged, and it should be the concern of people working in the criminal justice system to ensure that they are recognized and fulfilled. But completely different justifications are needed if it is claimed that victims have procedural rights in the criminal process. Should the victim have the right to be consulted on the decision whether or not to prosecute, on the bail/custody decision, on the acceptance of a plea to a lesser offence or to fewer offences, or on sentence? Some victims and victims' families want this kind of involvement, although many do not wish to have such burdens,[86] but the question here is whether there are good arguments for recognizing such claims as rights.

An essential first step is to consider what the role of the State should be in the criminal process. One familiar argument is that the State's leading role is a social necessity: if it were left to victims, their families and their supporters to deal with people who break the rules, this would open the way to revenge, retaliation, vigilantism, and serious injustice, if not anarchy. This consequentialist argument does not establish, however, why it should be the State—as opposed to local communities, for example—that should have the overall responsibility and power. For this, one needs a conception of the State's proper functions. John Gardner has argued that one of the

---

[85] For the culmination of a lengthy process of giving statutory recognition to rights of this kind, see the Domestic Violence, Crime and Victims Act 2004.

[86] Victim Support, *The Rights of Victims of Crime* (1995).

defining roles of the State should be to facilitate peaceful living among citizens, and to safeguard the basic means by which citizens can lead good lives.[87] He argues that this requires the State to control reprisals by individuals; it also requires rules to be authoritatively established, and to be reinforced by sanctions. The State has as one of its major functions the prevention or reduction of harm, and this includes responding to wrongs done by censuring those who commit them. The State can and should do this in a way that shows respect for the offender as a rational citizen (e.g. by conforming to human rights), and which adopts a fair and consistent approach to the task.[88] These last specifications have particular resonance for the criminal process, in the investigatory, pre-trial and trial stages: a major role of the State is as guarantor of the rights of all those involved, as well as providing official agencies (such as the police, public prosecutors and courts) to carry out the essential functions of law enforcement.

This may be regarded as a general argument of principle. It may have to give way, to some extent, if the reality is that a certain state is failing to perform its proper role—where, for example, there is widespread mistrust among the people because of long-running social divisions (perhaps Northern Ireland may be an example); or even where it is evident that there is a vitiating gulf between provision for wealthier citizens (who can afford extra security measures) and provision for the poor, a social problem that may be no less manifest in law enforcement than in health or education.[89] But the argument of principle—the starting-point, informed by the commitment to retributive justice—is that the primary interests in the application of the criminal sanction through the processes of the criminal justice system are those of the State and the suspect/defendant/offender. In respect of sentencing, the court should take a decision according to the law. The victim's personal view should be no more relevant to this than the personal view of any other individual. The rule of law, embodied in the Convention and other human rights documents, requires decisions to be taken by an independent and impartial tribunal according to settled rules announced beforehand. A particular victim may be vindictive or forgiving, demanding or afraid of the offender, and it would be an abdication of the State's responsibility to allow such individual feelings to influence the sentence. The same reasoning applies to the key stages of the criminal process, such as the decision to investigate, the decision to prosecute, and the acceptance of a plea to a different charge: the rule of law requires these decisions to be taken impartially and independently, and not influenced by the wishes of a particular individual. It is true that in practice the willingness of a victim or complainant to become involved, by making a statement or alternatively by declining to give evidence in court, can often determine whether an enquiry or prosecution is taken forward. But that fact does not alter the rights and wrongs, and indeed in

---

[87] J. Gardner, 'Punishment—in Proportion and in Perspective', in A. Ashworth and M. Wasik (eds), *Fundamentals of Sentencing Theory* (1998).

[88] See further A. von Hirsch and A. Ashworth, *Proportionality in Sentencing* (2005), Ch.2.

[89] For discussion and further references, see K. Roach, *Due Process and Victims' Rights: the New Law and Politics of Criminal Justice* (1999), 261; A. Ashworth, 'Responsibilities, Rights and Restorative Justice', (2002) 42 *BJ Crim.* 578, at 580–1.

some types of case (such as domestic violence) prosecutions may be brought without the victim's co-operation.[90]

The implication of this reasoning is that there are no convincing arguments for accepting that victims or victims' families have a right to influence any of the key decisions in the criminal process. Whether there is still good reason to say that the police or prosecutors should receive and 'take account of' victims' wishes before taking these decisions is a moot point: this could be criticized as a sham if at the same time we maintain that the decisions should not be *influenced* by the victim's wishes, because victims might feel they are being misled and might feel disappointed if their wishes are not followed.[91] However, this is the position reached in English law in respect of Victim Personal Statements, which may now be submitted by victims to the court, although the Lord Chief Justice's Practice Direction states that 'the opinions of the victim or victim's close relatives as to what the sentence should be are not relevant.'[92] Information contained in the statement may be relevant when assessing the consequences of the offence for the victim, and at the pre-trial stage the same would definitely be true at remand proceedings—there are cases where it would be important to know about the alleged victim's apprehensions about (further) violence or harassment. But this shows that a line is emerging between information from the victim (which may be relevant, subject to verification) and the opinions of the victim (which should not be relevant).

It is important now to re-assert that no part of this argument suggests that victims should be ignored or that they should be less well served. Just like defendants, they should be treated with dignity. The argument has been that they should not be granted procedural rights that enable them to influence decisions in the criminal process. This leaves untouched the need to review the rules relating to investigations, procedure and evidence in particular types of case—notably cases of sexual assault, where victims (whether male or female) remain open to questioning, in and out of court, on details of their past which are of questionable relevance to the proper interests of the defendant.[93] Similarly, all the arguments in favour of improved support, information and compensation for victims remain untouched. For example, it has been recognized for many years that victims are not always kept informed about the progress of 'their' case through the system, and sometimes hear about a plea of guilty to a lesser offence only at a much later stage. The appointment of a Commissioner for Victims and Witnesses, and the preparation of a code of practice for victims, are welcome steps taken under the Domestic Violence, Crime and Victims Act 2004. There are strong reasons why the Act should have gone further and established statutory rights to services for victims, but at least it promises a distinct advance in respecting victims' rights.

---

[90] See the discussion in Ch.7, below.

[91] See the research into the pilot project on submitting victim statements to prosecutors, discussed by A. Sanders, C. Hoyle, R. Morgan and E. Cape, 'Victim Impact Statements: Can't Work, Won't Work', [2001] Crim LR 447.

[92] *Practice Direction (Victim Personal Statements)* [2002] 1 Cr App R 69.

[93] See further J. Temkin, *Rape and the Legal Process* (2nd ed., 2002).

How do these conclusions on the role of the State and on victims' rights relate to new initiatives in restorative justice? In the precise sphere of this book, the implications are limited because it is usually a precondition of a defendant entering restorative justice that he or she admits guilt. Restorative justice is not put forward as a means of resolving factual disputes or a substitute for trials. What it challenges is the view that the State should have exclusive responsibility for the administration of criminal justice, and it argues in favour of 'restorative conferences' (composed of victims and their families, offenders and their families, and community representatives) to allow victims and offenders to come to terms with what happened and to determine the response to offences.[94] Although it is said to be essential that the offender consents to participate in the conference and can walk away at any time, it is plain that the conferences take place in the shadow of the formal legal system and that any consent is therefore somewhat bounded. Victims clearly have a significant role in deciding the outcome, and this goes against the rule-of-law principles of independent and impartial judgment by making it likely that outcomes will depend to some extent on whether the victim is vindictive or forgiving.[95] For advocates of restorative justice this is less important than whether the victim comes forth with an apology to the offender and whether the victim feels better for the experience of being able to enter into a dialogue with the offender. It is evident, finally, that we have travelled a long distance from Packer's two models of the criminal process (see p. 38 above), and that to interpret trends and tendencies from the victim's point of view one would need an entirely different model.[96]

Insofar as restorative justice is invoked to deal with cases at the lower end of the scale of seriousness, there may be advantages in experimenting with it to see whether it yields the benefits (in terms of community reintegration and crime prevention) that tend to be claimed for it. But as the seriousness of the offences increases, so the importance of maintaining rule-of-law standards and respecting the rights of defendants in the face of sanctions imposed upon them increases. This issue is pursued further in Part 6 below.

2.6 DISPOSITIVE VALUES

The discussion thus far has focused on values in the context of a theory of the criminal process, and it is now time to return to another aspect of pre-trial decisions—'dispositive' values. The focus here is on police cautions, conditional cautions, final

---

[94] See further G. Johnstone, *Restorative Justice* (2001); G. Johnstone, *A Reader on Restorative Justice* (2003).

[95] See the criticisms by A. Ashworth, 'Responsibilities, Rights and Restorative Justice' (2002) 42 *BJ Crim* 578, and the reply by A. Morris, 'Critiquing the Critics: a Brief Response to Critics of Restorative Justice', *ibid.*, 596.

[96] See K. Roach, 'Criminal Process', in P. Cane and M. Tushnet (eds), *Oxford Handbook of Legal Studies* (2003), 780–1.

warnings, discontinuance of cases, restorative justice conferences and other forms of diversion from the formal process.[97] To a large extent the values relevant here reflect the purposes at the stage of sentencing, which is the best-known and most widely publicized dispositive decision, but it is important also to retain a philosophical connection with the principles discussed above in relation to process values. In particular, the right of an innocent person not to be punished is relevant to both types of decision.

(a) PREVENTION OF CRIME

The prevention of crime is among the reasons for having a criminal justice system, with police, courts, and sentences. Indeed, in Part 5 above we argued that this should be a primary function of the State. It is also an underlying reason for diversion, but this is not to say that it should be determinative in individual cases. These two points should be kept separate. It is one thing to argue that the system of diversion should operate in such a way that it contributes to the overall prevention of crime, at least by dealing with offenders in ways that do not increase the chances of further law-breaking by them or by others. It is another thing to maintain that the prospect of a particular person not reoffending should be a necessary or sufficient reason for diverting that offender from the formal criminal process: that might conflict with the principle of proportionality (see (d) below). The point here is that, since dispositive decisions without trial may be regarded as part of or analogous to the sentencing system, they should certainly not be invoked in a way that increases the probability of people committing offences.

(b) CONSENT AND FAIRNESS

This principle has a direct connection with process values. The system should ensure that, as far as possible, a person's decision whether or not to accept diversion is a free and informed one, and that there is a right of access to a court if guilt is disputed.[98] The idea of a completely free decision may be regarded as illusory, in the sense that the alternative of going to court will often be perceived as more stressful, but there are ways of maximizing this freedom. For example, legal advice should be available so as to help a suspect with this decision, not least because cautions and final warnings are recorded and may be cited in subsequent proceedings, and also because restorative justice conferences may sometimes be less benign than they might seem.[99] It is essential to ensure that methods of diversion do not become methods of subversion, so far as fairness and the protection of the innocent are concerned, and therefore the statutory

---

[97] These were introduced in Ch.1 above, and will be discussed in detail in Ch. 6 below.

[98] As required under Article 6: *Ozturk v Germany* (1984) 6 EHRR 409.

[99] This is not to imply that legal advice necessarily leads to the best outcome for an accused person: see Ch. 3 on the ethics of defence lawyers, and Ch. 10 on lawyers' advice on plea.

requirement of an admission of guilt before the offer of a conditional caution is to be welcomed.[100]

(c) VICTIM COMPENSATION

Any arrangement for diversion should ensure that the victim does not thereby lose a right to compensation. The system should remain committed to victims' rights to support and services, for the reasons elaborated at p. 51 above. This does not necessarily mean that offenders should be required to pay full compensation to their victims in order to be eligible for diversion: as in formal sentencing proceedings, compensation should reflect the offender's means too. Again, the statutory requirements for conditional cautions appear to deal properly with this question, but for informal processes such as restorative conferences there is no legal framework.

(d) PROPORTIONALITY OF IMPOSITION

There should be a sense of proportion between the seriousness of the offence and that which the offender is asked to agree to as part of the diversion. This is not merely a means of ensuring that consent is as voluntary as it can be. It is also a basic element of desert in sentencing: a person who has committed an offence only deserves to be punished to an extent that may be described as appropriate to the seriousness of the offence committed, in terms of harm and culpability. Thus the impositions on those who are 'diverted' must be proportionate to one another, in the sense that more serious cases should involve more onerous requirements and less serious cases should involve less onerous requirements. The impositions should also be of modest severity overall, so that they can appropriately be ranked below court-imposed penalties.

In terms of the human rights discussed at pp. 30–35 above, why is proportionality of sentencing so important? Apart from the strong arguments of principle for ensuring that punishment is proportionate so as to deal fairly with individuals,[101] the European Court of Human Rights has insisted that punishments must not be so disproportionate as to constitute 'inhuman and degrading' punishment under Article 3;[102] the Charter of Fundamental Rights in the European Union, in force since 2003, declares in Article 49(3) that 'the severity of penalties should not be disproportionate to the criminal offence'; and there are other examples of human rights documents insisting on this limitation of State punishment.[103] In terms of human rights law, therefore, the right not to be punished disproportionately to the seriousness of the offence committed seems well established.

---

[100] Criminal Justice Act 2003, discussed in Ch. 6, below.

[101] For elaboration, see A. von Hirsch, *Censure and Sanctions* (1993), Chs. 1 and 2.

[102] *Weeks v United Kingdom* (1988) 10 EHRR 293, and other authorities discussed in Emmerson and Ashworth, *Human Rights and Criminal Justice* (2001), Ch. 16.

[103] See D. van Zyl Smit and A. Ashworth, 'Disproportionate Sentences as Human Rights Violations', (2004) 67 *MLR* 541.

One emergent difficulty, as suggested above, is that some processes which are intended to be beneficial to the offender will in fact be more onerous, in terms of the requirements they impose, than is justified by reference to the seriousness of the offence. This may be a problem with the outcomes of some restorative conferences, and there is therefore an argument in favour of taking steps to limit the impositions that may be made or 'agreed', or to require court approval of the outcome. The same difficulty may arise with some rehabilitative programmes offered as part of diversion: there is a developing range of programmes to tackle alcohol or substance abuse, to manage anger, etc., and the degree of commitment required may be considerable. Proponents of these programmes often claim that it is no use if offenders participate in them for less than the full course; but if this means months of attendance, and therefore considerable impositions by comparison with the seriousness of the offence, there are urgent questions of disproportionality to be addressed.

2.7   CONCLUSION: THE CRIMINAL PROCESS AND THE LIMITATIONS OF HUMAN RIGHTS

In this chapter we have begun to sketch a rights-based theory of the criminal process—that the process should have the twin goals of regulating the processes for bringing suspected offenders to trial so as to produce accurate determinations, and of ensuring that fundamental rights are protected in those processes. We have offered arguments for our belief that this approach should be adopted in England and Wales—both on principle and because it is implicit in international documents such as the European Convention on Human Rights that now play a fundamental role in English law. However, we have also recognized the need to supplement the Convention rights and to develop a fuller statement of rights that would include (for example) the rights of young people and the rights of victims. We have also proposed separate objectives for dispositive decisions, notably the decision to divert a person from the criminal process without trial. We have not overlooked the many conflicts that inevitably occur in the criminal process and the many difficult decisions those require: the human rights framework has been offered as a way of dealing with those conflicts that has a firmer moral and political foundation than consequentialist theories and has greater integrity and transparency than approaches that simply refer to 'balancing.' However, two limitations of rights theories must be kept firmly in view—the gap between the law in action and the law in the books, and the political volatility of criminal justice systems.

(a)   RIGHTS, RHETORIC AND REALITY

Theories of rights are essentially normative: they indicate what should or should not be done, what should be protected and when. To recognize a right is important, but to ensure that it is respected in practice is something different. Our approach to the criminal process based on human rights does not purport to be a description of the present system in operation. Thus we do not overlook the variable gap, sometimes small and sometimes large, between passing a law that recognizes and protects a right and ensuring that the right-holders are in a position to exercise that right as intended. Wherever relevant in this book we refer to empirical evidence that sheds light on whether certain rights or procedures are properly implemented in practice. We will argue that there are respects in which police decisions, decisions by Crown Prosecutors, decisions by magistrates at remand proceedings, and decisions on the acceptance of pleas of guilty (to take just four examples) fail to give due protection to established rights. When we refer with approval to the statutory framework for conditional cautions recently introduced under the Criminal Justice Act 2003, there is no assumption that the requirements will be observed in all cases in practice (see pp. 159–161). That remains to be seen, once there has been an opportunity for either empirical research on conditional cautions or for judicial review of decisions taken.

Generally speaking, what is required to ensure that declared rights are actually respected is not only an ethical commitment on behalf of the relevant agency to respecting those rights (see Chapter 3 below), but also proper information to suspects/defendants about their rights and ready access to legal advice relating to their predicament. The same applies to information about victims' rights, and access to support or information through Victim Support or the Witness Service. There have been several improvements in recent years, but it is a longstanding complaint that neither suspects nor victims and witnesses have all the information they are entitled to expect about their rights and how to exercise them. If they do not, it is likely that there will be a significant gap between the law as declared and the law in practice.

(b) THE POLITICAL VOLATILITY OF THE CRIMINAL PROCESS

In recent years the criminal justice system has increasingly become a focus for political posturing.[104] It is not so much that the two leading political parties have conflicting approaches, but rather that they are trying to outdo one another in the 'toughness' of their rhetoric. As the re-shaping of 'New Labour' began in the 1990s, 'weak' policies on law and order were identified as a potential threat to its other policies and to electoral success: even after the 1997 election victory, by a margin of some 180 seats, the Labour Government continued to regard any 'weakness' in its criminal justice policies as a danger to its popularity—an analysis that attributes considerable influence to the media, sections of which would seize on any apparently 'weak' policies. In the mid-1990s the Conservatives bolstered their political cause through the words and policies of the then Home Secretary, Michael Howard, who proclaimed that 'prison

---

[104] See D. Downes and R. Morgan, 'The Skeletons in the Cupboard: The Politics of Law and Order at the Turn of the Millenium', in M. Maguire, R. Morgan and R. Reiner (eds), *The Oxford Handbook of Criminology* (3rd ed., 2002); M. Tonry, *Punishment and Politics* (2004).

works.' A decade later the same man has returned, now as leader of the Conservative Party, with the same tough talking.[105]

The Government knows, from its own research, that a prison-led policy of public protection is highly unlikely to succeed, even if it were defensible on other grounds. So few offences are reported, so few detected, and so few prosecuted, that increasing the use of imprisonment for the two or three per cent of offenders who fall to be sentenced by the courts is a far less propitious route to public protection than investment in crime prevention policies.[106] Yet the Government's pronouncements, for example in the White Paper of 2002 that preceded the Criminal Justice Act 2003,[107] lay the greatest emphasis on the 'heavy end' of criminal justice—longer sentences for persistent criminals and for 'dangerous' offenders—and fail to set out and publicize a truly evidence-based policy.

Moreover, the Government's pronouncements contain virtually no reference to human rights issues. Although this Government introduced the Human Rights Act, its criminal policy statements tend to pay no attention to the issue, and often seem to make a virtue out of avoiding or minimizing human rights protections. When the Joint Committee on Human Rights examined the Criminal Justice Bill presented to Parliament in late 2002, it found many respects in which the Bill appeared to have been put together either in ignorance or in defiance of the Convention. For example, ss 9 and 10 of the Criminal Justice Act 2003, on taking fingerprints and intimate samples from all arrested persons irrespective of whether they are charged, raise issues under Article 8 and the protection of personal data.[108] The presumption against bail for those who have previously failed to surrender to bail (s 16) does not reflect the approach of Article 5 of the Convention or the Strasbourg Court's insistence on avoiding 'stereotyped' reasoning in favour of assessing the facts in the light of a presumption of liberty.[109] The Bill's provisions on character were strenuously attacked by the Joint Committee on Human Rights on three separate grounds, and it is questionable whether their objections have been met by the subsequent amendments.[110] The new hearsay provisions (ss 114 onwards) fail to ensure complete compatibility with the right of effective challenge in Article 6(3)(d), leaving it to judicial discretion to ensure that no conviction is based 'solely or mainly' on evidence that falls foul of the Article 6(3) right.[111] And among the reservations about the exception to the double jeopardy principle is a concern that ss 78 and 79 (on new evidence, and the interests of justice) fail to ensure compliance with Article 14.7 of the International

---

[105] See 'Howard Turns Clock Back on Crime Policy', *The Guardian*, 11 August 2004.

[106] A. Ashworth, 'Criminal Justice Reform: Principles, Human Rights and Public Protection', [2004] Crim LR 516.

[107] Home Office, *Justice for All* (2002).

[108] Joint Committee on Human Rights, *Criminal Justice Bill: Further Report* (11th Report of Session 2002–03), paras 40–54.

[109] *Ibid.*, paras 64–71.

[110] Joint Committee on Human Rights, *Criminal Justice Bill* (2nd Report of Session 2002–03), paras 11–21.

[111] *Ibid.*, paras 24–30.

Covenant on Civil and Political Rights.[112] It is one thing for the Government to try to justify this kind of rights-minimalism; it is quite another thing for it to fail to give explicit recognition to the issues in its policy statements.

If the Government were to try to defend this approach, it would probably be on the ground that it is well aware of the human rights issues, but that the challenge facing contemporary society is of a different order and therefore calls for exceptional measures. Rarely do the media or the Government talk about criminal policy in general. More commonly, they identify particular types of crime and criminal. More stringent or tougher measures are needed (we are told) for the fight against terrorism, for the war on drugs, to combat organized crime, and so forth. This might sound convincing if it were not placed in the context of a society that aspires to the rule of law and which has long proclaimed its adherence to various international treaties on human rights. It is, as we argued at pp. 46–48 above, a complete misconception to argue that human rights become less important whenever the detection and prosecution of serious crime is the objective. On the contrary, at a theoretical level human rights are rights against governments adopting arbitrary processes and failing to observe proper procedures and safeguards when dealing with suspects and defendants. And in terms of the jurisprudence of the Strasbourg Court, there are many pronouncements showing that governments cannot simply remove safeguards under Articles 5 and 6 in the name of the fight against terrorism or other serious crimes.[113] No Government statements on the criminal process discuss these issues in relation to new policies. The rhetoric is all about taking tough measures and protecting victims. There is nothing about upholding human rights (which is also in the public interest), and the rhetoric of protecting victims would not be sustainable on a proper analysis of the ways of protecting people that are likely to be most effective on the available evidence. Our rights approach indicates a framework for dealing with apparent conflicts between individual rights and 'the public interest'—one that urges greater transparency about the weighting of rights, and closer attention to claims about the need to diminish rights and the outcome of doing so, but no meta-principle that purports to resolve all difficult cases.[114]

---

[112] 11th Report (above, n 108), paras 27–38.   [113] See the cases cited in n 84 above.

[114] See also Waldron, above n 77.

3

ETHICS, CONFLICTS AND CONDUCT

Chapter 2 sketched a normative model of the criminal process in which the pursuit of a particular end—retributive justice—was constrained by respect for rights and other values. This chapter examines one way in which the demands of this rather abstract model can be put into practice: through the consideration of ethics. Ethics are important for a number of interconnected reasons: first, as we have just noted, ethical principles can help to close the gap between our aspirations and our day-to-day actions. This is reflected in the fact that ethical codes now exist to guide the conduct of a number of actors in the criminal process. Secondly, while the criminal process is structured by a framework of rules, discretionary decision making plays a crucial role. Rules always leave room for interpretation, and often deliberately preserve discretion. Such discretion should be exercised in an ethical way. A third reason why ethics are important is that the question of just what conduct is ethically right is often not a simple one to answer. It is not much use responding to someone who asks how to exercise their discretion by telling them to do so in a way that both pursues retributive justice and respects rights. This is in part because different actors in the criminal process play different roles, and we expect these roles to mould the way in which they act. Thus, to take the most obvious example, we expect the defence lawyer advising his client to act differently to the police officers who are questioning him. The consideration of ethics involves considering how such roles should guide conduct, and this is no simple matter: there is some room for debate about the correct principles.[1] Finally, ethics are important because actors in the criminal process are constantly tempted to subvert the rules and principles intended to govern their conduct, even when the rules leave little room for interpretation. The criminal process deals with people who have done, or—the qualification is significant—are alleged to have done, all manner of unattractive things, and judgments of 'moral character' may lure officials into bending the rules in order to ensure that such people are convicted, or treated harshly.[2] This is perhaps the greatest challenge to the pursuit of justice in the criminal process—

---

[1] Cf. the classic articles by W.H. Simon, 'The Ethics of Criminal Defense' (1993) 91 *Mich LR* 1703 and D. Luban, 'Are Criminal Defenders Different?' (1993) 91 *Mich LR* 1729.

[2] On judgments of moral character, see e.g. K. Hawkins, *Law as Last Resort* (2003), at 183, 243 and 334–5 on Health and Safety inspectors, and H. Parker, M. Sumner and G. Jarvis, *Unmasking the Magistrates* (1989) on the magistracy.

the temptation to seek justice summarily. It is not only police officers who are inclined to subvert the rules or to act in a way inappropriate to their role; as we will see, defence lawyers, prosecutors and judges all face the same temptation. A strong commitment to ethics, and a clear understanding of the ethical implications of one's role in the system, are therefore cornerstones of the criminal process.

The chapter opens with a brief discussion of the idea of ethical conduct. Next it outlines some *un*ethical practices, and then attempts to examine and reconstruct some possible justifications for such practices. Consideration is then given to the problems of displacing the occupational cultures and other influences which may lead to resistance against change. Formal accountability systems are also discussed, and the chapter concludes with a consideration of the prospects for bringing about changes in the conduct of practitioners within the system.

3.1 RULES, ROLES AND ETHICS

Is there any need to discuss ethics when there are so many legal rules, codes, and guidelines impinging on the work of law enforcement agents? Is there really any room for moral disputation when we have such documents as the Police and Criminal Evidence Act 1984 and its Codes of Practice, the Code for Crown Prosecutors, the Code for Victims, and countless recent statutes on criminal justice? Three good reasons may be offered for pressing ahead with ethical inquiries.

First, ethical principles should apply to those who lay down rules and guidelines as well as to those who are subject to them. Thus there should be no suggestion that ethical issues affect only the lower ranks: the decisions of members of the legislature, the Home Secretary, the Director of Public Prosecutions (the DPP), and the Lord Chief Justice should be equally subject to appraisal on ethical grounds. However, there should be no confusion between legal rules and moral or ethical principles. It is good that legal rules should be based on ethical principles, rather than (say) on short-term pragmatism, but the function of ethical principles is to supply strong reasons for adopting a particular rule. In so far as incorporation of the European Convention on Human Rights into English law imports a kind of higher law, which even legislators should respect, this constitutes one formal source of ethical principles for policy-makers. But, as we saw in Chapter 2, the Convention does not contain all the rights and principles that ought properly to be upheld.

Secondly, there is no warrant for the view that the criminal justice system is entirely covered by rules and clear-cut guidance. Recent years have seen greater efforts to introduce various forms of guidance and accountability, but there are still vast tracts of discretion, some of it deliberate so as to enable flexibility, some eked out by practitioners to allow them to follow their preferred practices. Wherever there is discretion, and even where there are rules, there may be choices between following ethical principles and following other policies or preferences.

Thirdly, it is well known that there are strong occupational cultures among the various professional groups in the criminal justice system. The point is clearest in relation to the police. For example, a study of detectives for the Royal Commission on Criminal Justice concluded that a necessary step towards improving the situation would be 'raising CID officers' awareness of the faults in the traditional "detective culture" ("macho" and "elitist" attitudes, belief that "rules are there to be bent", excessive secrecy and suspicion of outsiders, and so on) and the ease with which young officers are sucked into it, almost without realising it'.[3] In its report, the Royal Commission referred to 'the culture and approach of the Criminal Bar' as a possible obstacle to the success of some of its proposals for streamlining pre-trial procedure.[4] Research into the conduct of criminal defence lawyers has also shown how the culture of many solicitors' firms operates so as to adapt the law and the lawyer's role, in ways that differ from the formal rhetoric and procedures, and which result in less than full protection for suspect-defendants.[5] There is also evidence that judges sitting in the Court of Appeal were received into an occupational culture which, for many years, resulted in a particularly restrictive approach to the exercise of the Court's statutory powers.[6] In the face of such well-entrenched cultures, what are the prospects for rules, let alone guidelines or unfettered discretion? In practical terms these cultures seem to be direct competitors with ethical principles, partly because they often put sectional interests first, but partly also because they sometimes challenge the values of those who argue for the recognition of rights. Exploration of these occupational cultures will be one of the principal tasks in this chapter.

What kind of principle may be described as ethical? It should be a principle that is impartial as between persons, and for which one can give reasons which show a respect for the rights and interests that have a good claim to be protected. Impartiality in this context requires that no preference should be shown towards persons (whether suspects, victims, defendants, or whatever) on extraneous grounds such as wealth, social connections, sex, race, and so forth. It also forbids conduct based on the self-interest of the official or criminal justice practitioner, who ought to act out the ethical commitments attached to the assigned role (e.g. investigating officer, defence lawyer) and set aside personal convenience, profit, or other extraneous motivation. As for rights and interests, this refers not merely to the interests discussed in Chapter 2 above, but also to the fundamental orientation of the criminal process towards either an inquisitorial or an adversarial approach. Although several of the procedures in English criminal justice blur the line between the two, there is little doubt that the fundamental orientation is towards an adversarial model. This, in turn, invests various actors with certain role responsibilities.

Thus the duty of the defence lawyer is 'to promote and protect fearlessly and by

---

[3] M. Maguire and C. Norris, *The Conduct and Supervision of Criminal Investigations* (1992).

[4] Royal Commission on Criminal Justice, *Report* (1993), para 7.36 on preparatory hearings.

[5] M. McConville, J. Hodgson, L. Bridges and A. Pavlovic, *Standing Accused* (1994); M. Travers, *The Reality of Law* (1997).

[6] R. Nobles and D. Schiff, *Understanding Miscarriages of Justice* (2000), Ch. 3.

all lawful and proper means the lay client's best interests.'[7] In relation specifically to criminal defence, the lawyer must endeavour to protect the defendant 'from conviction except by a competent tribunal and upon legally admissible evidence sufficient to support conviction for the offence charged':[8] this requires the defence lawyer to contest all arguable issues, but not necessarily to take advantage of favourable errors made by the prosecutor or the court.[9] This is where the countervailing duty of the lawyer to the court, particularly the duty not to mislead the court, comes into play.[10] Thus when it is said that the defence lawyer's duty is that of 'obtaining an acquittal within the limits of lawful procedure',[11] the last six words demonstrate how the lawyer's duty to the court may override the duty to the client. The extent of the duty to the client is also bounded by the lawyer's personal responsibility for the way in which the defence is run (although the Court of Appeal will only overturn a conviction if the defence advocate was 'flagrantly incompetent').[12] There are several controversial issues in the ethics of defence lawyering, including those relating to the defence of someone who has admitted guilt, to defending where the prosecution or the court has made an error,[13] and to attacking the character of prosecution witnesses.[14] However, in this chapter we are concerned not only with the conflicts within the lawyer's role but also with the conflict between ethical principles and occupational cultures, as we will see in Part 2 below.

Whereas the defence lawyer's role is essentially partisan, that of the prosecuting lawyer should be impartial, not seeking convictions as such but taking on the role of a 'minister of justice'.[15] The prosecutor's goal should be to conduct the case dispassionately, seeking justice according to the law (not relying, for example, on inadmissible evidence) and disclosing to the defence all evidence that should be disclosed. As noted on p. 64 below, the failure of prosecuting lawyers to disclose evidence to the defence lay at the root of some of the notorious cases of miscarriage of justice. In the present context, the point about disclosure illustrates the way in which roles and ethics may be subject to alteration by statute: the disclosure rules were altered by the Criminal Procedure and Investigations Act 1996 and again by the Criminal Justice Act 2003, and the roles (and ethical duties) of both prosecuting and defending lawyers must change with them.

---

[7] General Council of the Bar, *Code of Conduct*, para 203(a).   [8] *Ibid.*, Annex H, para 12.1.

[9] It appears that the distinction lies between errors of law (which the defence lawyer should draw to the court's attention) and errors of fact (which may be allowed to persist): for references and discussion, see M. Blake and A. Ashworth, 'Some Ethical Issues in Prosecuting and Defending Criminal Cases', [1998] Crim LR 16. A recent example of the duty to draw an error of law to the court's attention as soon as it becomes apparent is provided by *Gleeson* [2004] Crim LR 579.

[10] General Council of the Bar, *Code of Conduct*, para 202.

[11] C. Humphreys, 'The Duties and Responsibilities of Prosecuting Counsel,' [1955] Crim LR 739, at 746.

[12] E.g. *Nangle* [2001] Crim LR 506.   [13] See further Blake and Ashworth, above n 9.

[14] See the research by J. Temkin, 'Prosecuting and Defending Rape: Perspectives from the Bar' (2000) 27 J Law & Soc 219.

[15] General Council of the Bar, *Code of Conduct*, Annex H, para 11.

3.2 IDENTIFYING 'UNETHICAL' PRACTICES

In order to provide a factual basis for the discussion in the rest of the chapter, it is now proposed to identify fairly briefly some seven presumptively unethical practices. Many of them are discussed in greater detail later in the book, but it is important at this early stage to illustrate the context in which ethical arguments take place. Whether the practices can properly be termed 'unethical' will not be determined until we have discussed the explanations for them, but they are discussed here because they appear to be unethical. There is no suggestion that all the practices are widespread, but it is believed that they occur on some occasions, and references are given to support this belief.

(a) 'HELPING THE POLICE WITH THEIR INQUIRIES'

One of the purposes of introducing new rules on detention in police stations under the Police and Criminal Evidence Act 1984 was to ensure that persons brought to police stations under arrest were only detained if it was necessary to do so, and if there was sufficient evidence for a charge.[16] Early research by McKenzie, Morgan, and Reiner showed that custody officers routinely authorized detention without an examination of the sufficiency of evidence, and did so by reference to the need 'to secure or preserve evidence or to obtain evidence by questioning'.[17] A more recent Home Office study found the same situation: 'it was exceptional for detention not to be authorised', and this happened in only one of some 4,000 cases.[18] This practice is unethical because it deprives suspects of protection against being detained unless that is absolutely necessary, a protection that Parliament intended to give them.[19]

(b) RIGHTS OF SUSPECTS

The 1984 Act and its Codes of Practice were also designed to lay down standards of fair treatment and to restate the courts' discretion to exclude evidence obtained in contravention of the standards. The reason behind these protections is to spare defendants intimidation, and to enhance the reliability of any evidence that is obtained. Yet the years since 1986 have seen a steady stream of cases in which police officers have been found to have departed from the Codes of Practice on Questioning and on Identification.[20]

---

[16] Police and Criminal Evidence Act 1984, s37.

[17] I. McKenzie, R. Morgan and R. Reiner, 'Helping the Police with their Inquiries: the Necessity Principle and Voluntary Attendance at the Police Station', [1990] Crim LR 22.

[18] C. Phillips and D. Brown, *Entry into the Criminal Justice System* (1998), 49.

[19] E. Cape, *Defending Suspects at Police Stations* (4th ed., 2003), 57–58, citing the statement of the Home Office Minister in 1984 that the detention must be necessary, 'not desirable, convenient or a good idea but necessary.'

[20] See generally Cape, *ibid.*, Ch. 8; among the examples are *Forbes* [2001] 1 AC 473 and *Harris* [2003] EWCA Crim 174.

(c) FAILURE TO INFORM SUSPECTS OF RIGHTS

Another purpose of the 1984 Act was to require the police to inform each suspect/defendant of certain rights—the right to make a telephone call from the police station, the right to have someone informed of one's detention, and the right to have legal advice that is free, independent, and given in a private consultation. After the implementation of the new law in 1986 it was found that not all suspects were being informed of these rights.[21] The relevant Code of Practice was altered in 1991, and further research showed that the rate of informing suspects had increased but was still less than complete; almost all suspects were told of the right to legal advice, but only 73 per cent were told that it is free, 56 per cent were told that it is independent, and hardly any were told that the consultation would be private.[22] A subsequent Home Office study confirmed that the statement of rights was made in different ways at different police stations, suggesting that this might be connected to the differing rates of take-up of legal advice that were found.[23] Insofar as police officers give the statement in an unclear or unduly rapid fashion, or emphasize the possible problems (such as delay) in summoning legal advice, they probably engage in unethical conduct. The motivation may be that they regard the law as impeding the most effective approach to investigation.

(d) FAILURE TO DISCLOSE RELEVANT EVIDENCE

Similar motivation may underlie the failure by the police to disclose to the prosecution or the defence certain evidence in favour of the defence, which was a reason for quashing the convictions in the cases of the Maguire seven, the Birmingham six, and Judith Ward.[24] The Attorney-General's Guidelines on disclosure were not in force at the time of the original trials in these cases, but the principle of disclosure did exist. Similarly, in the case of the Maguire Seven, the results of certain tests carried out by the Forensic Science Service, with results favourable to the defendants, were not notified to the defence. Non-disclosure of forensic evidence also occurred in the cases of the Birmingham Six and Judith Ward. These omissions can be regarded as unethical. Breaches of the disclosure rules were not confined to the 1970s, as subsequent appellate decisions demonstrate.[25] The rules on disclosure have since been changed twice, in 1996 and 2003.[26] Failure to follow statutory requirements conscientiously is unethical, whether it is the police, the prosecution, or the defence that is at fault.

---

[21] A. Sanders and L. Bridges, 'Access to Legal Advice and Police Malpractice', [1990] Crim LR 494.

[22] D. Brown, T. Ellis and K. Larcombe, *Changing the Code: Police Detention under the Revised PACE Codes of Practice* (1993).

[23] Phillips and Brown, above n 18, 61.

[24] For further details, see J. Rozenberg, 'Miscarriages of Justice', in E. Stockdale and S. Casale (eds), *Criminal Justice under Stress* (1993).

[25] E.g. *Fergus* (1994) 98 Cr App R 313.   [26] For discussion, see Ch. 9.2 below.

(e) FAILURE TO PROTECT A CLIENT AT INTERVIEW

One of the reasons for allowing suspects the right to consult a lawyer at a police station is to ensure that the conduct of the police towards the suspect is scrupulously fair. However, in some cases legal advisers are reluctant to intervene to protect their client, allowing hostile and hectoring modes of questioning to pass without comment.[27] In clear cases this is unethical conduct by the legal adviser, particularly where the lawyer's motivation for failing to intervene is not related to advancing the interests of the particular lay client.

(f) FAILURE TO DISCONTINUE A WEAK CASE

A primary reason for introducing the Crown Prosecution Service (CPS) was to bring a professional prosecutorial review into the system, to prevent weak or inappropriate cases from going to court,[28] and for this they were given a power of discontinuance.[29] Despite a discontinuance rate of around 13 per cent, there are still cases which the CPS fail to discontinue even though they know that there is insufficient evidence, perhaps to retain good relations with the police or out of a pro-conviction motivation inconsistent with the 'minister of justice' role that prosecutors are meant to adopt.[30]

(g) AVOIDANCE OF 'PRESUMPTIVE' MODE OF TRIAL

Under the existing system for determining mode of trial, various cases have arisen in which the prosecution has preferred an either-way charge, the defendant has elected Crown Court trial, and the prosecution has thereupon dropped the either-way charge and brought a charge that is triable summarily only, in a magistrates' court. Defendants have challenged these tactics by means of judicial review, and the Divisional Court has held that in general the choice of charge lies within the discretion of the prosecutor so long as the substituted charge is not inappropriate and there is no bad faith, oppression, or prejudice.[31] The CPS Code now instructs prosecutors not to prefer a higher charge in this situation, save in exceptional circumstances. It remains possible to alter the charges before the mode of trial proceedings have begun, which also raises ethical issues. It is one thing to lower the charge to ensure that the case is heard quickly (avoiding the waiting time for the Crown Court) if there are good reasons for this, perhaps connected with victims or other witnesses; it is quite another thing to do

---

[27] See, e.g. D. Roberts, 'Questioning the Suspect: the Solicitor's Role' [1993] Crim LR 368, and J. Baldwin, 'Legal Advice at the Police Station', [1993] Crim LR 371.

[28] Royal Commission on Criminal Procedure, *Report* (1981), para 7.6.

[29] Prosecution of Offences Act 1985, s23, discussed in Ch. 7 below.

[30] J. Baldwin, 'Understanding Judge Ordered and Directed Acquittals in the Crown Court', [1997] Crim LR 536, esp. at 550–2; see further Ch. 7 below.

[31] *R v Liverpool Stipendiary Magistrate, ex p Ellison* [1989] Crim LR 369; cf. the similar legal and ethical problems raised by preferring a new charge and thereby obtaining an extension of time limits, *R v Leeds Crown Court, ex p Wardle* [2001] UKHL 12 and *Wardle v U.K.* (2003) 4 EHRLR 459.

this in the hope of taking advantage of the higher conviction rate in magistrates' courts. Admittedly the ethical argument here is complex, but the temptations for prosecutors require careful assessment.

3.3 UNDERSTANDING 'UNETHICAL' BEHAVIOUR

The preceding section has set out some examples of behaviour that might be described as 'unethical', in the sense that it fails to show proper respect for citizens and often removes, circumvents, or weakens certain rights that should be accorded to the suspect or defendant. There may be other sources of miscarriages of justice, but the focus here is on conduct that may be said to involve some conscious circumvention of the rules. Suspending final judgment on whether these practices are to be termed unethical, we must first inquire into the reasons for them.

There is often a tendency to regard practices of this kind as the product of individuals, exercising a discretion unconstrained by context or by colleagues. This is the 'rotten apple' theory, assuming that a small number of 'rogue' individuals decide to defy the rules. This ignores the fact that these individuals work in a professional context in which several influences such as organizational rules and occupational pressures operate, sometimes fuelled by the unrealistic expectations of the public and others.[32] Thus research into the police has often concluded that much police behaviour is influenced by a 'cop culture' that is spread widely through the organization. There is no need here to enter into an extensive analysis of the findings of the various researchers. It is sufficient to mention four elements that seem to be at the core of 'cop culture':

(a) support for colleagues' decisions and the inappropriateness of close supervision;

(b) what is termed 'the macho image', which includes heavy drinking and physical presence, and may extend to sexist and racist attitudes;

(c) the sense of mission in police work; and

(d) the idea that rules are there to be used creatively and bent.[33]

The suggestion is that these and similar attitudes are widespread, not that they are universal. There may be differences from division to division, particularly between rural and urban areas. There may be individuals or groups, particularly women and some younger police officers, who accept few or no aspects of the culture. Senior

---

[32] K. Hawkins, 'The Use of Legal Discretion: Perspectives from Law and Social Science', in K. Hawkins (ed), *The Uses of Discretion* (1992), at 22.

[33] For detailed discussion, see e.g. J. Skolnick, *Justice without Trial* (1966); J. Chan, 'Changing Police Culture', (1996) 36 *BJ Crim* 109; D. Dixon, *Law in Policing: Legal Regulation and Police Practices* (1997); S. Choongh, 'Policing the Dross: a Social Disciplinary Model of Policing', (1998) 38 *BJ Crim* 623.

officers may argue that changes are taking place, but the stronghold of the culture has always been in the lower ranks. The phenomenon of police culture has been observed so frequently that its existence in some quarters cannot be doubted, even if it must be accepted that its form and intensity are variable.

In an attempt to unravel the reasons which underlie the culture, we may begin by considering (a) support for colleagues' decisions and the inappropriateness of close supervision. Two research studies for the Royal Commission on Criminal Justice in the 1990s found that the supervision of junior officers in the conduct of inquiries and in questioning was not the norm and was often regarded as a breach of the trust that should be shown in every officer's skills.[34] This is linked to the idea of police solidarity and the duty to support a fellow officer, although it may have a darker side, as the Royal Commission recognized in its reference to officers and civilian staff being 'deterred by the prevailing culture from complaining openly about malpractice'.[35] To some extent the isolated position of the police in society may breed a form of solidarity and defensiveness and the culture may reflect the differing perspectives of police officers 'at the sharp end' and those officers who are managers, with the lower ranks covering for one another and trying to shield from senior officers various deviations from the rules.[36]

There is well-established evidence of the existence in the British police of (b), what is termed the 'macho image', manifest in the physical dangers of the job, 'the alcoholic and sexual indulgences' of male police officers, and the struggle of women police officers to gain acceptance.[37] There are, however, important points to be made about this aspect of 'cop culture.' First, it does not follow that there is a precise correlation between the way the police talk and behave when off-duty, and their conduct of their duties.[38] The demanding nature of police work may be said to make it necessary to 'let off steam' when off-duty or in the canteen, and it does not necessarily mean that this translates into conduct at work.[39] Secondly, on the allegation that racism forms part of the police culture, Robert Reiner suggests that some interpretations fail to take proper account of the nature of police work in a society that places ethnic minorities at a disadvantage in many respects.[40] Indeed, Reiner argues more generally that, just as it is unrealistic to regard police malpractices as stemming from isolated individuals without reference to the wider police culture, it is equally unrealistic to focus on the culture without reference to the social structures that contribute to and sustain it. Account must be taken of the role assigned to the police in society—as a form of social

---

[34] J. Baldwin, *Supervision of Police Investigations in Serious Criminal Cases* (1992); Maguire and Norris, above n 3.

[35] RCCJ Report, para 2.65.   [36] R. Reiner, *The Politics of Policing* (3rd ed., 2000), 101–3.

[37] *Ibid.*, 97–98, for the evidence.

[38] C. Hoyle, *Negotiating Domestic Violence* (1998), Ch. 4, for a sustained discussion of both empirical evidence and theoretical interpretations.

[39] P.A.J. Waddington, 'Police (Canteen) Culture: an Appreciation', (1999) 39 *BJ Crim* 286.

[40] Reiner, above n 36, 98–99 and 124–134.

service that has to deal with the least advantaged people, as well as meeting targets that often imply a degree of control over social events that they simply cannot exert.

In a sense the typical elements of 'cop culture' may appear to be odd bedfellows of (c), the sense of mission in police work. This is a serious-minded, socially conservative cluster of attitudes which celebrate the position of the police as a 'thin blue line' standing between order and chaos. Of course it is not claimed that the mission, any more than the culture, is monolithic. Indeed, the conflict in police ideologies between advocates of 'zero tolerance' and advocates of the 'problem-solving' approach demonstrates one clear difference. The research evidence regards the mission as strengthened by seeing the police as being on the side of the right, serving society and ranged against offenders and other miscreants who are in the wrong. Reiner describes the subtle interplay of three themes: 'of mission, hedonistic love of action, and pessimistic cynicism' that constitute the core of the police outlook.[41] Many officers join the police with a sense of mission, in terms of defending society and its institutions against attack and disorder, and then develop a kind of cynicism about social trends that seem to threaten existing ways of doing things. The Royal Commission appeared to accept some such view:

'We recognize that police malpractice, where it occurs, may often be motivated by an over-zealous determination to secure the conviction of suspects believed to be guilty in the face of rules and procedures which seem to those charged with the investigation to be weighted in favour of the defence.'[42]

To be sceptical about the moral quality of this police mission would be easy: it certainly contains its contradictions, in that it purports to emphasize established moral values when there is evidence that some officers rejoice in various sexual exploits, and in that it adopts a puritanical attitude towards drug-users when police alcoholism is a long-standing problem.[43] Yet, these contradictions apart, there is a true sense in which the police are performing an essential and central social function. To this extent both the term 'police force' and its modern successor, 'police service', contain elements of realism. There is nothing unhealthy in having a sense of mission about that, any more than it is unhealthy for doctors, nurses, or even lawyers to have a sense of mission. Just as people are right to expect committed medical care when ill or injured, so citizens are entitled to expect committed official action when they fall victim to a crime or in the face of threats to good order. Often, this amounts to the protection of the weak against the predatory. But while the vital nature of this social function cannot be disputed, its definition can be—not least when it leads to forms of so-called 'noble cause corruption,' with officers succumbing to the temptation to seek justice summarily, as we put it in the opening paragraph of the chapter. Elements of police culture evidently define the police mission differently from Parliament, for example, since police officers often express contempt for 'legal restrictions'. There is

---

[41] *Ibid.*, 90.   [42] RCCJ Report, para 1.24.   [43] Reiner, above, n 36, 98.

no question that the maintenance of good order counts, but there is room for debate about what counts as the maintenance of good order.

This leads us directly to (d): the idea that rules are there to be used creatively and bent. The sense of mission may be so powerful that it displaces respect for the laws. There are two strands to this. The first emphasizes the use of the criminal law as a resource for legitimating or reinforcing police handling of a situation: the police officer has available a range of offences with which to support his or her authority, and may decide whether or not to invoke one of them as a reason for arrest and charge.[44] Of course this is hardly applicable to crimes such as murder, rape, and armed robbery, but it can be applied to the range of public order offences, obstruction and assault on police officers, and a number of other charges. The primary objective of the police may be to keep the peace and to manage situations; in this they use and exert authority; anyone who resists that authority may be arrested and even charged. The second strand concerns the various procedural rules about questioning, notably the Codes of Practice under PACE. The reason these rules are broken from time to time is that they are seen as unwise impediments to proper police work, standing in the way of vigorous questioning which will get at the truth, or (sometimes) will produce the results which senior police officers or the media seem to want. On the one hand there is pressure arising from the high expectations of others; on the other there is a belief that those expectations cannot be met when lawmakers fail to understand the realities of police work.

Compared with the police, rather less is known about the occupational cultures of other groups within the criminal justice system. But it should not be thought that other groups do not have working cultures which pull against the ethical discharge of their role responsibilities, and a few words can be said here about defence solicitors and crown prosecutors. In the detailed study of a number of criminal defence practices in England and Wales by McConville, Hodgson, Bridges, and Pavlovic, several unethical practices were discovered at various stages. Once again, the researchers do not claim that all criminal defence practices operate, or operated, in this way: indeed, they point out that some practices are well run and properly orientated. But they draw attention to some defence lawyers' failure to protect clients in police stations from improper questioning,[45] encouraging or even engineering a plea of guilty in spite of the client's inclinations,[46] 'selling out' clients in court by using a particular phraseology that makes it clear to magistrates that the lawyer believes that the client's instructions are unworthy of belief.[47] Why might defence lawyers and their staff indulge in these and other kinds of unethical behaviour? The research leads to various suggestions. One of these is that some of the practices are driven by financial considerations, arising from the structure of the legal aid system. There was also evidence that some

---

[44] For a classic study on this, see E. Bittner, 'The Police on Skid Row: a Study in Peacekeeping', (1967) 32 *American Sociological Review* 699.

[45] McConville *et al*, above n 5, 61–2, 112–5, and 124.

[46] *Ibid.*, 70 and 194ff; also Travers, above n 5, Chs. 5 & 6.

[47] *Ibid.*, 180–1; see also A. Hucklesby, 'Remand Decision Makers', [1997] Crim LR 269, at 278–9.

defence lawyers subscribe to what, in police language, may be termed 'toe-rag theory': that particular clients (or clients of a particular kind, or from a certain family or housing estate) are guilty anyway, are always committing crimes, and therefore it is pointless to go through the motions of a 'full and fearless defence'.[48] This approach may be underpinned by a desire to keep 'on the right side' of the police and the courts where possible, rather than losing credibility by mounting a vigorous defence of a presumptively guilty villain. This leads the authors to suggest that one of the defects may be in the training of solicitors, in that it fails to emphasize the centrality of human rights to the defence lawyer's role responsibilities. In other words, the adversarial system of criminal justice cannot work properly if and to the extent that lawyers fail to provide 'full and fearless' defence of their clients,[49] let alone if they allow their moral judgment of certain clients to detract from their proper role responsibility. And ethical constraints do not pull in a single direction: thus some defence lawyers may attack witnesses in a way or to a degree that strains the boundaries of ethics, sometimes to create a good impression with the client rather than because there really is a material inconsistency in a witness's story.[50]

It is interesting to speculate whether the advent of the Public Defender Service will alter these practices. At present the PDS operates only in eight areas, but preliminary research findings comparing its police station work with that of contracted private firms suggests that fewer PDS clients were charged or summoned than the clients of private firms.[51] This may tend to confirm the findings of the research by McConville and others which suggest that some firms may not always exert themselves on behalf of the client. The PDS itself argues that 'as we have no inbuilt financial incentive to prolong cases it helps us really to focus on our clients' needs.'[52] When the full findings of the research project are known, they may shed light on the motivation of private defence lawyers as well as the PDS.

Lastly, what about unethical behaviour by crown prosecutors? In this sphere there is considerably less research to draw upon, but there is some evidence that crown prosecutors sometimes resolve the conflicting pressures upon them by indulging in unethical conduct. One example already given is that prosecutors may fail to discontinue a weak case, even though aware of the weakness, for reasons which can only be described as unethical—for example, a desire to keep 'on the right side' of the police, or fear of an adverse reaction from the police, or even agreement with the police view that the defendant deserves to be put through a trial.[53] A closely-related example might be where a key exhibit or a vital witness goes missing at the eleventh hour: the ethical approach might be to discontinue, or at least to draw the predicament

---

[48] A. Mulcahy, 'The Justifications of "Justice" ', (1994) 34 *BJ Crim* 411.

[49] See further M. McConville, 'Plea Bargaining: Ethics and Politics', in S. Doran and J. Jackson (eds), *The Judicial Role in Criminal Proceedings* (2000).

[50] McConville *et al*, above n 5, 219; also P. Rock, *The Social World of an English Crown Court* (1993), Ch. 2.

[51] The interim research report is available at www.legalservices.gov.uk

[52] *Putting Clients First: Public Defender Service, Annual Report 2003–04* (2004), 4.

[53] Baldwin, above n 30; cf. also the discussion by McConville, above n 49.

to the attention of the defence, whereas continuing with the case in the hope that the loss will not come to light is surely unethical. If it is accepted that the role of the prosecutor, even in an adversarial system, is to act as a minister of justice, these and related practices should be condemned as unethical.

3.4 JUSTIFYING 'UNETHICAL' BEHAVIOUR BY CHALLENGING THE ETHICS

In the foregoing paragraphs we have discussed possible reasons for the occupational cultures of various criminal justice agencies and for resulting conduct which appears unethical. One element running through these explorations is that some, even many, of those who act in the ways described may argue that their behaviour is ultimately ethical. In other words, they may claim the moral high ground, and argue that the notions of ethics being relied upon here are flawed, limited, and inappropriate.

(a) ARGUMENTS FOR CIRCUMVENTING RULES

In order to establish the context for any such redefining of the ethical, we might consider three standpoints that appear to ooze practicality and good sense, particularly among those who work in particular parts of the criminal justice system. The first, already mentioned in one context, is the argument that certain rules should be circumvented because the rulemakers do not understand the practical problems. The second is that it is wrong to expect police, prosecutors, etc. to operate with 'their hands tied behind their backs'. And the third is that, when the CPS drops a case, or when a court gives a lenient sentence, or even when the Court of Appeal quashes a conviction, this is bad for morale in the criminal justice system. All these standpoints are connected, but they deserve brief discussion individually.

Is it right to circumvent rules on the ground that the rulemakers do not understand the day-to-day, on-the-ground problems of the criminal process? The claim is heard in various quarters. It is heard among some police officers in relation to PACE and its Codes of Practice: these are restrictions imposed by people who expect 'results' and yet do not understand the difficulties the police have to encounter. A similar claim might be heard among barristers who resent the procedural imperatives and preparation times associated with Plea and Directions Hearings and other pre-trial assessments.[54] There are three problems with a claim of this kind. First, there is the constitutional argument: any official or public organization that substitutes its own judgment for one reached through the appropriate democratic channels is behaving unconstitutionally. Both the police and lawyers' groups are well able to put their

---

[54] RCCJ Report, para 7.36; Auld Report, *Review of the Criminal Courts* (2001), 490–2.

points in political debate, and should therefore accept the outcome in their work. Secondly, there is the values argument: the claim assumes that crime control, in a fairly absolute form, is the only value that is in the public interest. It gives no weight to the protection of the rights of suspects. And thirdly, there is the evidential argument: is it really true that 'the job' cannot be done if the restrictions are observed? In fact this is less likely to be a matter of evidence than a question of values again, since the claim that the job cannot be done suppresses the unarticulated clause, 'within the prevailing culture'. If a different culture prevailed, perhaps the job could be done. One can only plausibly assert that it cannot be done if one assumes no change in the culture. These three arguments expose the weaknesses of the claim that it may be justifiable to circumvent rules made by out-of-touch rule-makers. They apply no less to the view said to obtain among some magistrates' clerks some years ago, that High Court rulings were there to be circumvented because 'the judges did not understand the practicalities, e.g. of dealing with truculent, often regular, customers, or a busy court schedule'.[55] This, again, seems to have been based on the assumption that the conviction of the 'guilty' is important above all else.

The second claim is similar in some respects. It is that society expects the police to combat crime with their hands tied behind their backs, or that society expects prosecutors to obtain convictions with one hand tied behind their backs. The precise formulation varies, but the target is always the 'restrictions' imposed, usually by the legislature but sometimes by the higher judiciary. The claim could be countered by means of the three arguments deployed above—the constitutional point, the values argument, and the question of evidence. However, another argument is worth raising here: the assumption that respecting the rights of suspects significantly diminishes the number of convictions and therefore the protection of the public and of victims. This is a complicated argument, requiring considerable space to develop and to rebut. Suffice it to say here that no clear evidence has been found that the adverse inferences from silence permitted for some ten years since the Criminal Justice and Public Order Act 1994 have produced a significant increase in convictions. They have produced changes in working practices within the criminal process, as Home Office research demonstrates,[56] but the failure to meet the objectives of increasing the number of convictions—and critics always argued that this might mean an increase in wrongful convictions—suggests that the rather complicated legal distinctions that have grown up around the 1994 Act are simply not worthwhile and that the adverse inference provisions should be abolished.[57] Thus giving protection to suspects does not necessarily mean fewer convictions: it is not a zero-sum game, as it were.

The third claim is that it is bad for police morale when the CPS decides against

---

[55] The words of a magistrates' clerk, quoted by A. Rutherford, *Criminal Justice and the Pursuit of Decency* (1993), 62.

[56] T. Bucke, R. Street and D. Brown, *The Right of Silence: The Impact of the Criminal Justice and Public Order Act 1994* (2000).

[57] D. Birch, 'Suffering in Silence: a Cost-Benefit Analysis of section 34 of the Criminal Justice and Public Order Act 1994', [1999] Crim LR 769.

pursuing a particular case, contrary to the wishes of the police. Parallel claims are sometimes heard when a court gives a low sentence on conviction, and there is also the suggestion that one reason why station sergeants tend not to refuse charges from officers who bring in arrestees is that it might affect morale. Now as an empirical proposition this claim may well be correct. Such events may reduce police morale, as may new restrictions on their questioning of suspects, changes in their pay and conditions, and several other matters. The problem here is whether one should defer to the conservatism that underlies the morale of many professions, including the police, a conservatism no doubt linked with a sturdy defence of the police mission. The police mission is therefore a crucial element in any attempt to redefine the ethical approach. What kind of ethics, it might be asked, could call into question the vigorous pursuit of the fundamental social functions of crime prevention and conviction of the guilty?

(b) RE-ASSESSING THE ETHICAL APPROACH

To answer this question, we might begin by constructing a model version of the mission. Some of the main elements have been described above, but there is a need for a rounded version that could fit the words and opinions of police officers. The key element is crime control: this is surely the point of the criminal justice system. It means that law observance should be maintained. In this the police are inevitably in the front line, having peace-keeping functions that (in terms of time spent) outstrip the processing of suspected offenders. A second element is that, where the interests of the defendant conflict with those of the victim or society, priority should be given to the latter. A third and connected element, following from the first two, is that the police should pursue this society-centred approach so far as is possible, exploiting any discretion left by the criminal justice system to further the conviction of those whom they believe to be guilty. Taken together, these elements of crime control and the protection of society may be treated as establishing a powerful case in favour of the police mission. If we are not to descend into anarchy, someone has to do it. Better that it be done in a committed way than without any sense of its social importance.

Assuming that there is some truth in this account, is it defensible? Almost every step suffers from confusion which, when examined, mixes overstatement with understatement and neglects important features of social life. It would be easy to claim that this is because this version of the police mission has been formulated in a way favourable to the thesis being advanced: but the counter-arguments below can be ranged against any other version of the police mission that keeps faith with what has been found by on-the-ground research.[58] The counter-arguments are these.

The first element refers to crime control as if it were to be pursued without regard to any other values. Is it plausible to advance such an uncomplicated notion? To take an extreme but telling example, does it suggest that the police should be free to use

---

[58] E.g. the findings of Maguire and Norris, above n 3.

repressive measures wherever they regard them as appropriate, or that torture should be available for use on those suspected of serious crimes? If the answers are negative, as they should be, then we need to adopt a more sophisticated and sensitive notion than 'crime control'. Many people might accept at first blush that crime control is the ultimate aim of the criminal justice system, but on reflection they would surely recognize that it ought not to be pursued without qualification. That would lead to a police state.

The second element is that priority should be given to the victim or society over the interests of the suspect/defendant. In the vernacular this might be called 'toe-rag theory', since its essence is that the interests of the 'innocent and good' should be preferred over those of the suspect or defendant. As one constable stated some years ago, 'Speaking from a policeman's point of view it doesn't give a damn if we oppress law-breakers, because they're oppressors in their own right.'[59] This seems to suggest that accused persons should have no rights, or few rights, or at least rights that can be overridden when that is necessary in the public interest (as interpreted by the police). This is to turn the idea of rights on its head. The whole idea of rights is that they respect the individual's autonomy and ensure that the individual is protected from certain kinds of inappropriate behaviour and is furnished with certain assistance when he or she is in the hands of public officials. As we saw in Chapter 2 above, rights are essentially anti-utilitarian claims, in the sense that they represent claims that the individual not be treated in certain ways even if that might handicap pursuit of some collective good. However, the idea of priority for 'the interests of society' seems to accord the individual suspect or defendant no particular rights, and to deny the whole legitimacy of human rights such as those incorporated in the European Convention and discussed at pp. 32–35 above.[60] Moreover, it does so at a stage before the suspect or defendant has been convicted, thereby affirming a strong presumption of guilt arising from the investigating officer's belief. Is it really acceptable to place so much emphasis on the judgment of one or more police officers, especially when one element in the cop culture is a mutual support and respect for the skills of others which frowns on routine supervision?

These arguments also show the weakness of the third element, always seeking to promote the interests of society against those of the suspect. This is flawed for various reasons. Suspects are members of society. Even members of society who are unlikely to be suspected of crime might accept that those who are suspected should be accorded some rights. Few would agree that it should be for the police to decide which suspects should be accorded rights and which not. The notorious cases of miscarriage of justice leave us well aware that police officers' judgments of someone's guilt or innocence should not be determinative. Surely the ethical approach for the police is to

---

[59] Quoted by Reiner, above n 36, 89.

[60] This is not to overlook the importance of victims' rights, which may on occasion conflict with those of suspects and defendants. But, again, there is a difference between victims' interests and the public interest: for further discussion, see pp. 48–52 above.

ensure that evidence is collected fairly and then presented to the court for its adjudication. Upholding the right to a fair trial requires fairness in the gathering of evidence and in the construction of the case.

The conclusion is therefore irresistible that the 'police mission' described above cannot claim the moral high ground: it is not a 'noble cause,' and does not justify officers in seeking to do justice summarily. It overstates the notion of crime control by assuming that this should be pursued either without qualification or with only such qualifications as the police deem appropriate. It assumes that respect for the rights of suspects is bound to detract from crime control, and does so for insufficient reason. In this it understates the importance of respect for human rights, even for those suspected or accused of a crime. And, like the 'balancing' approaches criticized in Chapter 2, it shows no appreciation of the subtlety and structures of arguments about the extent of human rights, and rather tends to assume that human rights should be overridden whenever it can be said to be in the public interest to do so.

Any challenge by prosecutors to the ethical approach might take a similar form: the essence would be that certain rules and procedures stand in the way of what is right in terms of crime control. For example, John Baldwin found that some crown prosecutors would run a relatively weak case where the charge was a serious one: he quotes one as saying that 'the more serious the case and the more finely balanced it is, the more you stretch the point'. He concludes that 'some CPS lawyers share a common value system with the police, a core element of which is that serious cases ought to be prosecuted, almost irrespective of considerations as to evidential strength'.[61] The supporting argument would be, therefore, that this is necessary to ensure that wrongdoers are brought to book, and that the 'stretching' of the rules is justified by that end. The counter-arguments are (a) that this is not the prosecutor's function in an adversarial system, since the prosecutor should act as a minister of justice who is not concerned to maximize the number of convictions but to ensure that the due process of the law is carried through; and (b) that the purported justification that 'there is a lot more at stake in letting a potential rapist, murderer or child abuser off the hook'[62] overlooks what is at stake for the individual defendant, which is why the Royal Commission of 1981 insisted that 'a realistic prospect of conviction', not simply a *prima facie* case, should be required before a defendant is put through a trial.[63]

3.5 DISCRETION AND ACCOUNTABILITY

It will be evident from the foregoing paragraphs that many of the decisions to be taken by criminal justice agencies are characterized by discretion rather than by binding rules. As Keith Hawkins puts it:

---

[61] Baldwin, above n 30, 551.   [62] A senior crown prosecutor, quoted by Baldwin, *ibid.*
[63] For further discussion, see Ch. 7 below.

'Discretion arising from a number of sources suffuses the processes of law enforcement and regulation. Discretion is plastic, shaped and given form to some extent by the institutions of law and legal arrangements and more substantially by decision-makers' framing behaviour. Systems of formal rules, for all their appearance of precision and specificity, work in only imprecise ways. Indeed, precision and consistent practice are not necessarily assisted by the drafting of ever more elaborate schemes of rules. The legal system is not neatly carved up by smoothly functioning institutional arrangements, but in reality, as a loosely coupled set of subsystems, is more messy, with internal inefficiencies and conflicts. Those enforcing rules may seek to attain the broad aim of a legal mandate in general terms, but the specific question of whether and how a particular rule applies in a particular circumstance will inevitably be reserved for, or assumed within, the discretion of the legal actor concerned.'[64]

Thus, as we have seen in this chapter, whether there are rules or areas of discretion, occupational cultures and working practices may exert an influence on how people with power in the criminal process actually operate. One way of trying to combat this is through codes of ethics, but their prospects of success are variable. One institutional approach to ensuring that the various authorities fulfil their functions and exercise their powers as they ought to is through systems of accountability. We have already seen how values such as the protection of declared rights (of victims and suspects or offenders) and the prevention of abuse of power by officials might be threatened if the policies or the practices of a law enforcement agency diverge from the purposes of the system. Methods of accountability should include proper scrutiny of general policies, rules, and/ or guidelines for decision making, active supervision of practice, avenues for challenging decisions, and openness rather than secrecy at key stages.

In a democratic form of society, issues of public policy should be decided by the legislature. However, in matters of law enforcement the tendency has been for Parliament to avoid such issues and to leave them to each agency itself, usually without any check other than the formal requirement to submit annual reports to the House of Commons. Thus agencies such as the Inland Revenue, Customs and Excise, and the Health and Safety Commission are relatively free to determine their own policies: although some of their procedures are authorized by statute, there is no overall body that reviews the policies and practices of these agencies, despite their tremendous significance for the reach of the criminal process. On the other hand, the tendency has been to draw the police increasingly under a system of central control. Although there remains a considerable degree of local accountability, the thrust of the first part of the Police Reform Act 2002 is to give statutory authority for increased central control, empowering the Home Secretary not only to set performance targets but also to issue a code of practice for chief constables, to bring certain operations under national control, and to exert greater control over the appointment and dismissal of chief constables.[65]

---

[64] K. Hawkins, *Law as Last Resort* (2003), 424–5.
[65] See further D. Ormerod and A. Roberts, 'The Police Reform Act 2002', [2003] Crim LR 141.

More generally, law enforcement bodies are subject to scrutiny from various government and parliamentary sources. The Select Committee procedure applies, and thus the Home Affairs Committee has examined the performance of such organizations as the police, the CPS, the Forensic Science Service, and the Prison Service. Within Government, there is also the role of the Audit Commission in assessing the performance of agencies. The existence of these bodies adds to accountability, even though their direct powers are limited. Perhaps of greater operational impact are the inspectorates in the criminal justice system. The police, the Probation Service, the Prison Service and now the CPS are overseen by Her Majesty's Inspectors, who issue annual reports that obtain considerable publicity. However, there are other major law enforcement agencies that stand outside any such system of independent inspection: neither the Inland Revenue, nor the Environment Agency, Health and Safety Commission or any of the other so-called regulatory agencies is subject to inspection, and there is certainly no such body to oversee the work of defence lawyers who receive criminal legal aid money, let alone the work of the judiciary.

Are law enforcement agencies accountable to the courts? There is a number of public law doctrines available, but the tendency has been to confine judicial review to the outer limits of unreasonableness (by applying the *Wednesbury* principle).[66] In recent years there have been some cases of successful judicial review of certain policies for and against prosecution,[67] but the prevailing attitude remains one of reluctance.

Accountability is an important feature of a criminal justice system. It encourages transparency, it may enhance the protection of the rights of individuals, and it helps to ensure that the power entrusted to law enforcement authorities is not abused. However, it is wrong to rely on *post hoc* accountability methods to secure these desirable goals. If more members of the public can be drawn into the criminal process, whether as lay visitors in police stations or through jury service, that increases transparency. But the key objective is to ensure that rules and guidelines are applied faithfully, and not limited in their practical effect because their purpose and spirit are not accepted by those who are supposed to apply them. It will therefore be argued that there is a key role for training and for ethical orientation.

3.6 CRIMINAL JUSTICE REFORM THROUGH ETHICS

Law enforcement agencies and the administration of criminal justice are governed by masses of legislative rules, and yet it is well established that: (i) even rules can be adapted, (ii) there are wide areas of discretion, and (iii) there must continue to be some areas of discretion. One step, to promote respect for 'rule of law' ideals and to

---

[66] See P. Craig, 'Grounds for Judicial Review: Substantive Control over Discretion', in D.J. Feldman (ed), *English Public Law* (2004).

[67] See Chs. 6 and 7 below.

avoid the kind of arbitrariness against which Articles 5 and 6 of the Convention are intended as safeguards, is to attempt to structure discretion by the use of guidance and guidelines. Other common features of reform proposals are better training of criminal justice personnel and better lines of accountability. Measures of this kind, espoused in various forms by such politically disparate groups as the 1993 Royal Commission on Criminal Justice after their review of criminal justice processes and by Michael McConville, Andrew Sanders, and Roger Leng at the end of their sharply critical research report on police and prosecution services,[68] are now recognized to be far more promising than mere changes in legal rules.

The reason for this is the strength of occupational cultures within such key agencies as the police, the CPS, the various regulatory inspectorates, defence solicitors, the criminal Bar, the Forensic Science Service, and so on. More has been said here about the occupational culture of the police, to some extent justifiably since they form the principal filter into the criminal justice system, but we have also reviewed evidence on occupational cultures within the CPS, among defence lawyers, and even among appellate judges. What is noticeable about at least some of the occupational cultures in criminal justice is that their concern is not simply to preserve established working practices or to defend traditional territories of influence, but also to see that 'justice' is done. This is the sense of mission. Everything turns, of course, on what one takes to be 'justice' in this context. We must refuse to accept references to 'the interests of justice', 'the public interest', and even (more emotively) 'the interests of victims'—unless it is carefully spelt out how exactly these rather sweeping claims have been arrived at. We need to identify the values that underlie such statements, and then consider what values should be recognized in criminal justice. But this essential part of the ethical approach cannot be treated in isolation: one cannot expect changes in the culture of lawyers, let alone in the culture of the police, so long as politicians and other key figures fail to show respect for the value of human rights and other ethical precepts.[69]

To expect those working in criminal justice to adopt an ethical approach, it is necessary to have some kind of code of ethics. To expect rules alone to change behaviour may be naïve, but without some rules or guidance it is unlikely that behaviour will be changed at all. So the priority must be to formulate and to develop codes of ethics that not only set out the proper spirit and orientation of those performing certain functions, but also give examples of points at which an ethical approach might differ from an unethical approach. In this respect, both the General Council of the Bar's *Code of Conduct for Barristers* and the Law Society's *Code for Advocacy* stand in need of some reconsideration: the use of examples could improve them significantly. Although the Bar's *Code of Conduct* includes some ethical

---

[68] M. McConville, A. Sanders and R. Leng, *The Case for the Prosecution* (1991), Ch. 10.

[69] See the powerful argument of J. Chan, 'Changing Police Culture', (1996) 36 *BJ Crim* 109 on the link between police culture and prevailing socio-political attitudes.

principles for prosecutors, these should be reconsidered and an ethical code for Crown Prosecutors developed in parallel.[70]

To formulate such principles, reflection on the proper roles of the various groups and agencies within the criminal justice system would be needed. The literature of English criminal procedure is replete with statements about the proper role of the prosecutor. In the nineteenth century it was said that the motivation of a prosecutor should be that of a Minister of Justice,[71] and this was elaborated by Sir Herbert Stephen when he wrote that the object of the prosecutor should be 'not to get a conviction, without qualification, but to get a conviction only if justice requires it'.[72] The rhetoric of this position recognizes that obtaining convictions should not be regarded as the sole or dominant aim of the prosecutor, and that the concept of justice also includes recognition of certain rights of defendants and of victims.[73] The CPS vision includes a commitment to 'prosecuting cases vigorously, robustly and fairly',[74] but this particular document stops short of giving guidelines or even examples of practices this would favour or disfavour. Somewhere the CPS should articulate guidance on ethical approaches to situations where, for example, the prosecutor realizes that the court has made an error in favour of the prosecution, or realizes that certain evidence may have been obtained unfairly, or enters into plea negotiations despite doubts that the charge(s) can be sustained in court, or is tempted to make representations at remand proceedings even though it is unclear that the statutory requirements for a custodial remand are fulfilled.[75]

In respect of defence lawyers the reasons for spelling out the ethical approach are no less pressing. It is insufficient to state, in a broad way, that the lawyer should seek to protect the client while not misleading the court. There must be a sharper statement of the defence lawyer's guiding function: where the objective of providing a 'full and fearless' defence conflicts with the lawyer's duty to the court, it is essential to spell out what course this indicates in a range of common situations. Among those would be the problems of defending a person believed to be guilty, particularly where the lawyer believes that perjury has been or will be committed; where the defence lawyer knows of an error of law, or alternatively an error of fact, in the proceedings which favours the defence; where advice has to be offered to a client who wishes to plead not guilty; where the client wishes the lawyer to make an application for bail against the lawyer's professional judgment; and so on.[76]

---

[70] For general analysis of these codes and their professional context, see D. Nicolson and J. Webb, *Professional Legal Ethics* (1999), Ch. 4.

[71] Crompton J in *Puddick* (1865) 1 F & F 497.

[72] H. Stephen, *The Conduct of an English Criminal Trial* (1926), 11.

[73] Cf. the somewhat ambivalent statement in the American book by C.M. Nissman and E. Hagen, *The Prosecution Function* (1982), 2: 'In pursuing his goal to seek justice, the prosecutor must punch through the tiresome criminal defender, whose goals are necessarily in conflict with the search for truth and justice.' The concept of justice carries much freight here.

[74] Crown Prosecution Service, *Annual Report 2002–03*, 4.

[75] See further Blake and Ashworth, above n 9.

[76] *Ibid.*; see also Nicolson and Webb, above n 70, Ch. 7, and Legal Services Commission, *Code for the Criminal Defence Service* (2005).

The reason for emphasizing the importance of giving examples is to try to give the ethical principles the greatest chance of practical success. While many lawyers are dismissive of rules of this kind, on the basis that 'each case depends on its own facts', this is not entirely true. Some situations and ethical dilemmas are common, and for those an orientation can be given; for unusual and controversial situations, only general ethical principles may be offered. However, ethical guidance that is as detailed as possible would help to confront those elements of occupational culture that are known to give priority to unethical motivations such as financial reward, preserving contacts, and distaste for particular suspect/defendants. Defining the role responsibility of a defence lawyer, prosecutor, or police officer is the first step. But no less essential is the further step of putting together examples of situations where there may be a divergence between the ethical and other approaches.

Once this has been done, the next step would be to inculcate the principles through training and other means. The main task would be to convey the reasons why these principles are worth adhering to, whether by abstract instruction or by means of role-play exercises, debates, etc. This approach must be integrated into a programme for retraining personnel at all levels, from senior management down to new recruits. Otherwise, a statement of ethical principles would be a poor match for a well-entrenched occupational culture. The key questions must be addressed convincingly: why must I show respect towards someone who admits to a dreadful crime? If I feel that I can solve a difficult case by deviating from the rules, is it not in the interests of society that I should do so? Both the democratic argument and ethical principles should be elaborated in reply.

These broad prescriptions should be no less applicable to other groups such as judges, court clerks, the Forensic Science Service, the so-called regulatory agencies and so on. No doubt some will be sceptical of the claims of the ethical approach, particularly when pitted against entrenched occupational cultures in certain spheres. Certainly no claim is being made here that, even if successfully defined and then inculcated, it would solve the problems of the pre-trial process. Rather the argument is that it ought to be recognized as a worthwhile part of altering the orientation of the system towards the ideals and values set out in Chapter 2 above. Simply declaring those principles, or other legal rules, is unlikely to work, for reasons that have been explained. The gap between the law in the books and the law in practice will become ever more visible in the chapters that follow, and it is the value-system of those people who dominate practice that emerges as the key element.

4

QUESTIONING

In 1992, the Court of Appeal quashed the convictions of the 'Cardiff three', three young men who had been convicted of murder. There is no doubt that the men were innocent: the actual killer was later located through a DNA match and pleaded guilty at his trial in 2003.[1] One of the pieces of evidence against the Cardiff three was the confession of one of them, Stephen Miller. Quashing the convictions, the Court of Appeal commented on the way in which Miller had been questioned by the police: 'Miller was bullied and hectored. . . . Short of physical violence, it is hard to conceive of a more hostile and intimidating approach by officers to a suspect.'[2] The case highlights one of the key problems that criminal procedure must address, which was identified in the previous chapter. In police detention, suspects like Miller can be subjected to serious abuses. Such abuses are unacceptable in themselves, but also undermine one of the key aims of the criminal process, which is to produce reliable evidence. Faced with police bullying, Miller confessed falsely, and this was one factor accounting for the wrong convictions at trial.

Police questioning is a key pressure point in criminal procedure partly because it is central to police investigative practices. Over the years, the powers of arrest available to the police have been extended, allowing them to rely on detention for questioning in a greater proportion of cases. During questioning, it is perhaps not surprising that the aim of the police will be to produce a confession. The majority of suspects—around 60 per cent—do make some form of confession, and confessions are powerful evidence, likely to secure a conviction at trial.[3] Suspects who are not forthcoming about their guilt may be seen as obstructing the police investigation. The reaction of the police may then be to put more pressure on the suspect, by detaining and questioning him for longer and by adopting a harsher tone.[4] This is doubtless the sort of process that led to the oppressive questioning of Miller. A further possibility is that, given that confessions are good evidence, police officers may 'verbal' suspects by falsely attributing incriminating statements to them. These

[1] 'Real Killer Jailed in Case of Cardiff 3' *The Guardian*, 5 July 2003.

[2] *R v Paris, Abdullahi and Miller* (1992) 97 Cr App R 99, 103.

[3] M. McConville, *Corroboration and Confessions: The Impact of a Rule Requiring that No Conviction Can Be Sustained on the Basis of Confession Evidence Alone* (1993), 32–33. In 98 per cent of cases where a confession was secured, the suspect pleaded or was found guilty.

[4] See S.M. Kassin *et al*, 'Behavioral Confirmation in the Interrogation Room: On the Dangers of Presuming Guilt' (2003) 27 *Law & Human Behavior* 187.

occurrences are constant dangers, ones which criminal procedure needs to erect safeguards against.

During the 1990s there were significant changes to the context of police questioning. The beginning of the decade saw considerable concern about false confessions. Although the regulation of police detention through PACE was often said to have made such concerns redundant, the Cardiff three case, and others, showed that serious abuses and false confessions could still occur.[5] There was considerable talk about a change in police interviewing practices, towards a style of 'investigative interviewing' in which the police did not assume guilt and were prepared to listen to the suspect's explanations.[6] Police investigative practices were also said to be changing in another way, becoming less reliant on confessions and more so on proactive policing, using intelligence and sting operations.[7] Some of these practices have problems of their own (see the discussion of surveillance in Chapter 5 and entrapment in Chapter 9) and it is not evident that they have led to much change in the way police question suspects.[8] Even if there has been a move away from aggressive interviewing, the 1990s saw other changes which have contributed to making the police interview room a more pressurized environment. In spite of the recommendation of the Royal Commission on Criminal Justice that the 'right to silence'—the rule that adverse inferences should not be drawn from a suspect's silence—be retained, soon after the Commission reported the Conservative Government announced that it would be seeking to abolish the right. Important changes to the right to silence were then introduced by the Criminal Justice and Public Order Act 1994. The legislation will be discussed in more detail below, but at this stage it is worth explaining that one of the key provisions is that, where a defendant relies at trial on a fact not mentioned to the police during interview, a court or jury may draw adverse inferences against him.[9] It is against this background that this chapter examines issues connected to police questioning.

[5] For other examples, see the case of George Heron, discussed in G. Gudjonsson, *The Psychology of Interrogations and Confessions: A Handbook* (2003), 96–106; and the case reported in 'Judge Brands Detectives as Liars after Collapse of Robbery Trial' *The Guardian*, 8 October 2003. See also *R v Smith* [2003] EWCA Crim 927.

[6] See T. Williamson, 'Reflections on Current Police Practice' in D. Morgan and G. Stephenson (eds), *Suspicion and Silence: The Right to Silence in Criminal Investigations* (1994); Home Office, *A Guide to Interviewing* (1992).

[7] M. Maguire and T. John, 'Covert and Deceptive Policing in England and Wales: Issues in Regulation and Practice' (1996) 4 *Eur. J. Crime, Criminal L. & Criminal Justice* 316.

[8] Research conducted in 1993–4 found that the majority of arrests were still based on reactive policing, with only 13 per cent based on 'surveillance/enquiries'. C. Phillips and D. Brown, *Entry into the Criminal Justice System: A Survey of Police Arrests and Their Outcomes* (1998).

[9] Criminal Justice and Public Order Act 1994, s 34.

4.1 QUESTIONING AND CONFESSIONS:
PSYCHOLOGICAL RESEARCH

One of the most important advances in the understanding of the process by which the police elicit confessions has been the development of a sophisticated body of psychological research on questioning. Such research has become increasingly important in the practice of the courts, with psychologists and psychiatrists often called to give expert evidence about the reliability of confession evidence in individual cases. Psychological research also offers more general lessons to the legal system as to how it should deal with the questioning process and the evidence that results from it.

Research on police questioning tells us something about the circumstances in which suspects confess to crime. A significant finding is that the questioning process itself does little to elicit confessions. Most suspects who confess do so at the outset of the police interview, rather than in response to being challenged by the police.[10] As to why some suspects but not others decide to confess, the most significant factor appears to be the strength of evidence against them. A suspect who knows that the police are likely to be able to prove his guilt has little to lose by confessing.[11] Are some types of defendant more likely to confess than others? Gudjonsson has attempted to answer this question. One, perhaps surprising, finding was that the mental characteristics of defendants do not appear to be linked to the likelihood of confession. Although many police suspects are intellectually disadvantaged, this does not necessarily make them more likely to confess to the police.[12] The only individual factor which was identified as being a good predictor of whether a suspect would confess was whether that person had taken illegal drugs in the 24 hours before arrest. 'The most likely explanation', Gudjonsson concludes, 'is that suspects who are dependent on illicit drugs are motivated by factors that they perceive as expediting their release from custody.'[13]

The factors described above do not distinguish between true and false confessions. It is obviously very difficult to conduct research into the reasons why people confess falsely, because the truth or falsity of a confession is often impossible to establish. Notorious cases such as that of Stephen Miller can provide some pointers. A major study of dubious confessions in the US concludes that false confessions are most likely to occur in serious cases where the police are under pressure and have little evidence against a suspect.[14] In such circumstances, the police may put a large amount of pressure on a suspect who—the lack of evidence suggests—could well be innocent. Gudjonsson has explored the explanations given by prisoners who claim to have confessed falsely. His findings again identify the pressure exerted by the police as a significant factor. But prisoners also claimed to have confessed falsely for reasons

---

[10] Gudjonsson, above n 5, 70, 133.   [11] *Ibid.*, 153.   [12] *Ibid.*, 73.   [13] *Ibid.*, 71.
[14] R. Ofshe and R. Leo, 'The Decision to Confess Falsely: Rational Choice and Irrational Action' (1997) 74 *Denver University L. Rev.* 979.

over which the police would have less control: out of fear of custody, and to protect other people.[15] Finally, psychological factors may contribute to false confession. Gudjonsson stresses that 'false confessions are not confined to the mentally ill and those with learning disability. . . . The view that apparently normal individuals would not seriously incriminate themselves when interrogated by the police is wrong.'[16] Gudjonsson has, however, pioneered research on the way in which the psychological factors of compliance and suggestibility can contribute to false confessions. Some people, who are not necessarily intellectually disadvantaged, may be particularly likely to comply with those in authority, or to accept suggestions (e.g. 'you hit him') put to them by other people. It may not be obvious to the police whether an individual is compliant or suggestible, though these characteristics can be measured by psychological tests.[17] These various findings should be borne in mind during the discussion that follows.

4.2 THE CONTEXT OF QUESTIONING

(a) ARREST AND DETENTION

In order to gain a full understanding of police questioning, we need to know something about the context in which it takes place. One reason for this should already be apparent: as has been noted, research suggests that it is in serious cases where there is little evidence against suspects that the danger of false confession is greatest. Ensuring that the police can only question suspects against whom there is reasonable evidence of guilt will reduce the risk of false confession. On the other hand, if it is made too difficult for the police to question suspects, they may be unduly impeded in their role of gathering evidence. We therefore begin by considering the circumstances in which suspects can be arrested and detained in police custody. Of course, there are other issues at stake here than the reliability of evidence gained through questioning: arrest and detention is an intrusion on the liberty of suspects and there is therefore potential for breach of Article 5 of the European Convention on Human Rights.

The usual process is that a suspect will be arrested and then taken to the police station where questioning is likely to ensue. PACE gives the police fairly wide arrest powers. The provisions are structured by a distinction between 'arrestable offences' and other offences, the former being more serious than the latter and involving wider arrest powers. Arrestable offences include all offences for which an adult offender can be sentenced to five years or more imprisonment, plus certain other specified offences.[18] In practice, the threshold of seriousness is not very high: arrestable offences include theft, criminal damage and all assaults, apart from common assault. PACE,

---

[15] Gudjonsson, above n 5, 176.   [16] *Ibid.*, 626.   [17] *Ibid.*, Chs 13–14.
[18] PACE, Sched 1A provides a list.

s 24 allows police officers to arrest anyone who is committing, has committed, or is about to commit an arrestable offence, or anyone reasonably suspected of the same. Reasonable suspicion is an objective standard, and means no more than that the officer suspects, on reasonable grounds, that the suspect is guilty; he need not actually believe that the suspect is guilty.[19] Section 24 leaves the officer with a discretion whether or not to arrest—he 'may' arrest in the circumstances described above—and there may be other, less intrusive ways of bringing a case against a suspected offender. For example, the police can proceed by way of summons,[20] but it seems that this is rare.[21] The discretion to arrest is a wide one, however, and it is unlikely that it could be successfully challenged. The House of Lords has held that arrest can be justified in order to dispel or confirm suspicion through questioning or seeking further evidence.[22] The Criminal Justice Act 2003 provides the police with another option when it comes at arrest: a power popularly known as the power to grant 'street bail' will allow the police to release an arrested person before they are taken to the police station.[23] The condition of release will be that the person attend the police station at some future time.[24]

There is a further power of arrest for offences that fall outside the arrestable category. The 'general arrest conditions' in section 25 give the police a power to arrest for non-arrestable offences where an officer has reasonable grounds to suspect that such an offence has been committed or attempted, or is being committed or attempted, and that the service of a summons is impracticable or inappropriate. The conditions include an officer not being satisfied that he knows the name and address of the suspect.

It is difficult to say how widely or justifiably these arrest powers are used. Research on police decision making 'on the street' emphasizes the flexibility of police powers, which allow coercive powers such as arrest to be used for a variety of purposes, some with little connection to crime investigation.[25] There does seem to be an increasing number of arrests year on year, even during periods of falling crime rates.[26] Some commentators suggest that PACE has led to arrests being carried out on a firmer evidential basis than was previously the case, but others doubt this.[27] As for the outcome of arrest, Phillips and Brown found that 40 per cent were eventually convicted; 50 per

---

[19] *Castorina v CC Surrey, The Times*, 15 June 1988.

[20] On this procedure, see J. Sprack, *Emmins on Criminal Procedure* (9th ed., 2002), 20–6.

[21] M. McConville, A. Sanders and R. Leng, *The Case for the Prosecution: Police Suspects and the Construction of Criminality* (1991), 38–40.

[22] *Holgate-Mohammed v Duke* [1984] 2 WLR 660.

[23] CJA 2003, s4, inserting a new s30A in PACE.

[24] See generally A. Hucklesby, 'Not Necessarily a Trip to the Police Station: The Introduction of Street Bail' (2004) Crim LR 803.

[25] See A. Sanders, 'From Suspect to Trial' in M. Maguire, R. Morgan and R. Reiner (eds), *The Oxford Handbook of Criminology* (3rd ed., 2002), 1037–44.

[26] See *Arrests for Notifiable Offences and the Operation of Certain Police Powers Under PACE, England and Wales 2002/03* (HOSB 17 2003).

[27] D. Brown, *PACE Ten Years On: A Review of the Research* (1997), 51–5.

cent were charged, 17 per cent cautioned, 20 per cent had no further action taken against them and 13 per cent were dealt with in other ways.[28] They also found evidence that black and Asian suspects were arrested on weaker evidence than white suspects.[29]

On being arrested, a suspect should be told that he is under arrest, and the grounds for the arrest.[30] He should also be cautioned, and taken to a police station.[31] At the police station detention is not, in theory, automatic: it must be authorized by the custody officer. PACE provides that a suspect can be detained where the custody officer reasonably believes that detention is necessary 'to secure or preserve evidence . . . or to obtain evidence by questioning him'.[32] Though the 'necessity' criterion might be thought to be relatively demanding, research shows that it is not. It is very rare for custody officers to refuse to permit the detention of suspects.[33] It will be apparent that both this provision, and the law on the discretion to arrest for arrestable offences, empower the police to detain suspects in order to question them even if there is little evidence against the suspect, or if there is sufficient evidence to permit the case to proceed to court without questioning. Despite the width of the current powers to arrest and detain suspects, proposed amendments to PACE would expand powers of police arrest.[34] The amendments abandon the seriousness threshold which currently governs arrest powers. Instead, a new set of general arrest conditions would enable arrest for any offence at all. The conditions include that arrest is necessary to 'allow prompt and effective investigation' of the arrestee's conduct and to confirm the person's name and address. Another condition which will allow arrest is where arrest will 'prevent any prosecution of the offence from being hindered by the disappearance of the person in question', which raises questions about how the police are to know whether a person will disappear. There is no evidence that current arrest powers are too restrictive—as noted above, the police are already provided with wide and flexible powers of arrest. It is difficult to see why a person suspected of a minor offence, such as common assault or careless driving, should be subjected to the coercive power of arrest just to enable questioning by the police. At least the current Bill has abandoned some of the worst aspects of the Home Office's original plans. Under these, arrest for a minor offence would have been possible simply to 'enable communication' with the suspect.[35]

Once arrested and taken to a police station, suspects can be detained for a considerable period before being charged. PACE again distinguishes between levels of offence: this time the key concept is 'serious arrestable offence'. Where an offence is

---

[28] C. Phillips and D. Brown, *Entry into the Criminal Justice System: A Survey of Police Arrests and Their Outcomes* (1998), xiv.

[29] *Ibid.*, 44.   [30] PACE, s28, Code C 10.3 and note 10B.   [31] PACE, s30, Code C 10.4.

[32] PACE s37(2).   [33] D. Brown, *PACE Ten Years on: A Review of the Research* (1997), 57–62.

[34] Serious Organised Crime and Police Bill, cl 101. For an attempt to justify the new powers in the meaningless language of modernization and community needs, see Home Office, *Policing: Modernising Police Powers to Meet Community Needs* (2004).

[35] Home Office, ibid.

not a serious arrestable offence, a suspect can be detained for 36 hours before being brought before a court: this period has been expanded from the previous limit of 24 hours by the Criminal Justice Act 2003.[36] During this period detention should be reviewed periodically by a senior officer: after an initial period of six hours, and then at nine hour intervals.[37] After 24 hours, further detention must be authorized by an officer of at least the rank of superintendent.[38] The evidence suggests that, especially during the initial 24 hours, the process of review is routinized and is not a very effective means of limiting detention to what is necessary.[39] After 36 hours further detention can only be authorized by the magistrates' court, and the offence must be a 'serious arrestable offence'. This category includes murder, manslaughter, rape, a number of firearms offences, and causing death by dangerous or careless driving while under the influence of drink. It also comprises a more flexible category: any arrestable offence which has led to, or is intended or is likely to lead to consequences such as death, serious injury or serious financial loss.[40] The magistrates can author-ize further detention, 36 hours at a time, up to a maximum of 96 hours.[41] In practice, detention is usually for a relatively short period: the average is around seven hours.[42] It should be noted that there are wider powers of detention for terrorist offences.[43]

It is possible for suspects to be questioned at the police station even if they have not been formally arrested. Some attend the police station 'voluntarily'. Research has found that voluntary attendance may be used quite frequently: at one police station a third of all suspects were dealt with as voluntary attenders.[44] This process avoids some of the regulations imposed by PACE, such as the detention time limits.[45]

(b) LEGAL ADVICE

The Royal Commission on Criminal Procedure saw access to legal advice in the police station as a fundamental part of its proposed regime for regulating the police station. Legal advice, it was hoped, would go some way to 'minimising the effects of arrest and custody on the suspect.'[46] The right to legal advice is guaranteed by s 58 of PACE. In strictly defined circumstances it can be delayed, but not denied, by the police. The courts have enforced a strict reading of s 58.[47] The right is supplemented by a scheme

---

[36] PACE, ss 41, 42 amended by CJA 2003, s7.   [37] PACE, s40.   [38] PACE, s42.

[39] D. Dixon *et al*, 'Safeguarding the Rights of Suspects in Police Custody' (1990) 1 *Policing & Society* 115.

[40] PACE, s116.   [41] PACE, ss43, 44.   [42] Phillips and Brown, above n 8, 109.

[43] Terrorism Act 2000, Sch 8.

[44] I. McKenzie, R. Morgan and R. Reiner, 'Helping the Police with their Enquiries: The Necessity Principle and Voluntary Attendance at the Police Station' [1990] Crim LR 22; D. Dixon, *Law in Policing: Legal Regula-tion and Police Practices* (1997), 113–15.

[45] There are some protections in PACE, s29 and Code C 3.21–2.

[46] Royal Commission on Criminal Procedure, *The Investigation and Prosecution of Criminal Offences in England and Wales: The Law and Procedure* (1981), para 4.77.

[47] *R v Samuel* [1988] 1 QB 615.

of duty solicitors, providing 24 hour advice across the country. Before PACE was introduced, around 10 per cent of suspects may have asked for legal advice.[48] Post-PACE the figure has crept up, and now stands at around 40 per cent.[49] Research has found that the police have some ability to manipulate suspects' requests for legal advice in the manner in which they inform them of it.[50] The most recent research on this issue found that around a third of suspects were not told that legal advice is free, and around a quarter were not informed about it clearly, both factors that are likely to influence uptake of legal advice.[51] There is some drop off between request and receipt of advice; because waiting for legal advice is likely to prolong custody, some suspects, especially those arrested during the night, cancel the request.[52] About 34 per cent of suspects now receive legal advice.[53] Some advice is given over the telephone, and some advisers attend the police station but not the interview.[54] Changes to the rules on legal aid mean that the proportion of advice given over the telephone is likely to increase.[55]

There have been problems with the quality of legal advice offered to suspects in detention. Some solicitors' firms have used representatives who are not legally quali-fied to give advice.[56] A qualification scheme has been introduced, and the quality of advice now seems to have improved.[57] But even solicitors are sometimes not particu-larly zealous in defence of their clients. The most telling example of this is that a solicitor sat through the abusive interviews of Stephen Miller without objecting to them. There was also remarkably little intervention during the oppressive interview-ing of George Heron.[58] In a more recent case, a confession was excluded on account of a solicitor's hostile and sarcastic interventions at interview.[59]

The lesson to draw from all this is that, while legal advice is undoubtedly an important safeguard for suspects, it would be a mistake to exaggerate its impact. The majority of suspects do not receive legal advice and do not have a legal adviser with them during police questioning.

---

[48] The figures in the literature vary considerably: see D. Brown, *PACE Ten Years On: A Review of the Research* (1997), 95.

[49] T. Bucke and D. Brown, *In Police Custody: Police Powers and Suspects' Rights under the Revised PACE Codes of Practice* (1997), 19; T. Bucke, R. Street and D. Brown, *The Right of Silence: The Impact of the CJPOA 1994* (2000), 21.

[50] A. Sanders and L. Bridges, 'Access to Legal Advice and Police Malpractice' (1990) Crim LR 494.

[51] D. Brown, T. Ellis and K. Larcombe, *Changing the Code: Police Detention Under the Revised PACE Codes of Practice* (1992), 26, 31.

[52] Phillips and Brown, above n 8, 64.   [53] Bucke and Brown, above n 49, 23.

[54] Bucke and Brown, *ibid.* at 32, found that a legal adviser was present at all interviews in 37 per cent of cases where suspects were interviewed.

[55] See E. Cape, 'The Rise (and Fall) of a Criminal Defence Profession' [2004] Crim LR 408.

[56] J. Hodgson, 'Adding Injury to Injustice: The Suspect at the Police Station' (1994) 21 *J. Law & Soc.* 85.

[57] L. Bridges and S. Choongh, *Improving Police Station Legal Advice* (1998).

[58] Gudjonsson, above n 5, 105.   [59] *M* [2000] 8 *Archbold News* 2.

(c) THE RULES

The legal regime governing the questioning of suspects is to be found in PACE, Code C and to a lesser extent in case law. The first rule worthy of note is that interviews should take place in the police station.[60] To allow suspects to be questioned outside the police station would be to provide a loophole through which the police station regime— including access to legal advice and the recording of interviews—could be evaded. There are exceptions to the basic rule to allow the police to ask questions if gaining information from a suspect is urgent.[61]

The rule against interviewing outside the police station depends on having a definition of 'interview'. Sometimes the police will question a person regarding an incident and have their suspicions raised through the response to their questions. If questioning continues, at some point a dividing line will be crossed and the questioning will become an interview. Code C defines an interview in terms of whether the questions asked are about involvement in an offence.[62] Nevertheless, there may be claims that a suspect has freely made admissions before arriving at the police station. In these circumstances, anything said should be put to the suspect at the beginning of the formal interview, giving him an opportunity to confirm or deny it.[63]

It is unclear how often suspects are interviewed outside the police station. One study conducted for the Royal Commission on Criminal Justice found a figure of 10 per cent, but this is not regarded as a reliable estimate:[64] the real figure is probably larger. The courts are alive to the problems in this area, and enforce the Code C definition of interview relatively strictly.[65] Nevertheless, the admission in court of statements made outside the police station is still a possibility. Given the concerns here, and the fact that an admission denied by the defendant will have little evidential value, this seems to be an area where a strict rule of inadmissibility—unless the statement is either recorded or later confirmed by the suspect—would be appropriate. Any decision to admit such evidence would create incentives for the police to try to gain admissions outside the police station regime.

The suspect should be cautioned at the start of the interview.[66] After the changes to the right to silence were introduced, the caution has been in the form: 'You do not have to say anything. But it may harm your defence if you do not mention when questioned something which you later rely on in court. Anything you do say may be given in evidence.'[67] The caution is relatively complex and, given the level of intel-lectual disadvantage among police suspects, there are considerable doubts about how well it is understood. One study found that none among a group of thirty suspects

---

[60] Code C, 11.1.   [61] *Ibid.*   [62] Code C, 11.1A, 10.1.   [63] Code C, 11.4.

[64] S. Moston and G. Stephenson, *The Questioning and Interviewing of Suspects Outside the Police Station* (1993).

[65] Eg *Okafor* [1994] 3 All ER 741; cf *R v Senior and Senior* [2004] Cr App R 215.

[66] Code C, 10.1.   [67] Code C, 10.5.

could give a correct explanation of the caution;[68] indeed, even police officers have difficulty in explaining the caution correctly.[69] Some officers attempt to explain the caution to suspects, but there is a fear that a technically inexact explanation, or an attempt to explain which reveals that the suspect really does not understand the consequences of not mentioning facts, might harm the case in court. Some training sessions have therefore advised officers not to attempt an explanation,[70] a good example of how concern about the admissibility of evidence can override ethical concerns. If there is evidence that a suspect does not understand the caution, then surely it is proper not to hold facts not mentioned in interview against him in court.

The issue of the caution has been further complicated by the decision of the European Court of Human Rights in *Murray v United Kingdom*.[71] Here it was held that a suspect's Article 6 right to a fair trial was breached when he was denied access to legal advice in a situation where adverse inferences could be drawn from his failure to mention facts at interview. The right to silence provisions have therefore been amended to prevent the drawing of adverse inferences from suspects who have not had access to legal advice, but this means that the standard caution will sometimes be misleading. Thus, if the suspect is to be interviewed outside the police station, or before consulting with a legal adviser who he has requested, or after he has been charged, the 'old' caution must be given: 'You do not have to say anything, but anything you do say may be given in evidence.' Some suspects, at different points in time, will be given first one caution and then the other. Code C contains a form of words to explain the change,[72] but there must again be doubts about comprehensibility.

An accurate record should be made of all interviews.[73] This is an important safeguard against verballing. The introduction of tape recorders in interview rooms has facilitated this process, and tape recording is now standard practice.[74] For some time there has been interest in video-taping interviews. The advantage is that this would give a more complete record of what occurred. There are concerns, though, about whether playing the tapes in court would be fair to defendants. Magistrates and jurors would no doubt be keen to read what they could into the defendant's demeanour during questioning—perhaps especially if the question whether to draw an inference from silence arises. But demeanour is a poor guide to veracity at the best of times, and will be even more so when the subject is seen under the stressful conditions of police questioning.[75] Video-taping is now covered by a new PACE Code of Practice (Code F), and is being piloted before a decision is made as to whether to introduce it nationally.

---

[68] S. Fenner, G. Gudjonsson and I. Clare, 'Understanding of the Current Police Caution (England and Wales) Among Suspects in Police Detention' (2002) 12 *J. Community & Applied Social Psychology* 83.

[69] I. Clare, G. Gudjonsson and M. Harari, 'Understanding of the Current Police Caution (England and Wales)' (1998) 8 *J. Community & Applied Social Psychology* 323.

[70] Bucke, Street and Brown, above n 49, 28.   [71] (1996) 22 EHRR 29.   [72] Code C, Annex C.

[73] Code C, 11.7.   [74] See generally PACE, Code E.

[75] S. Kassin and C. Fong, ' "I'm Innocent": Effects of Training on Judgments of Truth and Deception in the Interrogation Room' (1999) 23 *Law & Human Behavior* 499.

Whichever form of recording is used, there is the problem of producing a transcript or summary of the tape. The process is time consuming and often introduces inaccuracies.[76]

Another limitation to the recording of interviews is that in some cases the police may rehearse what is to be said on tape before the formal interview begins. This is a further reason for concern about what is said outside the police station. Inside the station, cell visits by officers are meant to be recorded, but it is difficult completely to ensure against rule-breaking.[77] As an antidote, the Royal Commission on Criminal Justice recommended video-taping custody areas, so that in the event of a dispute the movements of police officers could be checked.[78]

Prolonged interviewing of suspects is problematic. In a difficult or complex case it may be justified, but in some cases prolongation of the interview process may wear down and confuse the suspect. Stephen Miller was interviewed for 13 hours, and this doubtless contributed to his confessing falsely. Code C contains rules on breaks between interviews for refreshments and requires suspects to have at least eight hours rest in 24, free from questioning, but there is no cap on the cumulative length of questioning, other than the time limits on detention. These are not inconsiderable, as was seen above. Even with rules on the police station environment, the potential effects of custody on suspects should not be underestimated. Suspects are likely to be nervous and uncertain. They have little control over the environment in which they find themselves. Many complain of lack of sleep—something which has been found to impair the ability to cope with questioning.[79]

Code C does provide that questioning should end when the police have gathered a certain amount of information. The interview process should cease when the officer in charge of the investigation:

'(a) Is satisfied all the questions they consider relevant to obtaining accurate and reliable information from the suspect about the offence have been put to the suspect, this includes allowing the suspect an opportunity to give an innocent explanation and asking questions to test if the explanation is accurate and reliable, e.g. to clear up ambiguities or clarify what the suspect said;

(b) has taken account of any other evidence which is available; and

(c) . . . the custody officer reasonably believes there is sufficient evidence to provide a realistic prospect of conviction. . . .'[80]

This provision was modified in 2003; previously the Code had said little, other than that questioning should end when the officer believes that a prosecution should be brought and that there is sufficient evidence for it to succeed. Under this provision, courts had held that inferences could not be drawn from silence where questioning

---

[76] See Royal Commission on Criminal Justice, *Report* (1993), Ch 4 paras 73–80; Gudjonsson, above n 5, 85.
[77] M. McConville, 'Videotaping Interrogations: Police Behaviour on and off Camera' [1992] Crim LR 532.
[78] Above n 76, Ch 4, para 37.   [79] Gudjonsson, above n 5, 31.   [80] Code C, 11.6.

continued after the cut-off point.[81] The 2003 revision is doubtless a response to this; it appears to provide for a longer period of questioning than the earlier version. Questioning can continue beyond the point at which there is sufficient evidence to justify prosecution, in order to test the suspect's version of events and obtain accurate information from him. This might be said to signify a change in the nature of the questioning process, from an investigative one, where the aim of the police is largely to find out what happened, to a case-building one, where the suspect's version of events can be tested in more detail and his response, or lack of it, to the evidence against him will be significant. More will be said about the significance of this in the discussion of the right to silence, below.

PACE and the codes regulate the environment in which interviewing takes place. They say little, however, about how interviews should be conducted. Code C lays down some basic rules: questioning should not be oppressive, and the police should not offer inducements such as release on bail in return for a confession.[82] Beyond this, a few guidelines may be found in the case law. Again, oppression is outlawed, but the definition of oppression is pitched fairly high: confronting the suspect with disturbing information is not regarded as oppressive.[83] The repeated bullying questioning of Stephen Miller, though, was held to be oppressive. In addition, a confession may be excluded if it was obtained in conditions likely to lead to its being unreliable, or if admitting it is likely to make the trial unfair.[84] These requirements—discussed in more detail below—offer limited guidance to questioners. To gain more idea of how interviews are actually conducted, it is necessary to turn to the empirical research.

The most recent research on police questioning presents a mixed picture. Police officers are now trained in less aggressive 'investigative interviewing' techniques. The Royal Commission on Criminal Justice largely accepted that training in such practices was a panacea for concerns about police questioning.[85] The success of this initiative has been assessed by Clarke and Milne, who conclude that its impact is limited. While the majority of interviews studied were largely unproblematic, overall, police officers examining the interview sample thought that 10 per cent of interviews may have breached PACE requirements, though sometimes this was for technical reasons such as failure to caution.[86] Whether because of investigative interviewing training or not, studies do suggest that there have been changes to interviewing practices post-PACE. Where less serious crimes are concerned, interviews tend to be short (less than 20 minutes) and largely non-confrontational affairs.[87] Pearse and Gudjonsson concluded

---

[81] See E. Cape, 'The Revised PACE Codes of Practice: A Further Step Towards Inquisitorialism' [2003] Crim LR 355, 364.

[82] Code C, 11.5.

[83] PACE, s76, interpreted in *Fulling* [1987] 2 All ER 75; see also *Foster* [2003] EWCA Crim 178. A detailed review of the case law on oppression is M. Zander, *The Police and Criminal Evidence Act 1984* (4th ed., 2003), 316–20.

[84] PACE, ss76, 78.   [85] Above n 76, Ch 2, paras 13–24.

[86] C. Clarke and R. Milne, *National Evaluation of the PEACE Investigative Interviewing Course* (2001), 40.

[87] J. Baldwin, 'Police Interview Techniques: Establishing Truth or Proof?' (1993) 33 *Brit. J. Criminol.* 325.

that the interviews for non-serious crimes that they studied differed markedly from those described in the pre-PACE research, where manipulation and persuasion was common. In fact, they felt that police officers were too reluctant to challenge the suspect's version of events, and that training needed to address this.[88] As well as run of the mill cases, Pearse and Gudjonsson have also studied the interview tactics used in serious criminal cases, and here a very different picture emerges. When the stakes are high the police will resort to a number of pressurizing and manipulative tactics to gain a confession. This may result in confessions of dubious quality and censure by the courts.[89]

4.3 INTERVIEWS

(a) THE RIGHT TO SILENCE

It was noted earlier that, despite the recommendations of the Royal Commission on Criminal Justice, major changes to the right to silence were introduced by the Criminal Justice and Public Order Act 1994. This legislation does not require suspects to answer questions, either during interview or at trial: in that sense a right to silence remains. What the legislation does do is allow a court or jury to draw adverse inferences from silence in four situations. One of them—where a defendant does not testify at trial—will not be discussed here. Two of the other situations are relatively well defined. Under s 36, where a suspect fails to account for objects, substances or marks on him or in his possession, an adverse inference can be drawn against him at trial. Under s 37, the failure to account for his presence at a particular place is treated the same way. With these sections, an inference can only be drawn if a specific question about the object/mark/presence is put to the suspect. In contrast, s 34 is much more open-ended. Adverse inferences can be drawn where a defendant relies on a fact in his defence at trial which he failed to mention during police questioning. The fact must be one which he could reasonably have been expected to have mentioned during questioning. The discussion here will concentrate on s 34, although many of the points are also applicable to ss 36 and 37.

There are a number of arguments for and against this reform.[90] To start with some of the reasons why these provisions were introduced, it is often said that silence, of the sort targeted by s 34, is suspicious, and that it is only right to draw it to the attention of the fact-finder. There can of course be innocent reasons for not mentioning facts during police interview, which include feeling ill or intimidated, not trusting the

---

[88] J. Pearse and G. Gudjonsson, 'Police Interviewing Techniques at Two South London Police Stations' (1996) 3 *Psychology, Crime & Law* 63.

[89] Gudjonsson, above n 5, Ch 4.

[90] See the discussion in Morgan and Stephenson, above n 6.

police, and wanting to protect someone else.[91] But, so long as these possibilities can be effectively brought to the attention of the jury, and weighted in the evaluation of the evidence, there does not seem anything inherently wrong in asking it to consider drawing an inference from silence. Another reason given for reform was that defendants might gain acquittal at trial by producing an 'ambush' defence—one that the prosecution had no inkling of, and would not be able to rebut at trial. There was little evidence of ambush defences being a significant problem,[92] and in any case new provisions on defence disclosure—which were recommended by the Royal Commission on Criminal Justice—offer an equally appropriate way of dealing with defence ambush.[93] All the same, the argument that ambush defences were not a significant problem was hardly an argument for the status quo, unless some positive reasons for retaining the traditional scope of the right to silence could be mustered.

What reasons are there, then, for not permitting inferences from silence? Strong reasons of principle are sometimes mentioned, such as that adverse inferences conflict with the privilege against self-incrimination. That claim raises a number of complex issues which will be dealt with in Chapter 5. One problem with adverse inferences is that they put pressure on suspects to talk. This was something of concern to the Royal Commission on Criminal Justice, which worried that the pressure might lead to innocent suspects making incriminating statements. Here it quoted from the Report of the Royal Commission on Criminal Procedure, which had argued that adverse inferences 'might put strong (and additional) psychological pressure upon some suspects to answer questions without knowing precisely what was the substance of any evidence for the accusations against them. . . . This in our view might well increase the risk of innocent people, particularly those under suspicion for the first time, making damaging statements'.[94] Two comments can be made about this. First, the passage notes that any pressure brought to bear by the possibility of inferences will be additional to the existing pressures of police interview. There is little doubt that many suspects find detention and questioning an intimidating process. However, it is sometimes noted that those who are especially vulnerable to making false confessions are likely to do so anyway, even with the full protection of the right to silence. While there is some truth in this, the traditional right to silence allows legal advisers to counsel vulnerable suspects to remain silent without worrying that this may jeopardize the case in court. Allowing adverse inferences also gives an additional tool to the police, who might use inferences as a particular threat in some cases. There seems to be some merit, then, to the argument about the dangers of pressurizing suspects. A second point to make about the passage just quoted is that it gestures towards another reason for the traditional right to silence: it highlights the fact that at police interview,

---

[91] See M. McConville and J. Hodgson, *Custodial Legal Advice and the Right to Silence* (1993).

[92] R. Leng, *The Right to Silence in Police Interrogation: A Study of Some of the Issues Underlying the Debate* (1993).

[93] The provisions are to be found in the Criminal Procedure and Investigations Act 1996, discussed further in Chapter 9.

[94] Quoted in RCCJ, above n 76, Ch 2, para 23.

the suspect may not know the details of the evidence against him. At trial, most people would think it unfair to ask a defendant to defend himself without full knowledge of the prosecution case. It is arguable that similar concerns apply at interview, and that here suspects should not be asked to engage in discussion of the case against them unless they know its details.[95] The principle here might be linked to a more theoretical defence of aspects of the right to silence made by Kent Greenawalt. According to Greenawalt, it is a basic moral principle that one should not be expected to respond to accusations in the absence of reasonable suspicion.[96]

These, then, are some of the arguments for and against the changes to the right to silence brought in by the Criminal Justice and Public Order Act. The actual provisions in the Act were not the last word on just when adverse inferences could be drawn from silence. The provisions left considerable scope to the courts to interpret them and to add additional safeguards. It is therefore important to look at the case law before examining how the Act has changed the context of police interview. This is an area in which the European Court of Human Rights has been involved: it has cautiously accepted that the new law is compatible with the Convention. In *Murray*,[97] a decision on similar provisions in Northern Ireland, the Court found that the right to silence is not absolute. It found it permissible that the accused's silence, 'in situations which clearly call for an explanation from him, be taken into account in assessing the evidence adduced by the prosecution.'[98] It did, however, observe that in that case the question of what inferences to draw had been left to a professional judge, and that a number of other safeguards restricted the use of silence as evidence of guilt. It also held that the fact that Murray had been denied access to legal advice before police questioning led to a breach of Article 6: legal advice was seen as taking on particular importance in cases where inferences could be drawn from silence. This, as was seen earlier, led to changes in English law and to a new caution which has to be given where a suspect is questioned without access to legal advice. The Court considered the English silence provisions in more detail in *Condron v United Kingdom*.[99] Again, the provisions were found to pass muster so long as they were handled carefully. In particular, it was held to be crucial to instruct the jury in some detail on the nature of inferences that can be drawn from silence. The Court endorsed the model direction on inferences from silence given by the Court of Appeal, and found that the fact that part of it had not been given by the trial judge in *Condron* led to a breach of Article 6. A similar conclusion was reached in *Beckles v United Kingdom*.[100]

Under the current case law of the ECtHR and the Court of Appeal, then, a jury in an inferences from silence case must be given a number of directions.[101] It should be told that the defendant cannot be convicted solely or mainly on the basis of an inference from silence, and that an inference can only be drawn if it is satisfied that:

---

[95] A. Zuckerman, *The Principles of Criminal Evidence* (1989), 330.

[96] K. Greenawalt, 'Silence as a Moral and Constitutional Right' (1981) 23 *William & Mary L Rev* 15.

[97] Above n 71.   [98] *Ibid.*, para 47.   [99] (2001) 31 EHRR 1.   [100] [2002] Crim LR 917.

[101] See *R v Argent* [1997] 2 Cr App R 27; Judicial Studies Board Specimen Direction 40 (at www.jsboard.co.uk).

when interviewed, the defendant could reasonably have been expected to mention the fact in question; that the only sensible explanation for his failure to do so is that he had no answer at the time or none that would stand up to scrutiny; and that without the inference from silence, the prosecution's case is so strong that it clearly calls for an answer by the defendant.[102] The usual inference to be drawn is that the fact in question is false. What might be said about these requirements is that they are largely procedural. They tell the jury to eliminate innocent explanations for silence before drawing an inference, not to convict on an inference alone, and so on. The Court of Appeal has been rather more reluctant to lay down substantive requirements, about the type of factual situation where an inference may or may not be drawn.[103] For example, although defendants have argued that, given lack of disclosure by the police, it was not reasonable to expect them to mention particular facts during interview, the Court of Appeal has declined to lay down any clear rule here, simply leaving the issue to the jury.[104] This seems to be the position, too, with vulnerable suspects.[105] The most unsatisfactory case law from the Court of Appeal has been on the subject of legal advice. The Court has doubtless felt that it has had to be cautious here. It expressed a concern that ruling that legal advice not to answer police questions is a bar to adverse inferences would render s 34 'wholly nugatory'.[106] Initially, it seemed that in a case where a suspect had remained silent on legal advice, the jury would have to consider whether the reasons for the advice were good ones.[107] The Court of Appeal rethought its position in *Betts and Hall*, where it noted that what really mattered was whether the defendant had remained silent because of legal advice, not whether his decision was wise or whether the advice was good.[108] In an extraordinary decision the Court has now doubted this. In *Howell*, the defendant claimed that he would have been only too happy to explain himself to the police, but his legal adviser had counselled silence, and he had decided to follow this advice.[109] The Court of Appeal now held that an adverse inference could be drawn even if the defendant genuinely relied on his solicitor's advice. What was important, instead, was whether the suspect was behaving reasonably. 'There must always be soundly based objective reasons for silence, sufficiently cogent and telling to weigh in the balance against the clear public interest in an

---

[102] The notes to the JSB directions observe that there is some uncertainty as to the last of these requirements. Its endorsement by the ECtHR in *Beckles*, and by the Court of Appeal in *Chenia* [2003] 2 Cr App R 6, point to its being mandatory.

[103] This aspect of the case law is criticized in D. Birch, 'Suffering in Silence: A Cost-Benefit Analysis of s34 of the CJPOA 1994' [1999] Crim LR 769. An exception is seen in *Mountford* [1999] Crim LR 75 and *Gill* [2001] 1 Cr App R 160 (both doubted in *Gowland-Wynn* [2002] 1 Cr App R 569), but here the substantive requirement comes about because of the procedural requirement to eliminate innocent explanations.

[104] *Argent*, above n 101.

[105] This is the implication of the Court of Appeal's decision on heroin withdrawal in *Condron* [1997] 1 WLR 827, as well as of a case on s35 of the Act: *Friend* [1997] 2 Cr App R 231.

[106] *Condron and Condron* [1997] 1 Cr App R 185, 191.

[107] A good discussion is I. Dennis, *The Law of Evidence* (2nd ed., 2002), 156–9.

[108] [2001] 2 Cr App R 257; see also *Chenia*, above n 102.

[109] [2003] Crim LR 405, confirmed in *Knight* [2004] 1 Cr App R 9.

account being given by the suspect to the police.'[110] There seems to be a basic confusion here. While s 34 does refer to facts 'which . . . the accused could reasonably have been expected to mention', a determination of what it was reasonable to mention is only one part of the process of drawing an inference from silence. Innocent, as well as guilty, suspects can behave unreasonably. For silence to be evidence of guilt the reasons for silence are important, whether reasonable or not: specifically, whether silence was due to the suspect having no account to give, or none that would stand up to scrutiny. But if the reason for silence was that the suspect was relying on legal advice, no inference can be drawn.[111] *Howell* is an unfortunate decision, but one which perhaps indicates the difficulty of operating a workable regime of drawing inferences from silence while at the same time promoting the importance of legal advice.

What effect has s 34 had on suspects in practice? Research allows a number of conclusions to be drawn.[112] It appears that the changes to the right to silence have led to fewer suspects refusing to answer some or all of the questions put to them by the police: the number of suspects refusing to answer all questions has fallen from 10 to six per cent.[113] But this has not led to more confessions: some police officers feel they are just getting more lies from suspects.[114] This may be helpful if the lie can be shown to be false, but it is not necessarily an easy route to conviction. And where the conviction rate is concerned, the new provisions have made no discernible impact.[115] As for the concerns about s 34 which have been mentioned, it seems that in some cases disclosure is a problem. Although overall the police are said to be more forthcoming with their evidence, some officers continue to provide 'the bare minimum', and it is primarily the minority with legal advice who benefit from the more open attitude.[116] But there is concern in police circles that, in general, too much is being disclosed to suspects before interview, and that this enables them to fabricate exculpatory stories.[117] The future, then, may see reversal of any improvements in disclosure; this despite the fact that in *Murray* the ECtHR held that inferences from silence would only be permissible in circumstances which 'clearly call for an explanation' from the suspect.[118] Another concern highlighted by the research is that the new law, and the caution that goes with it, can be used as a weapon by the police. If a suspect has been advised to stay silent, the police can repeatedly refer to the terms of the caution to persuade the suspect to rethink his position, so driving a wedge between the suspect and his adviser.[119] Finally, some legal advisers have expressed concern about how the new law can bring pressure to bear on the vulnerable.[120]

---

[110] *Ibid.*, 24.

[111] There are complications in that in some cases the suspect may have mixed motives for remaining silent.

[112] T. Bucke, R. Street and D. Brown, *The Right of Silence: The Impact of the CJPOA 1994* (2000). Broadly similar conclusions about the operation of Northern Irish law are drawn in J. Jackson, M. Wolfe and K. Quinn, *Legislating Against Silence: The Northern Ireland Experience* (2000).

[113] Bucke, Street and Brown, *ibid.*, 31.   [114] *Ibid.*, 34.   [115] *Ibid.*, 67.   [116] *Ibid.*, 22–4.

[117] See HMIC, *Under the Microscope Refocused: A Revisit to the Thematic Inspection Report on Scientific and Technical Support* (2002), 10–11.

[118] See n 71 above, 47.   [119] Bucke, Street and Brown, above n 112, 27–30.   [120] *Ibid.*, 37–8.

There are, then, reasons for concern about the changes to the right to silence brought in by the Criminal Justice and Public Order Act. While the Court of Appeal and European Court of Human Rights have gone some way to erecting safeguards to prevent the jury putting too much weight on silence, rather less has been done to ensure that the inferences from silence regime does not operate unfairly in the police station. Requirements of disclosure before interview remain minimal[121] and, by not taking a firmer stand on the issue of legal advice, the courts have effectively diluted its authority, strengthening the hand of the police in cases where suspects are advised to stay silent. It is true that in *Murray* the European Court of Human Rights took a strong stand on the issue of access to legal advice before interview. In giving judgment, the Court noted that

'at the beginning of police interrogation, an accused is confronted with a fundamental dilemma relating to his defence. If he chooses to remain silent, adverse inferences may be drawn against him. . . . On the other hand, if the accused opts to break his silence during the course of interrogation, he runs the risk of prejudicing his defence without necessarily removing the possibility of inferences being drawn against him. Under such conditions the concept of fairness enshrined in Article 6 requires that the accused has the benefit of assistance of a lawyer already at the initial stages of police interrogation.'[122]

Yet most suspects still face this dilemma without the benefit of legal advice; all that is required is that they be given access to advice, something which, for various reasons, the majority still do not take up. In *Howell*, the Court of Appeal also observed that s 34 changes the context of police questioning: '[n]ow, the police interview and trial are to be seen as part of a continuous process in which the suspect is engaged from the beginning.'[123] More recently, as was noted earlier, the Code C rules on when questioning should end have been changed: under the revised Code, questioning—which can continue so as to test the suspect's account and can capitalize on this by using non-responses as evidence—might be thought to have taken on some of the nature of cross-examination. Given the new significance of questioning, it would seem right to strengthen the suspect's due process protections in the police station.[124] This would include stronger requirements on disclosure of the police case before interview, and perhaps better access to legal advice. Suspects cannot be forced to consult lawyers if they do not want to, but it is known that some refuse legal advice so as not to prolong their detention. Having legal advisers on hand in police stations has been suggested as a way to overcome this problem, and it is perhaps now time to give it more thought.

The point, then, is not that a regime which involves drawing inferences from silence in the police station is inevitably unfair. Its fairness is conditional on the environment in which questioning takes place, a point made well by the Royal Commission on

---

[121] *DPP v Ara* [2002] 1 Cr App R 16.   [122] See n 71 above, 67.   [123] See n 109 above, 23.

[124] See J. Jackson, 'Silence and Proof: Extending the Boundaries of Criminal Proceedings in the United Kingdom' (2001) 5 *E & P* 145.

Criminal Procedure. The Commission expressed concern that changes to the right to silence would require a suspect:

To answer questions based upon possibly unsubstantiated and unspecific allegations or suspicion, even though he is not required to do that at the trial. Such a change could be regarded as acceptable only if, at a minimum, the suspect were to be provided at all stages of the investigation with full knowledge of his rights, complete information about the evidence available to the police at the time, and an exact understanding of the consequences of silence.[125]

As has been seen, there are doubts about whether suspects gain anything like 'an exact understanding of the consequences of silence' from the current police caution. Nor is there any requirement of full disclosure on the part of the police.

The other problem that has emerged in the wake of the CJPOA is the way in which the courts deal with the issue of legal advice as a reason for silence. The judiciary are doubtless concerned that allowing legal advice to be a reason for silence that prevents adverse inferences would result in all solicitors counselling suspects to remain silent. This seems unlikely: after all, it was not what happened prior to the introduction of the CJPOA provisions. But even if this concern is realistic, it does not follow that the courts should take it into account. If they do—as seen in *Howell*—they will penalize defendants who follow legal advice. If that is the only way to make s 34 workable, then it would be better not to have the section at all. Again, the point is not that there is anything wrong in theory with drawing inferences from silence, but that if the scheme cannot be made to work fairly in practice, it would be preferable to abandon it.

4.4 INTERVIEWING VICTIMS

While the focus of this chapter is on the questioning of suspects, it is worth noting briefly that similar concerns apply to police questioning of victims and witnesses. Like suspects, victims and witnesses can be suggestible and compliant; they need to be questioned carefully. Whereas suspects have an interest in ensuring that what they say is not distorted by the police, victims and witnesses will often have less incentive to do so. They may feel that the best way they can help the police is by agreeing with any suggestions put to them, or by being as definite as possible about what they saw. It is therefore important to avoid putting leading questions to witnesses, or to disclose to them too much of the investigator's theory of the case.

For the police, the purpose of questioning victims and witnesses is generally to produce a statement—a written summary of their evidence. The statement plays an important part in the processing of the case: it will form part of the case file reviewed

---

[125] Royal Commission on Criminal Procedure, *The Investigation and Prosecution of Criminal Offences in England and Wales* (1981), 4.52.

by the CPS in deciding whether to continue the prosecution. Cases often come to court some months after the event in question. Witnesses may then have little memory about what they saw at the time. Their earlier statements are often used to 'refresh' their memory—which raises the possibility that inaccuracies in the statement will then be repeated in the witness's testimony. If there is an inconsistency between the statement and what the witness says in court, this may be used by defence counsel to undermine the witness, damaging the case.[126]

What is known about the questioning of victims and witnesses suggests that standards here are worse than where suspects are concerned. Studies indicate that police officers use questioning tactics which shape the evidence gained from witnesses.[127] In the most recent research, Clarke and Milne found little evidence of the impact of training in 'investigative interviewing' of witnesses. Leading questions were common, and the 'predominant use of closed questions and the view that interviewers were "just taking a statement" indicates that interviews were clearly highly interviewer driven, with a confirmatory bias.'[128] The majority of interviews succeeded in gaining only a partial account from the interviewee.

In some types of case, the problems may be more pronounced. When interviewing children, police officers have been found to be perceived as disbelieving.[129] The problems in rape cases were once notorious, but these have now been somewhat improved by better training and facilities.[130] There is currently concern, however, over the tactics used in investigations into cases of sexual and physical abuse in children's homes. The Home Affairs Committee was able to quote one victim who claimed he felt bullied and pressurized into making a complaint. The Committee found evidence of leading questions being asked in these very sensitive cases involving sometimes vulnerable witnesses.[131]

As with the questioning of suspects, better training can probably improve the questioning of victims and witnesses. But training alone is unlikely to change things dramatically. One of the instigators of change in the way suspects have been questioned has been the transparency associated with the tape-recording of interviews. If the same were to be required for interviews with witnesses, it would be easier to see whether the police had encouraged particular responses during interview. In some cases, this might well strengthen the evidence. Some police forces now record interviews with significant witnesses in the most serious cases, but the Home Office has not shown any interest in promoting the practice. Even where investigations into

---

[126] See A. Heaton-Armstrong and D. Wolchover, 'Recording Witness Statements' in A. Heaton-Armstrong, E. Shepherd and D. Wolchover (eds), *Analysing Witness Testimony* (1999), 224–7.

[127] E. Shepherd and R. Milne, 'Full and Faithful: Ensuring Quality, Practice and Integrity of Outcome in Witness Interviews' in *ibid.*, 134–5.

[128] See Clarke and Milne, above n 86, 58–59.

[129] J. Morgan and L. Zedner, *Child Victims* (1992), 101–2.

[130] J. Temkin, *Rape and the Legal Process* (2nd ed., 2002), Ch 5.

[131] Home Affairs Committee, *The Conduct of Investigations into Past Cases of Abuse in Children's Homes* (2002), paras 36–37.

abuse in children's homes are concerned, where the dangers are acute, the Government, mindful of resources, has not been prepared unequivocally to recommend tape-recording.[132] A rule requiring every single interview to be recorded would probably be unworkable.[133] But the quality of witness evidence is surely important enough for a national policy, at least for serious cases.

4.5 CONFESSIONS IN COURT

It has been seen that there remain concerns about the way in which suspects are interviewed by the police, especially given changes to the right to silence. In the worst case scenario, a false confession will be the result of the interviewing process. It is therefore important to have safeguards at court which will guard against a false confession leading to a conviction.

The key legal provision in this regard is s 76 of PACE. Under this section, a confession should be ruled inadmissible if it has been obtained by oppression (s 76(2)(a)), or 'in consequence of anything said or done which was likely, in the circumstances existing at the time, to render unreliable any confession which might have been made by him in consequence thereof' (s 76(2)(b)). There is a degree of overlap between this section and s 78, which applies to confessions as well as to other prosecution evidence. Section 78 allows evidence to be excluded where its admission would render the proceedings unfair; this provision is discussed in detail in Chapter 11. Section 77 requires a court to caution a jury about relying on confessions made by the mentally handicapped. Here, the focus will be on s 76(2)(b).[134]

The wording of this provision is convoluted. It is not a simple 'exclude if unreliable' rule, but instead requires the court to consider *hypothetical* unreliability: the confession should be excluded, 'notwithstanding that it may be true',[135] if it was obtained in circumstances conducive to unreliability. The reason for this is presumably that the provision is intended to sanction bad questioning practices, even if they produce a confession which can be proved to be reliable, for example by evidence corroborating it or even a further admission by the defendant.[136] But in *Proulx*, particular stress was put on the concept 'any confession'. This was held to mean 'any such confession', and to require examination of exactly what had been said by the suspect, an approach which comes close to looking at actual rather than hypothetical unreliability.[137] Other

---

[132] *The Conduct of Investigations into Past Cases of Abuse in Children's Homes—Government Response* (2003), paras 29–35.

[133] Heaton-Armstrong and Wolchover, above n 126.

[134] The oppression safeguard is important, but appears to be rarely applied. The confession of Stephen Miller seems to be the only example of an appeal court finding interviewing conduct oppressive. For more details, see Zander, above n 83.

[135] Section 76(2).   [136] As in *McGovern* (1991) 92 Cr App R 228.

[137] *R v Bow St Magistrates' Court, ex p Proulx* [2001] 1 All ER 57.

aspects of the section shift the focus away from even actual unreliability: the wording 'anything said or done' hints that only if the police do something wrong will the confession be excluded. There is a certain amount of uncertainty in the case law here, revolving around the question of how much emphasis should be placed on these words. For example, in *Goldenberg* the defendant had requested an interview with the police but claimed that the resulting confession was potentially unreliable because he was desperate to be bailed so as to be able to obtain heroin.[138] The Court of Appeal held that this could be ignored because he had not confessed in consequence of anything said or done by the police, but on his own initiative. This rather restrictive view was supported in *Crampton*[139] and *Wahab*,[140] but in a number of other cases factors such as a low mental age have been taken into account.[141] In *Foster*, however, the suspect's vulnerability was downplayed by the Court of Appeal because while it may have been known to the police, it had not been shown that the interviewing officers were aware of it.[142] *Crampton* also highlights the causal test in the section: the words 'in consequence of' appear twice in s 76(2)(b), and this again tends to focus the test on the role of misconduct in securing confessions. The Court of Appeal in *Crampton* referred to the pre-PACE case law, quoting from *Rennie*: 'very few confessions are inspired solely by remorse. Often the motives of an accused are mixed and include a hope that an early admission may lead to an earlier release or to a lighter sentence. If it were the law that the mere presence of such a motive, even if prompted by something said or done . . ., led inexorably to the exclusion of a confession, nearly every confession would be rendered inadmissible.'[143] In this way, the background factors, which put some pressure on all suspects to confess, can be ignored. The approach of the courts seems to be that only if the police draw the prospect of bail and the like to the suspect's attention will a confession be excluded.[144]

One criticism of s 76 and its case law is that the courts have retained a reasonable degree of latitude in individual cases by never settling on a definitive interpretation of the section. In *Proulx*, it is actual reliability which is highlighted. In cases such as *Goldenberg* and *Crampton*, the focus shifts away from reliability and towards wrongdoing. It was noted above that illicit drug taking is a factor predictive of confession, the likely explanation being that drug takers are anxious to escape from custody. It does not seem right, then, that this very real factor is ignored in the reliability determination. The emphasis on wrongdoing in the s 76 case law is not necessarily a bad thing: breach of the Code C rules will often disadvantage a suspect in some way. But a better way to scrutinize confessions would surely be for s 76(2)(b) to be focused purely on reliability, leaving concerns about fairness and wrongdoing to be dealt with through the application of s 78.

It has been seen that PACE and the Codes give little detailed guidance on what is and is not appropriate questioning. It should now be apparent that the s 76 case law

---

[138] (1989) 88 Cr App R 285.   [139] (1991) 92 Cr App R 369.   [140] [2003] 1 Cr App R 15.
[141] E.g. *Everett* [1988] Crim LR 826; *McGovern* above n 136.   [142] [2003] EWCA Crim 178, [63].
[143] (1982) 74 Cr App R 207, 212.   [144] See *Barry* (1992) 95 Cr App R 384; Code C 11.5.

adds little in the way of detail. Could more detailed guidelines be given? This is
something which it is probably very difficult to do. It is not easy to say what degree of
pressure it is appropriate to apply to suspects in order to gain admissions; and there
are so many different ways in which pressure can be applied that creating guidelines is
difficult.[145] However, one rule which has been suggested is a prohibition on deception
in police interviews.[146] Research on questioning in the US reveals that deception, in
the form of exaggerating the strength of evidence, or inventing the existence of evidence, is common.[147] It is in fact a tactic recommended by the leading US interrogation manual.[148] Such deception was found to be a common ploy in police questioning
prior to PACE,[149] and there are more recent examples of it being employed. For
example, when interviewing George Heron for murder, police exaggerated the strength
of eyewitness reports linking him to the scene of crime.[150] In *Mason*, the defendant
and his solicitor were led to believe that Mason's fingerprints had been found at the
crime scene.[151] In both cases, the tactics met with judicial disapproval. Might it be
appropriate to have a firm rule against exaggerating or inventing evidence? That
depends on whether there is anything wrong with deception as a questioning tactic.[152]
It was noted earlier that the strength of evidence against a suspect is thought to be one
of the most significant factors leading to a decision to confess. Incriminating evidence
puts pressure on suspects, but there is not necessarily anything wrong with that. If
Mason's fingerprints really had been found at the scene of crime, there could be no
objection to confronting him with that fact. The pressure to confess caused by
incriminating evidence, then, is not problematic in itself. But what may well be objectionable is facing suspects with such pressure where the evidence does not warrant
it.[153] The more evidence there is against a suspect, the more likely it is that he is guilty,
and the more justification there is to put some sort of pressure on him to confess. This
suggests a good reason for a 'no deception' rule: as far as incriminating evidence is
concerned, such a rule calibrates the degree of pressure placed on a suspect to the
likelihood of his guilt. A rule against exaggerating and inventing evidence, then,
overcomes some of the difficulties in crafting rules on the degree of pressure which
can be placed on suspects.

There is another rule which can be applied to confessions and which has similar
merits: a rule requiring that confessions be corroborated by supporting evidence. This
would mean that a defendant could not be convicted on the basis of a confession alone.
A majority of the Royal Commission on Criminal Justice rejected such a rule, settling

---

[145] For various examples of pressurizing tactics, see Gudjonsson, above n 5, Ch 4.

[146] A. Alschuler, 'Constraint and Confession' (1997) 74 *Denver U. L. Rev.* 957.

[147] Ofshe and Leo, above n 14.   [148] Gudjonsson, above n 5, Ch. 1.

[149] B. Irving, *Police Interrogation: A Study of Current Practice* (1980).

[150] Gudjonsson, above n 5, 98.   [151] [1988] 1 WLR 139.

[152] For further discussion of the ethical issues, see A. Ashworth, 'Should the Police be Allowed to Use
Deceptive Practices' (1998) 114 LQR 108.

[153] See A. Redlich and G. Goodman, 'Taking Responsibility for an Act Not Committed: The Influence of
Age and Suggestibility' (2003) 27 *Law & Human Behavior* 141.

instead for a requirement to warn the jury about the dangers of relying on a confession alone.[154] One reason given against a corroboration rule was that it would lead to the collapse of some cases which are at present successfully prosecuted. This 'would lead to some defendants walking free who would rightly be found guilty under the present rules. This could only be regarded as acceptable if it could be shown that the proposed corroboration rule gave sufficiently greater safeguards against wrong convictions than are now available.'[155] The problem with this way of putting things is that it focuses on right and wrong convictions. It is of course very difficult to know whether a conviction based on no more than a confession is right or wrong in the sense of true to the facts. A more principled way of resolving the debate is to ask whether unsupported confessions are, by their nature, sufficiently strong a sort of evidence to warrant conviction. Even a guilty person is not 'rightly found guilty' if that finding is based on weak evidence. Despite the improvements brought in by PACE and the awareness of the problems of false confessions, confessions remain a problematic sort of evidence. Given the context of detention in the police station, police questioning is always a process which applies pressure to suspects to confess. There are also the factors highlighted in *Rennie*: confessions will often be made in the hope that they will bring some advantage. Although a confession will almost certainly be excluded if it can be shown to have been made as the result of an explicit offer to grant bail or the like, research suggests that offers of lenient treatment can be communicated implicitly.[156] Suspects who are addicted to drugs may be particularly keen to bring their detention to an end. The court in *Rennie* is right that such factors alone should not result in the exclusion of a confession, but they do help to make the case for a corroboration rule. In sum, there are simply too many doubts about the processes which lead suspects to confess for a conviction on a confession alone ever to be justified.

4.6 CONCLUSIONS

The provisions of PACE and other reforms have done much to improve the environment in which questioning takes place. Suspects are now better aware of their rights, and are at less risk of being verballed. The courts have taken a fairly strong line against the worst examples of interviewing practice. It is not surprising, however, that the reform process has tended to change what is relatively easy to change. Little has been done to regulate the questioning process at a finer level, where more difficult questions emerge: how much should the police disclose to the suspect before interview? Exactly how much pressure can be put on suspects in order to secure a confession? There may be no good way of answering the second of these questions, but there are

---

[154] Above n 76, Ch 4, para 87.   [155] *Ibid.*, Ch 4, para 71.

[156] S. Kassin and K. McNall, 'Police Interrogation and Confession: Communicating Promises and Threats by Pragmatic Implication' (1991) 5 *Law & Human Behavior* 233.

rules—a ban on deception and a corroboration requirement—which can go some way to increasing the quality of confessions considered by the courts.

This chapter opened by observing the key role police questioning plays in the criminal process. This point has never been lost on the police, who long campaigned for changes to the right to silence so as to make questioning more effective. Now that the right to silence has been modified, it is not clear that the change has brought substantial benefits. There has been no discernible increase in confessions, nor in convictions. It is not surprising, then, to find new complaints about the effectiveness of questioning emerging. One is that too many suspects are responding to the inferences from silence regime by offering the police a prepared statement, after which they refuse to answer further questions.[157] Another is that questioning is insufficiently effective because disclosure of the police case allows suspects to construct false exculpatory stories. The conclusion to draw from this may be, not that more reforms are needed to make questioning more effective, but that there are simply limits to the effectiveness of questioning as an investigative strategy, at least if it is to be conducted fairly. Doubtless if all suspects were treated like Stephen Miller, more confessions would be gained; but no one could think that acceptable. If basic limits on the conduct of questioning are to be respected, there is probably little the police can do to gain a confession through questioning. And if inferences are to be drawn from silence at interview, there is a strong argument that those basic limits should include effective access to legal advice and adequate disclosure before questioning. Accepting that fair questioning is unlikely ever to produce admissions or significant silence from recalcitrant suspects would be an important step in ensuring that future reform of the process is not frustrating for all involved.

---

[157] Home Office and Cabinet Office, *PACE Review: Report of the Joint Home Office/Cabinet Office Review of PACE* (2002), 35; cf *Knight*, above n 109.

5

GATHERING EVIDENCE: RELIABILITY, PRIVACY AND BODILY INTEGRITY

The criminal process is, in large measure, an investigative process. It exists to prepare cases for effective trial. To this end, prosecuting authorities are given powers enabling them to gather evidence. But these powers can infringe various interests. Some may be the interests of the criminal process itself: the purposes of the process are undermined if unreliable evidence is gathered. Others will be values external to criminal process, such as liberty, privacy, freedom from humiliation and bodily integrity. This chapter examines the ways in which these concerns do, and should, mould the process of gathering evidence against suspects. The sections of this chapter are relatively unconnected, more freestanding than those in other chapters of this book. However, from this rather fragmented set of topics we hope there emerges a picture of the complexity of criminal process, showing the varied interests and constraints which affect it.

5.1 STOP AND SEARCH

Stop and search is one of the most controversial police powers. This is primarily because of long-standing concern that the power is used in a racially discriminatory manner.[1] Commenting on the evidence it heard from minority ethnic communities, the Stephen Lawrence Inquiry observed: 'If there was one area of complaint which was universal it was the issue of "stop and search" '.[2] Even ignoring the race issue, there is concern that the majority of stops and searches are carried out on flimsy grounds and that stop and search is a generally ineffective means of investigating and disrupting crime.

Section 1 of PACE provides a police officer with a power to stop and search persons and vehicles if he reasonably suspects that he will find stolen or prohibited articles—prohibited articles being weapons or items which can be used to commit offences of

---

[1] See, e.g., B. Bowling and C. Phillips, *Racism, Crime and Justice* (2002), Ch 5.
[2] *The Stephen Lawrence Inquiry* (1999), 45.8.

dishonesty or criminal damage.[3] A number of other statutes provide similar powers for other offences, most notably the Misuse of Drugs Act 1971, which permits searches for controlled drugs.[4] A code of practice issued under PACE, Code A, governs the use of all stop and search powers. There are also significant stop and search powers under the Criminal Justice and Public Order Act 1994, s 60 and the Terrorism Act 2000, s 44. Under the former, an area may be designated as one within which a general power of stop and search for offensive weapons will exist for 24 hours. When this occurs, a police officer may stop and search persons and vehicles for weapons 'whether or not he has any grounds for suspecting that the person or vehicle is carrying weapons'.[5] The power can only be used where a senior officer reasonably believes that serious violence will take place within the area. A similar power exists to designate an area and carry out searches for items connected with terrorism under the Terrorism Act 2000.[6]

Stop and search involves detaining a suspect in a public place for a short period in order to search his or her outer clothing.[7] The suspect can be made to remove a jacket and gloves, but any more intrusive search should be carried out by an officer of the same sex as the suspect and in private—for example, in a police van.[8] The most intrusive searches should only be carried out at a police station, and only if the suspect can be taken there quickly.[9] The distinction between the stop and the search is significant: the officer may question the suspect before carrying out the search: questioning may be used to dispel suspicion (as when the suspect gives an explanation for his suspicious behaviour), but it should not be used to generate reasonable suspicion where none already exists.[10] Many people will be stopped but not searched; a stop which does not result in a search is much less intrusive and humiliating than one that does. For the sake of simplicity, however, we will not draw the distinction in the discussion to follow, which will use the term 'stop' to designate both stops and searches.

Reasonable suspicion lies at the heart of stop and search: without it, a search is illegal. One of the key concerns about stop and search is that it is used on the basis of stereotypes, and over the years the definition of reasonable suspicion in Code A has been expanded to make it as clear as possible that this is unacceptable. There must be an 'objective basis' for the suspicion, 'based on facts, information, and/or intelligence'.[11] 'Reasonable suspicion can never be supported on the basis of personal factors alone'—for example, race, age, appearance, previous convictions.[12] 'Reasonable suspicion cannot be based on generalisations or stereotypical images of certain groups or categories of people as more likely to be involved in criminal activity.'[13] But a generalization based on the suspect's behaviour, as when the suspect appears to be

---

[3] Criminal Damage was added by the Criminal Justice Act 2003, s1.

[4] Section 23.   [5] CJPOA 1994, s60(5).

[6] Sections 44–7. See also s43. The power is considered by the Court of Appeal in *R (on the application of Gillan and another) v Commissioner of Police for the Metropolis* [2004] 3 WLR 1144.

[7] Code A 1.2, 3.3, 3.5.   [8] Code A 3.6; PACE s2(9)(a).   [9] Code A, 3.7, note 6.

[10] Code A, 2.11.   [11] Code A, 2.2.   [12] *Ibid.*   [13] *Ibid.*

hiding something, is permissible.[14] The latest version of the Code advises that reasonable suspicion 'should normally be linked to accurate and current intelligence', and
that searches are most effective when targeted 'in a particular area at specified crime
problems'.[15] 'The overall use of these powers is more likely to be effective when up to
date and accurate intelligence or information is communicated to officers and they
are well-informed about local crime patterns.'[16] No one reading the Code could be left
in doubt about the sensitivity of the issues involved in stop and search.

The police are required to make a record of the search—including the basis for
reasonable suspicion—and to provide the suspect with a copy. Researchers have found
that officers often resort to 'voluntary' or 'consensual' searches to avoid the Code
requirements—including that of recording.[17] Code A now provides that 'An officer
must not search a person, even with his or her consent, where no power to search is
applicable'.[18] A record should be made of even consensual searches. In a provision
currently being piloted, the Code goes even further, requiring a record to be made,
and a copy given to the suspect, every time a police officer asks a person to account for
themselves (e.g. 'what are you doing here?'; 'why are you carrying a cricket bat?').[19]

On the basis of the records made by police officers, the Home Office compiles
statistics on the use of stop and search powers, including information on the race of
those stopped. The figures are doubtless inaccurate owing to under-recording by the
police (data from the British Crime Survey suggest that a quarter of stops go
unrecorded)[20], but they tell us something about trends and about the racial disparity
in the application of the power. In 2002–3 there were around 895,000 recorded stops
in England and Wales.[21] This is similar to the figure in 1996–7, but in the late 1990s
the figure rose to over 100,000. There was then a drop to 714,000 in 2000–1, but the
figures have risen since then. The drop may well have been due to criticism of stop
and search powers made by the Lawrence Inquiry. The renewed upward drift, which
has been encouraged by David Blunkett,[22] suggests that police sensitivity over the
power is wearing off. There is some evidence, however, that the power is now being
used more effectively; as we saw above, Code A now emphasizes 'intelligence led' stop
and search. The proportion of stops resulting in arrest stood at 10 per cent in 1997–8,
but has now risen to 13 per cent.[23] The recent upturn in the use of the power has not
been accompanied by a decline in this figure. As often in the criminal process, these
overall figures mark considerable regional variation. Essex had a stop and search rate
of 458 per 100,000 of its population, compared with 6,378 per 100,000 in Cleveland.[24]

---

[14] Code A, 2.3.   [15] Code A, 2.4.   [16] Code A, 2.5.
[17] See D. Dixon, *Law in Policing: Legal Regulation and Police Practices* (1997), 93–104.
[18] Code A, 1.5.
[19] Code A, 4.11. The provision results from recommendation 61 of the Lawrence Inquiry, above n 2. For
criticism, see M. Fitzgerald, 'Stop and Think' *The Guardian*, 26 March 2002.
[20] *Arrests for Notifiable Offences and the Operation of Certain Police Powers Under PACE: England and
Wales, 2002/03* HOSB 17/03, paras 23–4.
[21] *Ibid.*, table PA.   [22] 'Race Row as Blunkett Backs Stop and Search' *The Observer*, 10 March 2002.
[23] *Ibid.*   [24] *Ibid.*, Table P1.

It is not surprising that Cleveland's 'zero tolerance' regime is not very effective, with only 8 per cent of stops leading to arrest, compared with 13 per cent (the national average) in Essex and 18 per cent in Nottinghamshire which, like Essex, searches relatively few of its population.[25]

The figures on race and stop and search are initially stark. In 2002–3 blacks were six times more likely to be searched than whites, a slightly greater racial disparity than in the previous year.[26] There was also a slight fall in the proportion of stops of blacks which led to an arrest: from 17 per cent to 16 per cent, while the figure for whites remained the same at 13 per cent.[27] There is some regional variation, but a degree of racial disparity is a near nationwide constant: only Northumbria and Durham stop a smaller proportion of their black population than their white population.[28] Many black people are searched more than once in a year. These figures on race need careful interpretation, however. The Home Office figures showing that blacks are six times more likely to be stopped than whites reflect the proportion of black and white people in the national or local population. Fewer blacks than whites are actually stopped; the disparity occurs because there are many fewer blacks than whites in the population. It can be argued, however, that taking the proportion of blacks and whites in the population as a whole as the basis for calculating the stop and search rate is not a good way of judging whether stop and search powers are being used in a discriminatory manner. The people most likely to be targeted for stop and search are young people who appear in public in areas with a high police presence. If blacks outnumber whites in this 'pool', then there may not be as much racial disparity as appears on the face of the figures. Research has been conducted on the population 'available' for stop and search, which tries to take this into account.[29] The general conclusion of this study is that when the population available for stop and search is used as the basis for the calculation, much of the disparity disappears. In fact, one general trend across the research areas was for whites to be stopped at a rate higher than their proportion in the available population.[30] This raises an obvious question: if stop and search is being targeted on particular areas—areas with large numbers of young black men on the streets—can this targeting be justified, or is it in itself discriminatory? The conclusion of the research was that stop and search was generally targeted on areas with high crime rates, and to that extent the targeting was justified. Beneath this general picture of racial equity, however, were found 'examples where those from minority ethnic backgrounds were stopped and searched more often than would have been expected from their numbers in the available population.' And 'stops and searches were targeted at some areas where there [were] disproportionate numbers of those from

---

[25] *Ibid.*

[26] Home Office, *Statistics on Race and the Criminal Justice System—2003*, 27. 'Black' is the term used in this report; figures for Asians are given separately. For more recent statistics, showing a disturbing upward trend in the stop and search of blacks in London, see Metropolitan Police Authority, *Report of the Scrutiny on MPS Stop and Search Practice* (2004), 29.

[27] Home Office, *ibid.*, Table 4.4.   [28] *Ibid.*, Table 4.2.

[29] MVA and J. Miller, *Profiling Populations Available for Stops and Searches* (2000).   [30] *Ibid.*, 84–5.

minority ethnic backgrounds, yet where the local crime rates did not appear to justify this attention.'[31] Even sticking to the general picture, research on 'available' populations does not give us a clear answer to the question whether there is racial bias in stop and search patterns. Knowledge of the available population does not tell us what proportion among blacks and whites in that population are behaving suspiciously. And even though high crime areas seem to be the ones targeted for high levels of stop and search, there may still be bias of some sort at work if stop and search itself is a power which is difficult to justify because, for example, it makes a minimal contribution to crime prevention and detection.[32] We turn to this issue shortly.

So far we have concentrated on stop and search under PACE and other statutes which require reasonable suspicion. The Home Office also collects statistics on stop and search powers which do not require reasonable suspicion: the general powers to search for weapons or terrorist equipment which we noted above. These powers are used with increasing frequency: in 2002–3 there were 50,000 recorded weapons stops under CJPOA, s 60 (compared to 20,000 in the previous year), and 32,500 terrorist stops under the Terrorism Act 2000, s 44 (compared to 10,000 in the previous year).[33] As would be expected, these stops generate fewer arrests than stops that do require reasonable suspicion: there were 3,000 arrests under the CJPOA (a six per cent success rate) and 380 under the Terrorism Act (a one per cent success rate).[34] Racial disparity is marked for these searches too: in London, the Metropolitan Police searched 3,500 whites, 2,700 blacks and 1,900 Asians under the CJPOA:[35] the disparity here is greater than with PACE stops. There can be little doubt that the power is largely targeted on minority ethnic groups. Under the Terrorism Act, the disparity is most marked where Asians are concerned: nationally 12 per cent of searches were of blacks and 20 per cent were of Asians; in 2002–3 the number of Asians searched under this power increased four-fold from the year before.[36] The 'success rate' under the Terrorism Act (the proportion of stops leading to arrest) is about the same for Asians as for whites, and somewhat higher for blacks.[37] A minority of these arrests (five per cent) is actually in connection with terrorism.[38]

Even if—owing to the racial make up of the populations 'available'—there is little racial disparity in the use of stop and search powers, there is considerable evidence that their use is corrosive of good relations between the police and the black community. The Police Complaints Authority found that while only 10 per cent of people making complaints against the police were black, 40 per cent of complaints about stop and search were made by black people.[39] The Authority found that 'black people experience a different kind of dissatisfaction about stop and searches than do white people, and that the incidents they complain about are intrinsically different'.[40] Other research on the experience of stop and search has found that those from minority

---

[31] *Ibid.*, 87.   [32] L. Lustgarten, 'The Future of Stop and Search' [2002] Crim LR 603, 616–17.
[33] Above n. 20, Tables PB, PC.   [34] *Ibid.*   [35] Home Office, above n 26, Table 4.5.
[36] *Ibid.*, Table 4.6.   [37] *Ibid.*, Tables 4.8, 4.10.   [38] *Ibid.*
[39] Police Complaints Authority, *Stop and Search Complaints 2000–2001, Summary Report* (2004), 12.
[40] *Ibid.*, 21.

ethnic communities do not feel that the power is being used fairly: some feel that they are stopped in situations where white people would not be, and some complain of racist language during the stop.[41] We noted above the concerns highlighted by the Lawrence Inquiry; these are mirrored in a recent report by the Metropolitan Police Authority which found continued dissatisfaction—even anger—among minority ethnic communities about the use of stop and search.[42] The experience of being stopped and searched can be frightening and humiliating. Being a target of stop and search has been found to be correlated with having less confidence in the police.[43] For that reason, the power may directly undermine police/community relations. By alienating young people, stop and search may actually be counter-productive.[44]

Stop and search makes some contribution to crime control, but not a very significant one. There has been speculation as to whether the rate of stop and search has a general deterrent effect on crime, but studies of the connection between crime rates and stop rates find no strong connection.[45] A visible police presence on the streets no doubt deters some crime, but beyond this the actual use of stop and search probably adds little. Stop and search does, however, play some role in detecting crime: as noted above, currently around 13 per cent of stops result in an arrest. About 40 per cent of these arrests are for drugs offences, probably most often for cannabis.[46] It is questionable whether tackling such low level offending is worth the cost to police-community relations that is extracted by stop and search.[47] Although cannabis is now downgraded to a class C drug,[48] possession of it remains an arrestable offence[49] and the police will still be able to use stop and search to control possession. If a policy decision were made not to use stop and search for cannabis, much might be gained; in London, drugs stops have a low success rate (seven per cent)—they may be particularly prone to being based on stereotype, and to producing the racial disproportion that is such a marked feature of stop and search.[50] More generally, and ignoring drugs offences, it has been estimated that for every 106 crimes committed which are susceptible to arrest via stop and search, one stop and search arrest is made.[51] Some crimes are disrupted by stop and search—for example a person may be arrested on their way to commit burglary, or car theft, via stop and search. But it is thought that only 0.1 per cent of crime is disrupted by use of the power.[52]

Stop and search powers can be used by the police in better and worse ways. As noted above, some forces have higher arrest rates from stop and search than do others. If stop and search is carefully targeted, there will be fewer stops and a higher arrest

---

[41] V. Stone and N. Pettigrew, *The Views of the Public on Stops and Searches* (2000), 17–19, 26.

[42] Above n 26.

[43] J. Miller, N. Bland and P. Quinton, *The Impact of Stops and Searches on Crime and the Community* (2000), 51–2.

[44] See also M. Fitzgerald, *Final Report into Stop and Search* (1999).

[45] Miller *et al*, above n 43, Ch 3; cf Fitzgerald, *ibid*.   [46] Above n 20, Table PA.

[47] See Fitzgerald, above n 44.

[48] Misuse of Drugs Act 1971 (Modification) (No 2) Order 2003 (SI 2003/3201).

[49] Criminal Justice Act 2003, s 3, amends PACE, Sched 1A to this effect.

[50] MPA, above n 26, 35–6.   [51] Miller *et al*, above, n 43, 23.   [52] *Ibid.*, 30.

rate, though a lower number of arrests overall (that is because the police sometimes 'get lucky' when conducting a poorly targeted search).[53] A well targeted stop is also less likely to alienate the person involved. People who are stopped are also sensitive to the manner in which the stop is carried out: when the police act politely and respect-fully—as Code A requires[54]—there is again less damage to community relations. At present, however, there is plenty of evidence that stop and search is not used in this ideal manner: as we have seen, there are complaints about its use, especially from blacks. The overall arrest rate, which even after the recent rise stands at only 13 per cent, is a clear indication that the grounds for stops are often flimsy. A 13 per cent chance of finding evidence of a crime would seem to fall some way below the standard of 'reasonable suspicion'. Research evidence confirms that stops often are carried out on the basis of hunches and poorly supported generalizations.[55] Indeed, everything we know about the way police discretion is used on the streets suggests that stop and search will be used in circumstances outwith the demands of PACE. It will be used by the police to assert authority over particular sections of the community, to break up groups of youths, and to gather intelligence.[56]

As currently practised, stop and search is objectionable for many reasons.[57] Yet the public generally support the existence of stop and search powers, and do not wish to see them abolished.[58] If the power to stop and search was taken away from the police there would probably be minimal impact on the prevention and detection of crime. But there might be other negative effects. Arrest can be justified on very similar grounds to stop and search—both powers hinge on reasonable suspicion.[59] The arrest power allows the police to take a suspect to a police station and to detain him for a considerable length of time. The greatest negative impact of removing stop and search powers, then, would probably be an increase in the number of low suspicion arrests. Stop and search probably works best, in terms of both crime control and impact on the community, when it operates as a prelude to an expected arrest.[60] Where the police have reasonable suspicion that a crime has been or is about to be committed, stop and search can allow that suspicion to be dispelled, by showing that, for example, the suspect is not in possession of stolen property. Stop and search enables the police to respond to suspected offending in a less coercive manner than arrest. It is unlikely, however, that this ideal can be attained. Police discretion on the street is difficult to control, and once the power to stop and search is given it is inevitable that it will be used more widely than envisaged. If we are to retain stop and search we probably have to accept that the power will continue to cause problems, especially in relation to minority ethnic communities.

---

[53] See, e.g., Fitzgerald, above n 44.   [54] Code A, 3.1.

[55] Most recently, P. Quinton, N. Bland and J. Miller, *Police Stops, Decision-Making and Practice* (2000).

[56] See *ibid.* and Fitzgerald, above n 44.   [57] See generally Lustgarten, above n 32.

[58] Stone and Pettigrew, above n 41, 52.   [59] See Ch. 4.   [60] Code A, 1.4.

5.2 SURVEILLANCE

It is widely agreed that the use of surveillance techniques by law enforcement agencies has increased considerably and is likely to increase further. Not only are more offences being committed by electronic means, but also the range of techniques and devices for the surveillance of citizens becomes ever wider and it is natural that law enforcement agencies should wish to take advantage of this technology in order to improve the detection of crimes. Surveillance techniques that involve (for example) electronic eavesdropping or imaging may promise a high degree of reliability. However, they also raise a number of human rights concerns, and it is these concerns that have led to some recent changes in English law.

The general approach of the common law to matters such as the interception of communications is that this is permissible unless specifically made unlawful. Thus until the 1980s, telephone-tapping was authorized by the Home Secretary, and there was no relevant law. When this was challenged in *Malone v United Kingdom*,[61] it was found to be in breach of Article 8. Paragraph 1 of that Article safeguards an individual's right to respect for private life, home and correspondence. Paragraph 2 permits interference with the right on certain grounds that make it 'necessary in a democratic society', but the interference must be 'in accordance with the law'—so as to ensure that interference is not arbitrary but has procedural safeguards built in. The UK had no relevant law, and soon after the decision the Interception of Communications Act 1985 was passed. This introduced a statutory authorization scheme for telephone-tapping, but failed to deal with surveillance generally. Other methods remained unregulated, save for Home Office guidelines.

Among the subsequent challenges was that in *Khan v United Kingdom*,[62] where police officers had placed a listening device on the wall of a private house and recorded incriminating conversations. The police officers had followed the procedure of obtaining the chief constable's authority, but there was no legislative framework in England and so the interference with the targeted person's right to respect for private life was not 'in accordance with the law.' The Government anticipated this ruling by promoting the provisions that became Part III of the Police Act 1997, which provides an authorization procedure for surveillance involving entry on to property. However, this piecemeal approach to legislation still failed to provide a general framework for all forms of intrusive surveillance, and adverse decisions from Strasbourg continued to come.[63]

Many of the points of principle about safeguarding human rights in the process of using surveillance were accepted in a White Paper that proposed new legislation,[64] and

---

[61] (1985) 7 EHRR 14.   [62] (2000) 31 EHRR 1016.

[63] E.g. *Govell v United Kingdom* [1999] EHRLR 121; *Halford v United Kingdom* (1997) 24 EHRR 523; and, also relating to an investigation in the 1990s, *PG and JH v United Kingdom* [2002] Crim LR 308.

[64] Home Office, *Interception of Communications in the United Kingdom* (Cm 4368 of 1999), prompted by JUSTICE, *Under Surveillance* (1998).

the result is the Regulation of Investigatory Powers Act 2000. Although much more general than previous legislation, it fails to integrate or incorporate the provisions in Part III of the Police Act 1997, which remain in force. In outline,[65] the first part of the 2000 Act replaces the Interception of Communications Act 1985 with a new framework that extends to communications on public and private networks. It provides a procedure whereby the Home Secretary may issue a warrant, and s 5(2) and 5(3) reflect the language of Article 8(2) of the Convention in referring to proportionality and to the various reasons for which interference may be held necessary in a democratic society. The second part of the 2000 Act, in outline, introduces a regulatory framework for three forms of surveillance. *Directed surveillance* is covert surveillance that is not intrusive in its method but is likely to reveal matters within the protection of Article 8(1). *Intrusive surveillance* is covert surveillance that does involve intrusion into private premises or a vehicle. *Covert human intelligence sources* are persons who maintain a close relationship with a target suspect and thereby obtain information falling within the ambit of Article 8(1). What the Act does is to require authorization by a senior police officer, on the statutory grounds, before directed surveillance or covert human intelligence sources are deployed; and to require authorization of intrusive surveillance at the level of chief constable or, if the matter is urgent, by a senior police officer. The Act establishes a Commissioner to review warrants issued and a Tribunal to deal with complaints. This is more or less a continuation of the previous system, and it is doubtful whether it is Convention-compliant. The Strasbourg Court has held more than once that a procedure for interference with Article 8 rights must require judicial authorization,[66] and it must be highly doubtful whether the procedures for authorization by middle-ranking police officers (in respect of directed surveillance, covert human sources and, in some circumstances, intrusive surveillance) satisfy this requirement. Moreover, there is room for argument about the vagueness of some key terms in the Act—such as 'serious crime'—now that the Strasbourg Court is taking a more stringent approach to cases of State interference with Article 8 rights.[67]

In conclusion, the Regulation of Investigatory Powers Act 2000 represents a significant step towards protecting human rights in the process of gathering evidence through surveillance methods. While it is unfortunate that the Government adopted such a minimalist view of the requirements of Article 8 on such questions as judicial authorization, defining the grounds for interference, and informing individuals that

---

[65] For discussion of the 2000 Act, see H. Fenwick, *Civil Liberties and Human Rights* (3rd ed., 2002), 670–726.

[66] E.g. most clearly in *Kopp v Switzerland* (1999) 27 EHRR 91, at para 74; cf. the reasoning of the Home Office in the White Paper (above, n 4) at para 7.2, which is unpersuasive insofar as many other European and Commonwealth countries require judicial authorization, as the JUSTICE report (above, n 4) points out.

[67] The Government relies on two decisions of the Commission, *Hewitt and Harman v United Kingdom* App. No. 20317/92 and *Christie v United Kingdom* (1994) 78–A DR 119, as confirming that the phrases 'in the interests of national security' and 'the economic well-being of the country' are sufficiently certain; but in recent years the Court itself has signalled a greater emphasis on certainty in decisions such as *Valenzuela v Spain* (1998) 28 EHRR 483 and *Amann v Switzerland* (2000) 30 EHRR 843.

they have been subject to surveillance, surveillance by law enforcement officers is now much more fully regulated than it was at the end of the last century. More evidence of how the 2000 Act is working in practice is now needed.

5.3 EYEWITNESS IDENTIFICATION EVIDENCE

Eyewitness identification evidence plays a significant role in the criminal process. An analysis of cases in the Crown Court found it to be very or fairly important in around a quarter of cases;[68] it is used more often in certain types of crime, such as robbery and burglary.[69] Yet eyewitness identification is a relatively frail type of evidence: it has played a significant role in a number of miscarriages of justice. Laszlo Virag, for example, was convicted of murder after eight witnesses picked him out at an identification parade. He was later exonerated and the case led to a review of identification procedures.[70] Writing in 1972, the Criminal Law Revision Committee suggested that mistaken eyewitness identifications were 'by far the greatest cause of actual or possible wrong convictions'.[71] In the US, the Innocence Project has used DNA evidence to overturn a number of convictions secured before DNA technology was widely available. A review of the exoneration cases suggests that eyewitness identification played an important role in about 75 per cent of these wrong convictions.[72]

The primary concern of the criminal process where eyewitness identification evidence is concerned is to secure reliable evidence. There are a number of factors that may affect the accuracy of a particular eyewitness identification. Some of these relate to the witness, such as eyesight, memory, the conditions in which the offence was observed: distance from the offender, duration of the incident, quality of light. These are factors which the criminal process has relatively little control over, though at the trial stage the court should obviously do its best to draw their importance to the fact-finder's attention. There are other factors, though, over which the criminal process has much more control. The most obvious of these relate to the way in which any identification procedure is carried out, for example whether an identification parade is held or whether the witness is simply asked to identify the suspect as the offender at trial, when he is standing in the dock. There are more subtle factors, too, which the process has some influence over, such as the amount of time that elapses between the crime and the identification procedure, and whether the witness might have seen pictures of the suspect in the press before being asked to make an identification. The

---

[68] M. Zander and P. Henderson, *Crown Court Study* (1993), para 3.3.1.

[69] G. Pike, N. Brace and S. Kynan, *The Visual Identification of Suspects: Procedures and Practice* (Home Office Briefing Note 2/02).

[70] P. Devlin, *Report to the Secretary of State for the Home Department of the Departmental Committee on Evidence of Identification in Criminal Cases* HC 338 (1976).

[71] Criminal Law Revision Committee, *Eleventh Report: Evidence (General)* Cmnd 4991 (1972), para 196.

[72] See http://www.innocenceproject.org/causes/index.php

discussion in this chapter concentrates on factors relating to the identification procedure, though something will also be said about the handling of identification evidence in court.

Because of the importance of eyewitness identification evidence, and the recognition of its potential frailty, there is a considerable body of psychological research which examines in some detail the criteria which affect its quality.[73] Reference to this literature will be made where appropriate. At this point, it is worth highlighting some of the more obvious factors which have been shown to influence eyewitness identification. In the typical situation, a person has observed a crime being committed, and is later shown a suspect by the police and asked whether the suspect is the person seen earlier. Memory plays a crucial role in this process: the witness is being asked to compare a remembered image with the person shown to her. Memory decays over time, so in general the earlier the procedure is held, the better. Memory, and the identification process, are also open to influence and suggestion. Identification procedures which suggest to the witness that a particular person is suspected to be the offender should therefore be avoided. For example, confronting the witness with a suspect and saying 'we think this is the person who attacked you' will rarely be appropriate, because such a process is very suggestive. It is better to provide the witness with an identification process which involves a choice being made between several people. An identification parade can achieve this, but it is still important to avoid suggestion. If the witness reports that the offender had black hair, and the suspect is the only person on the parade who has black hair, the parade is obviously biased against the suspect. Even if such obvious pitfalls are avoided, however, suggestion may still occur. If a police officer accompanying the suspect stares at the suspect, this may suggest to the witness who to pick—and this can even occur even if the police officer is not intending to draw attention to anyone.[74]

Identification procedures are governed by Code D, issued under PACE. A new version of Code D, containing important changes, was implemented in March 2003.[75] This latest version of Code D responds to problems which had emerged under the previous one. The earlier version, in paragraph 2.3, placed a rigid requirement on the police to hold an identification procedure 'whenever a suspect disputes an identification.' This would usually require holding an identification parade. It became apparent, however, that there were circumstances in which little was to be gained from doing so. Such a situation was considered by the House of Lords in *R v Forbes*.[76] The witness in this case had been the victim of an attempted mugging. The police arrived quickly and drove the witness round the area where the crime had occurred; the

[73] See, e.g., B. Cutler and S. Penrod, *Mistaken Identification: The Eyewitness, Psychology and the Law* (1995); G. Wells and E. Olson, 'Eyewitness Identification' (2003) 54 *Annual Review of Psychology* 277.

[74] M. Phillips *et al*, 'Double-blind Photoarray Administration as a Safeguard Against Investigator Bias' (1999) 84 *J. Applied Psychology* 940.

[75] The substantive changes were implemented in a 'consultation draft' of the Code which came into effect a year earlier.

[76] [2001] 1 AC 473.

witness spotted Forbes and identified him as the offender. Forbes was arrested, but denied being the offender. No identification parade was held, despite Forbes requesting one. In this case the police had no suspect until the witness identified Forbes; it was not a case where the police had found a suspect and wanted his identity verified by the witness. Arguably, then, an identification parade would not have been of any use. The identification had already occurred; if the witness attended a parade and picked out Forbes, this would probably only show that Forbes was the person he remembered having picked out on the street. If he did not identify Forbes, this might be thought to show that he had forgotten what the person he picked out looked like, rather than that his initial identification was inaccurate. Despite this, the House of Lords felt that it could do little to deviate from the clear wording of Code D. An identification parade should have been held. Some exceptions to this requirement, however, were recognized:

'If an eye-witness to a criminal incident makes plain to the police that he cannot identify the culprit, it will very probably be futile to invite the witness to attend an identification parade. If an eye-witness may be able to identify clothing worn by a culprit, but not the culprit himself, it will probably be futile to mount an identification parade rather than simply inviting the witness to identify the clothing. If a case is one of pure recognition of someone well-known to the eye-witness, it may be futile to hold an identification parade. But save in cases such as these, or other exceptional circumstances, the effect of paragraph 2.3 is clear . . .'.[77]

In addition to the *Forbes* situation, identification parades were causing other problems. It is not easy to set up an effective identification parade. The process requires finding at least eight people 'who so far as possible resemble the suspect in age, height, general appearance and position in life.'[78] Their attendance at the parade must be coordinated with that of the suspect, the suspect's lawyer (if requested), and any witnesses. Research suggested that around 50 per cent of identification parades had to be cancelled once arranged, causing inconvenience to all concerned.[79] The difficulty of arranging an identification parade also meant that there was often considerable delay in holding one—a factor which reduces the quality of identification evidence.[80] At the same time, technological advances meant that a good alternative to live identification parades—a process called video identification—was available.

The latest version of Code D distinguishes between two types of case: those where the suspect is known to the police, and those where the identity of the suspect is not known. In the former case, unlike the initial situation in *Forbes*, the police have a suspect for the crime.[81] If the suspect denies being the offender, the Code now states that 'an identification procedure shall be held unless it is not practicable or it would

---

[77] *Ibid.*, 27.   [78] Code D, Annex B, para 9.   [79] Pike *et al*, above n 69.

[80] Y. Tinsley, 'Even Better than the Real Thing? The Case for Reform of Identification Procedures' (2001) 5 *E & P* 99.

[81] The more technical definition in the Code is in terms of whether 'there is sufficient information known to the police to justify the arrest of a particular person for suspected involvement in the offence' (3.4).

serve no useful purpose'.[82] This, then, enlarges the exceptions allowed by the House of
Lords in *Forbes* and means that the police would now have some discretion whether or
not to hold an identification procedure on facts similar to those in that case. In
principle, though, it does seem right to have departed from the previous, stricter
requirement. In the *Forbes* situation, an identification procedure may be little more
than a test of the witness's memory of who they initially identified, as opposed to a
test of the identification itself. If so, allowing a suspect to insist on an identification
procedure would enable him to undermine the identification (in the case where the
witness fails to re-identify the suspect) while offering no opportunity to test its quality.
Nevertheless, the discretion involved in deciding whether an identification procedure
would be useful is potentially problematic; guidance from the courts is called for
here.[83]

Once it is decided that an identification procedure should be held, the Code provides a hierarchy of procedures. Under the previous Code, an identification parade
was the preferred procedure, but the parade has now been put on a par with video
identification. A video identification is basically a recorded version of an identity
parade: the witness is shown video images (usually moving images) of a suspect
'together with images of others who resemble the suspect'.[84] A system for putting
together video identifications, called VIPER, is being run by West Yorkshire police.[85]
The West Yorkshire bureau has a database of video images; when an image of a
suspect is sent to them, they can put this together with images of eight other look-
alikes ('foils'). This can be sent back to the original force, to be shown to the witness
potentially within a few hours of the crime being witnessed. Under Code D, a video
identification is normally more suitable than a live parade if it can be held more
quickly;[86] as this will almost always be the case once VIPER is widely available, video
identification will become the norm.[87] In addition to reducing delay, video identification may offer other advantages over live parades. Once a large database is built up, it
will probably be more effective in presenting a group of people who resemble the
suspect, making the procedure fairer. Another benefit is more subtle. In a video
identification the witness will see the image of each person sequentially, rather than
seeing them all together. The psychological research suggests that this process is preferable, because it encourages witnesses to make a judgment on the basis of identification—a decision whether a particular person is the culprit—rather than on the basis
of comparative resemblance: 'this is the person in the group who looks most like the
culprit'.[88] The Code, however, goes some way to undermining this advantage by

---

[82] Code D, 3.12.

[83] Police forces vary considerably in their approach to identification procedures in the *Forbes* scenario: see
Streets Ahead: A Joint Inspection of the Street Crime Initiative (2003), 60–1.

[84] Code D, 3.5.

[85] Home Office Press Notice 14/3/03. Another system, PROMAT, is used by some forces.

[86] Code D, 3.14.

[87] *Streets Ahead*, above n 83, 62, notes that some forces have virtually stopped using live parades.

[88] See Wells and Olson, above n 73.

allowing witnesses to see particular images, or the whole set, as many times as they want, and even stipulating that no decision should be made until the whole set of images has been seen at least twice.[89] Another point about sequential presentation is that it increases the dangers of suggestion. If the suspect's image stands out from the others, perhaps because it is filmed against a different background, or if anyone present does anything to draw attention to the suspect's image, such as shuffling their feet when it appears, the process will be biased against the suspect.[90] A final point about the pros and cons of video identification is that video has been said to produce more positive identifications than live parades. This has been touted as one of its advantages.[91] But this conclusion is a little too quick; what matters is not the number of identifications but their accuracy. It may be that because video identifications are easier to arrange than live parades, they are used to identify suspects against whom there is less evidence than there would be with a live parade. If that is the case, then the larger number of positive identifications with video might represent a higher ratio of false to true identifications, making video identification, overall, worse than live parades in terms of accuracy.[92]

Beneath the two preferred options—video identification and live parade—come two less satisfactory methods of identification: group identification and, the most problematic, confrontation. In a group identification the witness sees the suspect as part of an informal group, such as people leaving an escalator. Here, it is more difficult to control whether the suspect stands out from the group. Unfortunately, the new Code allows considerable discretion here, permitting a group identification to be offered 'where the officer in charge of the investigation considers that in the particular circumstances it is more satisfactory than a video identification or an identification parade.'[93] In a confrontation, a suspect is simply presented to a witness; it should only be used if none of the other options are practicable.[94]

The suspect is given a degree of input on identification procedures. In video and live parades the suspect gets an opportunity to object to the inclusion of other people or images. The suspect's consent also plays a role in the choice of identification procedure. A suspect may refuse to take part in a particular identification procedure, but there are possible costs to this. The refusal can be referred to at a subsequent trial, and the police can also proceed covertly in order to institute an identification procedure without consent.[95] This might involve, for example, covert video images of the suspect being taken and used as part of a video identification. This is potentially disadvantageous, as it makes it more likely that the resulting image of the suspect will differ from any other images used in a video identification, and so stand out. There

---

[89] Code D, Annex A, 11–12.

[90] See G. Wells *et al*, 'Eyewitness Identification Procedures: Recommendations for Lineups and Photospreads' (1998) 22 *Law & Human Behavior* 1, 31.

[91] Home Office Press Notice 14/3/03; *Streets Ahead*, above n 83, 62–3.

[92] On the role of prior suspicion in the overall accuracy of identification procedures, see Wells and Olson, above n 73.

[93] Code D, 3.16.   [94] Code D, 3.23.   [95] Code D, 3.17.

are again issues about the control of discretion here, but also a more basic question: should suspects be able to refuse to be subjected to an identification procedure? It would be strange if suspects were able to avoid any attempt to compare them to a witness's recollection, even in court. So long as a defendant has adequate opportunity to draw attention to the possible frailty of an identification procedure in court, there does not seem, then, to be a strong case for a right of refusal without adverse consequences. But it then becomes important that defendants are well informed about the possible consequences of refusal. The new Code, however, is less than satisfactory on this score.[96] Although the Code provides for an explanation of the various procedures to be made to a suspect, this does not extend to explaining the possible detrimental consequences of refusing to cooperate, in terms of the quality of covert video identification. What is more, any explanation at all can be withheld if the police have reasonable grounds to suspect that the suspect will, on hearing the explanation, take steps to avoid being seen by a witness.[97]

In cases where the suspect's identity is not known, the police have more discretion still. They may take a witness to a neighbourhood or place in an attempt to obtain an identification. The Code provides some guidelines on this process; the basic idea is that 'the principles applicable to the formal [identification] procedures . . . shall be followed so far as is practicable.'[98] For example, the police should try to keep witnesses separate and to avoid drawing their attention to any particular person. As in all identification cases, '[b]efore asking the witness to make an identification, where practicable, a record shall be made of any description given by the witness of the suspect.'[99] Because in such cases the record of the description will provide the only good way of testing a witness's subsequent identification, it would be appropriate to phrase this requirement more strongly, allowing identification to proceed without a record only in exceptional circumstances. Once an informal identification has been made, the suspect will be known to the police, and the requirements of Code D for such cases, discussed above, will apply. Thus a formal identification procedure might be held; but given the new discretion not to do so where it would not serve any useful purpose, this may now occur rarely.

How satisfactorily does Code D regulate the process of gathering identification evidence from eyewitnesses? Some of the problems of the new version relate to the degree of discretion allowed to the police. There is nothing wrong with discretion in itself, but it needs to be used appropriately and subjected to meaningful scrutiny by the courts. Given the sorts of pressure on the police identified in Chapter 3, there must be doubts about the appropriateness of leaving discretion to them at this crucial stage of the pre-trial process.[100] Another problem is the way in which the sequential nature of the video identification process is compromised by allowing

---

[96] A. Roberts and S. Clover, 'Managerialism and Myopia: The Government's Consultation Draft on PACE Code D' [2002] Crim LR 873.

[97] Code D, 3.20.   [98] Code D, 3.2.   [99] *Ibid.*

[100] See A. Roberts, 'The Problem of Mistaken Identification: Some Observations on Process' (2004) 8 *E & P* 100.

witnesses to review images. The Code might also be criticized for other respects in which it departs from best practice identified by psychologists.[101] For example, with video identifications and live parades, foils (the group of people in which the suspect's image is to be included) should be chosen to resemble the suspect.[102] The better advice seems to be that in most cases the foils should resemble the witness's description of the offender. In an optimal identification procedure the person conducting it should be 'blind'—that is, they should not know which of the group is the suspect, and the witness should be informed of their ignorance.[103] This will help ensure that the witness receives no suggestive cues. As was noted, the avoidance of suggestion is more important than ever now that video identification is becoming the norm. While Code D stipulates that the police officer conducting the identification procedure should not be involved in the investigation of the case,[104] it does not go as far as implementing blind procedures. Another improvement would be to ask the witnesses for an expression of confidence that they have identified the offender immediately an identification is made. Once a witness discovers that the case against the person picked is proceeding to trial, she is likely to feel more confident that she has made the right choice. Assessing confidence at the first opportunity, then, is the only way to secure important information about the identification, information which may be useful to either prosecution or defence at a later stage of proceedings.[105]

Another facet of Code D which needs to be understood concerns the consequences of its breach. It has been seen that in *Forbes* the House of Lords interpreted Code D relatively strictly. It portrayed it as a mandatory set of rules which the police should not be able to evade, except in fairly well-defined circumstances. Nevertheless, it held that in *Forbes* the evidence obtained in breach of Code D was properly admitted in court. It endorsed the Court of Appeal's observation that:

'The evidence was compelling and untainted, and was supported by the evidence (which it was open to the jury to accept) of what the appellant had said at the scene. It did not suffer from such problems or weaknesses as sometimes attend evidence of this kind: as, for example, where the suspect is already visibly in the hands of the police at the moment he is identified to them by the complainant.'[106]

The House of Lords did hold, though, that in such cases the jury should be informed that Code D has been breached and asked to consider the significance of the breach. In some cases a breach of the Code will result in exclusion of identification evidence. The case law here is part of the wider case law on s 78 of PACE, under which evidence may be excluded if it would render the proceedings unfair. Section 78 is discussed in

---

[101] See Wells *et al*, above n 90; J. Turtle, R. Lindsay and G. Wells, 'Best Practice Recommendations for Eyewitness Evidence Procedures: New Ideas for the Oldest Way to Solve a Case' (2003) *Canadian J. Police & Security Services* 5 March.

[102] See *ibid*.   [103] See Wells and Olson, above n 77.   [104] Code D, 3.11.

[105] See G. Wells, E. Olson and S. Charman, 'Distorted Retrospective Eyewitness Reports as Functions of Feedback and Delay' (2003) 9 *J Experimental Psychology: Applied* 42.

[106] Above n 76, [32].

more detail in Chapter 11. As far as Code D is concerned, the cases suggest that evidence will be excluded if there has been a 'significant and substantial' breach of its provisions. Factors taken into consideration include whether the police have acted in bad faith, and whether the defendant has been disadvantaged by the breach.[107] The case law shows that the courts are prepared to sanction the worst breaches of Code D. Nevertheless, there is something odd in *Forbes* about the emphasis on the mandatory nature of the Code requirements juxtaposed with the decision that it was fair to admit evidence gained by breaching them. It may be that the looser requirements of the new Code D will go some way to aligning breach of the principal sections of the Code with unfairness to the defendant, and thus with inadmissibility. At the same time, as has been emphasized, it is important that the greater discretion in the new Code is not allowed to disadvantage defendants: the courts should be prepared to exclude identification evidence where its quality could have been meaningfully tested by a particular identification procedure, even where the failure to hold one is not strictly in breach of the Code. At present, there is some concern that the courts are reluctant to take this approach.[108]

There is another safeguard against mistaken identification when a case comes to court. *Turnbull* requires judges to warn juries about the dangers of mistaken identification.[109] Whenever a case depends 'wholly or substantially' on identification evidence, the judge should warn the jury of the special need for caution before convicting on such evidence. The warning should go into a reasonable amount of detail, informing jurors that even convincing witnesses, or more than one witness, can be mistaken, and drawing their attention to the details of the identification in issue. In cases where the quality of identification evidence is poor—for example, an identification based on a fleeting glance 'or on a longer observation made in difficult conditions'—the judge should go further. The case should be withdrawn from the jury unless there is evidence to support the identification. If there is supporting evidence, then the judge should identify it for the jury.

Turnbull is a welcome safeguard, though it is not without its problems—it itself contains some ambiguity about the concept of 'poor quality' identification evidence. Quality is good 'for example when the identification is made after a long period of observation, or in satisfactory conditions by a relative, a neighbour, a close friend, a workmate and the like.' The example of poor quality evidence that is given is 'a fleeting glance or . . . a longer observation made in difficult conditions.' There is quite a gap between these examples: should a short, but not fleeting, observation in good conditions be classified as good or poor quality? It is not surprising to find in the case law some inconsistency as to when the *Turnbull* requirements on supporting evidence apply.[110] *Turnbull* also says nothing as to how factors such as the confidence of an

---

[107] For reviews of the case law, see I. Dennis, *The Law of Evidence* (2nd ed., 2002), 230–3; M. Zander, *The Police and Criminal Evidence Act 1984* (4th ed., 2003), 338–40.

[108] See *R v Williams* [2003] EWCA Crim 3200, discussed in Roberts, above n 100, 117–18.

[109] [1977] QB 224.

[110] Cf *Oakwell* [1978] 1 All ER 1223; *Curry* [1983] Crim LR 737; *Bowden* [1993] Crim LR 379.

eyewitness in an identification, or delay between observation and identification procedure relate to the good/poor quality distinction. An example of the discretion all
this leaves to judges is *Williams*, where a two-second observation of a person in a
moving vehicle was held not to be poor quality because it was made by a police
officer.[111]

It has been questioned whether the courts should rely at all here on the good/poor
quality distinction. The Court of Appeal's judgement in *Turnbull* came in response to
the recommendations of the Devlin committee on eyewitness evidence. This committee had not distinguished between good and poor evidence, and had recommended
directing juries in all cases that 'it is not safe to convict upon eye-witness evidence
unless the circumstances of the identification are exceptional or the eye-witness evidence is supported by substantial evidence of another sort.'[112] There is something to
be said for this approach. All the evidence suggests that there are limits to the strength
of eyewitness evidence. If the suspect looks somewhat like the offender, or if there are
flaws in the identification procedure, then a number of eyewitnesses may all make the
same mistake. Even if the eyewitness does identify the actual culprit, that does not
make the evidence especially powerful: someone asked to guess whether a tossed coin
landed heads or tails may guess correctly, but that does not make the guess evidence of
the outcome. The basic fact is that some types of evidence are simply not powerful
enough to justify conviction unless there is supporting evidence. It was noted earlier
that there is value in asking witnesses for an expression of confidence in their identification at the time it is made, because post-identification information may inflate their
confidence in the identification. Courts are doubtless prone to make a similar mistake:
to think that because there is other evidence to support an identification, that makes
the identification of particularly high quality. This may well have been the case in
Williams,[113] where the fact that the defendant was arrested close to the scene of the
crime soon after it was committed supported the identification evidence. What it does
not do is make the identification evidence, taken by itself, anything other than a most
dubious basis for conviction. Of course, even the Devlin committee recognized that a
rule with too bright a line might be problematic: exceptional circumstances would
justify conviction on an eyewitness identification alone. The sorts of situations
described in *Turnbull* as constituting good quality evidence might be thought to
justify a conviction when standing alone. But in all other cases, the Devlin committee's
approach seems appropriate.

---

[111] *The Times*, 7 October 1994.
[112] *Report to the Secretary of State for the Home Department on the Departmental Committee on Evidence of
Identification in Criminal Cases* (1976), 8.4.
[113] Above n 111.

5.4 VOICE IDENTIFICATION

In some cases, a witness may not have seen the offender's face, but only heard his voice. What procedures exist to govern voice identification? Voice identification only seems to have been recognized as an issue in recent years.[114] Code D is silent on the subject, as it only applies to visual identification.[115] So far, the courts have not laid down very clear guidelines on voice identification. There is support for use of a suitably modified *Turnbull* direction in voice cases, but no insistence that requirements such as those in Code D be followed.[116]

There is little doubt that voice identification raises many of the same concerns as visual identification: mistakes can occur, and even confident witnesses can make them. In fact, the psychological research suggests that voice identification is even less reliable then visual identification.[117] This lends support to developing safeguards similar to those used with eyewitnesses. Any such adoption of Code D procedures needs to proceed cautiously, however. It may be that the difficulties of selecting appropriate foils are more pronounced than with eyewitnesses; if so, a requirement to hold voice parades may simply lead to parades where the suspect obviously stands out. Further, if voice identification, particularly after a delay, is very unreliable, holding a voice identification procedure may be akin to subjecting the suspect to a random procedure, where he has a one in nine chance of being identified as the suspect. What is really needed is reflection on the problem, and choice of appropriate strategies in the light of the psychological literature. Code D and *Turnbull* show what can be done—even if both have their drawbacks. It would be depressing if it took the voice equivalent of a miscarriage such as *Virag* to produce similar safeguards for voice identification.

5.5 DNA SAMPLES

In recent years, DNA profiles have become an increasingly important source of identification evidence. DNA is, potentially at least, a very powerful form of evidence. In contrast to witness identification evidence, then, its use does not particularly raise concerns about evidentiary reliability.[118] Instead, rather different issues are raised, concerning privacy and bodily integrity.

In order to fulfil the potential of DNA evidence, various changes have been made to the criminal process. The police have been given wider powers to obtain DNA samples

---

[114] See D. Ormerod, 'Sounds Familiar?—Voice Identification Evidence' [2001] Crim LR 595.

[115] The only exception is Annex B, para 18, which provides for the situation where an eyewitness wishes to hear the members of an identification parade speak.

[116] *Gummerson* [1999] Crim LR 680.   [117] See Ormerod, above n 114.

[118] This was not the case during the early years of its use. See National Research Council, *DNA Technology in Forensic Science* (1992).

from suspects. Changes have also been made to the way in which information from such samples can be stored. A national DNA database has been set up, containing information about the DNA from large numbers of people investigated by the police. The database now contains around 2.8 million profiles,[119] and it will continue to grow. What concerns are raised by these developments?

An initial point is that the existence of a massive DNA database is not as sinister as it might sound.[120] DNA does contain personal information about such things as our susceptibility to disease. It might therefore seem very disquieting that the State should record and keep such information. However, the sections of the human genome used in forensic identification are often referred to as 'junk' or 'non-coding' DNA. This means that they are not generally thought to contain significant information about an individual: a forensic scientist cannot, by looking at a DNA profile on the database, tell anything about the individual concerned. To the extent that forensic DNA is non-coding, then, its retention raises no more concerns than does the retention of finger-prints. A little caution is appropriate here, however. Forensic DNA profiles do reveal information about who is related to whom. Further, relatively little is known about the areas of DNA used in forensic analysis, and it is possible that some of them do now or might in the future reveal potentially sensitive information. Indeed, in 2001 it was reported that one forensic DNA marker is weakly linked to susceptibility to diabetes.[121] At the moment, this is probably not enough to raise real concerns about privacy. It does, however, highlight the need to keep a careful eye on the information contained in the database and on who has access to it. A further point is that as well as retaining DNA profiles, DNA samples—biological material from which DNA can be extracted—are also retained. The reason for this is that future changes in DNA technology may make the profiles currently stored on the database redundant.[122] By keeping samples, forensic scientists will be able to generate a new set of profiles, using different areas of the genome than the current ones. Again, this emphasizes the need for proper regulation of the database. Although the Government has made some reassuring noises,[123] expansion of the database, rather than its control, appears to be its priority.

---

[119] See www.forensic.gov.uk

[120] See D. Kaye, 'Bioethics, Bench and Bar: Selected Arguments in *Landry v Attorney General*' (2000) 40 *Jurimetrics J.* 193.

[121] 'Fingerprint Fear' NewScientist.com, 2 May 2001.

[122] Arguably, this is not a good reason for keeping samples. The database could be run on the basis of the portions of DNA currently used to build profiles. It is already standard practice to run a more powerful confirmatory test, and this could continue to be the case if new technology developed.

[123] See Human Genetics Commission, *Comments to Inform the Government Response to the House of Lords Report on Genetic Databases* (2001). The House of Lords Science and Technology Committee recommended that 'the Government should establish an independent body, including lay membership, to oversee the workings of the National DNA Database, to put beyond doubt that individuals' data are being properly used and protected.' *Human Genetic Databases: Challenges and Opportunities*, Fourth Report 2000–01, para 1.27.

The more serious concerns about the DNA database relate to the way in which the power to take DNA samples has been expanded over the years. The current position is that intimate samples, such as blood, can only be taken with consent (refusal to consent, however, can lead to adverse inferences at trial).[124] DNA, though, can be obtained from a non-intimate sample, such as plucked hair and mouth swabs. These can be taken without consent.[125] PACE therefore allows a non-consenting person to be subjected to a minor assault in order to obtain a plucked hair for DNA analysis. This is not all that different from the situation that has long existed with fingerprints where, in the event of non-consent, a minor assault would also be required to obtain a record.[126] What is perhaps most problematic about DNA samples, however, is the width of the category of suspects from which they can be taken and retained. A non-intimate sample can be taken from anyone charged with a recordable offence, as well as from anyone in police detention where it is thought that the sample may confirm or disprove involvement in a recordable offence for which he is being investigated.[127] The Criminal Justice Act 2003 extends this power further by removing the requirement that the sample be of potential evidentiary value in the investigation for which the suspect is detained.[128] Prior to 2001, samples, and the DNA profiles derived from them, had to be destroyed in the event that a suspect was not convicted of the offence for which the sample was taken. This requirement was removed under amendments brought in by the Criminal Justice and Police Act 2001.[129]

These powers, which allow DNA profiles to be retained against those who have been suspected, but not convicted, of an offence, have been challenged in the English courts. *Marper* involved two appellants.[130] The case against one had been discontinued, while the other had been acquitted at trial. Both were informed that the fingerprints and samples that had been obtained from them would not be destroyed. They challenged this decision, invoking Articles 8 (privacy) and 14 (discrimination) of the ECHR. The House of Lords held that any infringement of privacy was justified as being necessary in a democratic society for the prevention of crime. It could find no discrimination. The arguments here are worth looking at in a little detail. To keep things in perspective, it is worth treating DNA as more or less on a par with fingerprints; as explained above, in terms of privacy and bodily integrity, there is not that much difference between them.[131] An exception is that with DNA, samples of biological material are retained, and these could be used for a large number of purposes, some of them involving—as our understanding of the human genome grows—very serious infringements of privacy. While this is a disturbing possibility, the House of Lords' response is fairly convincing: any future use of DNA samples will have to be

---

[124] PACE, s 62. Under powers in the Road Traffic Act, discussed below, it is an offence not to provide a blood sample.

[125] PACE, s 63.   [126] PACE, s 61.   [127] PACE, s 63.

[128] CJA 2003, s 10, amending PACE, s 63.   [129] PACE, s 64.

[130] *R v Chief Constable of South Yorkshire ex p LS/Marper* [2004] UKHL 39.

[131] Cf the judgment of Baroness Hale in *Marper, ibid.*, which, while rather unclear, suggests that DNA profiles may raise greater privacy concerns.

Convention compliant, and the courts will deal with this in the future should misuse occur.[132] Nevertheless, what was said earlier about the need for proper regulation of access to the database and to samples bears repeating.

A good entry to the issues raised in *Marper* is to ask: suppose the Government decided to create a truly national DNA or fingerprint database—i.e. one containing fingerprints or profiles of every member of the population—what objections might there be? In terms of privacy concerns, such a database might not seem especially problematic. DNA profiles and fingerprints do not allow anyone examining them to tell very much about us. There may be more subtle impacts on privacy, however. When people hold information about us, there may be a 'chilling effect'. Even though nothing untoward may be being done with that information, we may fear that it is, or that it will be used against us in some way. A fear about fingerprints or DNA profiles is that they will be used to track us even if we are not suspected of criminal activity: if we are involved with a certain political group, for example. A more direct intrusion on privacy could come about through false alarms. When a fingerprint or source of DNA is found at the scene of a crime, it will be compared against all of the other prints or profiles on the database. Especially if the print is partial or the profile degraded, there is the possibility that it will result in innocent people on the database being investigated for the crime involved.[133] Where the database is not completely inclusive, the problems are greater, because there is the possibility that the culprit will not be represented on the database, and that the only match will be to an innocent person.[134]

As well as raising issues of privacy, an inclusive national database of fingerprints or DNA profiles would also need to be squared with concerns about bodily integrity: the prints and profiles have to be collected somehow, and the non-consenting would have to be assaulted in order to obtain them.[135] Just why should someone who is not suspected of any criminal activity be subjected to such procedures? To raise these concerns is not to say that inclusive national databases cannot be justified. Such databases would provide considerable benefits in bringing cases to effective trial. With privacy, the concerns are somewhat speculative and involve relatively low level infringements. This might be the sort of example, then, where a relatively crude consequentialist calculation is called for, in terms of whether the benefits outweigh the costs. The bodily integrity objections, however, are more serious, and would require a far stronger case to be made in terms of the potential benefits of inclusive databases. There is, though, one good reason for developing a national database, beyond its obvious utility in detecting crime. Current arrangements, whereby a national database is built up by taking samples from all those arrested, will lead to a situation where groups who are particular targets of police suspicion will be

---

[132] *Ibid.*, 28.

[133] See the concerns of Alec Jeffreys, discussed in 'DNA Fingerprinting "No Longer Foolproof" ' *The Guardian*, 9 September 2004.

[134] The issues are explored in more detail in M. Redmayne, 'Appeals to Reason' (2002) 65 *MLR* 19.

[135] A possible way of avoiding this would be to develop a national database by taking DNA samples from children at birth.

over-represented in the database.[136] We have seen, earlier in this chapter, that there is
concern that stop and search powers are used disproportionately against black people.
There is also evidence that blacks are arrested on lower levels of suspicion than
whites,[137] thus they will more readily find their way onto the database. There is
something to be said for the 'equality of suspicion' that would be assured by a truly
national database.

In *Marper*, inclusive national databases were not in issue. Prints and profiles were
not being taken from the public at large, but from suspected offenders for the purposes of criminal investigation. The need to investigate crime effectively probably
justifies giving the police powers to take prints and samples without consent; indeed,
the appellants in *Marper* challenged the retention and not the taking of the information, and this only once the cases against them had failed or been dropped. To put this
in perspective, the Court of Appeal quoted what had been said by the Home Secretary
in debate on the new power to retain prints and profiles of those not convicted:

'When the police investigate a case, if they do not proceed with a prosecution or the suspect
is acquitted, they routinely retain all the records of the investigation, including the notes of
interviews with suspects. . . . That has always been the case. The police would not dream of
throwing away their memory on the off chance that the offender [sic] may or may not
commit a further offence. Yet the law requires that the most objective and powerful forms of
evidence—fingerprints and DNA—have to be destroyed if a conviction does not follow from
the taking of the sample in question.'[138]

Even ignoring the elision of suspect and offender, this is perhaps not the best analogy.
It is the inclusion of fingerprints and DNA profiles on a powerful database that raises
concerns, not their retention, say, at the back of some police officer's desk drawer, or
the possibility that a police officer will memorize a person's DNA profile. A better
analogy would be with information that is more easily disseminated and communicated, such as photographs and video images taken for the purposes of identification
procedures. The current rules are that these should be destroyed unless the suspect is
charged, cautioned or prosecuted.[139]

Objections are rarely raised to the retention of fingerprints, DNA profiles, and
photographs of the *convicted*.[140] This is the nub of the arguments in *Marper*: does it
make a difference that the defendants have not been convicted? The appellants framed
this as a point about discrimination: in the eyes of the law, they had not been convicted, yet they were not being treated like other unconvicted people because they
were included on databases. The House of Lords thought there was nothing to this
point.[141] However, under the law at the time, prints and samples could only be taken

---

[136] D. Kaye and M. Smith, 'DNA Identification Databases: Legality, Legitimacy, and the Case for
Population-Wide Coverage' (2003) *Wisconsin L Rev*, 413.

[137] C. Phillips and D. Brown, *Entry into the Criminal Justice System: A Survey of Police Arrests and
their Outcomes* (1998), 48; HM Crown Prosecution Service Inspectorate, *Report on the Thematic Review of
Casework Having a Minority Ethnic Dimension* (2002).

[138] *R v CC South Yorkshire* [2002] 1 WLR 3223, 37.   [139] Code D, 3.30, 5.22.

[140] Cf Kaye and Smith, above n 136.   [141] Above n 130, 42–53.

without consent before charge if they might help in the investigation of the offence for which the suspect had been arrested (though once obtained, they could be used to link the defendant to other crimes, through a speculative search of the crime scene database). To keep them in order to investigate future crimes is to use them for a rather different purpose, and this surely requires some justification. The discrimination point therefore needs to be faced. In the Court of Appeal, Sedley LJ had argued that any discrimination was justified, because those suspected of crime by the police are different from the rest of the population. He did allow, however, that in cases where the police became convinced that a suspect was genuinely innocent—for example, where another person was convicted of the crime—the suspect's prints and profile should not be retained.

Given what is known about how police suspicion operates—in particular in regard to minority ethnic groups—this argument is none too attractive.[142] There is much to be said for the view that it is conviction which should mark the dividing line between the guilty and the innocent, and therefore between those whose details can be retained and those whose can not. Conviction is by no means a foolproof guide to guilt and innocence, but it is a publicly accessible one and is used for many other purposes, such as criminal records. With the amendments introduced by the Criminal Justice Act 2003 the arguments are now somewhat different, for samples can be taken from arrestees even if they are of no use in the investigation of the crime for which the suspect has been arrested. This means that if, for example, a suspect is arrested on suspicion of theft, admits the case against him apart from the element of dishonesty, and is not convicted, his fingerprints and DNA can be taken without consent for the sole purpose of indefinite retention on databases, even if the police concede that the case against him was mistaken. This is close to being on a par with taking prints and samples from non-consenting members of the population for an inclusive national database. As noted earlier, this is difficult to justify.

5.6 THE PRIVILEGE AGAINST SELF-INCRIMINATION

Our final example of a principled constraint on the ability of the State to gather and use evidence against suspects is the privilege against self-incrimination. This example is in many ways more complex than those considered so far. While the privilege is recognized in international human rights documents,[143] and has been implied into the European Convention on Human Rights by the court in Strasbourg, its scope and underlying justification are difficult to pin down. Historical studies suggest that our

---

[142] See above n 137.

[143] International Covenant on Civil and Political Rights, Art 14; Inter-American Convention on Human Rights, Art 8.

understanding of the privilege has shifted over time.[144] While acknowledging those points, we should begin by noting that certain aspects of the privilege do appear to have universal support. In English law, the most fundamental application of the privilege occurs at trial, in the form of the rule that the defendant is not a compellable witness at his own trial. The significance of that is that he can refuse to testify, and cannot be held in contempt of court for this refusal. Witnesses other than the accused benefit from certain immunities,[145] but, in general, they can be held in contempt if they do not attend court and testify when summonsed to do so. Different jurisdictions deal with the accused's position at trial in different ways, but, while the accused may not be able to escape being questioned, it would appear to be a general principle that he cannot be punished for refusing to answer questions.[146]

In 1993 the European Court of Human Rights appeared to recognize the privilege as being part of the fair trial guarantee in Article 6. The applicant in *Funke v France*[147] was suspected of tax evasion. The authorities demanded that he provide them with details of his bank accounts; when Funke did not do so the French court fined him 50 francs a day. The European Court of Human Rights found that: 'The special features of customs law . . . cannot justify such an infringement of the right of anyone "charged with a criminal offence" . . . to remain silent and not to contribute to incriminating himself.'[148] Some years later it expanded on these rather cryptic comments in *Saunders v United Kingdom*.[149] Saunders had been investigated under the Companies Act 1985 after he had been suspected of illegally boosting the price of shares in his company. Under the Act, inspectors had the power to require that Saunders produce documents and answer questions put to him. Refusal could be punished as contempt of court and any information gained through this process could be used against Saunders at trial. The European Court of Human Rights found the latter point significant: its 'sole concern', it explained, was 'with the use made of the relevant statements made at the applicant's criminal trial'.[150] The fact that his statements had been used against him at trial put those proceedings in breach of Article 6. This time the court said something more about the justification for the privilege against self-incrimination:

'[The] rationale lies, *inter alia*, in the protection of the accused against improper compulsion by the authorities thereby contributing to the avoidance of miscarriages of justice and to the fulfilment of the aims of Art 6. The right not to incriminate oneself, in particular, presupposes that the prosecution in a criminal case seek to prove their case against the accused without resort to evidence obtained through methods of coercion or oppression in defiance of the will of the accused. In this sense the right is closely linked to the presumption of

---

[144] See R. Helmholz *et al*, *The Privilege Against Self Incrimination: Its Origins and Development* (1997); M. MacNair, 'The Early Development of the Privilege Against Self-Incrimination' (1990) 10 *OJLS* 66.

[145] Most significantly, spousal immunity: see I. Dennis, *The Law of Evidence* (2nd ed., 2002), 446–50.

[146] For example, in China the accused need not give sworn evidence; in France, the defendant cannot avoid being questioned, but, again, need not take an oath and need not answer. See C. Bradley, *Criminal Procedure: A Worldwide Study* (1999), 88, 176.

[147] (1993) 16 EHRR 297.   [148] *Ibid.*, 44.   [149] (1997) 23 EHRR 313.   [150] *Ibid.*, 67.

innocence.... The right not to incriminate oneself is primarily concerned, however, with respecting the will of an accused person to remain silent. As commonly understood in the legal systems of the Contracting Parties to the Convention and elsewhere, it does not extend to the use in criminal proceedings of material which may be obtained from the accused through the use of compulsory powers but which has an existence independent of the will of the suspect such as, *inter alia*, documents acquired pursuant to a warrant, breath, blood and urine samples and bodily tissue for the purposes of DNA testing.'[151]

This passage has been repeated, with minor variations, in several other cases.[152] Although the court here suggests that the scope of the privilege is restricted—it does not apply to physical material gained under compulsory powers—it has resisted arguments that the privilege has restricted force in those areas where it does apply. Just as it was noted in *Funke* that the 'special features of customs law' did not justify abrogation of the privilege, so the arguments that special powers are needed to investigate complex financial wrongdoing (*Saunders*)[153] or even terrorism (*Heaney and McGuinness v Ireland*)[154] have been rejected. The latter case does note that the privilege may not be absolute, but just what this concession means is unclear. It seems that any abrogation of the privilege must not destroy its 'very essence';[155] for the moment the fact that 'social necessity' arguments were rejected in these cases is more significant than the acknowledgement that the right may not be absolute.

The effect of *Saunders* in English law is that a number of statutes giving similar 'inquisitorial' powers to investigators have been modified by the introduction of 'use immunity'.[156] Use immunity means that, although a suspect can be subjected to sanctions—such as a fine, or being held in contempt of court[157]—for refusing to answer questions or provide information, the information so obtained cannot then be used in court. (This position, whereby investigators can gain information but not use it to gain a conviction, has been described as 'the worst of all possible worlds' by one commentator.[158]) In other areas, however, English law has been less receptive to Convention jurisprudence on the privilege against self-incrimination. The Road Traffic Act 1988 provides that those who do not provide a breath or blood sample when asked to do so by a police officer who suspects them of drunk driving commit a criminal offence, and are subject to a fine.[159] The same Act also requires the owner of a vehicle to declare who was driving it at a particular time and place; refusal is again a criminal offence, and there is no use immunity.[160] This particular provision was challenged before the Scottish courts in *Brown v Stott*.[161] As the case involved a 'devolution issue' (a point under Scottish law concerning the Human Rights Act) the case came before the Privy Council, which found that the Road Traffic Act was not in

---

[151] *Ibid.*, 68–9.   [152] Eg *JB v Switzerland* [2001] Crim LR 748.
[153] Above n 149, 74. Cf the dissenting judgment of Judge Martens.
[154] (2001) 33 EHRR 12.   [155] *Ibid.*, 55.
[156] Youth Justice and Criminal Evidence Act 1999, s 59.
[157] *IJL and others v United Kingdom* (29522/95, 19 Sept 2000).
[158] S. Sedley, 'Wringing Out the Fault: Self-Incrimination in the 21st Century' (2001) 52 *NILQ* 107, 120.
[159] Sections 6, 7.   [160] Section 172(2)(a).   [161] [2003] 1 AC 681.

breach of Article 6. A number of reasons were given in support of this conclusion. We have already noted that among them was the unsatisfactory argument that the aim of road safety 'outbalanced' individual rights in this instance, an argument which finds no support in the Convention case law on self-incrimination.[162] Another argument was that all that was required under the Road Traffic Act was the answer to a 'single, simple question'.[163] It is unclear, however, why this should be significant, especially given the potential legal consequences of an answer to that question. A more significant point was that Convention jurisprudence on the privilege against self-incrimination was 'unsatisfactory and less than clear'.[164] According to Lord Hope, a close reading of *Saunders* reveals 'defects in the reasoning'.[165] The criticism, and it is a common one,[166] is that it is obscure why there should be a distinction, in terms of the privilege, between things such as blood samples and documents, and things such as speech; yet that is what the key passage in *Saunders* implies. For Lord Steyn, it would be odd to use the privilege to forbid requiring an answer to the question about the driver, while requiring a suspect to give a blood sample, the latter being more invasive than the former.[167] On this point, the Strasbourg court is often said to be caught in inconsistency. After all, *Funke* involved documents, as have later cases such as *JB v Switzerland*.[168] The case law involves some other fine distinctions, too. In *King v United Kingdom*,[169] the applicant had been asked by the tax authorities to provide details of his acquisition of certain properties and his business records relating to them; he complied when threatened with a fine, and the information was used to calculate his tax liability. His application to the European Court of Human Rights was found inadmissible; it was held that he did not face criminal prosecution, but only a request for information so that the authorities could establish his liability. It is not easy to see the distinction between this case and *JB*. A further complexity in this area is that the European Court of Justice has recognized a privilege against self-incrimination with a far narrower scope than the one developed in the case law noted above.[170]

Although there is considerable criticism of the case law of the European Court of Human Rights in this area, we think that in some respects it can be defended as coherent and principled. When it comes to the distinction between speech and other material which may be gained by compulsion, the clue is already there in the passage from *Saunders*, quoted above. The privilege, it is suggested, 'does not extend to the use in criminal proceedings of material which may be obtained from the accused through the use of compulsory powers but which has an existence independent of the will of the suspect such as, *inter alia*, documents acquired pursuant to a warrant, breath, blood and urine samples and bodily tissue for the purposes of DNA testing.' *JB* and *Funke* did

---

[162] See Chapter 2.   [163] Above n 161, 705.   [164] *Ibid.*, 711.   [165] *Ibid.*, 721.

[166] See, e.g., Dennis, above n 145, 141; T. Ward and P. Gardner, 'The Privilege Against Self Incrimination: In Search of Legal Certainty' (2003) *European Human Rights L Rev* 387.

[167] *Ibid.*, 711.   [168] Above n 152.   [169] (2004) STC 911.

[170] See *Orkem v Commission* [1989] ECR 3283 and, generally, C. Harding and J. Joshua, *Regulating Cartels in Europe* (2003), 166–9, 189, 194–6.

not involve documents acquired pursuant to a warrant; the problem in those cases was that the applicants were threatened with fines if they did not produce the documents themselves. There would be no objection, so far as the privilege against self-incrimination is concerned, had the authorities acquired the documents pursuant to a warrant. What, then, of breath, blood and urine samples and bodily tissue? Here, the situation is more complicated. Like documents, these things can—arguably[171]—be obtained without engaging the suspect's will, and it may be that the court has this point in mind. However, getting these things without cooperation is obviously difficult, and may involve significant intrusion on bodily integrity and even acts of violence. Nevertheless, if the authorities did so, the suspect's privilege against self-incrimination would not be infringed—though there would, of course, be all sorts of other objections to the procedures used. In practice, then, the law deals with the problem of obtaining such material by threatening suspects with prosecution if they do not cooperate. It seems proper to classify this as a breach of the privilege against self-incrimination.

At this stage, something needs to be said about the value of the privilege against self-incrimination. This is not easy. There are many attempts to justify the principle, but most are problematic in some way.[172] On our account, a fairly basic justification is possible, and what has been said above has in fact taken the first step towards providing it. It has been suggested that the privilege applies to any material which is gained, in the context of a criminal investigation, by placing on a person a requirement to cooperate. This implies that the basic principle is that a suspect should not be required to cooperate with the authorities who are prosecuting him. This reflects the common intuition that the privilege is connected to the proper relationship between State and citizen. The principle is valuable in that it limits State power in criminal prosecution, and allows the suspect to preserve some distance between himself and the State. This sort of principle is sometimes said to be connected to the presumption of innocence; indeed, the European Court of Human Rights makes that connection in the passage from *Saunders*. It is often said that a corollary of the presumption of innocence is that the State has to make its case without any help from the defendant. In fact, it is best to say that this 'no assistance' principle is an application of the privilege against self-incrimination which is not connected to the presumption of innocence, if that rule is understood to be about requiring that the prosecution prove its case beyond reasonable doubt. There is perhaps another way in which people talk about the presumption of innocence, and we will deal with that shortly.

In the previous chapter, we briefly discussed the right to silence. At that stage, we did not mention the privilege against self-incrimination at all. What is the connection between the right to silence and the privilege against self-incrimination? Terminology

---

[171] Breath and urine samples are perhaps difficult to obtain without engaging the will. Nevertheless, it seems possible, if unpleasant, to do so.

[172] See D. Dolinko, 'Is there a Rationale for the Privilege Against Self-Incrimination?' (1986) 33 *UCLA L Rev* 1063; M Green, 'The Paradox of Auxiliary Rights: The Privilege Against Self-Incrimination and the Right to Keep and Bear Arms' (2002) 52 *Duke LJ* 113; I. Dennis, 'Instrumental Protection, Human Right or Functional Necessity? Reassessing the Privilege Against Self-Incrimination' (1995) 54 *Cambridge LJ* 342.

is one problem here. To this point, we have described the privilege against self-incrimination as a principle under which the State should not require a suspect to cooperate with a prosecution which is being brought against him. For the purposes of the discussion here, we would distinguish the right to silence as being the rule that inferences should not be drawn from a suspect's failure to mention facts at police interview or failure to testify at trial. The European Court of Human Rights has held that this rule is not required as part of a fair trial; in other words, inferences can be drawn from silence, as under the Criminal Justice and Public Order Act 1994, without conflict with Article 6 (see Chapter 4). The court has, however, emphasized the need to draw such inferences with care, and to offer legal advice to those held in the police station in a regime where their failure to mention facts can be used against them at trial.[173] As a matter of theory, this approach is fruitful: there is a good argument that there is no strong relationship between the right to silence, as just defined, and the privilege against self-incrimination. Drawing inferences from silence does not place a suspect under a requirement to speak; indeed, the words of the new caution begin: 'you do not have to say anything'. The Criminal Justice and Public Order Act may put a certain amount of pressure on suspects to speak, but this is not the same as requiring them to. However, as the Strasbourg court notes, it is important that the regime of inferences from silence is handled carefully. To the extent that silence is suspicious, it is appropriate to draw inferences from silence. But if inferences are drawn too readily, or given too much weight, the scheme of drawing inferences from silence will change from being one where suspects face the natural consequences of their suspicious behaviour, to one where the only rational explanation for inferences is that they are being used to encourage suspects to speak by penalizing non-cooperation. Once the inferences from silence regime operates in this manner, it does appear to be in tension with the privilege against self-incrimination. We also saw in Chapter 4 that there is evidence that the current caution is difficult to understand. If it is interpreted by suspects as meaning that they are required to speak, then in practice there would again be a conflict with the privilege against self-incrimination.

In Chapter 4 we drew attention to Greenawalt's argument that, as a matter of basic morality, one should not be expected to respond to accusations unless they are backed up with evidence.[174] This means that it is wrong to draw inferences from silence where there is not a reasonable basis for suspecting the person involved of wrongdoing. This principle might be said to reflect the presumption of innocence, where the presumption is understood not, as evidence lawyers tend to understand it, as a rule about the standard of proof in criminal cases, but as a rule about how the State should treat citizens. The State should not treat its citizens as suspects unless it can provide reasons for doing so; it should treat people with civility.[175] This principle might be seen as connected to the privilege against self-incrimination, in that at a deeper level both

---

[173] *Murray v United Kingdom* (1996) 22 EHRR 29; *Condron v United Kingdom* (2001) 31 EHRR 1.

[174] K. Greenawalt, 'Silence as a Moral and Constitutional Right' (1981) 23 *William & Mary L Rev* 15.

[175] See D. Nance, 'Civility and the Burden of Proof' (1994) 17 *Harvard J Law & Public Policy* 647.

principles are about the relationship between citizen and State. But for many purposes it is useful to separate the principles. The privilege is more fundamental in that even when it is appropriate to draw an inference from silence—when there is sufficient evidence against the suspect to justify doing so—the privilege holds that it is still inappropriate to require cooperation. For example, at trial an inference may be drawn from the fact that the accused does not testify after the prosecution has made out a *prima facie* case, but it would still be wrong to hold the accused in contempt of court for not testifying. The principles, however, overlap to this extent: if there is a situation where breach of the privilege might be justified—for example, to allow the police to obtain blood samples by imposing a penalty for non-cooperation, a possibility we turn to shortly—cooperation should not be required unless the person involved is reasonably suspected of wrongdoing.

Thus far we have been clarifying what we mean by the privilege against self-incrimination, and suggesting why the principle should be regarded as important. The discussion obviously raises a number of difficult questions. On the account developed here, the provisions of the Road Traffic Act, imposing fines on those who do not give breath etc samples or who refuse to say who was driving their vehicle at a particular time, breach the privilege against self-incrimination. Might it be argued that road traffic offences are a special case, where breach of the privilege against self-incrimination is acceptable? It does at least seem that in practice, road traffic offences are treated differently in English law. The police have no general power under PACE to require suspects to provide body samples. They are able to obtain non-intimate samples—including mouth swabs and hair—by force, which, as explained above, does not infringe the privilege. Blood (intimate) samples cannot legally be taken by force, nor can suspects be required to provide them. An inference can, however, be drawn against a suspect who refuses to provide a blood sample,[176] and here too there is no breach of the privilege so long as the inference is drawn on a rational basis. If road traffic offences are treated differently, is there any good reason for this? Here, it is important to avoid the argument, used in *Brown v Stott*, that road safety outbalances individual rights. That sort of argument would justify exceptions to the privilege in almost any domain: anyone suspected of serious crime might be required to give blood samples, or to state where they were at a particular time. A better way of justifying an exception in this area would be to argue that those who own or drive vehicles accept an obligation to account for their use, or for the state (degree of sobriety) in which they use them, so long as they, or their vehicle, is reasonably suspected of involvement in wrongdoing. Vehicle ownership is a heavily regulated activity, involving licences, MOTs and the like, and the obligations imposed by the Road Traffic Act might be seen as part of this regulatory structure. A similar argument might be used in respect of *Saunders*, where it could be said that those who run companies accept an obligation to cooperate with investigations into wrongdoing. Obviously, this sort of argument is potentially unruly: it might be used to justify all

---

[176] PACE, s 62.

sorts of exceptions to the privilege against self-incrimination. It will need careful assessment in any case in which it is used and a threshold of reasonable suspicion should always be met before there is any obligation to answer questions.

Another question about the privilege against self-incrimination is whether it is compatible with the regime of defence disclosure introduced by the Criminal Procedure and Investigations Act 1996. Do the disclosure obligations in that Act amount to requiring the defence to cooperate? We say more about that issue in Chapter 9. For now it is worth using the example to highlight the ambiguity in the word 'require' which we have so far been using to define the ambit of the privilege against self-incrimination. The disclosure regime is enforced by adverse inferences, and it could be argued that, as with inferences from silence, these do not 'require' the defence to cooperate. But just when do the negative consequences of not doing X mean that there is a requirement to do X? The European Court of Human Rights uses a different, but no less murky, concept, that of 'coercion', to limit the application of the privilege. The court has had difficulty in defining coercion in this context. In *Allen* and *King*,[177] for example, one of the reasons for finding no breach of the privilege against self-incrimination was that there was no coercion, because the applicants only faced limited fines (up to £300) if they refused to cooperate. These cases can be contrasted with *JB*, where a fine of around £700 was held to engage the privilege. We suggest that there is one clear set of cases where the privilege is breached: where non-cooperation is made a criminal offence, as it is under the Road Traffic Act. In this situation the suspect is placed under a duty to cooperate, and that is unacceptable unless strong reasons can be found for making an exception to the general principle. 'Punishment' for contempt of court, as in *Saunders*, is probably sufficiently similar that this too can be seen as a clear case of infringement. Beyond this, it is difficult to know where to draw the line. With inferences from silence, for example, it was suggested above that if inferences are drawn as a means of penalizing non-cooperation, rather than because silence is suspicious, then this could be seen as a requirement to cooperate and thus a breach of the privilege.

Another difficult question is whether use immunity should play such a central role in delimiting the privilege. In *Heaney*, the applicant challenged a law requiring him to give an account of his movements during the preceding 24 hours; his failure to do so was a criminal offence. Under Irish law, it was not clear whether his answers could be used against him at trial for the terrorist offence he was suspected of involvement in. The European Court of Human Rights held that the possibility of use at trial was sufficient to engage the privilege. It is worth reflecting on whether a guarantee of use immunity should play such a large role in the reasoning here: might it be objectionable to require that someone give an account of their movements, or a breath or blood sample, even if the information so revealed is not used against them at trial? It might perhaps be thought enough if the information would help the prosecution, for example by leading to other evidence that could be used at trial. One might also take

---

[177] *King v United Kingdom*, above n 169; *Allen v United Kingdom* (2002) 35 EHRR CD 289.

the view that the requirement is objectionable in itself, even if there was a guarantee that no prosecution would follow.

Finally, there may be situations where the privilege against self-incrimination does not apply, but where values similar to those that motivate the privilege suggest that there is a strong objection to the imposition of a duty to cooperate. Consider s 38B of the Terrorism Act 2000. Under this provision it is a criminal offence, punishable by up to five years' imprisonment, to fail to inform the authorities that another person is engaged in terrorist activity, when that other person is known or reasonably suspected to be engaged in such activity. That other person might, of course, be a spouse or sibling.[178] If we regard it as important to maintain some distance between us and the State, so that the State's ends cannot be made to become our ends, then this extra-ordinarily wide-ranging provision is as objectionable as any of those discussed above. The common law once rightly held that the citizen had no legal duty to cooperate with the police.[179] It is depressing to see this basic principle overturned in the name of the war on terror.[180]

[178] See 'Bomb Suspect's Relatives Remanded in Custody' *The Guardian*, 9 May 2003.
[179] *Rice v Connolly* [1966] QB 414.
[180] See also Serious Organised Crime and Police Bill cl 56–61.

6

GATEKEEPING
AND DIVERSION

The concern of this chapter is with those decisions that determine whether or not a case enters the criminal justice system and, if so, what course it is set upon. These decisions were described in the first chapter as dispositive, which indicates that decisions to divert a case from prosecution (by preferring one of the alternatives discussed in this chapter) are likely to dispose of the case and be the final way of dealing with the offender for this offence. Some of these offenders may breach the conditions of their diversion and be brought back into the criminal process, but in the vast majority of cases the diversion has a practical finality. This makes it particularly appropriate to explore the reasons why some cases are diverted and others are not.

Out of all the criminal offences committed in any one year, only a very low proportion result in formal proceedings being taken against a suspect/defendant. The process of attrition, as it has come to be known, is gradual and substantial. Figures derived from the British Crime Survey, dealing with eight of the most frequently committed types of indictable offences, suggest that no more than two per cent result in a conviction.[1] Starting with those offences actually committed, around half of them are never reported to the police. Members of the public may choose not to report an offence because they think the police unable to help, because they regard the offence as too minor to report, because the offence is regarded as a private or domestic matter, because of fear of reprisals, or for other reasons. Of the 43 per cent that are reported to the police, a significant proportion are not recorded as crimes. A variety of reasons may come into play here: the offence may be attributed to a child below the age of criminal responsibility, or the police may not accept the victim's account, or the incident may have been resolved quickly and informally. This reduces the number of offences remaining in the system to 28 per cent. The next difficulty is that only a proportion of recorded offences are 'cleared up', in the sense of being detected or otherwise resolved. In relation to the eight types of crime studied in the British Crime Survey, about one-fifth are cleared up and this reduces the percentage remaining in the system from 28 to 5.5 per cent. Some of the offences that are cleared up result in

---

[1] G.C. Barclay (ed), *Digest 4: information on the Criminal Justice System in England and Wales* (1999), 29. The offences are criminal damage, theft of a motor vehicle; theft from a motor vehicle; bicycle theft; burglary, wounding, robbery, and theft from the person.

nothing more than an informal warning or no further action at all, particularly when they are traced to young offenders. Thus only three per cent of the offences result in a formal caution or in prosecution. Almost one-third of those are cautions, which (in the form of reprimands and warnings) are widely used for younger offenders, leaving some 2.2 per cent to be sentenced by the courts.

This startling rate of attrition does not apply equally to all crimes. Among those studied in the British Crime Survey, offences of wounding resulted in a much higher rate of court appearance. A higher proportion of recorded offences were cleared up and were then dealt with formally, so that some 10 per cent of offenders were sentenced by the courts. Turning to rape, the attrition rate is much higher because, although the majority of cases were detected because the perpetrator was known to the victim, large numbers were not pursued because the complaint was withdrawn or was regarded as unfounded. A prosecution was commenced in only 29 per cent of recorded cases in Harris and Grace's sample, with convictions in 18 per cent of recorded cases.[2] Lea, Lanvers and Shaw found that 11 per cent of the rapes in their sample resulted in a conviction,[3] but these were reported rapes whereas Harris and Grace's sample was of recorded rapes, and so the findings are not necessaily divergent.

What are the implications of the rate of attrition? One is that it demonstrates the naïveté of expecting the sentences passed by the courts to act as a significant control on crime. Those sentences deal with a small proportion of offenders—although, for the most part, they will be the most serious offenders—and, even making allowances for the probability that the symbolic effect of those (few) sentences will be greater than their proportionate size, this suggests that a strategy for the prevention of crime should not place great emphasis on sentencing. This is not to deny that sometimes sentences may exert a specific and/or general deterrent effect, but it is to counsel caution against overestimating those effects in the context of low rates of reporting, detection, and so on. A second implication is that decisions taken by law enforcement agents have a considerable influence on the selection of cases that go forward into the criminal process. Their decisions have a qualitative as well as a quantitative effect: the offenders who find themselves convicted in court are not a random group of the totality of offenders, nor necessarily are they the most serious group.[4] They are chosen, when others are not, for a variety of reasons that will be explored below.

The focus of this chapter will be upon the decisions taken by the gatekeepers of the criminal process. The discussion of different types of gatekeeper will be less detailed than the extensive literature would permit, in order to facilitate the analysis of general

---

[2] J. Harris and S. Grace, *A Question of Evidence? Investigating and Prosecuting Rape in the 1990s* (1999), 17. Only half of the convictions were for rape, the remainder being for lesser offences.

[3] S. Lea, U. Lanvers and S. Shaw, 'Attrition in Rape Cases', (2003) 43 *BJCrim* 583, at 592; again, although 11 per cent resulted in conviction, only five per cent resulted in conviction for rape.

[4] Although it is probably true to say that many cases are not reported because they are thought too minor, one study of the victims of violence found that the probability of an offender being brought to court and convicted was not related to the objective seriousness of the assault: C. Clarkson *et al*, 'Assaults: the Relationship between Seriousness, Criminalisation and Punishment' [1994] Crim LR 4.

issues. The role of the police will be outlined first, followed by a comparison with the approach of regulatory bodies as agencies that select for official action certain types of person or situation, a selection that may lead either to prosecution and trial or to a form of diversion. The second section considers the range of formal responses to those who are believed to be offenders. The third section focuses on police cautioning and related practices, and the fourth on the role of the CPS. The fifth section examines accountability, and the sixth analyzes the values behind some of the differing policies.

6.1 REPORTING AND ENFORCING

There is a real sense in which society is self-policing. The vast majority of offences are brought to the attention of the police by members of the public, and so the police operate in a reactive role. The decision to report probably means that the victim or witness expects something to be done about the offence. However, as we saw earlier, about one-half of the eight common types of offence studied in the British Crime Survey are not reported, and prominent among the reasons are a belief that the crime was insufficiently serious to report, and a belief that the police would not be able to do anything about it. The latter reason may betray a pessimism about police effectiveness rather than a genuine judgment that no formal response is necessary. In practice, however, many of these cases will also involve the first reason—that the formal invocation of law enforcement machinery is not really necessary. To that extent, then, members of the public may be said to filter out of the system, at the earliest stage, many non-serious offences. This might be regarded as a primitive example of proportionality at work: the idea that, in order to justify reporting an offence to the police or other relevant authority, it has to achieve a certain level of seriousness.

   However, the notion of society as self-policing cannot be pressed too far. The police are not simply the agents of the public, reacting whenever requested and not otherwise. There are at least three respects in which the police or other agencies exert a powerful influence. First, we have seen that the police do not record as crimes all incidents that are reported to them as crimes. As many as two-fifths of all incidents reported as thefts, robberies, woundings, etc. are not recorded by the police as such.[5] Some of these incidents may be dealt with by invoking minor public order charges, such as breach of the peace, which are not recorded crimes. But many of them will not be recorded or will be 'no-crimed'. The result is that, although the police are largely dependent on the public to report offences, they do not always record what is

---

[5] The counting rules changed in 2002, as a result of the introduction of the National Crime Recording Standard, but the evidence shows that since 1995 there has been a steady increase in the proportion of reported crimes that are recorded as crimes by the police: J. Simmons and T. Dodd, *Crime in England and Wales 2002–2003*, 32.

reported. The police operate as a significant filter on public reports, and even though members of the public may want official action (and, implicitly, official recording of the offence), this may not be what occurs.

Secondly, the idea of society as self-policing does not account for the many offences, perhaps one-quarter of indictable crimes, that are discovered by the police themselves. Here the argument becomes complicated. Sometimes, when the police have a 'crack-down' on certain forms of offences, such as sexual soliciting or drug-dealing in a particular locality, this is a response to complaints from the public. Such cases may be regarded, partly at least, as examples of social self-policing. On the other hand there may be many cases in which the police themselves decide to have a 'campaign' against a particular form of offending: drug-dealing in clubs would be more likely to fall into this category, as would drink-driving. The police are operating proactively here, to some extent because the crimes are victimless and therefore there is no victim to make a complaint. In this context the patterns of law enforcement may largely reflect the availability of police officers and the preferences of those in oper-ational control: the police can only mount 'proactive' campaigns if they are not overwhelmed by the 'reactive' demands of crimes reported to them, and when they do adopt a proactive strategy there may be a choice of what type of offence to target. Long-term strategies may be evidenced by the establishment of a specialist squad to target a particular kind of offending (e.g. a drug squad, or fraud squad). Shorter term targets may sometimes reflect the concerns of the media and of influential members of the public, as well as the views of police officers.

A third difficulty with the idea of society as self-policing is that this overlooks, or at least over-simplifies, the nature of the police function. Thus far we have referred to police work as if its focus is enforcing the law by catching criminals, whether as a result of prompting by a member of the public or as a result of a police campaign. Research shows that these kinds of activity do not dominate everyday policing. Much of what the police do is to perform a kind of service function, attending to a wide range of incidents that require something to be done about them—from road acci-dents and rowdy parties to stray cattle and barking dogs. Into all these situations the police officer brings authority and the ability to draw upon coercive powers if needed. These powers become even more prominent when there is thought to be a risk of public disorder—for example, at a demonstration or march or football match. These are the occasions on which the function of the police as maintainers of order comes to the fore. Whether the police use their coercive powers depends on a number of contingencies. If there is a genuine threat to good order they may intervene to make one or more arrests. Studies of police behaviour have long maintained that a police officer is more likely to arrest and charge someone who threatens the officer's author-ity by means of insults or failure to comply with the officer's commands or requests.[6] This forms part of the working culture of the police, discussed in Chapter 3. Significant

---

[6] The classic study is by E. Bittner, 'The Police on Skid Row: a Study in Peacekeeping', (1967) 32 *Amer. Soc. Rev.* 699.

as that proposition is in explaining why certain types of person come to be arrested and charged, it should not be allowed to overshadow the probability that some people clearly threaten to cause public disorder and should therefore be prevented from going further.[7] In other words, the use of arrest and criminal charges by the police in incidents thought to threaten good order is likely to be an amalgam of some clearly justifiable cases and others that turn more on the disposition, pride, or self-image of particular officers. Any description that ignores one or the other lacks realism. Both types of case show the criminal law as a resource for the police, however. The notion that Parliament makes the laws and the police 'merely' enforce them finds no echo here. The police manage situations so as to maintain order, using the offences in the Police Act 1996 and the Public Order Act 1986 as resources to draw upon, to be invoked against those who threaten the police conception of what constitutes good order and how it should be achieved.

This general survey suggests that society or the community is self-policing only to an extent. Most decisions not to report an offence to the police mean that the offence never comes to light and there is no prospect of the offender being charged and prosecuted to conviction. To that considerable extent, society does police itself. However, the police may have their own priorities, some of which may be shaped by public expectations and concerns. Thus it is evident that the criminal law in action does not correspond with the criminal law on the statute books. The body of criminal legislation cannot be placed over social behaviour like a template, in the expectation that there will be a 'fit' with the actuality of law enforcement. Further, there is evidently a considerable element of discretion in decisions to invoke the criminal law, and this makes it important to scrutinize the reasons why the police and the regulatory agencies decide to proceed against some people and not against others.

Perhaps as many as one-quarter of all prosecutions are brought by agencies other than the CPS. For example, the Health and Safety Executive brings prosecutions for offences concerning safety at work and in transport systems; H.M. Customs and Excise bring prosecutions for offences relating to the evasion or attempted evasion of customs duties and Value Added Tax; the Environment Agency brings prosecutions for offences of pollution; the Department of Trade and Industry brings prosecutions for financial offences; local consumer protection officers bring prosecutions for trading offences committed by shops and businesses; and so on. One major difference between these agencies and the CPS is that all these agencies have both an investigatory function and the power to prosecute. Each of them therefore has control over all the relevant decisions. Another major difference between these agencies and the CPS is that there is no accountability structure for the various agencies. Each of them follows its own policies and practices, with no attempt at an overall strategy among different agencies, and few attempts to harmonize their policies with those of the police and the CPS.

Cranston's research into consumer protection departments found that prosecution

---

[7] See R. Reiner, *The Politics of the Police* (3rd ed., 2000), Ch.4.

is usually regarded as a last resort, after informal settlements and warnings.[8] A similar finding emerged from the study of the Pollution Inspectorate by Richardson, Ogus, and Burrows,[9] from the research by Hawkins into environmental health officers,[10] and from the research by Hutter into the approaches of the Factory Inspectorate, the Industrial Air Pollution Inspectorate, and environmental health officers.[11] The Inland Revenue has long pursued its aim, of the maximization of public revenue, by means of settlements and penalties outside the criminal process, with relatively rare resort to the courts.[12]

The Environment Agency may be examined by way of illustration. The functions of the Agency include the regulation of pollution, waste disposal, wildlife conservation, fisheries, and water resources. The Agency publishes its 'Enforcement and Prosecution Policy' and also a more detailed document on the functions of the Agency with respect to particular types of offence.[13] The reader is immediately struck by the difference in emphasis from the CPS:

'The Agency regards prevention as better than cure . . . The purpose of enforcement is to ensure that preventative or remedial action is taken to protect the environment or to secure compliance with a regulatory system.'[14]

Combined with this difference in outlook is a difference in powers. Unlike the CPS, the Environment Agency has full investigative powers, and also many powers short of prosecution—such as the power to issue enforcement notices and/or prohibition notices, and the power to suspend or revoke environmental licences. 'Where a criminal offence has been committed, in addition to any other enforcement action, the Agency will consider instituting a prosecution, administering a caution or issuing a warning.'[15] The guidance then goes on to list various 'public interest factors' which the Agency regards as relevant to the decision to prosecute.[16] This has now been expanded in a statement of 'Guidance for Enforcement and Prosecution Policy.'[17] This includes detailed guidance on enforcement action in respect of particular activities (e.g. water quality, waste management, flood defence, radioactive substances). It spells out a 'Compliance Classification Scheme', with four levels of non-compliance for which, taking account of the actual and potential environmental impact, there would normally be different levels of enforcement action. Breaches in categories 3

---

[8] R. Cranston, *Regulating Business* (1979), 107 and 168.

[9] G. Richardson, A. Ogus and P. Burrows, *Policing Pollution* (1982).

[10] K. Hawkins, *Environment and Enforcement* (1984).

[11] B. Hutter, *The Reasonable Arm of the Law* (1988).

[12] J. Roording, 'The Punishment of Tax Fraud', [1996] Crim LR 240.

[13] Access to these is simple through the Agency's website at www.environment-agency.gov.uk, with the detailed document at www.environment-agency.gov.uk/epns/pdf/functions.pdf

[14] Environment Agency (1998), paras 4 and 6.   [15] *Ibid.*, para 8.

[16] *Ibid.*, para 22. These factors are similar to those stated in the Code for Crown Prosecutors. Paragraph 20 of the document states that 'the Agency recognises that the institution of a prosecution is a serious matter that should only be taken after full consideration of the implications and consequences. Decisions about prosecution will take account of the Code for Crown Prosecutors.'

[17] www.environment-agency.gov.uk, Version 6, 01.04.04.

and 4 would normally attract no more than a formal warning, for example. Where prosecution is being considered, usually in a category 1 case and sometimes in a category 2 case, a range of relevant factors is set out for consideration (e.g. impact, intent, previous history, offender's attitude).

Similar policies and practices are to be found in the work of the Health and Safety Commission. One part of its mission statement sets the tone: 'to secure compliance with the law in line with the principles of proportionality, consistency, transparency and targeting on a risk-related basis.' The difference of emphasis from the police and CPS is soon apparent:

In most cases, information, guidance and advice are sufficient to ensure that health and safety requirements are complied with. Where formal action is appropriate, the issue of an improvement or a prohibition notice normally provides a quick and effective means of securing the necessary improvements. The HSC expects, through its Enforcement Policy Statement, that enforcing authorities will consider prosecution when, for example, there is judged to have been the potential for serious harm resulting from a breach, or when the gravity of a breach taken together with the general record and approach of the offender warrants it.[18]

It is clear on the face of this statement that the whole orientation of Health and Safety enforcement is different from police enforcement of the criminal law. In criminal justice terminology, the regulatory agencies are pervaded by a culture of diversion. Prosecution is regarded very much as a last resort: the priority is to ensure compliance with the appropriate standards of safety. This instrumental view of the Commission's enforcement powers means that prosecutions are relatively rare, and this in turn gives rise to criticisms of unevenness and consequent unfairness in the use of the criminal law. Some argue that the infrequency of prosecutions and the predominance of warnings and other remedial measures indicates that regulatory agencies have been 'captured' by big business, or that the structure of regulation is an attempt to persuade the public that enforcement is being taken seriously when it is not. The written policies of the various agencies do show that the approach to prosecution differs markedly from that of the police. But empirical research into the working practices of regulatory agencies also goes some way to explaining why the difference in approach has evolved and is sustained. The leading study by Keith Hawkins argues that Health and Safety inspectors are motivated, in their enforcement decisions, by considerations of morality (bad cases justify prosecution) and by considerations of commensurability (non-serious deviations from the required standards call for lesser responses than prosecution),[19] as well as being affected by staffing levels, workloads and inspectors' perceptions of public reactions. Hawkins also confirms that individual inspectors differ in their approaches, some being more willing to bring a prosecution than others.

---

[18] Health and Safety Commission (1999), para 1.107.
[19] K. Hawkins, *Law as Last Resort* (2003), 243 and 220–226.

The policies and practices of the regulatory agencies are, then, characterized by a preference for diversion. They tend to see their power to prosecute as something to be employed sparingly and instrumentally—as one method of achieving compliance. In some cases they may prosecute because an incident has gained wide publicity and because the public might expect a prosecution,[20] rather than because it meets their normal criteria; and Robert Baldwin has argued that there has been a significant shift towards readier resort to punitive sanctions in recent years, especially in financial and business regulation.[21] However, this punitive drift does not destroy the contrast between the police and the regulatory agencies: the latter are still predominantly orientated towards ensuring compliance through negotiation, with their inspectors dealing on a long-term basis with businesspeople, and regarding the background threat of prosecution as more effective than its frequent use. Moreover, their staffing resources would not permit them to prosecute suspected offenders to the extent that the police resort to prosecution: bringing a prosecution is a significant drain on an inspector's time.[22]

The Environment Agency and the Health and Safety Commission have been chosen as examples of the many agencies which pursue a preventive or 'compliance' approach to enforcement, as distinct from a 'deterrence' or 'sanctioning' strategy which places greater emphasis on prosecution.[23] Compared with the approach of the police and CPS, their much greater emphasis on diversion rather than prosecution raises acute questions of social justice. Companies, wealthy offenders, and middle-class offenders are more often dealt with by regulatory agencies, whereas the more disadvantaged members of society are more likely to find their conduct defined as a police matter. The different approaches are then likely to result in more frequent prosecution of disadvantaged people than advantaged people for offences that may be no different in terms of seriousness. This might be defended on the principles of parsimony, of minimum intervention, and of assigning greater priority to the goal of securing maximum compliance than to equality of treatment—on the assumption that the clients of regulatory agencies are more likely to adjust their conduct to conform to the law if diverted than the clients of the police would be. This assumption would seem difficult to prove,[24] but its grip has the effect of allowing middle-class or white-collar offenders to benefit from diversion and other alternatives to prosecution, while lower-class or blue-collar offenders are processed in the 'normal' way.

How should this inequality be tackled? To assimilate the treatment of the clients of regulatory agencies to that of the clients of the police would increase overall suffering, and some argue that it is wrong to insist on equality if it results in equality

---

[20] G. Slapper and S. Tombs, *Corporate Crime* (2000).

[21] R. Baldwin, 'The New Punitive Regulation', (2004) 67 *MLR* 351; the main concern of the article is to show how and why the change of policy is not having the desired effect on corporate behaviour.

[22] Hawkins, above n 19, 46, 300, 421–422.

[23] For further discussion, see the works at nn 10–11 above.

[24] It has been vigorously contested: Slapper and Tombs, above n 20, Ch. 8.

of misery.[25] However, there are surely other ways of tackling this inequality of treatment. Initiatives to decriminalize minor offences or to introduce fixed penalty schemes could be increased. More fundamentally, fresh thought needs to be given to the approach of the police and prosecution service to the cases that come to their attention. It is not enough to develop restorative justice responses, because there are prior questions about the effectiveness of warnings (police cautions appear to be relatively effective), about the need for such strong sanctions for non-compliance with conditional and/or preventive orders (the regulatory agencies have a more open approach to repeated non-compliance), and about the treatment of clients with whom the police interact regularly (as do regulatory inspectors in their work). There are strong objections to any system that allows different investigative and prosecution agencies to pursue such divergent policies in respect of offences of similar levels of seriousness, without any attempt to address the inherent issues of social injustice. But those issues are complex and tangled, as is evident if one brings into consideration (a) the policy of the Inland Revenue, which deals with people from a wide range of backgrounds (but perhaps mostly the middle classes), in pursuing settlements for fairly large amounts of underpaid tax and prosecuting in fewer than 100 cases each year,[26] when those who come to police attention for stealing lesser sums are routinely prosecuted; and (b) the co-option of the police into an approach to youth crime that has tended to rely on warnings rather than prosecutions.

6.2 THE RANGE OF FORMAL RESPONSES

The criminal law provides the framework for formal responses to alleged lawbreaking, and yet we have already seen that it sometimes functions merely as a resource to be invoked in situations where this is thought necessary so as to maintain order or to enforce compliance. Discretion appears to be a key element in what actually happens—whether a case is diverted or sent for prosecution; and, if it is diverted, what form of diversion is chosen. The main focus in the following paragraphs is on the police and their approach to suspected offenders, but there will be intermittent reference to the approach of the regulatory agencies.

As will be described more fully in Chapter 7 below, the role of the police is in transition. For many years they have taken most decisions whether or not to charge a suspect, and often they have decided on the charge too. The advent of the CPS in 1986 brought in prosecutorial review of their decisions to prosecute, and in recent years there has been a concerted move towards joint working ('collocation') between police officers and prosecutors to determine the appropriate charges to bring, now reinforced

---

[25] The argument of N. Morris and M. Tonry, *Between Prison and Probation* (1990) in respect of equality of treatment in sentencing, criticized by A. Ashworth, *Sentencing and Criminal Justice* (3rd ed., 2000), Chapter 7.

[26] Roording, above, n 12.

by the provisions in the Criminal Justice Act 2003 removing the power to charge from the police and giving it to the CPS for all but minor cases. Much more will be said about these changes in the next chapter, but for the present it is important to notice the new sharing of power between the police and the CPS.

What considerations, in principle, should determine whether a case should be diverted or sent for prosecution? In many European systems of law there is a doctrinal contrast between the principle of compulsory prosecution (sometimes called the principle of legality) and the principle of expediency (sometimes called the opportunity principle). Many systems, such as the German and the Austrian, have placed great emphasis on the principle of compulsory prosecution. This may be said to promote the principles of legality and equal treatment, to prevent political interference with the process of justice, and also to heighten general deterrence.[27] In theory all those who commit offences are brought before the courts for an open determination of guilt and (if convicted) for sentencing, and there is no broad discretionary power to avoid prosecution—on the grounds that this might lead to local variations, allegations of political motivation, or the undermining of law by expediency. If the administration of the criminal law produces unjust results, it is for the legislature to amend it and not for prosecutors to make their own policies. Thus s 152 of the German Code of Criminal Procedure requires the public prosecutor to bring a prosecution in respect of all punishable conduct, to the extent that there is sufficient evidence. In practice, of course, there are various exceptions to this, including s 153a, which allows conditional termination of proceedings.[28] There are financial pressures towards the streamlining of criminal justice systems, as well as an increasing realization that prosecution and sentence in court are stressful for all participants and are not necessarily more effective (in terms of reconviction rates) than forms of diversion. Another well-established system of prosecutorial waiver is that whereby Dutch prosecutors may ask defendants to pay a *transactie* in return for a promise of non-prosecution.[29] Prosecutor fines have also been introduced in Scotland.[30] The Council of Europe has developed this theme in its recommendations for the simplification of criminal justice.[31]

The number of exceptions to the principle of compulsory prosecution might be thought to support an argument that systems such as the German are really little different from the English. The one proclaims a principle of compulsory prosecution and then derogates from it in several ways, whereas the other recognizes from the outset that prosecution policy must be a question of expediency.[32] However, there is good reason to retain some respect for the principle of compulsory prosecution

---

[27] See, e.g. J. Herrmann, 'The Rule of Compulsory Prosecution and the Scope of Prosecutorial Discretion in Germany', (1974) 41 *U. Chi. LR* 468; P.J.P. Tak, *The Legal Scope of Non-Prosecution in Europe* (1986).

[28] Herrmann, above, n 27; J. Herrmann, 'Bargaining Justice: a Bargain for German Criminal Justice?', (1992) 53 *U Pittsburgh LR* 755.

[29] C. Brants and S. Field, 'Discretion and Accountability in Prosecution', in C. Harding *et al*, *Criminal Justice in Europe* (1995), esp. 134–136.

[30] P. Duff, 'The Prosecution System', in P. Duff and N. Hutton (eds), *Criminal Justice in Scotland* (1999).

[31] Council of Europe, *The Simplification of Criminal Justice*, Recommendation R(87)18 (1987).

[32] Cf. H. Jung, 'Criminal Justice: a European Perspective', [1993] Crim LR 237, at 241.

because of the values (the principles of legality and equal treatment) it upholds, even though in Germany the prosecutor enjoys wide discretion in practice. In the heavily pragmatic English system, fundamental values and principles have little explicit recognition, even as starting-points. Instead, the alternatives to prosecution have developed one by one, often without statutory foundations, and hardly constitute a 'system' of diversion. However, they are used in large numbers, and their form and their justifications need careful scrutiny.

In England and Wales there are at least five forms of diversion of a case in which there is sufficient evidence that a person has committed an offence:

(a) NO FURTHER ACTION

The police may decide to take no further action. This course should be taken where there is insufficient evidence, but our discussion here is limited to cases where there is sufficient evidence that the defendant has committed a crime. Even in some such cases the police may decide to take no further action because, for example, the defendant has already been sentenced to custody, or indicates a willingness to have the offence 'taken into consideration' in sentencing for another crime, or the offender is very young, or the offence is non-serious.

(b) INFORMAL WARNING

A second alternative is an informal warning, given by a police officer in circumstances where a formal caution is considered unnecessary or inappropriate. Such a warning might be given by an individual officer on the beat, so that the offender is not even taken to a police station. Motorists have often benefited from informal warnings of this kind. However, the use of informal warnings for other crimes varies between areas, with only between 11 and 18 of the 43 police forces using them regularly,[33] although the overall trend seems to be upwards. Inspectors working for the various regulatory agencies may also use informal warnings in some cases: for example, in the Guidance issued by the Environment Agency, there is recognition that inspectors may occasionally give informal warnings, and there is an intermediate form of warning called a 'site warning' that is noted on the site inspection report but does not result in the sending of a warning letter.[34]

(c) FORMAL POLICE CAUTIONS

A third alternative is the formal police caution. The police should only offer to caution an offender when there is sufficient evidence to prosecute: this is a caution for an

---

[33] Audit Commission, *Misspent Youth: Young People and Crimes* (1996), para 30; R. Evans and R. Ellis, *Police Cautioning in the 1990s* (1997), 3.

[34] Guidance, above, n 14, para 2.4.

offence, and should be distinguished from informal warnings given by individual officers. The police caution is usually delivered by a senior officer in uniform at a police station. There is no legislative basis for this kind of cautioning, but cautions should be recorded by the police and disclosed to the court in an antecedents statement when relevant.[35] A caution for a sex offence results in the offender being placed on the Sex Offender Register and subjected to the various notification requirements under the Sex Offenders Act 1997, now replaced by Part 2 of the Sexual Offences Act 2003. Cautions for young offenders were replaced, under the Crime and Disorder Act 1998, by a statutory scheme of reprimands and final warnings.[36] The Criminal Justice Act 2003 introduces the conditional caution for adult offenders (see (e) below), but it is clear that old-style police cautions will continue to be available for use.

(d) RESTORATIVE JUSTICE

A fourth alternative is to refer the offender to a restorative justice scheme. Such schemes vary from area to area. In the Thames Valley and some other areas they have been run by the police and combined with formal cautions: the restorative caution.[37] There are also schemes of restorative conferencing which are not led by or dependent on the police, although relatively few of them seem to be available before conviction. In many quarters there is a belief that this approach holds considerable promise for victims, for the community and for offenders,[38] and it is envisaged that the new scheme of conditional cautions (below) may be harnessed to participation in restorative justice.

(e) CONDITIONAL CAUTIONS

Sections 22–27 of the Criminal Justice Act 2003 introduce a new form of diversion, the conditional caution. Such a caution may only be given to a person aged 18 or over, against whom the CPS decides that there is sufficient evidence of guilt, and who has admitted guilt. The conditions will usually be related to participation in a rehabilitative programme or the making of reparation. Further details of this new measure are given in Part 4 of this chapter.

Like the measures in some of the continental European systems described earlier, the conditional caution may include a financial condition such as paying compensation to the victim or making a payment to a relevant charity. Some agencies, notably the Inland Revenue, have long possessed a power to require compounded penalties as an alternative to prosecution. This means that a person may be required to pay, say,

---

[35] Home Office Circular 59/1990, Annex B.

[36] For discussion of their use, see C. Ball, 'Youth Justice? Half a Century of Responses to Youth Offending', [2004] Crim LR 167.

[37] See R. Young and C. Hoyle, 'New, Improved Police-Led Restorative Justice?', in A. von Hirsch *et al*, *Restorative Justice and Criminal Justice* (2003).

[38] Home Office, *Restorative Justice: the Government's Strategy* (2003).

twice the under-paid tax under threat of being prosecuted otherwise. This approach is open to relatively few agencies, however (HM Customs and Excise being another). The bringing of a criminal prosecution remains the ultimate sanction. As we have seen, the tendency is for regulatory agencies to regard this as a last resort, whilst the police have tended to use it more widely and more routinely.

In one important respect all the forms of diversion mentioned here, both in this country and in others, are the same. All of them allow the defendant the alternative of contesting guilt in court, by declining to accept the official offer and leaving the authorities to prosecute. This is in accordance with the European Convention on Human Rights, Article 6(1) of which has been interpreted so as to require the possibility of recourse to a court for a person who contests the decision to impose a penalty.[39]

6.3 THE POLICE AND SELECTIVE ENFORCEMENT

Once the police have sufficient evidence against an offender, they may (in conjunction with the CPS) consider prosecution, or may consider one of the other alternatives just set out. This 'prosecute or divert' decision is a crucial stage in responding to offences and suspected offenders. To choose diversion is to ensure that, for this offence at least, the believed offender has minimal engagement with the formal criminal justice system—although the new conditional caution blurs the line deliberately. To choose prosecution is (where the CPS agree) to make it highly likely that the case will progress through the court system. The experiences of all relevant parties (suspected offenders, victims and others) will be markedly different according to the route chosen. So far as offenders are concerned, a prosecution is likely to bring labelling, stigma and other possible after-effects of sentencing (as well as its direct impact on liberty). The diversionary alternatives may originally have been designed to avoid these effects, but we will see below that the dividing line between the two approaches is no longer as clear as that.

The great push towards wider use of cautioning came in the 1980s: the Home Office made several attempts, in circulars in 1983, 1985, and 1990, to persuade the police to increase diversion and to reduce the proportionate use of prosecutions. These had considerable success, and not just in respect of juveniles. For adult males the cautioning rate rose from five per cent in 1984 to 18 per cent in 1991, and for adult females from 14 to 40 per cent.[40] The circular of 1990 went so far as to state 'that the courts should only be used as a last resort, particularly for juveniles and young adults'.[41] However, there was a hardening of policy in the mid-1990s, and a Home Office circular of 1994—promoted by the then Home Secretary, Michael Howard,

---

[39] *Le Compte, Van Leuven and De Meyere* (1981), A.43, para 23; *De Weer* (1980) A. 35, para 23.
[40] *Criminal Statistics, England and Wales* (1986 and 1991), Table 5.5.
[41] Home Office Circular 59/1990, para 7.

with the phrase 'your first chance is your last chance'—aimed to bring about significant reductions in repeat cautioning and in cautioning for indictable-only offences. The result has been a significant downturn in the overall cautioning rate, from 41 per cent in each of the years 1992–1995 down to 30 per cent in 2002. For males aged 21 or over the decline in cautioning was from a peak of 26 per cent in the mid-1990s to 19 per cent in 2002; for females of that age, from a peak of 46 per cent in the early 1990s to 32 per cent in 2002 (see Table 6.1).[42]

This change of policy means that many people who would have been cautioned in the mid-1990s are now being prosecuted. There has not been a total reversal, however, and there seems to be no question of returning to the low cautioning rates for adults (five per cent for men, 14 per cent for women) that obtained in the early 1980s. Diversion remains embedded in the English system. But the changes of policy do prompt renewed questioning of the justifications for prosecuting rather than diverting, and of the claims made for cautioning and other forms of diversion.

(a) THE FORMAL PRINCIPLES FOR POLICE CAUTIONING

The principles on which the police should take their gatekeeping decisions are set out as 'National Standards' in Home Office Circular 18/1994. This document has no legal significance; indeed, police cautioning is almost entirely a set of extra-legal practices. The National Standards do not explicitly lay down an order of preference: although it is stated that 'there should be a presumption in favour of not prosecuting certain categories of offender, such as elderly people or those who suffer from some form of mental illness or impairment, or a severe physical illness', it is made clear, on the one hand, that this does not 'afford absolute protection against prosecution', and, on the other hand, that in dealing with any offender the police must first decide that 'cautioning is the correct course'. The introduction to the National Standards adds that 'there is no intention of inhibiting the practice of taking action short of a formal caution by giving an oral warning . . .'. It is unfortunate that there is no clear commitment to the principle of minimum intervention: this could have been achieved, as in respect of identification procedures, by presenting the alternatives to prosecution in their preferred order of use.[43]

The National Standards reaffirm that a formal caution should not be offered unless there is sufficient evidence to prosecute, the offender admits the offence, and the offender gives informed consent. In his study of juveniles, Evans found that as many as 22 per cent of those who had been cautioned had uttered either a denial or a statement falling short of a confession,[44] which strengthens the argument for access to free legal advice at this stage.[45] Assuming, however, that those requirements are fulfilled,

---

[42] It is possible that the falling rate of cautions was connected with the fall in crime, with which it coincided, but the dynamics of such a relationship are unclear.

[43] Home Office, *Police and Criminal Evidence Act 1984, Code of Practice D.*

[44] R. Evans, *The Conduct of Police Interviews with Juveniles* (1993).

[45] See also the facts of *DPP v Ara* [2002] 1 Cr App R 159, discussed in Part 7 below.

Table 6.1 Offenders cautioned as a percentage of offenders found guilty or cautioned by type of offence, sex and age group, 1992–2002

England and Wales

Percentages

Year	All offenders	Males						Females					
		All ages	Aged 10–11	Aged 12–14	Aged 15–17	Aged 18–20	Aged 21 and over	All ages	Aged 10–11	Aged 12–14	Aged 15–17	Aged 18–20	Aged 21 and over
Indictable offences													
1992	41	36	96	86	59	29	23	61	99	96	81	50	46
1993	41	37	96	83	59	32	26	60	99	95	80	52	46
1994	41	37	95	81	56	34	25	59	100	94	77	50	44
1995	41	37	94	79	54	35	26	59	99	93	76	51	44
1996	40	36	94	77	51	35	26	56	99	91	72	50	44
1997	38	35	93	74	49	35	26	52	98	89	68	48	42
1998	37	33	91	72	48	34	24	51	97	88	67	46	39
1999	34	31	87	69	45	31	22	48	96	87	64	43	36
2000	32	29	86	68	43	29	20	47	95	86	63	41	34
2001	31	28	86	66	42	28	19	46	95	85	64	41	32
2002	30	27	83	63	41	29	19	44	94	84	62	41	32
Summary offences													
1992	18	22	96	84	57	26	16	9	99	91	68	25	6
1993	18	22	97	85	63	30	16	10	95	89	74	28	7
1994	18	21	97	82	60	29	15	9	99	86	67	27	6
1995	18	20	94	78	56	28	13	11	95	80	65	25	7
1996	16	19	95	79	55	29	12	10	97	82	60	23	6
1997	18	19	94	77	50	28	12	14	94	78	52	28	10
1998	17	18	92	73	47	26	11	15	98	79	53	28	10
1999	18	18	88	70	46	26	11	17	92	75	56	32	11
2000	15	16	86	67	44	24	9	12	92	75	56	26	7
2001	16	17	88	67	44	23	10	13	86	75	55	25	8
2002	14	15	85	63	41	22	9	13	92	72	54	25	8

the key issue is then one of 'public interest'. The factors to be taken into account may be divided into five groups:

(a) the nature of the offence;
(b) the likely penalty if convicted in court;
(c) the offender's age and state of health;
(d) the offender's previous criminal history;
(e) the offender's attitude to the offence.

The decision to caution is a dispositive decision, analogous to sentencing in some of its principles and effects. The seriousness of the offence is a major factor, with some offences being regarded as too serious for cautioning even where the offender fulfils conditions (c), (d), (e), or indeed all of them. On the other hand, less serious offences may result in a caution even though the offender cannot be brought within (c), (d), or (e). The reference in (b) to the likely penalty may be found in the Code for Crown Prosecutors and in the 1990 version of the National Standards for Cautioning, but in most police forces it has now been replaced by a list of 'gravity factors', issued by the Association of Chief Police Officers in 1995. This enables the police to identify aggra-vating and mitigating factors in cases, and then to calculate a score which may help to indicate whether the correct course is to prosecute, to caution, or merely to give an informal warning.[46]

The clearest and best-established reason for cautioning is where the offender is very young, or elderly, or suffering from ill health. Young offenders are now dealt with under separate legislation: s 65 of the Crime and Disorder Act 1998 introduced a 'stepwise' approach of reprimands and final warnings for offenders under 18, and these have now been operational for some years. Some 87,000 reprimands and final warnings were given in 2002, significantly fewer than the 98,000 given in 2001,[47] and a decline that may reflect both falling numbers of young people and a trend towards prosecution. Turning back to adults, elderly offenders are quite likely to receive a caution, often for theft from a shop. Where an offender is suffering from mental disorder or a severe physical illness, this is often a strong reason in favour of a caution.

Why should young, elderly and mentally disordered offenders attract this more lenient and/or constructive response? The link with culpability is rather uncertain, although it can be maintained that those who are very young or mentally disordered are less to blame than others. The same could be said of some elderly offenders. However, there is considerable support for the rehabilitative argument that the process of prosecution, conviction, and sentence may cause stigma and otherwise be less effective in turning a young offender away from crime than diversion. In the case of young offenders this approach merges into the argument that sentences may have a

---

[46] See the comments of the Audit Commission, above, n 33, 21.
[47] *Criminal Statistics England and Wales 2002*, Table 2B.

harsher impact on certain types of offender, and therefore that a lesser response would be appropriate in order to preserve proportionality. This is perhaps most significant in cases of elderly offenders. It therefore appears that three rationales—culpability as an element of seriousness, rehabilitation, and equality of impact—may support this ground for cautioning.

The relevance of factor (e) is more debatable. It includes 'the wilfulness with which it was committed', which is clearly related to the question of culpability. Deliberate acts are usually more serious than 'spur of the moment' excesses. It also includes 'a practical demonstration of regret such as apologising to the victim and/ or offering to put matters right as far as he is able'.[48] The difficulty here is that wealthy offenders might be able to buy themselves out of prosecution by offering payments to their victims, whereas impecunious offenders cannot. The law of sentencing contains clear declarations of principle against such inequality,[49] but the National Standards for Cautioning contain none. Moreover, the 1994 National Standards state not only that it is desirable to establish the victim's view of the offence, but also that:

'if the offender has made some form of reparation or paid compensation, and the victim is satisfied, it may no longer be necessary to prosecute in cases where the possibility of a court's awarding compensation would otherwise have been a major determining factor. Under no circumstances should police officers become involved in negotiating or awarding reparation or compensation'.

The guidance here is not absolutely clear, but in recent years there has been a distinct move towards providing a more formal framework for apologies, compensation and other offender-victim interactions. This forms part of the scheme for reprimands and warnings for young offenders under the Crime and Disorder Act 1998, and also part of the scheme for conditional cautions introduced by the Criminal Justice Act 2003.

We have already noted that the 1994 National Standards were intended to alter practice on the granting of cautions to those who had been cautioned previously. Commenting that 'multiple cautioning brings this disposal into disrepute', the guidance went on to state that a second or subsequent caution should only be considered 'where the subsequent offence is trivial or where there has been a sufficient lapse of time since the first caution to suggest that it had some effect'. The new system of reprimands and final warnings under the Crime and Disorder Act 1998 institutionalizes a 'stepwise' approach by ensuring that only one reprimand is given, and only one final warning, so that prosecution must be the response to the next offence committed after a final warning.[50]

---

[48] Above n 41, Note F.   [49] See Ashworth, *Sentencing and Criminal Justice* (3rd ed., 2000), Ch. 7.

[50] For comparison, the Code of Practice for Conditional Cautioning states that a conditional caution should not be 'regarded as the logical next step for an offender who has received a simple caution', and that a person who has recently been cautioned for a similar offence should not be given a conditional caution (para 3.3).

(b) FOR AND AGAINST CAUTIONING

We have noted the rise and (partial) fall of cautioning in recent years. What are the advantages claimed for cautioning, rather than prosecuting? The National Standards begin by stating three purposes of cautions:

(a) to deal quickly and simply with less serious offenders;

(b) to divert them from the criminal courts;

(c) to reduce the chances of their reoffending.

The first purpose refers to proportionality, implying that quicker and simpler responses are more appropriate for less serious offences. However, the undertones of economics are also evident here, and the words 'and more cheaply' are implicit. The same undertones might be detected beneath the second purpose, although that might also be seen as a gesture towards the principle of minimum intervention.[51] The third purpose makes a bold claim about effectiveness. Statistics show that some 85 per cent of those cautioned in 1985 and 1988 were not convicted of a serious offence within two years of their caution.[52] This reconviction rate of 15 per cent is much lower than that for offenders convicted at court, at least for first offenders, which is 29 per cent for those without any previous convictions.[53] It could be commented that any such comparison is flawed because the court group is likely to have a higher proportion of people with previous cautions, who are more likely to be reconvicted anyway. A small matched study of juveniles by Mott suggests that those cautioned are still less likely to reoffend than those sentenced in court.[54] However, those who adopt the principle of minimum intervention do not need to establish that cautions are more effective, in terms of reconvictions. It is sufficient to argue that they have not been shown to be less effective than conviction and sentence.

What are the disadvantages of cautioning? Four possible disadvantages merit brief discussion—the danger of net-widening, pressure on defendants to admit to offences, unfairness to victims, and failure to discourage repeat offenders.

(i) Net-widening

Net-widening is the process of using a new measure, not (or not only) to encompass the target group of offenders who would otherwise have been prosecuted, but also to drag into the net people who might otherwise have benefited from a lesser response. This danger was pointed out to the police in the 1985 circular, and there is little evidence that the considerable increases in cautioning during the 1980s were achieved through any significant net-widening.[55] Whilst there may have been some cases of

---

[51] Properly speaking, diversion from the criminal courts cannot be a purpose of cautioning. It is simply its effect. A 'purpose' would be a reason why offenders should be diverted in this way.

[52] Home Office Statistical Bulletin 8/94, *The Criminal Histories of those Cautioned in 1985, 1988 and 1991.*

[53] G. Philpotts and L. Lancucki, *Previous Convictions, Sentence and Reconviction* (1979), 16.

[54] J. Mott, 'Police Decisions for Dealing with Juvenile Offenders', (1983) 23 *BJ Crim* 249.

[55] M. McMahon, 'Net-Widening: Vagaries in the Use of a Concept', (1990) 30 *BJ Crim* 121.

this kind, the figures suggest a genuine transfer of offenders away from prosecution towards cautioning. However, the reversal of the trend towards cautioning in the mid-1990s, and the greater resort to prosecution in the late 1990s and early part of the present decade, is evidence of a movement towards net-tightening in respect of both young and older offenders. No detailed study has been made of the types of offender who benefited from cautioning in the 1990s and who are prosecuted now, but their numbers are significant.

(ii) Pressure on defendants

Where a caution is offered this may put pressure on a suspect to admit to an offence when it is not clear that he or she committed it. If the suspect denies knowledge of a certain fact, he or she might wish to decline a caution and have the point adjudicated in court; and yet the disincentives to taking that course are so great (delay, risk of not being believed, risk of conviction) that acceptance of the caution is likely. The National Standards state that 'a caution will not be appropriate where a person does not make a clear and reliable admission of the offence',[56] but there is evidence that the alternative prospect of prosecution may be used to obtain an 'admission' that is not genuine.[57] It would take a strong person to refuse a caution and implicitly to challenge the police to prosecute, but such cases do occasionally happen and refusals to accept a caution may be vindicated.[58] An additional problem is that the police may not fully understand the relevant law, such as the mental element required for the crime or the possible defences.[59] In effect, whenever a person knows or believes that there will be a choice between accepting a caution and risking a prosecution, there is bound to be pressure to accept the caution. The disadvantages of this must be minimized by ensuring, as far as possible, that cautions are only offered if the conditions are strictly met. This would require far greater supervision within the police, or the provision of legal advice, or the transfer of the function to the CPS. As will be argued below, the issue of safeguards is particularly important now that cautions are cited in court and relied upon for other purposes.

(iii) Unfairness to victims

Unfairness to victims has probably been one unfortunate consequence of cautioning. Figures over 20 years show that the number of offenders ordered to pay compensation by criminal courts was 129,400 in 1981, 112,800 in 1991, and 105,000 in 2002.[60] These figures partly reflect the declining numbers of convictions, but they also raise questions about whether the overall increase in police cautioning over this period

---

[56] Above, n 41, Annex B, note 2B.

[57] *R v Metropolitan Police Commissioner, ex parte Thompson* [1997] 1 WLR 1519.

[58] In one case a doctor who used force to defend himself refused to accept a caution for assault, was prosecuted, and was acquitted: *The Times,* 17 June 1998.

[59] For example, see the case discussed by R. Evans, 'Challenging a Police Caution using Judicial Review', [1996] Crim LR 104.

[60] *Criminal Statistics, England and Wales* for 1981, 1991 and 2002.

(even taking account of the recent downturn) operated to deprive some victims of compensation from their offenders. However, as we will see below, the new scheme of conditional cautions embodies an attempt to address this problem by making the payment of reparation an enforceable condition.

(iv) Repeat cautioning

A fourth argument, increasingly heard in recent years, is that cautioning (in particular, repeat cautioning) sends the wrong message to some offenders.

While some areas operate voluntary 'caution plus' schemes, in others there is no backup to try to prevent further crime. Inconsistent, repeated and ineffective cautioning has allowed some children and young people to feel that they can offend with impunity.[61]

The idea that a caution standing alone was insufficient was a major force behind the system of reprimands and warnings for young offenders under the Crime and Disorder Act 1998. The system allows no more than one reprimand, and no more than one final warning (which will 'usually be followed by a community intervention programme, involving the offender and his or her family to address the causes of the offending and so reduce the risk of further crime'). This stepwise approach applies even where the next offence may not otherwise be serious enough to warrant prosecution. Some will regard this as a significant step towards legality, in reducing the discretionary elements of the system and bringing the response to young offenders more into the open forum of the courts. Others will insist that discretion remains abundant, notably in giving informal warnings which do not invoke the statutory system, and may regard the stepwise approach as an unfortunate move away from a proportionality principle in youth justice.

(c) THE PRACTICAL IMPLEMENTATION OF NATIONAL STANDARDS

There has been long-standing concern about the apparent gap between national standards and local practices. One consequence of this is so-called 'justice by geography.' Despite the guidance set out in the three Home Office circulars of 1985, 1990 and 1994, Evans and Ellis concluded, on the basis of research in late 1995, that 'the circulars have not been successful in achieving greater consistency between forces'.[62] The Association of Chief Police Officers issued a document on 'gravity factors' in 1995, and this may have brought about some improvement. On the face of it, there are still significant differences in cautioning rates among police areas. Thus the 2002 figures show a national average cautioning rate of 30 per cent, and variations from 48 per cent in Northamptonshire and in Surrey, 41 per cent in Northumbria and Warwickshire, 33 per cent in the Metropolitan Police area, and then 17 per cent in

---

[61] Home Office, *No More Excuses: a New Approach to Tackling Youth Crime in England and Wales* (1997), para 5.10.

[62] Evans and Ellis, *Police Cautioning in the 1990s* (1996), 2.

Cheshire and in South Yorkshire, and 21 per cent in Cleveland, Merseyside and Humberside.[63] To some extent this may reflect different mixes of cases in different police areas. Since cautioning is much used for first offenders, the proportion of first offenders coming to police attention is highly likely to affect the cautioning rate. Evans and Wilkinson found that the percentage of first offenders did differ significantly among areas (from 46 to 64 per cent) and that it was related to the juvenile cautioning rate in the ten forces studied. However, they also found that further variation in cautioning was not explained by the different offence-mix: much cautioning is for shoplifting, and forces adopted differing policies towards this.[64] One of the conclusions of this study was that cautioning guidelines tend to say little about the most crucial factor in practice—the type and seriousness of the offence. The ACPO guidelines on gravity factors were probably the first general attempt to tackle this issue, in the sense that they list specific gravity factors for a range of offences, but it does not appear to have eradicated disparity.[65]

When criticisms of variations in criminal justice are voiced, the reply is often that police forces are responding to local conditions and particular problems. It is certainly true that many worthwhile initiatives in criminal justice have come about through local attempts to address local problems; but there is also the probability that some local variations stem from a stubborn and insular unwillingness to absorb new national policies and to change working practices. This is often possible because of the considerable latitude left to the police, particularly in the absence of legislation. The matter then becomes another instance of police discretion being exercised in various ways. Thus McConville, Sanders, and Leng, on the basis of their research in the late 1980s, argued that the cautioning guidelines are so broadly worded that they can easily be used by the police to justify decisions taken on other grounds.[66] These other grounds are likely to reflect the working practices and concerns of the police. They give examples of a case being prosecuted in response to the insistence of a local business, even though it fell within the cautioning guidelines, and of another case resulting in a caution when (as a theft in breach of trust) it fell squarely within the prosecution category. Similarly, Evans studied attempts to introduce new guidance for the cautioning of young adults in two London police divisions, and found again that it was attitudes and working philosophies rather than written rules that tended to determine outcomes.[67] A 'Caution Consideration Chart' was introduced, but it tended to be used in some police stations as a resource, to legitimate decisions taken by the custody officer on other grounds. Sometimes, too, victims' views were similarly

---

[63] *Criminal Statistics England and Wales 2002*, Table 2.4.

[64] R. Evans and C. Wilkinson, 'Variations in Police Cautioning', (1990) 29 *Howard JCJ* 155.

[65] The Metropolitan Police incorporated these into a 'Case Disposal Manual', excerpts from which are set out in the judgment of Schiemann LJ in *R v Metropolitan Police Commissioner, ex p Thompson* [1997] 1 WLR 1519.

[66] M. McConville, A. Sanders and R. Leng, *The Case for the Prosecution* (1991), 122 and Ch. 6 generally.

[67] R. Evans, 'Evaluating Young Adult Diversion Schemes', [1993] Crim LR 490.

manipulated, being ignored when inconvenient and cited when they supported a decision already taken. Overall, the probability is that some decisions result from a simple following of the guidelines, whereas others are motivated more by assessment of the 'moral character' of the offender or victim or by concerns related to the police mission.[68] It might also be observed that the police will sometimes take a decision that might be justifiable on the limited information available but that might cease to be justifiable when more information comes to light. Some of the 'public interest' criteria for not prosecuting depend on matters extraneous to the offence, of which the police may have no knowledge.

6.4 THE ROLE OF PROSECUTORS

Some of the objections to police cautioning—its largely discretionary nature; the absence of a legal basis; the disadvantage to some victims—now appear to have been remedied by the introduction of conditional cautions under the Criminal Justice Act 2003. Much depends, however, on how the new arrangements are operated. Police cautions of the kind just discussed (now termed simple cautions) will remain available, and so in many cases there will be a choice between a simple caution and a conditional caution as a means of diversion. The Code of Practice states that the key to determining whether a conditional caution should be given 'is that the imposition of specified conditions will be an appropriate and effective means of addressing the offender's behaviour or making reparation for the effects of the offence on the victim or the community.'[69] Simple cautions will be appropriate where 'no suitable conditions readily suggest themselves' or where the offender 'has forestalled what would otherwise be a suitable condition', for example by compensating the victim.[70]

One major difference is that the CPS will be involved in decisions on conditional cautions. Although conditional cautions (like simple cautions) will be administered by a police officer, it will be for a prosecutor to decide that there is sufficient evidence to charge the offender with an offence, and that a conditional caution should be given in the case. Section 23 of the Criminal Justice Act 2003 sets out five requirements that must be met before a conditional caution can be given. In summary they are:

(a) that a constable or other 'authorised person' must have evidence that the offender has committed the offence;

(b) that the prosecutor should decide that there is sufficient evidence to charge, and that a conditional caution should be given;

(c) that the offender admits the offence;

---

[68] See above, Ch.3.
[69] Code of Practice on Conditional Cautioning (13 July 2004, www.homeoffice.gov.uk), para 1.2.
[70] *Ibid.*, para 2.2.

(d) that the effect of the conditional caution is explained to the offender, together with the consequence of breach; and

(e) that the offender signs a document containing the details of the offence, his admission, his consent to the conditional caution, and the conditions attached.

These statutory requirements are welcome. The Code of Practice reinforces them by, for example, stating that 'the prospect of a conditional caution should on no account be mentioned until the suspect has made a clear and reliable admission,'[71] and that offenders should be advised of their right to seek legal advice before accepting the caution and its conditions, if they have not exercised their right earlier.[72] These are necessary steps towards bringing rule-of-law protections into this key area of disposi-tive decision-making, where a decision to divert (and a person's acceptance of that diversion) may have significant consequences. It remains to be seen whether their effects may be blunted by the continued existence of simple cautions: it is not clear how the two alternatives will work in practice, and the Code declares roundly that 'the issue of simple cautions . . . will continue to be a matter for the police.'[73]

What conditions may be set? A person's decision to accept a conditional caution may well depend on the nature and onerousness of the conditions. Section 22(3) states that the condition(s) must have as their object either the rehabilitation of the offender or the making of reparation for the offence or both. The Code of Practice also states that any conditions must be proportionate to the offence, achievable within the time set, and appropriate to the offence or offender.[74] Reparation may involve doing actual repairs or paying compensation to the victim. Rehabilitation may involve taking courses on behaviour modification, participation in a form of restorative just-ice, etc. Much will depend on the local availability of relevant schemes. Moreover, if it is decided that the best approach would be through restorative justice, and both the offender and the victim agree, the making of the caution and its conditions will be postponed until the restorative processes have taken place and suitable conditions have been identified.[75]

What are the consequences of non-compliance? Section 24 provides that failure without reasonable cause to comply with any of the conditions may result in the institution of criminal proceedings for the original offence. The caution is therefore confirmed as a form of conditional non-prosecution. However, the language of the statute is permissive, not mandatory, and so there remains an element of prosecutorial discretion in deciding what course to take. There may be circumstances (perhaps where the breach is relatively minor) in which it is decided not to abrogate the con-ditional caution. If a prosecution is brought, however, this terminates the conditional

---

[71] *Ibid.*, para 4.1; cf. the *Thompson* case in 1997, n. 90 below and accompanying text.
[72] *Ibid.*, para 4.1(ii); cf. the *Ara* case in 2002, n. 91 below and accompanying text.   [73] *Ibid.*, para 2.3.
[74] *Ibid.*, para 5.1.
[75] *Ibid.*, paras 2.6 and 8.2. It appears that the restorative processes will usually be facilitated by the police, but that any resulting agreement as to conditions will have to be approved as proportionate, achievable and appropriate by the CPS.

caution. Section 24(2) also provides that the document signed by the offender when accepting the conditional caution is admissible in the proceedings. It is not certain that this prevents the defendant in those proceedings from pleading not guilty to the offence. It clearly makes it difficult to succeed in such a plea, since that would involve the retraction of a signed admission, but we have already noted evidence of people feeling pressure to make such an admission in the hope of escaping prosecution with a caution.[76]

6.5 ACCOUNTABILITY

It is apparent from the discussion of the gatekeeping practices of the police and of regulatory agencies that discretion is the dominant characteristic. Apart from the new provisions on conditional cautions, there is little law relating to diversion from the criminal process, and what law there is aims merely to facilitate rather than to direct. Guidelines have been created, but these are so generally phrased and so lightly enforced that their impact is muted—they can readily be used so as to justify decisions taken on other grounds. To what extent, if at all, are these decision makers accountable? The question has to be answered on two different levels: accountability for general policy, and accountability for individual decisions.

The CPS will have a primary role in the new scheme of conditional cautions, and the next chapter examines the framework of its accountability (including the Inspectorate). The main decision makers on cautioning have always been the police, and there have been significant changes to their accountability. The traditional concept of constabulary independence, in which local chief constables have been answerable to the law and also subject to HM Inspectorate of Constabulary, has now been considerably watered down by the provisions in Part 1 of the Police Reform Act 2002. That Act gives statutory authority for far greater central direction in policing, although there remains considerable discretion in the hands of chief constables.[77] However, in respect of decisions on diversion from prosecution, the framework remains rather weak. The 'National Standards for Cautioning' are supported merely by a Home Office circular, the terms of which were agreed with the Association of Chief Police Officers and the Crown Prosecution Service. No doubt the terms of the circular are used as a basis for inspections by Her Majesty's Inspector of Constabulary. No doubt, also, there are possible financial implications for refusal to comply. However, as far as the law is concerned, the Chief Constable of each area is solely responsible for decisions on law enforcement in that area. Since the Court of Appeal has held that 'No Minister of the Crown can tell him that he must or must not prosecute this man or that one',[78]

---

[76] Above, p. 156.   [77] D. Ormerod and A. Roberts, 'The Police Reform Act 2002' [2003] Crim LR 141.
[78] *R v Metropolitan Police Commissioner, ex p Blackburn* [1968] 2 QB 118, *per* Lord Denning MR.

the National Standards cannot be binding in law. The 1993 Royal Commission recommended:

'that police cautioning should be governed by statute, under which national guidelines, drawn up in consultation with the CPS and the police service among others, should be laid down in regulations. These regulations should also govern the keeping of records of cautions so that information about whether a suspect has been cautioned can easily be transferred between police forces'.[79]

This important step has not yet been taken. Although the Crime and Disorder Act 1998 introduced a statutory scheme of reprimands and warnings for young offenders, and the Criminal Justice Act 2003 introduced conditional cautions, there is still no legislative regulation of what might be termed 'old style' police cautions. Without that, the prospects for curbing local variations are not good.

Accountability for individual decisions depends largely on the internal structure of the agency. Within the police, there may be local police traditions or cultures that lead to variations in interpretation, even if there is a clear force policy. It is a well-known characteristic of the police that the amount of supervision of constables is not great, and that they have much *de facto* discretion.[80] Historically this has not been true of cautioning decisions, since cases for caution have tended to be referred to inspector level for approval. But the interaction between the arresting officer and the station sergeant remains influential in determining what happens subsequently. And the effect of force policy on those interactions is likely to be variable. The extent of a police force's commitment to cautioning will determine whether or not it can overpower certain aspects of the occupational culture.

To what extent can police decisions at this stage of the process be challenged in the courts? The answer differs according to whether the decision is to prosecute or not to prosecute. If a person is charged, despite falling within one of the categories for cautioning outlined in the National Standards, it seems that judicial review may be possible but that this would be judicial review of the CPS if they decide to continue the prosecution rather than discontinuing it. This, the Divisional Court held,[81] was because the police are merely the initiators of proceedings, and the 'last and decisive word' on the issue lies with the CPS.[82] The CPS would take this decision within the framework of the Code for Crown Prosecutors (to be discussed in Chapter 7 below), which is similar in terms to the National Standards. However, the leading case of *L*[83] was expressly limited to decisions to prosecute juveniles and, although there is some authority in favour of extending the principle to decisions to prosecute

[79] RCCJ, *Report* (1993), para 5.57.

[80] M. Maguire and C. Norris, *The Conduct and Supervision of Police Investigations* (1993); B. Irving and C. Dunnighan, *Human Factors in the Quality Control of CID Investigations* (1993).

[81] *R v Chief Constable of Kent, ex p L* (1991) 93 Cr App R 416, *per* Watkins LJ at 426.

[82] As mentioned above, the Criminal Justice Act 2003 transfers the power to charge from the police to the CPS in most non-minor cases.

[83] *R v Chief Constable of Kent, ex p L* (1991) 93 Cr App R 416.

adults,[84] the House of Lords has decided that judicial review of decisions to prosecute should be confined to cases of dishonesty, bad faith or some other exceptional circumstance.[85] It remains possible to allege that a particular prosecution amounts to an abuse of process, and to apply for it to be stayed on that ground.[86]

What of the reverse situation, where the police decide not to prosecute a suspected offender but to administer a caution? It is established that in these circumstances an application for judicial review may succeed if it can be shown that the appropriate principles were not followed, whether the case concerns a juvenile or an adult.[87] Thus in the case of P,[88] judicial review of a juvenile caution was granted when the police had failed to explain the role of appropriate adult to the child's mother and had failed to explain the consequences of an admission. In the case of C,[89] judicial review of a decision not to prosecute an adult was granted when it was shown that the CPS had failed to have regard to a material consideration.

The caution itself may be challenged if the procedure leading up to the decision was unfair. Thus in *R v Metropolitan Police Commissioner, ex parte Thompson*[90] the Divisional Court granted an order of *certiorari* quashing a caution. Counsel for the defendant argued that, where the police appear to be offering a caution if the defendant were to admit the offence, this is an unfair inducement which, on an analogy with the exclusion of confessions, should nullify the acceptance of the caution. The Divisional Court agreed with this proposition. The ruling is significant in two ways: first, it emphasizes the need to ensure that cautions are only offered and accepted in appropriate cases; and secondly, it is important when cautions are recorded and may be relied upon subsequently. The ruling also shows why it is desirable to have access to legal advice before accepting a caution, a point reinforced by the decision in *DPP v Ara*.[91] In this case the police decided that a defendant was suitable for a caution as a result of what he had said during an interview. The defendant took legal advice subsequently, but his solicitor was not allowed by the police to have access to the tape recording of the interview. The Divisional Court upheld the decision of the justices to stay the prosecution on grounds of abuse of process, on the basis that a person should have access to legal advice before deciding whether to accept a caution, and the refusal to disclose the interview tape rendered informed legal advice impossible.

To what extent are the various regulatory agencies accountable for their very different enforcement policies? We have noted that the annual report is practically the only

---

[84] *R v Inland Revenue Commissioner, ex p Mead* [1993] 1 All ER 772, *per* Stuart-Smith LJ at 780. In principle, the availability of diversion for adults following the introduction of conditional cautions constitutes a strong reason for permitting judicial review of decisions to prosecute instead.

[85] *R v Director of Public Prosecutions, ex p Kebilene* [2000] 2 AC 326.

[86] For discussion of the doctrine of abuse of process, see Ch.12 below.

[87] *R v General Council of the Bar, ex p Percival* [1990] 3 All ER 137, discussed by C. Hilson, 'Discretion to Prosecute and Judicial Review', [1993] Crim LR 639.

[88] *R v Metropolitan Police Commissioner, ex p P* (1995) 160 JP 367, discussed by R. Evans, 'Challenging a Police Caution using Judicial Review', [1996] Crim LR 104.

[89] *R v Director of Public Prosecutions, ex p C* [1995] 1 Cr App R 136.   [90] [1997] 1 WLR 1519.

[91] [2002] 1 Cr App R 159.

means of being called to account for policy. There is no inspectorate for the regulatory agencies, no steering committee for the policies of the regulatory sector, and certainly no body charged with reviewing the relationship between regulatory policies and the approach of the police to law enforcement. As for accountability for individual decisions, research suggests that there are variations in the local culture of different parts of a single agency—one familiar finding is a divergence of approach between rural areas and urban areas.[92] The accountability of the individual inspector may depend on how paperwork is completed and how thoroughly it is supervised. Good training and retraining may be important factors, but on the other hand these have to fight against organizational culture, financial pressures, and other countervailing forces. In his study of Health and Safety inspectors Hawkins emphasizes 'the centrality of organizations', their norms, their goals and their culture, in determining the approach taken by individual inspectors.[93] Individual inspectors may vary in their preparedness to bring a prosecution on given facts, but part of the explanation for their behaviour may be organizational pressures. Moreover, an individual decision not to prosecute is unlikely to be reviewed, within most agencies, unless it is a case of particular sensitivity to which the attention of senior officials has been drawn. Judicial review of a decision not to prosecute would be available in theory, since most of these agencies have the 'last and decisive word' within their own sphere of operation, but there are few examples of challenges being brought in this way.

These uncertainties in the formal avenues of accountability assume greater significance when the consequences of the decisions are recalled. If a case is not prosecuted and the police decide on a simple caution, there may be lasting consequences, such as the recording and citing of cautions and the placement of anyone (of any age) cautioned for a sex offence on the Sex Offenders Register. A decision by the CPS to offer a conditional caution under the 2003 Act may also have significantly deleterious consequences for the defendant. Furthermore, from the public point of view, the only way to revive the case (apart from applying for judicial review) is by means of a private prosecution. Those are rare, and the immense investment of time and money needed to mount such a prosecution means that it cannot realistically be termed a method of accountability.

6.6 VALUES AND PRINCIPLES

The stages of decision making discussed here raise several questions of value that need further discussion. Is equality of treatment ensured? Are the interests of victims properly respected? Are the rights of defendants respected? Is there too great a sacrifice of crime control?

---

[92] See, e.g., B. Hutter, *The Reasonable Arm of the Law* (1988).   [93] Hawkins, above n 19, 330.

(a) EQUALITY OF TREATMENT

In the previous section we saw that the due execution of stated policies is not ensured by the law because legal accountability is rather sketchy in this sphere. The practices of cautioning and diversion operate in a world where there is little law, save at the extremes, and considerable discretion. Even after the introduction of reprimands and warnings for young offenders under the Crime and Disorder Act 1998 and the introduction of conditional cautions by the Criminal Justice Act 2003, there is still no statutory basis for simple cautions of those aged 18 or over, and all the difficulties set out in Parts 3 and 5 of this chapter will remain.

The predominance of discretion might be regarded as a contradiction of the principle of equality before the law and equal treatment. In many European countries, the considerable weight given to the principle of compulsory prosecution shows awareness of the values at stake. It is true that most countries do not regard this as an absolute principle, and in recent years have sought to allow scope to the principle of expediency whereby certain cases are diverted from the courts, usually by prosecutors. But these can be regarded as circumscribed exceptions to the principle that criminal justice should be dispensed in open court, after a full consideration of the issues, with reasons given. While these values are usually compromised in some way,[94] there is surely good reason to ensure that they are expressed and are accorded some respect. The decisions in this chapter are decisions that may profoundly affect the course of a suspect/offender's life: not only may prosecution itself be highly significant for the defendant in terms of anxiety and stress, damage to reputation, and possible loss of employment, but the choice of method of diversion may have significant implications for the offender. If discretion is to be bestowed on certain authorities, it should be carefully structured so as to achieve desired policies and properly controlled through channels of accountability. The few laconic remarks of the 1993 Royal Commission on this question were most unsatisfactory.[95]

Cautioning practices and diversion often seem to accord appropriately favourable treatment to vulnerable groups such as the mentally disturbed. The diversion of mentally disordered offenders is a well-established practice, although it has been argued that the ready referral of mentally disturbed suspects to the mental health services and hospitals may sometimes be a disproportionately severe response, or may deprive them of rights they would have if prosecuted, or both.[96] There is evidence that in some cases the incidence of mental disorder is not recognized by the police, or indeed by the police surgeon, and that therefore appropriate safeguards are not put in place.[97] Of those whose disorder is recognized, the rate of diversion and no further

---

[94] See, e.g. H. Lensing and L. Rayar, 'Notes on Criminal Procedure in the Netherlands', [1992] Crim LR 623; J. Hodgson, 'Codified Criminal Procedure and Human Rights: Some Observations on the French Experience', [2003] Crim LR 165.

[95] RCCJ, *Report*, para 5.59.

[96] D. Carson, 'Prosecuting People with Mental Handicaps', [1989] Crim LR 87.

[97] See C. Phillips and D. Brown, *Entry into the Criminal Justice System* (1998), 188–189.

action is relatively high.[98] For those taken to court, there is a growing number of court-based psychiatric schemes, one purpose of which is to identify and assess mentally disordered defendants and to see whether a form of diversion (such as immediate hospital admission) is possible and desirable.[99] A preliminary study of an Islington scheme showed that many of the mentally disordered defendants had problems with living accommodation, problems of substance abuse, and that there was an apparent over-representation of black people with psychotic illness.[100]

Apart from particularly vulnerable groups, does the system ensure equality of treatment? One obvious problem is the difference of approach to 'police' matters and to spheres of conduct that are regulated by the various non-police agencies. Companies, wealthy offenders, and middle-class offenders are more often dealt with by regulatory agencies whereas the more disadvantaged members of society are more likely to find their conduct defined as a police matter. The different approaches are then likely to result in more frequent prosecution of the disadvantaged than the advantaged for offences that may be no different in terms of seriousness. The argument of Norval Morris and Michael Tonry on sentencing might be applied here, to the effect that it is wrong to insist on equality if it means equality of misery.[101] The effect of this would be to allow middle-class or white-collar offenders to benefit from diversion and other alternatives to prosecution, even though lower-class or blue-collar offenders were processed in the 'normal' way, since to assimilate the treatment of the former group to that of the latter would increase the overall suffering. On a principle of parsimony, minimum intervention may thus be given higher priority than equality of treatment. However, the factual basis for this reasoning is the assumption that there is no practical way of extending forms of diversion to lower-class offenders who commit 'police' crimes. This is quite unsubstantiated. Thus, even without attacking their order of priorities, it can be argued that there is a need to devise further forms of diversion that can be operated swiftly for large numbers of small-time offenders.

A second problem of equality of treatment concerns racial discrimination. Several studies suggest that there is some discrimination against African-Caribbean people in respect of decisions to prosecute or caution. For example, Tony Jefferson and Monica Walker found that Asians were much more likely to be cautioned than any others, but that African-Caribbeans were less likely than whites to receive a caution.[102] The Commission for Racial Equality monitored the cautioning of juveniles in seven police forces and found that African-Caribbeans were more likely to be referred for prosecution than whites.[103] It seems likely that part of the difference in prosecution rates

---

[98] *Ibid.*

[99] See J. Peay, 'Mentally Disordered Offenders', in M. Maguire, R. Morgan and R. Reiner, *Oxford Handbook of Criminology* (3rd ed., 2002), at 759–760.

[100] E. Burney and G. Pearson, 'Mentally Disordered Offenders: Finding a Focus for Diversion' (1995) 34 *Howard JCJ* 291.

[101] N. Morris and M. Tonry, *Between Prison and Probation* (1990), 33.

[102] T. Jefferson and N. Walker, 'Ethnic Minorities in the Criminal Justice System' [1992] Crim LR 83, at 88.

[103] Commission for Racial Equality, *Juvenile Cautioning: Ethnic Monitoring in Practice* (1992).

revealed by these studies would disappear if account were taken of whether the individual was willing to admit the offence: more African-Caribbeans decline to admit the allegations against them, which removes their eligibility for a caution.[104] However, there are other studies indicating a lower cautioning rate for African-Caribbean people, notably a study of juvenile cautioning by Evans[105] and the broader Home Office study by Phillips and Brown.[106] The picture is complicated by the fact that 'no further action' was taken against a higher proportion of black and Asian suspects, because of 'their lower admission rate and their involvement in certain types of offence which typically have above average NFA rates.' More recently, Martina Feilzer and Roger Hood conducted a large survey for the Youth Justice Board which found that the chances of a case involving a mixed-parentage young male being prosecuted were 2.7 times greater than that of a white young male with similar case characteristics, and that the chances of a mixed-parentage young female being prosecuted were six times that of a similarly placed white female.[107] This evidence is, as the report puts it, 'consistent with discriminatory treatment.'

A third problem is posed by the differential cautioning rates for females, which are much higher than those for males—in 2002, 62 per cent for girls aged 15–17 compared with 41 per cent for boys, and 31 per cent for women aged 21 or over compared with 19 per cent for men.[108] The face-value interpretation would be that females are receiving unduly favourable treatment, but this fails to take account of the probability that offences of different types and different levels of seriousness would be found in the different groups. Thus Phillips and Brown found that 'females were more likely to be cautioned because they were far more likely than men to admit their offences and more likely to be arrested for less serious offences (typically shoplifting).'[109] However, research in the early 1990s found that, whereas a majority of both sexes had no previous criminal history, cautioned males were twice as likely as females to have been previously convicted[110]—suggesting that some men were being treated more leniently than women, perhaps benefiting from repeat cautioning when women were not. Again the picture is far from clear, but it would be unwise to assume that women are typically treated more leniently.

(b) VICTIMS' RIGHTS

Are the existing arrangements for diversion effective in securing the rights of victims? In relation to simple cautions, the National Standards refer to the views of the victim

---

[104] M. Fitzgerald, *Ethnic Minorities and the Criminal Justice System* (1993), 18.

[105] R. Evans, 'Comparing Young Adult and Juvenile Cautioning in the Metropolitan Police District', [1993] Crim LR 572.

[106] C. Phillips and D. Brown, *Entry into the Criminal Justice System* (1998), 92.

[107] M. Feilzer and R. Hood, *Differences or Discrimination?* (2004).

[108] *Criminal Statistics, England and Wales 2002*, Table 5.5.   [109] Phillips and Brown, above, n 106, 92.

[110] C. Hedderman and M. Hough, *Does the Criminal Justice System Treat Men and Women Differently?* (1994), 2.

as a factor in the decision whether or not to caution, but this is at odds with the principle embodied in the Code for Crown Prosecutors—which distinguishes between the interests of the victim (relevant) and the views of the victim (not determinative).[111] As noted above, the simple caution is not well adapted to ensuring the payment of compensation to the victim. However, reprimands and warnings for young offenders under the Crime and Disorder Act 1998 can include requirements to make reparation. Moreover, for adults the introduction of conditional cautions under the Criminal Justice Act 2003 will enable prosecutors to offer cautions on the condition that the offender makes reparation or pays compensation to the victim. The Code of Practice makes it clear that 'it is vital not to give the impression that the victim's views (if any) will be conclusive as to the outcome, which (it should be explained) is at the discretion of the CPS.'[112] However, it seems clear that the payment of compensation should always be considered as a possible condition. Conditional cautions may also include a restorative element, requiring the offender to participate in a restorative process in which the victim may also decide to become involved. This may be regarded as following on from the development of restorative cautioning by the Thames Valley Police: it gives the police a central role in facilitating restorative conferences, which may be held with offender and victim or (if the victim is not willing) in the victim's absence.[113] Thus the CPS now has a more prominent role in taking decisions on diversion, in relation to conditional cautions; and the role of the police in dispensing community criminal justice may be enhanced, since the police seem to be envisaged as facilitators of restorative conferences that flow from conditional cautions. There are objections of principle to the police having this role,[114] but no other group of trained facilitators is yet available.

(c) DEFENDANTS' RIGHTS

One common feature of diversion schemes is that the defendant can decline the offer made by the police or prosecution if guilt is disputed, leaving them to prosecute in court and have the matter decided there. Whilst this is sufficient to comply with the European Convention on Human Rights,[115] it none the less leaves to the defendant a choice that is not without pressure. The making of an offer of a caution before the defendant had admitted guilt of the offence constituted the unfair procedure in the *Thompson* case,[116] although it is true that some suspects may know or be advised of the possibility of a conditional caution if they admit the offence. In principle, however, the police should first decide what action is appropriate, and only then ask the defendant whether he admits the offence and is prepared to accept a caution. It still remains possible for the defendant to decline a caution, and for the police or CPS then

---

[111] Discussed in Ch. 7.5 below.   [112] Code of Practice on Conditional Cautioning, para 7.1.

[113] R. Young and C. Hoyle, 'New, Improved Police-Led Restorative Justice?', in A. von Hirsch *et al* (eds), *Restorative Justice and Criminal Justice* (2003).

[114] A. Ashworth, 'Responsibilities, Rights and Restorative Justice', (2003) 43 *BJ Crim* 578, at 591.

[115] Above, n 39.   [116] Above, p. 163.

either to drop the case or bring a prosecution. On the one hand, there is considerable temptation to accept a caution, even if one is innocent, since it avoids a court appearance. On the other hand, cautions are recorded and have various consequences. The advent of conditional cautions should mean that decisions to offer them are made in a more rigorous and considered manner, since the CPS have to apply the five requirements set out in the 2003 Act.[117] However, we have already seen plenty of examples of divergences between the rules in the books and the practices of criminal justice, and it remains to be seen whether the rights of defendants and of victims are better protected under the new arrangements.

(d) CRIME CONTROL

One of the objections frequently raised against forms of diversion is that they undermine crime prevention, simply because many offenders do not take them seriously. It is not uncommon to hear anecdotes about offenders, often young, who express themselves as if they have a 'licence to offend' because they know that nothing worse than a caution will result. As we saw earlier, this led to the introduction of a new scheme in the Crime and Disorder Act 1998 to replace cautions for young offenders—only one reprimand before a final warning, only one final warning before prosecution. It may also be one factor in the introduction of conditional cautions, which may contain various requirements to ensure that the conditional decision not to prosecute makes demands on the offender. However, it should not be forgotten that the reconviction figures for cautions have generally been more favourable than those for convictions in court, and that according to Government figures it is only after three offences that a prosecution is less likely to be followed by reconviction than a caution.[118] It is therefore important to resist the temptation to equate greater severity with greater crime control: cautions and other forms of diversion may have no less preventive efficacy, and possibly greater preventive efficacy, than the prosecution-conviction-sentence approach. Indeed, as we saw in Part 2 of this chapter, it is beliefs of this kind that make many regulatory agencies confident that their compliance-oriented approach is more effective than ready resort to the criminal courts.

6.7 CONCLUSIONS

There are good arguments in favour of the diversion of non-serious offenders from the criminal courts, but this should be done at the least possible cost to the rights of victims and of defendants. The strongest arguments in favour of diversion are that prosecution-conviction-sentence may be a disproportionate response to some less

---

[117] Discussed in Part 5 of this chapter, above.
[118] Home Office, *No More Excuses* (1997), para 5.9, referring to research by the Audit Commission.

serious forms of law breaking, and that in general the prosecution approach may be a less effective response in terms of reoffending and therefore prevention. A secondary argument—though often powerful with governments—is that diversion may hold out the prospect of saving time and money. The courts are not involved, and less preparatory work is required of the police and prosecutors. However, we have noted above that a drive towards cost-cutting and simplification may lead to neglect of the rights of victims and the rights of defendants, and it remains important to ensure that this does not occur in practice even when the formal rules are designed to safeguard rights.

What is diversion? One of the difficulties in advocating the greater use of diversion is to be clear about what it entails. If one defines diversion simply in terms of diversion from prosecution, such that a case does not go down the prosecution-conviction-sentence track, then that is clear. All the five forms of diversion set out in Part 3 of this chapter fall within this definition. But such a simple definition leaves out of account some of the other advantages claimed for diversion—less formality, fewer obligations, less engagement with the institutions of criminal justice, less stigma, less contact with more experienced offenders, and so forth. Are police cautions a form of diversion if they result in the recording of the caution, so that it is notified to the court if the offender should be prosecuted subsequently or if the offender is put forward as being of good character,[119] and so that the offender goes on to the Sex Offenders Register?[120] Are conditional cautions a form of diversion, if they impose significant obligations on the offender, and require him to engage with the police or the probation service? One response to these questions would be that we should keep to the simple definition of diversion, as a non-court measure, since that is the most important difference. However, the question might arise whether a prosecution followed by a plea of guilty and a small fine or conditional discharge does amount to an imposition that may be less onerous than, say, a conditional caution. The more restrictive and demanding the methods of diversion become, and the closer in substance to court disposals they appear, then the more important it is to ensure that the rights of defendants are properly secured.

Allied to this is the absence of a proper hierarchy of methods of diversion. It may well be that the threefold hierarchy of diversion measures for young offenders—no further action, reprimand, final warning—is insufficiently flexible. But it remains unfortunate that the arrival of the conditional caution as a method of diversion has been accompanied by the affirmation that conditional cautions should not necessarily be used for more serious offences than simple police cautions, and that a conditional caution will not be regarded as the next logical step for an offender after a simple caution. This creates an unfortunate ambiguity about the relative severity of these two dispositive measures. No doubt the reply will come that relative severity should not be the issue: suitability for the offender should be the key factor. But this is unpersuasive,

---

[119] R. May, 'The Legal Effect of a Police Caution', [1997] Crim LR 491.
[120] K. Soothill, B. Francis and B. Sanderson, 'A Cautionary Tale: the Sex Offenders Act 1997, the Police and Cautions', [1997] Crim LR 482.

for three reasons. First, there is vagueness about the circumstances in which a simple caution should be more suitable for an offender than a conditional caution, except for the fact that it is less demanding in the obligations it may impose. Secondly, the Code of Practice emphasizes that proportionality should be a feature of the obligations imposed. And thirdly, it is no answer to say that all methods of diversion depend on the offender's consent, since it is well known that in practice there is an element of coercion, sometimes in the background and sometimes (at least so far as it appears to the defendant) in the foreground, that renders this form of consent a rather impoverished species of the genus.

The ambiguity about the relative onerousness of the methods of diversion for adults, and the absence of a hierarchy, is paralleled by the rather confused role and responsibilities for diversion. Joint working between police and prosecutors may mean that many decisions to take no further action will be taken after discussion. But the Code of Practice states that the police retain the decision whether or not to divert a case to a simple caution, whereas the decision making body in respect of conditional cautions is the CPS. If joint working were a reality, then one might have thought that both sets of decisions should be taken in the same way as decisions to prosecute and decisions on the appropriate charge—by police and prosecutors working together, although in the knowledge that the CPS now have the last word. The only justification for the rather anarchic arrangements seems to be that this is one way of introducing the CPS to powers of a kind that they have not previously exercised. It has long been argued that the CPS, as a quasi-judicial element in the criminal justice system, ought to have control over diversion decisions.[121] One reply has been that the CPS lacks the experience that prosecutors in other countries have. The new arrangements for conditional cautions, running parallel to the power of the police over simple cautions, may offer an opportunity for the CPS to gain the experience that they have lacked for so long.

Apart from the role of the CPS there are the more general issues about social justice, touched on in various places above. In principle, the criminal justice system should respond consistently and proportionately to alleged offenders in a way that reflects the amount of harm foreseeably done and their culpability, and this principle should apply across the boundaries between the many different enforcement agencies. Why should there be differences in response to someone who pollutes a river, someone who defrauds the Inland Revenue, someone who fails to take proper precautions for the safety of employees, someone who steals property from another, someone who sells unsound meat, and so on? One reply is that it is impossible to compare the relative seriousness of these different offences, and hence each of them must be viewed in its separate context. That is an unsatisfactory reply, since it is possible to make some progress towards a ranking of the relative seriousness of offences,[122] and to identify rankings of offences that are clearly inappropriate. The difficulty of settling

---

[121] A. Sanders, 'The Limits of Diversion from Prosecution', (1988) 28 *BJ Crim* 513.
[122] For discussion, see A. Ashworth, *Sentencing and Criminal Justice* (3rd ed., 2000), Ch. 4.

on comprehensive criteria of offence-seriousness should not be deployed as an excuse for avoiding the broader questions of social justice that arise when relatively poor and powerless people are prosecuted whereas the better-connected are enabled to pay their way out of trouble without the stigma of a criminal conviction.[123]

One example of the case for differential treatment concerns fraud: the Royal Commission on Criminal Justice did not accept Levi's suggestion that regulatory mechanisms be used quite widely in fraud cases,[124] but it did recommend that some fraud cases and some of those handled by the Securities and Investments Board might receive different treatment:

'Where the offence is of a technical nature, there has been no specific loss or risk to any member of the public (or if there has, where restitution can be made), and the predominant issues relate to the protection of the integrity of the markets rather than to serious dishonesty as such, then it may be that regulatory action is both appropriate and sufficient'.[125]

The Commission insisted that the penalties 'must be sufficiently severe that it could not be alleged that so-called "white-collar crime" was being more leniently handled than other equivalent offences'. That recognizes the point of principle, in terms of consistent treatment, but hardly deals with it in a manner that convinces across the whole spectrum of crimes. What is necessary is a thorough review of the prosecution policies of the various regulatory agencies. At present there is virtually no accountability, and certainly no overall accountability to a single body that can oversee consistency in matters of prosecution. It is one thing to argue that the different contexts in which some agencies work make different approaches appropriate. It is quite another thing to argue that there should be no attempt at a common starting-point, and no concern with broader issues of social justice and the apparent unfairness of these differing arrangements. These fundamental issues of social justice are taken further in the next chapter, on prosecutions.

---

[123] Cf. A. Sanders, 'Class Bias in Prosecutions', (1985) 24 *Howard JCJ* 176; it is not simply a question of economic offences, however. Members of lower socio-economic groups may also be more likely to be prosecuted for 'public order' offences, whereas the higher socio-economic groups may have their private spaces in which to behave badly.

[124] M. Levi, *The Investigation, Prosecution and Trial of Serious Fraud* (1993).

[125] RCCJ, *Report*, para 7.63.

7

PROSECUTIONS

For many years the prosecution system in England and Wales has been organized differently from almost any other. The police have retained the original decision whether or not to prosecute, and the function of the CPS (since its establishment in 1986) has been largely one of prosecutorial review. This two-stage approach became characteristic of the English system: the police have retained considerable power in the initial phases, and the CPS has no right to require the police to ask particular questions or to pursue particular lines of enquiry. But in the last few years the allocation of responsibilities has begun to change. There is now more joint working between police and prosecutors from the earliest stages, and new provisions in the Criminal Justice Act 2003 ensure that the CPS will be responsible for most decisions on charging. Files will still be reviewed at a later stage, but the new statutory charging arrangements mark a significant reorientation of the English prosecution system.

This chapter begins by outlining the origins and functions of the CPS. It then moves on to a discussion of several aspects of the prosecutorial function in the criminal process, in the belief that the decision to prosecute someone is in itself a form of imposition by the State that requires justification: not only must there be sufficient evidence to warrant putting the person to the trouble of mounting a defence, but there should also be a professional system for weeding out evidentially weak cases so as to protect the innocent by removing the possibility of miscarriages of justice in such cases. Moreover, there must be good policy reasons for considering and deciding that it is in the public interest to bring the prosecution (i.e. this must be both a proportionate and an appropriate response). In the course of exploring these issues we raise questions about the standards and the performance of the CPS and other agencies in this respect. We also ask about the ethical orientation of English prosecutors: are they committed to the appropriate ethical standards, and how (if at all) is compliance with ethical principles monitored? How committed are prosecutors to ensuring that human rights are respected in their decision making? The principle of equality of treatment is discussed throughout the chapter, not least in relation to the differences of approach taken by different prosecuting agencies. Of all the offences in English criminal law, some are treated as the business of the police and others are treated as the business of various 'regulatory' agencies, as we saw in Chapter 6. It cannot be said that the former are invariably more serious than the latter. Questions therefore arise about the justifications for different treatment, at the stage of prosecution or diversion, of offences of similar gravity that are committed in different types of situation and therefore policed and prosecuted by different agencies.

7.1 THE CROWN PROSECUTION SERVICE

Whose task should it be to prosecute alleged offenders? For many centuries the victim of the alleged offence had to be the motivating force behind the decision to prosecute, largely because there was no other agency to do this. There was no organized police force and no other body appointed by central or local government to initiate or organize prosecutions. Eventually the police became more and more involved in prosecuting, and as the regular police force was formed in the early part of the nineteenth century, it became natural to expect them not only to detect and arrest suspected offenders but also to initiate their prosecution. Doubts were expressed at the time about the propriety of giving this power to the police,[1] but these were not voices in favour of the status quo. On the contrary, the task of prosecuting was a burden on victims, and even where there were prosecution associations at work the result would still be inconsistencies of practice and inefficiencies in criminal justice. There were some arguments in favour of an independent prosecuting service, for the constitutional reason that it was inappropriate to bestow this task on a group (the police) whose principal tasks were keeping order and investigating alleged crimes.[2] Those arguments did not prevail, and the police appear to have taken over prosecutions almost by default. However, there was little doubt about the propriety of charging a public body with this task rather than leaving it to victims, whether individually or in association with one another: as part of its role in protecting people from crime, the State should make arrangements for the prosecution of those whose (alleged) conduct is judged to warrant that response.

Prosecution arrangements in England and Wales were altered in the mid-1980s. Until then there were three principal prosecuting agencies. The police, as just mentioned, had brought most prosecutions since the mid-nineteenth century. By the early 1980s, many police forces had developed or begun to develop a prosecuting solicitors' department, but it was still the police who took most of the decisions since the prosecuting solicitors were in their employ. Secondly, the Director of Public Prosecutions had a small department in London, dealing with all murder prosecutions, and with a spread of other cases concerned with such matters as national security, public figures, and alleged offences by police officers. And thirdly, there were the various agencies such as the Inland Revenue, the Post Office, the Health and Safety Commission (including the Factory Inspectorate), the Pollution Inspectorate, local authorities

---

[1] See G. Dingwall and C. Harding, *Diversion in the Criminal Process* (1998), Ch. 2, for a brief history and further references.

[2] *Ibid.*, 32.

(including, for example, their environmental health officers), and so forth. These so-called 'regulatory agencies' (already mentioned in Chapter 6 in the context of law enforcement) mostly had their own prosecutors.

Arguments in favour of changing the system were heard at various times, but perhaps the most influential event was the publication in 1970 of a report by the British section of the International Commission of Jurists.[3] This report drew upon arguments of principle (that it was wrong for the police, who investigated crimes, to take decisions in relation to prosecution, which require impartiality and independence) and also more pragmatic arguments (that the police were experts at investigation, and it would be a better use of their time to focus on this rather than to undertake all these prosecutorial duties). This report was constantly referred to in the 1970s, but it took a spectacular miscarriage of justice to provide the impetus for reform. The report on the *Confait* case, published in 1977, made criticisms of several aspects of the criminal justice system, and proposed that changes in the prosecution system should be considered.[4] The arguments for and against change were then considered by the Royal Commission on Criminal Procedure. There was much discussion of the Scottish system, in which each area has a procurator-fiscal who directs the police in the investigation of crime, who interviews suspects and witnesses, and who has several powers similar to those of a continental examining judge.[5] On the other side there were vigorous arguments from the police that they should retain control over prosecutions, using their experience and local knowledge.

The Royal Commission reported in 1981 in favour of the establishment of an independent public prosecutor system, but one with far fewer powers than its Scottish counterpart. After debates about whether the system should be locally accountable or national,[6] the Crown Prosecution Service (CPS) was created by the Prosecution of Offences Act 1985. The Act created a national Crown Prosecution Service, headed by the Director of Public Prosecutions and formally accountable to the Attorney-General. The CPS has a duty to take over all prosecutions instituted by the police (except for certain minor offences), and has a power to take over other prosecutions. The CPS was therefore accorded a status independent of the police. Section 10 of the Prosecution of Offences Act 1985 lays upon it the duty to publish a Code for Crown Prosecutors and to report annually to Parliament on its work and the use of its powers. Notable among these is its power to discontinue prosecutions in the magistrates' courts.[7] Unlike public prosecutors in many other jurisdictions, it was not given powers to institute proceedings itself, to direct the police to investigate any matter, or to put questions to any person. However, as we will see, new arrangements for joint working between police and the CPS are claimed to be breaking down the division of

[3] JUSTICE, 'The Prosecution Process in England and Wales', [1970] Crim LR 668.
[4] *Report of an Inquiry by the Hon. Sir Henry Fisher into the circumstances leading to the trial of three persons on charges arising out of the death of Maxwell Confait and the fire at 27 Doggett Road, London SE6* (1977).
[5] Royal Commission on Criminal Procedure, *Report* (1981), Ch.7.
[6] See the White Paper, *An Independent Prosecution Service for England and Wales* (1983).
[7] Prosecution of Offences Act 1985, s. 23.

functions and enabling prosecutors to advise the police on lines of questioning and other evidential needs.[8]

The CPS has carried out its statutory obligation to publish its *Code for Crown Prosecutors*, and has revised it four times since. The Code was first published in 1986, with subsequent editions in 1992, 1994, 2000, and 2004. The revision in 1994 was intended to ensure that the Code was phrased in plain English suitable for lay persons to read, as well as making some changes of substance which will be referred to below. The changes made in the 2000 version were relatively minor. In the last few years there has been a welcome step towards openness, with the publication on the CPS website of considerable amounts of prosecutorial guidance previously confidential to crown prosecutors.[9] Much of what appeared in the five Prosecution Manuals in former years is now available, most notably lists of factors relevant to decisions whether or not to prosecute for specific offences. This increases transparency, and should enable greater public understanding as well as affording possible grounds for challenge where it appears that the guidance has not been followed. Integrated into this guidance are the various sets of 'Charging Standards', established jointly by CPS lawyers and the police in the late 1990s with a view to assisting the police in setting the charge at the right level initially and ensuring that the CPS has a common starting point when reviewing case files. It is fair to say that when the three sets of Charging Standards—on offences against the person (now revised), on motoring offences, and on public order offences—were first issued the reaction was mixed. Some regarded them as part of a cost-cutting exercise rather than as a mere attempt to foster greater consistency: thus it was argued that the borderline between the summary offence of common assault and the indictable offence of assault occasioning actual bodily harm has been set in a way that is legally debatable and is designed to ensure that as many cases as possible remain in the magistrates' courts. Certainly the legal definition of assault occasioning actual bodily harm would encompass some of the harms now stated to fall into common assault for prosecution purposes.[10] It should be added that the movement towards greater transparency in matters of policy has resulted in a wide range of other guidance documents being placed on the CPS website, dealing with such matters as consents to prosecution, international cooperation, domestic violence, the reinstitution of proceedings, evidential considerations, case preparation, witnesses, disclosure, and many others. This is much to be welcomed, and reference to the guidance is made at appropriate points below.

The crucial question, however, is whether the guidance is faithfully applied. Research findings on this are discussed as appropriate throughout the chapter. However, there have been significant changes in the organization and working of the CPS in recent years. When the Labour Government came to power in 1997, one of its

---

[8] For the early history of the CPS, see Lord Windlesham, *Responses to Crime: Volume 4* (2001), Ch. 4.

[9] See the second edition of this work, at 179.

[10] See F.G. Davies, 'CPS Charging Standards: a Cynic's View' (1995) 159 JP 203, and 'Ten Years of the Crown Prosecution Service: the Verdict' (1997) 161 *JP* 207.

earliest initiatives was to set up a review of the CPS, chaired by Sir Iain (formerly Lord Justice) Glidewell. The emphasis of that review turned out to be largely managerial, and there was a disappointing reluctance to discuss major issues of policy on prosecutions.[11] The significant changes in working practices that have resulted include the introduction of many CPS caseworkers, not legally qualified, to deal not only with the preparation of cases but also with the presentation of 'straightforward' guilty plea cases in magistrates' courts. The range of their potential duties was increased in April 2004 to include appearing at early administrative hearings and at hearings after a guilty plea where the court had ordered a pre-sentence report. These changes were said to form part of the 'modernization' of the CPS,[12] but they also mean that many roles that were originally intended to be fulfilled by qualified lawyers are now being carried out by (trained) laypeople.

This could be defended as part of a strategy to deploy CPS lawyers for more important tasks. In 2001 the Auld Review called for major changes in the powers and duties of the CPS:

'The prosecutor should take control of cases at the charge or, where appropriate, pre-charge, stage, fix on the right charges from the start and keep to them, assume a more direct role than at present on disclosure and develop a more proactive role in shaping the case for trial, communicating appropriately and promptly with all those concerned. For all this the Service needs greater legal powers, in particular the power to determine the initial charge, and considerably more resources, in particular trained staff and information technology, than it has had in the first fifteen years of its life and than presently proposed. The Government has recently committed itself to provide a "better resourced, better performing Crown Prosecution Service, more effective in prosecuting crime and progressing good quality cases for court."[13] These are fine words, but are reminiscent of previous expressions of intent that were not implemented.'[14]

After directing those strong words at the Government, Lord Justice Auld went on to recommend that the CPS 'should determine the charge in all but minor, routine offences or where, because of the circumstances, there is a need for a holding charge before seeking the advice of the Service.'[15] The relevant law was changed accordingly by ss 28, 29 and 30 of the Criminal Justice Act 2003, in combination with Schedule 2. Section 29 provides that 'a public prosecutor may institute criminal proceedings against a person . . .', save for those cases excluded by Schedule 2 (for which the Director of Public Prosecutions has the power to give guidance). It seems likely that decisions in the more difficult cases will be reserved for the CPS, and that decisions in many lesser offences of which the police have ample experience (public order, road traffic) will be left with the police under the old procedure. It remains to be seen

---

[11] Glidewell, *The Review of the Crown Prosecution Service: a Report* (1998), reviewed at [1998] Crim LR 517.

[12] 'Extended Role for CPS Caseworkers', press release of 29 April 2004, www.cps.gov.uk

[13] Home Office, *Criminal Justice: the Way Ahead* (2001), para 3.13 [footnote in original].

[14] Auld L.J., *Review of the Criminal Courts of England and Wales* (2001), 399.

[15] *Ibid.*, 412.

exactly what guidance the Director gives to custody officers on the offences that must be referred to the CPS for charging. For the last few years there has been more joint working between the CPS and the police, in an effort to ensure that charges are drawn up properly at the outset rather than brought by the police and subsequently altered on review by the CPS.

Thus the Criminal Justice Act 2003 now provides for what is known as the 'statutory charging scheme', whereby the CPS will take all charging decisions at the outset in respect of most offences other than a few excluded and relatively minor offences.

'The specific aims of the new charging arrangements may be summarised as follows: the elimination at the earliest opportunity of hopeless cases, the production of more robust prosecution cases, the elimination of unnecessary or unwarranted delays in the period between charge and disposal, and the reduction of the number of trials that "crack" through the offering and acceptance of guilty pleas to reduced charges at a late stage in the process.'[16]

There are some grounds for believing that, given a fair wind, some or all of these objectives can be met. An evaluation of the pilot project found that conviction rates increased and discontinuance rates declined in many pilot areas, without significant detrimental effects in other quarters.[17] However, the success of the new arrangements will inevitably turn on the commitment of the police and the CPS to implement the full spirit of the new division of responsibilities. To put the matter bluntly, the police have lost some of their power and the division of responsibilities established by the 1981 Royal Commission and the Prosecution of Offences Act 1985 has been dismantled. Although the reasons for the change are obvious, the police may need to change their outlook and the CPS may need to satisfy them of their competence to reach sound charging decisions.[18]

7.2 EVIDENTIAL SUFFICIENCY

It is wrong for a person to be prosecuted if the evidence is insufficient. The essence of the wrongness lies in the protection of the innocent: if this principle is taken seriously, it should mean not merely that innocent people are not convicted, but also that innocent people should not be prosecuted. That is important for two reasons: first, as a method of ensuring that innocent people are not subsequently convicted, by weeding out weak cases at an early stage; and secondly, because being prosecuted is a considerable inconvenience (as expressed in the dictum that 'the process is the punishment'),[19] often a source of profound worry, and sometimes a considerable expense,

---

[16] I. Brownlee, 'The Statutory Charging Scheme in England and Wales: Towards a Unified Prosecution System?' [2004] Crim LR 896, at 897.

[17] Crown Prosecution Service, *Annual Report 2003–2004*, 6, 12, drawing upon *Charging Suspects: Early Involvement by the CPS* available at www.cps.gov.uk

[18] Cf. Brownlee, above n 16, 906.   [19] M. Feeley, *The Process is the Punishment* (1979), Ch. 1.

and it may also lead to an element of stigma and loss of social esteem. The homely phrase, 'no smoke without fire,' might well be applied. There are therefore sound moral reasons for not prosecuting someone against whom the evidence is insufficient. There are also good economic reasons: it is a waste of police time in compiling a full file on the case, of prosecution time in reviewing the case, and of court time in dealing with the case. It is therefore desirable in general that weak cases should be eliminated as early as possible: it was for this purpose that the Royal Commission on Criminal Procedure recommended the introduction of a public prosecution service to provide independent review, and that the Auld Review recommended the extension of CPS powers to the initial laying of the charge.

There are at least three major issues to be discussed before the principle of evidential sufficiency can be translated into practice. One is the test of sufficiency—what should it be? Closely intertwined with this is the second question—should the test vary according to the stage the case has reached? And third, how can prosecutors, at the stage of prosecutorial review, be expected to assess cases on the basis of a written file? In discussing these issues, it must constantly be borne in mind that evidential sufficiency is only one of the factors relevant in prosecutions. Another is the lawfulness of the prosecution in procedural terms—have the appropriate formalities been completed? Have the time-limits been observed? Has there been a previous prosecution arising out of the incident, so as to raise considerations of double jeopardy? A further factor is the policy of diversion, discussed in the previous chapter in the context of the cautioning of offenders. Thus, even if a case satisfies the test of evidential sufficiency, there may be strong reasons of public policy or, as it is termed in England and Wales, 'public interest' in favour of dealing with the case by means other than prosecution. In practice, questions of evidential sufficiency and public interest often interact, but for clarity of exposition this part of the chapter is devoted chiefly to evidential sufficiency, and the issue of 'public interest' is left over until the following part.

(a) FORMULATING THE TEST OF EVIDENTIAL SUFFICIENCY

Until the early 1980s the test that the police were said to apply in deciding whether the evidence was strong enough for prosecution was the 'prima facie test': is there 'evidence on the basis of which, if it were accepted, a reasonable jury or magistrates' court would be justified in convicting'?[20] This often seemed to mean that as long as there was some evidence on the main points that need to be proved the defendant ought to be brought to court to answer the charge.[21] The weakness of the test was that it made no explicit reference to the strength and credibility of the evidence, nor to probable lines of defence. In his submission to the 1981 Royal Commission on Criminal Procedure, the then Director of Public Prosecutions denounced this test as inadequate: it

---

[20] RCCP, *Report*, para 8.8.
[21] Provided, of course, that the 'public interest' test was also satisfied: see below.

was wrong, he argued, that a person could be prosecuted when an acquittal was more likely than a conviction, and the minimum standard should require that conviction is more probable than acquittal.[22] The Director's approach was commended by the Royal Commission on the basis that a lower standard would be 'both unfair to the accused and a waste of the restricted resources of the criminal justice system'.[23] When the CPS came into existence, the first edition of the Code for Crown Prosecutors in 1986 required a 'realistic prospect of conviction', a test that remains unchanged today.

Paragraph 5.2 of the 2004 *Code for Crown Prosecutors* requires crown prosecutors to take account of 'what the defence case may be and how that is likely to affect the prosecution case', and to consider 'whether the evidence can be used and is reliable'. The admissibility of evidence is a matter of legal judgment: paragraph 5.4a suggests that decisions to prosecute should not be based on evidence that is likely to be excluded by the court, such as unfairly obtained evidence or some hearsay. If there is doubt about whether the evidence would be included, the CPS should obtain a ruling in court.[24] The reliability of evidence is said to turn on such matters as 'the defendant's age, intelligence or lack of understanding' (where a confession is relied upon), the background of prosecution witnesses (in terms of dubious motives or relevant previous convictions), and the strength of any identification evidence.

What is the legal basis for the 'realistic prospects' test, and what are its theoretical justifications? It is clearly predictive in nature: it requires the prosecutor to assess whether, on the evidence likely to be given at the trial, a conviction is more probable than an acquittal. This includes matters such as the admissibility of the evidence and the likely defence. Paragraph 5.3 of the Code states that 'a realistic prospect of conviction is an objective test'. There are two different ways in which this might be interpreted. One is a straight predictive approach: the crown prosecutor's task would be to predict how the court in which the case would be tried would react to the evidence. This might require the prosecutor to take account of the different conviction rates of magistrates' courts and the Crown Court, and of any local trends in willingness or unwillingness to convict in certain types of case. An alternative would be an 'intrinsic merits' approach, according to which the task of the prosecutor would be to judge the strength of evidence and to apply the law to it faithfully. On this approach, prosecutors would exercise the function of keeping cases away from the lay tribunal when they judge that the evidence is insufficient, even though they think that the tribunal might well convict, and correspondingly prosecutors would persevere with a case when they believe that the evidence is sufficient, even though they recognize that the local court is unlikely to convict. Thus on the predictive view the disposition of the local courts sets the standard, whereas on the 'intrinsic merits' view it is a legal standard applied by various prosecutors to case files that determines decisions.

Those who believe in the supreme importance of lay adjudications would favour

---

[22] RCCP, Vol.ii, *The Law and the Procedure* (1981), Appendix 25.
[23] RCCP, *Report*, para 8.9.   [24] CPS, *Explanatory Memorandum* (1996), para 4.20.

the predictive view. Magistrates and juries should be the central figures, and prosecutors should merely attempt to anticipate their decisions rather than to neutralize or even by-pass them. On the other hand, fidelity to law would favour the 'intrinsic merits' approach, since one might doubt whether there could be sufficient reason why a local bench or justices' clerk, or the juries of a particular neighbourhood, should be allowed to distort or disregard the law of the country as a whole. Thus the American Bar Association has stated that: 'In cases which involve a serious threat to the community, the prosecutor should not be deterred from prosecution by the fact that in his jurisdiction juries have tended to acquit persons accused of the particular kind of criminal act in question.'[25] This is also the view now set out in paragraph 5.3 of the Code: a 'realistic prospect of conviction' means that 'a jury or bench of magistrates, properly directed in accordance with the law, is more likely than not to convict the defendant of the charge alleged'. In the Explanatory Memorandum of 1996 a straight predictive view was rejected explicitly:

'Crown Prosecutors should not take into account any perceived local views of the bench or juries when considering whether there is a realistic prospect of conviction. The reason for this is simple: if local considerations of this nature were allowed to influence the decision to prosecute, the goal of consistent decision-making would be lost.'[26]

The Explanatory Memorandum went on to set out some of the points to be taken into account when making these judgments. It also included the extraordinary assertion that 'the quality of justice does not vary from courtroom to courtroom or between tiers of court'.[27] There is considerable evidence that it does, and that many crown prosecutors believe that it does.[28] In particular, it is widely believed to differ between magistrates' courts and the Crown Court, in which the acquittal rates are certainly different. The Memorandum would have been on firmer ground in saying that the quality of justice dispensed by the two levels of court ought not to differ.

The CPS is right to opt for the 'intrinsic merits' approach, demanding as it is on prosecutors' judgments, since it aspires to advance the purpose of the law rather than deferring to the reaction of the (local) courts. Even on this approach, prosecutors will need to assess the credibility of witnesses, and it remains true that prosecutors are handicapped because they have no direct opportunity to assess the witnesses. However, one aspect of the new system is that prosecutors will be involved in the original decision to charge and may hear more from the police about the credibility of witnesses etc (even though they will not be present at interviews).[29] They will still be heavily reliant on the police for information and assessments of the statements and

---

[25] ABA, *Standards Relating to the Prosecution Function* (1980), 3–3.9.
[26] CPS, *Explanatory Memorandum*, para 4.10.   [27] *Ibid.*, para 4.13.
[28] A. Hoyano *et al*, 'A Study of the Impact of the Revised Code for Crown Prosecutors' [1997] Crim LR 556, at 563.
[29] In 2003, following the Damilola Taylor case, the CPS issued *Pre-trial Witness Interviews by Prosecutors— a Consultation Paper* (available at www.cps.gov.uk) in which they asked for views about whether and at what stage prosecutors might be allowed to interview witnesses 'to assess the reliability of the evidence the witness can provide' (para 17). It is not clear what the outcome of this consultation was.

the evidence; they will be directly susceptible to persuasion by the police officers with whom they are 'collocated'; but in principle, and until we have research evidence on the matter, the prosecutor's new-found involvement in charging may more frequently enable accurate charges to be laid in the first place.

However, it is one thing for the CPS to proclaim an 'intrinsic merits' approach,[30] and another thing entirely for this to be the normal practice. After all, if prosecutors are criticized by judges for taking decisions which they believe to be legally correct but which a judge believes to be wrong, there will be a temptation to shift ground. Thus the John Report on possible racial bias in CPS decision making found that prosecutors' 'reluctance to bring [racially aggravated] charges or decisions to accept pleas to lesser offences are often the result of prosecutors' experience or perception of how certain judges/tribunals treat racially aggravated offences.'[31]

(b) EVIDENTIAL SUFFICIENCY AND THE STAGES OF THE CRIMINAL PROCESS

The Code for Crown Prosecutors formerly stated a single test of evidential sufficiency: whether there is a 'realistic prospect of conviction'. As argued in previous editions of this book, that test is not suitable for practical application at all stages of the criminal process.[32] For example, at the end of questioning the police may believe that they have sufficient evidence to justify remanding a defendant in custody before first appearance at court, and the CPS may take the same view at that stage; but it may not be possible to say that there is a realistic prospect of a conviction. Similarly, in many cases the prosecutor receives a file for the first time just before remand proceedings are due to begin. This may be the morning after the defendant's arrest. The prosecutor will have had no time to listen to any interview tapes, and so it is likely that the police summary will dominate. Both the police and the crown prosecutor may believe that they have (or will have) sufficient evidence to justify the charge, but they may still have witnesses to interview and forensic reports to receive. In strict terms, there may not yet be a realistic prospect of conviction. Can a remand in custody be justified in these circumstances? Even one week's loss of liberty—often spent in an overcrowded prison, with poor facilities, away from family, friends, and employment (if any), and without unrestricted access to legal advice—is a serious deprivation. As we shall see in Chapter 8, the Bail Act 1976 directs a magistrates' court to have regard to the strength of the evidence; but, again, this is usually taken on trust from the CPS, who in turn may take it on trust from the police.

The CPS has now taken the general point, and the 2004 version of the Code distinguishes between the Full Code Test, applicable in normal situations, and the Threshold Test, applicable in cases where 'it would not be appropriate to release a

---

[30] In fact the Code does not in all respects conform to this approach: at least two considerations are predictive—see n 44 below.

[31] Gus John Partnership, *Race for Justice* (2003), 27.   [32] See the second edition of this work, p. 184.

suspect on bail after charge, but the evidence to apply the Full Code Test is not yet available.' The new guidance is based on Article 5(1)(c) of the Convention, which states that no one shall be deprived of their liberty except on reasonable suspicion of having committed an offence. According to paragraph 6.4 of the 2004 Code, the prosecutor should consider whether there is 'at least a reasonable suspicion that the suspect has committed an offence' by reference to:[33]

  (a) the evidence available at the time;

  (b) the likelihood and nature of further evidence being obtained;

  (c) the reasonableness for believing that evidence will become available;

  (d) the time it will take to gather the evidence and the steps being taken to do so;

  (e) the impact the expected evidence will have on the case;

  (f) the charges that the evidence will support.

Recognition of the need for this threshold test is a significant step, but it should not be thought that the 'reasonable suspicion' standard is a particularly robust one: although it has occasionally led to findings in Strasbourg that an arrest was unjustified,[34] considerable latitude seems to be left to state authorities on the matter.[35] Moreover, 'reasonable suspicion' has long been the test used by the police when deciding whether to arrest a person, but the study by Phillips and Brown found that in only 61 per cent of cases did the arresting officer believe that there was enough evidence to charge the suspect,[36] and that some 20 per cent of all arrests ended in no further action being taken (including 10 per cent of those where the officer believed that there was enough evidence to charge).[37] The CPS might argue that their legally-informed conception of 'reasonable suspicion' might be more robust than that employed by many police officers, but that would be to ignore the other pressures to keep certain suspects in the system.

  Paragraph 6.6 recognizes these concerns:

'A decision to charge and withhold bail must be kept under review. The evidence gathered must be regularly assessed to ensure the charge is still appropriate and that continued objection to bail is justified. The Full Code Test must be applied as soon as reasonably practicable.'

The wording here ought to be stronger. The defendant's right to liberty under Article 5 should only be withheld temporarily on these grounds, and it would be better to see open recognition of the principle of urgency and of the importance of ensuring that a

---

[33] Addendum Issued by the Director of Public Prosecutions: application of the *Code for Crown Prosecutors* to charging decisions where suspects are to be detained in custody after charge: the Threshold Test, 21 May 2004, www.cps.gov.uk

[34] In *Fox, Campbell and Hartley v United Kingdom* (1990) 13 EHRR 157.

[35] See *O'Hara v United Kingdom* [2002] Crim LR 493 and commentary.

[36] C. Phillips and D. Brown, *Entry into the Criminal Justice System* (1998), 45.

[37] *Ibid.*, 90–91.

suspect should not be kept in custody any longer than absolutely necessary under the Threshold Test.

7.3 THE PUBLIC INTEREST

The discussion of regulatory agencies in Part 2 of Chapter 6 has already demonstrated that there are different conceptions of the public interest at work across the broad sphere of law enforcement. Many of the regulatory agencies regard their primary role as one of securing compliance with the standards laid down by law. They are often willing to take time to achieve this, and many agencies adopt an approach that may be termed accommodative or conciliatory—using persuasion, education, and negotiation as the principal methods, and leaving the power to prosecute as a background threat which is rarely invoked. There is evidence that some regulatory agencies are becoming more punitive in recent years,[38] but the prevailing orientation is still towards persuasion and negotiation.

The position of the CPS has been rather less constant. The 1986 and 1992 editions of the *Code for Crown Prosecutors* were phrased so as to suggest that a prosecution should only be brought if 'the public interest requires' it, a formulation which suggested that there should be a presumption in favour of diversion from prosecution, and that a good reason was needed for prosecuting. It is not clear whether this emphasis was intended, or indeed whether it was thus interpreted in practice. However, in the 1994 version of the Code there was a distinct shift in the language, reflecting the then Home Secretary's determination to reduce the frequency of cautioning,[39] and this was repeated in the 2000 edition.[40] However, the advent of conditional cautioning has led to a further change, since the CPS is now in the business of considering and giving effect to diversion (as we saw in Chapter 6 above). Thus paragraph 5.7 of the 2004 Code states:

'Although there may be public interest factors against prosecution in a particular case, often the prosecution should go ahead and those factors should be put to the court for consideration when sentence is being passed. A prosecution will usually take place unless there are clear public interest factors tending against prosecution which clearly outweigh those tending in favour, or it appears more appropriate in all the circumstances of the case to divert the person from prosecution.'

This is a rather inelegant combination of the previous Code's pro-prosecution stance and the CPS's new responsibilities for diversion. Thus paragraph 8.4 goes on to recognize that a conditional caution may be appropriate if 'the interests of the suspect,

---

[38] R. Baldwin, 'The New Punitive Regulation', (2004) 67 *MLR* 351.
[39] A. Ashworth and J. Fionda, 'The New Code for Crown Prosecutors: Prosecution, Accountability and the Public Interest', [1994] Crim LR 894; cf. R. Daw, 'A Response', [1994] Crim LR 904.
[40] *Code for Crown Prosecutors* (2000), para 6.2.

victim and community may be better served by the suspect complying with suitable conditions aimed at rehabilitation and reparation.' There is clearly a tension inherent in paragraph 5.7 that will need to be worked out in practice, depending on the extent to which the CPS do in fact use conditional cautions for people who would otherwise have been prosecuted.[41]

The 2004 version of the Code follows its predecessors in setting out lists of common factors for and against prosecution. Among the factors in favour of prosecution (paragraph 5.9) are the fact that the victim was vulnerable, or the offence was motivated by any form of discrimination, or the defendant has relevant previous convictions or cautions, or the defendant was a ringleader or organizer of the offence, and so on. Many of these are well known as factors which militate in aggravation of sentence.[42] Similarly many of the 'common public interest factors against prosecution' listed in para 5.10 are circumstances which might otherwise mitigate sentence. Some of these are factors personal to the offender which make it likely that prosecution and conviction will have a disproportionately severe effect: old age, mental or physical ill health, mental disorder, and cases where there is evidence that the strain of criminal proceedings may lead to a considerable worsening of the accused's mental health. The justification for tipping the scales against prosecution in these cases is presumably some notion of equity or mercy, in the sense that it would be unfair to continue with a prosecution if that would have an impact on the particular offender far greater than is warranted by the offence.[43]

What justifications may be suggested for the other 'public interest factors against prosecution'? Several of them seem to be related to the notion of proportionality, since they refer to types of case in which prosecution and sentence might be an inappropriately severe response to the offence committed. Where the offence is so minor that a court is only likely to impose 'a nominal penalty', prosecution might not be 'in the public interest'. This refers to cases where a discharge or low value fine seems likely: the wording of the Code indicates that this involves a predictive judgment about the courts' sentencing practice,[44] although in line with the 'intrinsic merits' approach to evidential sufficiency it ought to be a principled judgment, not a predictive one. The cases envisaged are ones in which the harmfulness of the conduct was relatively low, or where the offender's culpability was low, including cases of 'genuine mistake or misunderstanding' or minor harm 'caused by a misjudgment', and some cases where the offender is elderly or suffering from mental illness. These, then, are cases lying towards the foot of any scale of offence-seriousness. The argument is that many of them do not warrant the bringing of formal proceedings, and might be dealt with more appropriately by an informal warning, or no action at all,

---

[41] The phenomenon of 'net-widening' was discussed at p. 155 above.

[42] See A. Ashworth, *Sentencing and Criminal Justice* (3rd ed., 2000), Ch. 5.

[43] For discussion of this principle in sentencing, see *ibid.* 151–155 and 208–211.

[44] CPS, *Explanatory Memorandum*, para 4.37. Both here and in the first factor in favour of prosecution in para 5.9a of the Code ('a conviction is likely to result in a significant sentence'), the language of the Code is based on prediction rather than on the 'intrinsic merits.'

and perhaps not even a police caution or conditional caution. The theory of desert or proportionality,[45] combined with the established finding that the process of being prosecuted may itself involve inconvenience, anxiety, or pain,[46] supports the prop-osition that a line should be drawn beneath which prosecution as a response is disproportionate and heavy-handed.

One evident difficulty in a system in which the CPS is expected to take account of public interest factors for and against continuing with a prosecution is that there is likely to be more available information about many pro-prosecution factors (which tend to arise from the nature of the offence, or the defendant's previous record) than about many anti-prosecution factors (which tend to be personal or social factors). This is not always so, because the relative non-seriousness of the offence is often a powerful factor in favour of diversion. But it is true that anti-prosecution factors may not be routinely gathered. Some may come to light where a suspect is released on police bail and enquiries are made; in others, the CPS might have to initiate those enquiries if they are considering a conditional caution, or if the question arises at the stage of reviewing charges already laid. In the early 1990s an attempt to remedy this information deficit was made in the Public Interest Case Assessment schemes, intro-duced in four areas and staffed by probation officers. Cases in which there might be personal or other circumstances that might justify the discontinuance of a prosecu-tion on 'public interest' grounds were selected for further enquiries. An evaluation of the scheme by a Home Office Research Unit team showed that it was generally successful in targeting cases where such information might be uncovered, that the CPS felt that the extra information was helpful, and that discontinuance rates for cases where PICA reports were prepared were double those in other cases.[47] The research also estimated that savings to the criminal justice system amounted to only about one-fifth of the costs of the scheme, because of the Probation Service resources needed to staff it. However, one aspect of the PICA schemes was that there was evidence of a general rise in discontinuances at the time,[48] suggesting perhaps that the schemes may have brought to the attention of prosecutors (even those outside the schemes) a factor that many of them were not accustomed to considering deeply.

7.4 CPS POLICIES AND THEIR IMPLEMENTATION

Parts 2 and 3 of this chapter have concentrated on the Code for Crown Prosecutors, as the basic CPS policy document. However, a visit to the CPS website reveals that the

---

[45] See A. von Hirsch and A. Ashworth (eds), *Principled Sentencing* (2nd ed., 1998), Ch. 4.
[46] RCCP, *Report*, para 8.7; M. McConville and J. Baldwin, *Prosecution, Courts and Conviction* (1981).
[47] D. Crisp, C. Whittaker and J. Harris, *Public Interest Case Assessment Schemes* (1995).
[48] *Ibid.*, 28.

service has now promulgated a large amount of guidance relating to specific issues in prosecuting.[49] Among the detailed documents are those relating to domestic violence, sexual offences, racially and religiously aggravated offences, mentally disordered offenders, and youth offenders and child witnesses. There are also fact-sheets summarizing CPS policy on such matters as prosecuting for manslaughter, driving offences involving a fatality, and sexual offences. The CPS 'Instructions for Prosecuting Advocates' runs to over 100 pages and cover a wide range of procedural and substantive issues. In this part of the chapter we examine some of the principal CPS policies in the light of evidence about their implementation.

(a) PROSECUTING CASES OF DOMESTIC VIOLENCE

The investigation and prosecution of domestic violence has become a major area of re-assessment in recent years.[50] Several studies have drawn attention to the high rate of attrition of these offences, and the concern that a complainant's withdrawal of the original statement may be due to pressure or threats from the abuser which make it inappropriate to drop the case.[51] The CPS Policy on Domestic Violence (2003 version) emphasizes that prosecutors should not assume that calling the victim as a witness is the only way of proving a case; that the seriousness of the violence, or a history of such incidents, should mean that the public interest in prosecuting outweighs 'the victim's wishes'; that a prosecutor experienced in domestic violence should supervise the case; and so on.

In 2004 the CPS Inspectorate published the report of a joint thematic inspection with the Inspectorate of Constabulary, *Violence at Home*, which assesses the response of the police and the CPS to incidents of domestic violence.[52] Once again, the attrition rate was spectacular, despite all the initiatives to 'narrow the justice gap' by bringing a higher proportion of defendants to court:

- 463 incidents reported
- 260 potential crime reports
- 118 crimes recorded
- 71 arrests made
- 25 case files to CPS
- 13 (estimated) convictions.[53]

---

[49] www.cps.gov.uk

[50] See C. Hoyle, *Negotiating Domestic Violence* (1998).

[51] A similar phenomenon is also to be found in reported rape cases where victim and perpetrator had previously been in an intimate relationship, and where intimidation or economic dependence appear to be the reasons for victim withdrawal: S. Lea, U. Lanvers and S. Shaw, 'Attrition in Rape Cases', (2003) 43 *BJCrim* 583, at 596.

[52] HMCPSI, *Violence at Home: A Joint Thematic Inspection of the Investigation and Prosecution of Cases Involving Domestic Violence* (2004).

[53] *Ibid.* 77.

The study also examined 418 case files that did reach the CPS. Over a quarter (118) were discontinued, and some 59 were given a bind-over. Of the 238 prosecuted there were 210 convictions, the vast majority (186) stemming from guilty pleas. However, it is important to recall that this CPS sample represents only a small proportion of the cases processed by the police, as the above attrition table demonstrates.[54]

The Inspectorate report comments on the failure to recognize and hence to give special attention to a number of domestic violence cases (37 per cent originally, and 11 per cent ultimately). There were some cases where 'prosecutors proceeded with the case as it was strongly in the public interest to do so, but there was weak evidence', which may show enthusiasm for taking action combined with a failure to apply the policy properly. A case with weak evidence should not even reach the public interest stage, since it should fail the test of evidential sufficiency.[55] In some 44 per cent of the cases coming to the CPS the victim sought to withdraw the complaint.[56] The Inspectorate found shortcomings in information from the police about the reasons for and circumstances of withdrawals.[57] However, in nearly 40 per cent of the withdrawal cases there was no record of the CPS considering all the alternative ways of proceeding, as the Guidance requires.[58] Similarly, in over 40 per cent of cases in which the case had been discontinued there was no record of the CPS having taken all the steps required by the Guidance.[59] The Inspectorate's report contains several other comments and recommendations, but the recurrent theme is the CPS failure to record that the guidance has been followed—which may amount simply to poor record-keeping, or may be evidence of badly structured decision making. We will return to these themes below.

(b) PROSECUTING RACIALLY AGGRAVATED OFFENCES

Sections 29–32 of the Crime and Disorder Act 1998 introduced a number of racially aggravated versions of existing offences, with higher maximum penalties. At the time of their introduction concern was expressed that there would be few convictions of these offences because the CPS would accept a guilty plea to the ordinary (non-aggravated) version of the offence. The CPS soon asserted its intention not to do this, and the 2003 document, Guidance on Prosecuting Cases of Racial and Religious Crime, states in bold type that 'it is CPS policy not to accept pleas to lesser offences, or omit or minimise admissible evidence of racial or religious aggravation for the sake of

[54] Cf. Hoyle (above, n 50), who records (46) that some 27 per cent of the 224 men arrested following an incident of domestic violence were prosecuted.

[55] HMCPSI Report, above, n 52, 85.   [56] *Ibid.*, 86.

[57] This was a weakness highlighted by the previous CPS Inspectorate Thematic Report 2/98, *Cases involving Domestic Violence* (1998), 19–20.

[58] HMCPSI Report (above, n 41), 90; the 1998 Report (previous note), 22–29, found that many of those involved in CPS decision-making were unaware of the proper approach in these circumstances.

[59] *Ibid.*, 95.

expediency.'[60] Apart from that, the Guidance document emphasizes the social importance of enforcing the legislation. The Inspectorate's thematic report on these cases emphasized the need to flag racially aggravated offences for special scrutiny, and to train specialist prosecutors who could supervise the processing of these cases.[61]

The empirical evidence shows how these ideals might come to be compromised in practice. Burney and Rose studied the operation of racially aggravated offences, and their report demonstrates the relatively high level of discontinuance for these offences—over 40 per cent in 1999. CPS data cited insufficiency of evidence as the reason for 41 per cent of terminations, and witness refusal or non-appearance as the reason for 35 per cent.[62] Their conclusion was that 'the CPS is caught between the desire to be seen to be doing justice to the victims of racism, and a legal structure which increases the pressure to drop the racial aspect of the case when the substantive offence is admitted.'[63] The time-honoured response to research findings of this kind, in all criminal justice agencies, is to say that that might have been a correct description at the time but that practices have moved on since the research was completed. That response is not available here, because of the publication of subsequent reports. Appearing in late 2003 was the John Report, *Race for Justice*, which looked again at similar areas of decision making. The report included 33 case studies of racially aggravated incidents, and found that 25 of them were either discontinued or down-graded (by acceptance of a guilty plea) to a lesser offence. Acceptance of a plea to a non-racially aggravated offence:

'. . . occurred in no less than 12 of the 33 cases. The plea bargaining process in some cases involved an offer (that could be from either prosecution or defence) to plead guilty to another, usually less serious, charge if the race dimension is removed altogether. In the 12 cases mentioned, "public interest" was given as the main reason for the CPS decision. However, in some of these cases the assessment of the public interest made by prosecutors seemed questionable.'[64]

Significantly, the John Report goes on to praise the CPS Guidance whilst casting strong doubt on the Service's ability to ensure that it is implemented:

'Without structural changes to build in management accountability for the way racist and religious crime is prosecuted and recorded across the Service, there is no reason to believe that, excellent though it is, the Guidance will be followed such that there are consistent and common standards for the prosecution and recording of these offences.'[65]

---

[60] CPS, *Guidance on Prosecuting Cases of Racist and Religious Crime* (2003), 14. For present purposes, the category of religiously aggravated offences will not be discussed separately.

[61] HMCPSI, *Casework having a Minority Ethnic Dimension* (2002).

[62] E. Burney and G. Rose, *Racist offences—how is the law working?* (2002), 77.

[63] *Ibid.*, 85.

[64] The Gus John Partnership, *Race for Justice: a review of CPS decision making for possible racial bias at each stage of the prosecution process* (2003), para 95; details of some of the questionable decisions are given in the subsequent paragraphs of the report.

[65] *Ibid.*, para 143.

The John Report admits that the cases it examined were dealt with up to two years earlier, but makes the point that initiatives that are impressive on paper may simply not translate into practice. The CPS cannot be sure that what the John Report found 'is not being repeated in the day to day practice of prosecutors.'[66] This is a vital point that has been reiterated in several contexts in this book: having the law or the guidance right is a necessary first step, but there are powerful reasons for believing that policies announced at the top of large organizations are not always implemented by those who deal with matters on a day to day basis. It is naïve to assume that rules are followed to the letter in everyday practice, and thereby to discount the effect of occupational cultures, pressures from others, and a simple desire to ease one's working life.

The CPS Inspectorate published in April 2004 its follow-up report on cases with a minority ethnic dimension.[67] Although it concluded that CPS performance had improved in the preceding two years, it still found a considerable number of racially aggravated cases 'in which we considered that the charge was reduced inappropriately ... We still disagreed with the decision in more than one-fifth of cases in which the charge was reduced.'[68] The Inspectorate also noted variations in the willingness of prosecutors to take such offences to trial, and found that some areas had not yet designated and trained specialist prosecutors for these cases. Moreover, the Inspectorate was not convinced that there would be rapid progress at a time when the new arrangements for joint working with the police were claiming experienced staff and considerable resources.

(c) RECORDING DECISIONS AND REASONS

One finding common to the John Report and to the various HMCPSI reports is the poor quality of endorsements on CPS files. Thus the John Report questions whether prosecutors in their case studies were unaware of the Guidance or whether there were other factors influencing their prosecutorial review decisions: 'the file endorsements do not allow researchers to answer basic questions that are begged by such practices.'[69] The same considerations, of course, apply to internal supervision of prosecutors: if the files are not fully written up, how can there be proper monitoring of the quality of decisions? The Inspectorate's report on cases of domestic violence makes the same points. In relation to decisions not to prosecute, the Inspectorate observed that 'public interest considerations should be recorded, but in many cases they were not and there was little to show which factors had been considered, or the weight given to them, during decision-making.'[70] The Inspectorate devoted four paragraphs to this issue, of which this is the first:

---

[66] *Ibid.*, para 170.
[67] HMCPSI, *A Follow Up Review of CPS Casework with a Minority Ethnic Dimension* (2004).
[68] *Ibid.*, para 6.52.
[69] *Ibid.*, para 99. The report makes similar points at paras 22, 31, 92 and 115.
[70] HMCPSI, *Violence at Home* (2004), para 7.18.

'File endorsements were of inconsistent quality and in many cases inadequate. It was often difficult to ascertain the factors taken into account at various stages of the process, whether there had been compliance with the Code and the Policy, and sometimes the actual decision made.'[71]

While it remains possible that all these decisions were correctly taken and that these are merely failures of record-keeping, the two reports suggest strongly that this was not the case. The poor quality of file endorsement not only makes internal monitoring difficult, but also casts doubt on the training and the ethos of those taking these crucial decisions. In all these studies it was prosecutorial review that was being examined, and in the new era the crucial stage will probably be the initial decisions on whether to prosecute and, if so, what charge to bring. The findings set out above give no confidence that the reasoning behind these decisions will be clearly and faithfully recorded.[72]

(d) DOWNGRADING OF CHARGES

The Glidewell Review was specifically asked to examine the criticism that the CPS were 'downgrading' too many charges, either by reducing the charge to a lower level or by accepting a guilty plea to a lesser offence. In the event its examination of this issue was rather lame, since it failed to discuss the available research and simply concluded that there was a suspicion 'that charges, particularly in relation to offences of violence and associated offences, are downgraded on occasions when they should not be.'[73] It is well known that the ladder of offences of violence, provided by the Offences Against the Person Act 1861, gives ample opportunity for downgrading and charge bargaining: research by Moxon and Hedderman found that only one-fifth of cases initially charged under s 18 were eventually dealt with under that section,[74] and Cretney and Davis found an even lower proportion of s 18 cases that were not downgraded.[75] We have also seen that downgrading remains a matter for concern in relation to racially aggravated offences.

One reason for some downgradings may relate to mode of trial. When the CPS has received a case file from the police, it may conclude that the case ought to be tried in the magistrates' court. To achieve this it may drop the higher charge and substitute a lower one, although it is not supposed to do this after a defendant has elected Crown

---

[71] *Ibid.*, para 7.77.

[72] See also HMCPSI, *Report of a Joint Inspection into the Investigation and Prosecution of Cases Involving Allegations of Rape* (2002), para 8.48: 'We examined 125 files to ascertain the quality of review endorsements, and were disappointed with the standard we found. Evidential considerations were fully recorded in only 55 cases (44 per cent). Public interest considerations were fully recorded in 39 out of 68 relevant cases (57.4 per cent).'

[73] I. Glidewell, *Review of the Crown Prosecution Service* (1998), 85.

[74] D. Moxon and C. Hedderman, 'Mode of Trial Decisions and Sentencing Differences between Courts' (1994) 33 *Howard JCJ* 97.

[75] A. Cretney and G. Davis, *Punishing Violence* (1995), 137; cf. also research by Genders, discussed in Chapter 10 below; and R. Henham, 'Further Evidence on the Significance of Plea in the Crown Court' (2002) 41 *Howard JCJ* 151, revealing differences by circuit.

Court trial on an either-way charge. Paragraph 9.2 of the *Code for Crown Prosecutors* states that speed should never be the only reason for trying to keep a case in the magistrates' court, whereas any greater delays and stress on witnesses might be an adequate reason. As for the allegedly high rate of acceptance of guilty pleas by the CPS in exchange for reducing the charge(s),[76] it is difficult to find general evidence on this, although we saw that the John Report identified this tendency in respect of racially aggravated offences,[77] and it is quite possible that detailed analysis of other offences might yield similar results. This would hardly be surprising, since the structure of the English criminal justice system is such as to place considerable pressure on defendants to plead guilty, and the relatively high acquittal rate in the Crown Court may also incline prosecutors to accept a plea to a lesser offence. Paragraph 10.1 of the 2004 Code declares that:

'Crown Prosecutors should only accept the defendant's plea if they think the court is able to pass a sentence that matches the seriousness of the offending, particularly where there are aggravating features. Crown Prosecutors must never accept a guilty plea just because it is convenient.'

Notwithstanding this counsel of perfection, the known hazards of trials and the cost-effectiveness of guilty pleas combined with the significant structural pressure within the whole system (see Chapter 10 below) render it likely that the CPS take a flexible view of para 10.1 in practice. Thus Burney and Rose found that some 58 per cent of justices' clerks and stipendiary magistrates had experienced racially aggravated offences being reduced to other charges following discussions between prosecution and defence:

'In the perception of these observers, the CPS decision was more likely to be instrumental: to avoid a trial, to secure a conviction, to avoid Crown Court. On the part of the defence, this could be a tactic to avoid a custodial sentence.'[78]

Both practices may be perfectly understandable in the context. Indeed, one might say that the criminal justice system cannot have it both ways—a reduction of delays and costs through securing more guilty pleas, and a punctilious insistence that a plea to a lesser offence should only be accepted if the prosecutor believes that an adequate sentence may still be passed.[79]

   Reduction of charges may be justified if the defendant has originally been over-charged: the CPS would be performing their correct review function if they insisted on this. But this does not always happen. The HMCPSI report on domestic violence cases found that after CPS review the vast majority of cases proceeded on the

---

[76] For general discussion of 'charge-bargaining', see Ch. 10.3 below.

[77] Above, n 64 and accompanying text.

[78] E. Burney and G. Rose, *Racist offences—how is the law working?* (2002), 78.

[79] Note, here, that the language of paragraph 9.1 is not predictive (see Part 2 of this chapter). The prosecutor must believe that 'the court is able to pass a sentence' that is commensurate, not that it will do so. This seems to direct attention to the maximum sentence for the offence to which the guilty plea is contemplated.

correct charge, but they concluded that some nine per cent of cases had not proceeded on the correct charge even after CPS review of the file:

'Overcharging by the police, and no action by the CPS to address it in the early stages of the case, can raise the expectations of victims unnecessarily. It can have a particularly negative effect if the charge is reduced at a later stage, in terms of retaining the commitment of the victim to the prosecution.'[80]

However, the question of downgrading will henceforth arise in a different context. Although there will still be CPS review of case files, the HMCPSI report affirms that 'the new charging initiative is designed to overcome this problem.' The hope is that the initial setting of the charges will be more accurate when it is the responsibility of the CPS, and the CPS annual report identifies 'reducing the number of cases that are discontinued' as a major objective of the new arrangements.'[81] This might well be regarded as a step forward, but the empirical findings cited above demonstrate that merely creating guidance and putting new systems in place does not ensure that practices change as desired. When the Director of Public Prosecutions refers to pro-secutors 'increasingly working alongside police colleagues whilst holding to our values of fairness, impartiality and integrity,'[82] he is referring to an aspiration and not yet to a reality. There will often be considerable pressure on prosecutors from police 'colleagues', and it remains to be seen how the CPS copes with this on the ground.

(e) DISCONTINUANCE

Section 23 of the Prosecution of Offences Act 1985 gives the CPS the power to discontinue charges brought in the magistrates' courts. However, ever since the CPS was founded there has been criticism that the CPS discontinues too high a proportion of cases, and the White Paper of 2002 referred to the 13 per cent discontinuance rate in the context of 'what is not working' in the system.[83] If one consults the annual reports of the CPS, the percentage of cases discontinued in the magistrates' courts (including bind-overs)[84] stood at 16.2 per cent in 2001–02 and had declined to 13.8 per cent by 2003–04.[85] Many of the criticisms have failed to take proper account of the purpose of the CPS and the reasons for discontinuance. First, the CPS was created in order to review files passed to it by the police and to ensure that the case proceeded on the proper charges. Discontinuance may therefore reflect the frequency with which the initial police decisions were incorrect: if that is so, it is a criticism of the police rather than the CPS, and the changes under the Criminal Justice Act 2003 which transfer the authority to charge to the CPS should bring a reduction in

---

[80] HMCPSI, *Violence at Home* (2004), para 7.54.   [81] CPS, *Annual Report 2003–2004*, 10.
[82] *Ibid.*, 3.   [83] Home Office, *Justice for All* (2002), 51.
[84] That is, the figure now includes cases that were discontinued when the defendant agreed to be bound over to keep the peace for, usually, a year. This shadowy practice calls for principled examination.
[85] CPS, *Annual Report 2003–2004*, Annex A, 5.

discontinuances. The reduction from 16.2 to 13.8 per cent in the last three years may demonstrate the beginnings of such a change. Secondly, there has also been criticism that too many Crown Court cases end in acquittal, which might suggest that the CPS is not weeding out enough weak cases.

In order to disentangle the various strands, we must consider the reasons for discontinuance. A Home Office survey in the early 1990s found that, of non-motoring cases discontinued, some 58 per cent were dropped on evidential grounds, 34 per cent on public interest grounds, and among the remainder were some cases where the defendant could not be traced.[86] The CPS's own discontinuance survey in 1994 found that in 43 per cent of cases there was insufficient evidence to proceed, in 28 per cent a prosecution was not in the public interest, and in 19 per cent of cases the prosecution was unable to proceed, largely because of the non-attendance of a key witness.[87] A later Home Office study found that evidential reasons were the ground for termination in 57 per cent of the cases, and public interest reasons in some 31 per cent of cases.[88]

The next step is to focus on discontinuances for evidential reasons. Crisp and Moxon's survey found that the top three reasons were a lack of supporting evidence (39 per cent), unreliability of witnesses (35 per cent), and evidence lacking on a key element in the offence (19 per cent).[89] The survey by Phillips and Brown found that the main reasons for termination were lack of supporting evidence (33 per cent), no evidence on a key element of the offence (24 per cent), anticipated witness failure (20 per cent), and actual refusal by witness to give evidence (19 per cent).[90] These findings refer to the time when the CPS involvement was solely that of reviewer of case files. In practice, many of these case files would have been discussed with the police, upon whom the CPS reviewer may often have to rely for judgments about reliability. In his research for the CPS, John Baldwin found that many of the difficult cases turned on the evidence of a single witness, and judgment about whether to proceed was finely balanced.[91] It seems that in many of the cases discontinued on evidential grounds, the police would have been in agreement about the poor prospect of conviction. On the other hand, Baldwin's research uncovered a distinct tendency among some prosecutors to proceed with a case despite a probable or manifest weakness. At one level, this meant that 'some prosecutors remain stubbornly of the view that the defendant may do the decent thing and plead guilty even though the pro-

[86] D. Crisp and D. Moxon, *Case Screening by the Crown Prosecution Service* (1995), 19.

[87] National Audit Office, *Crown Prosecution Service* (1997), 42. Logically speaking, cases of non-attendance of a key witness are cases of evidential insufficiency. By not counting them as such, the survey implies that that 'evidential insufficiency' is confined to insufficiency identified before trial. Cf. the categorization used in the Phillips and Brown survey (next note), which draws such a distinction.

[88] Phillips and Brown, *Entry into the Criminal Justice System* (1998), 141.

[89] Crisp and Moxon (above, n 86), 19.   [90] Phillips and Brown (above, n 88), 143.

[91] J. Baldwin, 'Understanding Judge Ordered and Directed Acquittals in the Crown Court', [1997] Crim LR 536, at 546.

spects of conviction might look precarious on paper'.[92] At a deeper level, Baldwin confirmed that:

'some prosecutors share a common value system with the police, a core element of which is that serious cases ought to be prosecuted, almost irrespective of considerations as to evidential strength. Cases have developed a considerable momentum by the time of committal, and expectations build up that cases will proceed to the Crown Court. In such circumstances, it is easy to understand why some prosecutors, particularly when lacking in experience or self-confidence, hesitate in making hard decisions in complex or serious cases'.[93]

In offering three reasons why prosecutors may fail to take the proper decisions at case review stage (sharing the pro-prosecution values of the police,[94] inexperience, lack of self-confidence), Baldwin was concerned to examine why too few cases were discontinued. His sample of cases was constructed with a view to casting light on that issue, which will be discussed further below. It suffices to comment here that many of the cases that were discontinued should probably not have proceeded as far as they did, in so far as there was insufficient reliable evidence from the outset. The criticism that the CPS is discontinuing too many cases on evidential grounds is therefore hard to accept. To prosecute when the evidence is insufficient inflicts unjustified anxiety on the defendant and wastes public resources. Paragraph 4.1 of the CPS Code states clearly that 'if the case does not pass the evidential test, it must not go ahead, no matter how important or serious it may be'.

    However, we must now look to the new charging arrangements, in which prosecutors will be working alongside the police to decide on diversion or prosecution, and then in settling the charge(s) to be brought. This may be expected to cut down the proportion of discontinuances, by ensuring that the original charge is 'correct' (i.e. sustainable) in a higher proportion of cases—not in all cases, of course, because either the evidence or predictions of the behaviour of witnesses may alter. But Baldwin's warning about the value systems of prosecutors must be heeded: it is possible that the collocation of police and prosecutors may increase the influence of the police value system over prosecutors, rather than *vice versa*. Much depends on power relations at ground level. For example, Mhlanga's research showed that a much higher proportion of prosecutions brought against non-white defendants were discontinued than against white defendants, and that the grounds were mostly evidential, suggesting that more charges were brought against non-white defendants when the evidence was weak:[95] is collocation likely to result in more of those cases being charged correctly in the first instance?

---

[92] *Ibid.*, 548.   [93] *Ibid.*, 551.

[94] Reference to 'the police' does not imply a single value system in that large organisation: see above, Ch. 3.

[95] G. Barclay and B. Mhlanga, *Ethnic differences in decisions on young defendants dealt with by the Crown Prosecution Service* (2000). See further HMCPSI, *A Follow Up Review of CPS Casework with a Minority Ethnic Dimension* (2004), paras 11.13–11.23, suggesting that the over-charging of minority ethnic defendants remains an issue.

Further research will be needed in order to ascertain how independent prosecutors are able to be when they are rubbing shoulders with the police every day. It will also be important to keep a close eye on the proportion of cases dismissed on a submission of no case,[96] to see whether case preparation improves noticeably under the new charging arrangements.

This discussion of discontinuance should not omit reference to 'public interest' factors, which account for around 30 per cent of all discontinuances in the magistrates' courts. On CPS figures, half of these are cases in which a very small or nominal penalty is thought likely, and a further quarter are cases in which a caution is thought more appropriate.[97] In so far as it is these cases that are the source of the criticism that the CPS uses discontinuance too frequently, there is one comparative measure that should not be neglected. That is the proportion of sentences in court that are 'very small or nominal'. It is difficult to find a precise figure for this, since there is no record of the number of small fines handed down by the courts; equally, it could be argued that in some circumstances a conditional discharge is neither very small nor nominal.[98] But it is worth pointing out that the proportion of discharges granted for indictable offences has increased considerably since 1986, and that from 1996 to 2002 some 14 per cent of adult men have been discharged by the courts for indictable offences, and the figure for adult women was 28 per cent in 1996 and 24 per cent in 2002. At the very least, this suggests that there is scope for more discontinuances rather than fewer, even if we maintain that the proper criterion should be whether a court ought to respond to the offence with a very small or nominal sentence ('intrinsic merits') rather than whether it is likely to do so (predictive). Perhaps the availability to prosecutors of conditional cautions may enable more of these cases to be diverted earlier.[99]

(f) ACQUITTALS BY THE JUDGE

Whereas discontinuance rates have (often wrongly) been taken as a measure of CPS performance in summary cases, so in Crown Court cases the performance of the CPS has sometimes been measured according to how frequently cases end in an acquittal by the judge. Acquittals by judge are of two different types. A judge-ordered acquittal occurs where the prosecutor informs the court that the CPS does not wish to proceed, and the judge formally orders the jury to acquit. A directed acquittal occurs during or at the end of the prosecution's case in court, if the judge decides that there is insufficient evidence on one or more elements of the offence. Research by Block, Corbett, and Peay in the early 1990s suggested that dispassionate scrutineers could identify weak

---

[96] CPS, *Annual Report 2003–2004*, Annex A, 8.

[97] National Audit Office, *Crown Prosecution Service* (1997), 42.

[98] A conditional discharge may be for a period of up to three years: if the offender commits a further offence during the specified period, he is liable to be sentenced for both the new offence and the offence for which the conditional discharge was granted.

[99] See above, Ch. 6.5.

cases among those that ended in acquittals by the judge: a minimum of 22 per cent of acquittals occurred in cases that were regarded as foreseeably flawed in the opinion of a trained prosecutor,[100] and the researchers' own assessments led them to state that:

'although fewer than half of ordered acquittals were considered definitely or possibly foreseeable, three quarters of directed acquittals were so classified. This supports our view, derived from the study, that directed acquittals result largely from weak cases that should have been discontinued, whereas ordered acquittals result largely from unforeseeable circumstances'.[101]

Baldwin conducted a somewhat similar enquiry for the CPS in 1995, with a sample of around 100 cases ending in acquittal by judge and some seventy other cases. He found that the ordered acquittals occurred chiefly where a key witness retracted a statement or failed to arrive at court (48 per cent), the judge took the view at the outset that the case was too weak (16 per cent), or the case was terminated following the convictions of other people (14 per cent). The directed acquittals occurred chiefly because a key witness failed to come up to proof (34 per cent), or there were problems of law or admissibility of evidence (32 per cent), or the judge ruled the evidence insufficient (12 per cent).[102] The important question is how many of these were foreseeable and ought to have led to earlier discontinuance. Baldwin found that around 41 per cent of all cases resulting in acquittal had reservations of a prosecutor entered upon the file at an early stage, and a further 35 per cent of files mentioned reservations but discounted them. His conclusions ran along two main lines. One was the acute difficulty of judging witness credibility and reliability, on the basis of either case files or discussions with police officers on the case. The other was that three characteristics of some prosecutors—inexperience, lack of self-confidence, and the sharing of values with the police—meant that some cases were not terminated as early as they should have been.[103] They were allowed to 'run'. To the extent that some of these characteristics remain, judgment must be reserved on expectations that the new arrangements for police and prosecutors working together will lead to significant changes.

Baldwin also found that, especially in serious cases, some prosecutors were reluctant to make the 'tough' decision of terminating a weak case, but would rather pass the responsibility for the decision to the court. As one prosecutor commented, 'the proper forum for deciding whether a person is telling the truth is the jury'.[104] Baldwin comments that this attitude 'can often be a superficial cop-out', but it is at least worth acknowledging that the jury system can make this sort of reasoning attractive. A similar attitude surfaced in the Stephen Lawrence Inquiry.

The initial prosecution of the murder of Stephen Lawrence was discontinued, largely owing to problems with the eyewitness evidence in the case. The prosecutor's decision was challenged during the inquiry by counsel for the Lawrence family, who argued that in making the decision the prosecutor was taking over the role 'of the

---

[100] B. Block, C. Corbett and J. Peay, *Ordered and Directed Acquittals in the Crown Court* (1993).
[101] *Ibid.*, 100.   [102] Baldwin, above, n 91, 539.   [103] *Ibid.*, 551.   [104] *Ibid.*

judge or the jury', but the inquiry found that the decision had been perfectly proper.[105] One might find some support for the 'leave it to the jury' approach in the law of evidence: as we will see in Chapter 11, the *Galbraith* test does depict questions of credibility as being exclusively within the domain of the jury. When this is coupled with the ambiguity of the evidential sufficiency test (as between a predictive or intrinsic merits test), it is not surprising that prosecutors should allude to the role of the jury when continuing with a borderline case. Our view is that, however difficult the decision, the paramount principle is that weak cases should not go to court. Prosecutors should not dodge their responsibility by arguing that the decision is for the jury, since it is their prior decision whether the evidence is strong enough to justify putting the defendant on trial.

Returning to acquittals by judge, is it right to regard these as a measure of CPS efficiency? The CPS resists this on the ground that judge-directed acquittals may simply mean that a key witness failed to come up to proof when the prosecution believed that they would. Thus the CPS Inspectorate found in 1999 that some 78 per cent of cases in which a magistrates' court or judge dismissed the prosecution were cases which 'failed for reasons that the CPS could not have foreseen.'[106] It seems that judge-directed acquittals fell from 12 per cent of contested trials in 1991–92 to 7 per cent of contested hearings in 2002–03,[107] and this may be said to represent an improvement in both the quality of preparation of cases and assessments of whether witnesses will come up to proof. In 2003–04 some 15 per cent of cases sent to the Crown Court resulted in a judge-ordered acquittal when the CPS offered no evidence because the realistic prospect of conviction had gone, or where a defendant had serious medical problems; or when witnesses went missing; or where the defendant has already been dealt with for other offences.[108] In cases which are to be heard in the Crown Court the CPS has no other opportunity to drop the charges save by offering no evidence. Whether the weakness that leads to a change of mind should have been identified earlier is a matter on which the research by Baldwin and by Block, Corbett and Peay casts light, but the proportion of cases in which this is so cannot be identified with confidence.

(g) TARGET FATIGUE?

It is well known that Government agencies are now set PSA targets each year, and that they have to report on their performance as measured by those targets. In 2003–04 the CPS reported that it met its targets on bringing more cases to justice (in almost all of its areas), in reducing the proportion of unsuccessful outcomes in both magistrates'

---

[105] Sir W. Macpherson, *The Stephen Lawrence Inquiry* (1999), paras 39-30 to 39-32.

[106] CPSI, *Adverse Cases* (1999), para 2.4.

[107] CPS, *Annual Report 2002–03*, 34; the figures are presented differently in the *Annual Report 2003–2004*, Annex A, 8, but the total numbers of judge-directed acquittals are certainly not declining.

[108] *Ibid.*, Annex A, 8. These latest figures include defendants bound over to keep the peace, some of whom would be persons already dealt with for other offences.

courts and the Crown Court, in improving levels of public confidence in the CPS, particularly among ethnic minority communities, and in keeping the average time taken to deal with persistent young offenders below 71 days. The CPS also has targets on such matters as sending committal papers to the defence within 14 days, delivering briefs to counsel within 14 days, paying witness expenses promptly, complying with primary disclosure, complying with secondary disclosure, and on prompt payment of invoices, for example, but discussion of these was dropped from the latest CPS report.[109] It is easy to ridicule the plethora of targets imposed by Government, particularly in view of the way the targets are sometimes adjusted to take account of failures to attain them. But it must be said that most of the targets imposed on the CPS relate to decisions and acts which are meaningful in terms of their impact on the criminal process and on those involved in it (whether as victims, witnesses, or counsel).

7.5 THE ROLE OF THE VICTIM

Both the Code for Crown Prosecutors and the CPS 'Statement on the Treatment of Victims and Witnesses'[110] speak firmly of taking account of the interests of victims, rather than their wishes, when making decisions about prosecutions. Nothing could be clearer than paragraph 2.1 of the Statement:

'The CPS is an independent prosecuting authority. We take decisions about cases based on the strength of the evidence followed by an assessment of the public interest. This process is governed by the Code for Crown Prosecutors. The CPS does not act directly on behalf of individual victims or represent them in court in criminal proceedings because it has to take decisions reflecting the overall public interest rather than the particular interests of any one person. Nevertheless, the interests of the victim are very important when we make decisions'.

The Statement goes on to affirm that the CPS needs to 'know how the crime has affected the victim', but it contains no reference to the victim's wishes. In this respect it is consistent with the Lord Chief Justice's guidance to courts on dealing with Victim Personal Statements: 'the opinions of the victim or the victim's close relatives as to what the sentence should be are therefore not relevant, unlike the consequence of the offence on them.'[111] However the Code for Crown Prosecutors is less clear than the CPS Statement, directing that 'prosecutors should always take into account the consequences for the victim of the decision whether or not to prosecute, *and any views expressed by the victim or the victim's family*.'[112] Insofar as this suggests that those

---

[109] *Ibid.*, 7–11. Cf. *Annual Report 2002–2003*, 7–10.
[110] CPS, *Statement on the Treatment of Victims and Witnesses* (hereinafter, the Statement), available at www.cps.gov.uk/victims_witnesses/treatment.html
[111] *Practice Direction (Victim Personal Statements)* [2002] 1 Cr App R 69, at para 3(c).
[112] *Code for Crown Prosecutors* (2004), para 5.12.

views should have an influence on the decision for or against prosecuting, it should not be followed.[113] It is inconsistent with the Statement and with the general approach of criminal justice agencies, as expressed in the Lord Chief Justice's guidance on sentencing.

This is a particular locus of conflict in domestic violence cases in which a victim withdraws a complaint or statement, and wants the prosecution to be dropped. In her 1990s research Carolyn Hoyle found that 'the CPS rarely proceeded with a case once the victim had withdrawn.'[114] The CPS Inspectorate concluded in 1998 that, in cases of victim withdrawal, 'we are not satisfied that the policy is being applied correctly or, on occasions, at all'—the policy being to proceed if possible, without reference to the victim's wishes.[115] When the HMCPSI conducted its further review in 2004 to monitor progress in dealing with domestic violence, it found that around 44 per cent of withdrawal cases were proceeded with, but commented that this left 'scope for improvement' and that 'appropriate consultation with the police was not commonplace.'[116] These, then, are cases in which the victim's (expressed) wishes should certainly not hold sway.

However, there is one situation in which the victim's views ought to be heeded—where the victim wants compensation from the offender. The CPS Statement recognizes it as a prosecutor's duty to press for compensation where the victim expresses a wish for it, and to make sure that the necessary information is available; and the advent of conditional cautions (discussed in Chapter 6.4 above) provides prosecutors with a possible means of securing compensation to the victim without prosecuting.

The Statement goes on to set out other duties of the CPS towards victims and witnesses, including a commitment to 'introduce ourselves to witnesses, wherever possible' and to 'look after the interests of the witnesses as the trial progresses.' The CPS is involved in a number of projects to carry this forward, including the 'No Witness, No Justice' programme that will lead to the setting up of Witness Care Units in all areas.[117] Furthermore, the Domestic Violence, Crime and Victims Act 2004 introduces a statutory Code of Practice for Victims and also creates a Commissioner for Victims and Witnesses, whose task will be to promote the interests of victims and monitor the implementation of the Code of Practice. It is likely that the work of the Commissioner will have an impact on CPS practice in due course.

---

[113] Research findings from the early days of the CPS pointed to evidence of some willingness to defer to the wishes of 'important' victims such as local businesses: M. McConville, A. Sanders and R. Leng, *The Case for the Prosecution* (1991), 114.

[114] C. Hoyle, *Negotiating Domestic Violence* (1998), 170.

[115] CPSI, *Cases involving Domestic Violence* (1998), para 12.3.

[116] HMCPSI, *Violence at Home* (2004), Appendix 5, R12.

[117] CPS, *Annual Report 2003–2004*, 15–16.

7.6 ACCOUNTABILITY

To what authorities and to what extent are prosecutors accountable? The absence of clear and effective lines of accountability for many regulatory agencies was discussed in the previous chapter. The focus here will be chiefly upon the Crown Prosecution Service.

(a) ACCOUNTABILITY TO PARLIAMENT

The CPS is organized hierarchically, with its local branches, 42 areas, and a head-quarters. Internal lines of accountability end with the Director of Public Prosecutions. He or she is answerable to the Attorney-General, who has ministerial responsibility for the general policies pursued by the CPS but not in respect of decisions taken in individual cases. There is thus no accountability to Parliament for decisions in indi-vidual cases, but it is the practice of Members of Parliament to refer to the Director of Public Prosecutions individual cases brought to their attention by constituents or others. The Director will usually reply by letter, giving some reason for the decision (often, a decision to discontinue a prosecution). The CPS is also open to scrutiny by the Home Affairs Committee of the House of Commons and by the National Audit Office.[118] As we saw earlier, the Prosecution of Offences Act 1985 imposes on the Director a statutory responsibility to issue a code, and to report annually to Parliament. The annual reports now have to record the CPS's performance in relation to Government targets, but apart from that they tend to be written in the style of Voltaire's Dr Pangloss.

That marks a significant contrast to the reports of the principal source of CPS accountability, Her Majesty's Crown Prosecution Service Inspectorate. By the mid-1990s there was still no inspectorate of the CPS, unlike the established inspectorates of constabulary, probation and then the prisons, and it is to the credit of the CPS that it set up its own internal inspectorate, which issued several critical reports.[119] In 2000, HMCPSI was formally established, and it has continued to issue searching reports on the performance of local CPS areas and on a number of general themes across areas. We have quoted from its report on *Violence at Home* in Part 4 of this chapter. Atten-tion might also be drawn to the thematic review of rape cases, where the Inspectorate was critical of the quality of file endorsements (absence of reasons for decisions) and also detected elements of inconsistency in key decisions which led to a recom-mendation that all decisions to drop or substantially to reduce the charge should be discussed with a second specialist lawyer.[120] The report also notes plenty of good

---

[118] National Audit Office, *Crown Prosecution Service* (1997).

[119] E.g. the report on *Cases involving Domestic Violence* (n 115 above and accompanying text), and its report on *Central Casework Section* (1999).

[120] HMCPSI, *Report on the Joint Investigation into the Investigation and Prosecution of Cases Involving Allegations of Rape* (2002), para 8.54 and paras 8.69–8.78.

practice in dealing with these sensitive cases, but it certainly does not give the impression that everything is for the best, as the CPS annual reports tend to do.

(b) ACCOUNTABILITY TO THE COURTS

The courts have stated many times their willingness to review decisions not to prosecute. It was established in the first *Blackburn* case[121] that the courts would be prepared judicially to review a general policy not to prosecute for certain classes of offence, for example, all thefts with a value below £100. In the third *Blackburn* case,[122] Lord Denning MR suggested that the courts would also be prepared to review an individual decision not to prosecute, and this dictum has received subsequent judicial support.[123] The primary basis for judicial review would be that either the policy or the individual decision not to prosecute was unreasonable in a *Wednesbury* sense, that is, was such that no reasonable prosecuting authority would have adopted the policy or taken the decision.[124]

We saw in the last chapter that the Divisional Court has upheld such challenges to the decision not to prosecute and the decision to caution in several decisions.[125] In the *Manning* case,[126] the Divisional Court quashed a CPS decision not to bring a prosecution arising out of a death in custody. Lord Bingham CJ stated that the standard of review must not be set too high, on the ground that judicial review is the only means by which the citizen can seek redress against a decision not to prosecute. That is not entirely true, since it remains possible to mount a private prosecution. But such a prosecution requires considerable time and energy, and the whole purpose of a public prosecution system is to prevent citizens from having thus to exert themselves. The greater difficulty with the *Manning* decision is that it is confined to cases of death in custody: while Lord Bingham made it clear that the CPS ought to give reasons for not bringing a prosecution in such circumstances, there remains no general obligation to give reasons for non-prosecution. Where reasons are given, the path to judicial review (and therefore effective accountability) is much easier. Thus in the *Jones* case,[127] judicial review of a decision not to bring a manslaughter charge was granted on the ground that the DPP had failed to apply the law correctly to the facts. However, not until there is a general obligation to give reasons will effective accountability be achieved.

Accountability for decisions to prosecute raises different issues. In *R v Chief*

---

[121] *R v Metropolitan Police Commissioner, ex p Blackburn* [1968] 2 QB 118.

[122] *R v Metropolitan Police Commissioner, ex p Blackburn (No. 3)* [1973] 1 QB 241.

[123] *R v General Council of the Bar, ex p Percival* [1990] 3 All ER 137.

[124] *Associated Provincial Picture Houses v Wednesbury Corporation* [1948] 1 KB 223.

[125] See Ch. 6.5 above.

[126] *R v DPP, ex p Manning* [2001] QB 330, analyzed by M. Burton, 'Reviewing Crown Prosecution Service Decisions not to Prosecute', [2001] Crim LR 374; see also *R (on application of Joseph) v DPP* [2001] Crim LR 489.

[127] *R v DPP, ex p Jones* [2000] Crim LR 858.

Constable of Kent and another, ex parte L,[128] the Divisional Court accepted that an individual decision to prosecute a juvenile could be subject to judicial review if it were clearly contrary to a settled policy of the Director of Public Prosecutions, i.e. the Code for Crown Prosecutors. Stuart-Smith LJ in the Divisional Court in *R v Inland Revenue Commissioners, ex parte Mead*,[129] accepted that judicial review of a decision to prosecute would also be possible where the applicant was an adult; the other member of the court, Popplewell J, disagreed with this. Now the House of Lords in the *Kebilene* case,[130] has held that an action for judicial review of a decision to prosecute should not be entertained unless there is evidence of dishonesty, bad faith or other exceptional circumstances. The presumption is that, if a prosecution cannot be challenged either on these grounds or under the doctrine of abuse of process, it should go ahead and the court should be allowed to decide the case on its merits—an approach that accords little significance to the pains of being prosecuted.

(c) ACCOUNTABILITY TO VICTIMS

As we saw in Part 5 above, the CPS has issued a 'Statement on the Treatment of Victims and Witnesses' that promises proper respect for victims and their interests. That Statement does not mention the task of responding to complaints from victims, but one of the Government's targets for the CPS (see Part 4 of this Chapter) is 'to increase to 94 per cent the replies to complaints which are made within 10 days.' In 2002–03 the CPS reported that it had increased the proportion from 82 to 89 per cent, still falling short of the target.[131] Some letters do not come directly from victims and their families but rather from Members of Parliament, and this also provides an important method of accountability. However, it remains the case that the CPS should act in the public interest and not directly on behalf of particular victims.

7.7 PROSECUTORIAL ETHICS

The CPS includes, as part of its overall aim, 'the consistent, fair and independent review of cases' and 'their fair, thorough and firm presentation at court.'[132] The Code itself spells this out in a little more detail:

'Crown Prosecutors must be fair, independent and objective. They must not let any personal views about ethnic or national origin, sex, religious beliefs, political views or the sexual orientation of the suspect, victim or witness influence their decisions. They must not be affected by improper pressure from any source.'[133]

---

[128] (1991) 93 Cr App R 416.   [129] [1993] 1 All ER 772.   [130] [2000] 2 AC 326.
[131] CPS, *Annual Report 2002–2003*, 9. There is no mention of this target in the 2003–2004 Report.
[132] CPS, *Annual Report 2003–2004*, 5.
[133] CPS, *Code for Crown Prosecutors* (2000), para 2.2.

This aspect of an ethical orientation to prosecuting concerns fairness as impartiality, in terms of non-discrimination and non-susceptibility to pressures from others. It will be no less important in the context of the new charging arrangements, where prosecutors will be working more closely with the police, and where prosecutors will for the first time have direct responsibility for a form of diversion from prosecution (conditional cautions).

What about the specific ethical principles of prosecuting cases that have been charged? It may be claimed that each crown prosecutor, as a solicitor or barrister, is governed by the ethical code of the relevant professional organization.[134] In Chapter 3 we reviewed the various formulations of the prosecutor's role, as a kind of 'Minister of Justice' concerned with obtaining convictions without unfairness to defendants. Various international documents now deal with these broader questions about the prosecutor's role, including the United Nations Guidelines on the Role of Prosecutors (1990) and the standards agreed in 1999 by the International Association of Prosecutors. The role has been characterized in the US Supreme Court by stating that the prosecutor:

'is in a peculiar and very definite sense the servant of the law, the twofold aim of which is that guilt shall not escape or innocence suffer ... It is as much his duty to refrain from improper methods calculated to produce a wrongful conviction as it is to use every legitimate means to bring about a just one'.[135]

The importance of these statements lies in their endorsement of the argument, developed in Chapter 3 above, that the protection of rights should be regarded as part of the law, and not as standing in opposition to the proper role of police or prosecutors. Whilst it is true that defence lawyers have the primary task of securing the defendant's rights, prosecutors should neither indulge in nor condone unlawful or unethical practices. They should show no less respect for fairness and human rights, as embodied in principles such as those set out in Chapter 2, than for the obtaining of convictions of the guilty. Paragraph 2.6 of the Code enjoins prosecutors to apply the principles of the European Convention on Human Rights; but we have seen, particularly in Parts 3 and 4 of this chapter, that an organization that works closely with the police may—on some occasions at least—become 'prosecution-minded' to an extent that compromises this broader ethical position. One way of tackling this would be to draw up some practical ethical guidance directed at the kinds of situation in which conflicts of this kind are likely to arise. Guidance cannot always overwhelm occupational cultures and other more subtle pressures, but it is one step in that direction.

---

[134] See M. Blake and A. Ashworth, 'Some Ethical Issues in Prosecuting and Defending Criminal Cases' [1998] Crim LR 16.

[135] *Berger v United States* (1935) 294 US 78, *per* Sutherland J at 88.

7.8 CONCLUSIONS

This chapter has outlined the purpose and functions of the CPS, evaluated some of
the principles they proclaim, and examined empirical evidence of their performance
of their various tasks. We have noted that, as with other large organizations, formulat-
ing the principles and the guidance satisfactorily is not sufficient to ensure that they
are implemented in practice. Frank recognition of the gap between rhetoric and
reality is rare in the CPS's own documents, but the presence of the Inspectorate (and
the publication of a small number of research reports)[136] ensures that a more realistic
view of the prosecution system can be obtained.

In this concluding section we raise three general issues. First, will the new charging
arrangements lead prosecutors to reach judgments more or less independently than
under the previous system? It has always been a problem for the CPS that their
information comes almost entirely from the police,[137] who may construct a case in a
way designed to dispose the prosecutor towards a particular outcome. There have also
been many claims that the CPS is not sufficiently independent of the police, and
Baldwin's research in the mid-1990s contributed supporting evidence.[138] The question now is whether the joint working of police and prosecutors, together with the
transfer of the authority to charge from police to CPS, will militate for or against the
desired independence. Will prosecutors who have to deal with police officers on a day-
by-day basis come to adopt an anti-defendant and pro-prosecution philosophy, of the
kind that leads them to 'run' cases where in truth the evidence is weak? Or will they be
able to retain a professional detachment that allows them to insist that cases be
dropped or charges of a particular kind be preferred, when the police are arguing
strongly in the opposite direction? It remains to be seen whether the new charging
arrangements will yield the benefits intended.

Secondly, on what principles and with what success will the CPS exercise their new
dispositive powers? The Criminal Justice Act 2003 gives the CPS the power to offer
conditional cautions to offenders, and requires them to propose the conditions. The
police will, it seems, retain the power to offer a police caution or otherwise to divert
the case—it is not clear what input the CPS will have into those decisions.[139] The CPS
is unaccustomed to exercising this kind of power, although prosecutors in many
other countries have had similar powers for some years[140]—even in Scotland, where
the 'fiscal fine' established itself in the 1990s.[141] It is a dispositive power, akin to

---

[136] The CPS has published on its own website the fairly critical John report on possible racial bias: see n 64
above.
   [137] Cf. however the consultation paper on CPS interviews of witnesses, above, n 29.
   [138] See above, n 91. See also Brownlee, above n 16, at 906.
   [139] See the discussion in Ch. 6.4 above.
   [140] J. Fionda, *Public Prosecutors and Discretion: a Comparative Study* (1995); A. Selih, 'The Prosecution
Process', in Council of Europe, *Crime and Criminal Justice in Europe* (2000), 103.
   [141] For discussion, see P. Duff and N. Hutton (eds), *Criminal Justice in Scotland* (1999), Ch. 7.

sentencing, and clear guidance to prosecutors combined with close monitoring will be required. If the CPS exercises the power responsibly and accountably, then the case for giving it a more central role in pre-trial diversion will be strengthened. Since diversion is a dispositive function, it is appropriate that it be fulfilled by a quasi-judicial official such as a crown prosecutor and not by someone whose principal task is the investigation and prevention of crime. It is evident that the lack of enthusiasm in the two Royal Commissions for giving this responsibility to the CPS was based on lack of confidence in the ability of the CPS to discharge it;[142] the CPS now has the opportunity to demonstrate its suitability for this role through its handling of conditional cautions.

   Thirdly, there remains the need urgently to confront the fundamental issues of social fairness raised by the different enforcement and prosecution policies of the CPS and the so-called regulatory agencies. The arrival of conditional cautions gives the CPS the opportunity to re-assess its role in diversion. However, there remain broader issues of fairness that need to be tackled on a wider criminal justice canvas. The different policies of the CPS and the various regulatory agencies (which tend not to prosecute frequently, but to prefer forms of diversion) mean that citizens who commit offences that are of roughly equivalent seriousness may receive a very different response according to the agency that deals with enforcement. There is a need for a general review of the proper policies to be pursued by the so-called regulatory agencies, as well as the CPS, and also for a new system of accountability that applies the same standards to the CPS and the other agencies. If equality before the law and equal treatment are to be realistic aspirations, this glaring anomaly in English criminal justice must no longer be left unchallenged.

---

[142] See further the second edition of this work, 205–206.

8

REMANDS BEFORE TRIAL

The bail/custody decision raises some of the most acute conflicts in the whole criminal process. On the one hand there is the individual's right to liberty, safeguarded by Article 5 of the Convention, and the interest of a person arrested and charged with an offence in remaining at liberty until the trial has taken place. On the other hand, there is a public interest in security and in ensuring protection from crime. Some practitioners, politicians, and others have concluded that the way to deal with this conflict is in each case to balance the defendant's rights with the public interests. However, the vague notion of 'balancing' that is usually advanced in this context is manifestly inadequate. No judgment of balance can be properly reached until there is a clear appreciation of what rights defendants (and actual or potential victims) have at this stage, and fuller analysis of the content and legitimacy of the claimed public interests, and of the evidential foundations for predictions of risk. As will appear during the course of this chapter, there is a wide range of relevant considerations, combined with a dearth of practical information at some crucial stages. Because of the impact on the liberty of the defendant, the issues are too important to leave to wide expanses of little-regulated discretion, whether in the hands of police officers, magistrates, or judges. The focus in this chapter will be on the issues of principle raised by the law and practice.[1]

To grant a person bail is to accept their claim to liberty in the period before the next official proceedings; bail may be unconditional or conditional. To refuse bail means that the consequence is likely to be a remand in custody, i.e. in prison. Questions of remand on bail or in custody arise at various stages in the criminal process. First, there is the new phenomenon of what is called 'street bail', that is, the power of an officer who arrests a person for an offence to release the arrestee on bail, to report to a police station at a specified time.[2] Secondly, there is the possibility of police bail, granted at the police station, pending the first court appearance. Thirdly, there is the court's decision on remand between the first and the final court appearance. Fourthly, there is the question of remand after conviction and before sentence is passed, for example to allow time for the preparation of a report on the defendant. And fifthly, there is

---

[1] For full accounts of the law and practice, see P. Cavadino and B. Gibson, *Bail: The Law, Best Practice and the Debate* (1993), and N. Corre and D. Wolchover, *Bail in Criminal Proceedings* (2nd ed., 1999).

[2] See the discussion in Part 2 of this chapter, below.

the question of remand pending an appeal against verdict or sentence, which is the subject of a Practice Direction.[3] The fourth and fifth decisions will not be discussed here, and there will be only a few references to police bail and street bail. The principal focus is upon the court's decision whether to remand on bail or in custody between first appearance and trial.

8.1 REMANDS, RIGHTS AND RISK

What rights of a defendant are at stake here? Article 5(1) of the Convention declares the general right to liberty, but allows liberty to be taken away in six distinct situations, the third of which (in Article 5(1)(c)) is the lawful arrest or detention of a person in order to bring him before a competent legal authority on reasonable suspicion of having committed an offence.[4] Article 5(3) goes on to provide that persons detained under that paragraph shall be brought promptly before a court, and shall be entitled to trial within a reasonable time.[5] In applying these provisions, the European Court of Human Rights in Strasbourg has developed several distinct requirements. Its decisions have recognized four grounds for the refusal of bail: risk of absconding before trial, risk of interfering with the course of justice, risk of committing offences, and risk to public order.[6] More importantly, the Strasbourg organs have insisted on a number of procedural guarantees during remand proceedings, and we will see later in the chapter how these have affected or might affect English law.

For the present, our starting point is provided by three principles that stand out in the Strasbourg jurisprudence. The first is that the basis for considering the application of Article 5 should always be a presumption of liberty and a presumption of innocence (taken, of course, from Article 6(2)). Thus in *Caballero v United Kingdom*,[7] the Commission stated that the judge:

'having heard the accused himself, must examine all the facts arguing for and against the interest of a genuine requirement of public interest justifying, with due regard to the presumption of innocence, a departure from the rule of respect for the accused's liberty.'

The same passage goes on to articulate the second major principle prominent in the case law—the need to avoid stereotypical reasoning and to assess each case individually:

---

[3] *Practice Direction: Bail Pending Appeal* [1983] 1 WLR 1292.

[4] On 'reasonable suspicion', see Ch. 4 above.

[5] For discussion of the rather clumsy drafting of Article 5(3) and the Court's interpretation of it, see B. Emmerson and A. Ashworth, *Human Rights and Criminal Justice* (2001), Chapter 13B.

[6] For elaboration, see *ibid.*, Chapter 13C.

[7] (2000) 30 EHRR 643, at 652, endorsed by the Court at [21]. (The Commission decision was originally referred to as *C.C. v United Kingdom*, see [1999] Crim LR 228.)

'For example, the danger of an accused's absconding cannot be gauged solely on the basis of the severity of the sentence risked.[8] As far as the danger of re-offending is concerned, a reference to a person's antecedents cannot suffice to justify refusing release.'[9]

There is also authority for a third principle, evident in both the remand decisions and the decisions on trial within a reasonable time—that courts should take care to impose the least restrictive regime on a defendant pending trial. Before depriving a defendant of liberty, courts must consider 'whether there [is] another way of safe-guarding public security and preventing him from committing further offences,'[10] an injunction that points in English law towards conditional bail in one of its forms. Other judgments emphasize the need for 'special diligence' and speed where a defendant is remanded in custody, rather than on bail.[11]

It is not difficult to understand the reasons for the rights declared in the Convention. In principle, it is quite wrong that anyone, including agents of law enforcement, should be able to make an arrest, bring a charge, and then, without proving that charge in court, secure the immediate detention of the defendant.[12] Detention without trial is widely regarded as an incident of totalitarianism, or at least an expedient to be contemplated only in an extreme kind of national emergency.[13] It therefore follows that any argument for depriving unconvicted individuals of their liberty in civil society ought to have peculiar strength. Indeed, that point is reinforced when one considers the potential consequences for the defendant of a loss of liberty before trial—not just the deprivation of freedom to live a normal life, often compounded by incarceration under the worst conditions in the prison system, but also restricted ability to prepare a defence to the charge, loss of job, strain on family relations and friendships, and often appearance in court in a deteriorated or demoralized condition. The higher rates of suicide and self-injury for unconvicted rather than convicted prisoners may have much to do with these adversities.[14]

No doubt it was considerations of this kind that led the Supreme Court of the United States to declare that:

'this traditional right to freedom before conviction permits the unhampered preparation of a defence and serves to prevent the infliction of punishment prior to conviction. Unless this right to bail before trial is preserved, the presumption of innocence, secured only after centuries of struggle, would lose its meaning.'[15]

---

[8] Citing *Yagci and Sargin v Turkey* (1992) 20 EHRR 505, para 52.

[9] Citing *Muller v France* (17 March 1997), para 44.

[10] *Clooth v Belgium* (1991) 14 EHRR 717, Commission at para 75; reiterated by the Court in *Jablonski v Poland* (2003) 36 EHRR 455, at [84].

[11] *Punzelt v Czech Republic* (2001) 33 EHRR 1159, at [73].

[12] See R.A. Duff, *Trials and Punishments* (1986), 140, arguing that in principle custodial remands before trial are utterly inconsistent with respect for individual citizens as rational agents.

[13] This, of course, is a major reason why the provisions in ss 21–29 of the Anti-Terrorism, Crime and Security Act 2001, authorizing the detention without trial of 'suspected international terrorists', were held inconsistent with the Convention in *A. v Home Secretary* [2004] UKHL 56.

[14] A. Liebling and H. Krarup, *Suicide Attempts and Self-Injury in Male Prisons* (1993), 52.

[15] *Stack v Boyle* (1951) 342 US 1, *per* Vinson CJ at 4.

Yet this statement introduces another concept that needs careful inquiry. If remands in custody are to be permitted at all, can they fairly be described as 'the infliction of punishment'? From time to time it has been alleged that courts have indulged in 'punitive remands', remanding a person in custody when it is known full well that a custodial sentence would not be appropriate on conviction.[16] Remand for those reasons is plainly an abuse. But even in cases where the remand is not punitive, the hardship inflicted on the defendant is undeniable. However, definitions of punishment invariably link the element of hard treatment to conviction of an offence by a court.[17] Remand in custody inflicts hardship, as might a dog bite or a falling tree in a storm, but it cannot be regarded as punishment. It is, however, a gross abuse of power, since it involves a deprivation of liberty inflicted intentionally under cover of law.

The US Supreme Court rejected a challenge to the Bail Reform Act of 1984, which allows a judicial officer to authorize pre-trial detention if there is clear and convincing evidence that 'no condition or combination of conditions of pre-trial release will reasonably assure the safety of any other person and the community'—a formulation similar to the third principle frequently declared by the Strasbourg court (above). Rejecting the argument that the statute was unconstitutional because it imposed punishment before trial, the majority held that a statute on pre-trial detention is 'regulatory, not penal'.[18] The minority retorted that this approach 'merely redefine[s] any measure which is claimed to be punishment as "regulation" and, magically, the Constitution no longer prohibits its imposition'.[19] The reply scores a debating point, but leaves open the justifications for the detention of the mentally disordered, of persons subject to quarantine, of illegal immigrants pending deportation, as set out in Article 5.1 of the European Convention. There surely are circumstances in which the State is justified in depriving a person of liberty even though that person has not been convicted of an offence—indeed, is not even suspected of one. Clearly the justification for this must be strong and pressing, in view of the deprivation of liberty involved. Such detention may not amount to punishment, but it still needs urgent and compelling justification.

Thus far we have assessed the reasons for maintaining a strong presumption of liberty at the pre-trial stage. But in all judicial systems there is some provision for that presumption to be rebutted, and typical grounds for refusing bail are the risk that the defendant will not appear for trial; the risk that the defendant will commit offences unless placed in detention; and the risk that the defendant might interfere with witnesses or otherwise obstruct justice. All these grounds for pre-trial detention are phrased in terms of risk: the State is using its power by authorizing the detention of certain people to reduce certain risks to other citizens and to the criminal justice system. Are these separate grounds justifiable reasons for depriving a person of

[16] See e.g., the warning of Lord Hailsham LC against punitive remands in 1971–[1972] *The Magistrate* 21.

[17] The classic definition is that of H.L.A. Hart, *Punishment and Responsibility* (1968), 5.

[18] *United States v Salerno* (1987) 481 US 739. For an accessible discussion, see Lord Windlesham, 'Punishment and Prevention: the Inappropriate Prisoners', [1988] Crim LR 140, at 143–5.

[19] *United States v Salerno*, at 760 *per* Marshall and Brennan JJ.

liberty? If they are, do we have sufficient knowledge to be able to assess the risks accurately?

Let us consider the first of the three main grounds for refusing bail—that otherwise the defendant is unlikely to stand trial or, alternatively put, that there is a significant risk of absconding. In terms of justification, one key question concerns the relative social importance of ensuring that persons charged with offences attend their trial on the due date. Courts are rightly reluctant to hold a trial in a defendant's absence.[20] Presumably the police could be dispatched to arrest someone who failed to attend without offering a reasonable excuse, but there might be a greater anxiety over certain defendants who seem likely to flee the country or to hide themselves away. In principle, there is a greater public interest in securing the trial of those charged with more serious rather than less serious offences. As for the assessment of risk, we saw that the Strasbourg jurisprudence counsels against simply assuming that persons charged with serious offences will fail to appear at trial. There must be some ground for identifying a significant risk—perhaps that the defendant had on previous occasions failed to attend trial. Even then, the court must be satisfied that no other method of securing attendance at trial would be effective (deprivation of liberty must be a last resort).

A second main ground is the probability of committing offences if granted bail. In terms of justification, it is often asserted that there is a public interest in ensuring that people already charged with an offence do not commit offences during the period before their trial. The exact basis for this is unclear. Is it that the State is somehow responsible for the conduct of persons who have been charged but not yet tried, perhaps because it is the slowness of the machinery of criminal justice that creates the opportunities? Otherwise, in what way do remandees differ from, say, people with previous convictions who are walking the streets? Surely it cannot be that anyone who has been charged may be presumed guilty, and for that reason may be thought likely to commit a further offence if left at large before the formal trial: that reasoning, with its presumption of guilt, would contradict the presumption of innocence. Indeed, this was one of the grounds on which the Irish Supreme Court refused to recognize this as a legitimate ground for pre-trial detention, commenting that 'this is a form of preventative justice which . . . is quite alien to the true purpose of bail'.[21] Yet the trend undoubtedly is to deny this, and for governments to regard the period between arrest and trial as a time at which they must take action to control risks to citizens, and must endeavour to promote public safety by providing for some defendants to be deprived of their liberty.[22] One argument may be that the fact that a person has been charged with an offence is crucial. In some cases the defendant may well have confessed guilt

---

[20] But there may be circumstances in which this is permissible consistently with Article 6 of the Convention: see *Jones* [2002] UKHL 5, and *Jones v United Kingdom*, decision of 9 September 2003.

[21] *People (Attorney-General) v Callaghan* [1966] IR 426, *per* Walsh J at 516. In 1996 the Irish Constitution was amended so as to provide for pre-trial detention where reasonably necessary 'to prevent the commission of a serious offence by that person.' See further U. ni Raifeartaigh, 'Reconciling Bail Law with the Presumption of Innocence', (1997) 17 *Oxford JLS* 1.

[22] The Supreme Court of Canada reached a similar conclusion in *Morales* (1993) 77 CCC (3d) 91.

and indicated an intention to plead guilty, which may be taken to contradict the presumption of innocence; but defendants may change their intentions when the prosecution evidence becomes clear and they have received legal advice, so it would be unwise to build too much on those foundations. More generally, it could be argued that the laying of a charge ought to be attributed significance now that the Crown Prosecution Service has primary responsibility for such decisions; but that overlooks the need for the CPS frequently to take the charging decision before all the evidence is available. As we saw in Chapter 7, the 2004 version of the Code for Crown Prosecutors now propounds a 'threshold test' for cases where 'the suspect presents as a substantial bail risk if released from custody,' that test being one of reasonable grounds to suspect the defendant of having committed the offence.[23] That standard is, as argued in Chapter 7, significantly below the 'reasonable prospect of conviction' test that is normally required. The arguments here, then, are much weaker than is commonly supposed; and none of them is compatible with the fundamental presumption of innocence, since they tend in the direction of assuming guilt. The Strasbourg Court has indeed insisted that the existence of reasonable suspicion of the offence is a necessary precondition for any custodial remand,[24] and that there must be persuasive evidence for concluding that there is a significant risk of serious offences being committed. That does not confront the question of why liberty should be taken away before trial, but offers a procedure that gives some recognition to the presumption of liberty, if less to the presumption of innocence.

A third ground is the probability that the defendant might interfere with witnesses or otherwise obstruct the course of justice if released on bail. In some of these cases there is a distinct justification: the risk to the security of another person. Where the rights of another citizen are shown to be at risk, perhaps in a domestic violence case or some other instance of ongoing attacks, the protection of those rights may well provide a justification for restrictions and, in some circumstances, for the deprivation of liberty. The uttering of threats by the defendant towards the victim would be one way of demonstrating the risk. In contrast to the situation in the previous paragraph, threats offer evidence of a specific risk to a particular person. Therefore, if it appears to be a choice between the defendant's liberty or the victim's freedom from probable harm, detention pending trial may be easier to justify.[25] If there is thought to be a more general risk of interfering with witnesses or obstructing the course of justice, the

[23] *Addendum issued by the Director of Public Prosecutions: Application of the Code for Crown Prosecutors to Charging Decisions where Suspects are to be Detained in Custody after Charge: the Threshold Test* (May 2004); now incorporated in para. 6.4 of the Code for Crown Prosecutors (2004)—see Ch. 7.2 (b) above.

[24] 'The persistence of a reasonable suspicion that the person arrested has committed an offence is a condition *sine qua non* for the lawfulness of the continued detention': *Assenov v Bulgaria* (1999) 29 EHRR 652, at [154].

[25] In *CPS Policy on Prosecuting Cases of Domestic Violence*, para 8.2, the CPS states that it will draw to the court's attention, on any bail application, threats or other risks of danger presented by the defendant to the victim or witnesses. On the positive duty of a State to protect individuals under threat, see *Osman v United Kingdom* (1998) 29 EHRR 245, and B. Emmerson and A. Ashworth, *Human Rights and Criminal Justice* (2001), Ch. 18.

justification for restricting the defendant's liberty is to secure the integrity of the criminal justice system. But for any such restriction, and particularly for a deprivation of liberty, there must be persuasive evidence of the risk—perhaps evidence that the defendant may have been involved in such incidents before, or evidence of threats uttered.

The fourth ground for the refusal of bail recognized by the Strasbourg Court is where the nature of the crime and the probable public reaction to it are such that the release of the defendant might lead to public disorder. This justification may apply where it is considered right, exceptionally, to detain a defendant for his own protection.[26]

All these grounds for the refusal of bail turn on questions of predicted risk. In relation to the most frequent ground for refusal of bail—the risk of offences being committed in the period before trial—the 'risk' consists of the probability of an offence being committed if the defendant is granted bail, and the seriousness of any likely offence. A low probability of a very serious offence ought to have more weight than a high probability of a minor offence. Indeed, for non-serious offences, it will be argued, custodial remands should simply be ruled out. However, what we have seen in this section and will continue to see throughout this chapter is that the crucial issues are conspicuously under-determined. We have failed to identify a persuasive reason for the State to take power over defendants in the pre-trial period, to the extent of depriving them of liberty. We have argued that the well-known fallibility of predictions of dangerous conduct applies no less in the pre-trial sphere. These themes will now be developed more specifically in relation to the relevant English law.

8.2 THE LAW RELATING TO REMANDS

This part of the chapter, considers the history and current form of the law relating to remands, first in relation to court remands, and then in relation to remand decisions taken by the police.

(a) COURT REMANDS

In England and Wales the law relating to remands has developed in two distinct phases. The first phase focused chiefly on the problem of securing the attendance of the defendant at the trial. In *Robinson* (1854), Coleridge J held that this was the sole point to which the magistrates should give attention.[27] In *Rose* (1898),[28] Lord Russell stated that 'it cannot be too strongly impressed on the magistracy that bail is not to be withheld as a punishment but that the requirements as to bail are merely to secure the

---

[26] *Letellier v France* (1992) 14 EHRR 83.

[27] (1854) 23 LJQB 286. For summaries of the history, see A.K. Bottomley, 'The Granting of Bail: Principles and Practice' (1968) 31 *MLR* 40, and Corre and Wolchover (above, n 1), 11–19.

[28] (1898) 78 LT 119.

attendance of the prisoner at his trial'. It was not until the 1940s and 1950s that the English courts, with Lord Goddard as Lord Chief Justice, began to establish that an alternative ground for remanding in custody is that the defendant is likely to commit an offence if granted bail.[29] The Home Office took the unusual step of circulating to all magistrates the text of Lord Goddard's remarks in *Wharton* (1955).[30] Statutory confirmation came in the provisions of the Criminal Justice Act 1967, an Act which also introduced the possibility of granting conditional bail.

Two similar phases can be discerned in the American law. Until the 1960s the law and practice tended to concentrate on the problem of securing the attendance of defendants at trial: surveys showed that courts were mostly using financial bonds (sureties) as the means to this end, and that the result was the pre-trial imprisonment of people too poor to raise the money for such a bond.[31] Congress passed the Federal Bail Reform Act in 1966, legislating for 'release on recognisance' rather than financial bonds as the normal pre-trial order.[32] The second phase was marked by a growing anxiety about the commission of offences by people on bail, a concern that culminated in Congress passing the Bail Reform Act of 1984. Although the Act contains a number of procedural safeguards, its main provision is, as we have seen, based on a prediction of future danger.[33] Many other jurisdictions seem to have arrived at positions broadly similar to the English and American, although the provision in the Canadian Criminal Code still maintains that the primary ground for refusing bail is to secure attendance at the trial. However, the secondary ground (to be considered if the primary ground is inapplicable) refers to 'the protection or safety of the public'.[34]

The relevant law for England and Wales is now contained chiefly in the Bail Act 1976, as amended. In essence, a court has four main alternatives: release on unconditional bail, release on conditional bail, release on bail subject to a surety or security, and remand in custody.

Little needs to be said about unconditional bail. As for conditional bail, the Act makes provision for this in s 3(6). It appears that around one-quarter to one-third of defendants granted bail are placed under conditions:[35] Raine and Willson found that the most common condition is residence at a specified address (78 per cent of conditional cases), followed by not contacting named persons (46 per cent), not going to a certain address (24 per cent), curfew (21 per cent), and reporting at a police

---

[29] See *Phillips* (1947) 32 Cr App R 47; *Wharton* [1955] Crim LR 565 ('unless the justices felt real doubt as to the result of the case, men with bad criminal records should not be granted bail'); and *Gentry* [1956] Crim LR 120 (same policy reiterated).

[30] See Bottomley, above n 27, at 52.

[31] See C. Foote, 'Compelling Appearance in Court: Administration of Bail in Philadelphia' (1954) 102 *U. Pa. LR* 1031; on the subsequent research by the Vera Institute that led to the change in federal law, D.J. Freed and P. Wald, *Bail in the United States* (1964).

[32] For an outline, see P.R. Jones and J.S. Goldkamp, 'Judicial Guidelines for Pre-Trial Release: Research and Policy Developments in the United States', (1991) 30 *Howard JCJ* 140.

[33] See n 18 above and accompanying text.

[34] N. Padfield, 'The Right to Bail: a Canadian Perspective' [1993] Crim LR 510.

[35] P.M. Morgan and P. Henderson, *Remand Decisions and Offending on Bail* (1998), Ch.4.

station (18 per cent).[36] They found that many conditions are proposed by the defence (in the hope of deflecting the court from a custodial remand), rather than by the magistrates themselves. They also found that half their interviewees believed that bail conditions would not be enforced, a perception that clearly weakens the efficacy of conditional bail. The Bail Act also provides that a court may, subject to certain restrictions, require a surety to secure the defendant's attendance at court. It may also require a defendant to give security for surrender to custody before release on bail.[37] The danger with financial conditions, as the American experience shows, is that they may tend to exclude the less well-off from bail, and there is English evidence to suggest that some remands in custody occur because the levels of surety set by the courts are unrealistic.[38] This is quite wrong, being unfair discrimination against people of modest means.

The centrepiece of the Bail Act is s 4, which proclaims what has been described as a general right to bail or a presumption in favour of bail. Thus s 4(1) provides that 'a person to whom this section applies shall be granted bail except as provided in Schedule 1 to this Act'. Paragraphs 2–6 of Part I of that Schedule[39] list a number of 'exceptions to the right to bail', including custodial remands for the defendant's own protection[40] and (more doubtfully) custodial remands because the court does not yet have sufficient information to take a decision on bail. The main provision is paragraph 2, which must be quoted in full:

'The defendant need not be granted bail if the court is satisfied that there are substantial grounds for believing that the defendant, if released on bail (whether subject to conditions or not), would–

(a) fail to surrender to custody, or

(b) commit an offence while on bail, or

(c) interfere with witnesses or otherwise obstruct the course of justice, whether in relation to himself or any other person.'

These three grounds correspond broadly with those approved by the European Court of Human Rights in its development of Article 5(3), and have a loose affinity with those subsequently incorporated in the Bail Reform Act of 1984 in the US.[41] The Schedule to the English Act goes on to set out various considerations to which regard should be

---

[36] J. Raine and M. Willson, 'The Imposition of Conditions in Bail Decisions', (1996) 35 *Howard JCJ* 256; very similar percentages were found by Morgan and Henderson (previous note), at 42.

[37] See Cavadino and Gibson, above n 1, 40–6.

[38] *Ibid.*, 170, proposing a legislative requirement to take account of defendants' means and social background.

[39] Pt. II of the Schedule deals separately with non-imprisonable offences, which will not be discussed here.

[40] See above, n 26, for a relevant Strasbourg decision. Section 13 of the Criminal Justice Act 2003 introduces the possibility of alternatively granting conditional bail in such cases.

[41] The US Act refers to a serious risk that the defendant will flee or will obstruct justice; or where the case involves a crime of violence (very broadly defined), a major drug offence or any crime punishable by life imprisonment; or where the case involves a felony charge against someone previously convicted of two offences in the above categories.

had when taking bail/custody decisions. Among those is 'the defendant's record as respects the fulfilment of his obligations under previous grants of bail in criminal proceedings', a matter plainly relevant when the court is considering exception (a) to the right to bail.

Another consideration is 'the character, antecedents, associations and community ties of the defendant'. Community ties may be relevant to the probability that a defendant will attend his trial (exception (a)), since it may be argued that a person who is homeless or in temporary accommodation is more likely to abscond than someone with a permanent address (and a family) in the locality. However, it has been urged repeatedly that homelessness should not lead to a custodial remand without thorough exploration of other alternatives.[42] The 'character and antecedents' of the offender may give grounds for a prediction of whether he or she is likely to offend if given bail (exception (b)). This question has attracted surprisingly little legal analysis or empirical inquiry. One oft-quoted statement is that of Atkinson J in the Court of Criminal Appeal in *Phillips* (1947),[43] where he warned courts against granting bail to defendants with a 'record of housebreaking', and added that 'in 19 out of 20 cases it is a mistake [to] release young housebreakers on bail'. Statistical studies suggest that this is a considerable exaggeration.[44] The Strasbourg Court has signalled the need for courts to avoid stereotypical reasoning and therefore not to make assumptions simply on the basis of a criminal record:[45] previous convictions must be recent, relevant and of a certain seriousness before it will be proper to contemplate rebutting the presumption of liberty on this ground.

A further consideration listed in paragraph 9 is 'the nature and seriousness of the offence or default (and the probable method of dealing with the offender for it)'. The Strasbourg Court has warned against a general assumption that the seriousness of the charge increases the risk of non-appearance at trial, and there must be further and specific evidence of a risk of this defendant absconding.[46] The seriousness of the charge ought to be relevant to custodial remands on the second ground, in recognition that it would be wrong to remand in custody a person whose charge (if proved) would be unlikely to result in a custodial sentence. However, on the face of the Bail Act, and the exceptions to bail that it enumerates, the probability of further minor offences such as shoplifting could justify a custodial remand. The Act should be amended so that exception (b) refers to the likelihood of committing a *serious* offence whilst on bail, as does the law on custodial remands of juveniles, so as to make this principle clear.

The Convention has had some effect in curtailing attempts to 'toughen up' the law of bail in the 1990s. Section 25 of the Criminal Justice and Public Order Act 1994 sought to remove a court's powers to remand on bail any person charged with murder, attempted murder, manslaughter, rape, or attempted rape who already has a

---

[42] E.g. in Home Office circular 155/1975, *Bail Procedures.*   [43] (1947) 32 Cr App R 47.

[44] E.g. P.M. Morgan, *Offending Whilst on Bail* (1992).   [45] Above, n 7 and accompanying text.

[46] Above, n 8 and accompanying text.

conviction for such an offence. In *Caballero v United Kingdom*,[47] the Strasbourg Court confirmed that this was in breach of Article 5(3), because, as the Commission had put it, 'the exclusion from the risk assessment of a consideration of all the particular circumstances and facts of each accused's case (other than the two facts contained in s 25) exposes, of itself, accused persons to arbitrary deprivation of liberty.' Section 25 was amended[48] so as to provide that a court may only grant bail to such persons if satisfied that 'there are exceptional circumstances which justify it.' This may still be thought inconsistent with the presumption of liberty implicit in Article 5(3), since the re-worded s 25 establishes a presumption in these cases in favour of deprivation of liberty,[49] and the Strasbourg Court has held that the authorities, not the defendant, must bear the burden of proving the need for detention.[50] By adopting an interpretative approach that treats as an 'exceptional circumstance' the view that the defendant appears unlikely to commit a serious offence if not remanded in custody,[51] a court could find the substance of s 25 compatible, but not the burden of proof.

Following the Law Commission's report, two other provisions of the Bail Act have been amended in an attempt to produce Convention compatibility. Thus s 26 of the Criminal Justice and Public Order Act 1994 has been amended by s 14 of the Criminal Justice Act 2003, so as to establish a presumption that a person should not be granted bail if it appears that he has committed an offence whilst on bail for another charge, 'unless the court is satisfied that there is no significant risk of his committing an offence' if granted bail. Similarly, s 15 of the 2003 Act provides a presumption that a person who has failed to appear at court without reasonable cause should not be granted bail, again unless the court is satisfied that there is no significant risk of a further failure to surrender to bail. The 'no significant risk' formula is more directly linked to the rationale of each provision than 'exceptional circumstances', but it still reverses the general presumption of liberty. It also places great weight on assessments of risk, and ought to be interpreted as calling for sound, evidence-based reasons in favour of detention whereas, by virtue of the presumption, the defendant has to produce evidence-based reasons why there is no significant risk in granting him bail.

(b) POLICE REMANDS

The powers of the police to remand persons whom they have interviewed and may wish to interview again, and persons whom they have charged, pending their first

---

[47] (2000) 30 EHRR 643 (above n 6); the Government conceded after the Commission's opinion, and so the Court did not deliver a full judgment.

[48] By s 56 of the Crime and Disorder Act 1998.

[49] Cf. the unsatisfactory decision in *R v Crown Court at Harrow* [2003] 1 WLR 2756, criticized by A. Ashworth and M. Strange, 'Criminal Law and Human Rights', [2004] EHRLR 121, at 128–9.

[50] *Reid v United Kingdom* (2003) 37 EHRR 9, at [70].

[51] Adapting the Court of Appeal's sentencing judgment in *Offen (No.2)* [2001] 1 WLR 253; see Law Commission, *Bail and the Human Rights Act 1998* (2001), Part VIII.

court appearance, are contained in the Police and Criminal Evidence Act 1984, as amended by the Criminal Justice and Public Order Act 1994. The principal change in the 1994 Act was to confer on the police the power to grant bail with conditions: previously, they were only able to grant unconditional bail or to keep the suspect in custody overnight pending court appearance. One danger of granting such a power, well known to criminologists, is that it will be used in a net-widening manner. That is, a power intended to reduce the number of remands in custody will actually be used in cases where unconditional bail was previously allowed. In Raine and Willson's research at six police stations towards the end of 1995 this seems to have been the result. The introduction of conditional bail led to a small overall reduction in overnight detention of suspects by the police, but a significant drop in cases of unconditional bail. Where conditional bail was granted, the most frequent conditions were to keep away from a named place or a named person, sometimes for the protection of a witness or complainant. In view of the relatively slight drop in overnight detentions followed by court proceedings, it appears that the change has not contributed to a reduction in costs to the extent that was anticipated.[52] Raine and Willson also found that in some cases the police were using their bail powers as bargaining chips in their dealings with suspects, a finding that is hardly surprising[53] but which raises again the question whether such extensive powers over the liberty of individuals should be granted to the police.

The Criminal Justice Act 2003 introduces the concept of 'bail elsewhere than at a police station', which is likely to become known as street bail. The powers introduced by s 4 of the 2003 Act are discretionary, and the provisions on 'the right to bail' in the Bail Act 1976 do not apply here: police officers *may* release an arrested person on bail, and require that person to attend at a police station. No other requirement may be imposed, which means that other forms of conditional bail are not possible 'on the street.' It is not clear how these new powers will be used, and whether they will succeed in avoiding unnecessary processing of suspects at police stations and therefore in contributing to an increased police presence on the streets.

8.3 THE TREATMENT OF UNCONVICTED DEFENDANTS

The vast majority of cases in magistrates' courts do not involve any remand of the defendant, whether on bail or in custody, although the figures show a drift towards dealing with fewer cases at the first appearance:

---

[52] J. Raine and M. Willson, 'Police Bail with Conditions', (1997) 37 *BJ Crim.* 593.

[53] See the similar findings from Canada reported by G. Kellough and S. Wortley, 'Remand for Plea: Bail Decisions and Plea Bargaining as Commensurate Decisions', (2002) 42 *BJ Crim.* 186.

Table 8.1 Cases dealt with in magistrates' courts at first appearance[54]

	Summary motoring offences	Other summary offences	Indictable offences
1986	97%	92%	47%
1996	89%	82%	36%
2002	89%	80%	39%

This shows an overall decline in the proportion of cases dealt with at first appearance, although the figures appear to have stabilized in recent years. The vast majority of the indictable defendants in 2002 had been summoned rather than arrested.[55] Turning to those not dealt with on first appearance, custodial remands of those charged with indictable offences who were ultimately dealt with in a magistrates' court increased from seven per cent in 1986 to 10 per cent in 1996 and, after a rise in the late 1990s, returned to 10 per cent in 2002. Among those committed by magistrates for trial in the Crown Court, the proportion remanded in custody has risen from 22 per cent in 1986 to 25 per cent in 1996 and to 31 per cent in 2002. Research in the 1980s by Jones (1985) and in the 1990s by Hucklesby (1997) revealed wide variations in the use of custodial remands by courts in different areas, suggesting the persistence of local cultures on this issue.[56]

What is the position in the prisons? Remand prisoners have always tended to be placed in the most overcrowded conditions in the system, since they are sent to local prisons. When the Woolf Inquiry reported on conditions in Strangeways and other prisons which had seen disturbances in 1990, a considerable proportion of the report was devoted to improving the lot of remand prisoners—unconvicted, but bearing the brunt of poor conditions.[57] Moreover, the provision of legal advice to defendants remanded in custody is difficult and may impair their defence.[58] All of this is certainly inconsistent with the proper treatment of people who have not yet been convicted, even if it is not formally in breach of the presumption of innocence and the right to legal assistance. The number of people in prison on remand stood at approximately 12,000 in 2004, of whom some 8,000 were awaiting trial and 4,000 awaiting sentence.

---

[54] *Criminal Statistics, England and Wales 1986, 1996, and 2002.*

[55] *Criminal Statistics England and Wales 2002,* Table 5.2.

[56] P. Jones, 'Remand Decisions at Magistrates' Courts', in D. Moxon (ed), *Managing Criminal Justice* (1985); and A. Hucklesby, 'Court Culture: an Explanation of Variations in the Use of Bail at Magistrates' Courts', (1997) 36 *Howard JCJ* 129.

[57] *Prison Disturbances April 1990: Report of an Inquiry by Rt. Hon. Lord Justice Woolf and His Honour Judge Tumin* (1991), particularly Ch. 10.

[58] See the study of young remand prisoners by F. Brookman and H. Pierpoint, 'Access to Legal Advice for Young Suspects and Remand Prisoners', (2003) 42 *Howard JCJ* 452.

This constitutes a much lower proportion of the total prison population than in previous years, but that is because the number of convicted and sentenced offenders in prison has risen so steeply to beyond 60,000. The remand population remains high, particularly in respect of those who have not yet had their trial. Moreover, average waiting times for those remanded in custody between committal by magistrates and trial in the Crown Court have increased significantly in recent years: from around nine weeks for custody cases in the mid-1990s the average had risen to 12.7 weeks in 2002.[59]

Some improvements in the remand system may have taken place, but in the light of the fundamental right to liberty enshrined in Article 5 we must continue to examine whether it is necessary to have as many as 8,000 people in prison at any one time awaiting trial. One way of examining this issue is to consider the outcomes of the cases against those remanded in custody. According to the *Prison Statistics 2002*, one-fifth of both male (21 per cent) and female (20 per cent) remandees were either acquitted or had their cases discontinued. For males, 50 per cent received custodial sentences and 23 per cent non-custodial disposals. For females, 41 per cent received custodial sentences and 32 per cent non-custodial disposals.

These figures raise a number of serious questions. In the cases of those remanded in custody and subsequently acquitted or not proceeded against, the loss of liberty is particularly hard on the individuals concerned. It could be argued that these are not necessarily cases of malfunction in the criminal justice system: if a conscientious judgment was made about the probability that, if not remanded in custody, they would fail to attend trial, commit offences whilst on bail, or interfere with witnesses, none of those matters bears directly on the probability of conviction. However, the importance of these decisions for defendants means that two aspects of custodial remands require special attention. First, the Strasbourg Court has made it clear that the remanding magistrates must be satisfied of the continued existence of 'reasonable suspicion' (i.e. evidence) against the defendant,[60] and paragraph 9 of Schedule 1 to the Bail Act states that the strength of the evidence should be considered. To what extent are magistrates able to do this meaningfully? It is well known that decisions by magistrates tend to correspond with recommendations by the CPS, which in turn correspond with decisions by the police. The correlations are strong, but not invariable, and therefore do not necessarily lead to inferences of undue influence or failure of decision makers to examine issues independently. Thus Morgan and Henderson found that, in respect of those held in police custody, the CPS recommended custody for only 48 per cent, and 76 per cent of those recommendations were accepted; the CPS recommended conditional bail for a further 46 per cent, and magistrates accepted 90 per cent of those recommendations.[61] Since one-fifth of those remanded in custody are acquitted or not proceeded against, this ought to prompt inquiries into the reasons why they were remanded in custody. Morgan and Henderson identify a

---

[59] *Criminal Statistics England and Wales 2002*, Table 3B.   [60] Above n 25 and accompanying text.
[61] P. Morgan and P. Henderson, *Remand Decisions and Offending on Bail* (1998), 37.

number of characteristics that are strongly associated with decisions to remand in custody, notably the absence of a fixed address, seriousness of charge, and bail history. It is also important to know why cases were dropped, where that was the outcome, and why this could not have happened at an earlier stage. At the very least, the figures suggest that the pain of custodial remand, felt so acutely by those subject to it, does not always weigh so heavily with those who take decisions in respect of defendants.[62]

What about those who receive non-custodial sentences after being remanded in custody? This is the outcome for about a quarter of males and nearly one-third of all females remanded in custody before trial. Does it mean that they were unnecessarily remanded in custody in the first place?

At least four lines of argument cast doubt on this. The first is the one that most sentencers hasten to offer: that a court passing sentence must recognize the fact that the offender has already spent time in custody, and that a court may properly take this into account and impose a non-custodial sentence in a case where, if there had been no custodial remand, it would probably have imposed custody. The magistrates who pass sentence will rarely be the same individuals who refused bail and ordered the custodial remand, so the sentencing decision will be taken entirely *de novo*. There can be no objection to the court taking account of what has already happened: indeed, this may allow the court to adopt a more constructive approach than it might otherwise have felt able to do, by making a community order rather than imposing a custodial sentence. The implication of this argument is that the imposition of a non-custodial sentence does not necessarily suggest that the custodial remand was wrong, since in many cases if there had not been a custodial remand there would have been a custodial sentence. In theory this argument seems plausible. It is difficult, however, to determine how much substance it has in practice, since no research has been carried out into the reasoning of magistrates when sentencing offenders who have been in custody on remand. No one knows what proportion of the cases resulting in a non-custodial sentence are a response to the custodial remand, and what proportion imply that there need have been no custodial remand in the first place.

Moreover, this first argument may prove rather more than was intended. If it is true that sentencers tend to take account of the fact that an offender has spent time in custody on remand, it may be the case that some of those given custodial sentences are sentenced in that way simply so as to facilitate their immediate release. If the court learns that an offender has been in prison for two months awaiting trial, it may feel that he or she has already been punished quite sufficiently (or even too heavily) for the offence, and may therefore impose a sentence of four months' imprisonment so as to ensure immediate release.[63] Otherwise, the court might have chosen some kind of

---

[62] It should also be added that this country, unlike many of its European neighbours, does not have a statutory scheme for compensating those who are remanded in custody and then acquitted, although Article 5(5) of the Convention mandates 'an enforceable right to compensation.'

[63] This is said to be the approach of some courts in other European countries: see, e.g. W. Heinz, 'The Problems of Imprisonment', in R. Hood (ed), *Crime and Criminal Policy in Europe: Proceedings of a European Colloquium* (1989).

community order as a suitable sentence. It is not known how many courts would react in this way—some might grant a conditional discharge or other sentence in these circumstances. But the point is that the numbers of people remanded in custody who are subsequently given custodial sentences by magistrates' courts may also include some cases (we know not how many) where the court would not have imposed custody if there had been no custodial remand. To take the further step and assert that the numbers of those given non-custodial sentences who would have received custody but for the custodial remand are far greater than the numbers of those given custodial sentences who would have received non-custodial sentences but for the custodial remand is to advance into the realms of speculation. The proportions are not known.

A second argument against taking the figures at face value is that the criteria for granting or withholding bail are not directly related to the probability of a custodial sentence. The three criteria in para 2 of the Schedule to the Bail Act focus only on the period between first court appearance and trial. It is true that para 9 of that Schedule suggests that courts should also have regard to 'the nature and seriousness of the offence and the probable method of dealing with the offender for it', but it is not clear how much separate attention has been given to this provision. Where a defendant is remanded in custody because there are substantial grounds for believing that other- wise he or she may not attend the trial, or for believing that otherwise witnesses may be threatened, these reasons have nothing to do with the likely sentence in the case. The statistics are not sharp enough to determine the relative proportions of cases: in the Home Office's 1978 survey, the probability of committing an offence was given as a reason in 63 per cent of cases, and the probability of the defendant absconding was given as a reason in 51 per cent of cases. Exactly how many cases depended only on one or the other reason is unclear, but some evidently bear no relationship to the probability of a custodial sentence on conviction.

A third argument points to the divergence between the bail provisions and the relevant sentencing law. Section 152(2) of the Criminal Justice Act 2003 states that a court 'must not pass a custodial sentence' unless satisfied that the offence 'was so serious that neither a fine alone nor a community sentence can be justified for the offence.'[64] No such restrictions are to be found in the Bail Act and, except with reference to juvenile remands, there is no clear injunction that the court should adopt the least restrictive form of remand (unconditional bail; conditional bail) unless satisfied that the defendant would receive a custodial sentence if convicted as charged.

A fourth argument raises questions about whether the remand decisions taken in court really are considered and rounded determinations. We have already noted the findings of Morgan and Henderson that, in the majority of cases, magistrates tend to adopt the same course as that recommended by the CPS.[65] Hucklesby found that the vast majority of remand hearings were uncontested: only in nine per cent of cases

[64] A similar provision has been part of the law since 1991: see Criminal Justice Act 1991, s 1(2).
[65] Morgan and Henderson, above n 61; for experimental evidence to the same effect, see M. Dhami, 'Conditional Bail Decision-Making in the Magistrates' Court', (2004) 43 *Howard JCJ* 27, at 40.

was there a different view advanced by prosecution and defence. In most cases the CPS did not oppose bail, and in almost half of the cases where bail was opposed the defence did not contest this. At least two processes appear to be at work here. One is the influence of the police: if they grant bail from the police station, it is highly unlikely that a court is going to find that a custodial remand is needed, and the CPS would have difficulty in sustaining such an argument.[66] The other is the influence of court culture, which sustains different rates of remand in custody in different courts over prolonged periods of years.[67] Both influences tend to suggest that in some cases the CPS does not make the recommendation it might think appropriate, and Hucklesby's finding that generally nearly nine out of ten CPS recommendations are accepted by the court[68] shows that the CPS makes different recommendations on similar cases because they are to be heard in different courts, or even by differently-constituted benches. Moreover, this process of anticipating the decisions of other parties is also evident in the approach of some defence solicitors, who admit both to adapting their representations to the particular bench (sometimes not applying for bail if it would be 'hopeless' in view of the constitution of the bench), and to using various tactics or coded language in order to distinguish bail applications which they believe in from those which they make purely because the client has insisted. This is a clear example of unethical behaviour, with defence lawyers failing to do their best to advance a defendant's case or, as Hucklesby puts it, ranking 'their credibility and status with the court above the interests of their clients'.[69] Hucklesby found that the CPS usually failed to give reasons for its representations: indeed, in 60 per cent of cases where the CPS requested a custodial remand, no reasons were stated, and even in cases where the defence contested the hearing the CPS failed to give its reason (e.g. by referring to a reason in the Bail Act) in many cases.[70] Insofar as these practices persist, they constitute a clear demonstration of the way in which apparently open and formal processes mask the reality of informal decision making, anticipation of the decisions of others, and the drive to maintain professional respect. In the present context, the implication is that decisions result from possibly tacit or even unconscious local coalitions between police practice and bench traditions, with the CPS and defence solicitors operating in a way that sees them anticipating the decisions of others in many cases and only rarely standing up for a view that differs from that of other key participants. Of course, a high rate of concordance in decisions does not conclusively prove undue influence, since it remains possible that the police, the CPS, and then the courts are applying the same criteria independently and reaching mostly the same conclusions, but the evidence of the criminal justice practitioners interviewed by Hucklesby strongly suggests otherwise.[71]

---

[66] J. Burrows, P. Henderson and P. Morgan, *Improving Bail Decisions: the Bail Process Project* (1994); for similar findings in Canada, see Kellough and Wortley, above n 53, at 204.

[67] Hucklesby, above n 56; A. Hucklesby, 'Remand Decision Makers', [1997] Crim LR 269.

[68] *Ibid.*, 276; also Morgan and Henderson, above n 61, 35–36.

[69] Hucklesby, [1997] Crim LR 269, at 279.   [70] *Ibid.*, 280–1.

[71] Hucklesby, above n 56, at 137–40.

Consideration of the four lines of argument against a face-value interpretation of the statistics on trial and sentence therefore demonstrates a pervasive uncertainty about the use of bail and of remands in custody. We lack the detailed research necessary to establish which explanations account for what percentage of cases. What does seem to be clear, however, is that the terms of the law on remands ought to be re-examined. In principle, as the Strasbourg Court has emphasized, the strength of the case ought to be a primary factor, before one of the specific grounds for deprivation of liberty is considered. In practice this creates difficulties in cases where the full evidence may not have arrived by the first (or even subsequent) remand hearing, especially if the results of a forensic science test are being awaited. We saw earlier that the CPS has now acknowledged this point by lowering the standard of evidence required,[72] but it remains a key issue in custodial remands. In principle, too, the probable penalty, if the defendant is convicted as charged, ought to be a factor. The Bail Act should require the court to be satisfied that a custodial sentence would be appropriate, if the case were proved as alleged; and it should re-write the 'future offences' ground so as to state expressly that there should be no remand in custody unless there is a substantial risk of *serious* offences being committed if the defendant were left at liberty.[73] If risk is to be a criterion, there must be legislative guidance not only on the seriousness of the probable offence but on the degree of risk and the basis for inferring it. This raises the issue of the information provided to bail decision-makers, a topic taken up in Part 5 of this chapter.

8.4 THE TREATMENT OF VICTIMS AND POTENTIAL VICTIMS

This is a provocative heading, intended to raise starkly the question whether the public in general or victims in particular have received any benefit from having larger numbers of defendants in custody at any one time. It would be almost impossible to trace any effects on the crime rate, largely because (1) the 'crime rate' is itself an elusive phenomenon which even surveys of victims (which are more complete than official records) have difficulty in charting,[74] and (2) even if we had a reliable measure of the number of crimes committed each year, it would necessarily be a product of several interacting influences, and it would rarely be possible to attribute particular trends to particular causes. But the question can be approached from other angles. One is to inquire into the volume of offences committed by persons who have been granted bail, perhaps with a view to suggesting that either too few people or the wrong

---

[72] See the 2004 edition of the *Code for Crown Prosecutors*, discussed in Ch. 7.2 (b) above.

[73] The 1996 amendment to the Irish Constitution insists on risk of a serious offence (see n 21 above), and this is also evident in the Strasbourg jurisprudence (see n 23 above).

[74] See M. Maguire, 'Crime Statistics', in M. Maguire, R. Morgan and R. Reiner (eds), *Oxford Handbook of Criminology* (3rd ed., 2002), 348–58.

people are remanded in custody. Another is to inquire into the proportion of those remanded in custody who are subsequently given non-custodial sentences, with a view to suggesting that it was unnecessary to order their pre-trial detention to secure public protection.

The most direct sense of public protection is to protect someone who has been threatened with violence by the defendant or who has a well-grounded fear of violence. Such issues may arise in neighbourhood disputes or intra-family offences. The *Victim's Charter* states that any victim worried about attack should tell the CPS, who should inform the court. The police are then required to inform the victim if the suspect is released on bail, what conditions (if any) have been imposed, and what the victim can do if the conditions are broken.[75] The CPS policy on domestic violence cases refers to the possibility of courts responding to evidence of threats against victims or witnesses.[76] If the court is satisfied that the only way to remove the threat of violence is to remand the defendant in custody, then this should be done, for the reasons outlined earlier. There is also a prosecution right to appeal against the grant of bail, recently extended to all imprisonable offences.[77]

Turning to public protection in a more general sense, let us begin by considering possible bail failures. Of those bailed to appear at court in 2002 for indictable offences, some 19 per cent failed to appear on the due date at a magistrates' court, and some nine per cent at the Crown Court.[78] These may be regarded as wrong decisions in the sense that the court evidently thought that there were no substantial grounds for believing that they would fail to surrender to custody. However, no such grounds may have been apparent at the time, and in any event the courts could be said to have decided correctly in the vast majority of cases. Moreover, it does not follow that these remandees should have been placed in custody: for some of them, conditional bail may have proved effective, and for many of the absconders from magistrates' courts their offending behaviour would not be particularly serious.

Of greater public concern are those defendants remanded on bail who are found to have committed offences during the period of remand. A study by Morgan and Henderson of some 2,300 bail cases in 1993–94 found that 17 per cent of those bailed by the courts were convicted of an offence committed during the period of bail.[79] Most of them were convicted of only one offence committed on bail, and the factors most closely connected with offending on bail were:

(a) a wait of more than six months before trial;

(b) a charge of car crime, burglary or robbery;

---

[75] Home Office, *The Victim's Charter* (1996 edn), 10; s13 of the Domestic Violence, Crime and Victims Act 2004 now requires the Home Secretary to publish a Code of Practice for Victims, and the Act also provides for the appointment of a Commissioner for Victims and Witnesses.

[76] CPS *Policy on Prosecuting Cases of Domestic Violence*, Part 8.

[77] Criminal Justice Act 2003, s18, amending the Bail (Amendment) Act 1993.

[78] *Criminal Statistics England and Wales 2002*, Table 5.9.　　　[79] Morgan and Henderson, above n 61, 44.

(c) a previous custodial sentence;

(d) age under 18; and

(e) a previous breach of bail.

Where an offence was committed on bail, it was particularly likely to be the same type of offence as originally charged if that charge was theft or handling (54 per cent), burglary (46 per cent), or a serious motoring offence (35 per cent).[80] If public protection is to be an important purpose of the bail/custody decision, then there is a need to focus on two distinct issues. The first is whether we can predict with sufficient accuracy which offenders are more likely to offend on bail than not: the Home Office is not optimistic about this,[81] and in view of the relatively low percentage of bailed defendants proved to offend on bail (17 per cent) this is hardly surprising. Even if the general predictive tools were more accurate, the focus ought then to be on the offences committed on bail. If the majority happen to be offences of theft or car crime, this prompts the question whether custodial remands are appropriate in these cases. It has been argued above that other means of restricting those whose offending behaviour is not conspicuously serious should be tried. It is important not to move directly from regarding 'offending on bail' as a problem, which it is, to regarding the use of custody as an appropriate or (in more than the short term) effective remedy. Indeed, it seems that the easiest offences to predict are likely to be lower on the scale of seriousness, raising doubts about the justification for remands in custody to prevent them.

This makes the connection between the failures of remands on bail and the failures of remands in custody. Is the public best protected by the extensive use of custodial remands? It is true that custodial remand represents a guarantee that the defendant will not commit offences against most members of the public (except, of course, those who are in prison either on conviction or on remand themselves). But deprivation of liberty remains, in principle, an incursion into a person's rights and that requires strong justification. Protecting a person against threats of violence may (in the absence of conditions that would be effective) be a sufficient reason for custodial remand. But we should ask whether protecting the public against theft or car crime is sufficient to outweigh this fundamental right. Moreover, we should recall the discussion in Part 3 of this chapter, where it was shown that one-quarter of those remanded in custody are not convicted, and that around one-quarter receive non-custodial sentences. For the reasons there discussed, this raises serious questions about the need, from the point of view of public safety, to remand so many people in custody before trial.

---

[80] *Ibid.*, 46.

[81] *Ibid.*, 60; Morgan and Henderson's study reports on an initiative to reduce offending on bail which had only mixed results.

8.5 PROCEDURAL JUSTICE AND REMAND DECISIONS

We now move on to consider four aspects of procedure relevant to the fairness of remand decisions—access to legal advice; bail information schemes; the speed of court hearings; and appeals.

(a) ACCESS TO LEGAL ADVICE AND ASSISTANCE

The European Court of Human Rights has insisted that a person should have a right to legal assistance before being deprived of liberty, especially before trial.[82] English law contains various provisions to ensure access to legal advice, both on arrest and detention and then during any custodial remand. But research shows that in practice, particularly with young defendants, the path towards provision of this access is not always smooth. Young remand prisoners have practical difficulties contacting their lawyers, and the lawyers have practical difficulties in arranging visits to prisons, particularly within the constraints of their other obligations.[83] In view of the importance of such contacts to the preparation of a defence, and thus to respecting the right declared in Article 6(3)(b), this may amount to a significant handicap to those remanded in custody. The provision of legal advice at the police station is generally better, and in some 90 per cent of cases a defendant who requests a duty solicitor will see one within 45 minutes,[84] but the conditions for giving and receiving legal advice are not always sufficient to satisfy the Convention.[85] Strasbourg decisions on the Convention have helped to produce a recognition that there is a duty on the prosecution to make some disclosure to the defence before bail hearings, in order to satisfy the principle of equality of arms that is established as an element of the right to a fair trial.[86] The Attorney-General's Guidelines on Disclosure state that 'disclosure ought to be made of significant information that might affect a bail decision,'[87] although the extent of compliance with this guidance is not known.

(b) BAIL INFORMATION SCHEMES

The problem of obtaining relevant and verified information for remand courts has been recognized for some time. If remand decision makers have insufficient

---

[82] Emmerson and Ashworth, above n 5, 13–25.

[83] See the research summarized in F. Brookman and H. Pierpoint, 'Access to Legal Advice for Young Suspects and Remand Prisoners', (2003) 42 *Howard JCJ* 452, at 460–3.

[84] CPS, *Annual Report 2002–03*, 43.

[85] Compare the strong statement of principle and its application in *Brennan v United Kingdom* (2002) 34 EHRR 18, with the unsatisfactory domestic decision in *M and La Rose v Metropolitan Police Commissioner* [2002] Crim. LR 215.

[86] E.g. *Nikolova v Bulgaria* (1999) 31 EHRR 64; *R v DPP, ex parte Lee* [1999] 2 All ER 237.

[87] Attorney-General, *Disclosure of Information in Criminal Proceedings* (2000); see also Law Com. 269, *Bail and the Human Rights Act 1998*.

information on the defendant's personal and social situtation, the possibility of advancing cogent grounds for conditional or unconditional bail is diminished. The Vera Institute of Justice began programmes in the US in the early 1960s, aimed at supplying courts with some objective data on which they could base their decisions, in particular data about the defendant's 'community ties.'[88] The idea was taken up in England and Wales in the 1970s, and then revived in the late 1980s. The Home Office circular of 1988 reiterated the importance of information,[89] but most of the pioneering work in this revival was carried out by the London office of the Vera Institute of Justice.[90] Since then, bail information schemes have spread slowly to become part of the system. By March 2003 some 90 per cent of prisons holding remand prisoners had a bail information scheme, but only 65 per cent of magistrates' courts had a court-based bail information scheme.[91] More progress clearly needs to be made, to ensure adequate provision of bail information throughout the system. In many cases, of necessity, the information has to be gathered quickly, usually on the morning of the first remand hearing, but there seems to be general satisfaction with the reliability of the information obtained.[92] In those cases where the defendant seems in danger of being remanded in custody largely because of the absence of an address to stay at, the bail information officer may need to make an attempt to find a place in a bail hostel. This may take time, and may require a case to be put back in the list for hearing, but it is crucial to ensure that a custodial remand is not made because the defendant has no fixed address rather than because of any risk that he poses.

Bail information schemes probably do make a difference in practice, particularly if used in the way just discussed.[93] However, their limited bearing on remand decisions should not be overlooked. The reason behind the majority of decisions to remand in custody is the second statutory ground, the likelihood that the defendant would commit an offence whilst on bail. Bail information schemes are not concerned principally with this ground or this group of defendants, although they may sometimes yield information that enables a case to be made for conditional bail in some of these cases.

(c) SPEED AND DELAY

The police are the first agency to deal with all those who are arrested, and, as we have seen, they take an initial decision whether to detain the defendant in custody pending the court appearance or to grant police bail. The CPS is now responsible for making representations to the court about bail, but in many cases the Crown Prosecutor is likely to receive a large pile of case files on arrival at work in the morning (consisting

---

[88] See Jones and Goldkamp, above n 32, 1404.   [89] Home Office Circular 25/1988, *Bail*, para 5.

[90] C. Stone, *Bail Information for the Crown Prosecution Service* (1988).

[91] CPS, *Annual Report 2002–03*, 43; the target for magistrates' courts was 80 per cent by 2003, and this was therefore not met.

[92] HM Inspectorate of Probation, *Bail Information: Report of a Thematic Inspection* (1993).

[93] See the essay by G. Mair and C. Lloyd in F. Paterson (ed), *Understanding Bail in Britain* (1996).

of 'overnight arrests' by the police) and will have to present these cases to the court that very morning. In those circumstances the most likely course of events is for the prosecutor to rely on the notes appended by the police to each file, unless the bail information scheme has already yielded some useful points. Prior to the remand hearing there is unlikely to be much time for a detached review of the evidence in the case, and this is why, as we saw in Chapter 7, the CPS has introduced a modified test to deal with this preliminary stage in proceedings. However, there is evidence that the CPS do not merely follow police decision making: research by Morgan and Henderson in 1993–94 shows that, in respect of some 1,500 defendants refused police bail and held in custody overnight, the CPS recommended a custodial remand in only 48 per cent of cases, conditional bail in a further 46 per cent of cases, and unconditional bail in six per cent.[94] This suggests that, despite the speed at which decisions have to be taken, a degree of independent judgment is brought to bear.

The brevity of the hearings themselves has long given cause for concern, in view of the momentous consequence of loss of liberty in some cases. Doherty and East's Cardiff study in 1981 found that cases were processed in court with great rapidity, the clerk setting the tone by rattling through the necessary words. Even in cases where defendants were remanded in custody, some 38 per cent were concluded within two minutes and 87 per cent within ten minutes.[95] No doubt some of the former were remands of persons already in prison, whereas most of those taking longer than ten minutes were probably first hearings, but the figures still raise concerns in view of the seriousness of taking away liberty. It seems that many magistrates still make bail decisions in a few minutes,[96] and it is not known whether the extra emphasis on procedure resulting from training under the Human Rights Act has altered practice in this respect.

A further question on delay concerns the time taken to complete cases: the Strasbourg jurisprudence requires 'particular expedition' where a person is being held in custody.[97] In this respect, the lengthening average period of waiting time for trial (up to 12.7 weeks on average in 2002) is a matter for concern.[98] The much longer delays for certain defendants—the 2002 figures show 450 prisoners on remand for more than 12 months, and a further 900 on remand for 6–12 months[99]—may involve breaches of Article 5(3).

(d) APPEALS AND REAPPLICATIONS

When a court refuses bail or attaches conditions to it, there is an obligation to state the ground(s) on which the court relies and to give reasons for bringing the case within

---

[94] Morgan and Henderson, above n 61, 37.
[95] C. Doherty and R. East, 'Bail Decisions in Magistrates' Courts' (1985) 25 *BJ Crim.* 251.
[96] M. Dhami, 'Conditional Bail Decision-Making in the Magistrates' Court' (2004) 43 *Howard JCJ 27*, at 28.
[97] E.g. *Reid v United Kingdom* (2003) 37 EHRR 9, at [78].   [98] Above n 59.
[99] *Prison Statistics 2002*, Table 2.5.

that ground.[100] A defendant who is refused bail by a magistrates' court may make a reapplication to a judge in chambers. Correspondingly, the Bail (Amendment) Act 1993 introduced a prosecution power to appeal to a judge against the grant of bail by a magistrates' court in the face of representations by the prosecution, and the Criminal Justice Act 2003 has now extended that power to all imprisonable offences. The case for a defence right of reapplication is unanswerable in view of the enormity of the consequences of a decision to remand in custody. The case for a prosecution power of appeal is strong in cases where there is thought to be a clear danger to individuals if the defendant is granted liberty. Unless the power is shown to be used oppressively, it surely has a proper place in criminal procedure.

8.6 EQUAL TREATMENT IN REMAND DECISIONS

To what extent do remand decisions appear to discriminate against certain sections of the population? To what extent do they fail to recognize the special needs of certain groups? These questions warrant considerable discussion in their own right, and it is possible only to give some general indications here.

The findings of research into the impact of race on remand decisions prompt questions about discrimination. In his study of over 3,000 cases Roger Hood found that a higher proportion of defendants from an Afro-Caribbean background (26 per cent) than whites (20 per cent) were remanded in custody pending trial and that, even after taking account of variations in the key facts of individual cases, some apparent discrimination remained.[101] The John report on racial elements in CPS decision making found that the CPS opposed bail more frequently for African-Caribbeans than for other groups of defendants, especially on the ground of the risk of obstructing justice. File endorsements did not disclose the evidential foundations for many of the recommendations, suggesting that information from the police may have been passed on orally. The report concludes that it is probable that racial stereotyping was influencing some of these decisions.[102] In relation to young arrestees, Feilzer and Hood found higher rates of remand into secure conditions among black (10 per cent) and mixed parentage (13 per cent) young males than among those who were white (8 per cent) or from Asian or other ethnic groups (6 per cent). Moreover, 'as many as a

---

[100] Bail Act 1976, s5(3); for low rates of compliance in the early 1990s, see A. Hucklesby, 'Bail or Jail? The Practical Operation of the Bail Act 1976' (1996) 23 *JLS* 213—reasons only given for custodial remands in 47 per cent of cases.

[101] R. Hood, *Race and Sentencing* (1992), 146–50; see also M. Fitzgerald, *Ethnic Minorities and the Criminal Justice System* (1993), 19–21.

[102] The Gus John Partnership, *Race for Justice: A review of CPS decision making for possible racial bias at each stage of the prosecution process* (2003), paras 16 and 28; for similar suggestions in Canada, see G. Kellough and S. Wortley, above n 53, 196.

third of cases where a black male had been remanded in custody failed to result in conviction, compared with one in five cases involving white males.'[103]

Whereas the number of untried men in custody stood in 2002 at around 7,200, a similar figure to 1992, the average number of women in prison on remand increased from 264 in 1992 to 496 in 2002—almost double, in other words. Some 5,000 women were remanded at custody at some time during 2002. Since women tend to be convicted of less serious offences than men, this increase calls for special justification. It appears that 14 per cent of women remandees were charged with offences of violence, compared with 21 per cent for men. The largest proportionate differences were that 30 per cent of the women were charged with theft, compared with only 15 per cent of the men; and 19 per cent of the women were charged with drugs offences, compared with 12 per cent of the men.[104] The figures for theft give particular cause for concern, since it seems unlikely that they were all so serious as to call for a custodial sentence on conviction. Indeed, the figures suggest this: in addition to the 20 per cent of women remandees who were acquitted at their trial, a further 32 per cent received a non-custodial sentence on conviction.[105] Even bearing in mind the points raised in Part 3 above, it is a serious cause for concern that fewer than a half of women remanded in custody are thought to require a custodial sentence.

Special arrangements for the remand of mentally disordered defendants were introduced by the Mental Health Act 1983. However, the power to remand defendants to hospital for a psychiatric report, rather than to prison, appears not to have been widely used. Courts still remand defendants to prison for reports in large numbers. A study by Robertson and others in 1989 found that many custodial remands were made in cases where the offence was minor and the defendant had no fixed address. There were then delays before an assessment by an outside psychiatrist could take place, and often delays in hospital admission thereafter, although about a half of those seen by psychiatrists were offered a hospital bed. The authors comment that 'remands in custody [are] not only an inhumane, but an ineffective way of securing help and care for disturbed people'.[106] A 1993 survey by Kennedy and others confirmed that many mentally disturbed people remanded in custody did not have stable housing arrangements, and the authors argue that at least one-fifth of them could and should be accommodated in probation hostels rather than placed in prison.[107] Recent research suggests that mentally disturbed people are still represented in disproportionately large numbers among the remand population in prisons, and that mental problems connected with substance abuse are a growing concern.[108]

[103] M. Feilzer and R. Hood, *Differences or Discrimination?* (Youth Justice Board, 2004).

[104] *Prison Statistics 2002*, Figures 2.3 and 2.4, and Table 2.1.   [105] Above, pp. 220–224, for discussion.

[106] G. Robertson, S. Dell, A. Grounds and K. James, 'Mentally Disordered Remand Prisoners', (1992) 32 *Home Office Research Bulletin* 1.

[107] M. Kennedy, C. Truman, S. Keyes and A. Cameron, 'Supported Bail for Mentally Vulnerable Defendants' (1997) 36 *Howard JCJ* 158.

[108] D. Brooke, C. Taylor, J. Gunn and A. Maden, 'Substance Misuse as a Marker of Vulnerability Among Male Prisoners on Remand' (2000) 177 *BJ Psychiatry* 248.

8.7 CONCLUSIONS

The starting point for discussion of remands should be Article 5 of the Convention, which declares the right to liberty but provides for various circumscribed exceptions. In principle there are two ways of constructing a justification for depriving a defendant of that right. The first is to argue that there is a distinct risk to the rights of another citizen: this may arise if the defendant has already been charged with assaulting a person and there is evidence to suggest a risk of further violence (as is sometimes the case following incidents of 'domestic violence'). Alternatively it may arise where there is reason to believe that the defendant will threaten someone, especially a victim-complainant or witness. Previous threats could provide sufficient evidence. What emerges clearly is that such decisions should involve both principled reasoning and an assessment of risk. Although in practice much attention is often focused on risk, on the basis of submissions made by the prosecution or police, the issue of principle is no less critical. If the right to liberty is to be taken seriously, courts that do find a significant risk must still strive to preserve the defendant's liberty by seeking non-custodial means of responding to the risk through conditional bail.

A second strand of justification refers to overwhelming reasons of public interest. We have raised questions about the nature and strength of this public interest in the possible pre-trial conduct of persons who are presumed innocent,[109] but it seems to be a feature of many legal systems that the presumption of innocence weakens once a person has been charged by a public prosecutor. One element is the public interest in ensuring that defendants who have been charged attend their trials. Although it would be difficult to deny some such interest, it is questionable whether it is strong enough to justify taking away a person's liberty, particularly when the offence charged is not of the highest seriousness and absconding is not a certainty but a greater or lesser probability. This is, *par excellence*, a sphere in which non-custodial methods of securing attendance should be developed, particularly bail hostels and electronic tagging. And it should certainly be a precondition that the offence as alleged is 'worth imprisonment', before there is any question of imprisoning someone so as to ensure that the trial takes place.

Another element of public interest may be that of minimizing the number of offences committed by persons on bail. The foundations of this interest were discussed critically in Part 1 of this chapter, but the recent re-enactment of a provision requiring courts to treat offending on bail as an aggravating factor in sentencing demonstrates the political force of this concern.[110] However, the Bail Act's reference simply to the probability of committing 'an offence' whilst on bail is much too weak. At the very least, the law should insist that (a) the prosecution has satisfied the court that there is sufficient evidence against the defendant on the charge laid, and (b) that, if convicted as charged, the defendant would probably receive a custodial sentence.

---

[109] Above, p. 211.   [110] Criminal Justice Act 2003, s143(3).

Some oblique recognition of the latter point may be found in the recent Practice Direction on failure to surrender to bail.[111]

Once again, however, interacting with these issues of principle is the practical problem of risk assessment. In order to determine whether it is more likely than not that this defendant will commit an offence likely to result in imprisonment if granted bail, there is a need for a database for the prediction of offending, the like of which appears not to exist in England and Wales. There is a database for the probability of keeping the conditions of parole if released from prison, and there are some data on the probability of certain offenders committing so-called 'dangerous' offences. But here, unlike in the US, there is no database that can be used to predict offending, let alone serious offending, whilst on bail. The American research by Goldkamp and Gottfredson does contain some useful pointers—for example, that reoffending and non-appearance at trial are highly correlated so that to predict one is usually to predict the other; and that bailees are more likely to offend the longer the period awaiting trial[112]—but it remains true that the numbers of false positives would be high. The scattered research in England suggests the same, as we saw above: it is easy to say that people charged with taking cars are the group most likely to offend on bail, but most of them are not in fact detected in law-breaking whilst on bail. Similarly, it is easy to claim that courts should have greater regard to objections to bail advanced by the police, but the vast majority of those to whom the court grants bail in the face of police objections are not detected in law-breaking whilst on bail.[113]

None of these observations breaks new ground, and yet their significance for bail has been accorded little attention. Thousands of people are being deprived of their liberty every year on the basis of predictions which have insecure statistical foundations. All the criminological evidence in analogous fields points to the likelihood of considerable over-prediction. If it is emphasized that the primary concern is to prevent the commission of *serious* crimes in the period between arrest and trial, that makes the problem of protection harder, not easier. Serious crimes are rarer and therefore more difficult to predict than law-breaking in general, and the rate of false positives may well be very high.[114]

At a time when governments have shown an attraction to tougher policies on remands, it is essential to reassert fundamental principles: the courts should operate with a strong presumption in favour of liberty; this ought not to be displaced unless the court is satisfied that there is sufficient evidence to continue with the charge, a test which should become stricter as time progresses and should require careful judgments by the CPS; where a court finds evidence of significant risk, it should examine

---

[111] Practice Direction, *Bail: Failure to surrender and trial in absence*, *The Times*, 26 January 2004.

[112] J. Goldkamp and M.R. Gottfredson, *Policy Guidelines for Bail: An Exercise in Court Reform* (1985), based on research in Philadelphia courts.

[113] Above, n 81 and accompanying text.

[114] For a brief summary of the research on identifying dangerous offenders, see Ashworth, *Sentencing and Criminal Justice* (3rd ed., 2000), 180–9.

whether adequate protection can be provided by a form of conditional bail; before it remands a defendant in custody, it should be satisfied that the charge, if proved at the trial, would be likely to result in the imposition of a custodial sentence. When a court decides that a custodial remand is unavoidable, it should be for as short a period as possible. English law does have mechanisms to ensure this, including time-limits for cases where the defendant is remanded in custody,[115] but some defendants still spend more than six months (and a few more than 12 months) awaiting their trials in custody.[116] Although waiting times are longer in most other European countries, this should not distract attention from the lengthening delays here.

In conclusion, we make five points about remand decisions. First, they rely to a large extent on predictions, and the evidential foundations are rarely strong. That ought to counsel great caution: although it is common these days to refer to risk, public protection and public safety, this should not be allowed to conceal the fragility of many of these predictions. Secondly, the Convention framework as developed by the Strasbourg Court ought to be used instead of the more common references to 'balancing' the defendant's right to liberty against the need for public protection. In principle, the right to liberty should be respected, and only if there is strong evidence should one of the recognized exceptions be allowed to prevail. Moreover, the Strasbourg Court has emphasized the evidential basis for and the seriousness of the charge. As argued here, English law should be amended so as to require courts to consider the probability of a prison sentence being imposed if the facts alleged are proved, before a custodial remand is made. That requires the court to make a prediction of a different kind, but one that should be possible if there is coherent guidance on sentencing. This leads on to the third factor: there must be greater willingness among decision makers to question the decisions taken previously in each case, and to re-appraise the evidence and the approach to be taken. In particular, the CPS must be prepared to conduct a meaningful review of the police conclusion, and the court should likewise conduct a meaningful review of the CPS recommendation. Defence lawyers, too, must be prepared to offer a 'full and fearless' defence rather than trying to curry favour with the court or CPS, as Hucklesby's research suggests in some cases. Such changes will require alterations to the system, since decision makers cannot be expected to reach different decisions without (a) a little more time and (b) fresh information. Fourthly, the question of police remands must be revisited. It seems to be assumed that the only practical approach to deciding bail/custody decisions prior to a court appearance is to leave these to the police. However, that gives them considerable (bargaining) power over suspects, and a decision to refuse bail has strong correlations with subsequent decisions about loss of liberty. The question of conferring this power on a senior member of the CPS should be revisited urgently. And fifthly, courts must (continue to) adopt a more legalistic and rights-responsive approach to remand decisions. The right to liberty and the presumption of innocence should become part of the everyday

---

[115] Corre and Wolchover, above n 1, Ch. 12.   [116] Above n 99 and accompanying text.

currency of the courts, to make it clear how exceptional a remand in custody should be. This has little to do with overcrowding in the prisons: even if the prisons were empty, the argument for remanding an accused person in custody ought to be a strong one. At the same time, and for the same reason, efforts to develop non-custodial facilities for holding defendants in the community must be re-doubled.

9

PRE-TRIAL ISSUES: DISCLOSURE, DELAY AND ABUSE OF PROCESS

As a case proceeds to court, mechanisms need to be in place to ensure that an effective trial can take place. Much of this will be the business of the parties, who will prepare their trial strategies, ensure that witnesses are called and so on. But not everything can be left to the parties: in the run up to the trial, there are various procedural mechanisms to ensure that the eventual trial runs smoothly and fairly (things which may not be in the interests of the parties). In considering these mechanisms and how they function, we are drawn into consideration of one of the broadest—and most difficult—questions in the criminal process: in what circumstances can it be said that a criminal trial is fair?

The courts have various mechanisms available to them to promote trial fairness. Some of these are only available during the trial proper: devices such as exclusionary rules of evidence, and the power to find 'no case to answer' against the accused. These will be considered in the following chapter. During the pre-trial stage one device has come to increasing prominence in recent years: this is the power to stay a prosecution for abuse of process.[1] As we will see, the boundaries of this power are not exactly clear, but the basic idea is that it is used by the courts to stop the judicial process being abused. A good flavour of the thinking behind the doctrine is provided by Lord Griffiths in one of the leading authorities, *R v Horseferry Road Magistrates' Court, ex parte Bennett.*[2] Here, the defendant had been brought to Britain to stand trial, not through formal extradition procedures, but by being arrested and handcuffed to the seat of an aeroplane bound for London:

'In the present case there is no suggestion that the appellant cannot have a fair trial, nor could it have been suggested that it would have been unfair to try him if he had been returned to this country through extradition procedures. If the court is to have the power to interfere with the prosecution in the present circumstances it must be because the judiciary accept a responsibility for the maintenance of the rule of law that embraces a willingness to oversee executive action and to refuse to countenance behaviour that threatens either basic

---

[1] See generally A. Choo, *Abuse of Process and Judicial Stays of Criminal Proceedings* (1993).
[2] [1994] 1 AC 42.

human rights or the rule of law. . . . The courts, of course, have no power to apply direct discipline to the police or the prosecuting authorities, but they can refuse to allow them to take advantage of abuse of power by regarding their behaviour as an abuse of process and thus preventing a prosecution.'[3]

It was held that Bennett's prosecution should have been stayed by the magistrates as an abuse of process. The effect of staying a prosecution for abuse of process is that the case cannot proceed to trial. This is not quite the same as an acquittal, and it is possible that the authorities could attempt to prosecute the defendant again for the same offence. However, any such prosecution would almost certainly be stayed as itself an abuse of process.

9.1 FILTERING CASES PRIOR TO TRIAL

In preceding chapters it has been stressed that defendants should not face trial unless there is good justification for their doing so. This is partly because of the cost of trial procedures; partly because of the distress and inconvenience they impose on defendants; and partly to protect the innocent from mistaken conviction. Thus, at various stages of the criminal process, there are evidential barriers to filter out weak cases. There must be 'sufficient evidence' before a defendant is charged,[4] and the CPS must determine that there is a reasonable prospect of conviction before taking a case to court. As we saw in Chapter 7, the CPS should also ensure that prosecution is in the public interest. Even when the trial has commenced, there are evidential barriers to ensure that the defendant is not put in jeopardy of conviction without good reason. The judge should not let the case go to the jury unless there is sufficient evidence to enable a jury to find the crime charged to be proved beyond reasonable doubt;[5] there is a similar test in summary trial.[6]

A further filtering mechanism exists in the pre-trial stage. All cases start their lives in the magistrates' court, where issues such as bail can be given a speedy initial determination (see Chapter 8). But the more serious criminal cases are actually tried in the Crown Court. Historically, the process of committing these cases for trial in the Crown Court has been used to give defendants an opportunity to claim that there is insufficient evidence to justify bringing their case to trial. The mechanism for doing so used to be the institution of the grand jury, but the grand jury was abolished in 1930. For much of the last century defendants were able to use 'committal proceedings' before the magistrates to argue against the case proceeding to jury trial. Various committees and commissions recommended the abolition of committal proceedings, on the basis that 'paper committals' served no useful purpose and 'full committals'

---

[3] *Ibid.*, 150.   [4] See Ch 4 and E. Cape, 'Sufficient Evidence to Charge?' [1999] Crim LR 874.
[5] *R v Galbraith* [1981] 1 WLR 1039, discussed in Ch. 11.
[6] See *Blackstone's Criminal Practice 2003*, para D20.8.

put victims and witnesses under stress by requiring them to give their evidence twice,[7] and they were eventually abolished for cases triable only on indictment in 2001;[8] provisions to do the same for either way offences are included in the Criminal Justice Act 2003.[9] Cases are now transferred to the jurisdiction of the Crown Court by a relatively simple administrative mechanism, and defendants are now likely to wait for the trial proper before arguing that the prosecution case is weak. It is not easy to say why the filtering process operated by the magistrates gradually came to lose its significance in the criminal process. There may be a number of factors. A dry run of the case during committal would once have been the major opportunity for defendants to discover the details of the case against them. But improvements in disclosure rules—as well, perhaps, as something as banal as the invention of the photocopying machine—has meant that committal proceedings are no longer needed for this purpose. The creation of the CPS which, whatever its flaws, does review the strength of the case and does discontinue a considerable number of prosecutions (see Chapter 7), may also be part of the explanation.

The current procedures for transferring cases to the Crown Court are, in outline, as follows. There is an initial hearing in the magistrates' court to decide the question of bail. In either way offences there will also be a mode of trial hearing, and then, if the case is to be tried on indictment, it is simply transferred to the Crown Court without committal. This does not deprive the defendant of all means of challenging the case prior to trial. He can apply to the Crown Court to have the case against him dismissed.[10] The judge has discretion whether or not to hear oral evidence on the application. He should dismiss the case against the accused if he considers the prosecution does not have enough evidence to enable a reasonable jury to convict.[11]

9.2 PRE-TRIAL DISCLOSURE

(a) PROSECUTION DISCLOSURE

Disclosure of evidence before trial is a matter of some importance. From the point of view of efficiency, trials will run most smoothly when each side has some notice of the evidence and arguments that the opposing side will present at trial. But there are also more serious issues of justice at stake here. Non-disclosure of evidence was a common factor in many of the miscarriage of justice cases of the late 1980s and early 1990s.

---

[7] See Royal Commission on Criminal Justice, *Report* (1993), 89–91, discussing similar recommendations by the Royal Commission on Criminal Procedure (1981) and the Fraud Trials Committee (1987).

[8] Under the Crime and Disorder Act 1998, s 51.

[9] Section 41 and Sch 3.

[10] Crime and Disorder Act 1988, Sch. 3; Crime and Disorder Act 1998 (Dismissal of Charges Sent) Rules 1998 (SI 1998 No 3048).

[11] See J. Sprack, *Emmins on Criminal Procedure* (9th ed., 2002), 200–1.

Failures in prosecution disclosure continue to be a frequent ground of appeal to the Court of Appeal.

As far as the prosecution is concerned, there is a basic requirement that it disclose its case prior to trial. This will usually take the form of a bundle of witness statements presented after the case has been transferred to the Crown Court. Evidence not disclosed in this manner may not be admissible at trial. In the magistrates' court, there is a similar requirement of advance notice of the evidence as far as either way offences are concerned.[12] Remarkably, there is no legal requirement that the defence be advised of the prosecution case in advance in summary cases. Although the Divisional Court has held otherwise,[13] it is quite possible that this breaches Article 6 of the ECHR, which has been held to require equality of arms.[14] In light of this, guidelines on disclosure issued by the Attorney General now advise disclosure of the prosecution's case in summary cases.[15]

The foregoing deals with advance notice of the evidence the prosecution intends to call at trial. What of evidence that it does not intend to call? If, for example, a witness interviewed by the police fails to support the prosecution's version of events, it is unlikely that the prosecution would choose to call that person at trial. Yet knowledge of what the witness said might be of considerable importance to the defence. Rules requiring disclosure of such unused material were gradually developed by the courts.[16] In 1996 they were put on a statutory footing. The Criminal Procedure and Investigations Act 1996, along with the Code of Practice issued under it, lay out in some detail how prosecution disclosure should be managed and what tests should be applied to determine whether material should be disclosed. Aspects of the regime have been modified by the Criminal Justice Act 2003; although these provisions are not yet in force, for the most part we will deal with them as if they are. The first thing to say about prosecution disclosure of unused material is that it has long been controversial. This is partly because, as noted above, failures in prosecution disclosure are a common element in many well known miscarriage of justice cases; it is perhaps hardly surprising that the prosecution should sometimes be reluctant to disclose to the defence material which may undermine its case. It is also because the 1996 reforms were introduced as a result of claims by the police that the common law disclosure regime imposed too heavy a burden on them; the reforms were thus widely perceived as having restricted the defence's ability to access important information.

The CPIA regime imposes an obligation on the police to list and describe unused material in a 'schedule' (there is a separate schedule for sensitive information).[17] The

---

[12] Magistrates' Courts (Advance Information) Rules 1985.

[13] *R v Stratford JJ, ex parte Imbert* [1999] 2 Cr App R 276.

[14] For further discussion, see B. Emmerson and A. Ashworth, *Human Rights and Criminal Justice* (2001), 380–386.

[15] *Disclosure of Information in Criminal Proceedings* (2000).

[16] For an overview of the history, see R. Leng, 'The Exchange of Information and Disclosure' in M. McConville and G. Wilson (eds), *The Handbook of the Criminal Justice Process* (2002).

[17] CPIA, s 24.

schedule is crucial to the operation of the disclosure scheme. It forms the basis on which the CPS will make decisions as to what material should be disclosed to the defence; the non-sensitive schedule itself is disclosed to the defence, and is thus the primary means by which the defence can make a claim that material relevant to it has not been disclosed. Any material which 'might reasonably be considered capable of undermining the case for the prosecution or of assisting the case for the accused'[18] should be disclosed to the defence (there is an exception for sensitive material; more will be said about this below). This test should be kept under review.[19] Thus, as the facts change, and as more is learned about the defence case, further material may fall within the test and require disclosure.

In practice, there are a number of problems with the way this scheme works. Research on its operation by the CPS Inspectorate and by Plotnikoff and Woolfson shows that it is not working as intended and that there is near universal lack of confidence in it.[20] A major problem is that the schedules prepared by the police are poor: they contain insufficient detail to enable prosecutors to make informed decisions about what should be disclosed, and sometimes fail to mention significant information. The CPSI found defects in schedules in more than half of the cases it studied. Ideally, the CPS should scrutinize the schedules carefully, and ask for more information from the police where detail is lacking. But this does not happen. This may partly be due to a lack of resources. There may also be other reasons which are related to the structure of the disclosure regime and the CPS's own view of its role within the criminal justice system.

In Chapter 7 we saw that there are tensions affecting the role of the CPS. Although, ideally, the CPS should play a 'minister of justice' role, it may sometimes be tempted into adversarial game-playing. Research has noted that this sometimes occurs where the question of bail is concerned,[21] and we have seen in Chapter 7 that the risk of prosecutors identifying themselves with the police has recently increased with CPS charging and the location of prosecutors in the police station. It is possible, then, that prosecutors will be tempted to gain an advantage over the defence by disclosing as little information as possible. The CPSI certainly considered that in some instances prosecutors applied the disclosure test too strictly.[22] And here the structure of the Act and the political climate behind it can be seen to play a role. When the statutory regime was introduced, it was seen as responding to complaints by the police that prosecution disclosure had become too generous. The disclosure test was initially worded subjectively—material should be disclosed if, 'in the prosecutor's opinion [it] might undermine the case for the prosecution against the accused',[23] and this may

---

[18] CPIA, s 3(1)(a).   [19] CPIA, s 9.

[20] Crown Prosecution Service Inspectorate, *The Inspectorate's Report on the Thematic Review of the Disclosure of Unused Material* (London, 2000); J. Plotnikoff and R. Woolfson, *'A Fair Balance'? Evaluation of the Operation of Disclosure Law* (London, 2001).

[21] See C. Lloyd, *Bail Information Schemes: Practice and Effect* (Home Office Research and Planning Unit Paper 69, 1992), 17, 23–4.

[22] Above n 20, 4.118.   [23] CPIA 1996, original s 3(1)(a).

have encouraged a restrictive attitude. A restrictive attitude was also encouraged by another aspect of the statutory scheme. As we will see below, the legislation originally tied prosecution disclosure to defence disclosure. When the defence disclosed the details of its case, the prosecutor was to consider 'secondary prosecution disclosure', applying a test more clearly focused on the needs of the defence.[24] The Act was certainly capable of being read as making full prosecution disclosure something to be earned by the defendant's fulfilment of his own statutory obligations. The CPSI did criticize prosecutors for sometimes applying the test in this 'conditional', or 'tit for tat' manner.[25] Indeed, a revealing indicator of just how deep set is some sort of conditional reading of prosecution disclosure obligations is that the CPSI commented that certain basic information, such as crime reports and message logs, should be disclosed 'following a reasonable defence statement',[26] a view which itself suggests that disclosure of basic information is viewed as something to be earned rather than as a right. The reforms introduced by the CJA 2003 do de-emphasize conditionality,[27] but it would be naïve to think that this sort of attitude will not linger on.

The observations made in the preceding paragraph indicate the importance of ethics and principles in this area. The basic principles are surely uncontroversial. The defence has a right to disclosure of all relevant evidence; as the principle is sometimes put, the prosecution should be seen as the trustee, rather than the owner, of any information gathered during the police investigation.[28] The European Commission of Human Rights has expressed a similar idea in terms of equality of arms: the State's superior resources mean that the defence should have access to all relevant evidence that has been or could be gathered by the prosecution.[29] In the wider scheme of things, defence disclosure may be desirable, but that does not mean that prosecution disclosure should be conditional on what the defence discloses. It is true that once the defence discloses information about its case the prosecution will have more idea about just what would be relevant to that case, but the reluctance to disclose even basic information such as crime reports seems to reflect a deeper ambivalence about disclosure. What prosecutors may worry about is that defendants who benefit from generous disclosure before they have disclosed their own case will fabricate a defence that is tailored to the disclosed material. That is a more legitimate reason for restricting prosecution disclosure in some way, but it is still difficult to see how it justifies taking a restrictive attitude to such basic information as crime reports. The principles point towards wide disclosure, using a generous test of relevance.

In terms of reform, there is no 'magic bullet' which will improve prosecution disclosure practices. Plotnikoff and Woolfson concluded that the solution lay in training and funding of prosecutors, to enable them to make informed decisions about the material gathered during the police investigation. In some areas prosecutors

---

[24] CPIA, original s 7.   [25] Above n 20, 5.33.   [26] *Ibid.*, 4.75.
[27] See M. Redmayne, 'Disclosure and its Discontents' [2004] Crim LR 441, 444.
[28] P. O'Connor, 'Prosecution Disclosure: Principle, Practice and Justice' [1992] Crim LR 464.
[29] *Jespers v Belgium* (1981) 27 DR 61.

have instituted a practice of 'routine revelation' of certain categories of material. This should be encouraged, for it not only ensures that basic information reaches the defence, but also eases the prosecution's workload by avoiding the need to make individualized decisions about particular material. As in many areas, contemplation of ethics is important here. Understanding the importance of disclosure to a fair trial is a first step towards improving prosecution decision making on disclosure.

(b) DEFENCE DISCLOSURE

When it comes to defence disclosure, different principles apply. Before 1996, there was no general obligation on the defence to disclose details of its case before trial. There were limited exceptions to this general rule, applying to alibis, expert evidence, and serious fraud trials. The CPIA changed this, imposing an obligation on the defence to disclose details of its case following initial disclosure by the prosecution. Defence disclosure was expanded by the CJA 2003. As the law now stands the defence should provide a defence statement, setting out the details of its case, including any defences and points of law to be raised, and the matters on which it takes issue with the prosecution, as well as the reasons why it does so.[30] The defence should also provide a list with the names and addresses of witnesses it intends to call and of any expert witnesses it has consulted.[31]

Defence disclosure has certain parallels with the changes to the right to silence introduced by the Criminal Justice and Public Order Act 1994 (see Chapter 4). Both are enforced by adverse inferences. If a defendant fails to issue a defence statement, or if his defence at trial departs from what was disclosed, an adverse inference may be drawn against him. It must be said, however, that adverse inferences from non-disclosure are even less straightforward than those from silence. The defendant's failure to disclose a defence before trial is only suspicious because the law places an obligation on him to do so, and in that situation the inference that the defence is fabricated is surely a weak one. Indeed, where the defendant fails to disclose the name of a witness, or a point of law on which he relies, it is difficult to see how any adverse inference could be drawn at all. These problems no doubt partly explain why the defence disclosure provisions in the CPIA have had such little impact. In contrast to the mass of case law on the inferences from silence provisions, there are barely any reported cases on the conditions in which an inference from faulty disclosure can be drawn.[32] The research suggests that the majority of defence statements are insufficiently

---

[30] CPIA, s 5.

[31] These reforms were initially controversial, in part because there were fears that police would put undue pressure on witnesses: M. Zander, *Consultation on Proposals for Advance Disclosure of Defence Witness Lists and Unused Defence Expert Witness Reports* (2002). CJA 2003, s 40 now requires a Code of Practice to be drawn up to govern police interviews with defence witnesses. It is expected that the defence will be given the right to attend interviews.

[32] The principal decision is *Tibbs* [2000] 2 Cr App R 309. See also *Wheeler* [2001] 1 Cr App R 10; *R (Sullivan) v Crown Court at Maidstone* [2002] 1 WLR 2747.

detailed to meet the requirements of the Act, yet that judges and prosecutors are reluctant to make much of such failings. The changes brought in by the CJA 2003 do give sharper teeth to the enforcement mechanisms,[33] but, as with prosecution disclosure, it may well be that legislative change will make little difference to the practice of the courts.

There is a basic dilemma involved in the enforcement of defence disclosure, and it echoes one we came across with inferences from silence. The Government has signalled its intention to make defendants cooperate better with the disclosure regime.[34] But it is difficult to see how this can be done while at the same time maintaining fairness. Encouraging defence disclosure by rewarding it with full prosecution disclosure is one strategy, but, as noted above, it is inconsistent with principle. The defence's right to receive relevant evidence should not be made conditional on its fulfilment of a different obligation. There is some concession to this view in the CJA amendments to the CPIA,[35] but the new regime has instead shifted the focus to adverse inferences. Where disclosure is concerned, such inferences are not without their problems. The CJA reforms will certainly not mark an improvement in fairness if adverse inferences start being drawn incautiously. With inferences from silence, some courts have been rather more wholehearted about the regime than they have been with disclosure inferences. The similarity with disclosure lies in the fact that strict enforcement of the CJPOA provisions has sometimes been at the cost of fairness.[36] *R v Howell*[37] is the most obvious example of this; in this case involving silence based on legal advice, the Court of Appeal allowed an adverse inference to be drawn as a means of encouraging defendants to cooperate with the police (even when advised not to), rather than because there was any logical basis on which silence could be taken to have been an indicator of guilt. The law is being used instrumentally, to encourage certain behaviour on the part of defendants, rather than being applied with an eye to fairness to both sides. With both areas of the law, the moral is similar: if the provisions cannot be enforced fairly, it would be better not to have them at all.

Defence disclosure obligations raise further issues of principle. There has been a gradual move towards expecting more cooperation from the defence in the process of prosecution, and this raises questions about just how far the obligation to cooperate should be extended. A case which well illustrates the issues is *R v Gleeson*.[38] Here, the defence realized it had a technical defence to the charge made in the indictment. It waited until the end of the prosecution case, and then made a submission of no case to answer on the basis that the common law conspiracy charged by the prosecution was impossible (i.e. it claimed that the defendant had conspired to do something which was not actually an offence). The judge agreed that this was a sound defence, but

---

[33] CPIA, ss 6E, 11.

[34] See the White Paper which preceded the Criminal Justice Act 2003: *Justice For All* Cm 5563 (2002), Ch. 3.

[35] See M. Redmayne, 'Disclosure and its Discontents' [2004] Crim LR 441, 444–5.

[36] See D. Hamer, 'The Privilege Against Self-Incrimination and the Persistent Risk of Self-Incrimination' (2004) 28 *Criminal Law Journal* 160.

[37] [2003] EWCA Crim 01.   [38] [2004] Crim LR 579.

permitted the prosecution to redraft the indictment so that the charge was statutory conspiracy (to which impossibility is not a defence). The defence appealed on the basis that the judge should not have permitted this course of action. In dismissing the appeal, the Court of Appeal commented on the duties of the defence:

'A prosecution [should] not be frustrated by errors of the prosecutor, unless such errors have irremediably rendered a fair trial for the defendant impossible. For defence advocates to seek to take advantage of such errors by deliberately delaying identification of an issue of fact or law in the case until the last possible moment is, in our view, no longer acceptable, given the legislative and procedural changes to our criminal justice process in recent years.'[39]

The CJA amendments make defence obligations somewhat clearer than they were at the time of *Gleeson*. The CPIA now specifies that the defence should disclose any points of law to be relied on, though the sanction specified for failure is the drawing of adverse inferences rather than, as in *Gleeson*, the loss of a watertight defence. Whatever the legal position now is, the implications of *Gleeson* deserve some thought. Read literally, the passage just quoted could lead to extraordinary results. Suppose the prosecution fails to bring out some crucial fact while cross-examining one of its witnesses. Should the defence then be expected to inform the prosecution of its oversight, enabling it to make good the error before the close of its case? That might well be thought to involve the defence in doing the prosecution's work for it, and to undermine basic principles of adversarial justice. On the other hand, as the Court of Appeal points out, various changes in criminal procedure, such as the introduction of defence disclosure, do involve the defence in making the prosecution's job easier by alerting it to the issues which it will face at trial. Does this imply that all defence disclosure is unprincipled?

Various distinctions can be made in this area.[40] Where the prosecution is taken completely by surprise by a defence, it may be impeded in its ability to rebut the defence case. Alibi defences are an obvious example: if the defence produces an alibi at the last minute, the prosecution will not have had an opportunity to consider how best to challenge the alibi, and the jury may be too easily persuaded that the alibi creates reasonable doubt. It would therefore seem appropriate to have some mechanism to ensure that the prosecution is not caught by surprise. An alibi notice provision was in fact introduced in 1967; this enabled the judge to disallow the defence introduction of an alibi if the rules were not complied with.[41] This very serious sanction is out of proportion to the mischief at which it was aimed, and it is likely that judges did not often apply it.[42] One positive development in the CPIA was that the sanction was changed to adverse inferences, which—while bearing in mind what was said above

---

[39] *Ibid.*, [35].

[40] For extended discussion, see R. Mosteller, 'Discovery Against the Defense: Tilting the Adversarial Balance' (1986) 74 *California L Rev* 1567.

[41] Criminal Justice Act 1967, s 11.

[42] For some evidence on this point, see M. Zander and P. Henderson, *Crown Court Study* (1993), 74–6.

about the difficulty of such inferences—seems far more appropriate. It would also be appropriate to instruct the jury that the prosecution's inability to rebut the defence might be due to its having been caught by surprise.

One question which has arisen in connection with alibi notices is whether the prosecution can use the notice as part of its own case. (It might wish to do so, for example, if the alibi established the defendant's presence near the scene of crime, as in *Nathaniel*[43]). The Court of Appeal has held that in some circumstances this is permissible.[44] This is rather more controversial than a system of alibi notice backed up by adverse inferences. It brings things closer to the *Gleeson* situation in that the defence disclosure obligation has been used to enable the prosecution to make its *prima facie* case, rather than to respond to the defence case. At present, alibi notices remain exceptional in this respect; the Attorney General's guidance on disclosure recommends that prosecutors do not use defence statements in their cases in chief.[45]

A further controversial disclosure provision relates to expert evidence. The CPIA, as amended, now provides that the defence should provide to the prosecution the names and addresses of any expert witnesses it has consulted but does not intend to call.[46] This is a scaled back version of an original proposal which would have required the disclosure of unused expert reports. The argument against disclosure of reports is that it would have a 'chilling effect': the defence might be less willing to seek expert evidence in the first place if it felt that by doing so it could damage its own case. Because of the restrictions imposed by the law on legal professional privilege, the disclosure of just names and addresses will not normally allow the prosecution to strengthen its own case; usually it will simply allow the prosecution to rebut expert evidence called by the defence by informing the jury that the expert is just one of many consulted.[47]

It seems, then, that a distinction can be drawn between general provisions which use adverse inferences to encourage disclosure, and to enable the prosecution to respond to the defence case, and ones which use defence disclosure to improve the prosecution's case in chief. But is this distinction principled? The argument that it is would first draw on the principle that a defendant should not have to cooperate with the State when it is trying to convict him of a crime (in Chapter 5, this was identified as the essence of the privilege against self-incrimination). There are problems in defining this principle clearly—it might be argued that in the present context the defence is free not to cooperate—but in *Gleeson*, where the defendant is effectively denied a valid defence, it does seem that the Court of Appeal is coming close to placing the defendant under a duty of cooperation. A second reason for supporting the distinction is that once defence cooperation actually helps the prosecution make its own case, the defendant may feel that his trust in his lawyer is undermined, with the detrimental result that he will be less forthcoming about his defence. This is the sort of chilling effect which justifies non-disclosure of material—such as expert reports—discovered by the defence but which is detrimental to its case.

---

[43] [1995] 2 Cr App R 565.   [44] *Rossborough* (1985) 81 Cr App R 139, and *Nathaniel, ibid.*
[45] Above n 15, para 18.   [46] CPIA 1996, ss 6C, 6D.   [47] See Redmayne, above n 35, 453–4.

(c) PUBLIC INTEREST IMMUNITY

There are further complexities in the disclosure regime where sensitive material is involved. If the police investigation involved an informer, for example, the prosecution might well be reluctant to disclose this information to the defence. In this situation the prosecution can make a claim of 'public interest immunity'. In recent years, this area of the law has caused various problems. The basic principle is that PII claims need to be judged by the courts; the prosecution should not decide that certain material is sensitive and therefore not to be disclosed; non-disclosure needs the approval of the trial judge. Beyond this, the courts recognize three different types of PII claim. In type 1 claims, the defence will be alerted to the fact that a claim is being made and to the general nature of the material involved: for example that it relates to an informer but not the identity of the informer. In type 2 claims the defence will be notified of nothing more than that an application is being made; this might occur where telling the defence that the claim relates to an informer would make it obvious who the informer is. In type 3 claims the defence will not even be told that a PII application is being made.

The English courts, as well as the European Court of Human Rights, stress the importance of informing the judge whenever material is not being disclosed for PII reasons. The judge can then look out for the defence's interests during the trial. At the start of the trial, for example, it might seem that PII material is not relevant to the defence case; but the case might develop at trial in such a way that the material does become relevant and the decision to withhold it needs to be reassessed. There is less consensus on other issues. Type 2 PII hearings raise particular problems, for here the defence is not able directly to present argument on the key issue: the importance of the sensitive material to its case. In *Jasper v United Kingdom*,[48] the defence argued that in this situation the judge should appoint a 'special counsel', who could represent the defence during the PII hearing, being privy to the nature of the sensitive material but not reporting back to the defence on its exact nature. A majority of the court thought the English courts did not need to go this far to comply with Article 6, but a substantial minority dissented on this point. In *Edwards and Lewis v United Kingdom*,[49] the court seems to have come close to reversing its decision in *Jasper*. Both defendants made entrapment claims at their respective trials. Here the European Court thought it especially important that the defence should have some say about certain information that was not disclosed on PII grounds. This was because it was thought unfair to have the judge decide an issue—the validity of the entrapment claim—while in possession of information relevant to that claim about which the defence was not able to present adversarial argument. The solution, it was thought, was to appoint special counsel. This shows rather less trust in the impartiality of the judiciary than did the decision in *Jasper*.

---

[48] (2000) 30 EHRR 1.   [49] App nos 39647/98 and 40461/98, 22 July 2003.

Unsurprisingly, the decision in *Edwards and Lewis* threw the English courts into some turmoil. A few trial judges appointed special counsel, and the issue quickly came before the House of Lords. Its decision in *R v H and C*[50] is in some ways unhelpful. Rather than giving clear guidance on when special counsel should be appointed, it suggests that the issue should rarely arise because prosecutors can simply apply the test of disclosure found in the CPIA: if sensitive material assists the defence case or undermines the prosecution case, then it should (probably) be disclosed. If the prosecution cannot accept disclosure, it should terminate the prosecution. Where sensitive material does not meet the test in the CPIA, then it need not be disclosed. In neither case should the judge normally be troubled with the decision. While this may sound very sensible, it does not really confront the difficulty that prosecutors seem to encounter in practice. That they so often do bring PII issues to the judge's attention suggests that they do not find the basic CPIA test a simple one; rightly or wrongly, they do not trust their own judgment and would rather involve the judge. Keeping the judge out of the picture may make things simpler from the point of view of the appearance of justice and the concerns expressed by the ECtHR, but it may not be the fairest way of dealing with the issues. Beyond this, the House of Lords was prepared to say little more than that the appointment of special counsel should be exceptional. Its reticence may have been due, in part, to the knowledge that the Government had requested a referral of the decision in *Edwards and Lewis* to the Grand Chamber of the European Court of Human Rights. This request, however, was later withdrawn. In practice, the courts may find more useful guidance in the judgment of the Court of Appeal, which held that special counsel should be appointed whenever sensitive material is relevant to a 'preliminary determinative ruling', such as an application to stay proceedings, or where it is prejudicial to a defendant so that the judge does not feel able to make a decision involving the material without adversarial argument.[51]

There is another matter relating to PII on which judicial guidance has been disappointing. So far we have said nothing about the test the judge should apply when ruling on a PII claim. The basic question here is whether the judge should withhold relevant evidence from the defence in order to protect sensitive information. The ECtHR has suggested that this approach may be acceptable: 'The entitlement to disclosure of relevant evidence is not an absolute right. In any criminal proceedings there may be competing interests, such as national security or the need to protect witnesses at risk of reprisals or keep secret police methods of investigation of crime, which must be weighed against the rights of the accused.'[52] This view is a familiar one; it supposes that the defendant's rights are subject to being traded off against other values. The importance of those other values should not be slighted. An informer whose identity is revealed may be put in danger, and if they are to be protected this may involve very significant disruption to their life. Ordered to disclose the identity of

[50] [2004] 2 WLR 335.   [51] [2004] 1 Cr App R 17.
[52] *Edwards and Lewis v United Kingdom*, above n 49, 53.

such a person, the prosecution may feel it has no choice but to abandon the prosecution. Yet it is hardly palatable to withhold relevant evidence from the defence. There is
obviously a difficult dilemma here, but given that non-prosecution—rather than the
endangerment of the informer—is an option, one should be very wary of using the
sort of balancing language that the ECtHR appears to espouse. Another point to bear
in mind is that the prosecution may be able to avoid the dilemma described here by
not bringing a prosecution which depends crucially on an informer in the first place.
If a balancing test is to be used, then it is important to take a wide view of the issues
(Could the situation have been avoided? Why not abandon the prosecution?) rather
than one which simply weighs the importance of sensitivity against the defendant's
rights.

    Where PII is concerned, the English courts have tended to distance themselves from
the sort of balancing language used by the ECtHR. Yet they have managed to leave
considerable ambiguity as to the nature of the test to be applied. In *Keane* it was
suggested that material should be disclosed if it 'may prove the defendant's innocence
or avoid a miscarriage of justice.'[53] Of course, the basic rule is that the defendant does
not have to prove innocence. It is difficult to know whether this is just a careless choice
of words, or whether the test is intended to set a reasonably high threshold. In favour
of the latter interpretation, one might suppose that, had the court intended a simple
test of relevance to be applied, it would have said so. Things are not clarified by the
House of Lords in *H and C*. While the general thrust of the judgment is that relevant
evidence should be disclosed to the defence, there are dicta which suggest that it is
acceptable to withhold information so long as it will not be of significant help.[54]

    There may be good reason for some caution in setting the test for disclosure of PII
material. If the test is too wide—including, for example, material which '*may* be
relevant' to the defence case—then the judge at a preliminary hearing may feel the
need to disclose evidence which turns out not to be relevant to the defence case as it is
developed at trial. But the current test for disclosure in the CPIA—'material which
might reasonably be considered capable of undermining the case for the prosecution
or of assisting the case for the accused'—is sufficiently robust to avoid this problem.
Given the difficulty of justifying a balancing test where the defendant's ability to
defend himself is concerned, there is a good argument for applying this test at the PII
stage. Any material which meets this test should be disclosed. As for the vexed question of special counsel, the Court of Appeal's guidance in *H and C* appears to ensure
that special counsel will be appointed in cases where they are most needed, that is,
where the judge has a difficult decision to make and will benefit from adversarial
argument.

---

[53] [1994] 1 WLR 746, 751–2.   [54] Above n 50, [18], [37].

9.3 DELAY

Cases should generally be brought to trial as quickly as possible. There are several reasons why delay should be avoided. First, as we have observed on several occasions, the pre-trial stage involves considerable stress and uncertainty for defendants, as well as for victims. The case should be resolved as soon as possible so that all involved can get on with their lives. Where defendants are concerned, things are even more serious where bail has been denied. Every day between remand and trial is an extra day in custody; while time served on remand can be taken into account at the sentencing phase if the defendant is found guilty, no compensation is offered in the event of an acquittal. Secondly, human memory declines over time. The longer the period between the alleged crime and the trial, the less likely witnesses are to remember events clearly. Delay therefore makes the trial a less accurate means of adjudicating guilt and innocence. A third possible reason for avoiding delay has been highlighted in recent Government initiatives to bring defendants to trial as quickly as possible—sometimes within days of the alleged crime. It is thought that a speedy response to offending reinforces the connection between the crime and its punishment, bringing home to offenders the consequences of their offending behaviour. There may be something to be said for this, but it should be noted that there is some danger in going too far down the road to speedy trials: if a case is prosecuted too quickly the parties may not have time to prepare for trial. The 'Narey reforms' introduced by the Crime and Disorder Act 1998 are intended to speed up the court process, especially for less serious cases. Without going into detail, the idea is that in straightforward summary cases where the accused is expected to plead guilty the defendant will appear in court within days of being charged. The abolition of committal proceedings, discussed earlier, is also intended to bring cases to trial more quickly. Another mechanism for increasing efficiency is 'plea before venue' in either way cases (see Chapter 10). While there is some evidence that these reforms have resulted in faster throughput of cases, concerns have been expressed that they leave the defence too little time to prepare for court.[55]

There are three main contexts in which pre-trial delay becomes an issue for the courts. The first is where a number of years have elapsed between the alleged crime and its prosecution; this may happen, for example, in child abuse cases where the victim does not feel able to report the crime until adulthood. Secondly, where a defendant is remanded in custody, there are various time limits imposed to ensure that the case does not take too long to come to trial. The courts often have to deal with situations where the prosecution argues that there are good reasons for extending the time limits. Finally, the courts also concern themselves with delay between charge and trial, whether or not the defendant has been on remand. If the prosecution does not

---

[55] See D. Brown, *Reducing Delays in the Magistrates' Courts* Home Office Research Findings No 131 (2000); J. Robins, 'The Speed of Fight' *Law Society Gazette* 3 August 2000, 24.

bring the case to trial within a reasonable time, the court may stop the prosecution as an abuse of process. Each of these contexts will be dealt with in turn.

(a) DELAY AND 'STALE' OFFENCES

As far as stale offences are concerned, there is a very different approach between summary and indictable offences. For summary offences—the least serious offences, which can only be tried in the magistrates' courts—proceedings must be started within six months of the alleged offence having taken place.[56] Apart from such cases, in English criminal law, there is no statute of limitations. There is thus no bar to bringing a case to court 20, 30, 50 or even more years after the alleged crime was committed. Indeed, in passing the War Crimes Act 1991, Parliament intended that crimes committed during the Second World War should be prosecuted. A few prosecutions have been brought under this Act. For example, in *Sawoniuk*,[57] the defendant was tried for offences said to have been committed more than fifty years earlier.

A decision to prosecute an offence which occurred many years ago should obviously not be taken lightly. Quite apart from the difficulty of gathering reliable evidence, it may be argued that it is simply not right to hold someone to account for something which they did many years ago, given that their personality and circumstances may have changed completely during the intervening years. This is perhaps particularly pertinent where an adult is prosecuted for a crime committed during their youth. There is some recognition of this in the Code for Crown Prosecutors, which, among the public interest factors against prosecution, lists the situation where 'there has been a long delay between the offence taking place and the date of the trial.'[58] Of course, this should not always be a determining factor. Where, as in the case of war crimes, an offence is extremely serious, lapse of time by itself should not be a bar to prosecution. The CPS Code goes on to acknowledge counter-balancing factors, noting that staleness is not such a good reason against prosecution where 'the offence is serious; the delay has been caused in part by the defendant; the offence has only recently come to light; or the complexity of the offence has meant that there has been a long investigation.'[59] In the course of an inquiry into child abuse in children's homes the Home Affairs Committee considered whether a statute of limitations should be introduced to deal with the problems caused by delay.[60] It decided against it, and this seems right. Delay should not be an absolute bar to trial; it needs to be considered along with the counter-balancing factors in the individual case.

The primary concern of the courts in delay cases of this type is whether the defendant can have a fair trial, in the sense that he can adequately defend himself against the charges brought by the prosecution. There are two principal devices

---

[56] Magistrates' Courts Act 1980, s 127.   [57] [2000] 2 Cr App R 220.   [58] Para 6.5.
[59] *Ibid.*
[60] Home Affairs Committee, *The Conduct of Investigations into Past Cases of Abuse in Children's Homes*, Fourth Report 2001–2, paras 84–9.

available to the courts to deal with this problem. The first is a warning to the jury about the difficulties caused by delay. The Judicial Studies Board has issued a specimen direction on the issue.[61] The gist of this is that the judge should ask the jury to consider the reasons for delay—for example, whether it reflects on the reliability of the complainant. The jury should also be told to make allowances for the fact that the passage of time may have made it difficult for the defendant to defend himself: he may have little memory of events many years ago, and evidence once available to him—such as an alibi—may no longer be.

In some cases the courts will go further than this. They may stay the prosecution on the grounds that it is an abuse of process. For example, in *R v Telford Justices, ex parte Badhan*,[62] the defendant was prosecuted for a sexual offence some fifteen years after it was said to have occurred. The Divisional Court held that proceedings should have been stayed, because it was not possible for the defendant to receive a fair trial. Here, there was no abuse of process in the sense that the prosecution was at fault: it had not caused the delay. The delay was due to the complainant not having come forward for many years, for reasons which the court seemed to accept were good ones. Nevertheless, the feeling that the defendant was placed in a very difficult position—'to investigate an alibi for an unknown Saturday evening in a year commencing 16 years ago is a doomed enterprise'[63]—justified a stay. The case may be contrasted with *Wilkinson*,[64] where the defendant was charged with sexual assaults of his daughters some fifteen to thirty years earlier. Although the Court of Appeal noted that the defendant himself may have contributed to the delay—by swearing his daughters to secrecy—it put most emphasis on the criterion of whether a fair trial was possible. It was held that it was, the Court noting that in this case the allegation did not relate to a specific day, but to a continuing course of conduct. 'Accordingly, it is not a case in which inability, after many years, to establish a particular alibi for a particular day could have been an important factor.'[65] A third case on this issue is *R v B*,[66] where the defendant had been convicted, in 2002, of sexually abusing his stepdaughter between 1968 and 1972. The Court of Appeal's decision here is odd. It did not feel that any criticism could be made of the judge's decision to proceed with the case, and, indeed, to allow the case to go to the jury. Nevertheless, it decided to use what it referred to as its 'residual discretion to set aside a conviction if we feel it is unsafe or unfair to allow it to stand.'[67] The principal concern here again seems to be the difficulty the defendant faced in defending himself: 'All that the defendant could do was to say that he had not committed the acts alleged against him. . . . [W]hen faced with allegations of the sort that were made here, "I have not done it" is virtually no defence at all.'[68] Whatever the merits of the decision to quash the conviction, the judgment in *B* seems to be a deliberate attempt to avoid giving clear guidance on how to deal with delay.[69]

---

[61] Specimen Direction 37, available at www.jsboard.co.uk. Cf. *Brian M* [2000] 1 Cr App R 49.
[62] [1991] 2 QB 78.   [63] *Ibid.*, at 91.   [64] [1996] 1 Cr App R 81.
[65] *Ibid.*, at 86.   [66] [2003] EWCA Crim 319.   [67] *Ibid.*, 27.   [68] *Ibid.*, 28.
[69] The decision has apparently caused some consternation among prosecutors: see Home Affairs Committee, *The Work of the Criminal Cases Review Commission* (2004), at Q75.

A number of criticisms can be made of the case law on this area. The distinction between *Badhan* and *Wilkinson* is obscure. To be sure, Badhan would have little chance of producing an alibi, but surely Wilkinson would too. And if Wilkinson cannot respond to the allegations with an alibi, surely he is in just as difficult a position as Badhan and the defendant in *B*: reduced to arguing 'I did not do it'. Even if there were something to the alibi point, it is not obvious that the difficulty prejudices Badhan. The jury, surely, is unlikely to take a dim view of his case just because he cannot provide an alibi for a specific day 16 years ago: he simply would not be expected to remember such details; indeed, it might well be suspicious if he did claim to have an alibi. And while it is true that 'I did not do it' is not the strongest of defences, there are many defendants in cases that do not involve delay who have no other defence than this. Consent defence rape cases are notorious for coming down to being the defendant's word against the complainant's, but that, rightly, is never considered to be a reason for stopping the case.

If there is a difference between the cases it is that the evidence against Wilkinson is somewhat stronger: there are two complainants, and their testimony provides some mutual support. There are actually problems for the courts in admitting that this is the distinguishing criterion. As the Court of Appeal in *B* admits, whereas the law once required corroboration in cases of rape and sexual assault, the corroboration rules were abolished in 1994.[70] To decide that a prosecution should be stayed because a complaint is unsupported, then, would seem to undermine Parliament's decision that corroboration is not required for a conviction. Further, a judge should not refuse to let a case go to the jury just because he has doubts about the credibility of the witness. This is the rule in *Galbraith* (about which more will be said in the following chapter) that credibility is an issue for the jury. If judges have doubts about the credibility of the complaints in these cases, then, the only real option is to stay the proceedings on grounds of delay or, as in *B*, to allow an appeal on 'lurking doubt' grounds.

The cases discussed here obviously raise difficult issues. But it may be that the courts have, on occasion, been too ready to block a conviction on grounds of delay. Directing juries about the difficulties faced by defendants in these cases is clearly a sensible thing to do; once that is done, it is hard to see why the difficulty a defendant would have in producing an alibi is a relevant factor to take into account. If there are doubts about the credibility of the complainant, then that may be a good reason to halt the case. But that should prompt the courts to confront the *Galbraith* rule directly, rather than to circumvent it by other means.

(b) CUSTODY TIME LIMITS

Article 5 of the ECHR protects the right to liberty. Pre-trial detention is permissible, but a defendant so detained is 'entitled to trial within a reasonable time or to release pending trial.' Where indictable offences are concerned, English law has various

---

[70] See D. Birch, 'Corroboration: Goodbye to All That?' [1995] Crim LR 524.

provisions which help to ensure that defendants remanded in custody are brought to trial with reasonable dispatch. A defendant can only be remanded in custody for 28 days; after that period, a new decision must be taken. More importantly, the Prosecution of Offences Act 1985 and regulations issued under it contain provisions on custody time limits. Under these, for example, a defendant charged with an offence triable only on indictment is entitled to trial within 182 days of his case being transferred to the Crown Court.[71] If a time limit expires, a defendant is entitled to be released on bail, but the prosecution may apply for extension of the time limit before it expires. Section 22(3) of the Act provides that an extension should not be granted unless the court is satisfied that there is good and sufficient cause (the section lists the illness or absence of a judge or important witness as good causes, among others), and that the prosecution has acted 'with all due diligence and expedition'.

On the whole, the courts take custody time limits seriously and are reluctant to extend them.[72] One of the leading decisions is *R v Manchester Crown Court, ex parte McDonald*.[73] The Divisional Court indicated that it would not look favourably, when considering whether there has been due expedition, on 'pretexts such as chronic staff shortages, . . . overwork, sickness, absenteeism or matters of that kind.'[74] Factors such as the complexity of the case and the cooperativeness of the accused are relevant, however. In *McDonald* itself good reasons for the extension of custody were held to be the slow progress of enquiries conducted by the Spanish authorities, given that the English prosecutor had done all he could to move things on, and the fact that a judge scheduled to try a case had fallen ill. Such factors are no fault of the prosecuting authorities; some cases will always take longer to come to trial than others, and so long as the prosecutor has done all he can, an extension of the time limit seems appropriate. More controversial, though, is the decision in *R v Central Criminal Court ex parte Johnson (Orleander)*.[75] Here, delay was caused by the Forensic Science Service. The court held that as this was not the prosecutor's fault—again, he had done all he could to speed things up—the custody time limit could be extended. It refused to see the Forensic Science Service as being part of the prosecution for the purposes of the custody time limit rules. This is arguable: it seems clear that if delay is caused by lack of court or judicial resources in a routine case, time limits should not be extended.[76] The State should simply provide sufficient resources to enable timely prosecution. The Forensic Science Service, as the State's principal forensic science resource, should perhaps be seen in a similar manner. A similar issue arose in *R (Gibson) v Winchester Crown Court*.[77] Here, custody time limits were extended because of the unavailability of a courtroom in Winchester Crown Court (the main courtroom being occupied by a lengthy fraud trial). This was held to be good reason for the extension, but the decision may be contrasted with the forthright comments of May LJ in *R (Bannister)*

---

[71] Prosecution of Offences (Custody Time Limits) Regulations 1987 (SI 1987 No. 299), reg 5.
[72] See, generally, A. Samuels, 'Custody Time Limits' [1997] Crim LR 260.
[73] [1990] 1 WLR 841.   [74] *Ibid.*, 847.   [75] [1999] 2 Cr App R 51.
[76] See *R v Manchester Crown Court*, above n 73, 848.   [77] [2004] 2 Cr App R 14.

v Crown Court at Guildford. 'Parliament has set custody time limits for various obvious reasons. Parliament ultimately is also responsible for the provision of resources by
way of judges, recorders, courtrooms and staff, to enable cases to be heard within
those custody time limits.'[78]

What if a custody time limit is about to expire, and the prosecutor replaces the
original charge against the defendant with a new one? The literal effect of the time
limit rules is that a new time limit will start to run with the introduction of the new
charge; the obvious problem here is that this may allow the prosecutor to manipulate
the rules. This situation was considered in *R v Leeds Crown Court, ex parte Wardle.*[79]
The defendant had originally been charged with murder for causing death during a
burglary. When the custody time limit was about to expire, the prosecution substituted the murder charge for one of manslaughter. On appeal to the Crown Court, the
judge considered that, had the charge not been changed, an extension of the time limit
would not have been granted: the prosecution had not acted with due expedition.
Nevertheless, the effect of the new charge was to institute a new time limit, so the
defendant lost his automatic right to release on bail. The defendant was, of course,
free to make a new application for bail, but this was turned down because he had a
previous history of offending on bail and of not surrendering. The case eventually
reached the House of Lords. All of the judges expressed some concern about the way
the rules allow a new charge to institute a new time limit, but a majority held that the
law could not be interpreted in such a way as to allow the defendant's release in this
situation. Nor could there be said to have been an abuse of process. Wardle applied to
the European Court of Human Rights, claiming that his Article 5 rights had been
breached, but his application was ruled inadmissible. The Court considered that there
had been adequate judicial supervision of the decision to keep him in custody, and
that the prosecution had acted with sufficient expedition.[80]

Wardle leaves the law in an unsatisfactory state. The case seems to have involved
some shoddy performance on the part of the police and prosecutors. From the facts
given in the various judgments, it is difficult to see why a charge of murder was ever
considered appropriate. The victim, who had a weak heart, seems to have died from a
combination of shock and minor injuries, facts which do not suggest any intention to
kill or cause serious harm. One would have expected the charge to have been reduced
at a much earlier stage. There is also the Crown Court judge's finding that the prosecution had not acted with much urgency in disclosing witness statements and in
obtaining video evidence. The just result here would seem to involve blocking the
start of a new time limit, and a minority in the House of Lords (Lord Nicholls and
Lord Scott) did think that the rules could be read so as to achieve this. Another way of
protecting the defendant would be to stay the proceedings for abuse of process. There
was general agreement in the House of Lords that this device might be used in
extreme cases: where a new charge was substituted solely to introduce a new time

---

[78] [2004] EWHC 221 Admin, [11].   [79] [2002] 1 AC 754.
[80] *Wardle v United Kingdom* (2003) 4 EHRLR 459.

limit. But that was not felt to be the case here, because the charge had also been altered for good reasons, in that the evidence did not support the murder charge. Staying the trial for abuse of process would certainly be a drastic step in *Wardle*, for it would more or less ensure that Wardle could not be tried for a serious crime, so it is no surprise that all the judges were cautious about this remedy. Given that a stay was not thought appropriate in *Wardle*, it seems unlikely that there will be many cases where it will be justified; it will not be often that a prosecutor introduces a new charge *solely* to extend a time limit.

The discussion of abuse of process in *Wardle* is of some interest for what it tells us about the power to stay proceedings. It had been suggested in the Divisional Court that a stay was only appropriate in cases involving bad faith on the part of the prosecution, but the House of Lords distanced itself from this interpretation. According to Lord Hope, 'the essence of abuse of process in the context of criminal proceedings is that the prosecutor has sought to take advantage of a procedural rule for a purpose which can be described as improper or arbitrary'.[81] Lord Scott perhaps expressed the principle more broadly: abuse of process involves 'a use of court process for a purpose other than that for which the purpose in question was intended'.[82] When considering the prosecution of stale offences in the previous section, we saw that the abuse of process doctrine has been used, in cases such as *Badhan*, because of concerns about whether the defendant can receive a fair trial; that is hard to square with Lord Hope's formulation, and suggests, at least, a broader reading such as Lord Scott's. When we turn to consider entrapment we will find that there, too, the doctrine is being used in a broad manner. It is only relatively recently that the courts have made much use of the power to stay criminal proceedings for abuse of process: perhaps it is not surprising that the scope of the doctrine remains unclear.

(c) DELAY BETWEEN CHARGE AND TRIAL

There has been general acceptance in English and Commonwealth courts that there is a common law right to be tried without unreasonable delay or, to put the matter differently, that the courts have an inherent jurisdiction to prevent an abuse of their process where there has been unreasonable delay in bringing a case to trial.[83] This general right applies whether or not the defendant is in custody, and so can be distinguished from the issue of custody time limits discussed in the previous section. However, the English courts have insisted that the remedy of staying the prosecution for abuse of process should be invoked sparingly, and only where there has been clear fault on the part of the prosecution or where the delay has seriously prejudiced the defendant.[84] This approach prompts the question of the appropriate remedy for the

---

[81] Above n 79, 92.   [82] *Ibid.*, 155.

[83] See, e.g., the Privy Council in *Bell v DPP of Jamaica* [1985] AC 937, and the High Court of Australia in *Jago v District Court of New South Wales* (1989) 87 ALR 577.

[84] For magistrates' courts, see *R v Brentford JJ, ex parte Wong* [1981] QB 445; for the Crown Court, see *Attorney-General's Reference No. 1 of 1990* [1992] QB 630.

general run of cases in which delay occurs and whether, in those circumstances, what
we have is a right without a remedy. This difficult issue has been brought into sharp
relief by the Human Rights Act and by several recent decisions of the European Court
of Human Rights. Before returning to the question of remedies for breach, we consider the general approach of the Convention, and how the English courts have
interpreted and applied it.

The European Convention provides various guarantees of timely decision making
in criminal justice (e.g. Article 5.3, arrestee should be 'brought promptly before a
judge'; Article 5.4, person detained 'entitled to take proceedings by which the lawfulness of his detention shall be decided speedily by a court'), but the most relevant
for present purposes is the guarantee in Article 6.1—applicable equally to civil
and criminal cases—of a 'fair and public hearing *within a reasonable time* by an
independent and impartial tribunal.' It was established by the Court at an early stage
that the rationale for this right is that individuals should not be allowed to remain 'too
long in a state of uncertainty about their fate,'[85] although subsequently the Court has
emphasized more broadly 'the importance of rendering justice without delays which
might jeopardise its effectiveness and credibility.'[86] We may identify four key questions
about the extent and effect of this right—when time begins to run, to what decisions
the right applies, what amounts to a breach, and what remedies should be given.

(i) When does time begin to run?

For the purposes of both Articles 5 and 6, it was established by the Strasbourg Court
in *Deweer v Belgium*[87] that time begins to run from the point of charge, but that the
term 'charge' has an autonomous meaning in this context which approximates to
whether 'the situation of the [suspect] has been substantially affected.' The *Deweer*
approach was applied by the Court in *Heaney and McGuinness v Ireland*,[88] holding
that the applicants had been 'charged' for this purpose when served with a notice
requiring them to account for their movements, prior to being formally charged with
an offence.

However, in *Attorney-General's Reference (No. 2 of 2001)*[89] Lord Bingham, with
whom all their Lordships concurred on this point, held that time will usually begin to
run from the point at which a person is charged (in the English sense) or summoned,
adding mysteriously that this is not an inflexible rule. He referred to the Strasbourg
decision in *Howarth v United Kingdom*,[90] where the Court held that time began to run
from the point at which the applicant had been interviewed by the Serious Fraud
Squad, some four and a half months before he was charged. Without engaging with
that decision or the other Strasbourg jurisprudence, Lord Bingham commented that
'arrest will not ordinarily mark the beginning of that period. An official indication

---

[85] *Stogmuller v Germany* (1979) 1 EHRR 155, 5.   [86] *H v France* (1990) 12 EHRR 74.
[87] (1980) 2 EHRR 30.   [88] (2000) 33 EHRR 264.   [89] [2003] UKHL 68.
[90] (2001) 31 EHRR 861.

that a person will be reported with a view to prosecution may, depending on the circumstances, do so.'[91]

There are two obvious difficulties with the House of Lords' position. First, Lord Bingham appeared to depart from the Strasbourg approach without giving reasons for doing so—he is entitled to do this, but when s 2 of the Human Rights Act 1998 states that a British court 'must take into account' the Strasbourg jurisprudence one would expect a discussion of the relevant decisions and good reasons to be offered for taking a different approach. Secondly, Lord Bingham's speech leaves it unclear under what circumstances an English court may properly hold that time begins to run before the point of charge. This is manifestly unsatisfactory: should courts be guided by the Strasbourg decisions (such as *Deweer, Howarth* and *Heaney and McGuinness*), or is Lord Bingham signalling an approach that is more flexible from the prosecutor's point of view but different from the Convention jurisprudence?

(ii) To which stages of the criminal process does the guarantee apply?

The Strasbourg jurisprudence indicates that the 'reasonable time' guarantee applies from the time of arrest through to the final stage of appeals. Thus in *Howarth v United Kingdom*,[92] a two-year delay in dealing with an appeal was held to breach Article 6(1); in *Mellors v United Kingdom*,[93] a three-year delay between trial and appeal in Scotland was held unreasonable; and in *Reid v United Kingdom*,[94] the Court held that:

'The delays which appear in this case cannot be justified either by the complexity of the case or the exigencies of internal procedure. While one year per instance may be a rule of thumb in Art. 6(1) cases, Art. 5(4) concerning issues of liberty requires particular expedition.'

This contrast is not so much between the 'reasonable time' guarantees in the two Articles, as between whether the appellant was in custody or not—the Court has rightly insisted that custody cases call for greater expedition.

In *R (on the application of Lloyd) v Bow Street Magistrates' Court*,[95] the Divisional Court held that the guarantee covers the execution of a sentence or ancillary order made on conviction. Thus Dyson LJ found no difficulty in applying Article 6.1 to the enforcement of a confiscation order made on conviction for conspiracy to handle stolen goods: 'such proceedings are part and parcel of the confiscation proceedings, which in turn are part and parcel of the original criminal proceedings.'[96] It is therefore apparent that the question of unreasonable delay may be raised at any point between the initial charge (howsoever interpreted) and the final appeal or final act of enforcing orders of the court.

---

[91] [2003] UKHL 68, at [28].   [92] (2001) 31 EHRR 861.
[93] Judgment of 17 July 2003, App. 57836/00.   [94] (2003) 37 EHRR 211.
[95] [2004] Crim LR 136.
[96] The decision in *R v Chichester Justices, ex parte Crowther* [1998] All ER (D) 457, which went the other way, has been challenged in Strasbourg and the application has been declared admissible by the Court.

(iii) What amounts to a breach?

It is well established that the length of a delay must be considered in relation to the complexity of the case and the conduct of the public authorities (prosecution, court) and of the defendant.[97] As the Court put it in *Mellors v UK*:

'the reasonableness of the length of proceedings must be assessed in the light of the circumstances of the case and having regard to . . . the complexity of the case, the conduct of the applicant and of the relevant authorities, and the importance of what is at stake for the applicant.'[98]

In that case the delay of three years and two weeks in dealing with the appeal was held unreasonable: the case was not unduly complex, and although the defence contributed in a small way to the delays, the major problem was one of listing the appeal. Similarly in *Ahmed v Birmingham Magistrates' Court and the CPS*,[99] a Divisional Court held that a delay of some three years in enforcing a summons for dangerous driving and bringing the case to court breached Article 6.1. This was too long 'for the trial of a very simple, uncomplicated case of dangerous driving.' The causes lay in the court's failure to notice that it was sending letters to the wrong address, and in certain periods of unexplained inactivity, and there was no evidence that the defendant was trying to avoid or escape trial.

In *R (on the application of Lloyd) v Bow Street Magistrates' Court* it had taken some five years for proceedings to be brought against the applicant to enforce the confiscation order in respect of the unpaid portion. Among other delays were two years during which the receiver appointed by the court did nothing, and a further year's delay before the final summons could be heard at Bow Street. Dyson LJ stated:

'Convicted criminals who are the subject of confiscation orders do not attract sympathy, and are not entitled to favoured treatment. But there is nothing surprising about the requirement that, if the prosecuting authorities/magistrates court seek to enforce a confiscation order, they should do so within a reasonable time. It is potentially very unfair on a defendant that he should be liable to be committed to prison for non-payment of sums due under a confiscation order many years after the time for payment has expired, and long after he has been released from custody and resumed work and family life.'[100]

This is important in the way that it brings the discussion back to the reasons for respecting the right to be tried without unreasonable delay—the effects on people's lives and decision making about their future.

(iv) What is the appropriate remedy for breach?

The House of Lords has accepted in *Porter v Magill*,[101] that the right to trial within a reasonable time is a free-standing right safeguarded by Article 6(1): it is no answer to a breach of this right that other rights guaranteed by Article 6, such as the right to a fair trial before an independent and impartial tribunal, have been respected. The more

---

[97] *Konig v Germany* (1978) 2 EHRR 170.   [98] Above n 93, at [28].
[99] [2003] EWHC Admin 72.   [100] [2003] EWHC Admin 2294, at [25].   [101] [2002] 2 AC 357.

difficult question concerns remedies. The Strasbourg Court has acknowledged that breach of the right does not necessarily render the whole proceedings a nullity,[102] but because it operates after exhaustion of local remedies that Court has never had to consider the proper approach to a case which has been delayed so that the trial has not yet taken place. It has, however, held that each contracting state must have in place a remedy or range of remedies for breach of the right which are effective in law and in practice.[103] What remedies English law offers was the principal question before the nine members of the House of Lords in *Attorney-General's Reference (No. 2 of 2001)*.[104] The House of Lords held by a majority of 7–2 that it will rarely be appropriate to stay the proceedings if they have not yet begun, because there is a strong public interest in having charges tried. A court should therefore consider lesser remedies such as compensation or mitigation of sentence. Thus Lord Bingham held that:

'The appropriate remedy will depend on the nature of the breach and all the circumstances, including particularly the stage of the proceedings at which the breach is established. If the breach is established before the hearing, the appropriate remedy may be a public acknow-ledgement of the breach, action to expedite the hearing to the greatest extent practicable and perhaps, if the defendant is in custody, his release on bail. It will not be appropriate to stay or dismiss the proceedings unless (a) there can no longer be a fair hearing or (b) it would otherwise be unfair to try the defendant. The public interest in the final determination of criminal charges requires that such a charge should not be stayed or dismissed if any lesser remedy will be just and proportionate in all the circumstances. The prosecutor and the court do not act incompatibly with the defendant's Convention right in continuing to prosecute or entertain proceedings after a breach is established in a case where neither of conditions (a) or (b) is met, since the breach consists in the delay which has accrued and not in the prospective hearing.'

Does this amount to an effective remedy, in the sense 'either of preventing the alleged violation or its continuation, or of providing adequate redress for any violation that had already occurred'? Lord Bingham and the majority evidently thought that courts could be left to deal appropriately with this in individual cases. On the other hand, in a strongly worded dissenting speech Lord Hope went so far as to say that the majority's decision 'empties the reasonable time guarantee almost entirely of content.'[105] In his view, there are many cases where mitigation of sentence or compensation would not be sufficient recognition of the Article 6.1 right. Lord Bingham's condition (b) would presumably be satisfied by such things as bad faith, unlawfulness or executive manipu-lation of the kind seen in *R v Horseferry Road Magistrates' Court, ex parte Bennett*.[106] Lord Bingham did accept that there may be 'very exceptional' cases, lying outside categories (a) and (b) above, where a stay of proceedings might be appropriate, so the door is not absolutely shut for the defence. However, English law has taken a pragmatic approach that gives priority to the importance of ensuring that allegations of serious

---

[102] *Bunkate v Netherlands* (1993) 19 EHRR 477.
[103] *Kudla v Poland*, judgment of 26 October 2000, App. 30210/96, at [158].
[104] [2003] UKHL 68.   [105] *Ibid.* at [46].   [106] [1994] 1 AC 142.

crime are tried, and accords far less weight to the need to ensure that individuals are not kept uncertain about their fate for too long. The real question is whether it is sufficient to reduce a defendant's sentence slightly when there has been lengthy delay in bringing him to trial: Lord Hope believes that it is not, and the majority's view that the defendant's right can simply be 'balanced away' if the crime charged is a serious one is surely unacceptable in principle and unlikely to command support in Strasbourg.

9.4 ENTRAPMENT

Many of the pre-trial issues we have considered in this chapter are connected to the fairness of the trial: by regulating disclosure, and considering issues of delay, the pre-trial process offers an opportunity to ensure that the coming trial is as fair as possible. In extreme cases, as in those involving unreasonable delay, a stay for abuse of process can be used to prevent the trial from taking place at all. Our final topic in this chapter considers the use of pre-trial remedies as a response to entrapment. Here, the courts will sometimes prevent a trial from taking place because the police have gone beyond their law enforcement role by 'creating' the crime with which the offender is charged.

Although the majority of recorded offences are reported to the police by members of the public, who will often give useful information too, there are a minority of cases in which the police decide to adopt proactive methods. Typically, these are crimes without direct victims, such as drug-related crimes, or those involving a form of conspiracy or other organization. Intelligence-led policing may take different forms,[107] and our concern here is with approaches that rely on the deployment of undercover officers or participant informers. We saw in Chapter 5 above that the use of surveillance may impinge on the target person's right to respect for private life, and that this is why the European Court of Human Rights has insisted on certain safeguards, which the Regulation of Investigatory Powers Act 2000 attempts to translate into English law.[108] Proactive methods of law enforcement such as undercover policing and the use of participant informers raise similar questions about the right to respect for private life and the prevention of arbitrary interference by State officials, but they also raise a deeper question about the right to a fair trial under Article 6 of the Convention. If the State, through the police or a police-instigated informant, engages in an operation to test whether a person will commit a crime in a given situation, there is a point at which this becomes State-created crime; and for the State to create a crime and then to prosecute a person for that crime would be a gross abuse

---

[107] For discussion, see M. Maguire, 'Policing by Risks and Targets: Some Dimensions and Implications of Intelligence-Led Policing', (2000) 9 *Policing and Society* 315, and R. Billingsley, T. Nemitz and P. Bean (eds), *Informers: Policing, Policy, Practice* (2001).

[108] For comments on the extent to which this has been achieved, see Ch. 5.

of power. As we will see, the contention is that in this situation it would not be fair to try the defendant at all. This is how the point of principle was put in the leading English decision:

'It is simply not acceptable that the state through its agents should lure its citizens into committing acts forbidden by the law and then seek to prosecute them for doing so. That would be entrapment. That would be a misuse of state power, and an abuse of the process of the courts. The unattractive consequences, frightening and sinister in extreme cases, which state conduct of this kind could have are obvious. The role of the courts is to stand between the state and its citizens and make sure this does not happen.'[109]

This does not rule out all forms of proactive policing, as we will see. But it purports to set a limit to the exercise of police power and to create a realm of protection for citizens. And it does so both because citizens should not be tempted by State officials in this way, and because the integrity of the criminal justice system would be undermined if courts were to act upon the fruits of manifestly unacceptable practices by law enforcement agents or their informants. As the Strasbourg Court put it in the leading decision of *Teixeira de Castro v Portugal*:

'The Court concludes that the two officers' action went beyond those of undercover agents because they instigated the offence and there is nothing to suggest that without their intervention it would have been committed. That intervention and its use in the impugned criminal proceedings meant that, right from the outset, the applicant was definitively deprived of a fair trial.'[110]

Thus the leading decisions in both Strasbourg and London hold that the appropriate remedy for entrapment is that the proceedings should not take place at all—in England, this indicates a stay of the proceedings for abuse of process.

What form of activity by law enforcement agents amounts to entrapment and justifies this remedy? The House of Lords in *Looseley*,[111] concluded that it would be acceptable for the police to target an individual if three conditions are fulfilled. First, they must have reasonable grounds to suspect that person of involvement in the offence (or, more broadly, reasonable grounds for suspecting people who frequent a certain place of being thus involved). The notion of reasonable suspicion plays an important role in Article 5(1) of the Convention, in justifying restrictions of liberty such as arrest, and it is a wholly appropriate criterion here—even though interpretations of the phrase are sometimes rather broadly drawn.[112] The difficulty with this first condition is that using proactive techniques against anyone who happens to frequent a particular place amounts to a departure from the requirement of reasonable suspicion against the particular individual targeted.[113] Since this is not the only way of

---

[109] *Per* Lord Nicholls in *Attorney-General's Reference No. 3 of 2000; Looseley* [2001] UKHL 53. For analysis of the decision, see A. Ashworth, 'Re-drawing the Boundaries of Entrapment', [2002] Crim LR 161.

[110] (1999) 28 EHRR 101 at 39.   [111] Above n 109.

[112] See the discussion of arrest in Ch. 4.

[113] See D. Ormerod and A. Roberts, 'The trouble with *Teixeira*: developing a principled approach to entrapment', (2002) 6 *E & P* 38, at 51–52.

tackling this difficulty—it might, for example, be possible to set up a surveillance operation in order to determine which individuals might reasonably be suspected of involvement in offences—it may be argued that this extension of the condition is not Convention-compliant. The second condition is that the officers or informants should be duly authorized to carry out the operation in accordance with the Codes of Practice issued under the Regulation of Investigatory Powers Act 2000: this is a procedural requirement, and is intended to enhance supervision and to remove arbitrariness. For example, the Code of Practice makes it clear that proactive methods should not be used unless less intrusive methods of investigation are likely to be unsuccessful. And thirdly, if the first two conditions are fulfilled, the officer or participating informant must do no more than provide the suspect with an unexceptional opportunity to commit the offence. Formerly this was sometimes phrased in terms of passive rather than active involvement, but in practice, the officer or informant will often have to do some acts in order to provide the opportunity. The key factor is that the officer or informant should act normally, as a potential customer would do in a given situation, and not hold out any extra temptation.

How stringent these conditions turn out to be depends on their application in practice, of which little evidence has emerged in the few years since *Looseley*. But there are some obvious areas of contestability. The problematic issue of targeting premises or an area, rather than individuals, has already been mentioned. Another problem concerns persistence: how many times may the police properly give a suspect an opportunity to commit an offence? The House of Lords noted that some persistence may be necessary in drugs cases, but Lord Nicholls stated that 'the more forceful or persistent the police overtures, the more readily may a court conclude that the police overstepped the boundary.'[114] On the boundaries of 'reasonable suspicion', the Strasbourg Court regarded evidence of a person's 'predisposition' to commit the offence as a key factor,[115] whereas the House of Lords made the fair point that this may penalize those who have previous convictions. But it is not clear what approach the House of Lords would have taken towards cases of 'confirmation by subsequent facts', as where the police act on a hunch that turns out to have been correct: such cases appear to depart from the concept of reasonable (prior) suspicion.[116]

Two other types of police tactic that may border on entrapment are 'stings' and 'manna from heaven' operations. In *Christou and Wright*,[117] undercover police officers set up a bogus shop, Stardust Jewellers, trading normally in second-hand jewellery in the hope that stolen property would be offered to them. This was not so much a matter of tempting people to handle stolen goods as to obtain information about offences (usually, burglary) already committed. The Court of Appeal held that the officers had not overstepped the mark in anything they did or said: the whole operation was a form of deception, but (to use the language subsequently adopted in *Looseley*) the officers did no more than provide an unexceptional opportunity to

---

[114] [2001] UKHL 53, at [28].   [115] In the *Teixeira* decision, above n 110.
[116] See Ashworth, above n 109, at 172–173.   [117] (1992) 95 Cr App R 264.

people. Some of the Court's statements were unduly simplistic: when Lord Taylor stated that the defendants applied themselves to the trick, rather than having a trick applied to them, he made a rather unconvincing distinction.[118] But the use of decoys, for example where there have been attacks on victims of a particular kind in a certain area, seems acceptable if properly conducted. More controversial are 'manna from heaven' operations, of the kind employed in *DPP v Williams and O'Hare*.[119] The police parked a van full of cigarettes with its rear doors ajar and the cigarettes visible. The two defendants fell prey to the temptation. The Divisional Court held that this was not entrapment or otherwise objectionable, and the House of Lords in *Looseley* seemed to agree.[120] However, Lord Hoffmann also said that if a police officer were to leave a full wallet on a park bench to see who took it, that would be entrapment 'because the policeman is preying on the weakness of human nature to create crime for an improper purpose.'[121] The distinction between the two cases is not great, and should surely not turn on whether the officer was acting on personal initiative or as part of an authorized operation. It is therefore strongly arguable that the line should be drawn so as to protect citizens from 'manna from heaven' operations.

---

[118] For further debate, see A. Ashworth, 'Should the Police be allowed to use Deceptive Practices?', (1998) 114 LQR 108.

[119] (1994) 98 Cr App R 206.   [120] See Lord Hoffmann at [2001] UKHL 53, [65].   [121] *Ibid.*, [59].

10

PLEA

One of the key decisions for people who are prosecuted is how to plead. With the exception of special pleas such as *autrefois convict* and *autrefois acquit* in cases where the defendant pleads that he or she has previously been tried and cannot lawfully be re-tried for the offence,[1] and the rare plea of not guilty by reason of insanity, defendants have a choice of two: guilty or not guilty. In some cases the decision on plea may depend on the offence(s) charged, so that a plea of guilty may be offered to a lesser offence than the one charged or to only one or two offences where more offences are charged. In this connection, as we will see, the discussion of prosecutorial decision making in Chapter 7 above is particularly relevant. In some cases the decision on plea may depend on the mode of trial, i.e. the level of court in which the charge is likely to be heard. Summary offences are triable only in magistrates' courts, and indictable-only offences are tried in the Crown Court, but there is a large middle category of offences triable either way. In these cases defendants have a right to elect Crown Court trial: the Crown Court has a much higher acquittal rate than the magistrates' courts, but there is a longer delay before the trial and, where a conviction results, sentences in the Crown Court tend to be higher than in the magistrates' courts. The incentives are therefore mixed for defendants, whereas prosecutors tend to wish to have as many either way offences as possible dealt with in the magistrates' courts. The system for determining mode of trial is now designed to ensure that as many cases as possible, in the triable either way category, are dealt with by magistrates. Thus the 'plea before venue' system introduced under the Criminal Procedure and Investigations Act 1996 ensures that those who indicate an intention to plead guilty to an either way offence are dealt with in the magistrates' courts (subject to the possibility of committal to the Crown Court for sentence).

If the defendant pleads not guilty, the case goes to trial. If the defendant pleads guilty, there is no trial. Instead, the prosecution gives a statement of facts in court and, unless the defence disputes this statement to an extent that requires some form of hearing to resolve the matter,[2] the judge or magistrates will proceed to sentence the defendant. The European Convention on Human Rights declares that 'everyone is entitled to a fair and public hearing', that 'everyone charged with a criminal offence

---

[1] See the discussion of double jeopardy, below, Ch. 11.
[2] See the leading case of *Newton* (1982) 4 Cr App R (S) 388, and discussion by A. Ashworth, *Sentencing and Criminal Justice* (3rd ed., 2000), 307–311.

shall be presumed innocent until proven guilty according to law', and that everyone shall have the right 'to examine or have examined witnesses against him'.[3] A defendant who pleads guilty gives up these rights and does not put the prosecution to proof; as we describe below, the English criminal justice system contains an array of incentives designed to produce this outcome. In some countries those rights are thought so fundamental that they cannot be waived: the unavailability of the guilty plea is regarded as a guarantee of defendants' rights.[4] In France, for example, the plea of guilty has long been regarded as an alien concept: the court must examine the dossier to ensure that there is sufficient evidence of guilt. That rigid approach was called into question by the Delmas-Marty Commission,[5] and recently the French legislature approved the introduction of guilty pleas coupled with the incentive of a lesser sentence.[6] In the Netherlands there seems to be an increasing gap between legal theory and legal practice: the theory is still that the ascertainment of guilt is for public officials to accomplish, not for defendants to concede, and the court must review and check the dossier; in practice there are various possibilities of bargaining, and more summary procedures for those who do not contest their guilt.[7] In Germany there is no guilty plea, but there are forms of 'plea bargain' in which a defendant may confess to the judge in order to gain a reduction in the sentence.[8] Thus there is evidence of increasing Europe-wide recognition of guilty pleas coupled with reduced sentences. Any reduction in sentences seems to run counter to the trend for increasing severity against terrorism, organized crime and other serious types of offending; the suggestion is that pressures on resources are leading governments to find ways of reducing the number of trials taking place.

  In England and Wales guilty pleas were relatively unusual in the eighteenth century and did not become common until the nineteenth century, when defence lawyers were allowed to play a fuller part.[9] Nowadays there is not even the appearance of a review by the court where a guilty plea is entered, although in Crown Court cases the judge will read the papers quickly before passing sentence on a guilty plea. In essence, the guilty plea constitutes a waiver by the defendant of the right to be tried. The law

---

[3] See Ch. 2 above.

[4] M. Damaska, 'Evidentiary Barriers to Conviction and Two Models of Criminal Procedure: a Comparative Study', (1973) 121 *U. Pa. LR* 506.

[5] Commission Justice Pénale et Droits de l'Homme, *La Mise en Etat des affaires pénales* (1991), 10. See also the essay by Judge F. Tulkens in M. Delmas-Marty and J.R. Spencer (eds), *European Criminal Procedures* (2002).

[6] See 'Lawyers Protest as French MPs give police more powers', *The Guardian*, 12 February 2004.

[7] See N. Jorg, S. Field and C. Brants, 'Are Inquisitorial and Adversarial Systems Converging?', in C. Harding *et al, Criminal Justice in Europe* (1995), esp. 47–51.

[8] J. Herrmann, 'Bargaining Justice: a Bargain for German Criminal Justice?' (1992) 53 *U. Pittsburgh LR* 755; L. Leigh and L. Zedner, *A Report on the Administration of Criminal Justice in the Pre-Trial Phase in France and Germany* (1992), 43; H. Jung, 'Plea-Bargaining and its Repercussions on the Theory of Criminal Procedure' (1997) 5 *Eur. J. of Crime, Criminal Law and Criminal Justice* 112.

[9] M. Feeley, 'Legal Complexity and the Transformation of the Criminal Process: the Origins of Plea Bargaining', (1997) 31 *Israel LR* 183.

provides a strong incentive to plead guilty, in a provision that now appears in s 144 of the Criminal Justice Act 2003:[10]

'(1) In determining what sentence to pass on an offender who has pleaded guilty to an offence before that or another court a court must take into account:

    (a) the stage in the proceedings for the offence at which the offender indicated his intention to plead guilty; and

    (b) the circumstances in which this indication was given.'

The legislation does not state the amount of the discount, which judicial precedents set at up to one-third; and it avoids explicitly stating the well-established principle that, the earlier the plea, the greater the discount. But sentencing guidelines now deal authoritatively and in detail with these issues.[11]

This chapter begins with an inquiry into the percentage of defendants who plead guilty. It then considers some of the principal reasons for changes of plea, looking at charge bargains (where the defendant agrees to plead guilty in exchange for the prosecution reducing the level of the charge or the number of charges), at fact bargains (where the defendant agrees to plead guilty only on the basis that the prosecution will put forward a particular version of the facts), and at plea negotiation (where the change of plea is motivated by considerations of sentence). The tendencies evident in the English system are then evaluated in the light of defendants' rights and the supposed advantages to the public.

10.1 THE RATE OF GUILTY PLEAS

In the magistrates' courts the rate of guilty pleas is well over 90 per cent. Most of these are relatively minor matters, three-quarters being summary offences that almost always end in a fine. A contested trial in a magistrates' court is therefore fairly rare. Figures from the CPS show that in 2002–2003 some 5.8 per cent of their cases[12] heard in the magistrates' courts were contested, and around 28 per cent of those (or 1.7 per cent of the total) were dismissed.[13] These are the figures for cases heard in the magistrates' courts, excluding the 13 per cent of cases discontinued by the CPS. If we turn to

---

[10] The section was originally enacted as s 48 of the Criminal Justice and Public Order Act 1994. The changes in its terms are not significant for present purposes.

[11] Probably the leading authority was *Buffrey* (1993) 14 Cr App R (S) 511; see now Sentencing Guidelines Council, Reduction in Sentence for a Guilty Plea: Guideline (2004).

[12] Possibly a quarter of cases in the magistrates' courts are brought by other agencies, such as Trading Standards officers or the regulatory agencies. The CPS figures are therefore not comprehensive, but they are the best available.

[13] Crown Prosecution Service, *Annual Report 2002–2003*, 30. These figures are given in order to facilitate comparison with the *Criminal Statistics 2002*. There are more up-to-date figures in the CPS *Annual Report 2003–2004*, and they are similar: 5.4 per cent of magistrates' court cases contested, with 1.3 per cent resulting in acquittal.

the Crown Court, and again exclude the 15 per cent of cases not proceeded with, some 26.5 per cent of trials were contested, and of those just under 40 per cent resulted in acquittal.[14]

However, interpretation of the statistics is not straightforward. As will be apparent from the CPS figures just quoted, it is misleading to refer to 'the acquittal rate' in magistrates' courts or the Crown Court without making it clear how the rate has been calculated and, in particular, whether cases discontinued or otherwise withdrawn or dismissed are included. Thus the *Criminal Statistics 2002* record a guilty plea rate in the Crown Court of 66 per cent (compared with the CPS figure of 73.5 per cent), and record the acquittal rate in contested trials as 60 per cent (compared with the CPS figure of about 40 per cent). The figures come close together when it is revealed that the *Criminal Statistics* include cases where the judge ordered an acquittal because the prosecution was unable or unwilling to proceed (perhaps because a witness refused to testify), which amount to over a third of the 60 per cent.[15] There are also variations according to region and type of offence. Thus for many years the North Eastern circuit has had a far higher guilty plea rate than other circuits, whereas in the London courts the figure has been constantly below the national average. No clear explanation for these divergences has been found, and the acquittal rate of those who plead not guilty seems to be roughly the same among the various circuits. However, that is a percentage of a much larger number in London than in the North East. It is possible that the cultures of some provincial Bars could be different from that in London: if there are fewer barristers, they may be expected to know one another and to know the limited pool of judges rather well, and may therefore be able to give much more confident predictions of the outcome to their clients. The figures may also reflect the higher number of black defendants in London, it being well established that such defendants are less likely to plead guilty (and also more likely to be acquitted at trial) than others.[16]

Two other points must be made about the interpretation of guilty plea rates. First, there are differences in the counting of cases in which the defendant pleads guilty to some charges and not others. Secondly, the guilty plea rate differs according to the type of offence. Somewhat higher than the average of 66 per cent were the guilty plea rate for burglary (76 per cent), motoring offences (75 per cent) and drugs (73 per cent), whereas for offences of violence, the largest group in the Crown Court, the rate was 55 per cent and for sexual offences only 36 per cent.[17] These lower guilty plea rates may be related, in part at least, to the difficulty of ensuring that witnesses testify.

Why do so many defendants plead guilty and forgo their right to be tried? In the early 1970s Bottoms and McClean conducted interviews with over 200 defendants who pleaded guilty either at a magistrates' court or at the Crown Court. When they

[14] *Ibid.*, 33. Again, the figures for 2003–2004 are similar.   [15] *Criminal Statistics 2002*, 64–65.
[16] For discussion, see B. Bowling and C. Phillips, *Racism, Crime and Justice* (2002), Ch.7, and M. Tonry, *Punishment and Politics* (2004), Ch. 4.
[17] *Ibid.*, Table 3C.

asked why the defendant pleaded guilty, about two-thirds answered that it was because they were guilty. Indeed, some 70 per cent of these admitted to the police from the beginning that they were guilty.[18] A similar finding emerged from the later survey by Hedderman and Moxon, although 65 per cent of their respondents also said that the prospect of a lighter sentence was a reason for their decision.[19]

What about those who change their plea? There is little information about plea-changers in the magistrates' courts,[20] but for the Crown Court there are statistics on what are termed 'cracked trials'. A cracked trial is one that is listed as a not guilty plea, with court time set aside for a contested trial, and in which the defendant changes to a guilty plea after the case has been listed, i.e. at a fairly late stage. Some trials 'crack' on the day of the hearing, others a day or two before. Cracked trials cause unnecessary inconvenience and even anxiety to victims and other witnesses who are brought to court on what turns out to be a fruitless journey. They are also productive of inefficiencies in the criminal justice system, since they cause listing difficulties (even though there are usually one or two other trials waiting to come on) and consequently they may result in a wastage of scarce resources, namely court time, judicial time, and public money. The scale of the problem was evident from the findings of the Crown Court survey in the early 1990s: of the 65 per cent of cases that were guilty pleas, only three-fifths were originally listed as guilty pleas and the remaining two-fifths were made up of 'cracked trials' which were originally listed as not guilty pleas.[21] It is not clear that the spread of pre-trial hearings and the introduction of 'plea before venue', described in Part 5 of this chapter, have brought significant change in this respect. But the encouragement of earlier guilty pleas forms a major part of the official strategy for reducing the number of cracked trials.

10.2 PLEADING NOT GUILTY

We have seen that around six per cent of defendants in magistrates' courts plead not guilty throughout, but that in the Crown Courts it is just over a quarter who exercise their right to be tried. More do so in London, fewer in the North-East. Why do they persist in their pleas of not guilty, whilst others change their pleas? Once again, the most obvious answer is that they maintain that they are not guilty. It seems that around 60 per cent of defences involve a denial of the basic facts:[22] around one in six of these are alibi defences, and perhaps one-quarter are claims of mistaken identification.[23] The other 40 per cent of defences accept the basic facts but contest guilt on the basis of

---

[18] A.E. Bottoms and J.D. McClean, *Defendants in the Criminal Process* (1976), 115.

[19] C. Hedderman and D. Moxon, *Magistrates' Court or Crown Court? Mode of Trial Decisions and Sentencing* (1992), 24.

[20] J. Baldwin, *Pre-Trial Justice* (1986), 92–7.

[21] M. Zander and P. Henderson, *Crown Court Study* (1993), 95–6.   [22] *Ibid.*, 121.

[23] *Ibid.*, 75 and 92.

justification or lack of culpability. Some three-quarters of these seem to amount to a denial of *mens rea*, and almost all the remaining one-quarter claim self-defence.

Just as it seems likely that some people who are innocent eventually plead guilty, so it also seems likely that some who are guilty plead not guilty. They may do so for a variety of personal reasons, ranging from over-confidence to shame at the offence and an unwillingness to admit it publicly in any circumstances (e.g. with serious sexual offences). Some guilty defendants may be alive to the possibility that they have a chance of gaining an acquittal if prosecution witnesses fail to attend court to give evidence. Just as it is recognized that some defendants who change their pleas to guilty on the day of the trial do so because they see that the prosecution witnesses are at the court, so there may be others who, seeing that the prosecution witnesses have not arrived, persist in their plea of not guilty, with the result that the case collapses. While no study has identified the numbers involved, it seems entirely plausible that some defendants do benefit from windfalls of this kind. The Home Office refers to the view that 'delayed guilty pleas are a tactic employed in the hope that witnesses will lose patience and decide not to testify.'[24] The usual official response to this is to reinforce the incentives to plead guilty and to enter that plea early in the process. The difficulty is how to distinguish between the not-guilty pleaders who are guilty and the not-guilty pleaders who are not guilty, a key issue to which we return later. Moreover, account must also be taken of a third group—those who have an arguable point, such as whether a taking was dishonest or whether force was used reasonably in self-defence, and who wish to have that decided by a court.

10.3 CHARGE BARGAINS

The term 'charge bargaining' is used here to encompass two distinct kinds of case. The first is where a defendant faces two or more charges and signifies an intention to plead not guilty to them. It is then possible for the prosecution to drop one or more of the others, in return for a plea of guilty to one charge. Either the prosecution or the defence may suggest this way of resolving the matter. Many of these are cases where several distinct offences are alleged, but some will be cases in which the prosecution has charged a person with both theft and handling stolen goods in the expectation that there would be a conviction of only one offence. The second kind of case is where the defendant faces a serious charge and signifies an intention to plead not guilty to it. It may be possible for the prosecution to drop the serious charge in exchange for a plea of guilty to a less serious charge. Much depends on the criminal law. At some points the law seems to be ready-made for this kind of charge bargain: for example, a defendant might intend to plead not guilty to grievous bodily harm with intent, contrary to s 18 of the Offences Against the Person Act 1861, but might be

---

[24] Home Office, *Justice for All* (2002), 4.41.

willing to plead guilty to the lesser offence of recklessly inflicting grievous bodily harm contrary to s 20 of the same Act. The same applies if the original charge is under s 20, and the defendant is willing to plead to the lesser offence under s 47, assault occasioning actual bodily harm. Elaine Genders has demonstrated the way in which many s 18 charges come to be downgraded, partly because of the problems of proving intent unless the injury was particularly serious.[25] In her sample only 19 per cent of those charged under s 18 were eventually convicted under that section. Similarly, Ralph Henham found that some 62 per cent of those charged under s 18 pleaded guilty to a lesser offence.[26]

Defendants charged with murder sometimes offer a plea of guilty to manslaughter, particularly in cases of diminished responsibility. However, following the decision of the House of Lords in the case of *Morgan Smith*,[27] which broadened the defence of provocation, the Director of Public Prosecutions issued guidance to prosecutors to the effect that it would rarely be appropriate to accept a plea of guilty to manslaughter on grounds of provocation, and that the matter should be put before the jury.[28] To what extent this has been implemented remains to be established, because it is clear that simply issuing guidance does not necessarily produce the desired practices. This can be demonstrated by reference to the introduction of racially aggravated versions of several offences, under ss 28–32 of the Crime and Disorder Act 1998. It was obvious from the outset that this area would be ripe for charge-bargaining, with the possibility that defendants charged with the racially aggravated version of, say, assault or criminal damage would offer to plead guilty to the ordinary, non-aggravated offence of assault or criminal damage. The Director of Public Prosecutions gave an undertaking that such lesser pleas would not be accepted and instructed prosecutors accordingly. But, as we saw in Chapter 7 above, research found that downgrading of this kind occurred from the very commencement of the new law and still occurs in between one-fifth and one-third of cases.[29]

Apart from the specific types of offence just considered, in what proportion of cases do charge bargains take place? Most of the research focuses on the Crown Court, but charge bargains are by no means uncommon in magistrates' courts. Thus both Baldwin[30] and Mulcahy[31] found plenty of evidence of charges being reduced in number or in seriousness, followed by a change of plea to guilty. Such practices may be the result of a pre-trial review, whereby the defence lawyer discovers the likely

---

[25] E. Genders, 'Reform of the Offences Against the Person Act: Lessons from the Law in Action', [1999] Crim LR 689, at 691–3; see also A. Cretney and G. Davis, *Punishing Violence* (1995), 137–138.

[26] R. Henham, 'Further Evidence on the Significance of Plea in the Crown Court', (2002) 41 *Howard JCJ* 151, 153.

[27] [2001] 1 AC 146.   [28] Reported in *The Times*, 4 July 2003.

[29] CPS, *Guidance on Prosecuting Cases of Racist and Religious Crime* (2003); The Gus John Partnership, *Race for Justice* (2003), para 95; HMCPSI, *A Follow Up Review of CPS Casework with a Minority Ethnic Dimension* (2004), para 6.52; see above, Ch. 7.4 (b).

[30] J. Baldwin, *Pre-Trial Justice* (1986).

[31] A. Mulcahy, 'The Justification of "Justice": Legal Practitioners' Accounts of Negotiated Case Settlements in Magistrates' Courts' (1994) 34 *BJ Crim.* 411.

strength of the prosecution case; or they may emerge by the usual processes of inter-action between prosecution and defence lawyers, either around the court or even by telephone contact. Mulcahy's interviews with a small number of defence and prosecu-tion lawyers working in magistrates' courts led to the conclusion that trial avoidance is often thought desirable on both sides: if this is a fair representation of the general working culture,[32] to which there may of course be exceptions, then it is likely that there will be considerable pressure on some defendants in magistrates' courts to plead guilty. Similar findings emerge from the study of Health and Safety inspectors by Hawkins: although he found that there were some cases in which inspectors would not bargain, he discovered ample evidence of cases of 'pre-trial manoeuvring over number and type of charges.'[33] His conclusion, however, was that from the inspectors' point of view it was not simply a matter of speed and saving resources: 'while many of the bargains reveal a strong desire to expedite the matter, they also reveal a desire to achieve a commensurate penalty.'[34]

Turning to the Crown Court, as many as 77 of the 112 defendants in McCabe and Purves's sample who changed their plea at a late stage pleaded guilty to only part of the original indictment,[35] whereas in Baldwin and McConville's sample it was only 11 out of 121 late guilty pleaders[36] and in Bottoms and McClean's sample only three out of 68.[37] Most of the recent research on cracked trials does not provide details of the nature of any negotiation that took place, but some 51 per cent of those in Hedderman and Moxon's sample who changed their plea stated that they did so in the expectation that some charges would be dropped or reduced, resulting in a lighter sentence.[38] It may therefore be assumed that one or other form of charge bargain is a fairly frequent phenomenon.

What are the advantages and disadvantages for the prosecution? The chief benefit is that they are assured of at least one conviction, and do not have to risk the hazards of trial, more particularly in the Crown Court where as many as 60 per cent of contested cases end in an acquittal. In view of the possibility that witnesses may fail to turn up or may alter their story, or that the jury will be swayed by some non-legal factor, it is tempting for the prosecution to settle for the certainty of a conviction, albeit of a less serious offence (or fewer offences than charged). The Code for Crown Prosecutors (2004) states in paragraph 10.1 that in these cases:

'Crown Prosecutors should only accept the defendant's plea if they think that the court is able to pass a sentence that matches the seriousness of the offending, particularly where there are aggravating features. Crown Prosecutors must never accept a guilty plea just because it is convenient.'

---

[32] See also M. McConville *et al, Standing Accused* (1994), 194–8, and M. Travers, *The Reality of Law* (1997), Ch. 5 on defence solicitors.

[33] K. Hawkins, *Law as Last Resort* (2002), 105.   [34] *Ibid.,* 108.

[35] S. McCabe and R. Purves, *By-Passing the Jury* (1972).

[36] J. Baldwin and M. McConville, *Negotiated Justice* (1977), Ch. 2.

[37] Bottoms and McClean, above n 18, 126–7.   [38] Hedderman and Moxon, above n 19, 24.

This brief guidance reveals some of the conflicts besetting a prosecutor when taking a decision about accepting a lesser plea. The final words enjoin prosecutors not to give priority to 'convenience,' but presumably this means their own personal convenience in getting a file off their desk. If we revert to the fuller description provided by the 1992 version of the Code, we find a more frank acknowledgement of the conflicting forces at work:

'Administrative convenience in the form of a rapid guilty plea should not take precedence over the interests of justice, but where the court is able to deal adequately with an offender on the basis of a plea which represents a criminal involvement not inconsistent with the alleged facts, the resource advantages both to the Service and to the courts generally will be an important consideration.'[27]

Shorn of its double negatives, this seems to suggest that it is proper to accept a plea of guilty to a lesser offence if the maximum sentence for that offence is not too low compared with the seriousness of what the defendant did. Thus, for example, if in the Crown Court a defendant enters a plea of not guilty to a s 18 charge of causing grievous bodily harm with intent (which carries a maximum sentence of life imprisonment), and the defendant then offers to plead guilty to the lesser s 20 offence of inflicting grievous bodily harm (which carries a maximum sentence of five years' imprisonment), the prosecutor should reflect on whether the five-year maximum is appropriate for what was done. However, this guidance is rather naïve when viewed in the light of sentencing law. As Lord Bingham CJ stated, it is 'inconsistent with principle that a defendant should be sentenced for offences neither admitted nor proven by verdict.'[39] In the context of offences under ss 18 and 20, the maximum sentence of five years for s 20 offences must be reserved for the worst conceivable cases, and it would only be in rare cases that a sentence as far up the range as four years would be proper.[40] In practice, therefore, a prosecutor who accepts a plea to s 20 on an indictment charging s 18 would have to be satisfied that a sentence of two or three years would be adequate on the facts.

Acceptance of pleas is a controversial matter, and cases come to light each year in which the prosecution has manifestly not complied with the Code—for example *March*,[41] in which the prosecution accepted pleas of guilty to assault occasioning actual bodily harm and dropped charges of indecent assault in a case described by the trial judge as one of the most disgusting he had encountered, and a direct consequence of the acceptance of those pleas was to limit the court's sentencing power to two years' detention.[42] This and other cases suggest that savings of cost, preparation time and court time, together with the hazards of going to trial, inevitably tempt

---

[39] *Canavan and Kidd* [1998] 1 Cr App R (S) 243, at 247.   [40] *Simpson* [1998] 1 Cr App R (S) 197.
[41] [2002] 2 Cr App R (S) 448.
[42] This was because the offender was aged 17. If he had been convicted of indecent assault, however, the Crown Court would have had access to long-term detention under s 91 of the Powers of Criminal Courts (Sentencing) Act 2000.

prosecutors to accept pleas in circumstances where the sentence is plainly going to be lower than it might have been on conviction(s) as charged. That may be seen as an injustice—unless the charges were unduly high or numerous in the first place, which would constitute a different form of injustice. The Attorney-General's Guidelines state that 'the prosecution should be prepared to explain their reasons in open court' where they accept a plea, and that the prosecutor should 'whenever practicable speak with the victim or the victim's family, so that the position can be explained and their views and interests can be taken into account as part of the decision-making process.'[43] Transparency of this kind may sometimes operate as a counterweight to the pressures of expediency.

What are the advantages and disadvantages from the defendant's point of view? These depend on whether the defendant has committed an offence and, if so, what offence(s). It is easy to say that, if the defendant has really committed the higher offence, a plea of guilty to a lesser offence brings a benefit to the defendant in terms of a lower sentence. What is more debatable is the kind of case in which the defendant may be said to have been overcharged in order to put pressure on him or her to plead guilty to the lesser charge. In Chapter 7 we recorded evidence that this does occur, despite injunctions to the contrary in the Code for Crown Prosecutors. To the extent that it does happen, it means that some charge bargains hold no true advantage for the defence and only for the prosecution. By appearing to reduce the charge(s), the prosecutor obtains a plea of guilty to the offence that should really have been charged in the first place.

Much worse is the position of the defendant who maintains innocence of all charges. As we saw at the beginning of this chapter, English sentencing law holds out a massive institutional temptation, stemming from three sources—pleading guilty to a lesser charge should result in a lower sentence for the lesser offence, plus a further discount for pleading guilty, and if the defendant indicates an intention to plead guilty when brought before the magistrates on an either way charge the early plea may result in the magistrates passing sentence or at least committing the case to the Crown Court for sentence with a full discount. These institutional incentives may be known to the defendant, but they may be all the more powerful when conveyed by a lawyer who might be regarded as an expert. Thus if counsel's advice is that pleading guilty to a lesser charge is likely to result in a non-custodial sentence whereas conviction after a trial might result in custodial sentence, a defendant may well succumb to the pressure to forgo a perfectly reasonable defence. The dependence of the defendant on his or her legal representatives is considerable, and this brings issues of professional ethics to the fore.

---

[43] *Attorney-General's Guidelines on the Acceptance of Pleas* [2001] 1 Cr App R 425, paras 2 and 5. The reference to the views of the victim, as distinct from the interests, seems to be out of accord with principle and with most other statements about victim involvement: see Ch. 7.5 above.

10.4 FACT BARGAINS

Relatively little attention has been devoted to this class of case, which may be said to lie half-way between charge bargains and the straightforward plea bargains to be discussed in Part 5 below. There is, however, evidence that in some cases there has been an agreement by the defendant to change the plea to guilty on the faith of a promise by the prosecution to state the facts of the case in a particular way. An agreement not to mention a particular aggravating feature, for example, or not to mention the part played by another (such as a friend or spouse) may be sufficient to persuade the defendant to plead guilty. Again, the principal advantage for the prosecution is that it secures a conviction in the case, even though the 'public interest' may be said to suffer a loss because the sentence is based on facts less serious than those that actually occurred. There is also the discount for pleading guilty, which will lower the sentence further. The defendant, on the other hand, stands to benefit from these sentence reductions—although it can only be counted as a benefit if he or she is actually guilty of a more serious version of the offence than that put to the court.

In *Beswick*,[44] there was evidence that the offender had bitten the victim's ear and crushed his nose with his knee during an altercation. The indictment was for wounding with intent, contrary to s 18 of the Offences Against the Person Act 1861. Just before the trial the prosecution agreed not only to accept a plea of guilty to s 20 wounding but also to accept that plea on the basis that he merely 'bit at' the victim's ear, without mention of the facial injury. The prosecution statement of facts conformed to that agreement, but the judge refused to sentence on that basis and insisted on a *Newton* hearing at which witnesses were heard in order to determine the true facts.[45] The Court of Appeal approved the course taken by the judge, and stated that:

'The prosecution should not lend itself to any agreement whereby a case is presented to the sentencing judge to be dealt with so far as that basis is concerned on an unreal and untrue set of facts concerning the offence to which a plea of guilty is to be tendered.'

It is not known how closely this guidance is followed. Some would say that *Beswick* was an isolated case, but others have certainly come to light.[46]

In cases where the defendant wishes to put forward a plea of guilty on a version of facts that the prosecution is unable to accept, the Code for Crown Prosecutors states that 'the court should be invited to hear evidence to determine what happened, and then sentence on that basis.'[47] The CPS is also pledged to deal with any defence mitigation that 'contains unjust criticism of the character of the victim,' by stating its rejection of what has been said and inviting the court (where necessary) to hear

---

[44] [1996] 1 Cr App R (S) 343.   [45] On *Newton* hearings, see n 2 above.

[46] For example, *Attorney-General's Reference No. 44 of 2000 (Peverett)* [2001] 1 Cr App R 416 (discussed in Part 5 below), where part of the bargain was that the defendant's (less serious) version of the facts should be accepted (see the report at 418–419).

[47] Code, para 9.3; the guidance is qualified by the clause, 'where this may significantly affect sentence'.

evidence on the point.[48] In both instances, therefore, the judge should be asked to hold a *Newton* hearing. If the evidential findings at that hearing go against the defendant, 'some or even the whole of any discount to which he might otherwise have been entitled by reason of his plea of guilty' may be forfeited.[49]

10.5 PLEA BARGAINS

One of the main reasons for dealing first with charge bargains and fact bargains is that it leaves for separate consideration those cases in which the defendant begins by signifying a plea of not guilty to the charge and subsequently alters the plea to guilty. These are cases where there is no question of reducing the number or level of the charges, and no bargain about the factual basis on which the case will be put forward. The bargain, in effect, is with the law: it is only a bargain because the law holds out the incentive of a reduced sentence to those who plead guilty. The essence seems to be that the defendant trades a chance of acquittal for a lower sentence than would have been received in the event of conviction after a trial. There are five major ways in which the institutional incentives to plead guilty may have an impact on the defendant: the sentence discount itself, the 'plea before venue' system, indication of sentence, pre-trial hearings, and lawyer's advice. Together they amount to formidable pressure, but they will be examined separately at first. Most of the discussion here relates to the Crown Court, but the recent emphasis on granting the 'guilty plea discount' in magistrates' courts suggests that plea bargains, as well as charge bargains, may also be significant there.

(a) THE SENTENCE DISCOUNT

At the beginning of this chapter the wording of s 144 of the Criminal Justice Act 2003, on reduction of sentence for pleading guilty, was set out. Its broad and unqualified wording has now been the subject of guidelines from the Sentencing Guidelines Council: the discount applies to all courts (including magistrates' courts) and to all forms of sentence (including fines and community sentences). The provision also requires courts to state that they have reduced a sentence under that provision. The early evidence was that compliance with that requirement was variable,[50] but it is increasingly recognized as good sentencing practice to state how much of a reduction

---

[48] Crown Prosecution Service, *The Treatment of Victims and Witnesses*, para 3.6.

[49] *Beswick* [1996] 1 Cr App R (S) at 347.

[50] R. Henham, 'Bargain Justice or Justice Denied? Sentence Discounts and the Criminal Process', (1999) 63 *MLR* 515; cf. also his discussion of a small project in magistrates' courts, R. Henham, 'Reconciling Process and Policy: Sentence Discounts in the Magistrates' Courts', [2000] Crim LR 436. For criticisms of the methodology and conclusions of these projects, see A. Sanders and R. Young, *Criminal Justice* (2nd ed., 2000), 408–414.

in sentence has been given for the guilty plea.[51] Insofar as this practice is followed, it amounts to an authoritative form of communication to offenders and their lawyers, which is likely to heighten the influence of the discount.

To what extent are sentence reductions given in practice? Evidence shows that the overall differences in the Crown Court are considerable: thus in 2002 some 76 per cent of adult males pleading not guilty who were convicted received custodial sentences, compared with 62 per cent of those pleading guilty. This is a considerable difference, which surely demonstrates that a plea of guilty can make the difference between custody and community—a critical distinction, capable of exerting enormous pressure on defendants. For those sent to custody, the average lengths of sentence were 44 months and 27 months respectively.[52] This is an even wider differential than Roger Hood found in his 1989 sample of 3,000 Crown Court cases, but it is important to note that the 2002 figures are gross figures which take no account of previous convictions or mitigating factors. When Hood took account of the usual variables in analyzing his data, a difference of ten months was reduced to one of three months.[53] However, the gross figures in the *Criminal Statistics* are intriguing in other ways, since they continue to show that for some offences the average sentence on a plea of guilty is *higher* than on conviction after a trial. The 2002 figures are presented in Table 10.1.

What may be the explanation for the higher sentences for those who plead guilty to causing death by dangerous driving and to indecent assault, and the small difference for 'other woundings'? The commentary in the *Criminal Statistics* suggests that this may be a reflection of such factors as 'the timeliness of the guilty plea, the nature of the offence, and the circumstances and criminal history of the offender.' Hood's findings (above) certainly suggest that if all factors are taken into account the differences tend to diminish. But this does not explain why those factors should differ for these particular types of offence, although the commentary adds that 'for some offences, such as indecent assault on a female, those pleading guilty may originally have been charged with more serious offences (rape in this example) and are, therefore, at the more serious end of the offences within the class shown.'[54] A somewhat different explanation is required for the startling figures for causing death by dangerous driving. Perhaps it is that those who plead guilty are persuaded that there is really no point in contesting the case because the offence was such a bad one, whereas those who do contest it are those whose offence is at the lower end of the scale, just above the boundary between dangerous and careless driving.

The result of this discussion is that there is both statutory authority for, and broad empirical confirmation of, a significant discount for pleading guilty. In so far as the discount is known to defendants or is brought to their attention by lawyers, it is likely

---

[51] The Sentencing Guidelines Council has issued guidelines to this effect in *Reduction of Sentence for Guilty Plea*, at www.sentencing-guidelines.gov.uk. This was also the view of the High Court of Australia in *Cameron v R* (2002) 209 CLR 339.

[52] *Criminal Statistics 2002*, Table 4C.   [53] R. Hood, *Race and Sentencing* (1992), 125.

[54] *Criminal Statistics 2002*, para 4.27.

Table 10.1 Males aged 21 and over sentenced for indictable offences at the Crown
Court: plea rates and custodial sentencing for selected offences, 2002

England and Wales

Offence	Pleaded guilty (%)	Custody rate		Average sentence length (months)	
		Guilty	Not guilty	Guilty	Not guilty
Violence against the person					
Causing death by dangerous driving	75	87	(88)	42.1	33.1
Wounding or other act endangering life	58	90	94	46.9	57.7
Threat or conspiracy to murder	79	58	(71)	27.9	36.1
Other wounding	84	51	57	15.0	16.5
All violence against the person	79	55	72	21.6	34.9
Sexual offences					
Rape	39	96	99	80.4	90.6
Indecent assault on a female	63	65	83	28.2	28.5
Indecent assault on a male	69	72	84	33.2	32.1
All sexual offences	61	71	89	36.9	52.9
Burglary					
In a building other than a dwelling	95	74	69	18.8	28.5
In a dwelling	94	77	84	24.9	29.9
All burglary	94	77	82	24.3	34.0
Theft and handling stolen goods					
Other theft or unauthorised taking	91	55	(59)	12.8	22.2
Handling stolen goods	90	50	45	11.9	18.7
Theft from the person of another	91	61	58	12.7	16.7
Theft by an employee	89	42	(63)	14.1	17.3
Theft from shops	94	61	34	7.1	8.1
All theft and handling stolen goods	92	59	51	11.5	17.2
Fraud and forgery					
Other forgery	90	65	(73)	12.3	15.7
Other fraud	88	53	65	15.1	26.8
All fraud and forgery	88	53	65	14.2	23.7
Criminal damage					
Arson	88	62	(81)	33.3	48.0
All criminal damage	89	39	48	29.0	41.4
Drug offences					
Trafficking	84	77	92	35.0	58.9
Possession	95	28	(30)	10.7	11.7
All drug offences	86	70	89	36.1	65.8

to exert a considerable pressure towards pleading guilty. That, of course, is the purpose of the relevant law. It was formerly thought that the sentence discount did not apply in magistrates' courts, but the law is now clear and each page of the Magistrates' Courts *Sentencing Guidelines* now reminds benches that a timely plea should result in a sentence reduction.

(b) PLEA BEFORE VENUE

There is widespread recognition of the principle that, the earlier an intention to plead guilty is made known, the larger the sentence reduction should be. This follows from the leading rationale for the sentence discount, which is to save trouble and anxiety for victims and witnesses and to save public money.[55] To put this sentencing principle into practice means that the courts should be prepared to reserve the maximum discount for those who indicate a plea of guilty at the earliest possible stage. A significant change in the English system took place in 1997 with the introduction of 'plea before venue'. All defendants who are charged with triable either way offences are brought before magistrates and asked whether they intend to plead guilty. If they decline to intimate an intention to plead guilty, they may elect to be tried in the Crown Court or, if not, the magistrates will have the decision whether to commit them to the Crown Court for trial or to deal with the case themselves. However, the real incentive is for those who intimate an intention to plead guilty. The magistrates have the power to sentence them, if they decide that the case falls within their sentencing powers,[56] and this might mean a smaller and swifter sentence for the offender. However, that outcome is not certain, since the magistrates also have the power to commit the case to the Crown Court for sentence.

The 2002 statistics show that the change in practice since 1997 has been significant but not major: the rate of guilty pleas in the magistrates' courts has risen slowly, and committals to the Crown Court for trial have gone down from around 64,000 to some 50,000 per year, whereas committals for sentence have gone up from about 5,000 to some 18,000 per year.[57] The purpose of the system is to avoid late changes of plea and to have more cases dealt with cheaply in the magistrates' courts.[58] But in effect it places great pressure on defendants to plead guilty very early, perhaps before they have had disclosure from the prosecution and therefore properly grounded legal advice.

---

[55] In addition to the advice of the Sentencing Advisory Panel (above n 51), see also the High Court of Australia in *Cameron v R* (2002) 209 CLR 339 and the High Court of Justiciary in *Du Plooy v HM Advocate* 2003 SCCR 640, at [14].

[56] It was held in *R v Warley Justices, ex parte DPP* [1998] 2 Cr App R 307 that the magistrates' courts limit of six months' imprisonment for one offence could be used for cases that might justify a sentence of nine months at the Crown Court, if taking account of the discount meant that six months was the appropriate sentence. The maximum will be raised to 12 months by the 2003 Act.

[57] *Criminal Statistics 2002*, Figure 3.2.

[58] The Criminal Justice Act 2003, Sch. 3, takes this further by providing that plea and venue hearings may take place before a single magistrate.

The amount of pressure is increased by the Court of Appeal's decision in *Barber*,[59] to the effect that where a defendant intimates an intention to plead guilty before venue is determined, a discount of more than the 'usual' one-third may be appropriate. In that case the discount was some 40 per cent. This is an enhanced incentive to defendants, operative at a time when they have least information about the case against them. It is also confined to offences triable either way, although sentencing guidelines now state that the maximum discount should be available for all types of offence where the plea is intimated at the 'first reasonable opportunity.'[60] Whether a discount of more than one-third for pleading guilty is ever justifiable is a question to be discussed in the concluding part of this chapter.

(c) INDICATION OF SENTENCE

The screw is further turned by a new procedure introduced by the Criminal Justice Act 2003, indication of sentence in magistrates' courts. A defendant on an either way charge may request an indication of sentence—'an indication of whether a custodial sentence or non-custodial sentence would be more likely to be imposed if he were to be tried summarily for the offence and to plead guilty.'[61] The magistrates' court will then be informed of the defendant's record, and may or may not accede to the request. If it does give an indication, it must then give the defendant the opportunity to reconsider the plea; if the defendant decides on a plea of guilty, the court is bound by its indication. The aim of the new procedure is to put further pressure on the guilty to accept their guilt at an earlier stage. The Home Office recognized the danger to innocent defendants, and seemed to think that this is adequately covered by leaving it to the defence to make the request for sentence indication.[62] It is doubtful whether that procedural difference will outweigh the substantial incentive that will arise if magistrates then indicate that the sentence on a guilty plea will be non-custodial.

(d) PRE-TRIAL HEARINGS

Since the early 1980s some magistrates' courts have held pre-trial reviews of contested cases, with a view to facilitating an exchange of information between prosecution and defence, identifying issues so as to save time and perhaps bring about pleas of guilty. Following the spread of advance disclosure in the late 1980s some courts ceased to hold pre-trial reviews, but others have persisted with them. It seems that they may have modest advantages in cost-benefit terms: Brownlee, Mulcahy, and Walker found that they had little overall effect on the speed of case disposal, and resulted in relatively few changes of plea to guilty, but they still argue that there were overall cost-savings

---

[59] [2002] 1 Cr App R (S) 548; the issue of very early pleas was also at the heart of the decisions of the Australian and Scottish courts noted in n 55 above.

[60] Sentencing Guidelines Council (above n 51).

[61] Criminal Justice Act 2003, Sch. 3, substituting a new s 20 of the Magistrates' Courts Act 1980.

[62] Home Office, *Justice for All* (2002), para 4.43.

because the reviews were relatively inexpensive.[63] There is no legal framework for pre-trial reviews, the form of which varies according to the locality, and it is not known how many court areas still hold them. However, magistrates' courts now also have 'early first hearings' for cases in which there is likely to be a guilty plea, as well as the early administrative hearings where the plea before venue scheme operates.

Turning to the Crown Court, there has been a number of different initiatives designed to move cases forward more quickly by preparatory hearings before trial. The Auld Review identified four different types, running alongside one another:

'There are four separate, but largely similar, forms of procedure. First, there is the traditional non-statutory "plea and directions hearing", in which the judge can make non-binding rulings before the start of trial. Second, there is the statutory "pre-trial hearing" under Part IV of the Criminal Procedure and Investigations Act 1996 in which the judge can make binding rulings. Third is the now well established statutory procedures of "preparatory hearings", as the start and part of the trial, for serious and complex fraud cases under the Criminal Justice Act 1987, in which the judge can make binding rulings. Fourth is the similar and parallel form of "preparatory hearings" for other cases of complexity or length introduced by Part III of the 1996 Act.'[64]

The Auld Review was critical of this multiplicity of arrangements and also of the rigidity and bureaucracy sometimes associated with them. Its recommendation was for a more flexible single system, in the form of standard timetables with a 'pre-trial assessment' as part of the general case management responsibility of Crown Court judges. New criminal procedure rules will set out the details.

It is not yet clear whether the new system will still require counsel for the defence to complete a 'Judge's Questionnaire' about the case. The present document, in question 1(b), asks counsel at a pre-trial review whether the defendant's attention has been drawn to the statutory provision on reduction of sentence for a guilty plea (set out above). This is to ensure that those who maintain a plea of not guilty are made well aware of the law's considerable incentives to change their plea. This point is taken up in the next paragraph.

(e) THE *TURNER* RULES

The strong impression of one observer of pre-trial practice in the Crown Court in the early 1990s was that the identity and sentencing reputation of the judge or recorder were key factors in decisions on plea.[65] One might have thought that this variability should have lessened as more and more sentencing guidelines are being created, but the moves towards indications of sentence and other forms of pre-trial assessment

---

[63] I. Brownlee, A. Mulcahy and C.P. Walker, 'Pre-Trial Reviews, Court Efficiency and Justice: a Study in Leeds and Bradford Magistrates' Courts' (1994) 33 *Howard JCJ* 109; for earlier discussion, see J. Baldwin, *Pre-Trial Justice* (1986).

[64] Auld, *Review of the Criminal Courts of England and Wales* (2001), 481–2.

[65] J. Bredar, 'Moving Up the Day of Reckoning: Strategies for Attacking the Problem of "Cracked Trials" ', [1992] Crim LR 153.

suggest that it still remains important to know how *this* particular court views *this* particular case. Over 30 years ago in the leading decision of *Turner* (1970),[66] the Court of Appeal laid down various rules to govern the conduct of judges and counsel in these matters. The first rule is that defence counsel should be free to give advice to the defendant, if necessary in strong terms, about the best approach. The second is that defendants should have freedom of choice, having heard the advice. The third is that defence counsel should be able to see the judge, and vice versa, on matters relating to trial and sentence, but that this should only be done when really necessary. And fourthly, the judge should never indicate the likely sentence, except to say that the sentence will take the same form whether the defendant pleads guilty or is convicted.

The warning by Lord Parker CJ in *Turner* that visits by counsel to the judge's private room should be kept to a minimum has not always been heeded, and there has been evidence of non-compliance ever since. A survey in the early 1990s found that some judges were clearly doing what the Court of Appeal said they should not do, while other judges refused to see counsel for this purpose.[67] Moreover, there is a long series of Court of Appeal decisions quashing convictions for breaches of the rules. In 1990 the Court of Appeal again condemned the frequency of private meetings between counsel and the judge, with Lord Lane CJ stating that 'no amount of criticism, no number of warnings, and no amount of exhortation seems to be able to prevent that happening'.[68] At the start of the new millennium, the refrain in the Court of Appeal was strikingly similar:

'This case has a lamentable history . . . It illustrates what can, and too often does, happen, if, despite the repeated judgments of this Court to the contrary, counsel, in cases which are not wholly exceptional, have recourse to the judge, in his room, in order to discuss pleas and sentence.'[69]

What this reveals is not just a history of disobedience of the law by counsel and judges, but also a history of undue pressures imposed on defendants. This is because, if counsel discloses to the defendant that he or she has been to see the judge, any advice then given to the defendant may appear to be based on what the judge said. In *Pitman*,[70] the judge indicated that if the defendant changed his plea to guilty as charged there would be substantial mitigation, even though the defendant wished to argue that he was guilty not of reckless driving but of the less serious offence of careless driving. In *Turner* itself, counsel stated or implied that the judge had indicated that the sentence on the defendant would be non-custodial if he pleaded guilty, but custodial if convicted after a trial.[71] In both cases the Court of Appeal held that this placed improper pressure on the defendant in deciding on plea. In *Attorney-General's*

---

[66] [1970] 2 QB 321.

[67] JUSTICE, *Negotiated Justice: A Closer Look at the Implications of Plea Bargaining* (1993), 3.

[68] *Pitman* [1991] 1 All ER 468; for other examples, see *Smith* (1990) 90 Cr App R 413, and *Preston* (1994) 98 Cr App R 405.

[69] *Attorney-General's Reference No. 44 of 2000 (Peverett)* [2001] 1 Cr App R 416, *per* Rose LJ at 417.

[70] Above, n 68.   [71] Above, n 66.

Reference No. 44 of 2000,[72] there had been discussion between counsel about the defendant's pleas of not guilty to the 16 offences with which he was charged. Defence counsel intimated that the defendant might be prepared to plead guilty to some of the charges if the sentence were to be non-custodial. Defence counsel then requested a meeting with the judge in chambers, and both he and prosecuting counsel attended, together with a shorthand writer. Counsel put to the judge the proposed pleas of guilty to nine charges, and outlined some mitigation, in consequence of which the judge agreed that a suspended sentence of imprisonment would be appropriate. On this basis the defendant pleaded guilty and was given a suspended sentence, and Rose LJ condemned the process in the words quoted above.[73] It was accepted that the defendant would not have pleaded guilty to any of the offences if the suspended sentence had not been offered.

These decisions—and there are many others—demonstrate that there is a cultural belief among many counsel and judges (not all) that this is an acceptable way of dealing with a criminal case, despite the pressure it places on an innocent defendant. Rules have not succeeded in altering practices so far, and so one might be pessimistic about the *Attorney-General's Guidelines on the Acceptance of Pleas*, issued in December 2000 following the last-mentioned decision. The *Guidelines* seek to restrict meetings between judge and counsel in chambers to discuss plea and sentence to 'the most exceptional circumstances,' of which Rose LJ gave the example of a defendant who is dying but does not know that he is dying.[74] A full note of any meeting should be kept. If, however, there is a meeting and 'the prosecution advocate takes the view that the circumstances are not exceptional'—which seems to mean that the discussion should not, properly, be taking place—the *Guidelines* instruct the prosecutor to 'remind the judge of the relevant decisions of the Court of Appeal and dissociate himself or herself from involvement in any discussion on sentence.'[75]

The *Guidelines* seem to assume that there will still be meetings in the judge's chambers in cases that are not exceptional. In other words, the Attorney-General accepts that mere guidelines are unlikely to alter practices where Court of Appeal decisions have failed to do so. One reason for this may be practices at the Bar: Zander and Henderson found that some 70 per cent of those who changed their plea met the trial counsel only on the day of the trial.[76] Some 94 per cent of those who received legal advice on plea changed their minds followed the advice they received, often because it conformed with their own view, but sometimes because of persuasion by counsel.[77] One of the purposes of the various pre-trial hearings is to bring forward

---

[72] Above, n 69.

[73] The particular point in this appeal was whether the Attorney-General could then refer the sentence to the Court of Appeal as unduly lenient, given that prosecuting counsel had acquiesced in the arrangement. The Court refused to accept the reference, on the ground that the Crown's complicity raised an expectation that estopped it from seeking to resile from the arrangement subsequently.

[74] *Attorney-General's Reference No. 44 of 2000 (Peverett)* [2001] 1 Cr App R 416, at 417.

[75] *Attorney-General's Guidelines on the Acceptance of Pleas*, [2001] 1 Cr App R 425, at [4].

[76] Zander and Henderson, above n 21, 55.   [77] *Ibid.*, 96–8.

the time of meetings with counsel, although it is not known how 'successful' the various forms of hearing have been in applying pressure to defendants to change their plea to guilty.

What is the balance of advantages of plea bargains for the State? They contribute to the smooth running of the system by bringing speed and a reduction of the cost and resources needed to deal with the cases. They ensure a conviction, and avoid the hazards of trial which in 2002 produced an overall acquittal rate of around 60 per cent in the Crown Court. In the present system these advantages come at the price of a sentence reduction: it could be claimed that offenders who benefit from the sentence discount are receiving a lower sentence than they deserve (on the basis of harm and culpability), purely for reasons of speed and cost. Those who believe that sentencing should be based on preventive grounds, such as deterrence or incapacitation, would also regard the discount as detracting from its primary purpose. It would be difficult to calculate whether these losses to the system are justified by the advantages, because that would also involve a calculation of how many defendants would persist in a not guilty plea if there were no sentence discount for pleading guilty.

What is the balance of advantages for victims? In general guilty pleas spare victims the anxiety of having to give evidence in court, and the unpleasantness of hearing all the details of the crime analyzed at length in public. For those victims who do give evidence (a minority, because of the large numbers of guilty pleas), the process is often stressful.[78] However, research for the Sentencing Advisory Panel found that some rape victims resented the discount given for pleading guilty and said they would have been prepared to give evidence, if they had been given the choice, in order to ensure that substantial mitigation was not based on this factor.[79] It is not known whether a majority of victims feel this way, but the evidence is sufficient to raise questions about what some see as undeserved mitigation based on this ground—compounded, in some cases, by a reduction in the level of charge. In these cases it is particularly important that the victim or victim's family should be notified of such a significant step, but this does not always happen.[80]

What is the balance of advantages for defendants? The primary benefit is the discount for pleading guilty, which in general promises a substantial reduction in the length of a custodial sentence and (as the statistics in Table 10.1 strongly suggest) may in some cases result in the passing of a non-custodial rather than a custodial sentence. Such sentence reduction may be magnified by the defence lawyer's speech in mitigation: in general, it is much easier to construct a convincing mitigation for someone who has pleaded guilty than for someone who has contested guilt. It has often been said to be a further advantage that a defendant who was remanded in custody and who

---

[78] E.g. J. Morgan and L. Zedner, *Child Victims* (1992), 141–3; J. Shapland, J. Willmore and P. Duff, *Victims in the Criminal Justice System* (1985), 63–7.

[79] Sentencing Advisory Panel, *Advice to the Court of Appeal on Rape* (2002), at 41. The Panel drew attention to the possibility of making a Victim Personal Statement to this effect.

[80] For what should happen, see the *Code for Crown Prosecutors* (2004), para. 5.13. For what sometimes does, see *Wadsworth* [2004] 1 Cr App R (S) 109.

intended to plead guilty could delay the plea in order to benefit from the better conditions and more frequent visits available to remand prisoners,[81] but the recent emphasis
on larger discounts for early pleas may have lessened the attraction of this course.

These, however, are only advantages for the guilty defendant. From the point of
view of other defendants, these may be regarded as disincentives to a justifiable
challenge to the prosecution case. There are undoubtedly some innocent defendants
who feel pressure to plead guilty, because they believe there is a risk that they may not
obtain an acquittal and it might appear best to 'cut their losses' in the hope of
receiving a non-custodial sentence. Estimates of the number of innocent defendants
who take this course vary: Zander and Henderson's figures suggest that up to 11 per
cent of guilty pleaders claim innocence,[82] and earlier research suggested that an even
higher percentage of guilty pleaders were 'possibly innocent' of one or more charges.[83]
Not enough is known about the mental processes of people placed in this position,
but the research on false confessions should be sufficient to dispel any initial
reluctance to believe that people could indeed plead guilty when they were innocent.[84]
Moreover, the concept of innocence also needs careful attention: a defendant may
have a perfectly arguable defence and should, one might contend, have a right to put
the prosecution to disproof of the defence. Yet such a defendant may be advised
that running the defence is not worth the risk and the consequent loss of discount,
especially if this may make the difference between a custodial and a non-custodial
sentence. The sentencing discount positively discourages defendants from putting the
prosecution to proof of guilt. Of course the defence lawyer's ethical duty is not to
place any pressure on the defendant but to give a frank appraisal of the prospects and
of the advantages and disadvantages of continuing with a plea of not guilty. However,
even the *Turner* rules state the the lawyer should give advice 'if necessary in strong
terms,' and in practice it is hardly surprising if advice that is within the 'ethical rules'
is perceived by some defendants as overwhelming pressure.[85] The problem is not so
much the 'ethical rules' but rather the framework of criminal justice (notably the
sentencing discount) in which they find themselves situated.[86]

(f) NEGOTIATED DIVERSION

The focus of this discussion of plea bargains has been upon defendants whose
decision to plead guilty is influenced by the sentence reduction. However, another
form of bargain is where the possibility of a criminal charge acts as an incentive to
participate in some scheme of diversion. An example of this, mentioned in Chapter 6, is

---

[81] Cf. the discussion in the Auld Review (above, n 64), 434–444.

[82] Zander and Henderson, above n 21, 138–42.

[83] See the summary by P. Darbyshire, 'The Mischief of Plea Bargaining and Sentencing Rewards', [2000]
Crim LR 895, at 903.

[84] See below, n 115, on false confessions of guilt.

[85] See, e.g. J. Morison and M. Leith, *The Barrister's World* (1992), 132–7.

[86] For a forthright discussion, see M. McConville, 'Plea Bargaining: Ethics and Politics', in S. Doran and
J. Jackson (eds), *The Judicial Role in Criminal Proceedings* (2000), at 81–85.

the new system of conditional cautions, under which the CPS may agree conditionally not to prosecute a person if he or she agrees to certain conditions for a caution. Those conditions can impose some obligations, such as participation in a programme of work or treatment, and the threat of prosecution is suspended conditionally on compliance with the agreed terms. Thus the defendant may avoid a criminal conviction by agreeing to the terms for a conditional caution. As we noted,[87] one of the conditions for such a caution must be a free admission of guilt, but research suggests that innocent persons can be tempted to agree to a caution rather than face the threat of something more serious. This type of bargain therefore holds the same advantages and disadvantages as plea bargaining more generally.

10.6 POLICIES AND PRINCIPLES

There is much that is unsatisfactory in the rules and practices described in this chapter. Charge bargains are an unavoidable aspect of any system that includes graduated criminal offences (more serious, less serious) and that allows multiple charging. Graduated offences are right in principle,[88] and it is often justifiable to charge more than a single offence. But the result is to place pressure on defendants to plead guilty to something, as a kind of compromise. Fact bargains seem to have arisen through the absence of controls on the way in which the prosecution states the facts before sentence on a guilty plea: if the statement is unfairly adverse to the defendant the defence may challenge it, but if it is unfairly favourable, there seems to be little check. Plea bargains in the Crown Court have operated in a kind of half-light, and on the evidence of the last three decades it would be unwise to believe that the issuing of *Attorney-General's Guidelines* in 2000 or the spread of various forms of pre-trial hearing has brought widespread changes in the practices of lawyers and judges. Defendants may be given advice by their counsel, sometimes in strong terms, but the basis of this will often be a prediction of what the court will do. In effect, there is an element of gambling in the defendant's decision making here: the roulette wheel has taken the place of the rule of law. From the defendant's point of view, all three forms of bargain raise fundamental questions about the implications of the presumption of innocence and about the privilege against self-incrimination. They also raise questions about the quality of defence lawyering: what ought in theory to be 'full and fearless defence' within an adversarial system can become, in some courts and with some sets of lawyers, a series of negotiations based on preserving mutual respect and without always putting the client's interests first. From the public point of view, all of this may result in two kinds of unwanted consequences—the conviction (by guilty plea) of some people who are innocent, and the manipulation of criminal justice by

---

[87] Above, Ch. 6.4; simple police cautions offer the same possibilities for bargains.
[88] Cf. A. Ashworth, *Principles of Criminal Law* (4th ed., 2003), Ch.3, esp. 88–92.

some people who are guilty and who 'play the system', for example by waiting until the day of trial in order to see whether key witnesses attend before signifying their plea.

There has been no shortage of reform proposals in recent years, but all the official proposals have taken speed and economy as their objectives, and have sought to construct a system that places an even greater premium on pleading guilty. The Royal Commission on Criminal Justice in 1993 recommended a system of 'sentence canvass,' the essence of which would be that the judge should give an indication of the highest sentence on a guilty plea, if approached by defence counsel. This would have involved a reversal of one of the cardinal principles in *Turner*, but the Royal Commission was encouraged by the support of 88 per cent of defence barristers, 86 per cent of prosecution barristers, and 67 per cent of judges for a reform that would 'permit full and realistic discussion between counsel and the judge about plea and especially sentence'.[89] The Royal Commission started from the proposition that defendants are more interested in 'the actual sentence and in particular whether it will be custodial or not',[90] which shows again the importance of this borderline as distinct from the discount on the length or magnitude of a sentence. The Royal Commission accepted 'that to face defendants with a choice between what they might get on an immediate plea of guilty and what they might get if found guilty by the jury does amount to unacceptable pressure'.[91] Yet their proposal was, in effect, that defendants would be told the judge's view of what the highest sentence on a guilty plea would be, and that they would then ask counsel to predict what the sentence would be on a conviction after a trial, knowing that the sentence on a guilty plea would be significantly lower. In *Turner*, the court held that: 'a statement that on a plea of guilty he would impose one sentence but that on a conviction following a plea of not guilty he would impose a severer sentence is one that should never be made',[92] because this would constitute undue pressure on the accused. Thus the pressure would be unacceptable if the judge gave a view on both eventualities, but was thought to be acceptable if the judge gave one and counsel the other. The Royal Commission seemed to agree with this. No doubt counsel would perform the duty of advising the defendant not to plead guilty if he or she is not guilty, but this advice might well be overshadowed by the sheer weight of the incentives to plead.

The present Government has reaffirmed its objective of getting more defendants to plead guilty and to do so earlier, by means of a 'clearer tariff of sentence discount, backed up by arrangements whereby defendants could seek advance indication of the sentence they would get if they pleaded guilty.'[93] The benefit to witnesses and victims is acknowledged, but savings of court time and public money also loom large: 'if more defendants pleaded guilty early in the process, the courts and other agencies within the CJS would be able to concentrate on the remaining contested cases.'[94] This latest set of measures originates in the report of the Auld Review, which recommended a

---

[89] As reported by Zander and Henderson, above n 21, 145.   [90] RCCJ, *Report,* para 7.49.
[91] *Ibid.,* para 7.50.   [92] [1970] 2 QB 321, at 327.
[93] Home Office, *Justice for All* (2002), para 4.42.   [94] *Ibid.,* para 4.41.

clear set of graduated sentence discounts and a new system of advance indication of sentence, initiated by the defendant.[95] In reaching his conclusions, Auld LJ took account of a number of concerns raised in the second edition of this book. Those concerns relate to the difficulty of reconciling the various incentives to plead guilty with the framework of rights to which the United Kingdom is a signatory. The Royal Commission on Criminal Justice of 1993 spectacularly failed to make any reference to these rights. The Auld Review does so, but concludes that they do not stand in the way of the recommendations made.

The argument here is that the sentence discount for pleading guilty runs contrary to the spirit of at least four of the rights recognized under the European Convention on Human Rights, and possibly counter to their letter too. This argument starts by considering the rights of a defendant charged with a criminal offence, rather than starting with the objective of making the criminal justice system operate as smoothly and as cost-effectively as possible. The four rights to be considered are: the presumption of innocence, the privilege against self-incrimination, the right not to be discriminated against in the exercise of Article 6 rights, and the right to a fair and public hearing.

(a) THE PRESUMPTION OF INNOCENCE

Article 6(2) of the European Convention on Human Rights declares that 'everyone charged with a criminal offence shall be presumed innocent until proved guilty according to law'. One implication of this seems to be that a defendant has a right to put the prosecution to proof. No one should be recorded as guilty of an offence until the prosecution has proved that guilt, and 'any doubt should benefit the accused'.[96] The question is whether this right can be waived and, if so, under what conditions. The first part of the question may be answered by reference to a rather old decision of the European Commission on Human Rights, which held in 1972 that the possibility of pleading guilty does not infringe Article 6(2) so long as there are adequate safeguards against abuse, and that the judge is satisfied that the accused understands the effect of his plea.[97] The second part of the question is more difficult to answer, and the authorities indicate that the presence of a substantial incentive to give up the right to be tried—one-third or more off the sentence for the offence(s)—needs to be reviewed in Strasbourg.

In an early case entitled *X v United Kingdom*,[98] the trial judge had observed when passing sentence that a guilty plea would have constituted a mitigating circumstance. The applicants argued in Strasbourg that this amounted to the imposition of a heavier sentence on the grounds that they had contested the charge, and accordingly that

---

[95] Auld Review, above n 64, 443–444.

[96] *Barbera, Messegue and Jabardo v Spain* (1989) 11 EHRR 360, para 33.

[97] *X v United Kingdom* (1972) 40 CD 64, at 67, discussed by B. Emmerson and A. Ashworth, *Human Rights and Criminal Justice* (2001), 504–505.

[98] (1975) 3 DR 10, at 16.

the sentence was in breach of Article 6. In rejecting the application as manifestly ill-founded the Commission observed:

'It is clear from the statements by the trial judge that he did not increase the applicants' sentence on the ground that they had affirmed their innocence throughout the trial, but rather refrained from reducing what he deemed to be the proper sentence, having regard to the gravity of the offences concerned.'

This is consistent with the theory behind the guilty plea discount in English law,[99] even though it remains true that exercising one's right to be tried has a cost in the sense that the sentence passed in the event of conviction will be higher (possibly 50 per cent higher)[100] than the sentence on a guilty plea. Does the compatibility of a discount for pleading guilty depend on the extent of the inducement involved? In *Deweer v Belgium*,[101] the Court found a violation of Article 6 where the applicant had been offered the choice between paying a relatively modest fine by way of 'compromise' or facing lengthy criminal proceedings. If he had chosen to contest the charge his butcher's shop would have remained closed by administrative order, thus depriving him of income. The Court held that a procedure under which an accused can waive the right to a hearing on payment of a penalty is not necessarily inconsistent with Article 6, but that such a settlement must be free from 'constraint.' In the present case there was such disproportionality between the moderate fine and the substantial collateral consequences of contesting the proceedings that the settlement was tainted by constraint and therefore in breach of Article 6. In English cases the discount on a custodial sentence can be up to one-third,[102] and it is clear that a plea of guilty may make the difference between a custodial sentence and a community sentence.[103] Is a decision to plead guilty made in those circumstances sufficiently free from 'constraint', in the sense applied in *Deweer v Belgium*?

The magnitude of the English discount may suggest that it is not. It is one thing to offer a small inducement to plead guilty, in order to reinforce the proposition that those who are guilty should plead guilty and not try to 'play the system.' It is quite another thing if the extent of the inducement is so great as to 'drown out' that proposition and induce those who are not guilty to change their plea. This distinction has gained some recognition in Scotland, where the sentence discount for pleading guilty was only introduced in the mid-1990s into a system that had previously opposed it as inconsistent with the presumption of innocence.[104] In the leading

---

[99] See, e.g. *Harper* [1968] 1 QB 108.

[100] If the sentence after conviction is three years, and the sentence after an early guilty plea is two years (applying the one-third discount), then the former is 50 per cent higher than the latter.

[101] (1980) 2 EHRR 439.

[102] The Sentencing Guidelines Council's guidelines on Reduction in Sentence for a Guilty Plea (2004) limit the discount to one-third, overruling *Barber*, above n 59.

[103] *Howells* [1999] 1 Cr App R (S) 335, *per* Lord Bingham CJ at 337.

[104] In *Strawhorn v McLeod* 1987 SCCR 413 the Lord Justice-Clerk held that, because of its inconsistency with the presumption of innocence, 'no such inducement should be offered.' This was overruled by s 196 of the Criminal Procedure (Scotland) Act 1995.

decision in *Du Plooy v H.M. Advocate*,[105] the Lord Justice-General held that 'any practice of making an allowance has to be kept within bounds, so as to avoid discouraging, or appearing to discourage, accused persons from exercising their right to put the prosecution to proof.' Auld LJ, in his report, recognized the risk that some innocent defendants might be induced to plead guilty and commented that no system can guarantee that this will not happen. But his primary concern seemed to be that a sentencing system should not be tailored to encourage a defendant who knows he is guilty to 'try his luck', and this is why the sentence discount—and, on his view, a substantial one—is necessary.[106] In our submission, this approach ignores the force of the presumption of innocence and sacrifices it too readily to expediency.

The 1993 Royal Commission, not taking the nuanced view subsequently adopted by the Scottish courts, sought to deal with the problem of innocent defendants thus:

'Provided that the defendant is in fact guilty and has received competent legal advice about his or her position, there can be no serious objection to a system of inducements designed to encourage him or her so to plead. Such a system is, however, sometimes held to encourage defendants who are not guilty of the offence charged to plead guilty to it nevertheless . . . This risk cannot be wholly avoided and, although there can be no certainty as to the precise numbers . . . it would be naive to suppose that innocent persons never plead guilty because of the prospect of the sentence discount.'[107]

The only relevant point made subsequently is that 'against the risk that defendants may be tempted to plead guilty must be weighed the benefits to the system and to defendants of encouraging those who are in fact guilty to plead guilty. We believe that the system of sentence discounts should remain.'[108] This kind of 'balancing' argument, which appears to assign no particular weight to the presumption of innocence or any other recognized right, is quite unacceptable. Certainly it would be wrong for the advocates of rights to argue that it behoves us to take every possible step to ensure that innocent persons are never convicted. That would result in an immense investment of resources into criminal trials that might cripple the economy. But to dismiss that extreme position is not enough. As Dworkin argues, there is a strong case for maintaining that at all stages of the criminal process our procedures should put the proper value on the fundamental harm of wrongful conviction.[109] What the proper value is may be a matter for debate, but the argument here is that to hold out a substantial sentence discount as a standing incentive for defendants to waive their right to trial goes too far. It fails to give any special weight to the presumption of innocence, whereas its position as a fundamental right ought surely to require this.

---

[105] 2003 SCCR 640, at 644.   [106] Auld Report (above, n 64), 439–440.
[107] RCCJ, *Report*, para 7.42.   [108] *Ibid.*, para 7.45.
[109] R.M. Dworkin, 'Principle, Policy, Procedure', in C. Tapper (ed), *Crime, Proof and Punishment* (1981), 212.

(b) THE PRIVILEGE AGAINST SELF-INCRIMINATION

Although this privilege is not declared expressly in the European Convention on Human Rights, it is now established that the privilege and the related right of silence are implied rights that form part of the right to a fair trial in Article 6 of the Convention.[110] Leading Strasbourg decisions describe the privilege against self-incrimination as a 'generally recognized international standard' which lies 'at the heart of the notion of fair procedure under Article 6', and the same applies to the right of silence.[111] Both rights have been held to:

'presuppose that the prosecution in a criminal case seek to prove their case against the accused without resort to evidence obtained through methods of coercion or oppression in defiance of the will of the accused. In this sense the right is closely linked to the presumption of innocence contained in Article 6(2) of the Convention.'[112]

As we discuss elsewhere, the concept of coercion has been quite widely drawn by the Court.[113] The question here is whether the sentence discount for pleading guilty amounts to coercion in an analogous sense.

Two points may be made briefly. The first is that a substantial discount, of a third or more, may well amount to an inducement of the same magnitude as the financial penalties considered in cases such as *JB v Switzerland*[114] to infringe the privilege against self-incrimination. The second point is that there is a considerable literature on false confessions, as the Royal Commission on Criminal Justice recognized.[115] Difficult as it may be to imagine, some people who are innocent may be induced to plead guilty by the prospect of a non-custodial sentence and no further fuss. Just as the law holds that a confession should not be admitted if it was obtained in consequence of anything said or done which was likely, in the circumstances existing at the time, to render it unreliable, so one might argue that *pari passu* a plea of guilty should not be upheld if it was obtained in consequence of what might be described as a substantial inducement. Indeed, the argument would be that the legal system should not provide such an inducement, whereas English law, through its sentencing discount, clearly does.

(c) THE RIGHT NOT TO BE DISCRIMINATED AGAINST IN THE EXERCISE OF ARTICLE 6 RIGHTS

Article 14 of the European Convention on Human Rights declares that the rights in the Convention 'shall be secured without discrimination on any ground such as sex, race, colour'. Would this principle be breached, either in the letter or in the spirit, if it

---

[110] See Ch. 2 above.

[111] E.g. *Murray v United Kingdom* (1996) 22 EHRR 29 and *Saunders v United Kingdom* (1997) 23 EHRR 313, both drawing on Art. 14 of the International Covenant on Civil and Political Rights.

[112] *Saunders, ibid.* at para 68.   [113] Above, Ch. 5.6.   [114] [2001] Crim LR 748.

[115] RCCJ, *Report*, para 4.32.

were found that the operation of the criminal justice system routinely discouraged members of a particular ethnic minority from disputing their guilt?

Consider the available evidence in England and Wales. All studies that have included data on defendants' plea show that both persons from an African-Caribbean background and those from an Asian background tend to plead not guilty at a higher rate than whites. It also appears that African-Caribbeans are more likely to be acquitted, which may be regarded as vindicating their pleas.[116] The John Report found that 'defendants from African Caribbean and Asian ethnic groups are more likely to be acquitted than white defendants,'[117] suggesting that some of them are prosecuted when they should not be—which may explain the higher not guilty plea rate. Roger Hood found that not only do African-Caribbeans tend to plead not guilty more frequently than whites but that, when convicted, they tend to receive longer sentences largely because they have forfeited the discount for pleading guilty.[118] This can be regarded as a form of indirect discrimination: a general principle (the sentence discount) has a disproportionate impact on members of ethnic minorities simply because they exercise a right (the right to be tried and to be presumed innocent until convicted). The Royal Commission seemed to recognize this, but merely expressed its support for 'the recommendation made by Hood that the policy of offering sentence discounts should be kept under review'.[119] In fact, Hood argued that 'it is time [i.e. now] to consider all the implications of a policy which favours so strongly those who plead guilty'.[120] The Auld Review recognized that 'it is important to discover why one group of defendants, distinguished only by their ethnicity, should behave differently from others when faced with the same choices,'[121] and called for research to determine why this is so and whether the discount for pleading guilty was relevant to this. However, it appears that Auld was sceptical of these arguments, and took the general position that if members of ethnic minorities sought to exercise their right to be tried, they should take the consequence of a more severe sentence if found guilty. This overlooks the powerful argument about indirect discrimination, an argument that strongly favours the abolition (or substantial diminution) of the guilty plea discount.[122]

(d) THE RIGHT TO A 'FAIR AND PUBLIC' HEARING

Article 6(1) of the European Convention declares that 'everyone is entitled to a fair and public hearing', and goes on to describe the limited situations in which 'the press and public may be excluded from all or part of the trial'. One characteristic of cases in which

---

[116] For a summary of the early research, see M. Fitzgerald, *Ethnic Minorities and the Criminal Justice System* (1993), 26.

[117] Gus John Partnership, *Race for Justice* (2003), para 37.

[118] R. Hood, *Race and Sentencing* (1992), 125.   [119] RCCJ, *Report*, para 7.58.

[120] Hood, above n 118, 182.   [121] Auld Review, above n 64, 441.

[122] In M. Tonry, *Punishment and Politics* (2004), 75 and 87, it is argued that this reasoning should lead to the abolition of the guilty plea discount.

there is a guilty plea is that there is no real public hearing. An added characteristic of cases in which there is a plea bargain is that the crucial negotiation takes place in the absence not only of the public but also of the accused. The High Court of Australia spoke out strongly against these private meetings between judge and counsel, disapproving even the limited contact allowed by the *Turner* rules on the ground that this is inconsistent with 'the common law rule which requires a court to administer justice in public,'[123] and there is good reason to believe that a case determined in this way would not satisfy Article 6(1) of the Convention. Of course it may be replied that there is always some form of public hearing, at which the defendant pleads guilty, prosecution and defence speeches are made, and the judge decides on sentence. But if it can be established that the defendant's fate was determined by words spoken in private, of which only some were relayed to the defendant by counsel, this might cause some reconsideration of the Strasbourg approach.[124]

10.7 CONCLUSIONS

From the point of view of principle there are powerful arguments in favour of re-assessing the sentence discount for those who plead guilty. It is certainly against the spirit of four fundamental rights and freedoms recognized in the European Convention on Human Rights—the presumption of innocence, the privilege against self-incrimination, the right to equal treatment in the exercise of rights, and the right to a fair and public hearing—and is probably against the letter of two of them. The sentence discount sustains a number of perverse incentives that are liable to distort both the pursuit of truth and the protection of rights, in the context of charge, fact and plea bargains.

One major difficulty is the size of the sentence discount: it can often be as much as one-third (although less for a late change of plea), and can certainly make the difference between immediate custody and a non-custodial sentence.[125] These are formidable incentives, applicable both to those who are guilty and to those who are innocent. It has been argued here that discounts of this kind are so great that they place unfair pressure on those who maintain their innocence and wish to put the prosecution to proof—a strong temptation to 'cut one's losses' and plead guilty in exchange for a lesser sentence, particularly if it is non-custodial. A fairer system (assuming that the discount is to be retained) would be to offer a small incentive of no more than a 10 per cent reduction, aimed at preserving the freedom of choice of

---

[123] *Tait and Bartley* (1979) 24 ALR 473, at 488.
[124] See the case of *X v United Kingdom* at n 98 above, and accompanying text.
[125] Sentencing Guidelines Council, *Reduction in Sentence for Guilty Plea* (2004).

someone who mantains innocence and at ensuring that the exercise of the right to be presumed innocent until proved guilty does not have a significant cost.[126]

Another difficulty of the existing system is that so much often depends on the defence advocate's predictions of what the sentence may be on a guilty plea and if convicted at a trial. In a system where there is thought to be considerable variation in choice of sentence and sentence length between different magistrates' courts and different judges at the Crown Court, this injects an element of roulette into a system already loaded against a defendant who wishes to plead not guilty. One way of improving this situation is to increase consistency of sentencing, and to do so through the introduction of more guidelines, starting points and ranges. The work of the Sentencing Advisory Panel had led to the creation of guidelines for the sentencing of several types of offence in recent years,[127] and the Sentencing Guidelines Council has now begun to issue guidelines,[128] but it remains true that most offences are not covered by guidelines to an extent that makes the prediction of sentences possible even for advocates. The operation of the guidance on sentence reductions for guilty pleas will be difficult to monitor until there are guidelines for most of the common offences.

Both the Auld Review[129] and the Home Office in its White Paper[130] concluded that this problem of knowledge of the likely sentences, and the problem of innocent defendants who feel the pressure to plead guilty, should be dealt with by instituting a system in which it is for the defendant (through the defence advocate) to ask the court for an indication of the maximum sentence in the event of a plea of guilty at that stage and the possible sentence on conviction following a trial. The idea is that obtaining an indication of sentence from the court itself will remove much of the uncertainty about predictions made by advocates, and that requiring the defendant to take the initiative is a safeguard against undue pressures on the innocent. The latter point is unconvincing, since the decision to ask for an indication of sentence will usually be made after consultation with the defence advocate, who will give advice 'if necessary in strong terms.' Indeed, the Royal Commission of 1993 concluded that a system in which the judge gave such a sentence indication would amount to placing undue pressure on defendants, largely because the involvement of a judge made the pressure greater than simply the prediction of counsel. But Auld LJ disagreed:

'That comparison is precisely what a defendant considering admitting his guilt wants to know. He knows and will, in any event, be advised by his lawyer that a plea of guilty can attract a lesser sentence and broadly what the possible outcomes are, depending on his plea. So what

---

[126] Of course, any reduction in the amount of the discount would have to form part of a general re-appraisal of sentence levels and approaches to sentencing. We are certainly not arguing for any overall increase in the severity of sentences: other adjustments would have to be made.

[127] For an overview, see the Panel's reports at www.sentencing-guidelines.gov.uk

[128] The Sentencing Guidelines Council has also issued guidelines on general principles and on new sentences under the Criminal Justice Act 2003: see www.sentencing-guidelines.gov.uk

[129] Auld Review (above, n 64) 441–4.   [130] Home Office, *Justice for All* (2003), para 4.43.

possible additional pressure, unacceptable or otherwise, can there be in the judge, whom he has requested to tell him where he stands, indicating more precisely the alternatives?'[131]

Such a system of sentence indication may succeed in reducing the element of uncertainty, but it surely imposes additional pressure through the involvement of the authoritative figure of the judge. Given the magnitude of the possible difference between the two sentences, the real question is whether the pressure is so great as to impinge on the defendant's freedom of choice in the exercise of fundamental rights. If such an inducement were made to someone before he or she confessed a crime to the police, the confession might well be ruled inadmissible. False confessions do occur. Our submission is that the same considerations should apply in the context of changes of plea from not guilty to guilty.

Could the greater involvement of the judge, at the Crown Court, be used as a means of protecting the defendant's rights rather than imposing undue pressure? In Philadelphia, the fourth largest city in the US, there is no principle of sentence discount for pleading guilty. The result is that most defendants in felony cases do opt for trial, many of these being 'bench trials' by judge alone, which can be dealt with fairly quickly. This shows that, even in a country in which plea bargaining has come to be regarded as endemic, it is in fact merely a policy choice.[132] It could be eliminated or reduced substantially. That might entail costs, but it throws down the challenge to simplify criminal procedure generally. When the US Federal Sentencing Guidelines were introduced they were were designed to reduce the discount for pleading guilty and to place controls on plea negotiation: Schulhofer and Nagel concluded from their research that in the vast majority of cases (some 65 to 80 per cent) there was compliance with the guidelines and plea negotiations were not used as a means of circumventing them.[133] Alschuler, who has studied plea bargaining in the US extensively over a long period, argues that changes in criminal procedure could make for a fairer system that afforded the opportunity of trial to every defendant.[134]

No examination of these possibilities appears to have been conducted in this country. The overriding assumption is that it is necessary to increase the proportion of guilty pleas and of early guilty pleas, and any reference to the greater involvement of judges in assessing case papers and in ascertaining that innocent defendants were not being pressured into pleading guilty would probably be dismissed as too costly. But even if this is true—and until it has been thoroughly investigated, it would be unwise to make the assumption—then the question is plainly one of expense rather than respect for rights. In this chapter we have noted the strong structural incentives to plead guilty and to enter that plea at the earliest opportunity, and we have argued that

---

[131] Auld Review, above n 64, Ch. 10, para 112.

[132] S.J. Schulhofer, 'Is Plea Bargaining Inevitable?' (1984) 97 *Harv LR* 1037.

[133] S.J. Schulhofer and I. Nagel, 'Plea Negotiations under the Federal Sentencing Guidelines: Guideline Circumvention and its Dynamics in the Post-*Mistretta* Period' (1997) 91 *Northwestern ULR* 1284.

[134] Among his many writings, see particularly A. Alschuler, 'Implementing the Criminal Defendant's Right to Trial' (1983) 50 *U. Chi. LR* 931.

these incentives undermine safeguards for the innocent. Stephen Schulfhofer has advanced the same view in powerful terms:

Contractual exchange, under appropriate conditions, can leave both parties better off. But the converse is also true. When the conditions necessary for welfare-enhancing transactions are not met, contractual exchange can leave both parties worse off. In criminal justice, pervasive structural impediments to efficient, welfare-enhancing transactions have produced just this situation. With trials in open court and deserved sentences imposed by a neutral factfinder, we protect the due process right to an adversarial trial, minimize the risk of unjust conviction of the innocent, and at the same time further the public interest in effective law enforcement and adequate punishment of the guilty. But plea negotiation simultaneously undercuts all of these interests. The affected parties are represented by agents who have inadequate incentives for proper performance; prospects for effective monitoring are limited or non-existent; and the dynamics of negotiation can create irresistible pressure for defendants falsely to condemn themselves. As a result, plea agreements defeat the public interest in effective law enforcement at the same time that they deny defendants the benefits of a vigorous defence and inflict undeserved punishment on innocents who could win acquittal at trial.[135]

These words were written in an American context, and the somewhat optimistic description of trials seems rather overdone. Indeed, this point is taken up by Robert Scott and William Stuntz, who ask whether it is really desirable to push more innocent people to trial, on the basis that some of them will be convicted and will then receive harsher sentences than they would have done if they had pleaded guilty:

'This result stands every known theory of distributional justice on its head. We would think it common ground that losses, equally unjust losses, are better spread than concentrated, all else being equal. Schulhofer, like most critics of plea bargaining, seems to prefer a few innocent defendants serving long prison terms to a larger number serving a few years apiece.'[136]

Their view is certainly contestable: if all known theories of distributional justice point in the direction of more convictions for the innocent, then that is a good reason for not subscribing to them. From the rights perspective, the right of innocent persons not to be convicted ought to be recognized as a strong right with a high value, not something to be traded off simply for supposed efficiency gains. Scott and Stuntz would insist that, in a world where there are going to be convictions of innocent people, we must face the choice to which they refer, and not avoid it. Their approach, in the leading article on which Schulhofer was commenting, is to eschew both extremes—to argue both against the existing system of plea negotiation, and against the abolition of all plea negotiations—and to press the case for reconfiguring the bargaining process in order to make it fairer. They start from the position that modern criminal justice systems are so demanding of resources that, in most countries,

---

[135] S.J. Schulhofer, 'Plea-Bargaining as Disaster' (1992) 101 *Yale LJ* 1979, at 2008–9.
[136] R.E. Scott and W.J. Stuntz, 'A Reply: Imperfect Bargains, Imperfect Trials and Innocent Defendants' (1992) 101 *Yale LJ* 2011 at 2013.

there is an 'inability to test innocence claims at acceptable cost'.[137] Their proposals for reform, adapted to England and Wales, would include greater information for the defendant on the choice to be made, and clearer sentencing guidance to enhance predictability. Even as an interim position, however, this ought not to be followed in this country unless the size of the discount were significantly reduced. At present, the pressure is simply too great, the effect on innocent defendants (especially those from certain racial minorities) is unacceptable, and the system as a whole fails to place a sufficiently high value on preventing wrongful convictions.[138] The Auld Review and the present Government have failed to give priority to avoiding undue pressure on the innocent in their search for ways of achieving the efficiencies they desire.

[137] R.E. Scott and W.J. Stuntz, 'Plea Bargaining as Contract' (1992) 101 *Yale LJ* 1909, at 1951.
[138] Cf. the argument of Dworkin, above n 109 and accompanying text.

11

THE TRIAL

The trial is the focal point of criminal procedure. Case preparation in the earlier stages of the process will be carried out in the light of the possibility that the case may go to court. The rules governing trials therefore shape decisions made by police and prosecutors. While it is true that the majority of defendants plead guilty, and that the system encourages trial avoidance in this manner, the trial remains of importance because defendants' decisions on whether or not to plead guilty are often informed by what they believe to be the probability of conviction. Furthermore, in those cases where defendants do not plead guilty, a decision has to be made as to whether or not the defendant is actually guilty. The mechanism for making this crucial decision deserves detailed consideration.

Many aspects of the trial can only be understood through detailed consideration of the rules of evidence and fact-finding processes. Such a study is beyond the scope of the present work. We will merely present an overview of courtroom processes and consider some of the rules of evidence which are most closely connected to trial fairness.

11.1 MODES OF TRIAL

(a) MAGISTRATES' COURT AND CROWN COURT

There are two different levels of court with substantial differences in the trials that take place in them. The least serious cases are tried in the magistrates' courts and the more serious ones in the Crown Court; in practice, the vast majority of cases—at least 95 per cent—are dealt with in the magistrates' court. The principal distinction between the two courts is that cases in the Crown Court are tried by a professional judge sitting with a jury, and cases in the magistrates' court are tried by lay magistrates, or by a judge sitting alone. Lay magistrates are unpaid and hear cases on a part-time basis, usually sitting in court for half a day every week;[1] they typically sit in

---

[1] The standard requirement is a half day sitting each fortnight, but many magistrates sit more often than this, making the national average closer to a half day each week. There is considerable variation, however. See R. Morgan and N. Russell, *The Judiciary in the Magistrates' Courts* (2000), 18–19.

benches of three and are advised on legal points by a clerk. There is considerable debate about the relative merits of the two types of trial, and it is important to understand something about these issues before considering the way in which cases are allocated between the two types of court.

The first point to make is that there is nothing unusual about having two levels of court. Most jurisdictions have more elaborate procedures for trying the more serious cases.[2] Given limited resources, this is entirely appropriate. Accurate adjudication is more important in serious than non-serious cases, because the cost of error (of either mistaken conviction or mistaken acquittal) is greater. This does not, of course, mean that trials in the lower tier of court should be cursory, or that defendants tried there should face an undue risk of mistaken conviction. One of the concerns about the magistrates' court is that defendants do in fact face an unacceptable risk of false conviction. It is often remarked that the conviction rate is higher in the magistrates' court than in the Crown Court. According to CPS statistics, 70 per cent of defendants in contested trials in the magistrates' courts are convicted, compared with 56 per cent in the Crown Court.[3] This is a significant difference, but it is not obvious how to interpret it. In the inevitable absence of knowledge of the proportion of innocent and guilty defendants in each court, it is impossible to say whether one court is more accurate, or even lenient, than the other. It should also be noted that the cases dealt with in each court have different characteristics. Those tried in the Crown Court are more complex, and many summary offences have no *mens rea* element; it may therefore be that cases heard in the magistrates' courts are simply easier to prove.[4]

Moving beyond acquittal rates, there is a general perception among defendants and lawyers that trials in the Crown Court are fairer than magistrates' trials.[5] There are several reasons why Crown Court trial may be fairer. Juries typically come fresh to a case; they are not 'case hardened' in the way magistrates may be. Trial by judge and jury is also an effective way of keeping certain information—such as the fact that the defendant has previous convictions—away from the fact-finder.[6] Juries also tend to be more representative of the general population than magistrates, and in some circumstances this may make them superior fact-finders.[7] In referring to these as good reasons for thinking that jury trial is fairer, it is suggested that these reasons are

---

[2] Details of various jurisdictions can be gleaned from N. Osner, A. Quinn and G. Crown, *Criminal Justice Systems in Other Jurisdictions* (1993).

[3] *CPS Annual Report 2002–2003*, 29, 32. For the difficulty in obtaining accurate figures on this issue, see the discussion in Ch. 7.

[4] See P. Darbyshire, 'For the New Lord Chancellor—Some Causes for Concern About Magistrates' [1997] Crim LR 861, 869–72.

[5] See C. Hedderman and D. Moxon, *Magistrates' Court or Crown Court? Mode of Trial Decisions and Sentencing* (1992), 20, where 62% of defendants and 70% of solicitors are said to support the statement 'magistrates are on the side of the police'. See also Darbyshire, above n 4, 869.

[6] On the problems of achieving this in the magistrates' court, see M. Wasik, 'Magistrates; Knowledge of Previous Convictions' [1996] Crim LR 851; Darbyshire, 'Previous Misconduct and the Magistrates' Courts—Some Tales from the Real World' [1997] Crim LR 105.

[7] See M. Redmayne, 'Theorizing Jury Reform' in A. Duff *et al*, *The Trial on Trial: Volume 2. Judgment and Calling to Account* (forthcoming).

connected to the reason for having trials in the first place, which is, primarily, to make accurate decisions. There are of course other reasons why jury trial is thought to be fair, but there is likely to be more debate about the merits of such reasons. For example, juries are able to exercise 'jury equity' by reaching a verdict in defiance of the law. A case often used to illustrate this is the acquittal of Clive Ponting, who was charged for leaking information in breach of the Official Secrets Act for reasons which many would have regarded as reflecting the public interest. Although he had no defence in law, he was acquitted by the jury.[8] But jury equity is controversial, because it can shade into anarchy and defiance of the will of Parliament.[9] Jury trial is often praised for helping to ensure that the defendant is tried by his peers, but beyond the point that a representative jury may have advantages as a fact-finder (basically, because it will possess a wide range of knowledge[10]), it is unclear just what the merits of 'trial by peers' are thought to be.

It should be noted that jury trial has merits beyond those associated with the interests of defendants. The jury is, in various ways, a democratic institution. Jury trial gives citizens some input into the application of the criminal law.[11] The institution of the jury helps to ensure that the criminal law is expressed in terms comprehensible to ordinary people, and it also serves an educational and social function which, a recent survey suggests, should not be underestimated.[12] Bringing lay people into the court-room means that the pursuit of criminal justice is not a closed shop, dominated by lawyers and other professionals. It makes trials genuinely public and helps to prevent the State abusing its power. However, these merits are not the exclusive preserve of the jury; the use of lay magistrates brings similar benefits, though perhaps to a lesser extent.

As well as these general points about the respective institutional merits of magis-trates' and jury trial, there is research on magistrates' trials which does lend some support to the criticism that this is a cursory form of justice. Some time ago McBarnet commented on the 'ideology of triviality'[13] which she found prevailing in the magis-trates' courts: the presumption that the cases dealt with there were not important and that full due process protections were not appropriate. McConville *et al* were also critical of the quality of justice in magistrates' courts, commenting that defendants in the lower courts, rather than benefiting from a presumption of innocence, typically face an uphill struggle in persuading the court that the prosecution case is not made out.[14] In Morgan and Russell's study, only 30 per cent of regular court users

---

[8] See G. Drewry, 'The *Ponting* Case—Leaking in the Public Interest' [1985] *Public Law* 203.

[9] R. Schopp, 'Verdicts of Conscience: Nullification and Necessity as Jury Responses to Crimes of Con-science' (1996) 69 *S Cal L Rev* 2039.

[10] See Redmayne, above n 7.   [11] See *ibid.*

[12] See R. Matthews, L. Hancock and D. Briggs, *Jurors' Perceptions, Understanding, Confidence and Satisfac-tion in the Jury System: A Study in Six Courts* (2004), 64–6.

[13] D. McBarnet, *Conviction: Law, the State and the Construction of Justice* (1983), 144.

[14] M. McConville *et al*, *Standing Accused: The Organization and Practices of Criminal Defence Lawyers in Britain* (1994), Ch 9.

professed to having 'a great deal' or 'a lot' of confidence in lay magistrates, as compared to nearly 90 per cent with this level of confidence in professional magistrates.[15]
At the same time, only eight per cent said they had 'no' or 'very little' confidence in
the lay magistracy.

The differences between the two types of trial make the allocation of cases between
them an important issue. From the point of view of the Government, the question of
case allocation is particularly critical because it has significant resource implications.
A typical trial in the magistrates' courts costs around ten times less than a Crown
Court trial.[16] Measures which will keep more cases at the lower level therefore have the
potential to make considerable savings. The primary tool for case allocation is the
classification of offences into three types: summary, either way, and offences triable
only on indictment. The first and last categories are straightforward. Summary
offences, the least serious criminal offences, can only be tried in the magistrates' court.
Offences triable only on indictment, a category comprising the most serious offences,
can only be tried in the Crown Court. Things are more complicated with either
way (also referred to as 'indictable') offences. This large category comprises some
common offences such as theft and assault occasioning actual bodily harm. Here, a
decision must be taken as to where the case will be tried. The decision is for the
magistrates, and is taken at a mode of trial hearing. At the hearing, the magistrates
decide whether or not to try the case themselves; the decision will be based primarily
on how serious and complex the case is, but a Practice Direction details various other
considerations which are relevant to the mode of trial decision.[17] Magistrates have
limited sentencing powers, so the more serious either way offences are best dealt with
in the Crown Court, where they can be sentenced appropriately. As noted above, even
disregarding sentencing powers, the more elaborate fact-finding procedures of Crown
Court trial should be used in the most serious cases. If the magistrates decide to send
the case to the Crown Court, the case will be dealt with there. If, however, the decision
is to retain the case in the summary jurisdiction, that is not an end to the matter. The
defendant may override this decision by choosing to be tried in the Crown Court.
A complicating factor is that if the magistrates try the case themselves and find the
defendant guilty, they may commit the case to the Crown Court for sentencing if, on
reflection, they conclude that their sentencing powers are not sufficient; this power,
however, will be abolished when the relevant parts of the Criminal Justice Act 2003 are
implemented. This is discussed further below.

Over the years, a number of steps have been taken to ensure that as many cases as
possible are tried summarily. Some either way offences have been reclassified as summary, for example, common assault, driving whilst disqualified and criminal damage
up to a value of £5,000. The Practice Direction on mode of trial decision making is
now drafted so as to create a presumption in favour of summary trial, unless the court

[15] Above n 1, 60.
[16] Home Office, *Digest 4: Information on the Criminal Justice System in England and Wales* (1999), 69.
[17] [2002] 3 All ER 904, 51.

considers that the case contains an aggravating feature (various such features are listed in the guidelines), and that its sentencing powers are insufficient.[18] Moreover, in 1997 the 'plea before venue' arrangement was introduced.[19] This allows defendants to indicate whether or not they intend to plead guilty before the magistrates make the mode of trial decision. The idea here is that, if the defendant indicates that he intends to plead guilty, the magistrates will be more prepared to deal with the case themselves. Only if they consider that their sentencing powers are inadequate, after factoring in the sentence discount for a guilty plea at this early stage, will they commit the case for sentence in the Crown Court. The result has been a decline of some 15,000 cases a year committed to the Crown Court for trial, off-set in part by a rise of some 10,000 cases a year committed to the Crown Court for sentence.[20]

In addition to these policies, there has been one proposal about mode of trial decision making that has proved very controversial. In 1993 the Royal Commission on Criminal Justice suggested that defendants should no longer have the right to elect Crown Court trial in either way cases; this reform would mean that, in the absence of agreement between defence and prosecution, the magistrates' decision would be determinative.[21] In support of this proposal, it was argued that many defendants who elect Crown Court trial go on to plead guilty. They thus do not benefit from the arguably fairer trial procedures in the Crown Court, but are likely to be sentenced more harshly than they would have been in the magistrates' court. In this way, abolition of the right to elect could be said to be in the interests of defendants. This argument, however, has been disputed: there are no precise figures on the proportion of those electing Crown Court trial who go on to plead guilty. Even if many do, this may be the result of a charge bargain[22] offered by the prosecution which would not have been offered had the case remained in the magistrates' jurisdiction. Another argument used to support the reform was that it simply is not appropriate for defendants to choose trial venue; this allocative decision should be based on case characteristics which are suitably assessed by the magistrates.

The Royal Commission's proposal was immediately controversial, and the then Conservative Government did not attempt to introduce this particular reform; plea before venue was introduced instead as a means of reducing the number of indictable offences committed for Crown Court trial. It was eventually a Labour administration which attempted to remove the right to elect jury trial in either way cases. The proposal attracted considerable opposition.[23] Some of this was based on broad propositions about a right to jury trial. But there were also concerns about whether the mode of trial decision could be taken fairly by magistrates. The proposed legislation would have allowed defendants to argue their preference for jury trial before the magistrates. In making their decision, magistrates were to take into account the

---

[18] *Ibid.*   [19] See Ch. 10.   [20] *Criminal Statistics, England and Wales 2002*, Figure 3.2.
[21] Royal Commission on Criminal Justice, *Report* (1993), 87.   [22] See Ch. 10.
[23] A good account of the mode of trial saga is Windlesham, *Responses to Crime Volume 4: Dispensing Justice* (2001), Ch 7.

possible effect of a conviction on a defendant's livelihood and reputation. This might have involved considering whether the defendant had previous convictions, and therefore whether he had a reputation to protect which might have made a stronger case for jury trial. While it is something of a caricature, the thinking here seems to be that jury trial is especially valuable for middle class defendants charged for the first time with an offence such as theft. Unsurprisingly, such arguments are potentially socially divisive. In the event, such was the controversy that the original Mode of Trial Bill failed to win Parliamentary support. It was withdrawn, to be replaced by a Criminal Justice (Mode of Trial) (No. 2) Bill, which did not allow magistrates to take the defendant's reputation into account. This drew criticism from some of the supporters of the original bill[24] and, for various reasons, the second bill did not succeed either.[25]

It seems most unlikely that a government will attempt to remove the right to elect again in the foreseeable future. Misleading though they may be, headlines about the abolition of the right to jury trial do too much political damage. Instead, in the Criminal Justice Act 2003 the Government has now found a new way to reduce the number of cases proceeding to the Crown Court. The Act doubles magistrates' custodial sentencing powers from a maximum of six months for any one offence to a maximum of 12 months;[26] in future the limit may be raised to 18 months.[27] At the same time, magistrates' power to commit defendants to the Crown Court for sentencing in cases where they have accepted jurisdiction is to be removed.[28] Connected to this, and as we have seen in Chapter 10, defendants in cases where the magistrates have accepted jurisdiction will be able to ask the magistrates for an indication of whether a custodial sentence will be passed if they plead guilty at that stage.[29] A defendant who does this, and receives an indication that the sentence will be non-custodial, will have considerable incentive to plead guilty at that stage, for then the magistrates will be bound by their indication. Defendants are still free to elect Crown Court trial if they do not wish to plead guilty, but the knowledge that they are guaranteed a non-custodial sentence (if that is what has been indicated), may persuade more defendants to forego their right to Crown Court trial. In this way, and even more so than under the plea before venue procedure, the mode of trial issue is bound up with forms of plea-bargaining. The Criminal Justice Act also provides that magistrates should be informed of a defendant's previous convictions when determining mode of trial.[30]

It is perhaps surprising that the increase in magistrates' sentencing powers, integral to the strategy of keeping more cases in the lower courts, has received little criticism.[31]

---

[24] Most notably Michael Zander, who had been a member of the Royal Commission on Criminal Justice: see M. Zander, 'Why Jack Straw's Jury Reform Has Lost the Plot' (2000) 150 *NLJ* 723.

[25] See Windlesham, above n 23.   [26] CJA 2003, s154.   [27] *Justice For All* (2002), 72.

[28] CJA 2003, Sch 3 para 22 *et seq.*   [29] CJA 2003, Sch 3, para 6.

[30] CJA 2003, Sch 3, para 5, inserting a new s 19 into the Magistrates' Courts Act 1980.

[31] For a discussion of the new power, which notes that its effect may be limited in practice by the introduction of 'custody plus', see R. Ward and O. Davies, *The Criminal Justice Act 2003* (2004), 180–1.

Magistrates are essentially lay people, and it is questionable whether they should be entrusted with such significant powers over the liberty of defendants. As we have seen, there are doubts about the quality of justice in the magistrates' courts. In the sentencing sphere, these doubts are strengthened by research showing considerable variation in magistrates' sentencing practices.[32] While one should never be complacent about the workings of the courts, doubts about the magistrates' courts are arguably less significant so long as the magistracy's sentencing powers are curtailed. The greater the power of magistrates to remove liberty, the more we need to be assured that the summary courts reach high standards of due process. Connected to this argument is a further problem with the increase in magistrates' sentencing powers. The longer sentences available to magistrates should in theory be reserved for the most serious cases they deal with, those which would previously have been committed to the Crown Court for sentencing. But in practice there is a risk that these greater powers will 'drag up' other sentences by magistrates, affecting many defendants in the lower courts and placing further pressure on the prison system.[33]

Previous editions of this book have examined the debate about mode of trial and the right to elect Crown Court trial in some detail.[34] Now that the issue has moved out of the political spotlight, there is less need to examine the issues in depth. Briefly, however, there remains a reasonable argument for removing the right to elect jury trial in either way cases. Relatively few jurisdictions allow defendants a comparable choice,[35] and there is nothing like a right to choose trial venue in the European Convention on Human Rights. The argument that the decision is one for the courts to be taken primarily on grounds of case seriousness is a strong one. While there is something to the argument that certain types of case are especially suited to jury trial, regardless of their seriousness (an example is theft, which can involve the broad evaluative issue of dishonesty, defined in the case law in terms of the standards of ordinary and reasonable people[36]), there is a danger that in practice this argument will become the one that certain people (such as those without previous convictions) have a greater claim to jury trial than others, a contention that should be resisted. To say this is not to say that there is a strong case for removing the right to elect. Pressure for reform has been driven by the desire for efficiency, and there are reasons to regard efficiency-based arguments with caution. To the extent that jury trial is valuable—and above we have very briefly sketched some reasons for thinking that it is—any proposal to reduce the number of jury trials should be viewed sceptically. It should be noted, however, that jurors themselves consider that many of the cases they hear are too

---

[32] See Home Office, *Making Punishments Work: Report of a Review of the Sentencing Framework for England and Wales* (2001), App 2, Table 6.

[33] Cf M. Hough. J. Jacobson and A. Millie, *The Decision to Imprison: Sentencing and the Prison Population* (2003), 24–6.

[34] See Ch 8 of the previous edition.

[35] An exception is New Zealand: N. Cameron, S. Potter and W. Young, 'The New Zealand Jury' (1999) 62 *Law & Contemporary Problems* 103.

[36] *Ghosh* [1982] QB 1053.

trivial to justify the disruption to their lives involved in hearing them.[37] That view counts for something and suggests the need to reflect carefully on where and how we draw the line between summary and Crown Court jurisdictions. What is most disappointing about the mode of trial debates, however, is that they have been dominated by rhetoric[38] and have resulted in an increase in magistrates' sentencing powers which, while it may not make newspaper headlines, is arguably far more difficult to justify than the removal of the defendant's right to elect.

(b) TRIAL BY JUDGE AND JURY AND TRIAL BY JUDGE ALONE

Crown Court trial has traditionally been trial by judge and jury. But there has recently been interest in introducing other forms of trial in the Crown Court, and the Criminal Justice Act 2003 now allows for trial without a jury in cases of serious and complex fraud. There is a similar provision for cases where there is evidence of jury tampering.[39] As with the allocation of cases between Crown and magistrates' court, there may be mixed motives for the interest in reform here: efficiency concerns (trial by judge alone will be quicker and cheaper) sit alongside more principled reasons for the reforms.

Where cases of serious and complex fraud are concerned, s 43 of the Criminal Justice Act allows for trial by judge alone where the length or complexity of the trial make it unduly burdensome for a jury. This provision was controversial, and the Act specifically provides that it will not come into force without a further Parliamentary vote.[40] It seems that the Government will review the issues, and seek to persuade Parliament that suitable arrangements for non-jury trial are in place: this might involve, rather than trial by judge alone, a form of trial where the judge sits with advisers with some experience of relevant business practices.[41] Still, this is far removed from trial by jury, which involves a larger group (12) of randomly selected lay people who have full responsibility for findings of fact. The principal argument for reform in this area is that certain trials involve issues so complex that they are not well suited to lay fact-finding. Connected to this is the argument that fraud trials could be made to run more speedily were there no need to explain complex issues to the jury and that long trials place undue demands on jurors. The argument that juries cannot understand fraud cases in fact has very little empirical support.[42] It seems that in

---

[37] See Matthews *et al*, above n 12, 63.

[38] See, e.g., B. Houlder, 'The Importance of Preserving the Jury System and the Right of Election for Trial' [1997] Crim LR 875.

[39] CJA 2003, ss 44–6.   [40] CJA 2003, s 330(5).

[41] See 'Blunkett Saves Flagship Legislation with Climbdown on Trial by Jury' *The Independent*, 21 November 2003.

[42] See, e.g., T. Honess, M. Levi and E. Chapman, 'Juror Competence in Processing Complex Information: Implications from a Simulation of the Maxwell Trial' [1998] Crim LR 763; R. Lempert, 'Civil Juries and Complex Cases: Taking Stock After Twelve Years' in R. Litan (ed), *Verdict: Assessing the Civil Jury System* (1993); N. Vidmar, 'The Performance of the American Civil Jury: An Empirical Perspective' (1998) 40 *Arizona L. Rev.* 849.

practice a jury of 12 will include individuals who are perfectly capable of understanding the issues involved and of explaining them, where need be, to other jurors.
Further, the complexity of a trial is not fixed: measures can be taken to educate jurors
about business practices and to explain things to them simply and clearly, and cases
might be split into separate trials of distinct issues, although, of course, such measures
have efficiency implications.

Jury trial embodies many values; one should be wary of condensing the case for it
to a single point. But in the present context abstract appeals to the fairness of jury trial
are unhelpful; what are needed are more specific arguments. The strongest argument
for retaining jury trial in fraud cases is that such trials often boil down to the question
of dishonesty which (as was noted above) is an issue the jury is well placed to judge.
It is difficult to assess this claim. While the jury can relate its general sense of honesty
to everyday cases, it may in fact face difficulty in doing so where complex business
dealings are concerned, especially if the defendant argues that his actions were
standard practice in the business community. There are also reasons, apart from case
complexity, why jury trial may be problematic in complex cases. One of the strengths
of the jury is its ability to represent a wide range of experience and differing perspectives. But juries in longer trials are known to be less representative of the general
population;[43] this is unsurprising, because not everyone is able to set aside the time
required to hear a lengthy case. And some fraud trials are very long indeed: they
can last for several months. It must surely be questioned whether it is reasonable
to ask citizens to put their lives on hold for such long periods in order to judge a
criminal case.

There is, therefore, a fairly strong case to be made for some alternative to jury trial
in complex cases. But it is wise also to look beyond trial by judge alone in these cases.
Collegiate fact-finding has various advantages over fact-finding by an individual: it
brings wider experience and helps to ensure that arguments are carefully articulated.[44]
If some sort of combination of judge and expert assessors can be made to work, then
there is much to be said for that as a way forward. It also remains to be seen just how
ready judges will be to allow non-jury trial in complex fraud trials. It is to be hoped
that the decision to depart from the standard model will not be automatic, and will
look to the impact of a long trial on jurors as its justification, rather than poorly
supported arguments about the inability of lay people to understand complex issues.

The Criminal Justice Act 2003 originally contained a provision on 'jury waiver'.
This would have allowed defendants in the Crown Court to opt for trial by judge
alone. The choice of juryless trial could only have been refused in exceptional cases.
This provision was removed from the Act at a late stage in the legislative process.[45]
Letting defendants waive jury trial is, at first sight, an appealing idea.[46] But it is in fact

---

[43] Matthews *et al*, above n. 12, 26, 28, 71.

[44] See, generally, J. Abramson, *We, The Jury: The Jury System and the Ideal of Democracy* (1994).

[45] See 'Blunkett Furious as Lords Throw out Reform of Jury Trial' *The Guardian*, 20 November 2003.

[46] See J. Jackson and S. Doran, 'The Case for Jury Waiver' [1997] Crim LR 155.

potentially very radical. It would have allowed defendants effectively to bring the institution of trial by jury to an end: all it would take would be for every defendant to decline jury trial. Of course, it is extremely unlikely that this would happen: jury trial is often thought to be in the interests of defendants, and it is probable that sufficient numbers of defendants share this view that trial by judge alone would have remained exceptional. All the same, the theoretical possibility of *de facto* jury abolition should prompt us to look carefully at the jury waiver proposal.

The superficially appealing logic behind jury waiver is that, to the extent that jury trial is justified as being in the interests of defendants, there can be no objection to allowing defendants to forego it in favour of some other appropriate trial arrangement. There is no denying that defendants have legitimate interests in the means by which they are tried: interests in impartial and accurate fact-finding arrangements which adequately weight the presumption of innocence. But these things are also in the interests of the courts and of society as a whole. It is much more difficult to find legitimate interests defendants might have in a particular form of trial which are not shared in this manner (a similar argument was made above in respect of the allocation of cases between Crown and magistrates' court). If the argument is that trial by judge alone is somehow fairer than jury trial (perhaps because judges give reasoned decisions), then we seem to be questioning the institution of jury trial quite generally.

The best case that can be made for jury waiver seems to be this: in certain cases defendants might have respectable reasons for doubting the fairness of jury trial. If, for example, the case is one likely to arouse strong emotions,[47] or if the defence case will raise complex issues which the jury may have difficulty understanding[48] (though, as noted above, we should be wary of accepting that certain issues are too complex for jury trial), it may be appropriate to allow trial by judge alone. In such cases, non-jury trial would be in the general interests of society, and the defendant can be seen as representing society's and the courts' interests in a fair trial. The advantage of jury waiver is that defendants have a particularly keen interest in having their case heard by an unbiased tribunal, and are well placed to make the argument for it. Seen in this manner, jury waiver does not create such a deep tension with a general commitment to jury trial: the defendant will be permitted to elect trial by judge alone in those cases where the case for jury trial is weaker than normal. What this does imply, though, is that waiver should not be automatic: a defendant should be required to make a case for jury waiver. In some jurisdictions which allow waiver of jury trial, the prosecution is allowed to make representations on the issue;[49] given that the interests in mode of trial are not just the defendant's, that is appropriate. The provisions in the Criminal Justice Bill did not reflect these concerns, and to that extent, their rejection by Parliament can be supported. Another issue which bears thought in this context is whether

---

[47] See N. Vidmar, 'Generic Prejudice and the Presumption of Guilt in Sex Abuse Trials' (1997) 21 *Law & Human Behavior* 5.

[48] An example might be *R v Adams* [1996] 2 Cr App R 467.   [49] See Jackson and Doran, above n 46.

trial by a single judge is the best alternative to jury trial. Research on trial by judge alone in Northern Ireland suggests that it works well,[50] but group decision making does have advantages over decision making by an individual. An alternative of trial by a panel of two or three judges is well worth considering. This mode of trial would also allay any suspicions that jury waiver was being introduced simply as a means of cutting costs.

(c) RACE AND MODE OF TRIAL

So far we have not considered the implications of the defendant's race in the debates about mode of trial. Race is a complicating factor for many of the issues discussed so far. Defendants from minority ethnic groups may feel that a tribunal with members from their, or another, racial minority will afford them a fairer trial. To what extent should mode of trial decisions take this into account?

Something should first of all be said about how representative, in terms of race, the various forms of tribunal are. The magistracy as a whole seems to be racially representative of the country's population. That is, the percentage of black and Asian magistrates (to concentrate on the two largest ethnic minorities) is more or less the same as that of the national population. However, this picture breaks down when one looks at particular areas. As a rule, in urban areas where there is a large ethnic minority population, the local benches are unrepresentative.[51] With three lay magistrates sitting on a bench, however, there is of course more chance of a bench including a minority ethnic magistrate. A study by Hood, Shute and Seemungal found that 35 per cent of benches in the three urban areas they studied had at least one minority ethnic magistrate.[52] Where professional magistrates (District Judges) are concerned, five per cent were found to be from a minority ethnic group.[53] In the Crown Court, many fewer judges are from minorities: one per cent in the Hood *et al* study.[54] Just as with magistrates, the fact that the jury is a multi-member body makes it far more likely to contain minority ethnic members. The *Crown Court Study*, conducted in 1992, found that, overall, racial representation reflected that of the general population.[55] A more recent study in the London area also found that the make-up of juries was racially representative.[56] However, because juries are in principle selected randomly, there is no guarantee that a black or Asian defendant will be tried by a jury including a juror from a minority ethnic group. The *Crown Court Study* found that 65 per cent of juries were all white, so the odds are in fact quite low,[57] and similar to those for a bench of magistrates.

This situation has led to a proposal, made by both the Royal Commission on

---

[50] J. Jackson and S. Doran, *Judge Without Jury: Diplock Trials in the Adversary System* (1995).

[51] Morgan and Russell, above n 1, 14–15.

[52] R. Hood, S. Shute and F. Seemungal, *Ethnic Minorities in the Criminal Courts: Perceptions of Fairness and Equality of Treatment* (2003), 23.

[53] *Ibid.*   [54] *Ibid.*   [55] M. Zander and P. Henderson, *Crown Court Study* (1993), 241.

[56] Matthews *et al*, above n 12, 19–20.   [57] Above n 55, 242.

Criminal Justice and by the Auld review, that defendants in cases involving a minority ethnic dimension should be able to request ethnic minority representation on the jury.[58] This proposal has never found favour with policy-makers. In some cases, judges have tried to manipulate jury selection to increase the chances of minority representation, but the Court of Appeal has held that this should not occur.[59] If the proposal were to be implemented, it would face practical difficulties: would the defendant have a right to jurors from the same racial group, or just any minority ethnic group? And how would it be decided which cases involve a minority ethnic dimension? This latter point brings us to the empirical research, which lends some support to the argument that although white jurors may be somewhat biased against black defendants, that bias is likely to be least problematic in cases where there is a clear racial issue, for then the jurors will be prompted to monitor their prejudices.[60]

These practical issues apart, the case for departure from random selection is not very convincing. Here, some of the rhetoric surrounding the jury is unhelpful: if it is argued that a defendant should be tried by his peers,[61] and thus by a jury including members of his ethnic group, one has to ask just what is meant by peers, and just why it is thought that only our peers are well placed to judge us. The most convincing argument here is that, just as juries make good fact-finders because they include a wide range of expertise, so jurors including ethnic minorities may be especially good fact-finders in cases involving ethnic minority defendants because of their specialist knowledge. However, there are other ways of communicating such knowledge to the jury than the complex and haphazard one of manipulating jury selection. An argument in favour of the reform might also claim that defendants will have more confidence in the verdicts of a jury on which their ethnic group is represented. The evidence of lack of confidence in the current system is not very strong: Hood *et al* found that some ethnic minority defendants complained of jury bias (20 per cent of the black defendants tried by jury, though 14 per cent of white defendants were also 'unhappy with jury'), but only four per cent of Crown Court defendants identified an increase in the number of minority ethnic jurors as something to be done to increase confidence (the call for more minority ethnic judges was far more common).[62] The manipulation of jury selection might undermine the confidence of society as a whole in the system.[63] It might also change the dynamics of jury deliberation: jurors who know that they have been chosen specifically because a case involves

---

[58] Royal Commission on Criminal Justice, above n 21, 133; Auld LJ, *Review of the Criminal Courts of England and Wales: Report* (2001), 156–9. See also B. Bowling and C. Phillips, *Racism, Crime and Justice* (2002), 187–8.

[59] *R v Ford* [1989] 3 All ER 445; *R v Smith* [2003] 1 WLR 2229.

[60] S. Sommers and P. Ellsworth, 'How Much Do We Really Know About Race and Juries? A Review of Social Science Theory and Research' (2003) 78 *Chicago-Kent L. Rev* 997.

[61] H. Fukurai and R. Krooth, *Race in the Jury Box: Affirmative Action in Jury Selection* (2003), 138–48.

[62] Above n 52, 34, 39, 116. Cf Bowling and Phillips, above n 58.

[63] N. J. King, 'The Effects of Race-Conscious Jury Selection on Public Confidence in the Fairness of Jury Proceedings: An Empirical Puzzle' [1994] *Am Crim LR* 1177; L. Ellis and S. Diamond, 'Race, Diversity, and Jury Composition: Battering and Bolstering Legitimacy' (2003) 78 *Chicago-Kent L Rev* 1033.

a racial dimension might come to see their role differently—as representing a particular point of view, rather than the views of society as a whole.[64] In suggesting that the
arguments for minority ethnic representation are unpersuasive (at least on the evidence currently available), we are not advocating complacency about the present
system. Diverse juries are generally a good thing, for the reasons related to fact-finding
discussed above, and also because, perhaps linked to the point just made, they make
jurors feel more confident in their role.[65] There is every reason to ensure that juries are
as representative as possible, such as by looking beyond the electoral roll on which the
jury summons system is currently based. But the argument that such concerns should
go beyond the jury system as a whole, to attach to individual juries, is a much more
difficult one to sustain.[66]

The argument about general representativeness applies to judges and juries too.
The magistrates' and Crown Court benches should as far as possible reflect the social
characteristics of society as a whole, if only because everyone should have an equal
opportunity of sitting on the bench. However, when we come to look at the choice
between magistrates' and Crown Court, and between trial by jury and trial by judge
alone, race raises more complex issues. In some cases, minority ethnic defendants may
have concerns about possible jury bias. There are reported cases where jurors are said
to have made racially discriminatory remarks, and, because of the basic rule that jury
deliberations should remain secret, the courts have found it difficult to deal with this
situation.[67] If a defendant fears that the jury which tries him may be biased, then this
is just the sort of situation where there is a strong case for jury waiver: the defendant
may well prefer trial by a judge, where the verdict will be supported by reasons.

When it comes to the choice between magistrates' court and Crown Court, concerns about racial discrimination provide some support for the right to elect Crown
Court trial. There is evidence that black defendants are more likely to elect Crown
Court trial than are whites.[68] This should make us cautious about removing the right
to elect, because it may indirectly discriminate against black defendants. At its strongest, the argument is this: there is considerable evidence that black suspects are charged
by the police at lower standards of evidence than are white suspects.[69] As they enter
the system, then, the cases against blacks tend to be weaker, and to be charged at a
higher level than is merited (see Chapters 7 and 10). Black defendants may, therefore,
choose Crown Court trial for the better chance of acquittal offered there, and also
because the CPS are more likely to reduce charges in order to secure a guilty plea once
the case has gone to Crown Court. Removing the right to elect would thus deny black
defendants a means of protecting themselves against discriminatory police charging
practices. There is empirical research to support this view of the merits of the right to

[64] See Abramson, above n 44, Ch 3.   [65] Matthews *et al*, above n 12, 42–8.
[66] Abramson, above n. 44, Ch 3.
[67] *R v Quereshi* [2002] 1 WLR 518; *R v Connor, R v Mirza* [2004] UKHL 2.
[68] See M. Fitzgerald, *Ethnic Minorities and the Criminal Justice System* (1993), 21, 45.
[69] See C. Phillips and D. Brown, *Entry into the Criminal Justice System: A Survey of Police Arrests and Their Outcomes* (1998), 183–6.

elect,[70] but there is also evidence which cautions against over-simplifying the situation. As we saw above, Hood *et al* found that some black defendants were worried about jury bias; they also found that, overall, slightly more black defendants complained about unfair treatment in the Crown Court than in the magistrates' court.[71]

The possibility of indirect discrimination is a reason against removing the right to elect jury trial, at least until more is known about why ethnic minority defendants might favour this mode of trial. It also points to the importance of ensuring that proceedings in the magistrates' courts are as fair as possible. In the Hood *et al* study, around a third of minority ethnic defendants, when asked what could be done to improve things, pointed to the need for more minority ethnic District Judges and magistrates; magistrates themselves took the same view.[72] The authors suggest organizing magistrates' rotas so that, 'in those areas where a substantial proportion of defendants are from minority ethnic backgrounds, at least one magistrate from such a background will be sitting on the Bench'.[73] Random selection has never been the principle in the magistrates' court, therefore this proposal deserves serious thought.

(d) PROFESSIONAL AND LAY MAGISTRATES

A final issue about the way in which cases are allocated between different decision makers concerns the balance between lay and professional magistrates. Professional magistrates, previously known as stipendiaries, are now entitled 'District Judges'. There are around 100 full time District Judges in England and Wales, with around half of these sitting in London. Indeed, in London the majority of court appearances may be heard by District Judges.[74] There are significant differences between professional and lay magistrates: District Judges command more confidence from court users, they work more quickly, are less likely to grant adjournments, and sentence more harshly.[75] They are also less representative of the general population in terms of race and gender. In economic terms, there is probably not an awful lot to choose between lay and professional magistrates. Whereas District Judges are salaried, the fact that they work more quickly and rarely require advice from a clerk probably means that each mode of trial is equally efficient. At least, that is the case in terms of court work; to the extent that District Judges use custody more frequently than lay magistrates, they perhaps will impose greater costs on the criminal justice system.[76]

Despite the differences between the two types of magistrate, there is little formal policy on how cases should be allocated between them. In practice, District Judges tend to deal with the more complex and serious cases, and there is some potential here for resentment from their lay colleagues, who are apt to feel that they are missing out on the most interesting cases.[77] But there is no hard and fast rule and, especially in

[70] See L. Bridges, 'Taking Liberties' *Legal Action* 6 July 2000, 6.
[71] Above n 52, 31–5. The position was reversed for Asian defendants.   [72] *Ibid.*, 117, 131.
[73] *Ibid.*, 135.   [74] Morgan and Russell, above n 1, 26.   [75] *Ibid.*, 48–54.
[76] *Ibid.*, viii.   [77] *Ibid.*, 26–9.

London, District Judges deal with considerable numbers of routine cases. Morgan and Russell comment:

'What is unique about England and Wales is the way in which, within any one courthouse, the choice between adjudicators may be random. . . . We know of no jurisdictions other than England and Wales where moderately serious cases are allocated randomly within the same court tier between lay and professional judges.'[78]

An official policy of reserving the most serious cases for District Judges would probably face considerable opposition from lay magistrates. But the current *laissez-faire* policy is questionable in terms of principle. It also raises a more difficult question: should moderately serious cases (in which defendants will face up to a year's imprisonment) be dealt with by single decision makers? We have already noted that there are advantages to group decision making in fact-finding. Morgan and Russell's impression was that, while many other jurisdictions use the single judge model, it tends to be confined to less serious cases than in England and Wales.[79] Now that magistrates' custodial sentencing powers are to be increased to 12 months, the comparison is even more pertinent. There is evidence that the public have more confidence in group decision making than in decision making by a single individual.[80] An alternative model would be for the more serious cases in the magistrates' courts to be heard by a panel of two lay magistrates sitting with a stipendiary.[81] Such a system would involve the identification of a threshold of seriousness, or perhaps a sentencing limit, for the allocation of cases between the two types of magistrates' trial. A more radical proposal is for all trials in the magistrates' courts to be heard by such panels.[82] Whatever is thought of the merits of these various proposals,[83] the principal point is that we should be prepared to think imaginatively about modes of trial. The choice is not just between decision making by a single professional adjudicator and decision making by a lay panel; the option of adopting small mixed panels should not be dismissed.

---

[78] *Ibid.*, 100. See also P. Seago, C. Walker and D. Wall, *The Role and Appointment of Stipendiary Magistrates* (1995), 143–5.

[79] *Ibid.*, 103.

[80] *Ibid.*, 78–9; A. Sanders, *Community Justice: Modernising the Magistracy in England and Wales* (2001), 24–5.

[81] R. Morgan, 'Magistrates: The Future According to Auld' (2002) 29 *JLS* 308.

[82] See Sanders, above n 80; A. Sanders, 'Core Values, the Magistracy and the Auld Report' (2002) 29 *JLS* 324.

[83] Germany uses mixed panels, and the view there appears to be that the professional judges dominate proceedings. See S. Machura, 'Interaction Between Lay Assessors and Professional Judges in German Mixed Courts' (2002) 72 *International Rev Penal Law* 451; C. Renning, 'Influence of Lay Assessors and Giving Reasons for the Judgement in German Mixed Courts' (2002) 72 *International Rev Penal Law* 481. However, in England and Wales, where there is a tradition of independent decision making by magistrates, things might work out differently.

11.2 CROWN COURT TRIAL: JUDGE AND JURY

Crown Court trial involves a division of responsibility between judge and jury. Generally speaking, questions of law are for the judge and questions of fact are for the jury.
But this division is not rigid. The judge will often make factual evaluations when
deciding whether or not evidence is admissible. Judges also play a role in guarding
against false conviction by ensuring that a weak case does not go to the jury. We came
across this in Chapter 7 where, in discussing the role of the CPS, it was noted that
around a third of acquittals are on the basis of an order or direction from the judge to
the jury, rather than because the jury has acquitted of its own accord. Judges also have
some influence in cases that do go to the jury. At the end of the trial the judge sums up
on the facts, and can emphasize aspects of the evidence which he or she deems to be
important. Convictions are occasionally quashed because a judge has gone too far and
given a one-sided summing up.[84] Many cases nowadays will involve the judge giving
some direction to the jury on fact-finding: perhaps a warning about suspect evidence,
or a direction on how to draw an inference from a particular factual scenario. The
growing volume of standard directions published by the Judicial Studies Board attests
to the importance of the judge's role in guiding the jury.[85] There are some hints that
the European Court of Human Rights regards such directions as an important component of the right to a fair trial: given that the jury does not give reasons for its
decision, carefully stated judicial warnings are the best guarantee that the jury has
taken important factors into account.[86]

The principles underlying the division of roles between judge and jury are well
illustrated by the debates surrounding the test the judge should apply in deciding
whether there is a case to go to the jury. The leading case is *Galbraith*, which clarified
conflicts in the case law. Under *Galbraith*, the judge should direct a verdict of acquittal
if evidence to prove any element of the prosecution case is lacking. That much is
relatively simple; things are more difficult 'where there is some evidence but it is of a
tenuous character'. Here, the court identified two principles:

'(a) Where the judge comes to the conclusion that the prosecution case, taken at its highest, is
such that a jury properly directed could not properly convict upon it, it is his duty, upon a
submission being made, to stop the case. (b) Where however the prosecution evidence is
such that its strength or weakness depends on the view to be taken of a witness's reliability,
or other matters which are generally speaking within the province of the jury and where on
one possible view of the facts there is evidence upon which a jury could properly come to
the conclusion that the defendant is guilty, then the judge should allow the matter to be tried
by the jury.'[87]

A crucial issue is what is meant by the prosecution case 'taken at its highest'. The rest

---

84 *Wood* [1996] 1 Cr App R 207.   85 See http://www.jsboard.co.uk/criminal_law/index.htm
86 See *Condron v United Kingdom* (2001) 31 EHRR 1.   87 [1981] 1 WLR 1039, 1042.

of the quotation implies that the judge should assume that the witness is 'reliable', and apply the test on that basis. Of course, the defendant may suggest that the witness is lying or mistaken, but that is a matter for the jury. The usual criticism of this approach is that it affords insufficient protection to defendants. The judge may have serious misgivings about the reliability of a key witness, but unless the witness's evidence is self-contradictory,[88] the case should still be left to the jury. It is often pointed out that it seems odd that the trial judge should apply this test, while the Court of Appeal when reviewing the safety of a conviction applies a much broader test of whether the conviction is 'unsafe'. While the Court of Appeal shows great deference to the jury when applying this test, the 'unsafe' test does allow it to quash a conviction because of doubts about a witness.[89] The defence of *Galbraith* involves arguing that it is important to reserve some questions for the jury, and to avoid so far as possible the judge encroaching on the jury's domain. This policy, whereby issues of witness credibility are reserved for the jury, in fact underlies considerable parts of the law of evidence.[90]

The thin nature of the distinction involved here can be seen by examining the facts of *Hill*.[91] In this case, the defendant had been observed selling a 'small dark substance' to customers. Tried for supplying cannabis, *Hill* argued that the observations of the police officers were insufficient to make out a case for him to answer. The Court of Appeal agreed, and quashed his conviction. Without suggesting that there is anything wrong with this decision, it is not easy to articulate why the prosecution case, taken at its highest, did not warrant a conviction while, if we change the facts slightly, it would have done. If, for example, Hill's customer had testified that he had purchased from Hill a substance that was cannabis, the case would almost certainly have been strong enough to go to the jury.[92] No matter what doubts the judge had about the witness, he could not, within the confines of the *Galbraith* rule, have stopped the case. To answer that questions of credibility are for the jury is not immediately convincing: why, one might ask, should the nature of the substance which police officers saw Hill selling not be an issue for the jury? If there is a difference between the scenarios, it lies not in credibility, but in the degree of risk to which the defendant is exposed in leaving the case to the jury.

The *Galbraith* rule appears even harder to support when one notes that there are a number of seeming exceptions to it.[93] There are some credibility issues which judges do decide, and where a decision against the prosecution may bring the case to a halt. We have already come across examples: s 76 of PACE can result in the exclusion of a confession where the prosecution cannot convince the judge of its reliability (see Chapter 4), and the *Turnbull*[94] rule can result in a case depending substantially on poor quality eyewitness evidence being withdrawn from the jury (see Chapter 5).

---

[88] *Slippey* [1988] Crim LR 767.
[89] A good example is *R v B* [2003] EWCA Crim 319, discussed in Ch 9.
[90] See, e.g., *R v Turner* [1975] QB 834; *R v H* [1995] 2 AC 596.   [91] (1993) 96 Cr App R 456.
[92] The courts are prepared to recognize lay expertise in drug identification: *R v Chatwood* [1980] 1 WLR 874.
[93] See I. Dennis, *The Law of Evidence* (2nd ed., 2002), 95–6.   [94] [1977] QB 224.

The Court of Appeal has also held that unconvincing confessions from a mentally handicapped defendant should be withdrawn from the jury, even where the case does not raise a s 76 issue.[95] The Criminal Justice Act 2003 will require judges to direct an acquittal where the prosecution case is based on a statement made out of court which is thought to be unconvincing.[96] In practice, too, *Galbraith* is sometimes ignored: cases depending on the testimony of child witnesses are sometimes stopped when a judge has doubts about the witness's evidence.[97] It is possible to reinterpret *Galbraith* so as to reconcile these seeming exceptions with it: the situations just described, it might be argued, relate to doubts about the reliability of testimony, rather than about the sincerity of the witness (in the sense of whether the witness is deliberately lying). Although *Galbraith* itself seemed to raise both types of issue, it might be argued that the issue which really needs to be reserved to the jury is that of whether or not the witness is deliberately lying. There may be a policy reason for this distinction, though not, perhaps, a terribly convincing one in the criminal setting: judges are doubtless reluctant to say that they think a witness may be lying.[98] It is rather more diplomatic to leave this sort of decision to the secrecy of the jury room.

Galbraith involves an important issue: it determines just when a defendant will be put at risk of criminal conviction. It is difficult to find convincing reasons for the current rule, and the case law, as we have seen, recognizes a number of exceptions to it. It would be better, both in terms of consistency and of protecting defendants, to allow a judge to stop a case whenever it is thought that a conviction would be unsafe.[99]

11.3 THE EXCLUSION OF UNFAIRLY AND ILLEGALLY OBTAINED EVIDENCE

Where the police have obtained evidence against a suspect by unfair or illegal means, the courts face a difficult question: whether or not to admit the evidence. Sometimes, a decision to exclude such evidence will result in the collapse of the case against the defendant, and where the crime involved is a serious one, such as murder or rape, the court may be extremely reluctant to take this course. The issues involved here are complex, and to make any headway in considering them a number of distinctions must be drawn.

The police may engage in conduct which affects the reliability of the evidence against the accused. The most obvious examples here involve confessions. The police might, for instance, put undue pressure on a suspect by bullying him, lying to him,

---

[95] *Mackenzie* (1993) 96 Cr App R 98.   [96] CJA 2003, s125.

[97] See G. Davis *et al, An Assessment of the Admissibility and Sufficiency of Evidence in Child Abuse Prosecutions* (1999), 47–8.

[98] Cf Judicial Studies Board, Civil Bench Book, para 10.4.

[99] This was the recommendation of the Royal Commission on Criminal Justice: above n 21, 59.

denying him legal advice or, in the case of a juvenile, denying access to an appropriate adult. The police might also question a suspect outside the police station, so evading the protections offered by the PACE regime. Depending on the circumstances, these actions might affect the reliability of a resulting confession. For example, we saw in Chapter 4 that vulnerable suspects may confess falsely where they are bullied (as in the case of *Miller*[100]). A juvenile or an adult might feel overwhelmed by the experience of being detained, and without access to independent advice, might confess falsely. Where a suspect is questioned outside the police station, there may be no definitive record of what was said and so the very claim that a confession was made may be disputed. Where unreliability is the concern, there are good reasons for excluding the relevant confession. Section 76 of PACE provides a legal basis for doing so; it mandates the exclusion of confessions obtained in consequence of anything said or done which was likely to render the confession unreliable. The exclusion of unreliable evidence is not especially controversial (though it is certainly not easy to say just how unreliable evidence should be before it is a target for exclusion), and we will give little further attention to it in this chapter. That allows us to concentrate on the more difficult question of whether a confession, or other evidence, should be excluded where there are no doubts about its reliability. A defendant wrongly denied access to legal advice might be an intelligent adult, and might even admit the truth of the confession. Should the confession then be excluded? The first distinction to be drawn, then, is that between cases where reliability is a concern and those where it is not.

The examples given above allow further distinctions to be made. Where the police deny a suspect access to legal advice, they will usually be acting in breach of s 58 of the Police and Criminal Evidence Act 1984, which requires a suspect to be given access to legal advice except in very exceptional circumstances. But there are no clear rules about the amount of pressure a suspect can be subjected to.[101] The relevant Code of Practice rules out oppressive questioning,[102] but mild bullying might not amount to oppression, which the courts have tended to define quite narrowly.[103] Or, to use another example, the police might, as in *Mason*,[104] lie to a suspect about the existence of incriminating information. The usual objection to such conduct is not that it is in breach of the rules for conducting criminal investigations, but the rather vaguer complaint that it is somehow unfair.[105] Another example of unfairness, which we came across in Chapter 9, is entrapment. The principal objection to entrapment is not that it is in breach of any particular rules, but that in certain circumstances it is unfair. However, entrapment often will involve a breach of the criminal law. Where an undercover police officer asks a person to supply him with heroin, he will be committing a criminal offence: usually the inchoate offence of incitement, and perhaps also a drug possession offence. Other police practices will also involve breaches of the criminal

[100] (1992) 97 Cr App R 99. [101] See Ch 4. [102] Code C, 11.5.
[103] *Fulling* [1987] QB 426. [104] [1988] 1 WLR 139.
[105] It was argued in Chapter 4, however, that deception during questioning should be ruled out on reliability grounds. For more detailed discussion of why deception may be unacceptable, see A. Ashworth, 'Should the Police be Allowed to Use Deceptive Practices?' (1998) 114 LQR 108.

law. In *Khan*,[106] the police placed a bugging device on the outside of a house in order to obtain incriminating information. This probably involved the commission of criminal damage—although the damage was minor. The bugging operation also involved the breach of the right to privacy in Article 8 of the European Convention on Human Rights, and the interference could not be justified by reference to the prevention of crime because there was no legal framework regulating such police operations, as Article 8(2) requires. These various examples enable us to make the following distinctions: there may be an objection to police conduct because it breaches a statutory rule designed to protect suspects (e.g. denial of legal advice); because it is thought to be somehow unfair (e.g. lying to a suspect); because it breaches the criminal law (e.g. criminal damage); or because it breaches a broad human rights norm (e.g. the right to privacy). We will return to the possible significance of these distinctions in the discussion to follow.

In order to understand the arguments surrounding the exclusion of unfairly and illegally obtained evidence, it is useful to follow the literature in distinguishing four different approaches that the courts might adopt. The first is the disciplinary approach. The idea here is that evidence is excluded in order to deter future misconduct by the police. If the police gain a confession after improperly denying the suspect legal advice, then the court should exclude the confession in order to teach the police a lesson. The police will be less likely to deny legal advice in future cases if they are aware that any evidence they obtain from the suspect by questioning him cannot be used against him in court. However, this last assumption is questionable, and herein lies a significant objection to the disciplinary approach. Just as there are doubts about the deterrent effects of punishing criminals, there are doubts about the deterrent effect of excluding improperly obtained evidence. In future cases, the police may not be deterred if they are unaware of the relevant rules, if they think that the misconduct will not come to light, if they think that the suspect will plead guilty, or if for any other reason gathering evidence for use at trial is not what is motivating their conduct (the literature on policing makes it clear that much police conduct is motivated primarily by the goal of 'order maintenance').[107] While acknowledging this, it should be recognized that in some situations deterrence may be effective. The right to legal advice before questioning is an example. In the early days of PACE, the police frequently ignored this right. Judgments of the Court of Appeal, which in some cases overturned convictions based on confessions obtained after denial of legal advice, probably played a role in changing this situation.[108] The exclusion of evidence may have been particularly effective here because police questioning is usually centred on obtaining evidence rather than on other goals, such as order maintenance, and

---

[106] [1996] 3 All ER 289.   [107] See, e.g., R. Reiner, *The Politics of the Police* (3rd ed., 2000).

[108] Brown found that after the Court of Appeal decision in *Samuel* [1988] 1 QB 615, the power to delay access to legal advice was regarded as a 'dead letter' by detectives. D. Brown, *Investigating Burglary: The Effects of PACE* (1991), 76. See also D. Brown *et al*, *Changing the Code: Police Detention Under the Revised PACE Codes of Practice* (1992).

because the police station is a relatively well regulated area where rules can be enforced and misconduct will come to light. All the same, one should be wary of putting too much weight on this example: it is possible that the police responded to the exclusionary judgments by resorting to less visible forms of misconduct which still succeeded in neutralizing the benefits of legal advice.[109]

A second approach to illegally and improperly obtained evidence is the protective or remedial approach.[110] If the focus of the deterrence rationale is on the wrongdoer (the police), then the focus of the remedial approach is on the victim of the police misconduct: the defendant, against whom the prosecution seeks to introduce illegally or improperly obtained evidence. By excluding evidence under the remedial rationale, the courts seek to put the defendant back in the position he would have been in had his rights not been breached. This may involve a question of causation: if a suspect was denied access to legal advice, and then confessed, it will be legitimate to ask whether the confession came about as a result of the denial of legal advice. If the suspect would have confessed anyway, then excluding the confession will not restore the status quo. This may be a very difficult judgment to make. It is worth noting at this stage a substantial difference between the deterrent and protective rationales. Suppose that the police breach the defendant's rights, but do so in good faith: perhaps the defendant is held in custody for an extended period because it is thought that he is being held for a 'serious arrestable offence' (the definition of which is quite vague)[111], whereas the court later rules that the offence was not a serious arrestable one. Under the remedial approach, a court should exclude any confession made during the extended period of detention. This ensures that the defendant was not prejudiced by the breach of his rights. This result is not so obvious under the deterrence rationale. If the police acted in good faith, it might be argued that misconduct will not be deterred by exclusion, because if the police found themselves in the same position again (not knowing that they were acting wrongly), they would make the same decision. This approach has been taken in the US jurisprudence on the exclusionary rule in search and seizure cases.[112] Where the police in good faith obtain a search warrant which happens to be invalid, the fruits of the search will not be excluded. The police not being at fault, there is nothing to deter.

A common criticism of the remedial approach is that it is insensitive to 'comparative reprehensibility',[113] in that it leads to exclusion where there is a breach of a minor right when investigating a major crime. Suppose that a defendant who has been denied access to legal advice confesses to a series of murders. Excluding the confession might lead to the collapse of the case against him, something many people would feel very uncomfortable about. The deterrence approach might have the same effect. A third way of justifying the exclusion of illegally or unfairly obtained evidence

---

[109] A. Sanders and L. Bridges, 'Access to Legal Advice and Police Malpractice' [1990] Crim LR 494.

[110] A. Ashworth, 'Excluding Evidence as Protecting Rights' [1977] Crim LR 723. [111] PACE, s 116.

[112] C. Bradley, 'United States', in C. Bradley (ed), *Criminal Procedure: A Worldwide Study* (1999), 406.

[113] Y. Kamisar, ' "Comparative Reprehensibility" and the Fourth Amendment Exclusionary Rule' (1987) 86 *Michigan LR* 1.

avoids such outcomes by taking comparative reprehensibility as its central element. This is the moral legitimacy or integrity rationale.[114] There are different ways of theorizing this approach.[115] One is to appeal to the need for the verdicts of courts to appear legitimate in the eyes of the public. Citizens will not have faith in the courts if judges too easily overlook wrongdoing by the authorities; but nor will citizens be comfortable if they see serious criminals going free because of relatively minor wrongdoing. Judges should therefore bear in mind both the importance of convicting the guilty and the importance of sanctioning official wrongdoing when deciding whether or not to exclude improperly obtained evidence. The difficulty with this approach is that it puts too much emphasis on the reaction of the public. In crimes which attract widespread revulsion, such as the sexual abuse of children, the public might be perfectly happy to see the use of tortured confessions.[116] Most advocates of the integrity approach therefore distance themselves from 'public attitude integrity'. For example, whereas the Canadian Charter of Rights and Freedoms provides for the exclusion of evidence obtained in breach of Charter rights where its admission 'would bring the administration of justice into disrepute',[117] the Supreme Court has suggested that this involves thinking of the reaction of the 'average person in the community, but only when that community's current mood is reasonable.'[118] Another way to avoid an admissibility test which is hostage to public sentiment is to explain the idea of integrity in a different manner. Appeal might be made to a communicative theory of the criminal trial.[119] A criminal court is engaged in a moral dialogue with the defendant. Convicting the defendant involves censuring him, appealing to his ability to understand that he has engaged in wrongdoing. The message of censure, it can be argued, would be blurred if the prosecution relied on evidence gained by police wrongdoing.[120] Rather like the 'public attitude integrity' version of the theory, the communicative view also seems to rely on an empirical claim. But it is one which is even harder to judge, and could lead to all sorts of attitudes to exclusion. One might argue that the message of censure would be blurred if the prosecution relied on evidence obtained by even minor deliberate wrongdoing by the police. A more hard-headed approach would hold that the defendant's wrong-doing is sufficiently separate from any wrongdoing by the police that the message of censure will always be comprehensible, no matter how grave the police wrongdoing; perhaps especially so if alternative disciplinary mechanisms are available for police misconduct. A different approach to integrity avoids these problems by appealing to more abstract notions of integrity. What is important, it might be argued, is the

---

[114] See I. Dennis, *The Law of Evidence* (2nd ed., 2002), 85–9, and discussion in P. Mirfield, *Silence, Confessions and Improperly Obtained Evidence*, 23–8.

[115] For further discussion, see A. Ashworth, 'Exploring the Integrity Principle in Evidence and Procedure' in P. Mirfield and R. Smith (eds), *Essays for Colin Tapper* (2003).

[116] P. Mirfield, *Silence, Confessions and Improperly Obtained Evidence* (1997), 23–8, 364–70.

[117] Section 24(2).   [118] *Collins* [1987] 1 SCR 265, [44].

[119] See Ch 2, and R. Duff, *Trials and Punishments* (1986).

[120] See I. Dennis, 'Reconstructing the Law of Criminal Evidence' (1989) *Current Legal Problems* 21.

moral standing of the court. The courts' moral standing can be regarded as an objective matter, not affected by the views of the community or the ability of defendants to respond to censure. The courts should avoid tainting their moral status by relying on improperly obtained evidence, but they should also be sufficiently aware of their role as fact-finders that they should not acquit the guilty without good reason. Under the communicative theory, it might be said that the question is whether we have the moral standing to communicate censure to the defendant if we rely on the impugned evidence. There is considerable—though perhaps inevitable—obscurity in this sort of account, but the basic idea should be familiar. The courts somehow have to balance the wrongdoing involved against the importance of gaining a conviction in the case in hand.

A fourth approach, which might be termed the 'external' approach, would hold that the exclusion of improperly obtained evidence is never appropriate.[121] So long as the relevant evidence is reliable, the argument would go, the court should use it in its primary task of fact-finding. This is not to say that the police were right to beat the defendant up, or deny him a solicitor, or bug his house; nor is it to say that such impropriety should be overlooked. The argument is simply that a response to the impropriety should take place in a venue external to the present trial. The police could be prosecuted for assault, or disciplined for breaking the PACE rules, and in the bugging case an action for damages might be brought under the Human Rights Act. One difficulty with this argument, however, is that often those other remedies will be insufficient. There have been long-standing problems with police disciplinary proceedings, and if the authorities decide not to institute them there is little the victim can do. And while it is possible to prosecute the police for assault, this would involve further legal proceedings; there is something to be said, in terms of efficiency, for responding to the wrongdoing in the initial criminal trial.

The way the courts approach the exclusion of improperly or illegally obtained evidence can be evaluated on another dimension: that of the width of discretion given to the courts. On its face, there is little discretion involved under the protective rationale. Once it is decided that the defendant's rights have been breached, any resulting evidence should be excluded. Exclusion is automatic. Exclusion under the deterrence rationale also tends to be automatic: police wrongdoing must be punished. These two approaches will tend to result in clearer exclusionary rules. This is not the case with the integrity rationale, for here a difficult balancing exercise is central to the rule. This contrast should not be overstated. Under the protective rationale the courts will have considerable leeway in deciding whether the evidence in question was obtained as a result of police wrongdoing, and the integrity approach can gain structure through the development of case law or the use of multi-factor tests to constrain

---

[121] For this argument in the context of the Fourth Amendment to the US Constitution, see A. Amar, 'Fourth Amendment First Principles' in *The Constitution and Criminal Procedure* (1997). For further discussion of the external, or 'separation' approach, see Ashworth, above n 115, 113–15.

decision making.[122] Discretion can also be added to the protective and disciplinary rationales by allowing exceptions to be made in certain cases. Nevertheless, the basic distinction here is important in evaluating the approaches. The more one dislikes leaving considerable leeway to judges, the more one will favour the stricter rule-based approaches.

There is much more to say about these theoretical approaches to the exclusion of evidence. We will discuss them further after saying something about the case law that has developed on these matters in England and in other jurisdictions.

(a) THE ENGLISH CASE LAW

The approach of the English courts to illegally and unfairly obtained evidence has changed considerably since the introduction of the Police and Criminal Evidence Act 1984. The old common law approach was, basically, unsympathetic to the exclusion of such evidence. The words of Crompton J in *Leatham* are often quoted to illustrate the position: 'It matters not how you get it; if you steal it even, it would be admissible in evidence.'[123] There are dicta in some post war cases which suggest that judges might have a discretion to exclude improperly obtained evidence, but these dicta are obscure, and there are very few decisions where courts did use the discretion to exclude evidence.[124]

Section 78 of PACE provides that:

'In any proceedings the court may refuse to allow evidence on which the prosecution proposes to rely to be given if it appears to the court that, having regard to all the circumstances, including the circumstances in which the evidence was obtained, the admission of the evidence would have such an adverse effect on the fairness of the proceedings that the court ought not to admit it.'

This vaguely worded provision has led to a substantial change in the way the courts have approached illegally and unfairly obtained evidence. There is a considerable amount of case law, and it is not easily summarized, but the following observations can be made. PACE introduced a number of provisions regulating the treatment of suspects in the police station and the way in which evidence is gathered. The courts have been prepared to exclude evidence where these provisions have been breached, but exclusion is by no means automatic. A preliminary question is often whether the breach is 'significant and substantial'. A breach of s 58—the right to legal advice—for example, will be considered significant and substantial. But other breaches may be regarded as merely technical. In *Blackwell*, for example, there were various breaches of PACE Code C: among other things, the defendant was not reminded of his right to legal advice at the beginning of one of several interviews, and had been given breakfast

---

[122] As in the Australian approach, discussed below.   [123] (1861) 8 Cox CC 498, 501.

[124] For good summaries of the pre-PACE position, see Dennis, above n 120, 251–60; D. Ormerod and D. Birch, 'The Evolution of the Discretionary Exclusion of Evidence' [2004] Crim LR 767.

and a light lunch but was not offered a main meal; these were described as technical breaches.[125] That a breach is significant and substantial is not determinative of the admissibility issue. The courts put considerable importance on the question whether the defendant was disadvantaged by the breach of his rights. In *Samuel*,[126] for example, there was a wrongful denial of legal advice, and the defendant's solicitor testified that had he given advice it would have been to say nothing in the interview in which Samuel in fact confessed. But in *Alladice*, the defendant who was wrongly denied legal advice admitted that he was fully aware of his rights, and the court therefore found that allowing legal advice would have made little difference to him.[127] The confession in *Samuel* was excluded, but the one in *Alladice* admitted. Another factor which has been held to have some relevance is the question of bad faith. That the police breached PACE or the Codes in good faith will not necessarily prevent exclusion, but it has been said that bad faith is more likely to lead to exclusion.[128]

The case law discussed so far relates to breaches of PACE and the Codes of Practice. The rules involved are fairly clear and are generally designed to protect defendants. The judiciary seems to have adopted these rules and to be happy to enforce the rights contained in them. The wording of s 78 is far broader than the protection of such procedural rights; it refers simply to fairness. The courts are prepared to use s 78 in other situations, but it is probably fair to say that they are more cautious in doing so. One example is *Mason*,[129] where the defendant and his solicitor were falsely informed that his fingerprints had been found at the crime scene. Mason's confession was excluded; the court emphasized the fact that his solicitor was subject to the deception, so it may be that the exclusionary reaction here was connected to the court's desire to protect access to legal advice (what good is legal advice, after all, if that advice can be manipulated by deception?) In other cases involving some sort of deception, exclusion has generally not followed. In *Bailey*,[130] *Roberts*,[131] and (a different) *Mason*,[132] for example, suspects were encouraged to make incriminating admissions while in bugged cells. The admissions were not excluded, though in the latter case the court did call for clearer guidance on what was acceptable.[133] As for other sorts of deception, there are dicta suggesting that s 78 might be used in cases involving entrapment,[134] though, as we have seen, in such cases the more usual remedy is a stay for abuse of process.

There are also cases where the exercise of s 78 has been considered in relation to breaches of the European Convention on Human Rights. The best known example is *Khan*.[135] Here, the police covertly recorded incriminating statements made by the defendant. The House of Lords seemed prepared to accept that this involved a breach

---

[125] [1995] 2 Cr App R 625.   [126] [1988] 1 QB 615.
[127] (1998) 87 Cr App R 380. For other examples of the difficult causal decision involved, see *Oliphant* [1992] Crim LR 40; *Law-Thompson* [1997] Crim LR 674.
[128] *Samuel*, above n 108; *Walsh* (1990) 91 Cr App R 161.   [129] [1988] 1 WLR 139.
[130] [1993] 3 All ER 513.   [131] [1997] 1 Cr App R 217.   [132] [2002] 2 Cr App R 38.
[133] For further discussion of this sort of deception, see Ashworth, above n 105.
[134] *Smurthwaite and Gill* (1994) 98 Cr App R 437.   [135] [1996] 3 WLR 162.

of Article 8 of the Convention, which protects the right to privacy. This was held to be relevant to, though not determinative of, the s 78 question. The significance of the fact that the police have broken a law (here, the placing of the device may have involved criminal damage), or Convention right, would be determined by 'its effect, taken as a whole, upon the fairness or unfairness of the proceedings.'[136] In this case it was held that the trial judge had been right to decide that the evidence should not be excluded. The issues in *Khan* were considered by the European Court of Human Rights, which confirmed that there had been a breach of Article 8, but also held that relying on the evidence at trial did not breach the right to a fair trial in Article 6.[137] The Court of Appeal has considered a similar issue in the light of the introduction of the Human Rights Act 1998, and reached the same conclusion: although a breach of Article 8 is relevant to the s 78 question, evidence obtained in breach of that article need not be excluded.[138]

The discussion so far suggests that there has been a fair degree of consensus about the operation of s 78, at least so far as the courts are concerned. There are, however, significant differences of approach in the case law. In *Chalkley*, the Court of Appeal read s 78 as simply restating the old common law.[139] The result of this would be that, except in the case of confessions, s 78 would not enable evidence to be excluded unless the reliability of that evidence was in question. What was not appropriate, it was said, was for a judge to use the exclusionary discretion to express disapproval of the way in which evidence had been obtained—in *Chalkley*, by secretly placing a bugging device in the accused's flat. If such factors were to be considered, this should be in the context of the discretion to stay proceedings for abuse of process, not in the context of s 78.

The decision in *Chalkley* has been controversial.[140] It is not easy to reconcile with much of the other case law on the section, nor with the later decision of the House of Lords in *Looseley*.[141] As a matter of law, it is probably best disregarded. Nevertheless, one should at least try to appreciate why a narrow reading of s 78 might be attractive. The key question under the section is whether admission of evidence would have an adverse effect on the fairness of the proceedings. Unless evidence is unreliable, it might be argued that a decision to admit it cannot render the proceedings unfair. If there are no doubts about the reliability of the confession obtained through deception in *Mason*,[142] or the confession in *Samuel*,[143] or the covertly obtained statements in *Khan*,[144] just how can admitting them make the proceedings unfair?[145] Mason may

---

[136] *Ibid.*, at 175.   [137] *Khan v United Kingdom* (2001) 31 EHRR 45.

[138] *Mason* [2002] 2 Cr App R 38.

[139] [1998] QB 848. A similar view of s 78 (as only applying to potentially unreliable evidence) can be found in other cases, e.g. *Cooke* [1995] 1 Cr App R 318.

[140] For cogent criticism, see Dennis, above n 114, 81–4. See also A. Choo and S. Nash, 'What's the Matter with Section 78?' [1999] Crim LR 929.

[141] *Attorney General's Reference (No 3 of 2000)*; *R v Looseley* [2001] 1 WLR 2060.

[142] [1998] 1 WLR 139.   [143] Above n 108.   [144] Above n 106.

[145] For this view, see B. Robertson, 'The Looking Glass World of Section 78' (1989) *NLJ* 1223; N. Walker, 'What Does Fairness Mean in a Criminal Trial?' (2001) *NLJ* 1240.

have been treated unfairly when he and his solicitor were deceived, but that unfairness is not created by a decision to admit the evidence. There is, then, a certain logic to reading s 78 as being solely concerned with reliability. Against this view, one can argue that the key question is whether the proceedings—interpreted broadly as extending beyond the trial—are fair. Section 78 might be thought to give the courts the power to ensure that the proceedings as a whole are fair by refusing to admit evidence that has been improperly obtained. Some support for this interpretation can be found in the words 'including the circumstances in which the evidence was obtained' in the section. It might be thought that such circumstance can only be relevant to the admissibility decision if a broad view of fairness is taken. The European Convention on Human Rights is also relevant here: the Strasbourg Court views trial fairness as incorporating the fairness of pre-trial procedures.[146] Moving away from the wording of the section itself, the distinction might be put in terms of the questions whether the defendant can have a fair trial, and whether it is fair to try him. A defendant can have a fair trial so long as he is not exposed to an inappropriate risk of false conviction, such as might be produced by the admission of unreliable evidence; but it may not be fair to try a defendant where the authorities have acted unjustly towards him, even if he can receive a fair trial in the sense just described. When thinking about trial fairness, it is easy to get confused by moving between the fair trial/fair to try questions, and this may explain some of the ambiguity in the s 78 case law. In summary, the wording of s 78 is deeply ambiguous; similar ambiguity can be found in the normative question underlying the section (what makes a trial fair?). The issues raised in *Chalkley*, then, illustrate the difficulty of questions about the exclusion of evidence, and their controversial nature.

To point up some of the more controversial issues, we might consider the question of how the seriousness of the crime with which the defendant is charged relates to the s 78 exclusionary discretion. *Nathaniel* is an excellent example.[147] Here, the defendant was convicted of rape. The case against him relied on DNA identification evidence; however, the DNA in question had been retained by the police in breach of the then rules governing the retention of DNA profiles. The Court of Appeal quashed his conviction. It put some emphasis on the fact that when Nathaniel's DNA profile had originally been taken, he was informed that it would only be used in connection with the crime he was then charged with, which was not the rape he was eventually convicted of, and this 'breach of promise' might be thought to add a significant dimension to the case.[148] Nevertheless, the decision in *Nathaniel* draws divergent reactions. Dennis, who supports an integrity-based theory of the exclusionary rule, is critical, arguing that the rule in question does not reflect a fundamental norm. His reasoning may well reflect an appreciation of the seriousness of the crime with which

---

[146] E.g. *Teixeira de Castro v Portugal* (1999) 28 EHRR 101. [147] [1995] 2 Cr App R 565.
[148] Cf. *R v Croydon Justices ex p Dean* [1993] QB 769.

Nathaniel was charged.[149] However, Grevling, who appears to adopt a remedial theory, approves of the decision in *Nathaniel*.[150]

Cases such as *Nathaniel*, which involve cogent real evidence and serious offences, are interesting test cases for the exclusionary discretion. For this reason, it is worth saying something about the decision in *Attorney General's Reference (No 3 of 1999)*,[151] even though it raises somewhat different issues. At the relevant time, the rules in PACE on the retention of DNA profiles were that where a DNA sample had been taken from a defendant in relation to an offence of which he was acquitted, the sample and any information derived from it should be destroyed as soon as practicable. Further, under PACE, s. 64(3), in this situation information derived from the sample 'shall not be used (a) in evidence against the person [entitled to its destruction]; or (b) for the purposes of any investigation of an offence.' In the case giving rise to the reference, as in *Nathaniel*, the sample had not been destroyed when it should have been. The defendant was then connected to a violent rape through the DNA sample; he was arrested and a new DNA sample was obtained from him. It was this new sample that was used against him at trial. Because it was a new sample, its use did not fall foul of rule (a) above. The question for the House of Lords was whether rule (b) meant the DNA evidence should have been excluded from the trial. It held that it did not, because (b) does not refer to what the consequences of its breach should be; it says nothing about whether evidence should be excluded when a DNA sample is wrongly used to investigate an offence. In the House of Lords, argument was restricted to this issue of statutory interpretation. For this reason, there was little discussion of whether s 78 should be used to exclude evidence obtained in breach of rule (b). But Lord Hutton hinted heavily that, given the seriousness of the offence and the need to protect society, he would not have exercised the discretion in favour of the defendant.[152] We will return to the question of whether this is the right way to conceive of the exclusionary discretion; for now, it is worth making a further point about the decision. The interpretation of PACE given by the House of Lords has a certain literal logic to it: it is right that rule (b) says nothing about the effects of its breach. But it is nevertheless an odd interpretation of the rules. It is not what the Court of Appeal and the trial judge thought the provisions meant. Moreover, if (b) is not interpreted as being a rule of strict inadmissibility, it makes a mockery of (a), as the House of Lords later went some way to acknowledging.[153] There can be little point in saying that evidence obtained from a wrongly retained DNA sample cannot be used in evidence if the police can circumvent the rule by obtaining a new sample which is not covered by the exclusionary rule. The general lesson to draw from this is that the courts can be

---

[149] Above n 120, 265–7. For a similar view, see M. Hirst, *Andrews and Hirst on Criminal Evidence* (4th ed., 2001), para 14.22.

[150] K. Grevling, 'Fairness and the Exclusion of Evidence Under Section 78(1) of the Police and Criminal Evidence Act' (1997) 113 LQR 667, 683.

[151] [2001] 2 AC 91.   [152] *Ibid.*, at [43].

[153] The distinction drawn in the case 'did not reflect well on the law', according to Lord Steyn in *R v CC South Yorkshire ex p LS/Marper* [2004] UKHL 39, [33].

very sceptical of strict exclusionary rules when they are regarded as having undesirable results. Here, PACE is subjected to a strained interpretation in order to avoid such
results.

Moving beyond these DNA cases, there is relatively clear authority that crime
seriousness is relevant to the exercise of the s 78 discretion. We find this in the bugging
cases mentioned earlier.[154] And in *Khan*, Lord Nolan, while not expressly addressing
this point, commented that 'it would be a strange reflection on our law if a man who
has admitted his participation in the illegal importation of a large quantity of heroin
should have his conviction set aside on the grounds that his privacy has been
invaded.'[155] It is significant that these comments are found in cases dealing with
abstract fairness, rather than breach of the PACE rules. When one looks at the PACE
cases, one finds that the courts are fond of saying that 'fairness' in s 78 includes
fairness to the prosecution as well as to the defence. It is hard to tell just what is meant
by this, but it may simply imply that reliable prosecution evidence should not be
excluded without good reason. Apart from this, the PACE cases generally do not
suggest that the seriousness of the crime at issue is a factor to consider in deciding
whether to exclude evidence. The comments in the *Attorney General's Reference* are of
course an exception to this, to which we will return.

One final area of the law deserves brief discussion. The Road Traffic Act 1988 sets
out various rules for the taking of breath, blood and urine samples from suspects. The
Act makes it clear that prosecutions should not be brought where some of these
provisions have been breached, but is silent as to the effects of many of them. Nevertheless, the courts have taken a very strict approach to the Act, and held that evidence
should be excluded even where the police have deviated from the statutory regime in a
minor way, causing no obvious prejudice to the defendant in the process. The courts
in these cases do not refer to s 78, and the decisions are hard to reconcile with the
more general case law on that section.[156]

(b) OTHER JURISDICTIONS

A detailed analysis of exclusionary rules in other jurisdictions is beyond the scope of
this work, but it is worth looking briefly abroad to gain a wider perspective, before
returning to discuss the strengths and weaknesses of the approach of the courts in
England and Wales.

The US is well known for having a relatively strict exclusionary rule. The legal
position is complex, because much of the case law has been developed by the Supreme
Court in the context of different constitutional provisions:[157] there is no equivalent to

---

[154] See *Mason* (2002), above n 132 at 70, quoting with approval from *Bailey*, above n 130. See also *Latif and Shahzad* [1996] 1 WLR 104.

[155] Above n 135, 175.

[156] For discussion, and criticism, of the cases, see M. Hirst, 'Excess Alcohol, Incorrect Procedures and Inadmissible Evidence' (1995) 54 *Cambridge LJ* 600.

[157] Good overviews are Bradley, above n 112; Mirfield, above n 116, 319–39.

s 78 of PACE which, as we have seen, can be used in a wide range of circumstances. Concentrating on the Fourth Amendment, which guarantees security against unreasonable searches and seizures, the key decision is *Mapp v Ohio*.[158] *Mapp* requires the exclusion of any evidence obtained in violation of the Fourth Amendment. Later decisions appear to associate the exclusionary policy with a disciplinary rationale, but the decisions somewhat water down the strict exclusionary policy. Improperly obtained evidence need not be excluded if the police obtained an invalid search warrant in good faith,[159] or if the evidence would inevitably have been discovered by lawful means in due course,[160] and exclusion only applies to the prosecution's case in chief: the evidence can be used to rebut the defendant's evidence at trial.[161] It is often said, too, that strictness of the exclusionary rule leads trial courts to ignore breaches of the Fourth Amendment, for example by making a finding of fact that the police did have good grounds for conducting a search, and that it has led the Supreme Court to narrow down the Fourth Amendment.[162]

Outside the US, a number of jurisdictions openly embrace some version of the integrity rationale for the exclusion of illegally and unfairly obtained evidence. In Canada, for example, a number of rights are recognized in the Canadian Charter of Rights and Freedoms. Section 24(2) of the Charter provides that where evidence has been obtained in breach of a Charter right, it should be excluded from a criminal trial if its admission would bring the administration of justice into disrepute. As far as the case law is concerned, the exclusionary rule has two different aspects. Where evidence has been obtained in breach of the Charter in a way which involves the participation of the defendant ('conscriptive evidence'), evidence will be excluded automatically (the doctrine here reflects a broad interpretation of the privilege against self-incrimination).[163] Where evidence is not thought to be conscriptive, a wider balancing test will be applied.[164] This will involve looking at the seriousness of the breach of the charter (were the police acting in good faith?), the seriousness of the offence, and the importance of the evidence to the Crown's case. This leaves considerable discretion to trial judges, making it difficult to draw any general lessons from the case law.[165]

In Australia, it was recognized in *Bunning v Cross* that evidence can be excluded on grounds of 'public policy'.[166] The balancing test adopted by the High Court in this case has been adopted in the Evidence Act 1995, which states that illegally and improperly obtained evidence should not be admitted unless 'the desirability of admitting the evidence outweighs the undesirability of admitting evidence that has

---

[158] 367 US 643 (1961). For a detailed analysis of decisions on the Fourth Amendment, see R. Allen and R. Rosenberg, 'The Fourth Amendment and the Limits of Theory: Local Versus General Theoretical Knowledge' (1998) 72 *St John's L Rev* 1149.

[159] *US v Leon* 468 US 897 (1984).   [160] *Nix v Williams* 467 US 431.

[161] *US v Havens* 446 US 620 (1980).   [162] Mirfield, above n 116, 322.

[163] *Stillman* [1997] 1 SCR 8.   [164] *Collins* [1987] 1 SCR 265.

[165] See, eg, *Buhay* [2003] SCC 30.   [166] (1978) 141 CLR 54.

been obtained in the way in which the evidence was obtained.'[167] The Act goes on to list a series of factors to be taken into account, including the probative value and importance of the evidence, the difficulty of obtaining it without impropriety, and the nature of the offence for which the defendant is on trial. Research on the operation of s 138 predictably confirms that this gives the courts considerable latitude. Decisions are sometimes hard to reconcile with each other, and the courts are said to be reluctant to exclude evidence in cases where the crime charged is a serious one.[168]

In New Zealand there have been significant recent developments in the operation of the exclusionary rule.[169] New Zealand law recognized that judges have a relatively wide discretion to exclude evidence to promote the fairness of proceedings.[170] In 1990 New Zealand adopted a Bill of Rights and, as with the Canadian Charter, this affected the working of the exclusionary rule; but, unlike the Charter, the Bill of Rights itself is silent on how its breach should affect admissibility. On their own initiative the courts created what came to be known as the '*prima facie*' rule. Where police impropriety involved a breach of the Bill of Rights, there was a presumption in favour of exclusion.[171] In 2002, however, the Court of Appeal in *Shaheed* rejected the rule in favour of a broader balancing test, more akin to the Australian rule.[172] The balancing test acknowledges the seriousness of the offence as one of the factors to be taken into account, a factor which had previously been held to be irrelevant. *Shaheed* doubtless sends a message to trial judges that they need to exclude less evidence that has been obtained in breach of rights; but it would be wrong to jump to the conclusion that New Zealand law has now jumped dramatically in an inclusionary direction. Post-*Shaheed* one can find decisions where judges have been prepared to exclude cogent evidence that has been improperly obtained. *Maihi*[173] and *Rollinson*[174] are good examples; both cases involve improper searches for illegal drugs, and in *Maihi* it was found that the police were acting in good faith, a factor which in some jurisdictions would be a decisive factor in favour of admissibility. What is influencing the courts in these cases is partly a recognition of the importance of the right in issue—the right to be free from unlawful searches—and partly a candid recognition that the crimes involved (supplying drugs such as cannabis and amphetamines) are not especially serious. It is perhaps significant too that the language of vindication of rights features in *Maihi*: the court noted that were the evidence admitted there would be no vindication of Maihi's rights. The New Zealand courts, it seems, recognize the importance of rights, and this attitude plays a role in their exercise of the exclusionary discretion.

---

[167] Evidence Act 1995 (Australia) s138. There is an identical provision under s138 of the Evidence Act 1995 (New South Wales).

[168] See B. Presser, 'Public Policy, Police Interest: A Re-Evaluation of the Judicial Discretion to Exclude Improperly or Illegally Obtained Evidence' (2001) 25 *Melbourne ULR* 757.

[169] R. Mahoney, 'Abolition of New Zealand's *Prima Facie* Exclusionary Rule' [2003] Crim LR 607. For more detail, see P. Rishworth *et al*, *The New Zealand Bill of Rights* (2003), Ch 28.

[170] *Coombs* [1985] 1 NZLR 318.   [171] *Goodwin* [1993] 2 NZLR 153.

[172] [2002] 2 NZLR 377.   [173] (2002) CA181/02.   [174] (2003) CA434/02.

(c) EVALUATING THE APPROACHES

The foregoing discussion has illustrated a number of different approaches to the exclusion of illegally and unfairly obtained evidence, and highlighted many salient issues which need to be considered when analyzing this area of the law. We are now in a position to say a little more about the pros and cons of the various positions on the exclusionary rule, but we should begin with some words of caution. As we have seen, there are different rationales for the exclusion of improperly obtained evidence, but it is probably a mistake to think that one is necessarily better, or more logical, than the others. Although none of the jurisdictions surveyed take a stark external approach to the problem—which involves admitting improperly obtained evidence but granting the accused some other remedy, such as an action for damages, for breach of his rights—there is not anything obviously illogical about the external approach.[175] Those who favour some sort of exclusionary rule might claim that the external approach would lead to absurd results, such as the admission of a reliable confession gained through torture. But it is not clear why that result is absurd. The decision to admit such evidence does not necessarily endorse the behaviour of the authorities, and arguments that the court would be giving an incoherent verdict, or undermining its own moral authority, need not persuade everyone. The decision to endorse a particular approach to the exclusionary rule, then, is partly a political choice. It is not inevitable that we see our courts as giving approval to improper behaviour by the authorities when they admit evidence gained by such behaviour, but we can choose to see things this way if we want to. If we do, this will reflect a particular vision of the role of the courts: as having some sort of responsibility for the pre-trial process.

If it is accepted that the courts should have a degree of responsibility for the pre-trial process, that still leaves the decision as to just when they should exclude evidence. Again, it is not easy to argue that any one of the rationales explored above is more logical than the others. In fact, to the extent that different jurisdictions have chosen different rationales, those choices appear to underdetermine the actual decisions made by the courts. Canada, Australia and New Zealand can all be said to have adopted some version of the integrity rationale, but courts in Canada and New Zealand seem to be more prepared to exclude evidence than their Australian counterparts.[176] That might be explained by an awareness of the importance of rights in those jurisdictions.

Rather than arguing that one approach is necessarily better than the others, it seems more fruitful to proceed by looking closely at what the English courts appear to be doing, and evaluating that on its merits. The first thing to say—again, by way of warning—is that the English courts do not much refer to theories of exclusion when justifying their admissibility decisions. The most significant statement one can find is

---

[175] See A. Ashworth, 'Exploring the Integrity Principle in Evidence and Procedure' in P. Mirfield and R. Smith (eds), *Essays for Colin Tapper* (2003).

[176] The Scottish situation seems very similar to that in Australia: P. Duff, 'Irregularly Obtained Real Evidence: The Scottish Solution' (2004) 8 *E&P* 77.

a negative one: that the courts do not see their role as being to discipline the police.[177] Despite this, there does seem to be an overall pattern to the case law, one that is perhaps more coherent than it looks at first sight. When it comes to breaches of the PACE rules, the rationale appears to be remedial. The courts are concerned to ensure that defendants are not disadvantaged by breach of their rights, and the exclusionary rule is relatively strict. This can be seen by contrasting the decisions in *Samuel* and *Alladice*, where the question of disadvantage (would the defendant have confessed anyway?) is key. The different results in these two cases are often criticized,[178] but the decisions do reflect a morally coherent distinction. Of course, the protective rationale here involves a difficult question of fact: in determining whether the defendant was disadvantaged, the court must ask a 'what if?' question, and this opens the door to a certain amount of discretion in the decisions. But this discretion is probably unavoidable: discretion features in some way in any version of the exclusionary rule, as the US experience shows. But once the question of fact has been decided, the protective rationale does give a clear answer to the admissibility question: if evidence has been obtained as a result of breach of rights, it should be excluded.

A problem with the protective rationale is often said to be that it would allow exclusion of evidence after a technical breach of minor rights. In practice, however, this problem is overcome by stressing that exclusion is only required where evidence has been obtained as a result of a breach of the defendant's rights. Thus, in *Blackwell*,[179] where the PACE codes were breached because the defendant had only been given a light lunch, exclusion would not be appropriate because the defendant would presumably have confessed whatever size of meal he had had. Things might be different had this been one of a number of breaches which had plausibly worn Blackwell down so that he could not resist confessing. In that situation, exclusion would be appropriate. This distinction explains why the Road Traffic Act cases, mentioned briefly above, are difficult to justify. There the courts are prepared to exclude cogent evidence for just any deviation from the Act, even though it cannot have had any effect on the obtaining of a sample or on its quality.

A significant problem with this remedial reading of the case law is that the courts identify bad faith as a factor to take into account when deciding whether or not to exclude evidence. However, although several cases make this point, it may be less significant when it comes to the actual decisions made by the courts. We are not aware of any decision under s 78 where evidence is obtained in breach of a PACE right but is admitted owing to the absence of bad faith. Bad faith might operate to widen the scope of exclusion, in other words to sanction malpractice even where it is not clear that the defendant was disadvantaged as a result of the impropriety. There is no objection to that; what is important is that good faith is not used as a reason for

---

[177] Mirfield, above n 116, 139.

[178] See, e.g., F. Belloni and J. Hodgson, *Criminal Injustice: An Evaluation of the Criminal Justice Process in Britain* (2000), 71.

[179] Above n 125.

overlooking the fact that a defendant has been disadvantaged by a breach of his rights.

The case law discussed so far does not make a decisive case for the protective rationale. It could be explained as well under some version of the integrity principle. Where the two approaches are most likely to differ is in a case such as *Nathaniel*, where what might look to be a relatively trivial breach of the PACE rules results in the exclusion of cogent evidence of a serious crime. *Nathaniel* is in fact a very useful test case for thinking about the exclusionary rule. From the integrity perspective, the argument for admissibility would be that the court will undermine its moral standing if it excludes the evidence (though quite why this is so is, we have seen, very difficult to explain, unless one relies on the unruly notion of public confidence). The remedial argument against admissibility is that Nathaniel had a right not to have the evidence used to connect him to a crime. The only way to give that right significant force is to exclude evidence obtained in breach of it, and here the seriousness of the crime is not relevant.[180] It may be that the moral values underlying the PACE rule here are not especially weighty ones (we saw in Chapter 5 that the arguments for and against the destruction of DNA samples where a suspect has not been convicted are quite finely balanced), but what matters here are the rules set down by Parliament. It is not for the courts to rethink them, and to decide which deserve protection and which do not.

The integrity based argument for admissibility would proceed by pointing out that the rules in *Nathaniel* have been breached and that we have learned something very significant as a result: that Nathaniel committed a serious crime. We cannot now discard this knowledge,[181] and it would be wrong for the court to attempt to do so by excluding the crucial evidence. Although this argument has its attractions, close analysis suggests that there is something unsatisfactory about it. No one wants a rapist to go unpunished, but this was in fact an inevitable consequence of the rules on the destruction of DNA profiles in force at the time of the decision. If the police were applying the PACE rules at all, then, by destroying DNA profiles, they ensured that large numbers of people could not be linked to all sorts of crimes, including rape and murder.[182] That is undesirable, but Parliament presumably thought it an appropriate price to pay for upholding civil liberties. Once we grasp this, it might not seem so odd that *Nathaniel* is acquitted despite the very strong evidence against him. That is what Parliament decided should happen, and it is not for the courts to substitute their own decision. The same reasoning applies to *Attorney General's Reference No 3 of 1999*.[183] In that case, even accepting the interpretation of s 64 of PACE made by the House of Lords, the DNA evidence should have been excluded under s 78. Presumably, the

---

[180] On the inappropriateness of taking seriousness into account, see further A. Ashworth, *Human Rights, Serious Crime and Criminal Procedure* (2002), 108–18.

[181] See P. Roberts and A. Zuckerman, *Criminal Evidence* (2004), 152.

[182] When the law was changed to allow the DNA profiles of the acquitted to be retained on the DNA database, within four years profiles retained in such circumstances had been linked to 53 murders, 94 rapes and 63 aggravated burglaries. See *Marper*, above n 153, [8].

[183] Above n 151.

integrity theorist would argue against this by claiming that the fact that we have a defendant before us who we know has committed a serious crime should make the difference. But it is difficult to see why so much weight should be put on our clear knowledge of guilt in the case in front of us. Just why should this override the decision made by Parliament? It seems to us that the integrity theorist who objects to the exclusion of the DNA evidence in *Nathaniel* and *Attorney General's Reference* is really arguing that Parliament's policy choice was wrong. That is a respectable position to take, but it is slightly odd that those who argue for admissibility in breach of rights do not concentrate on wider arguments about the merits of the underlying law, but instead focus their criticisms on what is really far less significant—the importance of convicting the guilty defendant in the immediate case.[184]

In the earlier discussion, the 'PACE' case law was distinguished from a series of decisions under s 78 which involve wider issues of fairness, such as the use of deception or breach of the right to privacy in Article 8 of the ECHR. Here, it is more difficult to argue that the courts are following a remedial rationale. The courts might instead be characterized as being involved in a wider balancing exercise, where issues such as the seriousness of the crime charged are relevant. It is not surprising that the courts should take a different approach to this area. Where the PACE provisions are concerned, Parliament has laid down a reasonably clear set of rules, expressly protecting defendants. It is appropriate that evidence obtained in breach of those rules should be excluded. But the courts have little guidance on the situation in *Mason*,[185] where the police lied to the defendant and his solicitor. The bugging cases usually involve a breach of Article 8, but there are significant differences between this article and the PACE rules. The article is far broader and vaguer than the PACE provisions. Further, it is not so easy to argue that, through the Human Rights Act, Parliament has decided that people should not be convicted on the basis of investigative methods which breach Article 8. There is therefore some reason for the courts to be more cautious in these cases. A decision to exclude evidence involves the sort of broad policy factors which courts are often uncomfortable with. Significantly, in the case law one finds a number of pleas for Parliament to take the lead in this area by establishing clear rules on issues such as bugging.[186] And this is in fact happening: Codes of Practice under the Regulation of Investigatory Powers Act 2000 are now in force, and these establish rules—albeit rather vague ones—for the use of intrusive surveillance. This Code will be a test case for the courts. We would argue that the courts should protect defendants by excluding evidence which has been obtained in breach of it. Considerations such as case seriousness and whether or not the police were acting in good faith should then be treated as irrelevant to the admissibility decision.

In the meantime, there is some scope for criticism of the courts in this area. Beyond

---

[184] See n 182 above. Some commentators did address their criticisms to the underlying law: see M. Zander, 'All the Evidence Suggests that we Should Change our Minds over DNA' *The Times*, 30 May 2000.

[185] Above n 129.

[186] See *Mason* (2002), above n 132, [67]; *Bailey*, above n 130, 524; *Khan*, above n 106, 175–6.

the Codes established under RIPA, Parliament has shown little interest in laying down guidelines on the use of deception in the investigation of crime. The courts should be prepared to enter such regulatory lacuna by taking on the responsibility of developing guidelines—as in some situations they have done.[187] Overall, there seems to be considerable reluctance to exclude evidence gained in breach of Convention rights. This position can be contrasted with that in New Zealand where, as we have seen, the courts are prepared to take a reasonably tough line towards breaches of the Bill of Rights. Once again, there does not appear to be any logical answer to the question of which is the better approach. But we have argued throughout this book for greater attention to be given to rights in the criminal process. The recognition of the importance of rights suggests that those rights should play a greater role in admissibility decisions. While it is understandable that the English courts should be cautious in cases involving issues such as bugging, it would be appropriate for them to take a rather firmer line.

There is one last category of case to mention, although there is very little case law on it. In *Khan*,[188] it is possible that in placing the bugging device the police committed criminal damage. In *Cooke*,[189] the Court of Appeal was prepared to accept, for the sake of argument, that the police had assaulted Cooke in order to obtain a DNA sample from him. How should such breaches of the criminal law figure in the admissibility decision? Unlike the PACE rules, these laws were not designed with the protection of suspects in mind, so it might be argued that a remedial approach is less appropriate in this context. Further, there is some merit to the argument that the criminal law does not create rights against assault and against criminal damage, but rather weaker rights to a degree of protection from these infringements.[190] But in *Cooke*, if the sample was taken unlawfully it was taken outside the protective regime for the taking of DNA samples laid down by PACE, and so exclusion appears appropriate. Things are murkier in *Khan*, but it may be that this is a case where, rather than a remedial approach, it is proper to apply some sort of integrity rationale. Given the very minor nature of the illegality, the criminal offence here does not appear to give strong grounds for exclusion.

The exclusion of improperly obtained evidence is a difficult topic. While we have discussed it at some length, there are so many possible scenarios that might have to be considered by the courts that there is still much more to be said.[191] Recently, for example, the question has arisen whether evidence obtained from third parties by the

---

[187] Most notably, on entrapment: see *Looseley*, above n 141, though note the criticism of the current state of the law in Chapter 5. See also *Mason*, n 104 above.

[188] Above n 106.   [189] [1995] 1 Cr App R 318.

[190] The argument would be that a right cannot exist without a corresponding duty (as O'Neill puts it, duties are 'the business end of ethical and political requirements': O. O'Neill, *A Question of Trust* (2002), 29); and that it is unrealistic to place a duty of perfect law enforcement on the State. For a similar argument in a different context, see P. Roberts, 'Double Jeopardy Law Reform: A Criminal Justice Commentary' (2002) 65 *MLR* 393, 409–10.

[191] For more detailed discussion, see Rishworth *et al*, above, n 169.

use of torture is admissible.[192] As for the ground that has been covered, there are relatively simple conclusions to be drawn. The integrity rationale has received considerable support in the academic literature on the exclusionary rule. But there are reasons to think that it has been oversold. It is difficult to understand exactly what the basis for exclusion under the integrity rationale is;[193] this in turn can lead to considerable vagueness in the case law. Further, where the integrity theorist argues for the exclusion of evidence obtained in breach of rights by emphasizing the importance of convicting the guilty, there is a failure to appreciate that the policy choice underlying the relevant law simply is that guilty people should not be convicted in the relevant circumstances. Our view is that, at least where a protective regime such as PACE is concerned, the remedial or protective rationale provides a sounder basis for making admissibility decisions, and that the English case law by and large endorses it. The upshot of this is that, in general, factors such as case seriousness and good faith should not feature in admissibility decisions.

11.4 OTHER EXCLUSIONARY RULES OF EVIDENCE

It would be inappropriate to conclude a discussion of criminal trials without briefly noting the very significant changes to the rules of evidence introduced by the Criminal Justice Act 2003. The Act introduces dramatic changes to the rules of evidence in two important areas: hearsay and character evidence. Where hearsay is concerned, the general rule has been that statements made out of court are not admissible as evidence of the truth of their contents. Rather than presenting the court with second-hand evidence of what was said, parties should call the person who made the statement to court to give first-hand evidence. The common law hearsay rule was complex; there existed a number of exceptions to it, some introduced by statute, and a number of less clear-cut exceptions developed through fine distinctions made in the case law.[194] The Criminal Justice Act significantly relaxes the rule.[195] It provides a narrower definition of hearsay than the one that had developed at common law and extends the existing statutory exceptions to include oral as well as documentary evidence. Most importantly, perhaps, the Act provides judges for the first time with a discretion to admit evidence that does not fit within any of the exceptions.[196] Overall, the effect is likely to be that more hearsay evidence will reach the jury.

---

[192] *A, C, D v Secretary of State for the Home Department* [2004] EWCA Civ 1123. The Court of Appeal split on this question; because the case does not involve criminal proceedings, but the special situation of appeals to the Special Immigration Appeals Commission, we do not discuss it here.

[193] See Ashworth, above n 115.

[194] See A. Ashworth and R. Pattenden, 'Reliability, Hearsay Evidence and the English Criminal Trial' (1986) 102 LQR 292 and, more generally, A. Choo, *Hearsay and Confrontation in Criminal Trials* (1996).

[195] CJA 2003, ss 114ff. For an account of the new provisions, see D. Birch, 'Hearsay: Same Old Story, Same Old Song?' [2004] Crim LR 556; P. Roberts and A. Zuckerman, *Criminal Evidence* (2004), Ch 12.

[196] CJA 2003, s114.

The basic common law rule against bad character evidence was that evidence of a defendant's previous misconduct was inadmissible. Thus, if a defendant had previous convictions, the jury would not be informed of this fact. There were a number of exceptions to this rule. Some of these related to a rather obscure distinction between propensity and credibility: thus if a defendant gave evidence attacking the character of another witness, his previous convictions could be adduced to cast doubt on his credibility, but the jury would be instructed not to take them into account when assessing the likelihood that he had committed the crime. Another important exception allowed bad character evidence to be used by the jury in assessing the latter question (whether the defendant had committed the crime) in circumstances where the bad character evidence had particular probative value. It is particularly difficult to say what the effect of the Criminal Justice Act will be in this area, because the relevant provisions are obscurely worded, but, potentially at least, the new provisions are radical.[197] They allow the introduction of bad character evidence wherever it is relevant to an issue between the prosecution and defence, including the question whether the defendant has a propensity to commit the relevant crime.[198] The Act specifically provides that the defendant's propensity to commit the crime may be proved by adducing evidence that he has been convicted of the same offence before, or of an offence 'of the same category'; it will be up to the Home Secretary to determine what offences fall within the same category.[199] So far, theft and sexual offences against children have been identified as 'categories' where there will be a presumption of admissibility.[200] Judges will, however, have a discretion to exclude bad character evidence relevant to an important issue between the prosecution and defence where admitting it would have an adverse effect on the fairness of the proceedings.

The usual justification for excluding bad character evidence is that it is potentially very prejudicial to a defendant.[201] This is arguable: a previous conviction for a serious crime can have considerable probative value.[202] Previous convictions for less serious crimes are less informative, and it is therefore worrying to see theft identified as a category where there should be a presumption of admissibility: this proposal confuses recidivism rates (high for theft) with probative value (low for, in particular, minor theft).[203] There are also problems with the new law which go beyond the potential for prejudicing the jury against the defendant. Admitting previous convictions may well undermine defendants' confidence in the criminal justice system, and lead to their perceiving their treatment as unfair. In Hood et al's study of the perceptions of minority ethnic defendants, it is striking how often defendants complained about having their past held against them when, on their view, they had changed: they had

---

[197] Section 98ff. For an account, see C. Tapper, 'Evidence of Bad Character' [2004] Crim LR 533; Roberts and Zuckerman, above n 181, Ch 11.

[198] CJA 2003, s 101.   [199] CJA 2003, s 103.

[200] Draft Criminal Justice Act (Categories of Offences) Order 2004.

[201] See S. Lloyd-Bostock, 'The Effects on Juries of Hearing About the Defendant's Previous Convictions' [2000] Crim LR 734.

[202] M. Redmayne, 'The Relevance of Bad Character' (2002) 61 *CLJ* 684.   [203] See *ibid.*

stopped using drugs, or made a genuine attempt to change their youthful ways.[204] The routine use of previous convictions would certainly add to this perception. If the Act does lead to significant relaxation of the admissibility rules, issues of compatibility with the European Convention on Human Rights will be raised. Although one can only speculate, it is likely that, to make the new rules Convention compliant, juries will have to be carefully instructed on the inferences that can permissibly be drawn from bad character evidence, just as they are with inferences from silence (see Chapter 4). The long-term effect might then be a simpler set of admissibility rules, but a more complex task for the jury in analyzing evidence in the light of judicial instructions.

The reforms to the hearsay rule are in many ways less controversial. The traditional justifications for the hearsay rule have been that juries will give too much weight to hearsay evidence and that the opponent of the party introducing it is deprived of the opportunity to cross-examine the original maker of the statement. However, it has long been recognized that hearsay evidence is sometimes the best evidence available; further, the available evidence suggests that juries do not generally give very much weight to hearsay evidence.[205] For some, the complaint about the new rules in the Criminal Justice Act will be that they do not go far enough rather than that they go too far.[206] However, there are doubts about the compatibility of the new provisions with the ECHR. The European Court of Human Rights has held that defendants have a right to challenge witnesses against them:

'evidence must normally be produced at a public hearing, in the presence of the accused, with a view to adversarial argument. There are exceptions to this principle, but they must not infringe the rights of the defence. As a general rule, paragraphs 1 and 3 (d) of Article 6 require that the defendant be given an adequate and proper opportunity to challenge and question a witness against him, either when he makes his statement or at a later stage . . . where a conviction is based solely or to a decisive degree on depositions that have been made by a person whom the accused has had no opportunity to examine or to have examined, whether during the investigation or at the trial, the rights of the defence are restricted to an extent that is incompatible with the guarantees provided by Article 6'.[207]

The CJA reforms are not necessarily in tension with this view of trial fairness: courts in England and Wales can attempt to ensure compliance with the Convention by excluding hearsay evidence which infringes the terms of the Strasbourg case law. However, there are already signs that the Court of Appeal is unhappy with the strength of the right to challenge developed in Europe. In *R v M(KJ)*[208] it refused to believe that the case law meant that, where a witness refused to give evidence through fear, hearsay evidence of what that witness had said should be inadmissible because it deprived the defendant of the right to challenge witnesses against him.

---

[204] Above n 52.

[205] R. Park, 'Visions of Applying the Scientific Method to the Hearsay Rule' (2003) *Mich St L Rev* 1149; R. Park, 'Empirical Evaluation of the Hearsay Rule' in Mirfield and Smith, above n 175.

[206] See Birch, above n 195, for discussion of this view.

[207] *Luca v Italy* (2003) 36 EHRR 46 [39]–[40].   [208] (2003) 2 Cr App R 322.

The situation in Europe can be put in perspective by looking briefly at developments in the US. There, the Sixth Amendment to the Constitution guarantees a defendant's right to confront the witnesses against him, and the Supreme Court has recently interpreted this as a strong right.[209] In applying it to hearsay evidence, the reliability of the evidence no longer matters. A defendant simply has the right to see a witness stand up in court and make the incriminating statement there. This right might, however, be forfeited if the witness is unavailable owing to something done by the defendant. There is obviously room for debate about the wisdom of such a right, but the fact that a number of commentators view it as a fundamental component of a fair trial should make us think carefully about some of the amendments introduced by the Criminal Justice Act.[210]

In summary, three points can be made about the changes to the character and hearsay rules introduced by the Criminal Justice Act. The Government has tended to package these reforms as part of a movement to improve the lot of victims in the criminal justice system.[211] This is disingenuous. No one's lot is improved if bad character evidence simply prejudices juries against defendants, or if juries rely on unreliable hearsay evidence. Secondly, these reforms appear to be part of a general movement in the law of evidence away from strict rules of inadmissibility, and towards the use of judicial discretion to decide admissibility questions.[212] While many would see this as part of an inevitable process in which we finally come to trust juries fully, things may not be this simple. Where hearsay or character evidence is admitted, it is likely to be accompanied by warnings and instructions about its proper use, much as has happened with inferences from silence (see Chapter 4). This approach places considerable responsibility on the judge to ensure trial fairness by guiding the jury through the implications of the evidence. In some ways this may make the task of both judge and jury more complex, and certainly does not indicate unalloyed trust in the jury.

Finally, in so far as these reforms do show that, as a matter of policy, we are no longer so worried about placing too much trust in the jury, they prompt us to think more deeply about what it is that makes a trial fair. Hearsay raises questions about the defendant's right to confront witnesses, and with character evidence we need to ask whether dragging up a defendant's past is somehow unfair irrespective of the danger of prejudice.[213] Arguably, then, the criminal trial will come to be seen as structured by deeper and more complex notions of fairness than those associated with the unreliability of certain types of evidence. When discussing the exclusion of unfairly and

---

[209] *Crawford v Washington* 124 S Ct 1354 (2004).

[210] See R. Friedman, 'Confrontation: The Search for Basic Principles' (1998) 86 *Geo LJ* 1011; R. Friedman, 'Thoughts from Across the Water on Hearsay and Confrontation' [1998] Crim LR 697.

[211] J. Jackson, 'Justice for All: Putting Victims at the Heart of Criminal Justice' [2003] 30 *JLS* 309.

[212] See E. Swift, 'One Hundred Years of Evidence Law Reform: Thayer's Triumph' (2000) 88 *California L Rev* 2437.

[213] For some thoughts on this, see P. Tillers, 'What is Wrong with Character Evidence?' (1998) 49 *Hastings LJ* 781.

improperly obtained evidence we showed how notions of procedural fairness have come to be recognized as important aspects of the criminal trial, as well as how some of these ideas might be developed. The criminal trial is not just about getting the right result, in terms of accurately distinguishing between the innocent and the guilty; it is also about doing so in a proper manner. Only by thinking carefully about the demands of justice can we come to have a full understanding of the criminal trial and the rules that should govern it.

12

APPEALS

The appeals system serves many purposes. From the legal system's point of view, perhaps the most important purpose is the development and clarification of the law. A common law system could hardly exist unless appeals offered a means of reviewing the law. In performing this role, appeals allow the higher courts to exert some control over the lower courts. These are important functions of appeals and add much to an understanding of the forces shaping the appeals system. This chapter, however, tends to look at appeals from the point of view of litigants, for whom appeals offer a chance to challenge a result they are unhappy with. Such challenges have provided the criminal justice system with some of its most memorable images: the photographs of victims of long-running miscarriages of justice, such as the 'Guildford four' and the 'Birmingham six', celebrating their freedom on the steps of the Court of Appeal have a dramatic resonance. Like much media coverage of the criminal justice system, such images, if taken to be representative of what the appeals system is all about, are apt to mislead. For one thing, it is not only the Court of Appeal that hears criminal appeals. Further, while the criminal appeals system does play an important role in securing the acquittal of those who dispute the facts on which they were found guilty, the majority of appeals do not revolve around questions of fact. Most appeals involve legal issues. The legal issues vary: in a large number of appeals the question is solely about whether the sentence given by the court was correct.[1] Other appeals involve questions about the criminal law: whether, for example, the court applied the correct definition of some legal concept such as 'intention'. We will not consider such appeals in this chapter. The focus will be on the atypical, but important, appeals on questions of fact. We will also look at some appeals on questions of law, but only where the legal questions involve the defendant's procedural rights. These 'due process appeals' have given rise to difficult questions about when the courts should quash the convictions of the factually guilty.

Before moving on to consider these issues, it will be helpful to offer a brief overall sketch of the criminal appeals system. As well as the distinctions just mentioned, there is also a difference in the way prosecution and defence appeals are treated by the system: in general, prosecution appeals are more restricted than defence appeals, albeit that recent reforms have diminished this distinction. Bearing this in mind, both

---

[1] In 2003 the Court of Appeal heard 2,364 sentence appeals and 542 conviction appeals: *Judicial Statistics 2003*, 15.

prosecution and defence have rights of appeal from decisions of the magistrates' courts. The defence can appeal on questions of fact; here, appeal is to the Crown Court, which hears the appeal as a specially constituted panel of two judges sitting with a magistrate. This type of criminal appeal is unique in that it involves a rehearing of the case: the witnesses will be heard again, and their evidence assessed afresh. In most other appeals the court will hear argument from the parties, but it is rare for an appeal court to hear evidence from witnesses. Both prosecution and defence are also able to appeal from the magistrates' court on questions of law. Here, appeal is by way of 'case stated' to the Divisional Court: the magistrates are asked to supply a statement of the facts of the case as they have found them, as well as their legal conclusions; this will provide the basis on which the court hears the appeal. Both parties are also able to challenge the magistrates' decision on legal grounds by way of judicial review.[2] The case will be heard by the Divisional Court. From the Divisional Court, further appeal is possible to the House of Lords: leave will only be granted for points of law of general public importance.

From the Crown Court as a court of first instance, a defendant is able to appeal against a finding of guilt on grounds of either fact or law. Appeal is to the Court of Appeal, from where either party may appeal to the House of Lords. The prosecution has fewer appeal rights. Since 1987, it has been able to appeal certain pre-trial rulings to the Court of Appeal; this jurisdiction was originally confined to serious fraud cases, but was enlarged in 1996 to include all lengthy or complex cases.[3] The Criminal Justice Act 2003 will allow prosecution appeals on rulings made by the judge during the trial; if the prosecution is not successful in the Court of Appeal the effect will often be the acquittal of the defendant. These prosecution appeals involve points of law. Until recently, the situation was that the prosecution was not able to appeal against an acquittal in the Crown Court.[4] One (so far unused) exception to this rule was introduced in 1996, when the prosecution was given the power to challenge an acquittal that was tainted by, for example, threats of violence to jurors or witnesses.[5] The Criminal Justice Act 2003 takes things further, allowing appeals against acquittals in serious cases where significant new evidence of guilt emerges after the trial. With both these exceptions to the 'double jeopardy' principle there is a fairly complex process designed to ensure that an acquittal is not too easily challenged.

---

[2] The judicial review procedure would occasionally allow a decision of fact to be challenged, where the magistrates can be shown to have drawn an unreasonable conclusion.

[3] Under Criminal Justice Act 1987, s 9 and Criminal Procedure and Investigations Act 1996, ss 35–6. Section 309 of the CJA 2003 now adds 'seriousness' to the criteria for preparatory hearings under the CPIA.

[4] The Attorney General is able to obtain a ruling on a point of law arising in a case in which the defendant was acquitted, but this is not a true appeal as the defendant's acquittal is unaffected. The power is found in the Criminal Justice Act 1972, s 36.

[5] Criminal Procedure and Investigations Act 1996, s 54.

12.1 RESTRICTIONS ON APPEAL RIGHTS

The foregoing sketch is one-dimensional in that it illustrates the various avenues of appeal but says nothing about the conditions for appeal. A very important aspect of the appeal process is the way in which appeals are restricted and discouraged. All appeals from the Crown Court involve some sort of leave, either from the trial judge or from the Court of Appeal itself. This important filtering exercise will be discussed further below. Where the prosecution is concerned we have already seen that the appeal rights are on the whole less generous. Although the CJA 2003 extends prosecution appeal rights by allowing appeals from legal rulings by a Crown Court judge, prosecutors may well be discouraged from exercising this right by the possibility that, it they lose the appeal, the defendant will be acquitted.[6] Where defendants are concerned, there are also disincentives. For example, in the magistrates' court the appeal avenue to the Divisional Court by way of case stated or as an application for judicial review will generally only allow parties to appeal questions of law. A defendant who contends that the magistrates have made a factual mistake can appeal to the Crown Court. Although this right of appeal initially looks to be generous—the defendant does not need leave to appeal—there is a disincentive in that the Crown Court can increase his sentence. According to Pattenden, the power to increase sentence 'is not used very often'; however 'this fact is probably not well known'.[7] The power may well dissuade defendants from exercising their right of appeal; indeed, some commentators suspect that it exists partly for this purpose.[8] Another restriction on appeal to the Crown Court is that the right can only be exercised by those who have pleaded not guilty.[9] As we saw in Chapter 10, the vast majority of convictions at summary trial are achieved by way of guilty plea. This might not be troubling were it not for the fact that the guilty plea is not always a reliable indicator of guilt. The Crown Court has gone some way towards mitigating this rule by allowing a case where a guilty plea can be shown to be 'equivocal', or to have been made under duress, to be remitted to the magistrates for reconsideration. This, however, probably does not cover the situation where a defendant has pleaded guilty for a tactical reason (for example, because he thought his case was weak and he wanted to benefit from the sentence discount), or after 'forceful' persuasion from his lawyer which does not amount to duress.[10]

Turning to consider appeal to the Court of Appeal from trial in the Crown Court, we find a similar disincentive. Although the Court of Appeal does not have the power to increase sentence on a defence appeal, it can achieve something very similar. It may

---

[6] Though in this respect contrast ss 58 and 62 of the CJA 2003. These provisions are discussed in more detail below.

[7] R. Pattenden, *English Criminal Appeals 1844–1994* (1996), 219.

[8] *Ibid.*; J. Sprack, *Emmins on Criminal Procedure* (9th ed., 2002), 458.

[9] Magistrates' Courts Act 1980, s 108.

[10] 'Forceful' advice on plea is permitted under the Bar Code of Conduct. See the general discussion of guilty pleas in Chapter 10.

take several months for a defendant's appeal to be heard by the Court of Appeal. Many defendants will have spent this time in custody, and normally the time served in custody up to the failure of an appeal will be counted as part of the defendant's sentence. The Court of Appeal, however, has the power to rule that time served will not be subtracted from the sentence.[11] Effectively, then, the time served is treated as an additional punishment for defendants who are thought to be wasting the Court's time. Guidelines restrict the use of this power:[12] loss of time should normally not be ordered if the appeal has been supported by legal advice, unless the situation is that the application for leave to appeal was initially turned down but has been renewed.[13] In practice it appears that loss of time orders are rarely made, and are limited to 28 days loss of time. Nevertheless, as with the power to increase sentence in the Crown Court, it is likely that the possibility of loss of time acts as a significant deterrent to those minded to appeal, in part because it is not widely known that the power is used with restraint.[14] Indeed, the form to be completed by appellants brings the possibility of loss of time to their attention, but does not mention the constraints that have been developed.[15]

The loss of time rule and the power to increase sentence in the Crown Court are disturbing. Rather like the sentence discount for a guilty plea, their effect is to discourage defendants from pursuing their legal rights. As with the sentence discount, the justification for this is that such powers are necessary in order to prevent the courts from being overwhelmed by unmeritorious cases. In both areas this claim is difficult to assess: with the sentence discount there is some evidence to suggest that the flood of newly contested cases would not be that great.[16] With the loss of time rule, it appears that when the Court's intention to use the power was announced in a Practice Direction,[17] the number of appeals was halved.[18] What cannot be known, of course, is how many meritorious appeals are deterred. Where the Court of Appeal is concerned, the arguments are complicated by the system of leave to appeal. Leave offers a means of filtering out the weakest cases before they result in a full court hearing, and this might be thought to be a more rational way of dealing with the possible flood of appeals than the threat of extra punishment. However, even the leave process requires judicial time and, the argument goes, some deterrent is needed in order to ensure that the most meritorious cases are dealt with carefully and promptly.

The loss of time rule has been challenged before the European Court of Human Rights. The Court held that the rule did not infringe Article 6 (fair trial) nor, more surprisingly, Article 5(1) (right to liberty and security of person). The exception in

---

[11] Criminal Appeal Act 1968, s 29.
[12] *A Guide to Proceedings in the Court of Appeal Criminal Division* (1997), para 9.
[13] *Gayle, The Times*, 16 May 1986; *Wanklyn, The Times*, 12 November 1984.
[14] For an actual example, see *Morley, The Times*, 25 January 1995.
[15] CACD, Form NG. See also Practice Direction (Criminal: Consolidated) [2002] 3 All ER 904, [16]. Cf Royal Commission on Criminal Justice, *Report* (1993), Ch 10, para 19.
[16] M. Tonry, *Punishment and Politics* (2004), 87.   [17] [1970] 1 All ER 119.
[18] See *Monnell and Morris v UK* (1988) 10 EHRR 205, 30.

Article 5(1)(a), which allows 'lawful detention of a person after conviction by a competent court', was held to apply to the loss of time rule. This, it must be said, is puzzling. The ECtHR acknowledged that this exception does not permit just any lawful detention after conviction: there must be some rational connection between the conviction and the detention. Given that the time added to the sentence through the loss of time rule is not part of the punishment for the offence for which the defendant was convicted, it is not easy to see what this connection could be. The Court's explanation was that:

'Whilst the loss of time ordered by the Court of Appeal is not treated under domestic law as part of the applicants' sentences as such, it does form part of the period of detention which results from the overall sentencing procedure that follows conviction. As a matter of English law, a sentence of imprisonment passed by a Crown Court is to be served subject to any order which the Court of Appeal may, in the event of an unsuccessful application for leave to appeal, make as to loss of time.'[19]

The difficulty here is that this reasoning could be used to justify any further detention ordered after conviction: if, after an unsuccessful appeal, it was the practice of the Court of Appeal to toss a coin as a means of deciding whether or not to double the appellant's sentence, this too could be said to be one of the conditions understood to be imposed by a Crown Court sentence. Subsequent decisions of the Court have taken a rather tougher line to the use of detention as a means of controlling appeals processes, and the decision in *Monnell* might now be subject to rethinking.[20] To point out that the loss of time rule is very difficult to justify does not help the Court of Appeal with what is a difficult problem: the need to ration its procedures in order to make sure that it can function effectively. But it does underline the need to think carefully about the rule and its application, and the need to give the Court sufficient resources to deal with applications for leave to appeal.

As has been pointed out, the requirement for leave to appeal is in principle a more rational way of dealing with the problem of a flood of appeals. The system works as follows. A convicted defendant needs to obtain leave before his appeal will be heard by the Court of Appeal. This can be obtained from the judge who tried him, but, as the appeal will often involve some criticism of the judge, it is more common for appellants to apply to the Court of Appeal for leave to appeal. When an application is made, it will first be considered by a single judge. If the application is unsuccessful at this stage, it can be renewed; the renewed application is considered by the 'full court': a panel of two or three judges sitting in open court. If leave to appeal is granted, the appeal proceeds to a full hearing by the Court of Appeal. Table 12.1 gives a breakdown of the success rate at the various stages of this process for appeals against conviction over the last five years. In proportional terms, in 2003 about four per cent of all those convicted in the Crown Court sought leave to appeal against their convictions. Twenty

---

[19] *Ibid.*, 46.
[20] *Omar v France* (2000) 29 EHRR 210. See further B. Emmerson and A. Ashworth, *Human Rights and Criminal Justice* (2001), 522–3.

Table 12.1 Success Rates for Appeals Against Conviction.

		1999	2000	2001	2002	2003
Applications for Leave Received		2,104	2,068	1,943	1,914	1,787
Single Judge	Leave Granted	480	508	438	405	472
	Leave Refused	1,402	1,351	1,145	1,334	1,213
Applications Renewed to Full Court		637	551	422	457	561
	Leave Granted	123	144	150	140	138
Appeal Heard by Full Court	Appeal Allowed	171	150	135	166	178

Source: *Judicial Statistics 2003.*

six per cent of applications for leave were granted by the single judge. Of the 74 per cent that were refused, nearly half (46 per cent) made a renewed application to the full court. On this renewed attempt to get leave, a quarter were successful. From the 1,787 original applications, this gives an overall success rate in obtaining leave of 34 per cent. Of the 542 appeals heard by the full court that year, 33 per cent were successful. Of the original 1,787 applicants, then, about ten per cent would finally succeed in having their convictions quashed.

It is not obvious what to make of these figures: there is no telling whether or not ten per cent is a reasonable overall success rate. What is perhaps significant is that many who have their applications turned down by the single judge persist and have a reasonable chance of success on the renewed application to the full court. This suggests that the initial stage, where the application is considered by a single judge, is somewhat haphazard. Other evidence supports this. JUSTICE, a body with consider-able experience of miscarriage of justice cases, suggests that the process 'is regarded as particularly susceptible to inconsistency'.[21] It provides the following anecdote about one appeal against sentence: a solicitor mistakenly sent in two sets of appeal papers in the same case. 'Two single judge decisions followed, one granting and one refusing leave. Both decisions had been made, at different times, by the same judge.'[22] In his review of the criminal courts, Lord Justice Auld drew attention to some of the problems with the system: the single judge is required to consider applications for leave 'out of normal court sitting hours and in addition to preparatory work for each day's

---

[21] *Remedying Miscarriages of Justice* (1994), 8.   [22] *Ibid.*

sitting. . . . The norm is that they are done in the evenings, sometimes over the weekend and during vacation periods.'[23] It seems that the system is not properly resourced, and it is therefore not surprising that inconsistent decisions are made at the initial stage.

Returning to appeals from the magistrates' court to the Crown Court, it is worth looking at the available figures to see how they compare with those for the Court of Appeal. In 2003 there were nearly 12,000 such appeals: this represents less than one per cent of all those found guilty in the magistrates' courts. In 4,990 of these appeals (about 42 per cent), the appeal was allowed or the sentence varied.[24] The rate of appeal is very low: the figures given here combine appeals against verdict with appeals against sentence; using figures for 2000, Malleson and Roberts report that the rate of appeal against *verdict* to the Crown Court (which constitutes nearly all appeals where it is alleged that the magistrates have made a mistaken factual finding) is about 0.4 per cent. They note that it is hard to believe that there is a 99.6 per cent accurate conviction rate in the magistrates' court, and thus conclude that some unsafe convictions in that court are not being appealed against.[25] This may in part be due to the fear of an increased sentence and perhaps also to poor legal advice, but it may also be due to defendants simply not perceiving it worthwhile to appeal against a conviction, especially if the punishment has not been harsh. Beyond these figures, and the inferences that can be drawn from them, little is known about the appellate process in the Crown Court. This remains an under-researched area of the criminal process.

12.2 CHALLENGING JURY VERDICTS

Our focus now turns to the Court of Appeal, where it will remain for the rest of the chapter. When the Royal Commission on Criminal Justice reported in 1993, considerable critical attention was focused on the Court of Appeal. The Court was seen to have played a key role in the long-running miscarriage of justice cases that were finally rectified in the late 1980s and early 1990s. The Birmingham six and Guildford four had both had appeals dismissed by the Court soon after their convictions; the Birmingham six had also had a second appeal turned down in 1986. There was a widespread perception that the Court of Appeal had been unduly sceptical of claims of miscarriage of justice during the 1980s, and that some defendants had had

---

[23] Auld LJ, *Review of the Criminal Courts of England and Wales: Report* (2001), 639.

[24] *Judicial Statistics 2003*, 74–5. The success rate is in fact probably somewhat greater than this suggests: the available figures tell us that in about a quarter of appeals the appeal was abandoned or 'otherwise disposed'; among the latter category are cases remitted to the magistrates after an equivocal plea. If these cases are ignored, then the success rate is over 50 per cent.

[25] K. Malleson and S. Roberts, 'Streamlining and Clarifying the Appellate Process' [2002] Crim LR 272, 274.

their appeals dismissed unjustly.[26] Connected to this complaint that the Court has been over-sceptical is a criticism that it has tended to show too much deference to jury verdicts, in other words, that the Court is reluctant to interfere with a jury's decision to convict a defendant. There is a good deal of truth in the claim that the Court shows considerable deference to the jury.[27] Three possible reasons for this are worth identifying at this point. First, the Court of Appeal is at a disadvantage in relation to the jury. The jury will have seen and heard the witnesses in the case, whereas the Court of Appeal will only have access to the transcript of the original trial. While the Court may hear some live evidence, its role is restricted to that of reviewing the case, rather than rehearing it. Further, the jury does not give reasons for its decisions, thus the Court of Appeal lacks access to the precise reasons why the jury became convinced of the defendant's guilt. Secondly, the jury plays a crucial role in the criminal justice system, deciding whether or not defendants are guilty in the most serious contested cases. The criminal justice system puts considerable trust in the jury to make these decisions. If the Court of Appeal interfered with jury verdicts too readily, it would put itself in the uncomfortable position of questioning the ability of the jury to reach correct verdicts: it might be thought to be undermining the very system which it oversees. A third reason why the Court may be reluctant to interfere with jury verdicts is that this may be a by-product of a much more general reluctance of Appeal Courts to interfere with the decisions of trial courts.[28] Any legal system needs to be able to reach decisions with a reasonable degree of finality. There is considerable value in seeing the verdict as an authoritative ruling on a disputed issue: this allows interested parties to get on with their lives with a clear view of what their legal position is. If verdicts are too readily overturned, then this sense of finality will be eroded.

It is not surprising, then, to find the Royal Commission on Criminal Justice commenting that:

'In its approach to the consideration of appeals against conviction, the Court of Appeal seems to us to have been too heavily influenced by the role of the jury in Crown Court trials. Ever since 1907, commentators have detected a reluctance on the part of the Court of Appeal to consider whether a jury has reached a wrong decision. This impression is underlined by research conducted on our behalf. This shows that most appeals are allowed on the basis of errors at the trial, usually in the judge's summing up. We are all of the opinion that the Court of Appeal should be readier to overturn jury verdicts than it has shown itself to be in the past.'[29]

In the aftermath of the Royal Commission's report, there were a number of changes to the appeals system. A new body, the Criminal Cases Review Commission, was

---

[26] On the appeal of the Birmingham six, see C. Mullin, *Error of Judgement* (1990), Chs 41–4. More generally, see J. Rozenberg, 'Miscarriages of Justice' in E. Stockdale and S. Casale, *Criminal Justice under Stress* (1992); A. Zuckerman, 'Miscarriage of Justice and Judicial Responsibility' [1991] Crim LR 492.

[27] This is made plain in *Pendleton* [2001] UKHL 66.

[28] R. Nobles and D. Schiff, 'The Right to Appeal and Workable Systems of Justice' (2002) 65 *MLR* 676.

[29] Above n 15, 162.

established to take over the role of the Home Office in investigating miscarriages of justice and referring cases back to the Court of Appeal in cases where defendants have exhausted their normal appeal rights. There were also modifications to the Criminal Appeal Act 1968, which governs the powers of the Court of Appeal. The Act now provides that the Court of Appeal 'shall allow an appeal against conviction if they think the conviction is unsafe' and shall 'dismiss such an appeal in any other case'.[30] There were also changes to the Court's power to hear 'fresh' evidence. As noted above, the Court of Appeal is basically a court of review: it does not rehear cases. But sometimes new evidence will emerge after the conclusion of a trial, throwing doubt on the original verdict. Here, the question arises whether the Court of Appeal should hear such 'fresh' evidence. There is some concern that a defendant will simply fail to call important evidence at his initial trial, knowing that, should he be convicted, he will be able to challenge the verdict on appeal by revealing the evidence then. For this reason, the reception of fresh evidence is not automatic; the Court will be very reluctant to admit it if it could have been adduced at the original trial. The Royal Commission criticized the Court of Appeal for being too reluctant to admit fresh evidence; the Criminal Appeal Act now provides in s 23 that the Court should hear fresh evidence where this is 'necessary or expedient in the interests of justice', having regard to a number of factors such as 'whether the evidence appears to the court to be capable of belief' and 'whether there is a reasonable explanation for failure to adduce the evidence' at the original trial.[31]

The legal framework described in the previous paragraph obviously leaves considerable discretion to the Court of Appeal. Before examining how the Court approaches conviction appeals, one more aspect of its powers needs to be mentioned. If the Court decides that a conviction is unsafe, that does not necessarily mean that the appellant will go free. Since 1964 the Court has had the power to order a retrial.[32] Thus, if there remain doubts about the appellant's guilt, he can be retried by a new jury. This will not always be appropriate: there may have been such a lapse of time since the original trial that a retrial is no longer practical. In some cases, there will have been such media attention around the case that there will be doubts about the fairness of a new trial.[33] It has been held that the approach to the question of whether a conviction is unsafe should be cleanly separated from the retrial issue: the court should not be more ready to quash a conviction in a case where it knows that a retrial is a viable option than in a case where it is aware that it is making the final determination.[34] However, there can be little doubt that the retrial power has some affect on the way the court approaches its task. For one thing, the retrial power allows the court to combine a concern for the integrity of the original trial with respect for the jury as the final decision maker in the criminal process.

---

[30] Criminal Appeal Act 1968, s2(1). The amendments were introduced by the Criminal Appeal Act 1995.

[31] Criminal Appeal Act 1968, s23.

[32] The history of this reform is described in R. Nobles and D. Schiff, *Understanding Miscarriages of Justice* (2000), 62–4.

[33] On the approach to this, see *Stone* [2001] Crim LR 465.   [34] *Pendleton*, above n 27.

As we have seen, the Royal Commission urged the Court of Appeal to overturn jury verdicts more readily. One way of trying to assess whether there has been any change in the Court's attitude since 1993 is to look at the basic statistics. Here, it appears that the Court of Appeal is today actually quashing fewer convictions than it was ten years ago. In the early 1990s about 45 per cent of appeals heard by the full Court were successful. In 2000–2003 the figure was around 33 per cent. One should not jump to the conclusion that the Court of Appeal has, contrary to the wishes of the Royal Commission, become less receptive to appeals. There are a number of possible explanations for the change in success rate over the last decade. It may be that in the early 1990s the introduction of PACE and the CPS was still working through the system. Now that these changes have fully bedded in, the cases against defendants may simply be stronger, or at least harder to challenge. Changes in technology, such as the use of DNA evidence and CCTV, may also have played a role.

When it comes to the introduction of fresh evidence, it seems that the Court of Appeal's working practices have changed little. Roberts has replicated research carried out for the Royal Commission, by examining appeals heard by the Court in 2002. She found that fresh evidence was a ground of appeal in slightly more cases than it had been in 1990: 23 grounds of appeal from 300 cases in 1990 involved fresh evidence, compared with 37 from 300 cases in 2002.[35] Given that all of these cases had passed the leave stage, it suggests that the court is, in some sense, being more receptive to fresh evidence (this issue is very hard to be precise about, because the court sometimes hears fresh evidence '*de bene esse*', i.e. without specifying whether it passes the test in s 23, but may then declare the fresh evidence unconvincing). Against this, however, Roberts found that fresh evidence was a slightly less successful ground of appeal in 2002 than in 1990 (a 27 per cent success rate as compared to 35 per cent in 1990). Perhaps the court is hearing more fresh evidence but remains no more receptive to it as a ground for overturning a conviction.

It is obvious that an argument from fresh evidence is a relatively rare ground of appeal, making up only around seven per cent of grounds. As the Royal Commission noted, appeals are far more likely to be successful where it is argued that a (legal) error was made at trial. It is especially difficult for a defendant to mount a successful appeal when he can point to no error at trial and has no fresh evidence. Such appeals are often referred to as 'lurking doubt' appeals. The appellant is basically arguing that the jury made a mistake on the evidence as it was presented to it at trial, and here one would expect the court to be most sensitive about its role in relation to that of the jury. Roberts found this ground of appeal referred to in seven of the 300 appeals from 2002, and in only one of these was it successful. We briefly discussed a case of this sort in Chapter 9. In *R v B*, the court quashed a conviction for sexual abuse which was alleged to have occurred some thirty years before the trial.[36] There was no reference

---

[35] S. Roberts, 'The Royal Commission on Criminal Justice and Factual Innocence' (2004) 1 JUSTICE Journal 86, 91. There was a general growth in the number of grounds of appeal.

[36] [2003] EWCA Crim 319.

either to lurking doubt or to the Criminal Appeal Act; the Court simply justified its decision by referring to a 'residual discretion to set aside a conviction if we feel it is unsafe or unfair to allow it to stand.'[37] The ambivalence here (was the conviction unsafe or was the trial unfair?) indicates the difficulty lurking doubt cases can cause. If the prosecution case was demonstrably weak, then the appeal would not be a lurking doubt one but a challenge to the judge's (legal) decision to allow the trial to proceed after a submission of no case to answer.[38] In a lurking doubt case the Court is invited to quash a conviction without, perhaps, being able to explain exactly why it is doing so. As the lurking doubt test is described in *Cooper*: 'the court must in the end ask itself a subjective question, whether we are content to let the matter stand as it is, or whether there is not some lurking doubt in our minds which makes us wonder whether an injustice has been done. This is a reaction which may not be based strictly on the evidence as such: it is a reaction which can be produced by the general feel of the case as the court experiences it'.[39] The lurking doubt test seems to push the court beyond its ability to justify its decision with reasons, and it is therefore not surprising that it is reluctant to resort to it. What may happen, however, is that a feeling of lurking doubt will make the Court of Appeal more ready to allow the appeal on some legal ground. This can be seen in *R v B*: 'unfair' hints at a legal ground for allowing the appeal, something rather more substantial than the court's unease about the conviction on purely factual grounds.

In a fresh evidence appeal, an appellant is on slightly firmer ground. His argument is not that the jury simply got it wrong, but that there is evidence, never heard by the jury, which makes the conviction unsafe. This raises the question of how the Court of Appeal should react to the fresh evidence. The issue was considered by the House of Lords in *Pendleton*. The question is sometimes said to involve a choice between a 'jury impact' test and a test whereby the Court of Appeal concentrates on its own reaction to the evidence. The previous authority, *Stafford*, had rejected the jury impact test. The Court, it was held, should not ask whether the new evidence might have made a difference to the jury, but come to it its own view of the significance and credibility of the evidence. It is not always easy to see the difference between these two approaches. The sort of difference the test might make is alluded to in *Stafford*, where it was noted that the appellant had 'urged that the court should recognise that reasonable men can come to different conclusions on contested issues of fact and that, although the court came to the conclusion that the fresh evidence raised no reasonable doubt as to the guilt of the accused, they should nonetheless quash the conviction if they thought that a jury might reasonably take a different view.'[40] That there is an issue worth arguing about here is also hinted at by the Royal Commission, which contended that *Stafford* was open to criticism 'insofar as it concerns a decision by the court to hear and evaluate itself the fresh evidence and despite it to reject the appeal. In our view, once the court has decided to receive evidence that is relevant and capable of belief, and

---

[37] *Ibid.*, [27].   [38] *Galbraith* [1981] 1 WLR 1039, discussed in Chapter 11.
[39] *Cooper* [1969] 1 QB 267, 271.   [40] *Stafford v DPP* [1973] 3 All ER 763, 765.

which could have altered the outcome of the case, it should quash the conviction and order a retrial unless that is not practicable or desirable.'[41] Arguably, evidence can be capable of belief even if the court itself does not believe it. Under the Royal Commission's approach, it seems that the court would avoid taking a view on the credibility of a witness called to present fresh evidence (rather along the lines of *Galbraith*[42]). Where, however, a retrial is impracticable, the Commission thought that the only approach was to follow *Stafford*, and to allow the Court to decide the issue for itself.

The simplest thing to say about *Pendleton* is that it rejects the criticisms of the Royal Commission and follows *Stafford*. The outcome is that the Court should come to its own view of the safety of the conviction, and therefore the question of the practicality of a retrial does not arise until it is decided whether or not the conviction should be quashed. The appellant had argued that this approach undermined the role of the jury: only the jury impact test truly recognized the centrality of the jury in trial on indictment. The response of the House of Lords was that this got things the wrong way round: the real way to respect the jury was to be rather more reluctant to overturn its verdict. According to Lord Hobhouse, 'it is the appellant's argument which is unprincipled since it is he who is seeking to escape from the verdict of a jury merely upon the possibility . . . that the jury might have returned a different verdict.'[43] Beyond this, things get more complicated. It was emphasized that the question for the Court of Appeal is 'whether the conviction is safe and not whether the accused is guilty'.[44] The significance of this is not immediately clear; in most fresh evidence cases the defendant's argument will not be that there was some procedural irregularity which makes the defendant's conviction unsafe whether or not he is guilty. The argument will simply be that the fresh evidence raises doubts about the defendant's guilt. In *Pendleton* itself, however, it was argued that, had the fresh evidence been available at the time of trial, the defendant would have run a different defence, arguing not that he had observed but not participated in the murder, but that he had not even been present at the scene of crime. In this context, the safety/guilt distinction implies that something more akin to the jury impact test is being applied. As Lord Bingham commented: 'had the jury been trying a different case on substantially different evidence the outcome must be in doubt'.[45] This view is supported by the fact that Lord Bingham, while seeming to reject the jury impact test, nevertheless allowed that it could play a useful role: 'First, it reminds the Court of Appeal that it is not and should never become the primary decision-maker. Secondly, it reminds the Court of Appeal

---

[41] Above n 15, 175.   [42] [1989] 1 WLR 1039; see discussion in Chapter 11.

[43] Above n 27, 36.

[44] *Ibid.*, 19. In *Hakala* [2002] EWCA Crim 730 at 5, this was interpreted as a reference to the sort of situation in *Mullen*, where a factually correct verdict was tainted by abuse of process. From the context of the dicta in *Pendleton*, however, it is most unlikely that this is what the House of Lords had in mind. Dennis notes that there are similar dicta to those in *Pendleton* in *Hickey* (CA 30 July 1997), but observes that they are hard to reconcile with cases such as *Hanratty* [2002] 3 All ER 534, where the Court of Appeal heard fresh DNA evidence from the prosecution: I. Dennis, 'Fair Trials and Safe Convictions' (2003) 56 *CLP* 211, 223.

[45] Above n 27, 28.

that it has an imperfect and incomplete understanding of the full processes which led the jury to convict.'[46] Thus the Court would find it useful to test its own view by asking whether the fresh evidence might reasonably have affected the jury.

There is a further complication in *Pendleton*. A second judgment in the case was given by Lord Hobhouse, and there are differences between his approach and that of Lord Bingham. Hobhouse makes no mention of the jury impact test; if anything he distances himself from it.[47] Nevertheless, when he comes to address the safety of the conviction in *Pendleton*, his analysis is in terms of the impact that the new evidence, and the different defence it would have allowed the defendant to run, would have had on the jury. This suggests that the peculiar nature of the facts in *Pendleton*—the fresh evidence raised a new defence—may have made the issues especially amenable to analysis in terms of jury impact.

Evidently, *Pendleton* leaves some uncertainty over the question of what approach should be taken to fresh evidence cases. When we turn to look at what the Court of Appeal has made of this judgment, then, it is not altogether surprising to find that no consistent approach has emerged. One of the first cases to consider *Pendleton* was *Hakala*,[48] which associated itself with the more restrictive approach of Lord Hobhouse rather than the jury impact dicta of Lord Bingham. *Pendleton* was interpreted as simply confirming the decision in *Stafford*. In other cases it has been said that after *Pendleton* the test is whether the jury would inevitably have convicted.[49] That view echoes the jury impact line, but lies in stark contrast to Auld LJ's statement in *Maloney* that: 'The issue is not whether the Court considers, in the light of the proposed fresh evidence, that a jury might conceivably have reached a different decision if it had heard it. So, ... the Court should beware against adopting, consciously or unconsciously, a train of thought that unless they can be certain the jury would have convicted had they heard the proffered fresh evidence, the conviction must be unsafe.'[50] One might wonder how much is at stake here. The distinction between the narrow and wide views can appear very thin, so in practice these conflicting opinions may not amount to much. There are, however, cases where *Pendleton* has been used to justify a decision which might not otherwise have been made. An appeal in *Mills and Poole* had been heard by the Court of Appeal in 1996 and dismissed. In 2002 the Criminal Cases Review Commission referred the case back to the Court, giving as one of its reasons for doing so the recent decision in *Pendleton*. In considering the new appeal, which was allowed, *Pendleton* appears to have made the court particularly cautious about making its own judgments as to the credibility of witnesses.[51] In *R v Criminal Cases Review Commission, ex p Farnell*,[52] an application for judicial review of a decision by the CCRC not to refer a case to the Court of Appeal was successful; *Pendleton* was again used to justify the decision. The case in question

---

[46] *Ibid.*, 19.   [47] See *ibid.* at 38.   [48] [2002] EWCA Crim 730.
[49] See *Gray* [2003] EWCA 1001 at 13; *Ward* [2003] EWCA Crim 3191 at 9.
[50] [2003] EWCA Crim 1373 at 45.
[51] See *R v Mills and Another (No 2)* [2004] 1 Cr App R 7 at 79, 83.   [52] [2003] EWHC 835.

involved a claim of provocation. The Commission had expressed the view that the Court of Appeal was unlikely to find the defendant's actions excusable, but the High Court called attention to passages in *Pendleton* where the Court of Appeal was warned not to trespass on the jury's territory. It seems the Commission should have asked whether the Court of Appeal might find that *a jury* could consider Farnell's actions excusable. The wording of the Homicide Act,[53] which expressly reserves the decision on provocation for the jury, may have played a role in the High Court's sensitivity here, but it must be said that it is difficult for the Commission to decide which cases to refer to the Court of Appeal when that Court has taken no consistent line on how it will assess fresh evidence.

One can also speculate as to whether past cases might be decided differently under *Pendleton. Jones* is an interesting decision to consider in this respect.[54] Here the Court of Appeal heard fresh medical evidence about the victim's injuries in a murder case. The court decided that it was 'obliged to exercise its own judgment' as to whether the conviction was safe. Although it found the new evidence admissible, it considered it unconvincing and the conviction therefore safe. *Jones* was discussed very briefly in *Pendleton*, and was said to be compatible with the approach adopted there,[55] but it is obvious that a determined application of the jury impact test could have justified a different result in *Jones*. Indeed, in the aftermath of *Pendleton* there are cases involving fresh medical evidence where the jury impact test results in a different outcome. In *Jenkins*, for example, the conviction was quashed because the jury had never had the opportunity to consider the theory supported by the fresh evidence, and the evidence 'might reasonably have affected the decision of the jury to convict'.[56] But in other recent cases the Court has been prepared to take the *Jones* approach, turning down an appeal where it does not find fresh expert evidence convincing.[57]

This review of the Court of Appeal's case law in the aftermath of *Pendleton* might suggest that all is chaos. There is something to that view. Certainly the Court of Appeal, as well as the House of Lords, have found it difficult to explain how they approach fresh evidence. Beneath the conflicting dicta, however, there is probably a reasonable degree of consistency. Much depends on the overall strength of the case against a defendant. If the court has some doubt about the safety of the conviction, then, as in *Mills and Poole*, *Pendleton* may be used as a justification for allowing the appeal. To that extent, the Court is deciding whether the defendant is guilty. Where there is less doubt, the Court may feel no need to consider the jury's view of things. It may also feel able to decide for itself a reasonably self-contained issue, such as whether new expert evidence is convincing. But some appeals raise wider issues: in *Pendleton*, the defendant's defence had never been put before the jury, and in *Mills and Poole* there were questions about several aspects of the prosecution case. Here, the court is likely

---

[53] Homicide Act 1957, s3.   [54] [1997] 1 Cr App R 86.   [55] Above n 27, 18.

[56] *The Independent*, 20 July 2004.

[57] *Latimer* CA 9 Feb 2004, discussed in L. Elks, paper to Criminal Appeal Lawyers Association Conference, 2 October 2004.

to be aware of its role as a court of review: it cannot easily make judgments about witnesses it has never seen, or about how new lines of defence affect the case as a whole. Reference to the jury's perspective is a means of explaining this difficulty. 'It all depends on the facts' is often an unsatisfactory way of summarizing a complex area of case law, but there is considerable truth in it here. The facts of these appeals vary in many different ways, and it is not surprising that a rule such as the one in *Pendleton* cannot cope with the richness of the material to which it is supposed to be applied.

This leaves a question at a more conceptual level. The debate about *Stafford* and *Pendleton* is partly a theoretical one. Lord Devlin was highly critical of the decision in *Stafford* because he believed it undermined the role of the jury.[58] We saw earlier that the Royal Commission on Criminal Justice, too, thought the *Stafford* approach wrong. As a matter of principle, then, what approach should an appellate court take to a jury verdict that is challenged by means of fresh evidence? The argument that doubts about the appellant's guilt should, if possible, be resolved by the jury draws on the fact that, in trial on indictment, we do not have trial by professional judge but one where decisions about factual issues are made by the jury. Jury decision making is thought to be different, in various ways, from decision making by judges, and it is generally thought to be a valuable part of the criminal process. The argument, then, is that if we value jury decision making, and recognize that it is different from judicial decision making, we should not seek to avoid it in fresh evidence cases. In its strongest form, the argument would be put in terms of the defendant's right to be found guilty only on a verdict of the jury. A more refined version of the argument would proceed by pointing out that a number of rules of evidence, and in particular the rule in *Galbraith*[59] (discussed in Chapter 11), reserve issues of credibility for the jury. Where there is fresh evidence to support the defendant's case it could therefore be argued that appellate judges should not base a decision on the credibility of a witness but, if possible, order a retrial so that the credibility dispute can be resolved by a jury.

There are difficulties with these arguments that appellate judges should avoid resolving issues of guilt and innocence. In Chapter 9 we were critical of the rule in *Galbraith*, suggesting that judges should be prepared to prevent a case from going to the jury where a conviction would not be safe owing to doubts about the credibility of a witness. On appeal, too, we would argue that the focus should be on the safety of the conviction, the question of how convincing the case against the defendant is, rather than on concerns about whether particular issues should be reserved for the jury. Another problem with the argument against *Stafford* is that it would appear to lead to the following conclusion: where appellate judges are persuaded that a defendant is innocent, but nevertheless think that there is some chance that a jury would convict, the case should be sent for retrial so that the issue can be resolved by a jury. We regard that as unacceptable. In response, it might be argued that guilt and innocence should be treated differently. Thus, where the judges on appeal think that the defendant is innocent, they should resolve the matter themselves, but where they are convinced of

---

[58] Devlin, *The Judge* (1979), 148–76.   [59] See n 38 above.

his guilt, there should, if possible, be a retrial. The difficulty with this position is that it is hard to see how it could be justified. It is of course correct that in certain contexts guilt and innocence are treated differently. The 'error preference', discussed in Chapter 2, which views mistaken conviction as far worse than mistaken acquittal, is fundamental to the criminal process and is expressed in the burden of proof placed on the prosecution. The burden of proof is relevant to the appeals process insofar as appeal judges should be asking, not whether they think the defendant is guilty or innocent, but whether there is a reasonable doubt about guilt. But beyond that, there is no reason why the error preference should lead to a conclusion that the defendant is guilty being treated differently from a conclusion that he is innocent. If one is comfortable with appellate judges resolving factual issues to make a final acquittal, one should also be comfortable with them doing the same to reach a conclusion that a conviction should not be quashed. This is not to say that there is nothing useful in the 'jury impact' test: in many cases it is an appropriate way for the court to signal the limitations it faces as a court of review. But where the court is faced with a relatively simple dispute about the evidence in a case, as in *Jones*, there is nothing unprincipled about it resolving the issue itself.

There is an important sense in which the debates surrounding *Stafford* and *Pendleton* are side issues in arguments about how well the Court of Appeal is performing. When the Royal Commission reported in 1993, there was genuine concern that the Court had been unduly reluctant to quash convictions in certain cases. When one studies the arguments in the unsuccessful 1988 appeal of the Birmingham six, this reluctance is apparent. The Court seemed prepared to go to any length to find interpretations of the evidence which would uphold the convictions.[60] In particular, it was not prepared to contemplate that police officers had been guilty of gross misconduct, an attitude notoriously displayed in Lord Denning's reference to the 'appalling vista' that would unfold were a civil action by the Birmingham six against the police allowed to succeed.[61] It was the culture of upholding flimsy convictions at any cost which was the important thing to change in 1993, not the legal test for fresh evidence cases, which is a rather more refined matter of doctrinal principle. It is in terms of its general attitude and culture that the Court of Appeal should be judged as a means of determining whether things have improved since the 1980s. This is very difficult to determine. The statistics discussed earlier, which show a ten per cent drop in the rate of successful appeals since 1993, are worrying, but we cautioned against jumping to conclusions on the basis of them. Beyond such indicators, all one is left with is a very subjective impression of the court's general work. Very cautiously, we would suggest that there has been some improvement in the Court's attitude. The judges in the Court of Appeal are prepared to allow the possibility of police corruption, and are less likely to go to extreme lengths to find explanations for evidence which has been undermined by the arguments of the defence on appeal.

---

[60] See R. Nobles and D. Schiff, *Understanding Miscarriages of Justice* (2000), Ch 5.
[61] *McIlkenny v CC West Midlands Police Force* [1980] 2 All ER 227, 239–40.

12.3 DUE PROCESS APPEALS

In the previous section we concentrated on cases where the appellant's argument is basically that he is innocent, and that the jury came to a mistaken factual conclusion. In this section we discuss another type of appeal, where the defendant's principal contention is that there has been a failure of due process at trial and that, because of this, his conviction should be quashed whether or not he is guilty. Appeals of this type are dealt with under the same statutory framework as the 'fact' appeals considered above: in other words, the Court of Appeal should quash the conviction if it is 'unsafe'. This is a slightly strange test to apply to due process appeals. Before 1995, the test was in terms of whether the conviction was 'unsafe *or unsatisfactory*'. The new wording came about as a result of a recommendation of the Royal Commission and was intended to simplify the language of the statute. It was not intended to change the practice of the Court of Appeal which had previously been prepared to allow due process appeals.[62] In the event, however, the new test has led to some uncertainty about the Court of Appeal's powers. The tensions in the case law reflect not just differing views on the statutory language, but also deeper matters of principle. The questions here are similar to ones we discussed in Chapter 11 when looking at the power of the courts to exclude illegally or improperly obtained evidence.

The issues are well illustrated by the facts and decision in *Chalkley and Jeffries*.[63] The defendants were charged with conspiracy to rob. The principal evidence against them was a tape recording of their conversations, which had been obtained by placing a bugging device in Chalkley's home. The trial judge refused to exclude this evidence, and this led the defendants to plead guilty. On appeal it was held that, even if the trial judge's ruling as to the admissibility of the evidence had been wrong, the convictions were not unsafe. One of the issues here concerns the effect of a guilty plea on an appeal against conviction. It was held that, unless it could be shown that a mistaken decision by the judge left the accused with no alternative in law but to plead guilty, a guilty plea would normally preclude a successful appeal.[64] (The caveat—'normally'— is aimed at cases where a plea was made by mistake or without intention to admit the truth of the charge.) A further issue concerned the interpretation of the Criminal Appeal Act following the 1995 amendments. Auld LJ's conclusion was that: 'The Court has no power under the substituted section 2(1) to allow an appeal if it does not think the conviction unsafe but is dissatisfied in some way with what went on at the trial.'[65] Thus what we are here referring to as 'due process appeals' should, on Auld's view, no longer be allowed.

Chalkley, then, gives a simple answer to the question we are considering. However, other cases take a different view of the Court of Appeal's powers under the amended

---

[62] J. Smith, 'The Criminal Appeal Act 1995: Appeals Against Conviction' [1995] Crim LR 920; D. Schiff and R. Nobles, 'Criminal Appeal Act 1995: The Semantics of Jurisdiction' (1996) 59 *MLR* 573.
[63] [1998] 2 Cr App R 79.   [64] *Ibid.*, 94.   [65] *Ibid.*, 98.

Criminal Appeal Act, and the consensus now seems to be that *Chalkley* was wrongly decided.[66] For example, in *Mullen*, the Court of Appeal held that the defendant's trial had involved an abuse of process and that, whether or not he was guilty, his conviction should be quashed.[67] Similarly, in *Davis, Johnson and Rowe* it was recognized that: 'A conviction may be unsafe even where there is no doubt about guilt but the trial process has been "vitiated by serious unfairness . . .".'[68] There are many other dicta to like effect.

It is accepted, then, that the Court of Appeal should allow due process appeals and that the Criminal Appeal Act permits it to do so. However, what is not clear is just when it should quash a conviction on due process grounds. What can be said with a good deal of certainty is that if the original trial was vitiated by an abuse of process, then an appeal will be successful. However, 'abuse of process' is a relatively narrow category. It covers cases where a defendant has been entrapped, where he has been prejudiced by undue delay between charge and trial, cases of disguised extradition, situations where the prosecution has reneged on an agreement, and various other things. As we saw in Chapter 9, with the example of delay, the Court of Appeal is anxious to restrict the use of stays for abuse of process as far as possible, and they will only be available in cases where the prosecutor's conduct falls seriously below acceptable standards, as in the situations just described. This prompts the question: where a trial has been unfair in some way which does not amount to an abuse of process, should the defendant's conviction nevertheless be quashed? While statements such as the one made in *Davis*, quoted above, suggest that the answer to this question is 'yes', the case law has not yet made it clear just when unfairness short of abuse of process results in 'unsafety', nor is there agreement among commentators as to how this question should be answered.[69]

A complicating factor here is Article 6 of the European Convention on Human Rights, brought into English law by the Human Rights Act 1998. Article 6 guarantees the right to a fair trial, and the precise content of that right is determined largely by the judges in Strasbourg rather than by the English judiciary. This means that the Court of Appeal is no longer able to define trial fairness in such a way that its own conception of unfairness coincides with just those cases where it is prepared to quash a conviction irrespective of guilt. The Court of Appeal has, as it were, lost control of the definition of fairness. And, to complicate things further, the ECHR demands that a remedy be provided to anyone whose rights—including fair trial rights—are infringed.[70] An obvious remedy would be the quashing of a conviction. If this approach were taken, the concept of unsafety in the Criminal Appeal Act would be identical to the ECHR concept of fairness: whenever a trial was unfair under Article 6, the Court of Appeal would quash a defendant's conviction. At first sight, this is an

---

[66] *Hakala*, above n 44 at 5, states that *Chalkley* is not to be followed on this point.

[67] (1999) 2 Cr App R 143.   [68] [2001] 1 Cr App R 115, 132, quoting *Smith* (1999) 2 Cr App R 238.

[69] See Dennis, above n 44; N. Taylor and D. Ormerod, 'Mind the Gap: Safety, Fairness and Moral Legitimacy' [2004] Crim LR 266.

[70] ECHR, Article 13.

attractive approach. The Courts have flirted with it: in *Togher* it was said that 'if a defendant has been denied a fair trial, it will be almost inevitable that the conviction will be regarded as unsafe.'[71] In *R v A* it was said that the 'guarantee of a fair trial under Article 6 is absolute: a conviction obtained in breach of it cannot stand'.[72] But in *Davis* we find a rather more cautious tone: 'the duty of the ECHR is to determine whether or not there has been a violation of the Convention . . . it is not within the remit of the ECHR to comment upon the nature and quality of any breach or upon the impact such a breach might have had upon the safety of the conviction.'[73] The argument that breach of Article 6 automatically leads to the quashing of a conviction was rejected.

One can begin to understand the caution in *Davis* by bearing in mind that this case involved non-disclosure of evidence to the defendants. Non-disclosure of any relevant evidence will almost certainly be a breach of Article 6. In the event, in *Davis* the non-disclosure was sufficiently serious that the conviction was held to be unsafe, but in other cases the material not disclosed might seem relatively inconsequential. An example would be non-disclosure of the fact that a prosecution witness has previous convictions in a case where the evidence against the defendant is otherwise over-whelming.[74] Here, the Court of Appeal might well be reluctant to make the equation between Article 6 and unsafety. There are other scenarios where a distinction between fairness and unsafety might appear desirable. Dennis gives *Thompson and Venables*[75] as an example: here the European Court of Human Rights found a breach of Article 6 because the defendants had been tried in an adult court without sufficient modifica-tions to trial procedure being made to take account of their young age. While the defendants found the proceedings extremely unsettling, it has never been suggested that they were wrongly convicted in a factual sense. It is hard to imagine the convic-tions being quashed by the Court of Appeal should the case ever be referred back to it, and in this case it does seem that that course of action would be too drastic a means of acknowledging the unfairness of the trial. A less emotive example is *Condron*.[76] Here too the defendants were found to have had an unfair trial by the European Court of Human Rights, in this case because the judge's instruction to the jury on inferences from silence was insufficiently detailed. The Court of Appeal did not find the convic-tions unsafe in 1996,[77] and if the case were to be referred back to it in the light of the European Court's decision, it is unlikely that the result would differ. This too appears defensible.

We noted above that the scheme of the European Convention requires domestic remedies for Convention breaches. The Convention, however, says nothing about what the remedy should be, and it seems perfectly consistent with the Convention for the remedy to be something other than the quashing of a conviction. It has been pointed out that in cases like the ones just described the remedy could be in terms of a

---

[71] *R v Togher and Others* [2001] 3 All ER 463, 33.   [72] [2002] 1 AC 45, 25.   [73] Above n 68, 134.
[74] *Togher*, above n 71, is a possible example. See also *Underwood* [2003] EWCA 1500, though in that case the prosecution, through no fault of its own, had not known about the previous convictions.
[75] (2000) 30 EHRR 121.   [76] *Condron v United Kingdom* (2001) 31 EHRR 1.
[77] *R v Condron* [1997] 1 WLR 827.

financial award, a reduction in sentence, or a simple declaration that there has been a breach of rights.[78] Damages and simple declarations are in fact the common remedies awarded by the ECtHR itself. One can imagine the Court of Appeal accepting this approach, but there is a possible problem here. The court might begin to use such remedies as the 'easy way out', resorting to them in all cases of unfairness not amounting to abuse of process where there were no doubts about guilt. Taylor and Ormerod suggest that this approach 'fails to elevate human rights to their proper status in the overall context in which decisions are to be made.'[79] On this view, the court should be prepared to quash some convictions gained in breach of Article 6 even if the defendant is plainly guilty. This brings us back to the question asked earlier: in which cases should this occur?

It will be obvious that what is at stake in due process appeals is very similar to the issues surrounding the exclusion of illegally and improperly obtained evidence. In both contexts there is a tension between the role of the courts as fact-finders, and their role in upholding the moral integrity of the criminal process. We will not revisit all the issues discussed in Chapter 11; suffice it to say that in developing a framework for considering when unfair convictions should be quashed and when upheld we are not attracted by solutions which put significant weight on such vague concepts as legitimacy and moral integrity, unless more is said about exactly what these terms mean. Our approach would be the one we took to the exclusion of improperly obtained evidence: a protective, or remedial approach. Defendants should not be disadvantaged by breach of their rights. Where a conviction is gained via a breach of Article 6, therefore, that conviction should be held to be unsafe and quashed. Key here, as it was with improperly obtained evidence, is a causal question. The Court will have to ask whether, if Article 6 had not been breached, the defendant would have been convicted. As before, this will sometimes prove difficult to answer. But it is not altogether different from a question we have seen the Court is already asking under *Pendleton*: whether, if the jury had heard fresh evidence presented by the appellant, he would still have been convicted. There will doubtless be a temptation to find, in cases where defendants have obviously committed serious crimes, that the Article 6 breach did not cause the conviction. That is something we hope the Court of Appeal will guard against. In some cases a retrial will be possible, and that offers a way out of some of the more difficult dilemmas the court may face.

We doubt whether the explicit adoption of the remedial approach to breaches of Article 6 will greatly change the practice of the Court of Appeal. The most significant change would be in cases, such as *Chalkley* and *Togher*, where the defendant has pleaded guilty. The guilty plea in *Chalkley* was obviously caused by the judge's decision to admit the challenged evidence. Were this decision to be found in breach of Article 6, or to infringe the domestic conception of fairness under s 78, then on our account the conviction should be quashed. This would result in the factually guilty walking free, but if our commitment to fair trials is to mean anything, that is surely an

---

[78] Dennis, above n 44; Emmerson and Ashworth, above n 20, 17–33.   [79] Above n 69, 279.

appropriate outcome: it is what would have happened had the defendants' rights been respected in the first place. In *Togher* the decision is not so straightforward: there would be a difficult decision as to whether the undisclosed material, which went to the credibility of prosecution witnesses, might have caused the jury to acquit. If it might have, the conviction would, on our account, be unsafe. In *Togher*, unlike in *Chalkley*, a retrial would probably be a viable option.

12.4 POST-APPEAL REVIEW OF CONVICTIONS: THE CRIMINAL CASES REVIEW COMMISSION

Many defendants will find that their appeal is unsuccessful. Others will not appeal; after a certain time (28 days where appeals against conviction in the Crown Court are concerned), their right to appeal will lapse. In these situations, normal appeal rights have been exhausted. However, that is not quite an end to the matter. It is possible to have a conviction referred back to the Crown Court or Court of Appeal.[80] This may occur where, for example, new evidence emerges to throw doubt on the conviction. The system used to be that a decision on whether or not to refer a case back to the Court of Appeal was made by the Home Secretary, on advice from civil servants in the Home Office.[81] In the wake of the Royal Commission on Criminal Justice, a new body was set up to take over this role. The Criminal Cases Review Commission started work in 1997.

The CCRC investigates claims of miscarriage of justice and refers cases back to the appropriate appeal court. Although the Commission's powers involve both magistrates' and Crown Court cases, and challenges to sentence as well as verdicts, we here concentrate on the most common situation, where an application is made to have a conviction referred back to the Court of Appeal. The usual procedure is that an application will be made to the CCRC. The Commission will consider whether the application is eligible: it may only exceptionally make a reference if the applicant did not appeal at the time of his original conviction, and many applications are rejected because the applicant did not.[82] If eligible, the application will be investigated. In some cases this can be done fairly rapidly, but others will involve considerable work. The Commission has the power to commission police investigations. At the end of the process, a decision is made whether or not to refer a case to the Court of Appeal. If a preliminary decision is made not to make a referral, the applicant or his lawyer will usually be informed of the proposed reasons for non-referral and invited to comment. The Criminal Appeal Act 1995 sets out the criteria for making a referral, which should not be made unless 'the Commission consider that there is a real possibility that the

---

[80] There also remains the possibility of a pardon. See Pattenden, above n 7, 378–84.
[81] See Pattenden, above n 7, Ch 10.
[82] Criminal Appeal Act 1995, s 13. Criminal Cases Review Commission, *Annual Report 2002–2003*, 13: about a quarter of applications are found to be ineligible.

conviction . . . would not be upheld'. The grounds on which the conviction would not be upheld must involve 'an argument, or evidence, not raised in the proceedings which led to it or any appeal or application for leave to appeal against it', unless there are exceptional circumstances.[83]

It is obvious that at the centre of the Commission's task is a predictive exercise. It should not make a referral just because it thinks there has been a miscarriage of justice, but only if it believes that the Court of Appeal may quash the conviction. Thus its decision must be informed by the Court of Appeal's working practices. The Criminal Appeal Act underlines this by requiring a new argument or evidence, but even without this provision something new would generally be needed, because that is what the Court of Appeal itself demands. The referral criteria have been discussed by the Divisional Court, in a case involving judicial review of a CCRC decision.[84] Significantly, the judgment was given by Lord Bingham, who was then Lord Chief Justice. The 'real possibility test' he explained, 'plainly denotes a contingency which in the Commission's judgment is more than an outside chance or bare possibility but which may be less than a probability or likelihood or racing certainty'.[85] In cases concerning fresh evidence, 'the Commission must ask itself a double question: do we consider that . . . there is a real possibility that the Court of Appeal will receive the fresh evidence? If so, do we consider that there is a real possibility that the Court of Appeal will not uphold the conviction?'[86] A little more guidance is available to the Commission in the form of statements made by the Court itself in referral cases. The Court has on occasion been critical of the Commission for referring to it cases which it regards as a waste of its time.[87] Less bluntly, the Court has been prepared to give the Commission a lesson on the law, commenting in *Sharp*, a case that apparently came 'nowhere near' the criteria for the admissibility of fresh evidence, that 'had the Commission had its attention drawn to the authorities that we have set out in this judgment, which it does not appear to have had before it, it would have taken a very different view of Mr Sharp's application'.[88]

As will be obvious from the material already covered in this chapter, the Commission's predictive task is not an easy one. There is a fair degree of unpredictability in the Court of Appeal's approach to appeals, as in the *Pendleton* and *Chalkley* case law. Despite this, the Commission is reasonably good at predicting what the Court will do: about 70 per cent of its referrals are successful. As with many of the statistics in this chapter, there is no good way of judging whether this is too high, too low, or about right.[89] One can be reasonably sure, however, that were the success rate to fall far

[83] Criminal Appeal Act 1995, s 13.
[84] *R v Criminal Cases Review Commission, ex p Pearson* [2000] 1 Cr App R 141.   [85] *Ibid.*, 149.
[86] *Ibid.*, 150.   [87] *R v Ellis* [2003] EWCA Crim 3930; *R v Gerald* [1999] Crim LR 315.
[88] [2003] EWCA Crim 3870 at 33. See also the criticism of the Commission at 26.
[89] The Commission view it as about right, but others think it too high: see Home Affairs Committee, *The Work of the Criminal Cases Review Commission, Oral and Written Evidence Tuesday 27 January 2004*, Q 27, 74; cf the Memorandum submitted to the Home Affairs Committee by the Criminal Appeal Lawyers Association. See further R. Nobles and D. Schiff, 'The Criminal Cases Review Commission: Reporting Success?' (2001) 64 *MLR* 280.

below 50 per cent the Court of Appeal, mindful of being 'burdened with a mass of hopeless appeals',[90] would use its criticisms of referrals to prompt a more careful approach from the Commission. As for the Commission's caseload, this is not negligible: since 1997 it has dealt with nearly 6,000 cases. Around four per cent are referred to the Court of Appeal.[91] It refers more cases to the Court of Appeal than the Home Office did.[92]

The CCRC has been a welcome addition to the criminal justice landscape. It appears to have a reputation for careful investigation and to do its job well.[93] In the future, its experience of the workings of the criminal process should prove valuable: while its role is at present largely reactive, it has announced an intention to play a more strategic role by using its knowledge to suggest ways in which miscarriages of justice can be avoided.[94] One should not, however, expect the CCRC to perform miracles. Its ability to correct miscarriages of justice in its referral role is limited by factors largely beyond its control. In its early years, the CCRC claimed that it was underfunded.[95] The situation has now improved, but it will remain the case that the CCRC can only do as much as its resources allow. The CCRC's role is also, as we have seen, limited by the Court of Appeal's interpretation of its own powers. To the extent that the Court takes a sceptical view of fresh evidence and lurking doubt arguments, miscarriages of justice will go unremedied.

12.5 PROSECUTION APPEALS

We saw above that the structure of the appeals process reveals a marked asymmetry between prosecution and defence appeal rights. Prosecutors have fewer opportunities to appeal than defendants. Where prosecutors do have appeal rights, as in the magistrates' court, these tend to be restricted so as to allow appeals on points of law, rather than challenges to fact-finding. Recently, however, the appeal rights of prosecutors have been extended: the Criminal Justice Act 2003 gives the prosecution ways of challenging decisions as to points of law made by judges in the Crown Court. Most significantly, the same act allows the reopening of jury acquittals when they are challenged on factual grounds. The creation of this exception to the double jeopardy principle has been controversial. Even with these developments, however, the picture remains asymmetrical. In order to understand the law in this area, then, we need to begin by thinking about the reasons for this asymmetry. Because double jeopardy raises particular issues of principle, we discuss it separately in the next section.

---

[90] *Ex p Pearson*, above n 84, 149.   [91] Home Affairs Committee, above n 89, Q 34.

[92] Nobles and Schiff, above n 89, 282–3.

[93] See A. James, N. Taylor and C. Walker, 'The Criminal Cases Review Commission: Economy, Effectiveness and Justice' [2000] Crim LR 140.

[94] Home Affairs Committee, above n 89, Q 23; CCRC, above n 82, 32, 37.

[95] James *et al*, above n 93, 145.

We want the courts to make good decisions: to find facts accurately, to interpret the law properly and apply it to the facts in an appropriate manner. In general, appeals offer a means of enhancing these values: the trial court's conclusions can be checked and reassessed. Where questions of law are concerned, the process also allows appeal courts to develop and clarify the law, for the benefit of all trial courts. There are reasons for restraining and filtering appeals: appeal courts cannot work effectively if overloaded, trial courts need to retain some independence, and there is value in coming to a final decision reasonably quickly. While nothing in this picture yet explains why we should want appeal rights to be asymmetrical, the last point mentioned—that there are reasons for restraining appeals—does point us towards an explanation. Because mistaken convictions are much more serious than mistaken acquittals, the need to rectify a mistaken conviction carries far more weight in overcoming the reasons for restraining appeals. Nevertheless, this insight does not provide a very clear picture of how an appeals process might be structured: it explains why we might find asymmetry in an appeals system, but does not *require* asymmetry. If, for example, we decided that the restraint reasons were not very compelling, we might want to give prosecutors and defendants equal appeal rights. This position would be perfectly compatible with an acknowledgment that there are better reasons to permit defence appeals than prosecution appeals. There is, however, one further reason for asymmetry, which applies particularly to jury trial. Jury equity, or jury nullification, is the practice whereby a jury acquits a guilty defendant for reasons of principle. Jury equity is seen by some as being an important value in jury trial. Allowing appeals against jury acquittals might allow prosecutors to undermine jury equity. This argument will not persuade everyone; as we saw in Chapter 11, jury equity is controversial. There might also be some way of distinguishing nullification cases from others, and allowing appeals in the latter but not the former. Another argument that often emerges in the debates around appeals is that prosecution appeals should be avoided because they subject defendants to stress and uncertainty. While this point should not be overlooked, again it does not give us a very clear picture of how we should structure appeal rights. As a matter of practice, it is not taken to rule out all prosecution appeals. Even when a defendant appears to have secured a victory, as in having his acquittal quashed in the Court of Appeal, he may still face a retrial or further appeal to the House of Lords. Further, defence appeals too may impose stress and uncertainty on victims, or even on an 'alternative suspect' who may fear that, once the conviction is overturned, he will be prosecuted for the crime.[96]

It is not surprising, then, to find that the asymmetry in appeal rights is unstable, and that new avenues of prosecution appeal are being created. The foregoing discussion suggests that the best way to assess these changes is to examine them individually.

---

[96] As in the case of the murder of Wendy Sewell, for which Stephen Downing had his conviction quashed in 2001: see 'Guilty Secret of Town with Blood on its Hands' *The Observer*, 11 February 2001; 'Bakewell Killer Hunt Reopens After 25 Years' *The Observer*, 14 April 2002. Cf 'Cleared of Murder—But Still the Sole Suspect' *The Guardian*, 28 February 2003.

The discussion here will focus on the issues in broad outline, rather than the technical detail. The Criminal Justice Act 2003 for the first time gives prosecutors rights of appeal during trial on indictment. Previous appeal rights, which themselves were recent creations, were restricted to preparatory hearings in serious and lengthy cases. Under s 58, the appeal can relate to any ruling made up to the start of the summing up, including a submission of no case to answer. However, the Act has found a practical way of restricting such appeals to rulings which severely affect the prosecution case. If the Court of Appeal confirms the judge's ruling, the outcome will be the acquittal of the defendant; the prosecution must also agree to the defendant's acquittal if it abandons the appeal or if leave is refused. As this implies, prosecution appeals, like defence appeals, require leave, either from the trial judge or the Court of Appeal. The Court of Appeal cannot allow the appeal just because it disagrees with the judge's exercise of a discretion: the decision must be wrong in law or unreasonable.[97] A practical problem with allowing 'interlocutory' appeals—appeals during the course of a trial—is that proceedings will be suspended, creating delay and prolonging the defendant's stress. Provisions allow for the more urgent appeals to be expedited,[98] but in practice a jury, once empanelled, cannot be kept waiting for very long. The usual result of a successful prosecution appeal, then, will be that the Court of Appeal will order a retrial, but it may only do so if this is in the interests of justice.

A more wide-ranging power of appeal is to be found in s 62 of the Act, though this section only applies to certain serious offences, such as rape, murder, robbery and arson.[99] This allows the prosecution to challenge any evidential ruling, and here an unsuccessful appeal does not result in acquittal. It would be unsatisfactory if the trial could be put on hold over just any ruling with which the prosecution disagrees—a decision not to allow an inference from silence, for example—and the act has a solution of sorts to this problem. The evidentiary ruling must 'significantly weaken' the prosecution case. While the s 62 appeal is far wider than that in s 58, it is significant that there is some caution about its introduction. Section 58 will be introduced first; only if it works satisfactorily will s 62 be implemented.[100]

In principle, there is little to object to in these powers: widening prosecution appeal rights serves the ends of justice by allowing the scrutiny of the decisions of trial judges. It may also be of use in avoiding the situation where the law develops in a lopsided manner. If only defendants can appeal legal rulings, an anti-defendant bias in the application of the law may be prevented, but a pro-defendant bias may remain hidden. It is also worth noting that there is a significant number of cases in which the new powers might be used. Stays for abuse of process appear to be increasingly common, and a large number of cases collapse before they reach the jury, many of them because a submission of no case to answer succeeds.[101] Many of these decisions

---

[97] CJA 2003, s 67.   [98] CJA 2003, s 64.

[99] Schedule 4, Part 1 contains a list of around 30 serious offences.

[100] See R. Taylor, M. Wasik and R. Leng, *Blackstone's Guide to the Criminal Justice Act 2003* (2004), 83–4.

[101] B. Block, C. Corbett and J. Peay, *Ordered and Directed Acquittals in the Crown Court* (1993), esp 70–4; M. Zander and P. Henderson, *Crown Court Study* (1993), 124–5.

will be uncontroversial, but it is surely worth giving prosecutors the right to challenge them, given that they prevent a case from going any further.

There have been some concerns about the new powers, however. The Law Commission, when reviewing this area of the law, was initially cautious about creating prosecution rights of appeal, and would not have allowed appeal against a successful submission of no case to answer.[102] It expressed the concern that the defence might be discouraged from making such a submission by the fear that, if successfully appealed, there would be a new trial and thus a loss of any tactical advantage gained during the original trial. This emphasis on tactical factors did not impress commentators.[103] The Commission also expressed some concern over equality of arms, noting that given that the defence has no interlocutory appeal rights, it might seem odd to provide the prosecution with them. The response to this is that prosecution interlocutory appeals are the equivalent of defence appeals after the jury verdict, which prosecutors do not possess.

The principal objection to the new appeals in the Criminal Justice Act may well turn out to be practical. Dealing at the moment largely with defence appeals post-trial, we have seen that the Criminal Division of the Court of Appeal is already stretched in terms of resources, and that this may affect the quality of decision making at the leave stage. No one seems able to predict how many prosecution appeals these new provisions will attract,[104] but if the effect is to reduce the quality of appellate review available to defendants, they should not be viewed with equanimity. Linked to this is the question of delay. Compared to its European counterparts, English criminal procedure has generally resolved criminal matters speedily. This is due partly, no doubt, to the 'concentrated' nature of criminal proceedings in this jurisdiction, with the key stage being the trial.[105] Interlocutory appeals are a threat to this tradition. The net result may well be defendants spending longer on remand, and in a state of uncertainty about the outcome of the proceedings against them. Perhaps resources will be concentrated on interlocutory appeals in order to resolve them speedily, thus avoiding challenges under the Article 6 right to trial within a reasonable time. But if the knock on effect of this is that resources are taken from the process for hearing post-trial defence appeals, then, too, it will be difficult to see the new appeals as a good thing.

Reform of criminal procedure rarely stands still for long. Once we have prosecution appeals during the trial, attention may well turn to prosecution appeals post verdict, which might involve a challenge to the judge's directions to the jury on the substantive

---

[102] Law Commission, *Prosecution Appeals Against Judges' Rulings*, Consultation Paper No 158 (2000). This stance was modified in Law Commission, *Double Jeopardy and Prosecution Appeals*, Law Com No 267 (2001), in which it was proposed that appeals be allowed on the first, but not the second, limb of *Galbraith* (ie on a decision whether there is no evidence to support part of the prosecution's case, but not on whether such evidence as there is, taken at its highest, is sufficient to convict).

[103] See R. Pattenden, 'Prosecution Appeals Against Judges' Rulings' [2000] Crim LR 971; I. Dennis, 'Prosecution Appeals and Retrial for Serious Offences' [2004] Crim LR 619.

[104] See Law Commission, *Double Jeopardy and Prosecution Appeals*, above n 102, 86–9.

[105] M. Damaška, *Evidence Law Adrift* (1997), Ch 3.

law. Indeed, if interlocutory appeals under s 62 of the CJA come to disrupt trials by regularly throwing them into hiatus, it may well be argued that the appropriate place for those appeals is at the end of the trial. The Law Commission saw no case for post-verdict prosecution appeals,[106] but Lord Justice Auld did raise the question of the power to appeal perverse jury verdicts (this turned out to be one of the most controversial proposals in his report).[107] Some jurisdictions—Canada is an example[108]—allow the prosecution to appeal points of law after a jury acquittal. Although such appeals raise difficult issues, they should not be ruled out of contemplation.

12.6 DOUBLE JEOPARDY

The traditional double jeopardy principle meant that jury acquittals were final, as were acquittals by the magistrates once the appeals process was over. In addition, the principle protects defendants from retrial for an offence of which they have already been convicted. The law here involves some technical issues, because it needs to establish when a new charge is the 'same' as one for which the defendant has already stood trial.[109] In effect, if the new trial involves substantially the same facts as a prior one, the defendant will not be retried. We will not discuss these technical points; as before we concentrate on the arguments of principle.

In 1996 an exception to the double jeopardy principle was introduced, allowing an acquittal to be quashed and a new trial to take place in cases where the acquittal is found to be 'tainted' by the commission of an 'administration of justice offence involving interference with or intimidation of a juror or witness'.[110] This power has never been used.

The Criminal Justice Act 2003 goes much further. It creates a 'fresh evidence' exception to the double jeopardy principle.[111] The basic idea is that, where new evidence emerges throwing doubt on an acquittal, an application can be made to the Court of Appeal to quash the acquittal and order a new trial. The Court should only do so if there is 'new and compelling' evidence.[112] 'New' is defined in terms of whether it was adduced in the proceedings resulting in the acquittal, and 'compelling' in terms of whether the evidence is substantial, reliable, and 'in the context of the outstanding issues [i.e. the issues in dispute at the trial], it appears highly probative of the case against the acquitted person'.[113] If this test is satisfied, the acquittal will not necessarily be quashed: first, an interests of justice test must be considered. The considerations here include whether a fair trial is possible (it may not be, owing to, for example, media coverage or delay), and 'whether it is likely that the new evidence

---

106 Law Commission, above, n 102.   107 Auld, above n 23, 636–7.
108 See K. Roach, 'Canada', in C. Bradley, *Criminal Procedure: A Worldwide Study* (1999), 77.
109 See *Connelly* [1964] AC 1254; *Beedie* [1998] QB 356.
110 Criminal Procedure and Investigations Act 1996, s 54.   111 Criminal Justice Act 2003, Part 10.
112 CJA 2003, s 78.   113 CJA 2003, s 78(3)(c).

would have been adduced in the earlier proceedings against the acquitted person but for a failure by an officer or by a prosecutor to act with due diligence or expedition.'[114] A very significant point about the power to quash acquittals is that it is retrospective: it applies to acquittals secured before the new power is implemented as well as those secured after implementation. The power is also restricted to a number of serious offences, including murder, manslaughter and serious sexual and drug offences.[115]

The first thing to say about the new double jeopardy provision is that, in the opinion of the Joint Committee on Human Rights, it probably conflicts with the UK's international human rights obligations.[116] The International Covenant on Civil and Political Rights does not permit 'retrial' after an acquittal. In exceptional circumstances, however, 'reopening' of a trial will be acceptable. The distinction is that reopening would involve new evidence, not evidence that was available to the prosecutor at the original trial. The position under the ECHR is less clear: Article 4 of Protocol 7, which the UK has declared its intention to sign, permits a retrial on evidence of 'new or newly discovered' facts. It is not clear whether this would allow the use of evidence known to be available at the time of the first trial. While the provisions in the Criminal Justice Act allow the Court of Appeal to refuse to quash a conviction under the interests of justice test if the new and compelling evidence was originally available, as the Joint Committee argued, it does not appear acceptable to rely on discretion to protect human rights.

There are, of course, much deeper issues at stake here than whether or not the new law is compatible with the ICCPR. Reform of the law was controversial;[117] we need to ask whether any change to the double jeopardy provision can be justified. Put another way: what is the value of the double jeopardy principle? Most people would share the intuition that it is wrong for the State to have unlimited power to question acquittals. If a defendant is acquitted, the State should not be permitted to have another go, to see whether on the next occasion a conviction can be achieved. What is not so obvious, however, is exactly why this is regarded as wrong, nor whether there should be exceptions to the general principle. The intuition presumably has something to do with the importance of having limits on State power, but this idea needs a good deal of unpacking. The State is powerful in all sorts of ways. To pick one comparison which is particularly germane to the present discussion, there is no limitation on the number of times a person can be tried for different crimes. If a person is acquitted of burglary, there is nothing to stop the State from immediately charging him with burglary again, so long as the charge relates to a different burglary. In this way, a person's life could be made a constant misery by serial prosecution. It is true that where the new charge is for exactly the same crime, the prosecution will find it easier to bring the case: having established a case to answer once, it could easily put the defendant in genuine

---

[114] CJA 2003, s 79(2)(c).   [115] Schedule 5, Part 1 contains a list of 29 'qualifying offences'.
[116] Joint Committee on Human Rights, Eleventh Report 2002–3, *Criminal Justice Bill: Further Report*, 27–38.
[117] See in particular P. Roberts, 'Double Jeopardy Law Reform: A Criminal Justice Commentary' (2002) 65 *MLR* 393.

jeopardy of conviction again. But, especially when one bears in mind the power of the State to manufacture evidence, this distinction is not sufficiently absolute to rob the comparison of its force. In thinking abut double jeopardy, then, it is worth asking why we object to that rather than to serial jeopardy.

Some of the reasons given for the double jeopardy principle are not especially convincing.[118] It is true that, in general, repeated prosecution increases the risk of false conviction.[119] However, this applies to serial jeopardy as much as to double jeopardy. What is more, the risk can be controlled by devices such as the requirement for 'compelling' new evidence. It is also suggested that the new trial will cause distress to the accused,[120] but we are prepared to accept that in ordering retrials after successful appeals and, again, serial jeopardy surely causes equal distress. Finality is perhaps a more promising value to draw on in order to support the double jeopardy principle.[121] There is value to the parties, and to society as a whole, in accepting that a contested issue has been resolved. We are prepared to put aside concerns about finality when there is evidence that an innocent person has been convicted, but this can be seen to reflect the fact that, as explained above, the conviction of the innocent is a much more serious wrong than acquittal of the guilty. While there is much to be said for this explanation, it would not rule out the creation of exceptions to the double jeopardy principle. Finality might sometimes be thought worth sacrificing in order to secure the conviction of the guilty.

Ian Dennis has made much of this last point.[122] He cautiously supports the new double jeopardy exception in the Criminal Justice Act, and justifies it by appeal to the value of legitimacy, which he takes to be the controlling value of, if not the whole of the criminal process, at least the trial. On his account, when new evidence emerges to throw doubt on an acquittal, the verdict risks losing its legitimacy. Verdict legitimacy can be restored, however, by a new trial. The strength of Dennis's account is that it recognizes that the criminal process does not exist just to protect the interests of defendants. However, the key role that legitimacy plays here is at least questionable. As we have observed before, legitimacy is a rather vague value. An opponent of double jeopardy reform could as easily argue that the value of finality is such that it is never appropriate to reopen an acquittal (while eschewing the language of legitimacy, this, in effect, is Paul Roberts' argument against the reform).[123]

We think an argument for the double jeopardy principle can be put in slightly different terms than the ones explored so far. When the State invokes the machinery of criminal process against a defendant, it puts him at risk of conviction; in some cases, of false conviction. In order to have the moral authority to do this, the State

---

[118] For further discussion, see P. Roberts, 'Justice for All? Two Bad Arguments (and Several Good Suggestions) for Resisting Double Jeopardy Reform' (2002) 6 *E & P* 197.

[119] Law Commission, *Double Jeopardy*, Consultation Paper No 156 (1999), 37.

[120] Law Commission, above n 102, 37–8.   [121] *Ibid.*, 35–8.

[122] I. Dennis, 'Rethinking Double Jeopardy: Justice and Finality in Criminal Process' [2000] Crim LR 933; Dennis, above n 103.

[123] Above n 117.

should consider its trial procedures to be generally reliable; to the extent that it thinks they are not, it lacks the moral authority to use them to put people in jeopardy of conviction.[124] This suggests that the State is bound by the verdicts of its trial procedures; it is, we might say, estopped from calling them into question. To demand that a defendant face the jeopardy of conviction a second time is for the State to admit that its trial procedure is unreliable, and this undermines its authority to demand that the defendant stand trial again. This does not, of course, prevent defendants from calling a verdict into question: there is no inconsistency when this occurs.

We suggest that this account has some value in explaining the contours of the double jeopardy principle. The brief discussion of the ICCPR framework, above, implies that there is particular antipathy towards retrying an acquitted defendant by using evidence that was in the possession of the prosecution all the time. In this situation, the estoppel principle should bite with full force. Where new evidence emerges after the trial—by chance, as it were—there is perhaps an argument that things are different. The failure in the trial procedure might be said to be outside the State's responsibility. There is reason to be cautious about this argument: one can always imagine future technological breakthroughs that will give us new evidence, and in that sense trials will never be as reliable as they could be. Nevertheless, courts have to operate within the realm of present day possibility; the State should not be able to distance itself from trial verdicts by saying that things may be different in the future. In the same way, when new evidence does emerge to throw doubt on an acquittal, the State should not be able to revisit it.

We saw above that the initial exception to the double jeopardy principle in England and Wales was the 'tainted acquittal' procedure introduced by the Criminal Procedure and Investigations Act. On the account sketched above, this is none too objectionable. Where the trial process has been undermined in some way, especially by the defendant, it could be said that the State has less reason to be committed to the verdict (another explanation would be that the defendant himself is estopped from questioning the reopening of the trial). It is worth noting that the New Zealand Law Commission, which examined the double jeopardy rule around the time that the Law Commission for England and Wales was doing so, concluded that only an exception along the lines of the tainted acquittal procedure was acceptable.[125] Its proposals were in some ways narrower than the English provisions: the exception would only apply where the accused himself had tainted the acquittal. But in other respects they go further: perjury at the original trial would be included among the administration of justice offences that can trigger reopening of the verdict. In terms of theoretical coherence, there is a lot to be said for reform along these lines.

We hope that the account sketched here goes some way to capturing the basic value of the double jeopardy protection. We would not claim that it proves the Criminal Justice Act reforms to be unacceptable: things are rarely so neat when it comes to

---

[124] For something like this argument, see R. Nozick, *Anarchy, State and Utopia* (1974), 102–8.
[125] New Zealand Law Commission, Report 70, *Acquittal Following Perversion of the Course of Justice* (2001).

theoretical defences of fundamental principles. We hope, however, that it underscores
the sort of objection that can be made about the new law. Points of principle do not
exhaust the objections: as with prosecution appeals, there are more practical concerns
too. We have little idea how the power to quash a conviction will change the criminal
justice landscape. Once the new law is implemented, there is likely to be an initial rush
of cases taken to the Court of Appeal[126]—cases where the police will, for some time,
have been eyeing the possibility of a second go, perhaps using advances in DNA
technology to prove the guilt of an acquitted offender. Once this initial surge is
disposed of, the provision may be rarely used. Now that DNA technology is already
immensely powerful, there should be no new acquittals where it can be harnessed
without the objection that the evidence was available at the original trial. But it is also
possible that the power to reopen an acquittal will change the way police, prosecutors
and victims act. After a high profile acquittal the police may come to view the initial
trial as a 'first round', and look for ways to challenge the verdict. Victims may come to
structure their lives around the hope that 'their' offender can be brought to justice,
hiring private detectives or seeking to bug the suspect's home in the search for new
evidence. The media may launch campaigns against those regarded as having escaped
justice. These possibilities again raise the question of whether it was right to change
the law on double jeopardy. Just what will be gained from it? It is very hard to tell.

[126] Under CJA 2003 s 79, the interests of justice test includes a consideration of whether there has been
lack of due diligence or expedition since the original offence was committed. Delay in applying to the Court
of Appeal will therefore count against having the acquittal quashed. There may already be plans to make
certain applications once the new law is implemented: see ' "Killers" Fear Justice at Last' *The Observer*,
11 March 2001; 'Police Have a Hit List, Says Former Law Lord' *The Guardian*, 6 January 2004. Cf 'Double
Jeopardy "No Threat to Lawrence Suspects" ' *The Guardian*, 1 August 2002.

13

CRIMINAL PROCESS VALUES

Chapters 4 to 12 of the book have discussed various key stages of decision making in the criminal process, making reference to issues of policy and principle in the relevant law and practices. It is time now to reflect more generally upon the values that appear to dominate the English criminal process, the values that ought to dominate it, and how change might be brought about.

13.1 THE AVOIDANCE OF CRIMINAL TRIALS

Early in Chapter 1, a distinction was drawn between three types of decision at the pre-trial stage: processual decisions, which are concerned with the progress of the case from arrest through to court, or as far as the case goes; dispositive decisions, which divert a case from the process of prosecution and trial and which may dispose of the case through some kind of undertaking or penalty; and the temporizing decision, remand, which determines whether or not the defendant should be at liberty between first court appearance and trial. While there is often a tendency to regard these decisions as discrete rational determinations, it will have become apparent that they cannot be assessed properly without having regard to the system or process of which they form part. Thus, for example, each decision is shaped by the flow of information to the decision maker and by the way in which 'facts' and opinions are selected, constructed, and communicated—all of which may be influenced as much by power relations between the parties as by the law. Additionally, each decision maker may be not only subject to rules or guidelines, as the case may be, but also influenced by an occupational culture and by the expectations of others both within and outside the system. It is therefore important not to neglect the serial view of decisions, noting that decisions by the public and by ordinary police officers or by the personnel of regulatory agencies may have considerable implications for later determinations; that decisions on charge may have implications for mode of trial; that decisions on mode of trial may have implications for remand and for plea; and so forth. Moreover, events which occur early in the process—a mistaken identification, a false confession—can have profound implications later on. The fragility of various types of evidence should caution us to view claims about the 'facts' of cases, or about innocence and guilt, with a degree of scepticism.

Little has been said, in the foregoing chapters, about the differences between accusatorial and inquisitorial systems of criminal justice. The English criminal process is fundamentally accusatorial in orientation, eschewing the idea of an impartial inquiry into the case by a neutral official in favour of the notion that a fair result emerges from an adversarial process in which the prosecution constructs a case for convicting the defendant and the defendant attempts to undermine or discredit that case. One reason for not dwelling on this contrast is the complexity of the adversarial/ inquisitorial distinction, both in theory and in practice.[1] Another reason may be found in what may be termed the 'theory of convergence'—suggesting that the trend in Europe has been away from a clear dichotomy of approaches and towards a unified framework.[2] The convergence is said to have been assisted by the European Convention on Human Rights and the judgments of the Court: the Convention emphasizes the rights of the individual defendant, in a way that typifies accusatorial systems (for example, the various rights enumerated in Article 6, including the right to confront each witness), but it also promotes some principles associated with an inquisitorial approach, such as equality of arms and the duty of disclosure. It may be added that, quite apart from any influence exerted by the European Convention, the 'ideal type' of an accusatorial or an inquisitorial criminal procedure is hard to find. The example of forms of plea bargaining in France and Germany was given in Chapter 10, and the introduction of adversarial elements into the Italian system in 1989 is another example.[3] However, care must be taken in the interpretation of these and other trends. So much depends on the legal traditions and social culture of different countries that there can rarely be any simple comparison between the elements of two different criminal justice systems.

It has also become evident that, whereas the rhetoric of English criminal procedure tends to place emphasis on trial by jury according to the laws of evidence, the practice is otherwise. Most cases are heard in magistrates' courts, not in the Crown Court with a jury. The vast majority of cases—over 90 per cent in magistrates' courts and some two-thirds in the Crown Court—proceed on a plea of guilty, which means that no trial of guilt ever takes place. In no sense is this a 'natural' or 'unavoidable' phenomenon: the system is structured so as to produce it. There are incentives towards the avoidance of trials, incentives that do not exist in some other legal systems. The most notable of these is the sentence discount for a plea of guilty, up to one-third off the sentence that would otherwise be given for the offence. There are also disincentives to

---

[1] The best-known work is by M. Damaška, *The Faces of Justice and State Authority* (1976), and 'Evidentiary Barriers to Conviction and Two Models of Criminal Procedure: a Comparative Study' (1973) 121 *U. Penn LR* 506.

[2] For further discussion, see N. Jorg, S. Field and C. Brants, 'Are Inquisitorial and Adversarial Systems Converging?', in C. Harding *et al*, *Criminal Justice in Europe* (1995); M. Delmas-Marty and J.R. Spencer (eds), *European Criminal Procedures* (2002).

[3] See V. Grevi, 'The New Italian Code for Criminal Procedure: a Concise Overview', in A. Pizzorusso, *Italian Studies in Law* (1994); E. Grande, 'Italian Criminal Procedure: Borrowing and Resistance', (2000) 48 *Am J Comp L* 227.

appealing against court decisions, introduced for similar reasons. In recent years there have been increasing fiscal pressures towards having fewer cases dealt with in the Crown Court and more in the magistrates' courts, manifested in such changes as the reclassification of certain offences as 'summary only' in 1988, the introduction of the 'plea before venue' system in 1997, and the raising of magistrates' sentencing limits by the Criminal Justice Act 2003. However, in addition to these structural factors there are also cultural influences pulling in the same direction. We have noted evidence that defence lawyers and prosecutors may act co-operatively at some stages, particularly in plea negotiations, to the extent of subverting the ethics of adversarialism.[4] What ought to be different ethical orientations may thus become submerged beneath the working practices and occupational cultures of the local groups of professionals.

It is not only for cases that are pursued to conviction that the system tends strongly towards trial-avoidance. The trend towards diversion is designed to take cases out of the formal criminal process and to dispose of them separately. Prominent among these dispositive decisions are the police caution, conditional cautions, and the various warnings and compounded penalties used by the 'regulatory' agencies. The Crime and Disorder Act 1998 introduced a more rigid statutory regime for the diversion of offenders under 18, by way of reprimands and final warnings. Under that statute and by other means, various forms of restorative justice have also become available as means of diverting cases by agreement between victim, offender and 'community.'[5] The continued vitality of diversion, despite a generally repressive penal climate, seems to stem from the confluence of some very different arguments—that the painful consequences of being prosecuted may themselves be too severe a response to some forms of wrongdoing; that there is scant evidence that formal court processes are more effective in preventing re-offending; that encounters with the court system may create stigma and disadvantage that makes future law-abidance more difficult; and that diversion is far less expensive than court proceedings. Although some may suspect that considerations of cost weigh most heavily with policy-makers, the result may also be to advance the other arguments in favour of diversion.

It would be wrong, however, to overlook the disadvantages. On a general plane, a widely used discretion not to prosecute may be regarded as undermining the principle of legality and the idea of the rule of law. For example, the Sexual Offences Act 2003 creates several offences that criminalize perfectly normal acts of friendly touching between teenagers:[6] the Government's response is that no prosecutions will be brought for such conduct, and the CPS has drawn up guidelines to that end.[7] The official view is that these broad offences are needed to catch the minority of wicked sexual predators, but the counter-argument is that if guidelines for prosecutors can be

---

[4] See Ch. 3 above, and M. McConville, 'Plea Bargaining: Ethics and Politics', in S. Doran and J. Jackson (eds), *The Judicial Role in Criminal Proceedings* (2000).

[5] See the discussion above, Ch. 6.

[6] J.R. Spencer, 'The Sexual Offences Act 2003: Child and Family Offences' [2004] Crim LR 347.

[7] See www.cps.gov.uk

drawn up, then the law itself should be drafted so as to decriminalize normal and friendly acts. The law should not give such discretion to prosecutors to determine the effective ambit of a widely cast law. On a more specific plane, existing methods of diversion are often inseparable from incentives for the suspect or defendant to accept them. Rather like the discount for pleading guilty, the incentive to accept a caution or conditional caution—combined, of course, with a statement that the suspect must not admit to anything that he or she did not do—may prove a powerful practical induce-ment to terminate one's involvement with the criminal justice system quickly and without the anxiety of a court appearance. However, the European Court has insisted, and English law generally provides, that anyone who does not wish to accept diversion can decline and invite the prosecution to bring the case before a court.[8] This has some importance now that cautions, conditional cautions, reprimands and final warnings are recorded nationally and are liable to be cited in court if the defendant is sub-sequently convicted of an offence. Proper safeguards, such as access to legal advice, should be made available, and there should be a principle that any sentence the court passes on a subsequent finding of guilt should not be more onerous than the penalty voluntarily rejected by the defendant.

These remarks are at a general level, and the practical operation of the system may vary to some extent according to the type of crime alleged. In the previous chapters we have noted the special difficulties arising in certain types of case: for example, the problems of investigating and prosecuting offences of 'domestic' violence and serious sexual assaults have led to changes in law and in practice that may be said to create special sub-systems for such cases.[9] There is certainly a sub-system for cases of serious fraud, following the Criminal Justice Act 1987 and the operations of the Serious Fraud Office. While in principle it is right to contemplate separate procedural approaches to circumvent practical difficulties arising in certain types of case, there is a danger that the social concerns (sometimes expressed in terms of victims' interests or rights) motivating these changes may lead to a neglect of fundamental rights for suspects and defendants. Politicians are particularly fond of claiming that a new method of com-bating a particular type of crime is called for, and that the best approach is to curtail the rights of suspects and defendants, which they then purport to justify as being in the greater public interest or for public protection.[10] This form of assertion is most frequently encountered in the context of the 'war against terrorism', with the provi-sions of the Anti-Terrorism, Crime and Security Act 2001 being a prime example. More recently this style of reasoning has been used in the context of organized crime, where the Government is proposing the greater use of coercive powers to question witnesses and further changes to the pre-trial and trial processes.[11] Such reasoning may also be found outside the context of serious crime, as in recent proposals to extend powers of arrest and search (in a document that contains not one reference to

---

[8] *Ozturk v Germany* (1984) 6 EHRR 409.   [9] See particularly Ch. 7.
[10] See the discussion of such arguments in Chs. 1 and 2 above.
[11] Home Office, *One Step Ahead: A 21st Century Strategy to defeat Organised Crime* (Cm 6167 of 2004).

human rights).[12] We have argued in Chapter 2 that it is quite wrong for a country that has signed the European Convention on Human Rights to make such proposals without a thorough analysis of the rights implications; that this does not mean that there may not be situations of vivid danger where public interest arguments may justify some curtailment of a right under Articles 5 or 6 (but no more than absolutely necessary, and preserving the essence of the right); but that the factual premise needs to be established by clear evidence, rather than assuming that reducing the rights of offenders or increasing the rights of victims will necessarily be effective.

Implicit in those arguments is the principle that there are general norms of the criminal process which apply to all offences, and therefore that any difference of legal framework for particular types of case calls for justification. In Chapters 6 and 7 we argued that the English criminal process lacks an overall strategy for pre-trial justice. Different agencies continue to operate in different ways: the police and the CPS may be converging in their operations, but the regulatory agencies continue to follow their differing paths and priorities. These variations, not to mention the discretionary powers that go with them, leave open the possibility of differences of approach that may discriminate on improper grounds such as class, social position, race, and gender. What is absent from pre-trial justice is a common starting-point for all types of case: there is no conception that people who commit offences of similar seriousness should receive similar responses (unless there are strong grounds for doing otherwise), and no real attempt to provide guidance on the relative seriousness of the various types of offence. The so-called regulatory agencies have policies that are markedly different from those of the police, not to mention the differences among the different agencies, and this means that offences of a similar degree of seriousness may receive different responses according to the context (in a public place, on company premises, in a shop, in a customs shed at a channel port, and so forth). The responses differ at the point of enforcement and investigation, and also in the various forms of diversion used. Like sentencing, diversion decisions are dispositive. Unlike sentencing, there are no open hearings and there are no general principles applicable across the diverse contexts of tax, customs, health and safety, pollution, and so on.

The absence of an aspiration to promote general norms and consistency of treatment is also manifest in local variations of policy. We saw in Chapter 6 that, despite national standards, the statistics show the persistence of variations among police force areas in the use of police cautions, most of which follows longstanding patterns. To what extent the introduction of conditional cautions will follow the same pattern remains to be seen: in organizational terms the CPS is a national agency with a national hierarchy, but working alongside the police in a local criminal justice culture may have the effect of reproducing traditional patterns. Local variations in remand decisions, in plea rates, and in the practices of some regulatory agencies are also longstanding. It is true that several worthwhile innovations in the criminal process have originated in local schemes (e. g. bail information systems, Public Interest Case

---

[12] Home Office, *Policing: Modernising Police Powers to meet Community Needs* (2004).

Assessment schemes), and the ability to experiment should be preserved in some form. What should not be tolerated are declarations of local independence in matters of criminal justice policy. It is unjust that a person who is (rightly or wrongly) suspected of a certain offence in one area should be treated in a significantly different way from a similar person in another area. Local variations in practice should be monitored and local variations in policy should only be permitted if clear justifications can be found: this would expose the unwarranted whilst enabling experimental schemes to be introduced.

Both processual and dispositive decisions, as we have seen, tend towards the avoidance of trials. One feature of pre-trial processes that has become evident from the foregoing chapters is the tendency of some decisions to be taken in anticipation of the decisions of other agencies. There are, in fact, several influences flowing in different directions. Almost all the 'input' received by the CPS has come from the police, who have therefore exerted considerable practical influence through their construction of case files; to what extent this alters with the collocation of police and CPS remains to be seen. We have noted how some of the working practices of the CPS (in relation to bail and mode of trial decisions, for example) may be shaped by local magistrates or justices' clerks or the local judiciary. Equally some defence solicitors will tailor their approach on bail and other matters to the particular prosecutor, justices' clerk, or bench of magistrates. Magistrates may sometimes defer to the police or to the CPS rather than applying their judgment independently on remands or mode of trial. It is not always easy to be sure of the existence of undue influence in these relationships: it is sometimes theoretically possible that two different parties are applying the same test and reaching the same conclusion, but the research cited on prosecutions (Chapter 7), on remands (Chapter 8), and on mode of trial (Chapter 11) is strongly suggestive of other, less ethical approaches.

Two people who have less central roles than may be thought appropriate are the defendant and the victim. We have seen that, under existing practice in both the Crown Court and magistrates' courts, the defendant is excluded from plea negotiations and has to depend on the mediated words of legal representatives.[13] Direct information for the defendant at this often crucial stage is relatively rare, and this places much emphasis on the quality of legal representation. There is growing evidence that this is variable, and that it is not always motivated by a desire to secure the defendant's rights but is sometimes diluted by a desire to curry favour with the police, or to obtain the maximum fee for the minimum work, or not to 'pull the stops out' for a client deemed unworthy.[14] In the face of strong structural and cultural pulls towards trial avoidance and negotiated outcomes, an independent and ethical approach from the defence lawyer is vital to protect the suspect-defendant.

Victims, too, may be marginalized as the criminal process moves forward. Although it has long been known that the flow of information to victims about 'their' cases has

---

[13] J. Baldwin, *Pre-Trial Justice* (1986); A. Mulcahy, 'The Justifications of Justice', (1994) 34 *BJ Crim.* 411.

[14] M. McConville *et al.*, *Standing Accused* (1994), 273 and 281; M. Travers, *The Reality of Law* (1997), Ch. 5.

not been good, efforts to improve it have not been wholly successful. Decisions on prosecution and non-prosecution, bail, and acceptance of pleas are not always communicated to the victim. However, as argued in Chapter 2, while the case for greater support and information for victims is a strong one, the arguments for victim involvement in decision making are not.

13.2 THE PRINCIPLED APPROACH

The scourge of many debates about criminal justice policy is the concept of 'balance'. As it is often expressed, notably in the report of the 1993 Royal Commission, the 'balancing' of conflicting interests is presented as if there is no particular weighting of or priority among the interests. They are all matters to be taken into consideration, and somehow a 'balance' emerges. Sometimes the process is given an apparent respectability by quoting probabilities that a certain consequence will ensue—for example, the low risk of innocent people being convicted. The existence of a low risk on one side of the equation may be presented as if it tips the scales in that direction. However, as argued in Chapter 2 above, this would be to short-circuit the course of reasoning and to ignore the strength of some of the authoritatively recognized rights. It is time, now, to re-state the argument in the light of the material in the intervening chapters.

The principled approach to criminal justice—unlike Packer's two models—is explicitly normative. The purpose of the criminal process is to bring about accurate determinations through fair procedures. The approach therefore emphasizes various rights and principles that ought to be safeguarded: some rights, such as the right not to be wrongly convicted, may be defended on a philosophical basis, but the rights declared by the European Convention on Human Rights are recognized authoritatively and indeed brought into English law by the Human Rights Act 1998. The European Convention is largely about fair procedures, and its rights are designed to eliminate arbitrariness and to promote fairness rather than to achieve particular outcomes. The effect of the 1998 Act may therefore be described as the constitutionalization of the criminal process, insofar as the Act recognizes the fundamental status of Convention rights in English law through, for example, the courts' duty to take decisions compatibly with the Convention (s 6) and to interpret statutes 'so far as possible' compatibly with Convention rights (s 3). Thus the Act has had significant effects on the shape of the English criminal process, in matters such as disclosure and public interest immunity, adverse inferences from silence, pre-trial remands, the use of various forms of surveillance, entrapment and so on. However, it was argued in Chapter 2 that the British courts and some politicians have paid insufficient attention to the differing strengths of the Convention rights, and have made the mistake of treating rights under Article 6 as if they were qualified in the same way as those in Articles 8–11. Rectification of this mistake, which has led to the importation of broad 'balancing' notions into fair trial guarantees by way of a modified concept of proportionality, should lead to a further sharpening of the human rights approach.

None of this is to suggest that the Convention should be regarded as a solution to the ills of the criminal process. Both in Chapter 2 and subsequently, attention has been drawn to various shortcomings of the Convention. Its coverage of rights is incomplete and patchy: if one were drawing up such a document for the new millennium, there would be several obvious candidates for inclusion that find no place in the 1950 Convention—for example, victims' rights, protection for witnesses, special rights for young people and for women (whether as defendants, victims or witnesses), fault requirements for criminal convictions, and so on. The Convention has been treated by the Strasbourg Court as a living instrument, so that the Court has developed certain implied rights—such as the privilege against self-incrimination and the principle of equality of arms—and has applied other rights in a creative fashion. There have also been Protocols that have added rights to the Convention on matters such as double jeopardy, capital punishment and the right to personal property. But the document as a whole is much less comprehensive than, say, the Charter of Fundamental Rights of the European Union; and the future of that charter deserves careful attention.

13.3 DISCRIMINATION AND NON-DISCRIMINATION

The principle of equality before the law, or non-discrimination, ought to be respected as a fundamental element in the administration of justice. In its present form, the Convention does not declare it to be so: Article 14 declares a right not to be discriminated against in the exercise of other Convention rights, but only the declaration and ratification of a new Protocol on Non-Discrimination will achieve the wider recognition of the principle. It would then be necessary to use the principle as the basis for positive obligations that would recognize the case for special treatment of certain groups. We have noted in previous chapters that special procedures to protect the mentally disordered must be introduced to assist and to protect them in the criminal process.[15] The same should apply to members of minority ethnic groups, in respect of whom we have noted evidence that people from an African-Caribbean background may be disadvantaged in decisions to prosecute or caution and in the process of plea negotiation.[16] Increases in the number of people from ethnic minorities in the legal profession and the various criminal justice agencies are necessary, but they are unlikely to solve the above problems, at least in the short term. The extent of discrimination on grounds of gender is unclear, and some might argue that the discrimination favours rather than disfavours women. However, studies of sentencing

---

[15] See Ch. 6 on diversion.   [16] See Chs. 7 and 10.

suggest that it would be unwise to take at face value the apparently lenient treatment of women and girls, and remand decisions appear to bear this out.[17]

In relation to young suspects and defendants, a case for positive discrimination has long been recognized. However, the special procedures introduced for child defendants after the decision in *V and T v United Kingdom*[18] and for child witnesses under the Youth Justice and Criminal Evidence Act 1999 stand in contrast to the increasingly tough rhetoric used in relation to young defendants. In this country the spirit underlying the United Nations Convention on the Rights of the Child does not pervade Government pronouncements on youth justice, and the desire for vote-winning headlines seems to be thought more important.[19]

Another source of discrimination that is growing, and that is connected partly with the demonization of young people, is the spread of anti-social behaviour orders. The Government has announced repeated initiatives against anti-social behaviour, a loose concept that encompasses a range of conduct from relatively minor inconveniences to some fairly major crimes. It is not just the vagueness of the concept that is objectionable, but the response to it. The first response is to regard it as a matter for civil procedure resulting in a preventive order, which may contain as many as 10 or 12 restrictive conditions: this aspect of the Crime and Disorder Act 1998 was upheld by the House of Lords, although they held that the standard of proof required should be equivalent to the criminal standard.[20] The second response is that breach of any condition of the civil order renders the offender liable to up to five years' imprisonment, a higher maximum than for many crimes. The discrimination involved in this statutory regime consists of depriving people of proper legal safeguards, when the ultimate penalty is substantial. This is not the same as introducing non-criminal penalties for minor offences and calling them administrative offences.

A further source of discrimination, discussed at several points in the foregoing chapters, may be found in factors connected with social class or wealth. It is evident from Chapters 6 and 7 that any systematic examination of the prosecution policies of the police compared with those of the so-called regulatory agencies would reveal a diversity of approaches, amounting in general to a less formal, less public, and less severe response to law-breaking by employers, taxpayers, and others in established ways of life. It is hardly surprising that statistics about the social background of offenders show a predominance of those from the lower socio-economic groups when the enforcement process is skewed against those groups and in favour of those from the higher occupational categories. However, changing this would present a structural problem of immense proportions for the English criminal justice system. Those who adopt a desert or retributive approach would probably argue that the first task should

---

[17] Prison Reform Trust, *Justice for Women: the Need for Reform* (2000), paras 5.4–5.13.

[18] (2000) 30 EHRR 121; cf. *S.C. v United Kingdom* [2005] *Crim LR* 130, where a further breach was found.

[19] M. Tonry, *Punishment and Politics* (2004), esp. Ch. 2.

[20] *Clingham v Royal Borough of Kensington and Chelsea; R (McCann) v Manchester Crown Court* [2003] 1 AC 787, discussed briefly in Ch. 1 above.

be to decide on the relative seriousness of all these offences, whether 'white-collar', 'normal', 'financial', 'commercial', 'domestic', or however they may be labelled. The second task might then be to ensure that the criminal law may only be invoked at a certain level of seriousness, whatever the context of the offence, and not below that level. This would represent an attempt to achieve equality before the law, in the hope of preventing the use of the criminal process (or anti-social behaviour orders) for relatively minor offences by impecunious or poorly connected defendants when at the same time ensuring that corporate or wealthy defendants do not benefit from a less vigorous approach where their offences are serious. That change of emphasis would not be easy to achieve, however, for many reasons—the need for a significant shift of resources to allow equivalent enforcement of regulatory offences, the need to reconsider the ways in which certain regulatory offences are drafted, and the possibility that wealthy or corporate 'deviants' might deploy their considerable resources to devise means of 'creative compliance' with the law.[21]

An alternative approach would be to adopt a form of restorative justice, abandoning the search for equivalent measures of punishment and instead requiring corporations who offend to make due reparation to those harmed by their offending behaviour.[22] This approach is premised not only on a rejection of the retributive paradigm for punishment but also on the difficulty and expense involved in holding companies responsible according to traditional criminal procedures and doctrines. Thus Braithwaite and Fisse argue that companies should be served with a notice that presumes liability and requires them to state what remedial measures they propose to take, in respect of both any individual victims and the wider community. In their scheme this would release resources otherwise devoted to prosecuting corporate crime and enable law enforcement agencies to devote more resources to dealing fairly with other forms of crime.[23] Thus companies would be taken out of the criminal process and their offences dealt with by different procedures, not so much on principle but rather as a means of controlling scarce resources. An alternative might be to keep companies within the criminal process and to raise the threshold for dealing with individual offenders, putting fewer inadequate and minor offenders in prison.

Important as it is to tackle unfair discrimination in the criminal law, in the enforcement process, and in criminal procedure, it remains supremely difficult to do so within a society many of whose institutions and practices may be said to lean towards unfair discrimination. The criminal process should not be regarded as something separate from wider social issues and capable of separate treatment. Discrimination on grounds of race, gender, age and other stereotypical criteria will be hard to remove from the criminal process for so long as its manifestations are present in

---

[21] See D. McBarnet and C. Whelan, 'The Elusive Spirit of the Law: Formalism and the Struggle for Legal Control', (1991) 54 *MLR* 848.

[22] B. Fisse and J. Braithwaite, *Corporations, Crime and Accountability* (1993).

[23] For which the authors also have proposals based on restorative justice, reinforced by strong sanctions: J. Braithwaite and P. Pettit, *Not Just Deserts: A Republican Theory of Criminal Justice* (1990), discussed critically in A. von Hirsch and A. Ashworth (eds), *Principled Sentencing* (2nd ed., 1998), Ch. 7.

everyday social life.[24] This is not to deny the importance of efforts to remove discrimination from the criminal process, but it is to argue that there are structural factors that make it likely that some discriminatory effects might be found even if law enforcers were scrupulously fair in their own actions.

13.4 PROMOTING THE PRINCIPLES

How should the principled approach outlined in Chapter 2 and in this chapter be put into practice? Lawyers would tend to look to a network of rules or to a system of legal regulation as the means of advancing the desired principles. It has often been remarked that many stages in the criminal process are characterized by wide swaths of little-regulated discretion, from which it is assumed that the path of reform involves restrictions on or the complete removal of discretion. However, this would be naïve. It would be to assume that the existence of rules eliminates the practices that discretion allows. There are plenty of examples of rules being circumvented or neutralized, for instance by the police (Chapter 3), by Crown Prosecutors (Chapter 7), and by counsel and judges (Chapter 10). Thus the mere enactment of rules in primary legislation should not be regarded as sufficient, or even as more effective than discretion complemented by guidelines. Working practices need to be changed, and this is where questions of ethics and of training come to the fore.

We noted in Chapter 1 that the origins of many of the miscarriage of justice cases of recent years lie in the early parts of the criminal justice system, particularly the stage of investigation by police and forensic scientists. One of the most welcome developments has been the creation of the Criminal Cases Review Commission, discussed in Chapter 12 above. The CCRC is, however, currently a remedial rather than a preventive mechanism,[25] and it remains necessary to focus attention on the working practices of the police and other law enforcement agencies, and also the CPS and defence lawyers, at the early stages in the process. The criminal process in England and Wales has made significant advances in the treatment of certain fragile forms of evidence—notably confessions and eyewitness evidence—but further improvements should be made to eyewitness identification procedures, and thought needs to be given to new issues such as voice identification. Good legal advice should be available in these early stages, and this means ensuring that the system of payment for defence solicitors rewards early advice and case preparation appropriately,[26] and that the Public Defender Service develops along the right lines.

Moreover, it is not just the prosecution of some weak cases that is a cause for

---

[24] Cf. the argument of J. Chan, 'Changing Police Culture', (1996) 36 *BJ Crim.* 109.

[25] The CCRC has frequently stated that it will use its experience of miscarriage of justice cases to make recommendations for improving the criminal process, so in the future it may play a more proactive role.

[26] See House of Commons Constitutional Affairs Committee, *Draft Criminal Defence Service Bill* (Fifth Report of Session 2003/4).

concern, or unwarranted arrests followed by detention. The attrition rate is also in
need of constant scrutiny, and may embody miscarriages of justice of a different kind
inasmuch as guilty people are not prosecuted or are acquitted because the system is
organized in a way that fails to prevent that result. Thus there is a need to review
procedures for witness protection and for encouraging witnesses to give evidence by
the increased availability of video links and other mechanisms, subject to proper
safeguards for the defence. Unfortunately, however, some of the recent changes to
criminal procedure savour more of reducing the rights of the defence for symbolic
reasons rather than of improving the position of victims: as argued in Chapter 2,
the Government's notion of 're-balancing the system in favour of victims' is utterly
flawed.

What should happen when a breach of one or more pre-trial procedures is
uncovered? Much has been made, by some academics[27] and even by some British
judges,[28] of the 'integrity principle'. The argument is that the integrity of the court, or
more widely of the criminal justice system, would be compromised if it were to act on
evidence that had been obtained as a result of a departure from proper procedure. At
one level the argument is persuasive, and the imagery of 'tainting' or 'the fruit of the
poisoned tree' seems apposite. Yet in other respects the integrity principle leaves
certain questions unanswered. Should every departure from procedure, no matter
how small or inconsequential, be regarded as calling into question the integrity of a
court or the whole system? If not, by what criteria can we tell whether integrity is
compromised? Questions of this kind raise a doubt whether the integrity principle
can be a satisfactory operating standard for the courts: attractive as it is in clear and
gross cases, it needs considerable refinement if it is to be suitable for the general run of
situations.[29] More relevant to the objective of promoting a principled approach to
criminal justice is the protective principle: that a court should not act on evidence if
that would deprive the defendant of a protection that should have been assured. In
other words, a deviation from procedures may only be overlooked if the evidence in
question was not obtained as a result of its breach. The defendant should not be
disadvantaged by an investigator's non-observance of the procedures.

Of course, that leaves the question of just what procedures are proper. Once we
move away from the rules in PACE which give suspects various rights, there are a host
of difficult questions: when, if ever, is deception, or covert recording, or entrapment
proper? There is simply no avoiding the fact that, in general, an evaluation of the
criminal process involves difficult questions about what values should be respected.
Other examples are questions such as: When might a breach of the privilege against
self-incrimination be appropriate? When is it appropriate to keep a suspect's DNA
profile on a database? How wide should arrest powers be? Human rights documents

---

[27] E.g., I. Dennis, *Criminal Evidence* (2nd ed., 2002), Ch. 2E.

[28] E.g., Lord Lowry in *R v Horseferry Road Magistrates' Court, ex parte Bennett* [1994] 1 AC 42, and Lord
Nicholls in *R v Looseley* [2001] UKHL 53.

[29] For fuller analysis, see A. Ashworth, 'Exploring the Integrity Principle in Evidence and Procedure', in
P. Mirfield and R.J. Smith (eds), *Essays for Colin Tapper* (2003).

will not always provide clear, or convincing, answers to such questions, and there is room for reasonable disagreement on them. But our argument is that any attempt to answer these questions must involve careful analysis of the values at stake. All too often this does not happen.

The promotion of a principled approach requires not only the provision of appropriate remedies in cases where the principles are not put into practice, but also programmes of training and supervision and guidance for the professionals concerned. No doubt it would be argued that there are professional organizations to take care of such matters, and the role of the Law Society and the Bar Council will be cited. However, the discussion of occupational cultures which began in Chapter 3 and continued in subsequent chapters makes it plain that there is, at the very least, a risk not only that simply changing the rules will fail but also that leaving the task of changing practices to the professional organizations is unlikely to succeed. The risk of failure would be greatest where the particular occupational culture is adverse and strong. It is therefore necessary to attempt to reshape the occupational cultures of some of those working within the criminal process. As a first step, more detailed ethical principles need to be drawn up which spell out the role responsibilities of prosecutors and defence lawyers, and the constraints on their pursuit of these goals. The ethical principles should ideally be supported by examples of situations in which they are intended to bite. This would be a means of challenging occupational cultures in a direct way. In order to do that, of course, it would be necessary to have a reasonably accurate impression of the operation of occupational cultures in practice, and the available research (discussed in foregoing chapters) provides some evidence of unethical practices (without suggesting that all members of the various groups follow these practices). Ideas such as 'society expects us to fight crime with our hands tied behind our backs' must be carefully and persuasively unpicked. Thus it is vital to incorporate into training the reasons for respecting rights, and to reorient professional goals and official performance indicators in a way that reveres and rewards respect for rights over the mere obtaining of convictions.

None of this means that convicting the guilty is unimportant; rather, it emphasizes that this worthy goal should be achieved by fair processes. This is not just a matter of ensuring that Parliament, the courts and public authorities uphold Convention rights, although that is constitutionally important after the Human Rights Act. There is also evidence that people in general regard fair procedures as an essential element in a criminal justice system. To set against the belief of some politicians that public confidence in the system would be threatened by thoroughgoing respect for human rights (not that it is often thus expressed) are the findings of social psychologists such as Tom Tyler that people place as much emphasis on the fairness of procedures (notably, having a fair hearing) as on their outcomes.[30] Although some of Tyler's conclusions

---

[30] T. Tyler, *Why People Obey the Law* (1990).

may seem overblown,[31] there is good reason to accept his fundamental point that fair processes matter.

13.5 THE CRIMINAL PROCESS OF THE FUTURE

Any detailed reform proposals such as those advanced in this book are likely to have a modest effect if other aspects of the criminal justice system remain little changed, and any changes in the criminal justice system may have a modest effect if various social structures and policies remain little changed. Moreover, considerations of cost and public expenditure must be taken into account by anyone who forsakes the cover of academic discussion to venture some policy proposals. Recognizing cost as a constraint does not, however, argue against fundamental change. A decade ago, the Report of the 1993 Royal Commission was a missed opportunity in criminal justice reform—not only because of its abject failure to discuss Convention rights and their implications for criminal justice, but also because it considered expenditure in relation to discrete stages in the process rather than the whole. A more creative approach would be to take the annual budget of the whole system—including police, prosecutors, courts, legal aid, prisons, and so forth—and to consider a five-year reorientation of expenditure which would enhance human rights to the greatest extent without increasing the overall budget.[32] Rather than resorting to the imagery of 'balance' at each stage of the process, the challenge would be to ensure or maximize respect for rights while enhancing convictions of the guilty, looking critically at the roles of the various professional groups, at their powers, and at their practices. In addition to debating the rights of victims, the approach would be to examine wider social methods of preventing crime that promise fewer victims (and fewer offenders), such as the increased availability of pre-school education, improved housing, and other changes in social policy. It is unlikely that changing the criminal process itself will make much difference to crime rates and the safety of citizens: altering the rules of the criminal process is attractive to governments, not least because it is much easier than tackling fundamental issues of social policy, but also because the symbolic effects of appearing 'tough on crime' are expected to have favourable electoral consequences.

Thus one obvious feature of debates on the criminal process in the last decade is the increased politicization. A Government that began in 1997 by advocating evidence-based changes quickly forsook that approach in favour of announcing changes that

---

[31] E.g., at p. 101: 'if people receive fair procedures, outcome is not relevant to their reactions. If they do not, it is.'

[32] As argued in previous editions, the inquiry must necessarily take in spheres of expenditure other than criminal justice. Even if the debate could be confined within criminal justice, this approach would place the benefits of, say, pre-trial legal advice in a proper perspective rather than simply seeing it as an extra expense. See also K. Roach, 'The Criminal Process', in P. Cane and M. Tushnet (eds), *Handbook of Legal Studies* (2003).

appear tough and anti-defendant and thus court no danger of losing the political initiative to the opposition. In this climate there is a dire need for an attractive replacement discourse if rights—also advocated by this Government in its early days, prior to the enactment of the Human Rights Act—are to be respected properly in the criminal process. We have witnessed an unfortunate backsliding on human rights, to the extent that recent Home Office policy papers have rarely even discussed the issue in the context of new proposals for 'reform.' The human rights approach to criminal justice advocated in Chapter 2 of this book therefore runs counter to much contemporary policy, although it has its basis in the UK's international obligations (notably the Convention). However, neither the Convention nor other international instruments—nor, it may be added, any known general theory—provides a comprehensive set of principles for the criminal process. In practice there will always be some choices to be made, and some trade-offs to be agreed. What is distinctive about the approach advocated here, and elaborated in Chapter 2 is that it insists on a weighted approach, with justifications given for the different priority given to different rights. It also insists on evidence rather than rhetoric, and on evidence of actual enhancements in prevention or protection rather than evidence of reductions in the risk people believe they face.[33]

[33] For recent argument to the same effect on criminal justice policy and sentencing, see Tonry, above n 19.

BIBLIOGRAPHY

ABRAMSON, J. (1994), *We, The Jury: The Jury System and the Ideal of Democracy*, New York: Basic Books.

ALLEN, R., and ROSENBERG, R. (1998), 'The Fourth Amendment and the Limits of Theory: Local Versus General Theoretical Knowledge', *St John's L Rev.*, **72**: 1149.

ALSCHULER, A. (1983), 'Implementing the Criminal Defendant's Right to Trial', *U. Chi. LR*, **50**: 931.

—— (1997), 'Constraint and Confession', *Denver U. L. Rev.*, **74**: 957.

AMAR, A. (1997), *The Constitution and Criminal Procedure*, New Haven: Yale University Press.

ASHWORTH, A. (1977), 'Excluding Evidence as Protecting Rights', *Crim LR*, 723.

—— (1998), 'Should the Police be Allowed to Use Deceptive Practices?', *Law Quarterly Review*, **114**: 108.

—— (2000), *Sentencing and Criminal Justice*, 3rd edn., London: Butterworths.

—— (2002), *Human Rights, Serious Crime and Criminal Procedure*, London: Sweet and Maxwell.

—— (2003), 'Responsibilities, Rights and Restorative Justice', *BJ Crim.*, **43**: 578.

—— (2003), 'Exploring the Integrity Principle in Evidence and Procedure', in Mirfield and Smith, eds., q. v.

—— (2004), 'Social Control and "Anti-Social Behaviour": the subversion of Human Rights?', *Law Quarterly Review*, **120**: 263.

—— (2004), 'Criminal Justice Reform: Principles, Human Rights and Public Protection', *Crim LR*, 516.

——, and FIONDA, J. (1994), 'The New Code for Crown Prosecutors: Prosecution, Accountability and the Public Interest', *Crim LR*, 894.

——, and PATTENDEN, R. (1986), 'Reliability, Hearsay Evidence and the English Criminal Trial', *LQR*, **102**: 292.

——, and STRANGE, M. (2004), 'Criminal Law and Human Rights', *EHRLR.*, 121.

——, and WASIK, M., eds. (1998), *Fundamentals of Sentencing Theory*, Oxford: Oxford University Press.

AUDIT COMMISSION (1996), *Misspent Youth: Young People and Crime*, London: Audit Commission.

AULD, R. E. (2001), *Review of the Criminal Courts of England and Wales; Report*, London: The Lord Chancellor's Department.

BAKER, E. (1998), 'Taking European Criminal Law Seriously', *Crim LR*, 361.

BALDWIN, J. (1986), *Pre-Trial Justice*, Oxford: Oxford University Press.

—— (1992), *The Supervision of Police Investigations in Serious Criminal Cases*, Royal Commission on Criminal Justice Research Study No. **4**, London: HMSO.

—— (1993), 'Police Interview Techniques; Establishing Truth or Proof', *Brit. J. Criminol.* **33**: 325.

—— (1993), 'Legal Advice at the Police Station', *Crim LR*, 371.

—— (1997), 'Understanding Judge Ordered and Directed Acquittals in the Crown Court', *Crim LR*, 536.

——, and McCONVILLE, M. (1977), *Negotiated Justice*, Oxford: Martin Robertson.

BALDWIN, R. (2004), 'The New Punitive Regulation', *MLR*, **67**: 351.

——, and HAWKINS, K. (1984), 'Discretionary Justice: Davis Reconsidered', *Public Law*, 570.

BALL, C. (2004), 'Youth Justice? Half a Century of Responses to Youth Offending', *Crim LR*, 167.

BARCLAY, G. C., ed. (1999), *Digest 4: Information on the Criminal Justice System in England and Wales*, London: Home Office.

——, and MHLANGA, B. (2000), *Ethnic Differences in Decisions on Young Defendants Dealt with by the Crown Prosecution Service*, Section 95 Findings 1, London: Home Office.

BELLONI, F., and HODGSON, J. (2000), *Criminal Injustice: An Evaluation of the Criminal Justice Process in Britain*, London: Macmillan.

BILLINGSLEY, R., NEMITZ, T., and BEAN, P., eds. (2001), *Informers: Policing, Policy, Practice*, Devon: Willan Publishing.

BIRCH, D. (1995), 'Corroboration: Goodbye to All That?' *Crim LR*, 524.

——, (2004) 'Hearsay: Same Old Story, Same Old Song?', *Crim LR*, 556.

——, 'Suffering in Silence: a Cost-Benefit Analysis of Section 34 of the Criminal Justice and Public Order Act 1994', *Crim LR*, 769.

BITTNER, E. (1967), 'The Police on Skid Row: a Study in Peace-Keeping', *American Sociological Review*, 32: 699.

BLAKE, M., and ASHWORTH, A. (1998), 'Some Ethical Issues in Prosecuting and Defending Criminal Cases', *Crim LR*, 16.

BLOCK, B., CORBETT, C., and PEAY, J. (1993), *Ordered and Directed Acquittals in the Crown Court*, Royal Commission on Criminal Justice Research Study No. 15, London: HMSO.

BOTTOMLEY, A. K. (1968), 'The Granting of Bail: Principles and Practice', *MLR*, 31: 40.

BOTTOMS, A. E., 'Five Puzzles in Von Hirsch's Theory of Punishment', in Ashworth and Wasik, q. v.

——, and McCLEAN, J. D. (1976), *Defendants in the Criminal Process*, London: Routledge.

BOWLING, B., and PHILLIPS, C. (2002), *Racism, Crime and Justice*, Harlow: Longman.

BRADLEY, C. (1993), 'The Emerging Concensus as to Criminal Procedural Rules', *Michigan J. Int. Law* 14: 171.

—— (1999), *Criminal Procedure: a Worldwide Study*, Durham NC: Carolina Academic Press.

BRAITHWAITE, J., and PETTIT, P. (1990), *Not Just Deserts: a Republican Theory of Criminal Justice*, Oxford: Oxford University Press.

BRANTS, C., and FIELD, S. (1995), 'Discretion and Accountability in Prosecution', in Fennell, Harding, Jörg, and Swart, eds., q. v.

BREDAR, J. (1992), 'Moving up the Day of Reckoning: Strategies for Attacking the Problem of Cracked Trials', *Crim LR*, 153.

BRIDGES, L. (2000), 'Taking Liberties' *Legal Action*, 6 July 2000.

——, and CHOONGH, S. (1998), *Improving Police Station Legal Advice*, London: Law Society.

BROOKE, D., TAYLOR, C., GUNN, J., and MADEN, A. (2000), 'Substance Misuse as a Marker of Vulnerability Among Male Prisoners on Remand', *BJ Psychiatry*, 177: 248.

BROOKMAN, F., and PIERPOINT, H. (2003), 'Access to Legal Advice for Young Suspects and Remand Prisoners', *Howard JCJ.*, 42: 452.

BROWN, D. (1997), *PACE Ten Years On: A Review of the Research*, Home Office Research Study 155, London: Home Office.

—— (2000), *Reducing Delays in the Magistrates' Courts*, Home Office Research Findings No 131, London: Home Office.

——, LARCOMBE, K., and ELLIS, C. (1993), *Changing the Code*, Home Office Research Study 129, London: HMSO.

BROWNLEE, I., MULCAHY, A., and WALKER, C. P. (1994), 'Pre-Trial Reviews, Court Efficiency and Justice: a Study in Leeds and Bradford Magistrates' Courts', *Howard JCJ*, **33**: 109.

BUCKE, T., and BROWN, D. (1997), *In Police Custody: police powers and suspects' rights under the revised PACE codes of practice*, Home Office Research Study 174, London: Home Office.

——, STREET, R., and BROWN, D. (2000), *The Right of Silence: the Impact of the Criminal Justice and Public Order Act 1994*, Home Office Research Study 199, London: Home Office.

BURNEY, E., and PEARSON, G. (1995), 'Mentally Disordered Offenders: Finding a Focus for Diversion', *Howard JCJ*, **34**: 291.

——, and ROSE, G. (2002), *Racist offences—How is the Law Working?*, Home Office Research Study 244. London: Home Office.

BURROWS, P., HENDERSON, P., and MORGAN, P. (1994), *Improving Bail Decisions: the Bail Process Project*, London: Home Office Research and Planning Unit.

BURTON, M. (2001), 'Reviewing Crown Prosecution Service Decisions not to Prosecute', *Crim LR*, 374.

CAMERON, N., POTTER, S., YOUNG, W. (1999), 'The New Zealand Jury', *Law & Contemporary Problems*, **62**: 103.

CANE, P., and TUSHNET, M., eds. (2003), *Oxford Handbook of Legal Studies*, Oxford: Oxford Univeristy Press.

CAPE, E. (1999), 'Sufficient Evidence to Charge?' *Crim LR*, 874.

——, (2003), *Defending Suspects at Police Stations*, 4th edn., London: Legal Action Group.

—— (2003), 'The Revised PACE Codes of Practice: A Further Step Towards Inquisitorialism', *Crim LR*, 355.

—— (2004), 'The Rise (and Fall) of a Criminal Defence Profession', *Crim LR*, 408.

CARSON, D. (1989), 'Prosecuting People with Mental Handicaps', *Crim LR*, 87.

CAVADINO, P., and GIBSON, B. (1993), *Bail: the Law, Best Practice and the Debate*, Winchester: Waterside Press.

CHAN, J. (1996), 'Changing Police Culture', *BJ Crim.*, **36**: 109.

CHOO, A. (1993), *Abuse of Process and Judicial Stays of Criminal Proceedings*, Oxford: Oxford University Press.

—— (1996), *Hearsay and Confrontation in Criminal Trials*, Oxford: Oxford University Press.

——, and NASH, S. (1999), 'What's the Matter with Section 78?', *Crim LR*, 929.

CHOONGH, S. (1998), 'Policing the Dross: a Social Disciplinary Model of Policing', *BJ Crim.*, **38**: 623.

CLARE, I., GUDJONSSON, G., and HARARI, M. (1998), 'Understanding of the Current Police Caution (England and Wales)', *J. Community & Applied Social Psychology*, **8**: 323.

CLARKE, C., and MILNE, R. (2001), *National Evaluation of the PEACE Investigative Interviewing Course*, London: Home Office.

CLARKSON, C., CRETNEY, A., DAVIS, G., and SHEPHERD, J. (1994), 'Assaults: the Relationship between Seriousness, Criminalisation and Punishment', *Crim LR*, 4.

COMMISSION FOR RACIAL EQUALITY (1992), *Juvenile Cautioning: Ethnic Monitoring in Practice*, London: CRE.

COMMISSION JUSTICE PÉNALE ET DROITS DE L'HOMME (1991), *La Mise en Etat des Affaires Pénales*, Paris: la Documentation Francaise.

CORRE, N., and WOLCHOVER, D. (1999), *Bail in Criminal Proceedings*, 2nd edn., London: Fourmat.

COUNCIL OF EUROPE (2000), *Crime and Criminal Justice in Europe*, Strasbourg: Council of Europe.

CRAIG, P. (2004), 'Grounds for Judicial Review: Substantive Control over Discretion', in Feldman, q. v.

CRANSTON, R. (1979), *Regulating Business*, Oxford: Oxford University Press.

CRETNEY, A., and DAVIS, G. (1995), *Punishing Violence*, London, New York: Routledge.

CRIMINAL LAW REVISION COMMITTEE (1972), *Eleventh Report: Evidence (General)*, Cmnd. 4991, London: HMSO.

CRISP, D., and MOXON, D. (1995), *Case Screening by the Crown Prosecution Service: How and Why Cases are Terminated*, Home Office Research Study 137, London: HMSO.

——, WHITAKER, C., and HARRIS, J. (1995), *Public Interest Case Assessment Schemes*, Home Office Research Study 138, London: HMSO.

CROWN PROSECUTION SERVICE (2003), *Annual Report 2002–03*, London: CPS.

—— (2003), *Guidance on Prosecuting Cases of Racist and Religious Crime*, London: CPS.

—— (2004), *Annual Report 2003–04*, London: CPS.

CUTLER, B., and PENROD, S. (1995), *Mistaken Identification: The Eyewitness, Psychology and the Law*, New York: Cambridge University Press.

DAMAŠKA, M. (1973), 'Evidentiary Barriers to Conviction and Two Models of Criminal Procedure: a Comparative Study', *U. Pa. LR*, 121: 506.

—— (1976), *The Faces of Justice and State Authority*, New Haven: Yale University Press.

—— (1997), *Evidence Law Adrift*, New Haven: Yale University Press.

DARBYSHIRE, P. (1997), 'For the New Lord Chancellor: Some Causes for Concern about Magistrates', *Crim LR*, 861.

—— (1997), 'Previous Misconduct and the Magistrates' Courts—Some Tales from the Real World', *Crim LR*, 105.

—— (2000), 'The Mischief of Plea Bargaining and Sentencing Rewards', *Crim LR*, 895.

DAVIES, F. G. (1995), 'CPS Charging Standards: a Cynic's View', *Justice of the Peace*, 159: 203.

—— (1997), 'Ten Years of the Crown Prosecution Service: the Verdict', *Justice of the Peace*, 161: 207.

DAVIS, G., HOYANO, L., KEENAN, C., MAITLAND, L., and MORGAN, R. (1999), *An Assessment of the Admissibility and Sufficiency of Evidence in Child Abuse Prosecutions*, London: Home Office.

DAW, R. (1994), 'The CPS Code—a Response', *Crim LR*, 904.

DELMAS-MARTY, M., and SPENCER, J. R., eds. (2002), *European Criminal Procedures*, Cambridge: Cambridge University Press.

DENNIS, I. (1989), 'Reconstructing the Law of Criminal Evidence', *Current Legal Problems*, 21.

——, (1995), 'Instrumental Protection, Human Right or Functional Necessity? Reassessing the Privilege against Self-Incrimination', *Cambridge LJ*, 54: 342.

——, (2000), 'Rethinking Double Jeopardy: Justice and Finality in Criminal Process', *Crim LR*, 933.

——, (2002), *The Law of Evidence*, 2nd edn, London: Sweet and Maxwell.

——, (2002), 'Fair Trials and Safe Convictions', *CLP*, 56: 211.

——, (2004), 'Prosecution Appeals and Retrial for Serious Offences', *Crim LR*, 619.

DEVLIN, P. (1976), *Report to the Secretary of State for the Home Department of the Departmental Committee on Evidence of Identification in Criminal Cases*, London: HC.

DEVLIN, (1979), *The Judge*, Oxford: Oxford University Press.

DHAMI, M. (2004), 'Conditional Bail Decision-Making in the Magistrates' Court', *Howard JCJ.*, 43: 27.

DINGWALL, G., and HARDING, C., *Diversion in the Criminal Process*, London: Sweet & Maxwell.

DIXON, D. (1997), *Law in Policing: Legal Regulation and Police Practices*, Oxford: Oxford University Press.

——, (1990), 'Safeguarding the Rights of Suspects in Police Custody', *Policing & Society*, 1: 115.

DOHERTY, C., and EAST, R. (1985), 'Bail Decisions in Magistrates' Courts', *BJ Crim.*, 25: 251.

DOLINKO, D. (1986), 'Is there a Rationale for the Privilege Against Self-Incrimination?' 33 *UCLA L Rev.*, 33: 1063.

DORAN, S., and GLENN, R. (2000), *Lay Involvement in Adjudication*, Belfast: The Stationery Office.

——, and JACKSON, J. D. (1997), 'The Case for Jury Waiver', *Crim LR*, 155.

——, ——, eds. (2000), *The Judicial Role in Criminal Proceedings*, Oxford: Hart Publishing.

DOWNES, D., and MORGAN, R. (2002), 'The Skeletons in the Cupboard: The Politics of Law and Order at the Turn of the Millenium', in Maguire, Morgan and Reiner, eds., q. v.

DREWRY, G. (1985), 'The Ponting Case—Leaking in the Public Interest', *Public Law*, 203.

DUFF, P. (2004), 'Irregularly Obtained Real Evidence: The Scottish Solution', *E&P*, 8: 77.

——, and HUTTON, N., eds. (1999), *Criminal Justice in Scotland*, Aldershot: Ashgate.

DUFF, R. A. (1986), *Trials and Punishment*, Cambridge: Cambridge University Press.

——, (2001), *Punishment, Communication and Community*, New York: Oxford University Press.

——, FARMER, L., MARSHALL, S., and TADROS, V., eds. (forthcoming), *The Trial on Trial: Volume 2. Judgment and Calling to Account*, Oxford: Hart Publishing.

DWORKIN, R. M. (1981), 'Principle, Policy, Procedure', in Tapper, ed., q. v.

ELLIS, L., and DIAMOND, S. (2003), 'Race, Diversity, and Jury Composition: Battering and Bolstering Legitimacy', *Chicago-Kent L Rev*, 78: 1033.

EMMERSON, B., and ASHWORTH, A. (2001), *Human Rights and Criminal Justice*, London: Sweet & Maxwell.

EVANS, R. (1993), *The Conduct of Police Interviews with Juveniles*, Royal Commission on Criminal Justice Research Study No. 8, London: HMSO.

—— (1993), 'Evaluating Young Adult Diversion Schemes in the Metropolitan Police District', *Crim LR*, 490.

—— (1993), 'Comparing Young Adult and Juvenile Cautioning in the Metropolitan Police District', *Crim LR*, 572.

—— (1996), 'Challenging a Police Caution using Judicial Review', *Crim LR*, 104.

——, and ELLIS, R. (1997), *Police Cautioning in the 1990s*, Home Office Research Findings No. 33, London: Home Office.

FEELEY, M. (1979), *The Process is the Punishment*, New York: Russell Sage Foundation.

——, (1997), 'Legal Complexity and the Transformation of the Criminal Process: the Origins of Plea Bargaining', *Israel LR*, 31: 183.

FEILZER, M., and HOOD, R. (2004), *Differences or Discrimination*, London: Youth Justice Board.

FELDMAN, D. (2002), *Civil Liberties and Human Rights in England and Wales*, 2nd edn., Oxford: Oxford University Press.

——, (ed) (2004), *English Public Law*, Oxford: Oxford University Press.

FENNELL, P., HARDING, C., JORG, N., and SWART, B., eds. (1995), *Criminal Justice in Europe*, Oxford: Clarendon.

FENNER, S., GUDJONSSON, G., and CLARE, I. (2002), 'Understanding of the Current Police Caution (England and Wales) Among Suspects in Police Detention', *J. Community & Applied Social Psychology*, 12: 83.

FENWICK, H. (2002), *Civil Liberties and Human Rights*, 3rd edn., London: Cavendish.

FIONDA, J. (1995), *Public Prosecutors and Discretion: a Comparative Study*, Oxford: Clarendon.

FISSE, B., and BRAITHWAITE, J. (1993), *Corporations, Crime and Accountability*, Sydney: University of Sydney Press.

FITZGERALD, M. (1993), *Ethnic Minorities and the Criminal Justice System*, Royal Commission on Criminal Justice Research Study No. 20, London: HMSO.

——, (1999), *Final Report into Stop and Search*, London: Metropolitan Police Service.

FOOTE, C. (1954), 'Compelling Appearance in Court: the Administration of Bail in Philadelphia', *U. Pa. LR*, 102: 1031.

FRASE, R. (1999), 'France', in Bradley, q. v.

FRAUD TRIALS COMMITTEE (1987), *Report* ('The Roskill Report'), London: HMSO.

FREED, D. J., and WALD, P. (1964), *Bail in the United States*, New York: Vera Institute of Justice.

FRIEDMAN, R. (1998), 'Confrontation: The Search for Basic Principles' (1998), *Geo LJ*, 86: 1011.

——, (1998), 'Thoughts from Across the Water on Hearsay and Confrontation', *Crim LR*, 697.

FUKURAI, H., and KROOTH, R. (2003), *Race in the Jury Box: Affirmative Action in Jury Selection*, Albany NY: State University of New York Press.

GARDNER, J. (1998), 'Punishment—in Proportion and in Perspective', in Ashworth and Wasik, q. v.

GENDERS, E. (1999), 'Reform of the Offences Against the Person Act: Lessons from the Law in Action', *Crim LR*, 689.

GLIDEWELL, I., (1998), *Review of the Crown Prosecution Service: a Report*, Cm. 3960, London: The Stationery Office.

GOLDKAMP, J. and GOTTFREDSON, M. R. (1985), *Policy Guidelines for Bail: an Exercise in Court Reform*, Philadelphia: Temple University Press.

GRANDE, E. (2000), 'Italian Criminal Procedure: Borrowing and Resistance', *Am J Comp L*, 48: 227.

GREEN, M. (2002), 'The Paradox of Auxiliary Rights: The Privilege Against Self-Incrimination and the Right to Keep and Bear Arms', *Duke LJ.*, 52: 113.

GREENAWALT, K. (1981), 'Silence as a Moral and Constitutional Right', *William & Mary L Rev.*, 23: 15.

GREVI, V. (1994), 'The New Italian Code of Criminal Procedure: a Concise Overview', in Pizzarusso, q. v.

GREVLING, K. (1997), 'Fairness and the Exclusion of Evidence Under Section 78(1) of the Police and Criminal Evidence Act', *LQR*, 113: 667.

GUDJONSSON, G. (2003), *The Psychology of Interrogations and Confessions: A Handbook*, Chichester: Wiley.

GUS JOHN PARTNERSHIP (2003), *Race for Justice*, London: CPS.

HALLIDAY, S. and SCHMIDT, P., eds. (2002), *Human Rights Brought Home: Socio-Economic Perspectives on Human Rights in the National Context*, Oxford: Hart Publishing.

HAMER, D. (2004), 'The Privilege Against Self-Incrimination and the Persistent Risk of Self-Incrimination', *Criminal Law Journal* **28**: 160.

HARDING, C., FENNELL, P., JÖRG, N., and SWART, B., eds. (1995), *Criminal Justice in Europe: a Comparative Study*, Oxford: Oxford University Press.

——, and JOSHUA, J. (2003), *Regulating Cartels in Europe*, Oxford: Oxford University Press.

HARRIS, D., and JOSEPH, S., eds. (1995), *The International Covenant on Civil and Political Rights and United Kingdom Law*, London: Butterworths.

HARRIS, J., and GRACE, S. (1999), *A Question of Evidence?*, Home Office Research Study 196, London: Home Office.

HART, H. L. A. (1968), *Punishment and Responsibility*, Oxford: Oxford University Press.

HAWKINS, K. (1984), *Environment and Enforcement*, Oxford: Oxford University Press.

——, ed. (1992), *The Uses of Discretion*, Oxford: Oxford University Press.

——, (2003), *Law as Last Resort*, Oxford: Oxford University Press.

HEATON-ARMSTRONG, A., SHEPHERD, E., and WOLCHOVER, D., eds., (1999), *Analysing Witness Testimony*, London: Blackstone Press.

HEDDERMAN, C., and HOUGH, M. (1994), *Does the Criminal Justice System Treat Men and Women Differently?*, Home Office Research Findings No. 10, London: Home Office.

——, and MOXON, D. (1992), *Magistrates' Court or Crown Court? Mode of Trial Decisions and Sentencing*, Home Office Research Study 125, London: Home Office.

HEINZ, W. (1989), 'The Problems of Imprisonment', in Hood, q. v.

HELMHOLZ, R. (1997), *The Privilege Against Self Incrimination: Its Origins and Development*, Chicago: University of Chicago Press.

HENHAM, R. (1999), 'Bargain Justice or Justice Denied? Sentence Discounts and the Criminal Process', *MLR*, **63**: 515.

—— (2000), 'Reconciling Process and Policy: Sentence Discounts in the Magistrates' Courts', *Crim LR* 436.

—— (2002), 'Further Evidence on the Significance of Plea in the Crown Court', *Howard JCJ*, **41**: 151.

HERRMANN, J. (1974), 'The Rule of Compulsory Prosecution and the Scope of Prosecutorial Discretion in Germany', *U. Chi. LR*, **41**: 468.

—— (1992), 'Bargaining Justice: a Bargain for German Criminal Justice?', *U. Pittsburgh LR*, **53**: 755.

HIRST, M. (1995), 'Excess Alcohol, Incorrect Procedures and Inadmissible Evidence', *Cambridge LJ.*, **54**: 600.

—— (2001), *Andrews and Hirst on Criminal Evidence*, 4th edn., Bristol: Jordan.

H.M. CROWN PROSECUTION SERVICE INSPECTORATE (1998), *Cases Involving Domestic Violence, Thematic Report*, London: HMCPSI.

—— (1999), *Adverse Cases*, London: HMCPSI.

—— (1999), *Central Case Work Section*, London: HMCPSI.

—— (2000), *The Inspectorate's Report on the Thematic Review of the Disclosure of Unused Material*, London: HMCPSI.

—— (2002), *Report of a Joint Inspection into the Investigation and Prosecution of Cases involving Allegations of Rape*, London: HMCPSI.

—— (2002), *Report on the Thematic Review of Casework Having a Minority Ethnic Dimension*, London: HMCPSI.

—— (2003), *Streets Ahead: A Joint Inspection of the Street Crime Initiative*, London: HMCPSI.

—— (2004), *A Follow Up Review of CPS Casework with a Minority Ethnic Dimension*, London HMCPSI.

——, and H.M. INSPECTORATE OF CONSTABULARY (2004), *Violence at Home, Thematic Report*, London: HMCPSI and HMIC.

H.M. INSPECTORATE OF PROBATION (1993), *Bail Information: Report of a Thematic Inspection*, London: Home Office.

HODGSON, J. (1994), 'Adding Injury to Injustice: The Suspect at the Police Station' *J. Law & Soc.*, **21**: 85.

—— (2002), 'Human Rights and French Criminal Justice', in Halliday and Schmidt, q. v.

—— (2003), 'Codified Criminal Procedure and Human Rights: Some Observations on the French Experience', *Crim LR*, 165.

HOME AFFAIRS COMMITTEE (2002), *The Conduct of Investigations into Past Cases of Abuse in Children's Homes*, 4th Report, HC 836.

HOME OFFICE (1996), *The Victim's Charter*, London: Home Office.

—— (1997), *No More Excuses: a New Approach to Tackling Youth Crime in England and Wales*, London: Home Office.

—— (1998), *Speaking Up for Justice*, London: Home Office.

—— (1999), *Interception of Communications in the United Kingdom*, Cmnd. 4368, London: Home Office.

—— (2001), *Criminal Justice: the Way Ahead*, Cmnd. 5074, London: Stationery Office.

—— (2001), *Making Punishments Work*, London: Home Office.

—— (2002), *Narrowing the Justice Gap*, London: Home Office.

—— (2002), *Justice for All*, Cmnd. 5563, London: Home Office.

—— (2003), *Statistics on Race and the Criminal Justice System*, London: Home Office.

—— (2003), *Restorative Justice: the Government's Strategy*, London: Home Office.

—— (2003), *Crime in England and Wales 2002/2003*, London: Home Office.

—— (2004), *One Step Ahead: a 21st century strategy to Defeat Organised Crime*, Cmnd. 6167, London: Home Office.

—— (2004), *Policing: Modernising Police Powers to Meet Community Needs*, London: Home Office.

——, and CABINET OFFICE (2002), *PACE Review: Report of the Joint Home Office/ Cabinet Office Review*, London: Home Office, Cabinet Office.

HONESS, T., LEVI, M. and CHAPMAN, E. (1998), 'Juror Competence in Processing Complex Information: Implications from a Simulation of the Maxwell Trial', *Crim LR*, 763.

HOOD, R. G., ed. (1989), *Crime and Criminal Policy in Europe: Proceedings of a European Colloquium*, Oxford: Centre for Criminological Research.

—— (1992), *Race and Sentencing*, Oxford: Oxford University Press.

——, SHUTE, S., and SEEMUNGAL, F. (2003), *Ethnic Minorities in the Criminal Courts: Perceptions of Fairness and Equality of Treatment*, Lord Chancellor's Department Research Series No. 2/03, London: Lord Chancellor's Department.

HOUGH, M., JACOBSON, J., and MILLIE, M. (2003), *The Decision to Imprison: Sentencing and the Prison Population*, London: Prison Reform Trust.

HOULDER, B. (1997), 'The Importance of Preserving the Jury System and the Right of Election for Trial', *Crim LR*, 875.

HOYANO, A., HOYANO, L., DAVIS, G., and GOLDIE, S. (1997), 'A Study of the Impact of the Revised Code for Crown Prosecutors', *Crim LR*, 556.

HOYLE, C. (1998), *Negotiating Domestic Violence*, Oxford: Oxford University Press.

HUCKLESBY, A. (1996), 'Bail or Jail? The Practical Operation of the Bail Act 1976', *Journal of Law and Society*, 23: 213.

—— (1997), 'Remand Decision Makers', *Crim LR*, 269.

—— (1997), 'Court Culture: an Explanation of Variations in the Use of Bail by Magistrates' Courts', *Howard JCJ*, 36: 129.

—— (2004), 'Not Necessarily a Trip to the Police Station: the Introduction of Street Bail', *Crim LR*, 803.

HUGHES, G., PILKINGTON, A., and LEISTAN, R. (1998), 'Diversion in a Culture of Severity', *Howard JCJ*, 37: 16.

HUMPHREYS, C. (1955), 'The Duties and Responsibilities of Prosecuting Counsel', *Crim LR*, 739.

HUTTER, B. (1988), *The Reasonable Arm of the Law*, Oxford: Oxford University Press.

IPP, D. A. (1998), 'Lawyers' Duties to the Court', *LQR*, 114: 63.

IRVING, B. (1980), *Police Interrogation: A Study of Current Practice*, London: HMSO.

——, and DUNNIGHAN, C. (1993), *Human Factors in the Quality Control of CID Investigations*, Royal Commission on Criminal Justice Research Study No. 21, London: HMSO.

JACKSON, J. D., (2001), 'Silence and Proof: Extending the Boundaries of Criminal Proceedings in the United Kingdom' *E & P*, 5: 145.

——, (2003), 'Justice for All: Putting Vicitms at the Heart of Criminal Justice?', *JLS*, 30: 309.

——, and DORAN, S. (1995), *Judge without Jury*, Oxford: Oxford University Press.

——, —— (1997), 'The Case for Jury Waiver', *Crim LR*, 155.

——, WOLFE, M., and QUINN, K. (2000), *Legislating Against Silence: The Northern Ireland Experience*, Belfast: Northern Ireland Office.

JACKSON, S. (1998), 'Family Group Conferences in Youth Justice? The Issues for Implementation in England and Wales', *Howard JCJ* 37: 34.

JAMES, A., TAYLOR, N., and WALKER, C. (2000), 'The Criminal Cases Review Commission: Economy, Effectiveness and Justice,' *Crim LR*, 140.

JEFFERSON, T., and WALKER, M. (1992), 'Ethnic Minorities in the Criminal Justice System', *Crim LR*, 83.

JOHNSTONE, G. (2001), *Restorative Justice*, Devon: Willan Publishing.

—— (2003), *A Restorative Justice Reader*, Devon: Willan Publishing.

JONES, P. R. (1985), 'Remand Decisions at Magistrates' Courts', in Moxon, q. v.

——, and GOLDKAMP, J. S. (1991), 'Judicial Guidelines for Pre-Trial Release: Research and Policy Developments in the United States', *Howard JCJ*, 30: 140.

JOINT COMMITTEE ON HUMAN RIGHTS (2003), *Criminal Justice Bill, 2nd Report of Session 2002–03*, London: HC.

—— (2003), *Criminal Justice Bill: Further Report, 11th Report of Session 2002–03*, London: HC.

JORG, N., FIELD, S., and BRANTS, C. (1995), 'Are Inquisitorial and Adversarial Systems

Converging?', in Fennell, Harding, Jörg, and Swart, eds., q. v.

JUNG, H. (1993), 'Criminal Justice: a European Perspective', *Crim LR*, 237.

—— (1997), 'Plea-Bargaining and its Repercussions on the Theory of Criminal Procedure', *European Journal of Crime, Criminal Law and Criminal Justice*, 5: 112.

JUSTICE (1970), 'The Prosecution Process in England and Wales', *Crim LR*, 668.

—— (1993), *Negotiated Justice: a Closer Look at the Implications of Plea Bargains*, London: JUSTICE.

—— (1994), *Remedying Miscarriages of Justice*, London: JUSTICE.

—— (1998), *Under Surveillance*, London: JUSTICE.

KASSIN, S. M. (2003), 'Behavioural Confirmation in the Interrogation Room: On the Dangers of Presuming Guilt', *Law & Human Behavior*, 27: 187.

——, and FONG, C. (1999), ' "I'm Innocent": Effects of Training on Judgments of Truth and Deception in the Interrogation Room', *Law & Human Behavior*, 23: 499.

——, and McNALL, K. (1991), 'Police Interrogation and Confession: Communicating Promises and Threats by Pragmatic Implication', *Law & Human Behavior*, 5: 233.

KAMISAR, Y. (1987), 'Comparative Reprehensibility and the Fourth Amendment Exclusionary Rule', *Michigan LR*, 86: 1.

KAYE, D. (2000), 'Bioethics, Bench and Bar: Selected Arguments in *Landry v. Attorney General*', *Jurimetrics J.*, 40: 193.

——, and SMITH, M. (2003) 'DNA Identification Databases: Legality, Legitimacy and the Case for Population-wide Coverage', *Wisconsin L Rev*, 413.

KAYE, T. (1991), *Unsafe and Unsatisfactory?*, London: Civil Liberties Trust.

KELLOUGH, G. and WORTLEY, S. (2002), 'Remand for Plea: Bail Decisions and Plea Bargaining as Commensurate Decisions', *BJ Crim.*, 42: 186.

KENNEDY, M., TRUMAN, C., KEYES, S., and CAMERON, A. (1997), 'Supported Bail for Mentally Vulnerable Defendants', *Howard JCJ*, 36: 158.

KING, N. J. (1994), 'The Effects of Race-Conscious Jury Selection on Public Confidence in the Fairness of Jury Proceedings: An Empirical Puzzle', *Am. Crim. L.R.*, 1177.

KYMLICKA, W. (2002), *Contemporary Political Philosophy: An Introduction*, 2nd edn., Oxford: Oxford University Press.

LANGER, M. (2004), 'From Legal Transplants to Legal Translations: the Globalization of Plea-Bargaining and the Americanization Thesis in Criminal Procedure', *Harvard Int. LJ.*, 1.

LAW COMMISSION (2000), *Prosecution Appeals Against Judges' Rulings*, Consultation Paper No. 158, London: Stationery Office.

—— (2001), *Bail and the Human Rights Act 1998*, Consultation Paper No. 157, London: Stationery Office.

—— (2001), *Double Jeopardy and Prosecution Appeals*, Report No. 267, London: Stationery Office.

LEA, S., LANVERS, U., and SHAW, S. (2003), 'Attrition in Rape Cases', *BJ Crim.*, 43: 583.

LEIGH, L. H., and ZEDNER, L. (1992), *A Report on the Administration of Criminal Justice In the Pre-Trial Phase in France and Germany*, Royal Commission on Criminal Justice Research Study No. 1, London: HMSO.

LEMPERT, R. (1993), 'Civil Juries and Complex Cases: Taking Stock After Twelve Years', in Litan, ed., q. v.

LENG, R. (1993), *The Right to Silence in Police Interrogation*, Royal Commission on Criminal Justice Research Study No. 10, London: HMSO.

—— (2000), 'The Exchange of Information and Disclosure', in McConville and Wilson, eds., q. v.

LENSING, H., and RAYAR, L. (1992), 'Notes on Criminal Procedure in the Netherlands', *Crim LR*, 623.

LEVI, M. (1993), *The Investigation, Prosecution and Trial of Serious Fraud*, Royal Commission on Criminal Justice Research Study No. 14, London: HMSO.

LIEBLING, A., and KRARUP, H. (1993), *Suicide Attempts and Self-Injury in Male Prisons*, Cambridge: Institute of Criminology.

LITAN, R., ed. (1993), *Verdict: Assessing the Civil Jury System*, Washington DC: The Brookings Institution.

LLOYD-BOSTOCK, S. (2000) 'The Effects on Juries of Hearing About the Defendant's Previous Convictions', *Crim LR*, 734.

LOADER, I., and SPARKS, R. (2002), 'Contemporary Landscapes of Crime, Order and Control' in Maguire, Morgan and Reiner q. v.

LUBAN, D. (1993), 'Are Criminal Defenders Different?', *Mich LR*, **91**: 1729.

LUSTGARTEN L. (2002), 'The Future of Stop and Search', *Crim LR*, 603.

McBARNET, D. (1983), *Conviction: Law, the State and the Construction of Justice*, London: Macmillan.

——, and WHELAN, C. (1991), 'The Elusive Spirit of the Law: Formalism and the Struggle for Legal Control', *MLR*, **54**: 848.

McCABE, S., and PURVES, R. (1972), *By-Passing the Jury*, Oxford: University of Oxford Penal Research Unit.

McCONVILLE, M. (1992), 'Videotaping Interrogations: Police Behaviour on and off Camera', *Crim LR*, 532.

——, (1993), *Corroboration and Confessions*, London: The Stationery Office.

——, (2000), 'Plea Bargaining: Ethics and Politics', in Doran and Jackson, eds., q. v.

——, and BALDWIN, J. (1981), *Prosecution, Courts and Conviction*, Oxford: Oxford University Press.

——, HODGSON, J., BRIDGES, L., and PAVLOVIC, A. (1994), *Standing Accused*, Oxford: Oxford University Press.

——, and HODGSON, J. (1993), *Custodial Legal Advice and the Right of Silence*, Royal Commission on Criminal Justice Research Study No. 16, London: HMSO.

——, SANDERS, A., and LENG, R. (1991), *The Case for the Prosecution*, London: Routledge.

——, and WILSON, G., eds. (2002), *The Handbook of the Criminal Justice Process*, Oxford: Oxford University Press.

McKENZIE, I., MORGAN, R., and REINER, R. (1990), 'Helping the Police with their Inquiries: the Necessity Principle and Voluntary Attendance at the Police Station', *Crim LR*, 22.

McMAHON, M. (1990), 'Net-Widening: Vagaries in the Use of a Concept', *BJ Crim.*, **30**: 121.

MACHURA, S. (2002) 'Interaction Between Lay Assessors and Professional Judges in German Mixed Courts', *International Rev Penal Law*, **72**: 451.

MACNAIR, M. (1990), 'The Early Development of the Privilege Against Self-Incrimination', *OJLS*, **10**: 66.

MAGUIRE, M. (2000), 'Policing by Risks and Targets: Some Dimensions and Implications of Intelligence-Led Policing', *Policing and Society*, **9**: 315.

——, and JOHN, T. (1996), 'Covert and Deceptive Policing in England and Wales: Issues in Regulation and Practice', *European Journal of Crime, Criminal Law and Criminal Justice*.

——, and NORRIS, C. (1992), *The Conduct and Supervision of Criminal Investigations*, Royal Commission on Criminal

Justice Research Study No. 5, London: HMSO.

——, MORGAN, R., and REINER, R., eds. (2002), *Oxford Handbook of Criminology*, 3rd edn., Oxford: Oxford University Press.

MACPHERSON, SIR. W. (1999), *The Stephen Lawrence Inquiry: Report of an Inquiry*, Cm. 4261, London: Stationery Office.

MALLESON, K., and ROBERTS, S. (2002) 'Streamlining and Clarifying the Appellate Process,' *Crim LR*, 272.

MATTHEWS, R., HANCOCK, L., and BRIGGS, D. (2004), *Jurors' Perceptions, Understanding, Confidence and Satisfaction in the Jury System*, Research Development and Statistics Directorate, Findings 177, London: Home Office.

MAY R. (1997), 'The Legal Effect of a Police Caution', *Crim LR*, 491.

METROPOLITAN POLICE AUTHORITY (2004), *Report of the Scrutiny on MPS Stop and Search Practice*, London: Metropolitan Police Authority.

MILLER, J., BLAND, N., and QUINTON, P. (2000), *The Impact of Stops and Searches on Crime and the Community*, Police Research Series, Paper 127.

MIRFIELD, P. (1997), *Silence, Confessions and Improperly Obtained Evidence*, Oxford: Oxford University Press.

——, and SMITH, R. (eds) (2003), *Essays for Colin Tapper*, London: LexisNexis.

MOHONEY, R. (2003), 'Abolition of New Zealand's *Prima Facie* Exclusionary Rule', *Crim LR*, 607.

MORGAN, D., and STEPHENSON, G. eds. (1994) *Suspicion and Silence: The Right to Silence in Criminal Investigations*, London: Blackstone Press.

MORGAN, J., and ZEDNER, L. (1992), *Child Victims*, Oxford: Oxford University Press.

MORGAN, P. M. (1992), *Offending While on Bail: a Survey of Recent Studies*, London: Home Office Research and Planning Unit.

——, and HENDERSON, P. (1998), *Remand Decisions and Offending on Bail*, Home Office Research Study 184, London: Home Office.

MORGAN, R. (1996), 'The Process is the Rule and the Punishment is the Process', *MLR*, 59: 306.

——, (2001), 'International Controls on Sentencing and Punishment', in Tonry and Frase, eds. q. v.

——, (2002), 'Magistrates: The Future According to Auld' *JLS*, 29: 308.

——, and RUSSELL, N. (2000), *The Judiciary in the Magistrates' Courts*, Home Office and LCD Occasional Paper 66, London: Home Office.

MORISON, J., and LEITH, P. (1992), *The Barrister's World*, Oxford: Oxford University Press.

MORRIS, A. (2002), 'Critiquing the Critics: a Brief Response to Critics of Restorative Justice', *BJ Crim*. 42: 578.

MORRIS, N., and TONRY, M. (1990), *Between Prison and Probation*, New York: Oxford University Press.

MOSTELLER, R. (1986), 'Discovery Against the Defense: Tilting the Adversarial Balance', *California L Rev.*, 74: 1567.

MOSTON, S., and STEPHENSON, G. (1993), *The Questioning and Interviewing of Suspects outside the Police Station*, Royal Commission on Criminal Justice Research Study No. 22, London: HMSO.

MOTT, J. (1983), 'Police Decisions for Dealing with Juvenile Offenders', *BJ Crim.*, 23: 249.

MOXON, D. (ed.) (1985), *Managing Criminal Justice*, London: HMSO.

——, and HEDDERMAN, C. (1994), 'Mode of Trial Decisions and Sentencing Differences between Courts', *Howard JCJ* 33: 97.

MULCAHY, A. (1994), 'The Justifications of Justice', *BJ Crim.*, 34: 411.

MULLIN, C. (1990), *Error of Judgement*, Dublin: Poolbeg Press.

MVA, and MILLER, J. (2000), *Profiling Populations Available for Stops and Searches*, Police Research Series, Paper 131, London: Home Office.

NANCE, D. (1994), 'Civility and the Burden of Proof', *Harvard J Law & Public Policy*, 17: 647.

NAREY, M. (1997), *Review of Delay in the Criminal Justice System ('The Narey Report')*, London: Home Office.

NATIONAL AUDIT OFFICE (1997), *The Crown Prosecution Service*, London: National Audit Office.

NEWTON, T. (1998), 'The Place of Ethics in Investigative Interviewing by Police Officers', *Howard JCJ*, 37: 52.

NICOLSON, D., and WEBB, J. (1999), *Professional Legal Ethics*, Oxford, New York: Oxford University Press.

NISSMAN, C. M., and HAGEN, E. (1982), *The Prosecution Function*, Washington: Lexington.

NOBLES, R., and SCHIFF, D. (2000), *Understanding Miscarriages of Justice*, Oxford: Oxford University Press.

——, —— (2001), 'The Criminal Cases Review Commission: Reporting Success?', *MLR*, 64: 280.

——, —— (2002), 'The Right to Appeal and Workable Systems of Justice', *MLR*, 65: 676.

O'CONNOR, P. (1992), 'Prosecution Disclosure: Principle, Practice and Justice', *Crim LR*, 464.

OFSHE, R., and LEO, R. (1997), 'The Decision to Confess Falsely: Rational Choice and Irrational Action' *Denver University L. Rev.*, 74: 979.

O'NEILL, O. (2002), *A Question of Trust*, BBC Reith Lectures, Cambridge: Cambridge University Press.

ORMEROD, D. (2001), 'Sounds Familiar?—Voice Identification Evidence', *Crim LR*, 595.

——, and BIRCH, D. (2004), 'The Evolution of the Discretionary Exclusion of Evidence', *Crim LR*, 767.

——, and ROBERTS, A. (2003), 'The Police Reform Act 2002', *Crim LR*, 141.

——, —— (2002), 'The Trouble with *Teixeira*: Developing a Principled Approach to Entrapment', *E & P*, 6: 38.

OSNER, N., QUINN, A, and CROWN, G. (1993), *Criminal Justice Systems in Other Jurisdictions*, The Royal Commission on Criminal Justice, London: HMSO.

PACKER, H. (1968), *The Limits of the Criminal Sanction*, Stanford, CA: Stanford University Press.

PADFIELD, N. (1993), 'The Right to Bail: a Canadian Perspective', *Crim LR*, 510.

PARK, R. (2003), 'Visions of Applying the Scientific Method to the Hearsay Rule' *Mich St L Rev.*, 1149.

—— (2003), 'Empirical Evaluation of the Hearsay Rule' in Mirfield and Smith, q. v.

PARKER, H., SUMNER, M., JARVIS, G. (1989), *Unmasking the Magistrates*, Milton Keynes: Open University Press.

PATERSON, F., ed. (1996), *Understanding Bail in Britain*, Edinburgh: Scottish Office Central Research Unit.

PATTENDEN, R. (1996), *English Criminal Appeals, 1844–1994*, Oxford: Oxford University Press.

—— (2000), 'Prosecution Appeals Against Judges' Rulings', *Crim LR*, 971.

PEARSE, J., and GUDJONSSON, G. (1996), 'Police Interviewing Techniques at Two South London Police Stations', *Psychology, Crime & Law*, 3: 63.

PEAY, J. (2002), 'Mentally Disordered Offenders', in Maguire, Morgan and Reiner, eds., q. v.

PETTIT, P., and BRAITHWAITE, J. (1998), 'Republicanism in Sentencing: Recognition, Recompense and Reassurance', in von Hirsch and Ashworth q. v.

PHILLIPS, C., and BROWN, D. (1998), *Entry into the Criminal Justice System: A survey of Police Arrests and Their Outcomes*, Home Office Research Study No. 185, London: Home Office.

PHILLIPS, M. (1999), 'Double-blind Photo-array Administration as a Safeguard Against Investigator Bias' *J. Applied Psychology*, **84**: 940.

PHILPOTTS, G. J. O., and LANCUCKI, L. B. (1979), *Previous Convictions, Sentence and Reconvictions*, Home Office Research Study 53, London: HMSO.

PIZZARUSSO, A., ed. (1994), *Italian Studies in Law, vol. II*, Dordrecht: Martinus Nijhoff.

PLOTNIKOFF, J., and WOOLFSON, R. (2001), *'A Fair Balance'? Evaluation of the Operation of Disclosure Law'*, London: Home Office.

PRESSER, B. (2001), 'Public Policy, Police Interest: A Re-Evaluation of the Judicial Discretion to Exclude Improperly or Illegally Obtained Evidence', *Melbourne ULR*, **25**: 757.

PRISON REFORM TRUST (2000), *Justice for Women: the Need for Reform*, London: Prison Reform Trust.

PUBLIC DEFENDER SERVICE (2004), *Putting Clients First: Public Defender Service, Annual Report 2003/4*, London: Legal Services Commission.

QUINTON, A., ed. (1967), *Political Philosophy*, Oxford: Oxford University Press.

QUINTON, P., BLAND, N., and MILLER, J. (2000), *Police Stops, Decision-Making and Practice*, Police Research Series, Paper 130.

RAIFERTAIGH, U. NI (1997), 'Reconciling Bail Law with the Presumption of Innocence', *Oxford JLS*, **17**: 1.

RAINE, J., and WILLSON, M. (1996), 'The Imposition of Conditions in Bail Decisions', *Howard JCJ*, **35**: 256.

—— (1997), 'Police Bail with Conditions', *BJ Crim.*, **37**: 593.

REDLICH, A., and GOODMAN, G. (2003), 'Taking Responsibility for an Act Not Committed: The Influence of Age and Suggestibility', *Law & Human Behavior*, **27**: 141.

REDMAYNE, M. (2002), 'Appeals to Reason', *MLR*, **65**: 19.

—— (2002), 'The Relevance of Bad Character', *CLJ*, **61**: 684.

—— (2004), 'Disclosure and its Discontents', *Crim LR*, 441.

—— (2004), 'Theorizing Jury Reform', in Duff, Farmer, Marshall, and Tadros, q. v.

REINER, R. (2000), *The Politics of the Police*, 3rd edn., Hemel Hempstead: Wheatsheaf.

RENNING, C. (2002), 'Influence of Lay Assessors and Giving Reasons for the Judgement in German Mixed Courts', *International Rev Penal Law*, **72**: 481.

RICHARDSON, G., OGUS, A., and BURROWS, P. (1982), *Policing Pollution*, Oxford: Oxford University Press.

RISHWORTH, P., HUSCROFT, G., OPTICAN, S., MAHONEY, R. (2003), *The New Zealand Bill of Rights*, Auckland: Oxford University Press.

ROACH, K. (1999), 'Canada', in Bradley, q. v.

—— (1999), *Due Process and Victims' Rights: the New Law and Politics of Criminal Justice*, Toronto: UTP.

—— (2003), 'The Criminal Process', in Cane and Tushnet, eds., q. v.

ROBERTS, A., (2004), 'The Problem of Mistaken Identification: Some Observations on Process', *E & P*, **8**: 100.

——, and CLOVER, S. (2002), 'Managerialism and Myopia: The Government's Consultation Draft on PACE Code D', *Crim LR*, 873.

ROBERTS, D. (1993), 'Questioning the Suspect: the Solicitor's Role', *Crim LR.*, 368.

ROBERTS, P., (2002) 'Double Jeopardy Law Reform: A Criminal Justice Commentary', *MLR* **65**: 393.

——, and ZUCKERMAN, A. (2004), *Criminal Evidence*, Oxford: Oxford University Press.

ROBERTS, S. (2004), 'The Royal Commission on Criminal Justice and Factual Innocence', JUSTICE Journal, **1**: 86.

ROBERTSON, B. (1989), 'The Looking Glass World of Section 78', *NLJ*, 1223.

——, DELL, S., GROUNDS, A., and JAMES, K. (1992), 'Mentally Disordered Remand Prisoners', *Home Office Research Bulletin*, **32**: 1.

ROCK, P. (1993), *The Social World of an English Crown Court*, Oxford: Clarendon Press.

——, (2004), *Constructing Victims' Rights: the Home Office, New Labour and Victims*, Oxford: Clarendon Press.

ROORDING, J. (1996), 'The Punishment of Tax Fraud', *Crim LR*, 240.

ROYAL COMMISSION ON CRIMINAL JUSTICE (1993) (chair: Viscount Runciman), *Report*, Cmnd. 2263, London: HMSO.

ROYAL COMMISSION ON CRIMINAL PROCEDURE (1981) (chair: Sir Cyril Phillips), *Report*, Cmnd. 8092, London: HMSO.

ROZENBERG, J. (1993), 'Miscarriages of Justice', in Stockdale and Casale, eds., q. v.

RUTHERFORD, A. (1993), *Criminal Justice and the Pursuit of Decency*, Oxford: Oxford University Press.

SAMUELS, A. (1997), 'Custody Time Limits', *Crim LR*, 260.

SANDERS, A. (1985), 'Class Bias in Prosecutions', *Howard JCJ*, 24: 176.

—— (1988), 'The Limits to Diversion from Prosecution', *BJ Crim.*, **28**: 513.

—— (2001), *Community Justice: Modernising the Magistracy in England and Wales*, London: IPPR.

—— (2002), 'Core Values, the Magistracy and the Auld Report', *JLS*, **29**: 324.

—— (2002), 'From Suspect to Trial', in Maguire, Morgan, and Reiner, eds., q. v.

——, and BRIDGES, L. (1990), 'Access to Legal Advice and Police Malpractice', *Crim LR*, 494.

——, HOYLE, C., MORGAN, R., and CAPE, E. (2001), 'Victim Impact Statements: Can't Work, Won't Work', *Crim LR*, 447.

——, and YOUNG, R. (2000), *Criminal Justice*, 2nd edn., London: Butterworths.

SAURON, J.-L., (1990), 'Les Vertus de l'Inquisitoire, ou l'Etat au Service des Droits', 55 *Pouvoirs* 53.

SCHIFF, D., and NOBLES, R. (1996), 'Criminal Appeal Act 1995: the Semantics of Jurisdiction', *MLR*, **59**: 573.

SCHOPP, R. (1996), 'Verdicts of Conscience: Nullification and Necessity as Jury Responses to Crimes of Conscience', *S. Cal. L. Rev.*, **69**: 2039.

SCHULHOFER, S. (1984), 'Is Plea Bargaining Inevitable?', *Harv. LR*, **97**: 1037.

—— (1992), 'Plea Bargaining as Disaster', *Yale LJ*, **101**: 1979.

——, and NAGEL, I. (1997), 'Plea Negotiations under the Federal Sentencing Guidelines', *Northwestern ULR*, **91**: 1284.

SCOTT, R. E., and STUNTZ, W. J. (1992), 'Plea Bargaining as Contract', *Yale LJ*, **101**: 1909.

——, —— (1992), 'A Reply: Imperfect Bargains, Imperfect Trials and Innocent Defendants', *Yale LJ*, **101**: 2011.

SEAGO, P., WALKER, C., and WALL, D. (1995), *The Role and Appointment of Stipendiary Magistrates*, London: CCJS Press and Lord Chancellor's Department.

SEDLEY, S. (2001), 'Wringing Out the Fault: Self-Incrimination in the 21st Century', *NILQ*, **52**: 107.

SELIH, A. (2000), 'The Prosecution Process', in Council of Europe, q. v.

SHAPLAND, J., DUFF, P., and WILLMORE, J. (1985), *Victims in the Criminal Justice System*, Aldershot: Gower.

SHEPHERD, E., and MILNE, R. (1999), 'Full and Faithful: Ensuring Quality, Practice and Integrity of Outcome in Witness Interviews', in Heaton-Armstrong, Shepherd, and Wolchover, eds., q. v.

SIMON, W. H. (1993), 'The Ethics of Criminal Defense,' *Mich. LR*, **91**: 1703.

SKOLNICK, J. (1966), *Justice without Trial*, New York: Wiley.

SLAPPER, G., and TOMBS, S. (2000), *Corporate Crime*, London: Longman.

SMITH, J. C. (1995), 'The Criminal Appeal Act 1995: Appeals against Conviction', *Crim LR*, 920.

SOMERS, S., and ELLSWORTH, P. (2003), 'How Much Do We Really Know About Race and Juries? A Review of Social Science Theory and Research', *Chicago-Kent L. Rev.*, **78**: 997.

SOOTHILL, K., FRANCIS, B., and SANDERSON, B. (1997), 'A Cautionary Tale: the Sex Offenders Act 1997, the Police and Cautions', *Crim LR*, 482.

SPENCER, J. R. (2004), 'The Sexual Offences Act 2003: Child and Family Offences', *Crim LR*, 347.

SPRACK, J. (2002), *Emmins on Criminal Procedure*, 9th edn., London: Blackstone Press.

STEPHEN, H. (1926), *The Conduct of an English Criminal Trial*, London: University of London Press.

STOCKDALE, E., and CASALE, S., eds. (1993), *Criminal Justice Under Stress*, London: Blackstone Press.

STONE, C. (1988), *Bail Information for the Crown Prosecution Service*, London: Vera Institute of Justice.

STONE, V., and PETTIGREW, N. (2000), *The Views of the Public on Stops and Searches*, Police Research Series Paper 129, London: Home Office.

SWIFT, E. (2000), 'One Hundred Years of Evidence Law Reform: Thayer's Triumph', *California L Rev*, **88**: 2437.

TAK, P. J. P. (1986), *The Legal Scope of Non-Prosecution in Europe*, Helsinki: HEUNI.

TAPPER, C., ed. (1981), *Crime, Proof and Punishment*, London: Butterworths.

——, (2004) 'Evidence of Bad Character', *Crim LR*, 533.

TAYLOR, N., and ORMEROD, D. (2004), 'Mind the Gap: Safety, Fairness and Moral Legitimacy', *Crim LR*, 266.

TAYLOR, R., WASIK, M., and LENG, R. (2004), *Blackstone's Guide to the Criminal Justice Act 2003*, Oxford: Oxford University Press.

TEMKIN, J. (2000), 'Prosecuting and Defending Rape: Perspectives from the Bar', *J Law & Soc.*, **27**: 219.

——, (2002), *Rape and the Criminal Process*, 2nd edn., Oxford: Oxford University Press.

TILLERS, P. (1998) 'What is Wrong with Character Evidence?', *Hastings LJ*, **49**: 781.

TINSLEY, Y. (2001), 'Even Better than the Real Thing? The Case for Reform of Identification Procedures' *E & P*, **5**: 99.

TONRY, M. (2004), *Punishment and Politics*, Cullompton: Willan.

——, and FRASE, R., eds. (2001), *Sentencing and Sanctions in Western Countries*, Oxford: Oxford University Press.

TRAVERS, M. (1997), *The Reality of Law*, Aldershot: Ashgate.

TURTLE, J., LINDSAY, R., and WELLS, G. (2003), 'Best Practice Recommendations for Eyewitness Evidence Procedures: New Ideas for the Oldest Way to Solve a Case', *Canadian J. Police & Security Services*, 5 March.

TYLER, T. (1990), *Why People Obey the Law*, New Haven, CT.: Yale University Press.

VAN BUEREN, G. (1998), *The International Law on the Rights of the Child*, Leiden: Brill Academic Publishing.

VAN ZYL SMIT, D., and ASHWORTH, A. (2004), 'Disproportionate Sentences as Human Rights Violations', *MLR*, **67**: 541.

VICTIM SUPPORT (1995), *The Rights of Victims of Crime*, London: Victim Support.

VIDMAR, N. (1997), 'Generic Prejudice and the Presumption of Guilt in Sex Abuse Trials', *Law & Human Behavior*, **21**: 5.

—— (1998), 'The Performance of the American Civil Jury: An Empirical Perspective', *Arizona L. Rev.*, **40**: 849.

VON HIRSCH, A. (1993), *Censure and Sanctions*, Oxford: Oxford University Press.

——, and ASHWORTH, A., eds. (1998), *Principled Sentencing: Readings in Theory and Policy*, 2nd edn., Oxford: Hart Publishing.

——, and ASHWORTH, A., (2005), *The Proportionate Sentence*, Oxford: Oxford University Press.

——, ROBERTS, J., BOTTOMS, A., ROACH, K., and SCHIFF, M., eds. (2003), *Restorative Justice and Criminal Justice*, Oxford and Portland: Hart Publishing.

WADDINGTON, P. A. J. (1999), 'Police (Canteen) Culture: an Appreciation', *BJ Crim.*, **39**: 286.

WALDRON, J. (2003), 'Security and Liberty: the Image of Balance', *J. Political Philosophy*, **11**: 191.

WALKER, C. (2004), 'Terrorism and Criminal Justice—Past, Present and Future', *Crim LR*, 311.

WALKER, N. (2001), 'What Does Fairness Mean in a Criminal Trial?', *NLJ*, 1240.

WARD, A., and PEERS S., eds. (2004), *The E.U. Charter of Fundamental Rights*, Oxford: Hart Publishing.

WARD, T., and GARDNER, P. (2003), 'The Privilege Against Self Incrimination: In Search of Legal Certainty', *European Human Rights L Rev.*, 387.

WARD, R., and DAVIES, O. (2004), *The Criminal Justice Act 2003*, Bristol: Jordans.

WASIK, M. (1996), 'Magistrates: Knowledge of Previous Convictions', *Crim LR.*, 851.

WELLS, G. (1998), 'Eyewitness Identification Procedures: Recommendations for Line-ups and Photospreads', *Law & Human Behavior*, **22**: 1.

WELLS, G., and OLSON, E. (2003), 'Eyewitness Identification', *Annual Review of Psychology*, **54**: 277.

——, ——, and CHARMAN, S. (2003), 'Distorted Retrospective Eyewitness Reports as Functions of Feedback and Delay', *J Experimental Psychology: Applied*, **9**: 42.

WILLIAMSON, T. (1994), 'Reflections on Current Police Practice', in Morgan and Stephenson, eds., q. v.

WINDLESHAM, LORD (1988), 'Punishment and Prevention: the Inappropriate Prisoners', *Crim LR*, 140.

—— (2001), *Responses to Crime, Volume 4: Dispensing Justice*, Oxford: Oxford University Press.

WOOLF, L. J., and TUMIN, J., (1991) 'Prison Disturbances April 1990: Report of an Inquiry', Cmnd. 1456. London: HMSO.

YOUNG, R., and HOYLE, C. (2003), 'New, Improved Police-Led Restorative Justice?', in von Hirsch, Roberts, Bottoms, Roach, and Schiff, eds., q. v.

——, WALL, D., eds. (1996), *Access to Criminal Justice*, London: Blackstone Press.

ZANDER, M. (2000), 'Why Jack Straw's Jury Reform Has Lost the Plot', *NLJ*, 150: 723.

——, and HENDERSON, P. (1993), *Crown Court Study*, Royal Commission on Criminal Justice Research Study No. 19, London: HMSO.

—— (2003), *The Police and Criminal Evidence Act 1984*, 4th edn., London: Sweet and Maxwell.

ZEDNER, L. (2002), 'Victims', in Maguire, Morgan and Reiner, q. v.

ZUCKERMAN, A. A. S. (1989), *The Principles of Criminal Evidence*, Oxford: Oxford University Press.

—— (1991), 'Miscarriage of Justice and Judicial Responsibility', *Crim LR*, 492.

INDEX

abuse of process
  appeals 354–8
  power to stay proceedings 255
  scope of 355
  stale offence, prosecution of
    251
  staying prosecution for 237
acquittal
  appeal against 339
  directed 196–8
  double jeopardy *see* double
    jeopardy
  finality 364
  judge, by 196–8
  ordered 196–7
  prosecution appeals 360–4
  remand in custody, following
    220
administration of justice
  equality before the law,
    principle of 376
alibi
  notice of 244–5
anti-social behaviour order
  breach of 14
  civil procedure, application
    under 13–14
  introduction of 13
  offence, without evidence of
    14
  spread of 377
appeals
  acquittal, challenge to 339
  asymmetric rights 360–1
  burden of proof, relevance of
    353
  conviction, against 7
  Court of Appeal, to 339–41 *see*
    also Court of Appeal
  criminal 338
  Crown Court, from 339–41
  custody pending 341
  detention as means of
    controlling 342
  disincentives 370–1
  Divisional Court, to 339–40
  due process 354–8
  higher courts, control by 338
  House of Lords, to 339
  increase of sentence on 340–1

jury verdict, challenging
  344–53
lapse of right to 358
leave, requirement of 340,
  342–4
legal issues, involving 338
legal rulings, from 340
loss of time rule 341–2
lurking doubt 347–8
magistrates' court, from 339
prosecution, by
  asymmetry 360–1
  caution as to 363
  double jeopardy *see* double
    jeopardy
  equality of arms 363
  evidential ruling,
    challenging 362
  issues 362
  objection to 363
  post verdict 363–4
  rulings affecting
    prosecution case, as to
    362
  trial on indictment, during
    362
questions of fact, concerning
  338
questions of law, on 361
remand pending 208
restriction on rights of 340–4
rights of 339
sentence, against 7
success rate 343
system
  criminal 338–9
  purposes of 338
arrest
  arrestable offence 3, 84–5
  caution on 86
  discretion 85
  extension of powers, proposed
    372–3
  general arrest conditions 85
  grounds, informing suspect of
    86
  PACE, powers under 9
  police questioning on 84–7
  powers of 84–6
  reasons for, right to know 31

attrition
  process of 138
  rate of 139, 380

bail
  appeal against grant of
    229–30
  claim to liberty, acceptance of
    207
  conditional 214–15, 234
  court, decision of 207
  criteria for grant or refusal,
    relation to possibility of
    custodial sentence 222
  decision, conflict in 207
  decisions, factors in
    character, antecedents,
      associations and
      community ties 216
    nature and seriousness of
      offence or default 216
    statutory provisions
      215–16
  defendants committing
    offences during 225–6
  elsewhere than at a police
    station 218
  European Convention on
    Human Rights,
    compatibility with 217
  exceptional circumstances
    justifying 217
  financial conditions 215
  general right to 215
  information systems 227–8
  law, toughening up 216
  police 207
    grant by 218
  presumption in favour of
    215
  reapplications for 229–30
  refusal
    consequences of 207
    failure to appear at court
      217
    grounds for 208, 215
    interference with witnesses,
      risk of 212
    obstruction of course of
      justice, risk of 212

offences during bail period,
  risk of 211–13, 217,
  232–3
predicted risk, question of
  213, 233–4
presumption of liberty,
  rebutting 210
public disorder, release of
  defendant leading to 213
public interest reasons 232
risk of absconding, where
  211
remand on, failures of 226
representations 228–9
risk of absconding, gauging
  209
street 5, 207
sureties 214
trial, securing attendance at
  213–14
uncertainty as to use of 224
unconditional 214
burden of proof
  appeal, relevance in 353
  criminal trial, in 24
  innocence, presumption of 33

caution
  arrest, on 86
  caution plus schemes 157
  challenge to 163
  conditional 149–50, 159–61,
    170–1, 184, 206, 285
  introduction of 4
  effectiveness of 146
  formal 148–9
  judicial review of decision 163
  offences resulting in 139
  police cautioning
    accountability 161–4
    arguments for and against
      155–7
    change of policy 151
    conditional 149–50,
      159–61, 170–1
    defendants' rights 168–9
    defendants, pressure on
      156
    elderly or ill offenders 153
    equality of treatment
      165–6
    factors taken into account
      153
    females, of 167
    formal 148–9

formal principles 151–4
local variations 157–8
mentally disordered
  offenders 153
multiple 154
National Standards,
  practical implementation
  of 157–9, 161
net-widening 155–6
purposes of 155
racial discrimination 166–7
rate of 150
repeat 151
statistics 152
victims' rights 167–8
victims, unfairness to
  156–7
wilfulness of offences,
  relevance of 154
wrong message, sending
  157
young offenders 153
police interview, at start of
  89–90
purposes of 155
wider use, push to 150
charge bargaining
  advantages and disadvantages
    of 273
  Crown Court, in 271–2
  magistrates' court, in 270–1
  policies and practices 285–92
  practice of 269–73
  unsatisfactory nature of 285
child
  UN Convention on the Rights
    of the Child 28, 45, 48
  witness, as 13
communications
  authorization 114
  interception of
    challenges to 113
    common law, approach of
      113
    new framework for 114
    statutory provisions 113
    telephone-tapping,
      authorization 113
companies
  human rights provisions,
    application of 48–9
  reparation by 378
confession
  bullying, obtained by 81
  circumstances of 83

corroboration 103–4
degree of pressure to obtain
  103
denial of legal advice, effect of
  317
drug taker, by 102
false 82–4
inadmissible
  hypothetical unreliability
    101–2
  oppression, obtained by
    101
jury, direction to 104
oppression, obtained by 101
powerful evidence, as 81
psychological research 83–4
reliability of 315
consequentialism
  criminal process, in 43–5
conspiracy
  impossibility 243–4
consumer protection
  prosecution as last resort
    142–3
conviction
  appeal against see appeals
  crimes resulting in 3
Court of Appeal
  appeal to 7
  Crown Court, appeal from
    339–41
  discretion of 346
  due process appeals 354–8
  fresh evidence, hearing
    346–52, 359
  jury verdict, appeals
    challenging 344–53
  lurking doubt appeals in
    347–8
  miscarriage of justice cases,
    role in 344–5
  performance of 353
  quashing conviction, statistics
    347
  retrial, power to order 346,
    353
  unsafe conviction, allowing
    appeal against 346,
    348–9
crime
  attrition rate 2–3
  control 38–40
    diversion, effect of 169
  conviction, resulting in 3
  formal response to 2

prevention 21
prevention of 53
recorded 2
reported 2
state response to 21
white-collar 172
Criminal Cases Review
    Commission
  convictions, post-appeal
      review of 358–60
  establishment of 345–6
  funding 360
  judicial review of decision of
      350–1
  miscarriage of justice,
      investigation of 345–6,
      358, 379
  powers of 358
  predictive exercise, task as 359
  referral criteria 359
  referral to 7
  reputation 360
criminal courts
  Auld Review 14–15
Criminal Defence Service
  contracts 6
criminal justice
  agencies 21
  balancing, metaphor of 40–3
  consequentiality theories 43–5
  institutions, attack on 1
  New Labour, policies of 11–12
  policy
    forces shaping 16–17
    shift in 11
  political parties, position of
      16
  race, problem of 12–13
  reform, political climate
      10–12
  summary 59–60
  system 17
criminal justice agencies
  Audit Commission, scrutiny
      by 77
  discretion, exercise of 75–7
  policy issues, deciding 76
criminal justice system
  accountability 77
  accusatorial and inquisitorial
      370
  balance in 375
  ethics, reform through 77–80
  groups and agencies within,
      proper roles of 79

occupational cultures within
    69
  practical operation of 372
  principled approach 375–6
  professional cultures within
      61
  rules and clear-cut guidance,
      not covered by 60
  termination of involvement
      with, indictment 372
  theory of convergence 370
criminal law
  application of 21
criminal procedure
  assembly line, not 22
  cases, filtering 23
  function of 22
  human interests, infringing
      22–3
  rule of law, serving 21
  trial-centred theory 23
  values moulding 37
criminal process
  basic values 20
  consequentialism in 43–5
  crime control model 38–40
  discrimination in 376–9
  diversion from 21 see also
      diversion
  due process model 38–40
  evaluation
    balancing, metaphor of
        40–3
    consequentialism 43–5
    Packer's models 38–40
    rights perspective,
        development of 45–8
  framework for evaluation of
      19
  future, of 382–3
  gatekeepers 139
  general norms of 373
  human rights, application of
      13
  impartiality, requiring 50
  internal and external values
      20, 26–8
  investigative nature of 106
  issues in 1
  lack of consistency in
      373–4
  normative theory of 23
  officials, power of 18
  political volatility 56–8
  politicization 382–3

pre-trial justice, lack of
    strategy for 373
  principles, promoting 379–82
  purposes of 21
  reference to 17
  reform 9–16
  rights, importance of 27–8 see
      also human rights
  rights-based theory 55
  single normative model 20
  stages in 2–8
  State, role of 49–50
  State response to crime, as
      21
  theory of 19–26
  trial-based theory, objection
      to 25
  values reflected by 21
  victims, suspects and
      defendants, impinging
      on 17
Crown Court
  acquittal rate 264
  appeal from 339
  charge bargains in 271–2
  committal for sentence to 6
  preparatory hearing in 6
  transfer to 238
  trial in 6, 297–304
    black defendants, selection
        by 310
    election followed by guilty
        plea 301
    fairness of 298
    judge alone, by 304–7
    judge and jury, division of
        responsibility between
        312–14
Crown Prosecution Service
  accountability 175, 203
    courts, to 202–3
    Parliament, to 201
  acquittals by judge,
      performance measured
      by 196–8
  caseworkers 177
  charge, determining 6
  Charging Standards 176
  Code for Crown Prosecutors
      175–6, 184–5
  conditional cautions, decisions
      on 159–61
  creation of 175
  criminal proceedings,
      institution of 177

decision against pursuing case, effect on police morale 72–3
decisions and reasons, recording 190–1
decisions to prosecute, review of 146
disclosure of evidence, decisions on 240–1
dispositive powers, exercise of 205–6
diversion, responsibilities for 184, 206
ethics 203–4
fair, independent and objective, to be 203–4
files, endorsements on 190–1
guidance from 187
Inspectorate 201
Instructions for Prosecuting Advocates 187
judicial review of 162–3
lack of consistency in 373–4
law enforcement agencies compared 142
lawyers, deployment of 177
minister of justice role 240
organization and working, changes in 176
police, independent from 175
policy
   charges, downgrading 191–3
   decisions and reasons, recording 190–1
   discontinuance of charges 193–6
   domestic violence, prosecuting 187–8
   guidance on 187
   racially aggravated offences, prosecuting 188–90
prosecution, responsibility for 10
prosecutorial review by 173
public confidence, levels of 199
remand representations
   lack of reasons for 223
   making of 228–9
review of 12, 177
status of 175
targets 198–9
victim, interests of 199–200

weak case, failure to discontinue 65
working practices, shaping 374
custodial sentence
   criteria for 222
custody sheet
   details recorded on 3
Customs and Excise
   compounded penalties, requiring 149–50
   investigation by 4
   prosecutions by 142

deception
   investigation of crime, in 332
decision making
   dispositive 138
   professional context, in 8
   stages in 2–8
   trial, as function of 23–4
   types of decision 8–9
   values, questions of 164–9
defence
   alibi, disclosure of 244–5
   cooperation from 243
   disclosure of documents to 47
   disclosure of evidence by 242–5
   enforcement of disclosure 243
   expert evidence, disclosure of 245
   outline of case by 11
   points of law, disclosure of 244
   statement, failure to issue 242
   technical, submission of 243–4
defence lawyers
   culture of 61
   disclosure of evidence to 62
   duty of 61–2
   ethical approach of 79
   interview, failure to protect client at 65
   lawful procedure, duty to secure acquittal within 62
   toe-rag theory, subscription to 70
   unethical practices 69–70
defendant
   plea bargain, balance of advantages for 283–4
   plea negotiations 374

priority of interests of victim over 74
silence, drawing inferences from 11
unconvicted, treatment of 218–24
delay
   charge and trial, between
      abuse of process, stay of proceedings for 255
      breach, factors amounting to 258
      common law right 255
      reasonable time guarantee, where applying 257
      remedy for 255–6, 258–60
      time beginning to run 256–7
   jury, warning to 251
   pre-trial 249
   stale offences 250–2
Department of Trade and Industry
   prosecutions by 142
detention
   arrest, following 86
   charge, before 87
   Code of Practice 9
   custody time limits 252–5
   further, authorization of 87
   helping police with inquiries 63
   liberty and security of person, right to 31–2, 48
   period of 3
   questioning, for 3, 86
   suspects held in, length of 1
   suspicion, on 32
   trial, without 209
   United States, authorization in 210
Director of Public Prosecutions
   Crown Prosecution Service, heading 175
   former role of 174
discretion
   equality of treatment 165–7
   gatekeeping practices, dominant characteristic of 161
   processes of law, in 75–7
dispositive values
   pre-trial decisions 52–3
district judges
   cases heard by 310–11

diversion
  alternative to contesting guilt,
    as 150
  arguments for 169–70
  breach of conditions 138
  conditional caution 149–50,
    159–61, 170–1
  consent to 53
  crime control, effect on 169
  crime prevention 53
  Crown Prosecution Service,
    responsibilities of 184,
    206
  defendants' rights 168–9
  discretion, element of 146
  disincentives 372
  equality of treatment 165–7
  fairness 53
  formal police caution 148–9
  hierarchy of methods, absence
    of 170
  informal warning 148
  meaning 138, 170
  negotiated 284–5
  no further action 148
  offenders not taking seriously
    169
  proportionality of imposition
    54–5
  racial discrimination 166–7
  regulatory agencies, emphasis
    of 145
  relative onerousness of
    methods 171
  restorative justice scheme,
    reference to 149
  social justice, issues of 171–2
  trend towards 371
  victim compensation, and 54
  victims' rights 167–8
DNA evidence
  forensic profiles 125
  identification by 124
  junk 125
  national database 125–8
  non-coding 125
  privacy issues 127
  retention of profiles 126
  samples
    bodily integrity, concerns
      about 127
    power to obtain 124, 126
    public at large, from 128
    retention, objections to
      128–9

  unfair use of 323–4
  use of 126
domestic violence
  charges, downgrading 192–3
  Code of Practice for Victims
    200
  prosecuting cases of 187–8
  victim, interests of 200
double jeopardy
  acquittal, reopening 360
  argument for 366–7
  contours of 367
  exception to principle of 360
  finality, in interests of 366
  fresh evidence exception 364,
    366
  interests of justice test 364
  international human rights
    obligations, and 365
  new and compelling evidence,
    effect of 364
  new rules, use of 367–8
  reasons for rule 366
  reform of rule 16
  tainted acquittal procedure
    364, 367
  traditional principle 364
  value of principle 365

entrapment
  activity amounting to 261
  authorisation 262
  conditions for 261–2
  decoys, use of 263
  direct victims, crimes without
    260
  improper procedures 380
  justification 261
  manna from heaven
    operations 262–3
  pre-trial remedies 260
  premises, targeting 262
  proactive method of 260
  reasonable suspicion, notion
    of 261
  stings 262
  unfairness of 315–16
Environment Agency
  Compliance Classification
    Scheme 143–4
  functions of 143
  Guidance for the Enforcement
    and Prosecution Policy
    143
  investigative powers 143

  prevention, function of 143,
    145
  prosecutions by 142–3
equality of arms
  principle of 33, 363
escape
  use of force to prevent 30
ethics
  challenging 71–5
  circumventing rules,
    arguments for 71–3
  codes 59
  criminal justice reform
    through 77–80
  importance of 59
  principles, practical success 80
  prosecutorial 203–4
  re-assessment of approach
    73–5
  roles, as to 60–2
  rules 60–2
  training in 80
  unethical behaviour
    criminal defence lawyers, of
      69–70
    crown prosecutors, by 70
    identification of 63–6
    interview, failure to protect
      client at 65
    justifying 71–5
    practices being 63–6
    presumptive mode of trial,
      avoidance of 65
    relevant evidence, failure to
      disclose 64
    suspects, rights of 63–4
    understanding 66–71
    weak case, failure to
      discontinue 65
ethnic minorities
  guilty pleas 290–1
  non-discrimination, principle
    of 376–9
evidence
  bad character, of
    admissibility 334
    changes to rules 336
    common law rule 334
    exclusion, justification of
      334
    human rights provisions
      335
  charge, sufficient for 4
  DNA 124–9 *see also* DNA
    evidence

exclusionary rules 333–7
hearsay
    changes to rules 336
    general rule 333
    other jurisdictions, in 336
    reforms, justification 335
    statutory provisions 333
    witness, right to confront
        335–7
identification *see* identification
inadmissible 27
non-disclosure 238
    unfairness of 356
pre-trial disclosure
    Crown Prosecution Service,
        decisions by 240–1
    defence, by 242–5
    prosecution, by 238–42
public interest immunity
    246–8
relevant, failure to disclose 64
unfairly and illegally obtained,
        exclusion of
    arguments surrounding
        316
    Australia, in 326–7
    bugging cases 331–2
    Canada, in 326
    comparative
        reprehensibility 317–18
    confessions *see* confession
    deception, use of 332
    decision of court 314
    deterrent effect 316
    DNA sample, unfair use of
        323–4
    due process appeals, issues
        in 357
    effect on proceedings
        322–3
    English case law 320–5
    entrapment, obtained by
        315–16
    European Convention on
        Human Rights, breach
        of 321–2
    evaluation of approach
        319–20
    evaluation of approaches
        328–33
    examples 315
    exclusionary discretion 324
    external approach 319
    fairness, issues of 331
    New Zealand, in 327

oppressive questioning,
        obtained by 315
    other jurisdictions, in
        325–7
    PACE, provisions of 320–1
    possible scenarios 332–3
    procedural fairness, notions
        of 337
    protective approach 317,
        329–30
    public, reaction of 318
    public attitude integrity
        318–19, 330, 333
    rationales 328
    reliability, effect on 322–3
    remedial approach 317–18,
        329
    right to privacy, breach of
        321–2, 325
    road traffic offences, taking
        of samples in 325
    seriousness of crime,
        relevance of 323–5
    significant and substantial
        breach of provisions
        320–1
    torture, obtained from third
        parties by 332–3
    United States, in 325–6
unused, listing 239–40
witness statement 99–100
expert evidence
    disclosure 245

financial penalties
    prosecution, without 5
fingerprints
    bodily integrity, concerns
        about 127
    database of 127
    privacy issues 127
    public at large, from 128
    retention, objections to 128–9
fraud
    judge alone, trial by 304–7
    legal regime 7
    penalties 172
    regulatory mechanisms, use of
        172

guilty plea
    acceptance of 272–3
    contractual exchange 295
    delayed 269
    disposal of case by 25

duress, made under 340
election for Crown Court trial,
        following 301
equivocal 340
ethnic minorities, members of
        290–1
fact bargains 274
fair and public hearing, right
        to 291–2
fair trial, giving up right to
        265
incentives 265–6
judge, involvement of 294
lesser offence, to 264, 269–73
magistrates' court, in 266, 278
manslaughter, to 270
mitigating circumstance, as
        287
other countries, in 265
procedure on 264
rate of 266–8, 370
reasons for 267–8
reform proposals 286
review by court, absence of
        265
sentence discounts 287–9, 370
    prediction of 293
    re-assessment, arguments
        for 292
    size of 292
sentence following 7
types of offence, rates for 267

Health and Safety Commission
    compliance with law, ensuring
        144
    enforcement, orientation of
        144–5
    mission statement 144
Health and Safety Executive
    prosecutions by 142
human rights
    admissibility of evidence of
        bad character, issues of
        335
    Charter of Fundamental
        Rights 28–9
    companies, application to
        48–9
    consequentialism, theories of
        43–5
    convention rights
        breach, domestic remedies
            for 356–7
        derogation from 36

hierarchy 46
overview 30–5
prima facie 36
priority of 35–7
qualified 36
strong 37, 46
criminal process
application to 13
central to 27–8
influence on 375–6
double jeopardy exception,
effect of 365
equality of arms, principle of
33
European Convention
breach, admission of
evidence in 321–2
coming into force 29
decisions of British courts
applying 41
individual petition, right of
29
normative framework for
criminal process, as part
of 45
proportionality, concept of
41
provisions in defiance of 57
ratification 29
extension of powers or arrest
and search, proposed
372–3
fair and public hearing, right
to 32–4, 41
rights of witnesses, and
47–8
fair trial, right to see trial
gathering of evidence through
surveillance, in case of
114
Human Rights Act 1998 29
innocence, presumption of 33
International Covenant on
Civil and Political Rights
28
liberty and security of person,
right to 31–2
liberty, right to
bail provisions,
compatibility of 217
exceptions 232
presumption 208, 210
situations for loss of 208
life, right to 30
limitation of 55–8

non-discrimination 35,
376–9
obligations 28–9
priority of 35–7
private and family life, right to
respect for 34–5, 113
prosecution decisions, place in
173
public interest considerations,
balanced against 37
respect in practice 56
rights perspective,
development of 45–8
self-incrimination, privilege
against 129–37 see also
self-incrimination,
privilege against
standards 48
strong 37, 46
torture or inhuman or
degrading treatment or
punishment,
prohibition 30–1
UN Convention on the
Rights of the Child 28,
45, 48
victim, of 42
war or public emergency, in
time of 36

identification
Code of Practice 9
DNA samples, by 124–9 see
also DNA evidence
eyewitness evidence
breach of Code,
consequences of 121–2
frailty of 115
gathering 120
memory, role of 116
parades, use of 116–17
procedures, Code of
Practice 116
quality criteria 116
reliability 115
role of 115
suspect known to police,
where 117–20
suspect's identity not
known, where 120
group 119
image, use of 118–21
jury, warning to 122
mistaken, safeguard against
122

parades
hierarchy of procedures
118
problems with 117
procedure 117
use of 116–17
poor quality evidence 122–3
procedure
Code of Practice 116–17
flaws in 123
hierarchy of procedures
118
refusal to be subjected to
120
suspect, input of 119–20
video 118, 120–1
voice 124
information
laying of 4
innocence, presumption of
European Convention,
provisions of 287–9
generally 33, 208
guilty plea discount, and
288–9
inducement to plead guilty
288–9
nature of rule 134
right to put prosecution to
proof 287
interviews
rape cases, in 100
suspects, of see police
questioning
victims, of 99–101
witnesses, of 99–101

judge
Crown Court trial,
responsibility in 312–14
district 310–11
occupational culture 61
judicial review
Criminal Cases Review
Commission, decisions
of 350–1
Crown Prosecution Service, of
162–3
decision to caution, of 163
decisions as to prosecution, of
202–3
scope of 77
jury
accuracy of decisions 299
credibility issues, deciding 352

dangers of mistaken identity, warning as to 122
delay, warning as to 251
democratic institution, as 299
directions to
    confession, reliance on 104
    remaining silent, inferences drawn from 95–6
equity 299, 361
fairness of trial by 298
findings of fact, responsibility for 304, 312–14
fraud cases, in 304–5
lay fact-finder, as 26
racial bias 309
racially representative 307–8
silence, drawing inferences from 11
trial by
    abolition, possibility of 302–3
    alternative to 304–7
    Auld Review 15
    emphasis on 370
    indirect discrimination, possibility of 310
    middle class defendants, value for 302
    right to 301–2
    right to elect, attempts to remove 12
    trivial 304
    values 305
verdict
    challenging 344–53
    defiance of law, in 299
    legitimacy 366
    reasons, absence of 345
waiver 305
juvenile offenders
criminal process 7
decision to prosecute 162–3

law enforcement agencies
courts, whether accountable to 77
legislative rules governing 77
occupational cultures within 78
scrutiny, subject to 77
surveillance see surveillance
legal advice
defendants on remand, access by 227

denial of access to 90, 315–16, 321
police questions, not to answer 96–9
remanded prisoners, for 219
right to 87–8, 98
legal aid
criminal cases, in 5–6
legal assistance
availability of 5

magistrates
district judges 310–11
lay 297–8, 303, 310–11
lay fact-finder, as 26
professional 310–11
racially representative 307
stipendiary 310
magistrates' court
appeal from
    rate of 344
    right of 339
applications in 237
charge bargains in 270–1
contested trial in 298
cursory form of justice in 299
discontinuance of charges in 193–6
downgrading of charges for hearing in 191–2
first appearance, cases dealt with at 218–19
guilty plea, rate of 266, 278
indication of sentence in 279, 293–4
lack of confidence in 300
legal aid, grant of 5
pre-trial hearings 279–80
quality of justice in 299
sentencing powers 300, 302
summary offences, trial of 6
summons, hearing 5
trial in 297–304
manslaughter
guilty plea on murder charge 270
provocation, defence of 270
mentally disordered defendants
remand 231
police cautioning 153
mentally disordered person
criminal process involving 7
miscarriage of justice
appeal, defendants freed on 338

cases of 10
Court of Appeal, role of 344–5
Criminal Cases Review Commission, role of 345–6, 358
criminal procedure reform in response to 9
dealing with 10
non-disclosure of evidence 238
origins of 379
racism 12
reform, leading to 16
misconduct
civil processes, dealt with through 14
motoring offences
legal regime 7

not guilty plea
generally 268–9, 273
insanity, by way of 264

offences
arrestable 3, 84–5
clear up rate 138
conviction, resulting in 138
crimes, not recorded as 138
definition, certainty of 34
either way, limitation of right to elect 301
formal proceedings, resulting in 138
indictable 300
investigation into 22
police authority, supporting 69
police, discovered by 141
public, reported by 140
racially aggravated, prosecuting 188–90
regulatory 378
relative seriousness, ranking 171–2
stale 250–2
summary, reclassification as 300
offenders
persistent 15

Philips Commission
report 9
plea
    autrefois acquit 264
    autrefois convict 264

change of 268
charge bargaining 269–73
decision on 264
ethnic background, statistics
    on 291
fact bargains 274
guilty *see* guilty plea
innocence claims, testing 296
not guilty 268–9, 273
not guilty by way of insanity
    264
plea bargains *see* plea bargains
policies and practices 285–92
reform proposals 286
venue, before 301
plea bargains
argument against 295
defendant
    balance of advantages for
        283–4
    freedom of choice of 281
essence of 275
half-light, in 285
innocent defendant, pressure
    on 282
judges and counsel, conduct
    of 280–4
magistrates' court, indication
    of sentence in 279,
    293–4
negotiated diversion 284–5
other jurisdictions, in 370
policies and practices 285–92
pre-trial hearings 279–80
process of 7
sentence discount 275–8
State, advantages for 283
Turner Rules 280–4
venue, before 278–9
victims, balance of advantages
    for 283
police
accountability 161–4
authority, offences
    threatening 141
bail, grant of 218
cautioning *see* caution
Conservative administration,
    preference for 11
cop culture, elements of
    66–8
decision to prosecute, given
    174
decisions, challenging 162
detective culture 61

discontinuance of case, effect
    on morale 72–3
effectiveness, pessimism about
    140
entrapment *see* entrapment
fellow officers, duty to
    support 67
helping with inquiries 63
investigation and prosecution,
    separation of 175
investigative practices, changes
    in 82
macho image 67
malpractice 68
mission 68–9, 75
occupational cultures within
    78
off-duty behaviour 67
offences discovered by 141
offences supporting authority
    69
power, limits to 261
proactive 260–1
proactive campaigns 141
prosecutors, joint working
    with 146, 173
public, offences reported by
    140
    filtering 141
questioning *see* police
    questioning
racism in 67
reliability of evidence, conduct
    affecting 314
remand, powers of 217–18
repressive measures by 73–4
respect for laws, displacement
    of 69
responsibility for prosecutions,
    removal of 9–10
restrictions on 72
results expected from 71–2
role assigned to 67–8
role of, in transition 146
selective enforcement 150–9
unused evidence, listing
    239–40
police questioning
arrest, on 84–7
bullying 315
central role of 81
Code of Practice 89, 102–3
confessions *see* confession
context, changes to 82
context of 84–93

deception as tactic in 103
detention for 86
environment, improvement in
    104
evidence, exaggerating 103
interview
    cautioning 89–90
    ending 91–2
    environment for 92
    prolonged 91
    silence, right to 93–9 *see also*
        silence, right to
    tactics 93
    tape recording 90–1
    video-taping 90
oppressive 92, 315
outside police station 89
pressured environment, in 82
psychological research 83–4
role of 105
rules for 89–93
techniques, training in 92
victims, of 99–101
witnesses, of 99–101
police station
legal advice in 87–8
voluntary attendance at 87
pollution
prosecutions *see* Environment
    Agency
pre-trial disclosure
defence, by 242–5
prosecution, by 238–42
prison
conditions in, human rights
    31
remand conditions 219
privacy
DNA or fingerprint evidence,
    database of 127
right to 34–5
prosecuting lawyers
disclosure of evidence by 62
ethical approach, challenge to
    75
impartiality, requirement of
    62
proper role of 79
unethical practices 70
prosecution
accountability of prosecutors
    courts, to 202–3
    Parliament, to 201
    victims, to 203
acquittals by judge 196–8

agencies 174
case, disclosure of 239
charges, downgrading 191–3
common factors for and
        against 185–6
compulsory, principle of
        147–8, 165
discontinuance 193–6
domestic violence cases 187–8
ethics 203–4
evidential sufficiency
    evidence likely to be
        excluded 180
    Full Code Test 182
    innocent, protection of 178
    intrinsic merits approach
        181–2
    issues 179
    judgments of, factors in
        181
    need for 178–9
    new guidance 182–3
    realistic prospects of
        conviction 180–1
    stages of criminal process,
        varying in 179, 182–4
    test of 179–82
    Threshold Test 182–3, 212
human rights, respect for 173
other means, dealing with case
        by 179
procedural lawfulness of 179
public interest requirement
        184–6
racially aggravated offences
        188–90
regulatory agencies, by 142–5,
        174–5
stale 250–2
statutory charging system 178
system
    change in 174–5
    issues 205
    organization of 173
    police and prosecutors,
        joint working 173
    Royal Commission report
        175
targets 198–9
victim, role of 199–200
Public Defender Service
    establishment of 5
    operation of 70
    unethical practices, potential
        impact on 70

public disorder
    threat of 142
public interest immunity
    claim of 246–8
    test of sensitive information
        247–8
public policy
    issues, deciding 76
punishment
    remand in custody as infliction
        of 210

race
    mode of trial, and 307–10
    plea, statistics on 291
racial discrimination
    equality of treatment 166–7
racism
    institutional 12–13
    police, in 67
    remand decisions, equal
        treatment in 230–1
rape
    attrition rate 139
    conviction, number resulting
        in 139
regulatory agencies
    accountability 163–4
    Crown Prosecution Service,
        comparison with 142
    diversion, emphasis on 145
    inequality of treatment by
        145–6
    investigation by 4
    paths and priorities of 373
    policies and practices of 145
    prosecution by 142, 174–5
remand in custody
    acquittal following 220
    American law 214
    appeal, pending 208
    appeals 229–30
    bail information systems
        227–8
    black males, of 230–1
    considered decisions on 222–3
    conviction, after 207
    court, by 207, 213–17
    decision
        conflict in 207
        characteristics relating to
            220–1
        conclusions on 234
        equal treatment in 230–1
        delay in cases, effect of 229

first court appearance, before
        5
    infliction of punishment, as
        210
    initial decision 228
    innocence, presumption of
        208
    law of 213–18
    legal advice and assistance,
        access to 227
    legal advice, provision of 219
    liberty, presumption of 208,
        210, 233
    loss of right to liberty,
        justification 232
    mentally disordered
        defendants, of 231
    non-custodial sentence
        following 221–2
    official proceedings, before
        207
    police, by 217–18
    prison conditions 219
    procedural justice 227–30
    proceedings, procedural
        safeguards 208
    public interest reasons 232
    public protection, for 225–6
    punitive 17–18, 210
    reapplications for bail
        229–30
    rights of defendant at stake
        208
    risk assessment 210
    statistics 219–20
    taking into account on
        sentence 221–2
    time limits 252–5
    trial, securing attendance at
        213–14
    uncertainty as to use of 224
    victims and potential victims,
        treatment of 224–6
    women, of 231
restorative justice
    equality before the law,
        approach for 378
    forms of 371
    rights of victims, and 52
    scheme, reference to 149
    theory of 25
rights
    criminal process, central to
        27–8 see also human
        rights

road traffic offences
  self-incrimination, privilege
    against 131–2, 135
rule of law
  criminal procedure serving 21
  ideals, respect for 77
  impartiality, requiring 50
rules
  circumventing, arguments for
    71–3
  criminal process, of 21
  ethical principles 60–2
Runciman Commission
  report 10, 40–1

search
  extension of powers, proposed
    372–3
self-incrimination, privilege
  against
  absolute, not 46
  company investigation, in
    context of 130
  Convention jurisprudence
    132
  defence disclosure,
    compatibility with
    regime of 136
  duty to cooperate, and 137
  evidence, constraint on ability
    to gather 129
  fair trial guarantee, as part of
    33, 130
  guilty plea discount, and 290
  human rights documents,
    recognition in 129
  immunity, role in delimiting
    136
  international standard, as 290
  justification 135
  material obtained through
    compulsory powers, use
    of 132–3
  right to silence, and 94, 133–4
  road traffic offences 41, 131–2,
    135
  scope of 131
  State and citizen, connection
    to relationship between
    133–5
  tax authorities, material
    required by 132
  understanding of, shifting 130
  use immunity 131
  value of 133

sentencing
  Crown Court, committal to
    6
  desert-based theory 26
  graduated discounts 287
  guilty plea, effect of 7, 266
  increase on appeal 340–1
  judge, reputation of 280
  magistrates' court, indication
    of sentence in 279,
    293–4
  magistrates' court, power of
    300, 302
  plea bargain, discount on
    275–8
  proportionality of imposition
    54–5
  sex discrimination 376–7
  trial, as function of 26
Serious Fraud Office
  powers of 7
sex offenders
  normal acts, criminalization
    of 371–2
  Sex Offender Register,
    placement of persons
    cautioned on 164, 170
sexual harm order
  offence, without evidence of
    14
silence, right to
  adverse inferences, drawing
    90, 242
    effect of 97
    fairness of 98–9
    jury, directions to 95–6
    nature of rule 134
    solicitor's advice, reliance
      on 96–9
  caution 89–90
  changes to 93
    arguments for and against
      93–5
    concerns as to 97–8
  fair trial, as part of 33
  guilty plea discount, and 290
  international standard, as
    290
  legal advice not to answer
    questions 96–9
  privilege against self-
    incrimination, and 94,
    133–4
  reasons for remaining silent
    93–4

social class
  discrimination on grounds of
    377–8
social justice
  issues of 171–2
society
  self-policing 140–2
stop and search
  Code of Practice 107
  consensual search 108
  crime control, contribution to
    111
  drugs offences 111
  intrusive search 107
  objectionable, being 112
  PACE, powers under 9
  population available for 109
  power of 106–7
  public place, in 107
  public support for 112
  racial disparity 109–11
  reasonable suspicion, not
    requiring 110
  reasonable suspicion, on 107
  record of 108
  statistics 108–10
  terrorism provisions, under
    107, 110
  use of powers 111–12
  voluntary search 108
Street Crimes Initiative 15
summons
  hearing case on 5
  issue, procedure for 4
surveillance
  challenges to 113
  common law, approach of 113
  human rights, safeguarding
    113–14
  increase in 113
  interception of
    communications see
    communications
  law enforcement agencies, use
    by 113
  regulatory framework for 114
  right to respect for private and
    family life, and 113
  statutory provisions 114
  techniques 113
  use of 260
suspect
  building case against 4
  catching red-handed 4
  coercive powers over 22

detention, length of 1
identification of 3
legal advice, right to 87–8
police pressure on 81
prepared statement by 105
priority of interests of victim over 74
promotion of interests of society against 74
punishment, treatment equivalent to 17
questioning *see* police questioning
remand in custody 5, 17–18
see also remand in custody
rights of 63
failure to inform of 64

telephone-tapping *see* communications
terrorism
duty to cooperate with authorities 137
new methods of dealing with 372
post-11 September legislation 15
stop and search powers 107, 110
terrorist offences
legal regime 7
torture
evidence obtained by 332–3
prohibition, Convention rights 30–1
trial
adversarial system 26–7
allocation for 300
avoidance of 369–75
charge bargaining 269–73
charges, downgrading 191–3
committal for 237–8
cracked 268
Crown Court, in 297–304
right to elect 6
transfer to 238
see also Crown Court
decision making by 23–4
defendant pending, imposition of least restrictive regime 209
delay before 249

delay between charge and
abuse of process, stay of proceedings for 255
breach, factors amounting to 258
common law right 255
reasonable time guarantee, where applying 257
remedy for 255–6, 258–60
time beginning to run 256–7
detention pending, custody time limits 252–5
due process, failure of 354–8
effective, mechanisms for 236
error preference 24
fair, right to 32–4, 41
appeals 355–6
legal advice, denial of access to 90
promotion of 236
rights of witnesses, and 47–8
scope of 355
self-incrimination, privilege against 129–37 *see also* self-incrimination, privilege against
stale offence, of 250–2
fair and public hearing, right to 291–2
fairness, principles of 24
fallibility 24
filtering prior to 237–8
focal point of criminal procedure, as 297
inquisitorial system 27
jury *see* jury
magistrates' court, in 297–304
see also magistrates' court
modes of 6, 297–311
determining 264
Narey report 12
objects of 22
pre-trial decisions 369
pre-trial hearings 279–80
pre-trial procedure, breach of 380
presumptive mode, avoidance of 65
race, implications of 307–10
reasonable time, within 208

retrial, power to order 346, 353
sentencing as function of 26
two levels of court, in 297–8
unfairly and illegally obtained evidence, exclusion of *see* evidence
verdict, legitimacy 24–5

utilitarianism
theory of 43

victim
accountability of prosecutors to 203
attack, fear of 225
balance of justice tipped against 1
Code of Practice 51
compensation 54, 200
decision to prosecute, as motive force behind 174
diversion, effect on rights of 167–8
domestic violence cases, in 200
growing concern for 13
marginalization 374–5
personal view of 50
plea bargain, balance of advantages for 283
interviewing 99–101
police cautioning of offender, unfairness of 156–7
priority of interests of 74
progress of case, keeping in touch with 51
prosecution, role in 199–200
prosecution without co-operation of 51
protection 225
protection of interests of 18
questioning 4
remand of defendants, impact of 224–6
rights of 42
Council of Europe recommendations 49
Declaration 49
secondary victimization 18
services, right to 49
sexual cases, in, cross-examination 42
statement by 99–100

statutory rights of 15
taking account of 51
Victim Personal Statements
51

witness
child, treatment of 13
defence, provision of list of
242

eyewitness identification
evidence 115–23 *see also*
identification
interference with, refusal of
bail on risk of 212
police questioning 99–101
protection of interests of 18
rights of, balancing right to fair
trial 47–8

statement by 99–100
vulnerable
cross-examination 42
treatment of 13

young offenders
police cautioning 153
reprimand and formal
warnings, scheme of 4